JB JOSSEY-BASS

EVALUATION THEORY, MODELS, AND APPLICATIONS

Daniel L. Stufflebeam
Anthony J. Shinkfield

BICENTENNIAL
1807
WILEY
2007
BICENTENNIAL

John Wiley & Sons, Inc.

Published by Jossey-Bass
A Wiley Imprint
989 Market Street, San Francisco, CA 94103-1741   www.josseybass.com

Readers should be aware that Internet Web sites offered as citations and/or sources for further information may have changed or disappeared between the time this was written and when it is read.

Jossey-Bass books and products are available through most bookstores. To contact Jossey-Bass directly
call our Customer Care Department within the U.S. at 800-956-7739, outside the U.S. at 317-572-3986,
or fax 317-572-4002.

Jossey-Bass also publishes its books in a variety of electronic formats. Some content that appears in print
may not be available in electronic books.

Library of Congress Cataloging-in-Publication Data

Stufflebeam, Daniel L.
  Evaluation theory, models, and applications / Daniel L. Stufflebeam, Anthony J. Shinkfield. — 1st ed.
    p. cm.
  Includes index.
  "A Wiley Imprint."
  ISBN-13: 978-0-7879-7765-8 (cloth)
  ISBN-10: 0-7879-7765-9 (cloth)
1. Evaluation research (Social action programs) I. Shinkfield, Anthony J. II. Title.
  H62.S79624 2007
  001.4–dc22

                                                 2006036605

Printed in the United States of America
FIRST EDITION
HB Printing   10 9 8 7 6 5 4 3 2 1

CONTENTS

Contents

General Standards   •   Fieldwork Standards for Performance Audits   •   Reporting
Standards for Performance Audits

**PART TWO: AN EVALUATION OF EVALUATION
APPROACHES AND MODELS 131**

TABLES, FIGURES, AND EXHIBITS

Tables

Figures

Exhibits

ACKNOWLEDGMENTS

This book presents a broad array of concepts and procedures required to ensure valid, ethical, and effective evaluation practice. Such an ambitious venture has required the help and encouragement of others. We thank Jossey-Bass, our publisher, for delineating so clearly, following its marketing analysis, what emphases should be given in a book on program evaluation. The initial encouragement by Andrew Pasternack set us on an appropriate course to pursue, and the ongoing cooperation of Seth Schwartz gave us confidence that a first-rate production would eventuate. Seth worked closely with our immediate editor, Sally Veeder, of the Evaluation Center, Western Michigan University. We are indebted to Sally for her highly skilled and sustained editorial work—and for her unflagging good humor, even when difficulties arose (as they inevitably do). Finally, we are grateful to Jackie Shinkfield for providing secretarial assistance throughout the lengthy course of the book. We are fortunate to have had such a fine support team.

ABOUT THE AUTHORS

Daniel Stufflebeam is a Western Michigan University (WMU) Distinguished University Professor, McKee Professor of Education, and founder of the Evaluation Center. He established the center at Ohio State University in 1965, moved it to WMU in 1973, and directed it until 2002. At Ohio State he developed more than one hundred standardized achievement tests, including eight forms of the GED tests, and created the CIPP Evaluation Model. At WMU, he founded the Joint Committee on Standards for Educational Evaluation, chaired it through 1988, and led the development of standards for program and personnel evaluations. He also established and directed the national Center for Research on Educational Accountability and Teacher Evaluation and, more recently, designed WMU's interdisciplinary doctoral program in evaluation. He has received more than $20 million in grants and contracts; conducted evaluations in education, community development, housing, military personnel evaluation, state and national assessment, and other areas; lectured and consulted in twenty countries; and advised and assisted many organizations in the United States and abroad. He serves on the U.S. General Accounting Office Advisory Council on Government Auditing Standards. His publications include twenty-four books and monographs and about a hundred journal articles and book chapters. He received the American Evaluation Association's Paul Lazersfeld prize for contributions to evaluation theory, WMU's Distinguished Faculty Scholar Award, and the CREATE Jason Millman Award. His latest book, edited with Thomas Kellaghan of Ireland, is the

International Handbook of Educational Evaluation (2003). Stufflebeam holds a bachelor's degree from the University of Iowa and master's and Ph.D. degrees from Purdue University.

Anthony J. Shinkfield's professional experience has been predominantly in educational administration and the evaluation of social institutions and systems and of their personnel. This book is the third he has written in collaboration with Daniel Stufflebeam after *Systematic Evaluation* (1985) and *Teacher Evaluation* (1995). There is remarkable coincidence of both approaches to evaluation and writing styles, particularly as they live and work hemispheres apart. But their paths have crossed often, initially when Shinkfield was completing a doctoral degree at Western Michigan University in the mid-1970s and when he was invited to be a board member of the Center for Research on Educational Accountability and Teacher Evaluation (CREATE), 1992–1997.

After early years as a high school teacher and principal, he became a superintendent of secondary education in South Australia and, significantly, the first Australian headmaster at St. Peters College, Adelaide, for a period of 14 years (after the school had been in existence for 131 years). This school is one of three leading Australian independent schools. Since stepping down from that position in 1992, apart from work with CREATE, he has evaluated sections of universities, independent schools, and business houses. He has been deeply involved in a range of federal and state organizations and community activities, for which in 2001 he was accorded Australia's second highest honor, Officer of the Order of Australia. He remains a lifetime aficionado of cricket; "the rest are merely sports."

INTRODUCTION

We have planned and developed this book to aid and enlighten especially those who evaluate, or intend to evaluate, programs. In addition, the book includes guidance and examples related to evaluations of personnel and personnel evaluation systems. The book is intended particularly for use by practicing evaluators and students in graduate programs focused on evaluation theory and practice, but its handbook nature should prove useful to evaluation clients and others with an interest in learning about evaluation.

Evaluation studies must be directed to help clients and other stakeholders use findings well and particularly to improve and certify the value of the services. This is a heavy professional responsibility. In this book, we have drawn together information from the evaluation literature and a wide range of practical experience in order to guide, advise, and demonstrate that success in the worthwhile pursuit of systematic evaluation is both essential and clearly possible.

Evaluation is a vital component of the continuing health of organizations. If evaluations are conducted well, organizations and their people will have the satisfaction of knowing with confidence which elements are strong and where changes are needed. Evaluation therefore is a positive pursuit.

This book is designed as both a textbook for graduate courses concerned with the critical analysis and application of program evaluation theory, approaches and models, and methods and more widely as a handbook for use in planning, conducting, and assessing program evaluations. The book builds and expands on the widely circulated 2001 American Evaluation Association's *Evaluation Models,* no. 89 in the New Directions for Evaluation series (Stufflebeam, 2001). At this writing, the compact *Evaluation Models* had sold more copies than any other New Directions for Evaluation volume, most of which were on the market much longer than *Evaluation Models.*

Throughout this book, we typically refer to evaluation *approaches* (rather than *models*) as the generic term to cover all generalized ways of designing and conducting evaluations. We selected this term because it encompasses illicit as well as commendable ways of doing evaluations and includes all good approaches, whether or not they are labeled models.

We undertook this writing project at the urging of a number of colleagues and representatives of Jossey-Bass and initially sought only to update *Evaluation Models.* However, leaders at the publishing company convinced us of the need for an updated, extended treatment of *Evaluation Models* plus practical guidelines and procedures for applying the best models. In this book, we address these needs and also discuss the foundational topic of evaluation theory. Our goal has been to write a book on evaluation theory, models, and applications with all the elements of both a sound textbook and a practical handbook to guide evaluation practice. While the heart of the book is an updated, expanded treatment of *Evaluation Models* (found in Part Two), this core content is now embedded in a broader discussion of theoretical and practical topics. A unique feature is the book's discussion of personnel evaluation, an important topic usually avoided in program evaluations and not found in most books on program evaluation. We have focused the book on helping evaluators and others strengthen their theoretical understanding and working knowledge of evaluation. We believe the book should be useful in a succession of two semester-long courses in program evaluation and that evaluators and their clients can selectively apply its contents in intensive evaluation institutes, contracted evaluation projects, and self-evaluations.

Intended Audience

Since program evaluation is such a pervasive concern in society, we have designed the book to serve the needs of a broad range of those who need to use evaluations to assess, ensure, or improve the quality of programs. The book can be useful to graduate students, evaluation and research instructors, evaluators, program administrators, businesses, specialists in research and evaluation methodology, professionals, and other service providers who must meet requirements for public accountability and those who commission program evaluations. The book treats program evaluation across the disciplines and thus is intended for use in such fields as nursing, community development, housing, education, medicine, psychotherapy, disease control, business administration, jurisprudence, national defense, engineering, social services, philanthropy, and international development, among others. Evaluators and others in such fields can use the book to acquire knowledge of evaluation approaches and models that are available for evaluating programs, the concepts and theories undergirding different evaluation approaches, principles for guiding the work of evaluators, standards for judging evaluations, how to address the sensitive issue of personnel evaluation in the context of program evaluations, evaluations of twenty-six evaluation approaches, detailed information about six evaluation approaches, techniques for carrying out the full range of steps in any program evaluation, and sources of additional information and practical tools for program evaluations. Moreover, the book portrays the developing evaluation profession and requirements for its advancement.

Overview of the Book's Contents

Faced with a growing array of program evaluation approaches and models, evaluators need competence to assess and choose wisely among the options and then confidently and effectively apply the approach they selected. Overall, we chose topics to give instruction about the general nature of evaluation, provide an overview and comparative analysis of alternative approaches to evaluation, provide in-depth instruction—with examples—in each of six ways of conducting credible program evaluations, provide practical guidelines for choosing among approaches, and to design and carry out an evaluation from beginning to end.

Two dominant factors intertwine throughout the book, and are underlined by six themes: the *theoretical* and *practical* essentials of evaluation. The first theme is

> *The evaluation discipline must have a solid foundation in theory that offers a coherent set of conceptual, hypothetical, pragmatic, and ethical principles to guide the study and practice of evaluation.*

The second theme is

> *Practical imperatives demand that evaluations inform decision making and hold service personnel accountable for the displayed value of these services. As an extension of practicality, the evaluator must plan, develop, and deploy a distinctive evaluation methodology that is technically sound and responsive to clients' needs.*

Part One of the book introduces program evaluation in four chapters that set out the fundamentals of evaluation. Chapter One discusses the role of evaluation in society; defines evaluation and other key evaluation concepts; denotes the principal uses of program evaluations; identifies different, complementary methodological approaches; describes the evaluation profession in its historical context; and discusses different jobs in the evaluation enterprise. In general, this opening chapter offers an overall perspective on the evaluation field and background information for use in studying the ensuing chapters. Chapter Two looks closely at the nature of evaluation theory, particularly program evaluation theory. It defines evaluation theory, distinguishes between evaluation models and evaluation theories, identifies criteria for judging theories, and lists illustrative hypotheses for research on program evaluation. Stressing that nothing is as useful as a sound theory, the chapter calls for increased and improved efforts to generate and validate program evaluation theories. Chapter Three reviews and discusses principles and standards for use in guiding and assessing program evaluations. It begins with a discussion of a professionally generated set of standards for educational program evaluations (Joint Committee on Standards for Educational Evaluation, 1994) that require evaluations to meet conditions of utility, feasibility, propriety, and accuracy. Subsequently, the chapter summarizes and discusses the American Evaluation Association's *Guiding Principles for Evaluators* (American Evaluation Association Ethics Committee, 2004). These principles are focused on ensuring that competent evaluators will serve the general and public welfare by conducting evaluations that are methodologically sound, competently conducted, ethical, respectful of involved and affected persons, and in the public interest. The chapter concludes with a discussion of the U.S. *Government Auditing Standards* (Comptroller General of the United States, 2003). These standards cover program evaluation, as well as financial auditing, across the full range of government programs and services. Importantly, they include a 2002 amendment on independence, designed "to better serve the public interest and to maintain a high degree of integrity, objectivity, and independence for audits of government entities" (Comptroller General of the United States, 2002, p. 1). Part One concludes with Chapter Four, on personnel evaluation. While program evaluators typically have avoided the highly sensitive, sometimes volatile issue of personnel evaluation, in doing so they avoid a key factor in any program's success: the performance of its personnel. The chapter considers the problems and possibilities of conducting program evaluations that appropriately and effectively take account of the performance of program personnel and concludes with a general perspective on personnel evaluation.

In Part Two, readers are aided in identifying, analyzing, and judging twenty-six approaches thought to cover most program evaluation efforts. Readers will learn to discriminate between five illicit approaches, termed *pseudoevaluations,* and twenty-one legitimate approaches, which are divided into four categories: quasi evaluations, improvement- and accountability-oriented evaluations, social agenda and advocacy evaluations, and eclectic evaluations. Since no evaluation approach is always best, the analysis in Part Two is designed to assist evaluators in choosing that one or combination of approaches that best fits particular evaluation assignments. Part Two concludes with a consumer report–type assessment of eight of the most promising or likely to be used evaluation approaches against the requirements of the Joint Committee's *Program Evaluation Standards* (1994). Our assessments in this part are keyed to the book's next two themes. Closely connected, these are

> *Evaluators can choose from a defensible range of evaluation approaches.*
> *Evaluators should employ professional standards to ensure and assess the quality*
> *of evaluation approaches and particular evaluations.*

Part Three extends the development of these two themes by summarizing an evaluation case drawn from housing and community development to help illustrate the application of six selected evaluation approaches that we deem especially acceptable and noteworthy. We advise readers to keep this case in mind as they consider possibilities for applying each of six evaluation approaches. Subsequently, Part Three presents details and illustrates the application of these widely discussed and used evaluation approaches: the experimental design approach; the case study approach, Daniel Stufflebeam's CIPP Model; Michael Scriven's consumer-oriented evaluation approach; Robert Stake's responsive evaluation approach; and Michael Patton's utilization-focused evaluation approach. Some of these are included because we judge them to be the best available approaches. Others are discussed in depth because of their importance in the history of evaluation, as well as the likelihood of their continued use. In Part Three, readers will learn the backgrounds and orientations of the evaluation leaders who authored each approach, the approach's theoretical and philosophical underpinnings, pertinent evaluation methods and tools, and illustrations of its use.

Part Four of the book offers practical assistance, guidelines, and checklists for applying any defensible approach to evaluation. We offer down-to-earth procedures that are applicable to any sound evaluation approach. We discuss and provide illustrations on how to carry through a sequence of essential evaluation tasks: identifying and assessing evaluation opportunities; designing, budgeting, and contracting evaluations; collecting, analyzing, and synthesizing information; and reporting and facilitating appropriate use of findings. In explaining and illustrating these tasks, Part Four emphasizes that all aspects of an evaluation must satisfy the requirements of credible standards. Moreover, this part emphasizes the book's fifth theme:

> *Evaluators should involve stakeholders in the evaluation process to hear and consider their inputs and enhance prospects for their wise use of findings.*

Part Four concludes by giving particular emphasis to the importance of evaluating evaluations, the book's sixth theme:

> *As professionals, evaluators must subject their evaluations to evaluation.*

At the end of many chapters are review questions and group exercises to help readers check and increase their understanding of the material. The book is also supplemented by reference to the Western Michigan University Evaluation Center Web site (www.wmich.edu/evalctr), which includes checklists for guiding evaluations according to different approaches, illustrative evaluation reports, information about evaluation training opportunities, and topical papers of the Western Michigan University Evaluation Center. This Web site is an invaluable reservoir of information of relevance to this book. Readers can greatly enhance their learning of this book's contents by regularly consulting and making good use of tools and information on the Evaluation Center's Web site.

Study Suggestions

This book is a textbook, but its basic design is that of a handbook. Readers can turn to any chapter, independent of the others, to obtain information on a particular topic. The book may be studied in groups or independently. It can be worked through from beginning to end, or its chapters can be used selectively as handbook chapters. In our desire to serve graduate education, we have sought to provide sufficient content to support a sequence of two three-semester-hour courses.

Part One is oriented to providing readers an in-depth understanding of the evaluation discipline. The material in Part Two is especially useful in making choices among alternative approaches to evaluation, since it provides comparative analyses of alternative evaluation approaches. When you need to gain in-depth knowledge of a selected evaluation approach, that is, one that is already being applied in evaluating a given program or one you have selected after a review of alternatives, we advise you to see if that approach is discussed in Part Three. If it is, you can benefit by studying the pertinent Part Three chapter. Approaches not treated in Part Three can be studied in depth by consulting the references provided at the ends of the chapters. When you need practical suggestions for planning and carrying out the various steps involved in applying any evaluation approach, we suggest that you consult the procedurally oriented chapters in Part Four.

We also have a word of advice for graduate students and evaluation researchers who are seeking topics for research projects on evaluation. We suggest that you carefully review Chapter Two on evaluation theory and consider designing and conducting studies to test hypotheses such as those found in that chapter. Also, you could make valuable contributions by conducting and publishing case studies on applications of given evaluation approaches discussed in Part Three or comparative studies of two or more approaches. Other useful research and development projects could entail validation of selected evaluation procedures presented in Part Four (such as the traveling observer technique or the feedback workshop method) and development and validation of new evaluation checklists (for example, for evaluations in certain fields, such as parks and recreation, consumer products evaluation, organizational development, restaurant management, amusement parks, zoos, mail delivery, and foster care services). Finally, consider conducting and publishing metaevaluations (evaluations of evaluations).

Summary

In summary, we offer the following steps to guide your study of this book:

- Read Chapter One to gain an overview of the evaluation field, an introduction to program evaluation, a historical perspective on the development of the program evaluation area, the different roles one can play in the evaluation field, and sources of information about evaluation.
- Read Chapter Two to gain a perspective on the importance and status of theory in the program evaluation field and of the work needed to study and improve evaluation theories.
- Read Chapter Three to develop familiarity with the principles and standards for guiding and assessing evaluations.
- Read Chapter Four to identify the problems as well as the possibilities of evaluating personnel in the context of program evaluations and to gain an overall perspective on personnel evaluation.
- Study the chapters in Part Two to distinguish proper from improper evaluations, identify the range of available creditable evaluation approaches, and see consumer report evaluations of selected approaches.

• In Part Three, develop familiarity with the evaluation case and use it to selectively study the details of particular evaluation approaches of interest.

• Study the chapters in Part Four to identify practical procedures for carrying out the various steps in an evaluation and for evaluating evaluation plans and reports.

• For the book as a whole and each chapter, list what you see as your high-priority learning objectives, keep notes on your progress in achieving the objectives, and ultimately evaluate your learning gains.

• At the end of chapters with review questions and group exercises , respond to make sure you have grasped the chapter's main points, and then reread chapter material as appropriate.

• Consult the Western Michigan University Evaluation Center Web site and the references at the ends of most chapters to enhance your understanding of program evaluation theory, approaches, and applications.

We recommend that you try your hand at applying your new knowledge by designing evaluations of programs of interest; evaluating published evaluations; teaching others about evaluation theory, approaches, and procedures; and designing and conducting research on evaluation. Good luck!

References

American Evaluation Association Ethics Committee. (2004). *Guiding principles for evaluators.* Fairhaven, MA: American Evaluation Association. Available at http://www.eval.org/ Guiding%20Principles.htm.

Comptroller General of the United States. (2002, January). *Government auditing standards: Amendment No. 3 independence.* Washington, DC: U.S. General Accounting Office.

Comptroller General of the United States. (2003, June). *Government auditing standards: 2003 revision.* Washington, DC: U.S. Government Accountability Office.

Joint Committee on Standards for Educational Evaluation. (1994). *The program evaluation standards.* Thousand Oaks, CA: Corwin Press.

Stufflebeam, D. L. (Ed.). (2001). *Evaluation models.* New Directions in Evaluation, 89. San Francisco: Jossey-Bass.

PART ONE

FUNDAMENTALS OF EVALUATION

Part One provides information on the foundations of evaluation. The following four chapters give an overview of the evaluation field, analyze the state of theory in the field, describe the field's guiding principles and standards, and discuss the sensitive issue of evaluating a program's personnel. These chapters offer an appreciation of the history and status of the evaluation discipline and some of the key theoretical and professional issues facing its theoreticians and practitioners.

CHAPTER ONE

OVERVIEW OF THE EVALUATION FIELD

The term *evaluation* has been in the English language for centuries, and it has had diverse functions and meanings during that time. Only in recent decades, in particular the latter part of the twentieth century, has more precision been given to the term, including specificity to basic concepts and more explicit explanations about its aims as a functioning entity. This book's four central purposes are to help those who are studying, commissioning, and conducting evaluations to (1) become knowledgeable about the evaluation profession, including its vocabulary, functions, main methods, organizations, standards, guiding principles, specialized evaluation jobs, and sources of information about evaluation; (2) gain a perspective on evaluation theory; (3) understand and assess the major approaches for conducting program evaluations; and (4) acquire knowledge of procedural guidelines for applying evaluation approaches.

In this opening chapter, we are seeking answers to two questions: What is evaluation in today's terms? and What should it achieve? Basically, the chapter provides an overview of program evaluation. It discusses the relevance of evaluation to society and its pervasive character. It defines evaluation and other key concepts of the evaluation profession and contrasts the evaluation profession to other professions. Evaluations may involve multiple values of individuals, organizations or societies, and these may compete. However, we suggest that when there is a clear knowledge of the generic qualities underlying all good evaluation procedures and precepts, diverse elements may be satisfactorily encompassed in reports.

The chapter also identifies generic evaluative criteria, different ways of defining and applying program standards, and main uses of evaluation. It distinguishes between comparative and noncomparative evaluations and between informal and formal evaluations. It discusses the responsibilities of organizations and individual professionals and other service providers to evaluate and improve their services. It identifies major evaluative methodologies. It characterizes the evaluation profession and how it has developed, references guiding principles and professional standards for evaluations (discussed in detail in Chapter Three), and defines a range of evaluation-related jobs. In general, this chapter aims to acquaint readers with the basics of evaluation as a field of study and practice. The chapter is organized around key questions about evaluation that should be of interest to those relatively new to the field, seasoned evaluators who need to explain their profession to others, and evaluation instructors.

As do most other chapters, this one concludes with a set of review exercises and group discussion questions. After reading the chapter, we suggest you complete them as a means of assessing and confirming your mastery of the chapter. Also, you may find it useful to discuss your responses to the chapter's main organizing questions and review exercises with colleagues or fellow students. We suggest further that you enrich your understanding of this chapter's material by consulting the references listed at the end of the chapter and the Western Michigan University Evaluation Center Web site (www.wmich.edu/evalctr).

Why Is Evaluation Important?

Evaluation arguably is society's most fundamental discipline. It is oriented to assessing and helping to improve all aspects of society. Proper objects for evaluation cover a wide range of entities: school programs, libraries, museums, hospitals, physicians, immunization programs, continuing medical education programs, courts, lawyers, judges, universities, schools, university curriculum, instructors, construction projects, ladders, food and other consumer products, telecommunication services, postal services, government agencies, transportation services, parks and recreation programs, agricultural extension services, environmental policies, disease prevention and control programs, national defense, border control, research plans and findings, theories, and many more. These examples illustrate that evaluation is ubiquitous. It permeates all areas of scholarship, production, and service and has important implications for maintaining and improving services and protecting citizens in all areas of interest to society. Evaluation is a process for giving attestations on such matters as reliability, effectiveness, cost-effectiveness, efficiency, safety, ease of use, and probity. Society and individual clients are at risk to the extent that services, products, and other objects of interest are poor. Evaluation serves society by providing affirmations of worth, value, improvement (and how and when this should happen), accreditation, accountability, and, when necessary, a basis for terminating bad programs.

What Are Appropriate Objects of Evaluations and Related Subdisciplines of Evaluation?

We refer to the object of an evaluation as the *evaluand* or (in the case of a person) the *evaluee* (Scriven, 1981). Evaluands may be individuals, programs, projects, policies, products, equipment, services, concepts and theories, or organizations. Although this book concentrates on program evaluation, one can refer to a range of other areas of evaluation: personnel evaluation, product evaluation, institutional evaluation, student evaluation, and policy evaluation. The scope of evaluation applications broadens greatly when one considers the wide range of disciplines to which it applies. Among others, one can speak of educational evaluation, social services evaluation, arts evaluation, city planning and evaluation, real estate appraising, engineering testing and evaluation, hospital evaluation, drug testing, manufacturing evaluation, consumer products evaluation, agricultural experimentation, and environmental evaluation. Much of this book's material, including the concepts and methods in this chapter, is applicable across the full range of evaluation areas.

Are Evaluations Enough to Control Quality, Guide Improvement, and Protect Consumers?

The presence of sound evaluation does not necessarily guarantee high quality in services or that those in authority will heed the lessons of evaluation and take needed corrective actions. Evaluations provide only one of the ingredients needed for quality assurance and improvement. There are many examples of defective products that have harmed consumers, not because of a lack of pertinent evaluative information but because of a failure on the part of decision makers to heed and act on rather than ignore or cover up alarming evaluation information. One clear example was the continued sales of the Corvair automobile after its developers and marketers knew of its rear-end collision fire hazard. Here we see that society has a critical need not only for competent evaluators but for evaluation-oriented decision makers as well. For evaluations to make a positive difference, policymakers, regulatory bodies, service providers, and others must obtain and act responsibly on evaluation findings.

We have thus aimed this book not only at evaluators or those studying to become professional evaluators, but also at the users of evaluations. We believe that everyone who plays a decision-making role in serving the public should obtain and act responsibly on evaluations of their services. Fulfilling this role requires each such decision maker to take appropriate steps to become an effective, conscientious, evaluation-oriented service provider. The production and appropriate use of sound evaluation is one of the most vital contributors to strong services and societal progress.

How Does the Field of Evaluation Relate to Other Professions?

As a profession with important roles in society, evaluation has technical aspects requiring thorough and ongoing training. It possesses an extensive and rapidly developing professional literature containing information on evaluation models and methods and findings of research on evaluation. Its research material evolves from, and is closely connected to, the wide range of evaluations conducted in all fields, such as those referred to earlier in this chapter. Evaluation has many professional organizations (including the American Evaluation Association and other state and national evaluation associations, with more than twenty in countries outside the United States) and university training programs (among them, the interdisciplinary doctoral evaluation program at Western Michigan University and other evaluation graduate programs at Claremont Graduate University, the University of Illinois, Ohio State University, the University of Minnesota, the University of North Carolina, the University of Virginia, and the University of California at Los Angeles). The field also has standards for evaluation services (including the Joint Committee 1988, 1994, and 2003 standards, respectively, for evaluating personnel, programs, and students) and the U.S. *Government Auditing Standards* (Government Accountability Office, 2003), plus the American Evaluation Association's *Guiding Principles for Evaluators* (2004). Moreover, as discussed in Chapter Two, the evaluation profession possesses concepts and tools required to examine both evaluation theory and evaluation practice.

As a distinct profession, evaluation is supportive of all other professions and in turn is supported by many of them; no profession could excel without evaluation. Services and research can make progress and stand up to public and professional scrutiny only if they are regularly subjected to rigorous evaluation and shown to be sound. Also, improvement-oriented self-evaluation is a hallmark of professionalism. Program leaders and all members of any profession are obligated to serve their clients well. This requires that they regularly evaluate, improve, and be accountable for their contributions. In the sense of assessing and improving quality and meeting accountability requirements, all professions (including evaluation) are dependent on evaluation. In the latter instance, we refer to the evaluation of evaluation as *metaevaluation* (addressed in Chapter Twenty-Seven). On the other side, evaluation draws concepts, criteria, and methods from such other fields as philosophy, political science, psychology, sociology, anthropology, education, economics, communication, public administration, information technology, statistics, and measurement. Clearly it is important for evaluators to recognize and build on the symbiotic relationship between evaluation and other fields of study and practice.

We believe that the more systematic, more thorough, and the more disciplined the evaluation procedures are, the more beneficial and enduring will be the changes in the evaluand. This is particularly the case with formal evaluations. As mentioned in this book from time to time, evaluators can only do their best; despite strenuous efforts to involve clients in evaluations, there is no certainty that clients will heed and act on sound evaluation findings. Later chapters refer to the necessity for evaluators to pursue disciplined design, information gathering, organization of information, analysis of information, and communicating outcomes in sound reports. Evaluations that lack these kinds of disciplines typically are fruitless, wasteful, and misleading. Again, as later chapters show, there is no single best method or model to carry out evaluations. Nonetheless, the alternative approaches all require vigorous and objective applications of sound methods to reach valid conclusions.

What Is Evaluation?

Mainly because there have been different approaches to evaluation over the years, definitions of the term *evaluation* have themselves differed. In earlier times, for example, evaluation was commonly closely associated with assessing achievement against behavioral objectives or conducting norm-referenced testing. Then, particularly during the 1970s, emphasis was given to professional judgment. Since that time, an increasing number believe that evaluation is the collection and analysis of quality information for decision makers. These and other "definitions" of *evaluation* have elements of credibility, depending often on the type of evaluation study being undertaken. We take the stance in this book that no one method of evaluation is necessarily the best or most appropriate and that an eclectic approach may well be the most suitable to a particular context. It now remains to see whether it is possible to arrive at a definition, or definitions, that satisfactorily cover the often complex array of approaches and activities that constitute evaluation.

Evaluation has been defined in different ways. One of the earliest and still most prominent definitions states that it means determining whether objectives have been achieved. We reject this definition, because following it can cause evaluations to fail. One of its problems is that some objectives are unworthy of achievement. Surely evaluators must avoid judging a program as successful solely because it achieved its own objectives. The objectives might well be corrupt, dysfunctional, unimportant, not oriented to the needs of the intended beneficiaries, or mainly reflective of profit motives or other conflicts of interest of those in charge of the program. Another problem is that this definition steers evaluations in the direction of looking only at outcomes. Evaluations should also examine a program's goals, structure, and process, especially if the evaluation is to contribute to program improvement or adoption and adaptation by other service providers. Moreover, a focus on objectives might cause evaluators not to search for important side effects, which can be critically important in determining whether a product or other entity is safe. In addition to these deficiencies, evaluations employing the objectives-based definition provide feedback only at the end of a program. Evaluations also have an important role in helping to plan and guide programs toward successful outcomes. These defects and limitations are sufficient for us to reject the objectives-based definition of evaluation.

We also reject definitions that equate evaluation with any one methodology. Sometimes evaluations based on experimental designs can provide consumers with useful information on the comparative outcomes of competing programs, products, or services. However, in many evaluations, a controlled experimental approach would not be feasible, would be counterproductive, or would fail to address key questions about needs, goals, plans, processes, side effects, and other topics. Similarly, other useful techniques—such as surveys, standardized tests, site visits, or self-studies—are far too narrow in the information they yield to provide a sufficient basis for most program evaluations. Evaluation should not be equated with any one methodology. Instead, it should encompass all methods that are necessary and useful to reach defensible judgments of programs or other entities, and evaluators should selectively apply given methods.

In this book, we advocate a basic definition of evaluation[1] put forth by the Joint Committee on Standards for Educational Evaluation (1981, 1988, 1994, 2003). We present three variations of the definition. First, we present the definition as the Joint Committee stated it. Its definition is general. It calls for evaluations to be systematic and focused on determining an object's value. We subsequently extend the general definition to highlight a range of important, generic criteria for consideration when assessing programs. Finally, we expand the definition further to outline the key steps involved in carrying out a sound evaluation and to stress the importance of obtaining both descriptive and judgmental information. We see the Joint Committee definition as especially appropriate and useful when conversing with lay audiences and focusing their attention on the essence of evaluation. The second rendition can be helpful when discussing with clients the values that should be referenced when evaluating a particular program, institution, or other object. The third version is especially appropriate when planning the required evaluation work.

Joint Committee Definition of Evaluation

The Joint Committee's (1994) definition states that "evaluation is the systematic assessment of the worth or merit of an object" (p. 3). Advantages of this definition are that it is concise, consistent with common dictionary meanings of *evaluation*, and has the imprimatur of the prestigious Joint Committee on Standards for Educational Evaluation. This is the definition to use when discussing evaluation at a general level. Below we unpack the Joint Committee's definition to note and discuss its key concepts.

Evaluation's root term, *value*, denotes that evaluations essentially involve making value judgments. Accordingly, evaluations are not value free. They need to be grounded in some defensible set of guiding principles or ideals and should determine the evaluand's standing against these values. This truism presents evaluators with the need to choose the appropriate values for judging an evaluand. For example, in evaluating U.S. public services, evaluators should be true to, and sometimes specifically invoke, precepts of a democratic society such as freedom, equity, due process of law, and the need for an enlightened population. The Joint Committee's definition partially addresses the need to determine values by denoting that evaluations should assess merit or worth. Scriven (1991) points out the nontrivial differences between these two concepts and their important role in determining an evaluand's value. Table 1.1 summarizes the characteristics of these concepts, with further discussion below.

Merit. Generally one needs to look at the merit or quality of an evaluand. For example, does a state's special program for preparing middle school history teachers succeed in producing teachers who confidently and effectively teach middle school students about pertinent areas and periods of history? In general, does an evaluand do well what it is supposed to do? If so, it has good merit. The criteria of merit reside in the standards of the evaluand's particular discipline or area of service. In the example here, an evaluator might base her or his assessment of merit on published standards of effective teaching and a state's required content for middle school history programs. Graduates of the program would thus be assessed on knowledge of the required history content and effectiveness in teaching the

TABLE 1.1. CHARACTERISTICS OF MERIT AND WORTH.

Merit	Worth
May be assessed on any object of interest	Assessed only on objects that have demonstrated an acceptable level of quality
Assesses intrinsic value of object	Assesses extrinsic value of object
Assesses quality, that is, an object's level of excellence	Assesses an object's quality and value or importance within a given context
Asks, "Does the object do well what it is intended to do?"	Asks, "Is the object of high quality and also something a target group needs?"
References accepted standards of quality for the type of object being evaluated	References accepted standards of quality and data from a pertinent needs assessment
Conclusions rate the object on standards of quality and against competitive objects of the same type	Conclusions note the object's acceptable level of quality and rate it on importance and value to a particular consumer group
Assessments of merit may be the comparison of an object with standards or competitive objects	Assessments of worth may be comparative or noncomparative

content. The subject program would be judged high on merit to the extent that graduates scored high on pertinent measures of content knowledge and teaching competence.

Worth. An evaluand that has high merit might not be worthy. By *worth*, we refer to a program's combination of excellence and service in an area of clear need within a specified context. Suppose the middle school program was a special emergency program developed and funded at a previous time when the state's colleges and universities were graduating too few history teachers to meet the needs of schools in the state. Suppose further that more recently, the state's universities had increased their production of competent middle school history teachers, and many of these new teachers could not find jobs. Arguably, the state would no longer need the special emergency program, because the state's universities were now supplying more qualified middle school history teachers than the schools could employ. In this situation, although the state's special program has good merit, it now has low worth to the state and does not warrant continued investment of the state's scarce resources. We see in this example that the program's worth could be gauged only after an assessment had been made of the needs for the program's graduates. Here we see that assessments of worth have to be keyed to assessments of need within the context of a particular setting and time period.

Needs. By a *need*, we refer to something that is necessary or useful for fulfilling a defensible purpose. We define a *defensible purpose* as a desired end that has been legitimately defined consistent with a guiding philosophy, set of professional standards, institutional mission, mandated curriculum, national constitution, or public referendum, for example. Other terms for defensible purpose are *legitimatized mandates, goals*, and *priorities*. In the middle school illustration, presumably the state curriculum required that all students in the state be well educated in designated areas of history. This "defensible purpose" required further that school districts employ competent history teachers, which fits our definition of an entity that is necessary or useful for fulfilling the defensible purpose of sound history instruction—that is, a need. Since the state found this need was now being fulfilled by state colleges and universities, a proposal to retain this excellent special program would have met the criterion of merit but not the criterion of worth. In reaching judgments of something's worth, evaluators should first identify needs and determine whether they are being met or are unmet in the context of interest.

Needs may be of either the outcome or treatment variety. An *outcome need* is a level of achievement or outcome in a particular area required to fulfill a defensible purpose, such as preparing students for higher education. For example, high school students need to develop competencies in mathematics, science, social studies, and language arts in order to enter top-notch colleges and universities. A *treatment need* is a certain service, service provider, or other helping agent required to meet an outcome need. To continue the example, a school district needs an appropriate curriculum and competent teachers (the treatment needs) to help students attain areas and levels of competence (the outcome needs) required for admission to high-level colleges and universities. One assesses both treatment and outcome needs to determine whether they are being met or unmet and whether they are consonant.

Typically, though, the meeting of outcome needs is conditional on the meeting of treatment needs. For example, a dentist would be unlikely to check patients with no tooth decay for use of fluoridated water or toothpaste. Here the outcome need (for cavity-free teeth) is being met, and it is not necessary to check on the treatment need related to fluoridation.

Needs Assessments. In general, a *needs assessment* is a systematic assessment of the extent to which treatment or outcome needs are being met (Stufflebeam, McCormick, Brinkerhoff, & Nelson, 1985). One might posit that comprehensive high schools should serve the defensible purpose of developing students in all areas of human growth and development: intellectual, psychological, social, physical, moral, vocational, and aesthetic. In an appropriate range of curricular areas, a comparison of students' scores on standardized achievement tests to standards or norms would give an indication of whether students' intellectual outcome needs were being met. However, considering the school's intention to develop students also in physical, aesthetic, psychological, social, moral, and vocational areas, the achievement test scores would be insufficient to assess the full range of questions concerning students' outcome needs. To ensure that needs assessments are valid, they have to be keyed to the full range of intended outcomes. Some needs assessments will have a narrow scope and appropriately be assessed against a quite restricted construction of outcome needs.

Even in a narrowly focused program, it can be important to consider a broad range of outcome and associated treatment needs. For example, school-based instrumental music programs contribute to students' development in such areas as social relations, psychological well-being, discipline, and employment. In general, an assessment of a program's worth should gauge examinations of program quality and outcomes against the assessed outcome and treatment needs of beneficiaries. Table 1.2 offers a convenient summary of key concepts related to needs assessment.

TABLE 1.2. CONCEPTS RELATED TO NEEDS ASSESSMENT.

Concept	Definition	Example
Defensible purpose	A desired end that has been legitimated	Students' development of basic academic skills
Need	Something that is necessary or useful for fulfilling a defensible purpose	Competent, effective instruction in the basic skill areas
Outcome need	An achievement or outcome required to meet a defensible purpose	Students' demonstration of proficiency in specified areas, such as twelfth-grade math, science, and language arts
Treatment need	A certain service, competent service provider, or other helping agent	Competent instructors in twelfth-grade courses in math, science, and language arts
Needs assessment	A systematic assessment of the extent to which treatment or outcome needs are being met	Examination of students' scores on national tests and evaluation of the involved teachers

Evaluations Should Be Systematic. Beyond its focus on merit and worth, the Joint Committee's definition of evaluation requires evaluations to be *systematic*. We acknowledge that the broad meaning of *evaluation* encompasses haphazard or unsystematic evaluations as well as carefully conducted evaluations. In this book, we are advocating for and discussing the latter. Indeed, this book is a countermeasure to careless inquiry processes that masquerade as evaluations and often lead to biased or otherwise erroneous interpretations of something's value. Instead, we seek the kind of evaluation that is conducted with great care—not only in collecting information of high quality, but also in clarifying and providing a defensible rationale for the value perspectives used to interpret the findings and reach judgments and in communicating evaluation findings to the client and other audiences.

An Extended, Values-Oriented Definition of Evaluation

While the Joint Committee's definition of evaluation has the positive features just noted, it omits mention of other key generic values. We thus extend the definition of evaluation as follows: evaluation is the systematic assessment of an object's merit, worth, probity, feasibility, safety, significance, and/or equity. We see the values referenced in this definition as particularly important in a free and democratic society, but also acknowledge that we might have included additional values. Of course, evaluators have to engage in a good deal of values clarification as they plan their studies. Those included in our extended definition of evaluation are a good set to consider, but evaluators and their clients often should invoke additional values that pertain to the contexts of particular studies and interests of stakeholders. Nonetheless, many sound and defensible evaluations will be strongly influenced by some or all of the five values we have added to merit and worth. Below we discuss each of the values noted in the extended definition of evaluation.

Probity. During the writing of this book, there was a rash of public scandals in which major U.S.-based corporations defrauded shareholders and others out of billions of dollars. Moreover, at least one major audit firm that contracted to evaluate a corporation's financial conditions and lawful operations was found to have complicity in that corporation's fraud. This audit firm compromised its independence and credibility. Not only did it fail to report on the probity of the corporation's accounting practices, it also was alleged to have distorted and covered up information to hide the company's unethical, unlawful practices. Here we see that the company cheated its shareholders, workers, and ultimately the public, and that the audit company was charged with aiding and abetting the fraud. On another front, there have been despicable scandals across the globe in which clergy and teachers were found to be pedophiles.

Clearly, the public interest requires that evaluations address considerations of probity: assessments of honesty, integrity, and ethical behavior. Unless there is no prospect for fraud or other illicit behavior, evaluations should check on a program's uncompromising adherence to moral standards. However, when probity breaches are found, there is cause to err on the side of too much consideration of probity in evaluations of programs and institutions. To the extent required to form a defense against unethical behavior, probity considerations should be part and parcel of many evaluations of programs and of evaluations of evaluations.

Feasibility. While a service might be of high quality, directed to an area of high need, and unimpeachable on ethical grounds, it still could fail the criterion of feasibility. For example, it might consume more resources than required or cause no end of political turmoil. If either is the case, the service should at least be modified in these areas to make it more feasible. Obviously a good evaluation of the service should speak to this issue and, where appropriate, provide direction for making the service easy to apply, efficient in the use of time and resources, and politically viable. Evaluation of a program's feasibility sometimes justifies a cancellation decision. This argument in favor of assessing feasibility seems applicable to all programs.

Safety. Many evaluations focus squarely on the issue of safety. Obvious cases are evaluations of new pharmaceutical products, laboratory equipment, meat and other food products, automobiles, stepladders, electrical equipment, and insecticides. Consumers are at risk to the extent that such commodities are manufactured and sold without rigorous safety checks and appropriate cautions. Moreover, many programs also require evaluations that examine the safety of facilities, equipment, activity regimens, crowd control, and others. To see the importance of safety evaluations in programs, one only need recall head injuries in football, lost teeth in ice hockey, heat strokes in a variety of outdoor sports, fires and explosions in school laboratories, fires resulting in many deaths due to improper fire escape exits and or fire drills, and fatalities due to faulty school buses or incompetent bus drivers. The criterion of safety applies to evaluations in all fields and to evaluations of programs as well as products.

Significance. Another criterion that sometimes comes into play is a program's *significance:* its potential influence, importance, and visibility. Many programs are of only local or short-term interest. When they have far-reaching implications, evaluators should look at and make judgments about the significance of their mission, structure, and outcomes. Such an assessment can be especially important in deciding whether and how far to disseminate lessons learned and helping interested parties make sound decisions concerning adopting and adapting a program or parts of a program. Evaluators should often consider the possibility that a program under study has far-reaching implications outside the local arena and possibly should be evaluated for its significance over time and in other settings.

Equity. The last generic evaluative criterion to be mentioned here is *equity*, which is predominantly tied to democratic societies. It argues for equal opportunities for all people and emphasizes freedom for all. In the United States, an educational evaluation would be incomplete if it did not assess whether a public educational service is provided for, and made available to, public school students from all sectors of the society. This concept of equity is complex. It is not enough to say that public education services may be sought and used by all people. As Kellaghan (1982) has argued, when educational equality truly exists, there will be seven indications of equity:

1. A society's public educational services will be provided for all people.
2. People from all segments of the society will have equal access to the services.
3. There will be close to equal participation by all groups in the use of the services.
4. Levels of attainment, for example, years in the education system, will be substantially the same for different groups.
5. Levels of proficiency in achieving all of the objectives will be equivalent for different groups.
6. Levels of aspiration for life pursuits will be similar across societal groups.
7. The education system will make similar impacts on improving the welfare of all societal groups in their community environments.

Operationalizing Our Definition of Evaluation

The extended definition of evaluation has provided an expanded look at key generic criteria for evaluating programs. From the discussion, we can see that the Joint Committee's definition of evaluation and our adaptation focused on generic evaluative criteria are deceptive in their apparent simplicity. When one takes seriously the root term *value*, then inevitably one must consider value perspectives of individuals, groups, and organizations, as well as information. The combining of these in efforts to reach determinations of the value of something cannot be ignored. To serve the needs of clients and other interested persons, the supplied information should reflect the full range of appropriate values.

We now expand the definition further to outline the main tasks in any program evaluation and denote the types of information to be collected. Our operational definition of evaluation states that evaluation is the systematic process of delineating, obtaining, reporting, and applying descriptive and judgmental information about some object's merit, worth, probity, feasibility, safety, significance, and/or equity. One added element in this definition concerns the generic steps in conducting an evaluation. The other new element is that evaluations should produce both descriptive and judgmental information.

It is important to note that the work of evaluation includes both interface and technical steps. In the former, evaluators communicate with clients and other stakeholders in the interest of planning relevant evaluations; conveying clear, timely findings; and aiding and abetting use of the findings. The technical steps are concerned with the research aspects of an evaluation: the collection, organization, analysis, and synthesis of information. Evaluators need to be competent in both the interface and technical aspects of evaluation. This is best accomplished through formal courses and experiences in planning, conducting, and reporting a wide range of evaluations. We have characterized the work of evaluation in four steps: delineating, obtaining, reporting, and applying. Part Four of this book addresses these process steps in detail. We end by discussing the final major feature of our operational definition of evaluation, which concerns the nature of information included in evaluations.

Delineating. The delineating step entails the evaluator's interacting with the client and other program stakeholders. The aim here is to focus the evaluation on key questions, identify key audiences, clarify pertinent values and criteria, determine information requirements, project needed analyses, construct an evaluation budget, and effect contractual agreements to govern the evaluation work. Basically, the delineating step encompasses effective, two-way communication involving evaluator, client, and other interested parties and culminates in negotiated terms for the evaluation. Particular areas of needed expertise include audience analysis, listening, the ability to develop rapport, interviewing, content analysis, values clarification, conceptualization, proposal development, negotiating, contracting, and budgeting. The results of this step should set the stage for the ensuing data collection work. In fact, delineating activities extend throughout the evaluation in response to changing circumstances in the program, identifying new audiences, continuing interaction with stakeholders, and emerging needs for information. Moreover, a delineation process that is carried out thoroughly and professionally establishes a basis for essential trust and rapport between an evaluator and client group.

Obtaining. The obtaining step encompasses all of the work involved in collecting, correcting, organizing, analyzing, and synthesizing information. Key areas of required expertise are research design, sampling, measurement, interviewing, observation, site visits, archival studies, case studies, focus groups, photography, database development and management, statistics, content analysis, cost analysis, policy analysis, synthesis, and computer technology. Program evaluators need expertise in these and related technical areas in order to provide clients with sound, meaningful, and creditable information. Results of the obtaining work are grist for preparing and presenting oral and printed evaluation reports.

Reporting. In the reporting step, the evaluator provides feedback to the client and other audiences. Typically such work includes preparing and delivering interim oral and printed reports, multimedia presentations, press releases, printed final reports, and executive summaries. The point of all such reporting activities is to communicate effectively and accurately the evaluation's findings in a timely manner to interested and right-to-know audiences and to foster effective uses of evaluation findings. Reporting activities occur throughout and after completion of an evaluation. Particular areas of needed expertise are clear writing, the ability to format reports, competent editing, information technology, effective oral communication, and dissemination skills. Effective reporting sets the stage for applying the evaluation findings.

Applying. The applying step is under the control of clients and other users of the evaluation. Nevertheless, the evaluator should at least offer to assist in the application of findings. Such assistance might be follow-up workshops, critique of the client group's plans to apply findings, or responses to questions from the client or other users. We have found that this kind of assistance from evaluators is highly regarded by clients. It is seen as a continuation of the evaluation itself provided that the initiative comes from the client after the evaluator offers this "rounding-off" service. Assisting in the sound use of evaluation findings requires forethought and funding. Therefore, in starting an evaluation, the evaluator and client should consider the possibility of the evaluator's involvement in the applying stage and should plan, budget, and contract for such follow-up assistance as appropriate. To be effective in supporting the application of evaluation findings, evaluators need to be knowledgeable of principles and procedures of effective change and research on utilization of evaluation (see Alkin, Daillak, & White, 1979; Patton, 1997). Also, they need skills of communication, consulting, group process, and counseling.

Descriptive and Judgmental Information. The final major feature of our operational definition of evaluation concerns the nature of information included in evaluations. From experience, we know that sound, useful evaluations are grounded in descriptive and judgmental information. In general, audiences for evaluation reports want to know what program was evaluated and how good it is.

This requires the evaluator to collect and report both descriptive and judgmental information.

Descriptive Information. A final evaluation report should describe the program's goals, plans, operations, and outcomes objectively. As much as possible, the descriptive information should be kept separate from judgments of the program. Relatively pure, dispassionate descriptions of a program are needed to help evaluation audiences know such matters as what the evaluated program was like, how it was staffed and financed, how it operated, how much time was required for implementation, how much it cost, and what would be required to replicate it. The evaluator also has a vested interest in getting a clear view of the program apart from how observers judged it. This is especially important when interpreting a program's outcomes and judging its success. For example, in judging the effects of a community's immunization program on childhood diseases, the evaluator needs to determine and report the extent to which the pertinent inoculations were administered to all the targeted children as planned. If not, the deficient outcome more likely is due to poor program implementation than defects in the program plan.

Judgmental Information. Beyond the collection of descriptive information, it is equally important to gather, assess, and summarize judgments of the program. According to the above definition of evaluation, evaluations inevitably involve valuing, that is, judgment. Judgment-oriented feedback can be a vital, positive force when it is integral to development, directed to identifying strengths as well as weaknesses, and focused on improving the evaluand. Appropriate sources of judgments include program beneficiaries, program staff, pertinent experts, and, of course, the evaluator, among others.

How Good Is Good Enough? How Bad Is Intolerable? How Are These Questions Addressed?

Many evaluations carry a need to draw a definitive conclusion or make a definite decision on quality, safety, or some other variable. For example, funding organizations regularly have to decide which projects to fund, based on their relative quality and importance compared with other possible uses of available funds. For a project already funded, the organization often needs to determine after a funding cycle whether the project is sufficiently good and important to continue or increase its funds. In trials, a court has to decide whether the accused is guilty or not guilty. In determinations of how to adjudicate drunk-driving charges, state or other government agencies set decision rules concerning the level of acceptable alcohol in a driver's blood. These examples are not just abstractions. They reflect true, frequent circumstances in society when evaluations have to be definitive and decisive.

The problem of how to reach a just, defensible, clear-cut decision never has an easy solution. In a sense, all protocols for such precise evaluative determinations are arbitrary, but they are not necessarily capricious. While many decision rules are set carefully in the light of relevant research and experience, the rules are human constructions, and their precise requirements arguably could vary. The arbitrariness of cut scores is also apparent in different alpha and beta levels that investigators invoke for determining statistical significance and statistical power. Typically, the alpha level is set, by convention, at .05 or .01, but might as easily be set at .06 or .02. (See Chapter Twenty-Five for a discussion of statistical significance.) In spite of the difficulties in setting and defending criterion levels, societal groups have devised workable procedures that more or less are reasonable and defensible for drawing definitive evaluative conclusions and making associated decisions. These procedures include applying courts' rules of evidence and having juries of peers vote on a defendant's guilt or innocence, setting levels for determining statistical significance and statistical power, using fingerprints and DNA testing to determine identity, rating institutions or consumer products, ranking funding proposals or job applicants, employing cut scores on students' achievement test scores, polling constituents, grading school homework assignments, contrasting students' tested performance to national norms, appropriating and allocating available funds across competing services, and charging an authority figure or engaging an expert panel to decide on a project's future. Although none of these procedures is beyond challenge, as a group they have addressed society's need for workable, decision-making tools.

Some of these procedures have advance setting of cut scores, standards, or decision rules in common. For example, in the United States, it is known in advance that all twelve members of a jury must vote guilty for a defendant in a criminal trial to be found guilty beyond a reasonable doubt. Advance determinations of criteria and acceptable levels are also part and parcel of evaluations of new drugs; drunk-driving convictions; and certification of safe levels in water, air quality, food products, and bicycle helmets, for example.

When it is feasible and appropriate to set standards, criterion levels, or decision rules in advance, a general process can be followed to reach precise evaluative conclusions. The steps would be approximately as follows: (1) define the evaluand and its boundaries; (2) determine the key evaluation questions; (3) identify and define crucial criteria of goodness or acceptability; (4) determine as much as possible the rules for answering the key evaluation questions such as cut scores and decision rubrics; (5) describe the evaluand's context, structure, operations, and outcomes; (6) take appropriate measurements related to the evaluative criteria; (7) thoughtfully examine and analyze the obtained measures and descriptive information; (8) follow a systematic, transparent process to reach the needed evaluative conclusions; (9) subject the total evaluation to an independent assessment; and (10) confirm or modify the evaluative conclusions.

Although this process is intended to provide rationality, rigor, fairness, and transparency in reaching evaluative conclusions, it rarely is applicable to most of the program evaluations treated in this book. This is so because often one cannot precisely define beforehand the appropriate standards, evaluative criteria, and defensible levels of soundness for each one and for all as a group. So how do evaluators function when they have to make up their plans, identify criteria, and interpret outcomes without benefit of advance decisions on these matters? There is no single answer to this question. More often than not, criteria and decision rules have to be determined along the way. We suggest that it is often best to address the issues in defining criteria through an ongoing, interactive approach to evaluation design, analysis, and interpretation.

What Are Performance Standards?
How Should They Be Applied?

Often evaluation is characterized as comparing a performance to a standard. This concept is perhaps clearest in the judging of livestock, cats, and dogs, where associations of breeders publish the standards for particular breeds. Similarly, the sports of diving, gymnastics, and figure skating have published standards against which to judge performances by athletes. However, observers often view with disdain the lack of transparency, reliability, and validity of rendered judgments. The problems are even more acute in most standards-based program evaluations where there are no juried, published standards for particular classes of programs. In such cases, evaluators and clients often have to concoct and agree on standards by which to judge particular programs.

Sometimes the participants define behavioral objectives that, among other things, specify cut scores for distinguishing good performance from poor performance on each variable of interest. Many problems follow from this practice. The objectives are arbitrary and often unrealistic. They may not reflect the assessed needs of the intended beneficiaries. They may be more appropriate for average performers than very high or low performers. For example, beneficiaries who already far exceed the cut score standard may find a disincentive for improvement in the program's low level of expectation. At the other end of the distribution, beneficiaries who are far below the standard may believe it is futile to reach the cut score standard, and consequently they give up. Also, cut score standards have a tendency to narrow a program's focus; lock it in to predetermined objectives; and inhibit it from responding over time to emergent needs, developments, and insights.

An alternative to this narrow, preordinate approach to standards-based evaluation is to view a program standard as a requirement for continuing improvement. Deming (see Walton, 1986) sold this idea to Japanese automobile manufacturers in the 1970s and helped spawn an amazing trend of continuing improvement in the quality of automobiles that eventually spread throughout the world. Deming's notion was not to attain and continue to achieve at any given level of quality but continually to strive for better and better quality. In the education field, Sanders and Horn (1994) argued similarly that the standard for educational programs should be continued growth and improvement for every student, whatever her or his prior level of achievement. It makes no sense to close the gap between high and low achievers, since sound education that helps all students reach their fullest potential will inevitably widen the achievement gap. This claim can be rejected only if one also rejects the claim that humans vary in abilities and capacities. To do the latter would require discarding society's huge store of evidence from research on individual differences.

Why Is It Appropriate to Consider Multiple Values?

Many evaluations face the challenge of multiple value perspectives. This is part and parcel of the world's increasingly pluralistic societies. Addressing competing and often conflicting values of different members of an evaluation audience is a necessary and difficult task in evaluations. We would argue that it is the shared and differential needs of the clients of a given service that should be ascertained as a basis for determining what information to collect and what standards to invoke in determining the worth of a service.

Sometimes an evaluator should address the value conflict issue by separately interpreting process and outcome information against each main set of values or priorities of different segments of the stakeholder population. In other cases, the evaluator might serve better by seeking out and assessing multiple programs or services while considering that each might better address one set of values than another set.

In planning evaluations, evaluators should deal directly with the important matter of choosing and applying pertinent values. They should determine what sets of values will be referenced in interpreting findings and sometimes in searching for and analyzing program options. Such determinations require the evaluator to work within her or his basic philosophical convictions, that is, to act with integrity. Evaluators should also take into account a program's mission and the pertinent values, needs, and priorities of the program's leaders as well as the beneficiaries and other stakeholder groups. In issuing evaluative conclusions or putting forward assessments of alternative programs, evaluators should report the employed values and explain why they were chosen.

Addressing conflicting values is not an easy task for evaluators, if for no other reason than they are not the sole arbiters of one set of values over another. Our advice is, first, never to take the side of one group rather than another and, second, to take a dispassionate view of the needs of differing value groups and work toward the formulation of a sound set of guiding values that reflects integrity and the interests of the different parties to the evaluation.

Should Evaluations Be Comparative, Noncomparative, or Both?

Evaluations may focus on a single product or service or compare it with alternatives. Depending on the circumstances, an evaluation legitimately may be comparative or noncomparative. A main consideration is the nature of the audience and what evaluative information it needs. If the audience is composed of consumers who need to choose a product or service, the evaluation should be comparative and help consumers learn what alternatives are available and how they compare on critical criteria. If the audience includes developers or consumers who are already committed to the development or use of a given program, the evaluation might focus intensively on the workings of the program and provide direction for improving it. Periodically, however, even if a group is firmly devoted to a certain service or product, it might get a better version from the provider of this service or find a better alternative by opening consideration to other providers.

In general, we think that evaluations should be comparative before one purchases a product or service or starts a program, noncomparative during program development or use of a service, and periodically comparative after development or sustained use in order to open the way for improvements or radical alternatives. Whether an evaluation should be comparative depends on the intended uses of the evaluation.

How Should Evaluations Be Used?

We see four main uses of evaluations: improvement, accountability, dissemination, and enlightenment.

Formative Evaluations for Improvement

The first use is to provide information for developing a service, ensuring its quality, or improving it. Evaluations to serve this use typically are labeled *formative evaluations*. Basically, they provide feedback for improvement. They are prospective and proactive. They are conducted during development of a program or its ongoing operation. Formative evaluations offer guidance to those who are responsible for ensuring and improving the program's quality and, in doing so, should pay close attention to the nature and needs of the consumers. Formative evaluations assess and assist with the formulation of goals and priorities, provide direction for planning by assessing alternative courses of action and draft plans, and guide program management by assessing implementation of plans and interim results. Information from all such formative evaluations is directed to improving operations, especially those that are in the process of development. In the main, formative evaluations serve quality assurance purposes. In formative evaluations, the evaluator should interact closely with program staff and provide guidance for decision making. The evaluation plan needs to be flexible and responsive. When the main aim is to improve an existing program, the evaluation should resemble a case study more than a comparative experiment. In fact, locked-in, controlled experiments, requiring random assignment of program participants to alternative program treatments and treatments to be kept stable and unchanging, prevent the evaluator from giving to program personnel the ongoing feedback for improvement that is the essence of formative evaluations.

Summative Evaluations for Accountability

The second main use of evaluation is to produce accountability or summative reports. These are retrospective assessments of completed projects, established programs, or finished products. Summative evaluations typically occur following development of a product, completion of a program, and end of a service cycle. They draw together and supplement previously collected information and provide an overall judgment of the evaluand's value. Summative evaluations are useful in determining accountability for successes and failures, informing consumers about the quality and safety of products and services, and helping interested parties increase their understanding of the assessed phenomena. Summative evaluation reports are not aimed primarily at the development staff but at the sponsors and consumers. The reports should convey a cumulative record of what was done and accomplished and an assessment of the evaluand's cost-effectiveness. Information derived from in-depth case studies and field tests is of interest to the audience in such situations. Field tests can make productive use of comparative experiments. In the medical field, for example, results from double-blind studies comparing a newly developed treatment or other evaluand to a placebo or another competitive treatment can help potential users decide whether to use the new contribution. Whereas in general we argue against the use of experimental design in formative evaluations, it can be useful in some summative evaluations. This is especially the case in evaluations designed to undergird dissemination of a final product, service, program, or other evaluand. But even then, a comparative experiment is only a part of a sound summative evaluation. The full range of dimensions involved in summative evaluations is seen in Michael Scriven's Key Evaluation Checklist (accessible at www.wmich.edu.evalctr and outlined in Chapter Sixteen).

Table 1.3 summarizes main features of formative evaluation and summative evaluation.

Relationship Between Formative and Summative Evaluations

Both formative and summative evaluations are needed in the development of a product or service or, in the case of personnel, help in developing potential and gauging the extent to which required criteria for certification, tenure, promotion, and the like are met. Too often, summative evaluation is carried out only for judging programs or personnel. This restricts development processes and may lead to inadequate or even incorrect conclusions. Subjecting a trainee nurse to an accountability assessment while ignoring the obvious advantages of fostering improvement through formative methodologies is foolish. Similarly, when a wine-sealing machine is being built, the lack of formative information covering cost, efficiency, faults, and potential marketing would be disastrous to the manufacturers. Evaluations delayed until the near completion of a training or probationary period or a project's development may be too late to promote and assist successful outcomes.

The relative emphasis of formative and summative evaluations will change according to the nature and circumstances of the evaluand. In general, formative evaluation will be dominant in the early stages of a program and less so as the program matures. Summative evaluation will take over as the program concludes and certainly after it is completed. However, all concerned in these evaluations should have a clear understanding of when and in what circumstances formative evaluation may give way to summative evaluation. The conclusion should not be drawn, nonetheless, that all evaluations fall into one or both categories. Many of the evaluation approaches depicted later in this book can be used for formative or summative purposes or both.

Robert Stake (1969) made an interesting observation, apropos the relationship between formative and summative evaluations, that formative evaluations are

TABLE 1.3. FORMATIVE EVALUATION AND SUMMATIVE EVALUATION.

Descriptors	Formative Evaluation	Summative Evaluation
Purpose	Quality assurance; improvement	Provide an overall judgment of the evaluand
Use	Guidance for decision making	Determining accountability for successes and failures; promoting understanding of assessed phenomena
Functions	Provides feedback for improvement	Informs consumers about an evaluand's value, for example, its quality, cost, utility, and safety
Orientation	Prospective and proactive	Retrospective and retroactive
When conducted	During development or ongoing operations	After completion of development
Particular types of service	Assists goal setting, planning, and management	Assists consumers in making wise decisions
Foci	Goals, alternative courses of action, plans, implementation of plans, interim results	Completed projects, established programs, or finished products; ultimate outcomes
Variables	All aspects of an evolving, developing program	Comprehensive range of dimensions concerned with merit, worth, probity, safety, equity, and significance
Audience	Managers, staff; connected closely to insiders	Sponsors, consumers, and other interested stakeholders; projected especially to outsiders
Evaluation plans	Flexible, emergent, responsive, interactive	Relatively fixed, not emergent or evolving
Typical methods	Case studies, observation, interviews, not controlled experiments	Wide range of methods including case studies, controlled experiments, and checklists
Reports	Periodic, often relatively informal, responsive to client and staff requests	Cumulative record and assessment of what was done and accomplished; contrast of evaluand with critical competitors; cost-effectiveness analysis
Relationship between formative and summative evaluation	Often forms the basis for summative evaluations	Compiles and supplements previously collected formative evaluation information

closely connected to "insiders," that is, program developers, while summative evaluations are of more interest to "outsiders," that is, the potential users of the developing (or developed) programs. This does not assume that formative evaluations are necessarily undertaken by internal personnel or that summative evaluations are always conducted externally. A wide array of factors such as time lines, finance, and the competency of personnel to undertake evaluations will often determine whether evaluations, either formative or summative, are internal or external. The dominant question to be answered is whether the process and findings are credible.

Finally, formative evaluations often form the basis for summative evaluations. If this is to occur, those who commission the studies and the evaluators must make it clear to all involved that this will occur. It should also be recognized that on occasions, the merit or worth of a formative evaluation may be strengthened by the intervention of summative evaluations (usually carried out by external personnel) at critical points of a program's development. Such procedures require sound professional collaboration, which is a hallmark of good evaluation practice. (For other dimensions of this topic, see the section entitled "Why Are Internal Evaluation Mechanisms Needed?" later in this chapter.)

Evaluations to Assist Dissemination

The third use of evaluations is to help developers disseminate proven practices or products and help consumers make wise adoption or purchasing decisions. Here the evaluator must critically compare the service or product with competitors. Perhaps the best example of evaluations aimed at serving dissemination and informing adoption decisions are those found in *Consumer Reports*. Each issue of this well-known monthly magazine provides independent evaluations of alternatives for consumer products and services: alternative automobiles, insurance policies, mortgages, breakfast cereals, chain saws, refrigerators, restaurant chains, supermarket chains, hotel chains, and house paints, to name just a few. The unique feature of evaluations for dissemination is their focus on questions of practical interest to consumers. In Part Two, we describe Scriven's consumer-oriented evaluation approach. Note that many sound consumer-oriented evaluations do not employ experimental designs; however, under the right circumstances, experiments can be a useful means to meeting some of the information needs of consumers.

Evaluations to Foster Enlightenment

The fourth use of evaluations is to foster enlightenment, that is, new understandings arising from revelations. Basically, evaluation and research are different enterprises. The former attempts to consider all criteria that apply in determining value, while the latter may be restricted to the study of selected variables that are of interest in theory development or policy formation. Evaluations typically involve subjective approaches and are not as tightly controlled and subject to manipulation as is the typical research investigation. However, efforts over a period of time to evaluate a program or set of similar programs may produce information of use in evolving and testing theory. Certainly the results of evaluations often should and do lead to focused, applied research efforts and sometimes to development of institutional or social policies. Hence, we believe that in planning studies, evaluators should consider how their findings might contribute to new insights in matters of interest to theorists and policymakers. With some forethought, careful planning, and appropriate budgeting, evaluations may serve not only to guide operating programs, sum up their contributions, and disseminate effective products and services, but also to address particular research, theory, or policy questions.

Why Is It Important to Distinguish Between Informal Evaluation and Formal Evaluation?

To this point, it should be clear that program evaluation is a demanding field of practice. At the same time, everybody evaluates essentially all the time, whether making choices about the trivial or the critical. We believe it is important to distinguish formal evaluation from informal evaluation. In fact, the distinction is at the root of the need for and emergence of the evaluation profession. Just as most individuals employ home remedies and over-the-counter medications in addressing their minor ailments, almost everybody recognizes that some health issues require diagnosis and treatment by competent physicians in accordance with the standards of the medical profession. Similarly, many evaluations can and must be conducted on an informal basis, while others require a rigorous, systematic approach, including an independent perspective.

Informal Evaluations

Everybody performs informal evaluation whenever judging and making decisions about the things observed, thought about, interacted with, or being considered for purchase. For example, we do this when purchasing food, cars, tools, refrigerators, computers, computer programs, over-the-counter medications, stocks, correspondence courses, insurance policies, or termite protection services. Depending on the nature of the evaluand, one might look for options, read labels, consult friends who have pertinent experience, form a committee or task group to deliberate on the evaluative questions of interest, call the Better Business Bureau, consult other consumer information sources, or try out something before deciding to keep it. These are all good and appropriate evaluative moves and fit within our general concept of informal evaluation. However, the conduct of informal evaluations is prone to haphazard data collection, crediting and using propaganda and other forms of misinformation, errors of judgment, strong influence by salespersons, acting on old preferences or prejudices, relying on out-of-date information, or making expedient choices. In many cases, the steps in an informal evaluation are unsystematic, lacking in rigor, and based on biased perspectives. Thus, informal evaluations typically offer a weak basis for convincing decision makers and others of the validity of evaluation findings and appropriateness of ensuing conclusions and recommendations. We can get by with weak informal evaluations when only we have to pay the price and abide by the consequences. Better, more formal evaluations are called for when there is a need to inform critically important decisions, especially ones that will affect many people, require substantial expenditures, or pose substantial risk.

Formal Evaluations

In accordance with the definition of *evaluation* given earlier, formal evaluations should be systematic and rigorous. By systematic, we refer to evaluations that are relevant, designed and executed to control bias, kept consistent with appropriate professional standards, and otherwise made useful and defensible. Especially, we define formal evaluations as ones that are held up to scrutiny against appropriate standards of the evaluation profession. The kind of formal evaluation we are promoting requires systematic effort by one or more persons who have the requisite evaluation competencies. We do not disparage the informal evaluations that are part and parcel of everybody's daily life, any more than we would advise people not to make prudent use of home remedies and over-the-counter medications. Moreover, not all formal evaluations need to be conducted by outside evaluation experts. What is required is that those conducting the evaluation meet the standards of the evaluation field. In Chapter Three we summarize professionally developed guiding principles for evaluators, professional standards for program evaluations, and the 2003 U.S. Government Auditing Standards. Building on these principles and standards, this book is designed to help students and practicing evaluators attain the perspectives and basic level of proficiency required to implement defensible formal evaluations.

How Do Service Providers and Their Organizations Meet Requirements for Public Accountability?

We cannot stress too much that society is dependent on sound evaluations to obtain safe, high-quality goods and services from a wide range of professionals and other service providers. Any operatives should deliver services that are of high quality, up-to-date, safe, efficient, fairly priced, honest, and, in general, in the public interest. In order to meet accountability requirements, each profession, public service area, and society should regularly subject services to formal evaluations. Some of the evaluation work is appropriately directed at regulation and protection of the public interest. It should be conducted by independent bodies, including government agencies, accrediting boards, and external evaluators. Equally important are the formative and summative evaluations of services that professionals and other service providers and their organizations themselves conduct or commission. These internal or self-evaluations are an important aid to continually scrutinizing and improving services and also supplying data needed by the independent or external evaluators.

Accreditation

A wide range of accrediting organizations periodically assess the performance of member organizations against formally established standards. Typical accrediting evaluations are grounded in clear accreditation criteria and guidelines for self-assessments. The institution or program to be evaluated proceeds by conducting a lengthy process of self-assessment, typically lasting at least a year. A team of external evaluators, appointed by the accrediting organization, then reviews the self-report, conducts a site visit, and writes an independent evaluation report. The accrediting organization subsequently uses the report to make decisions on whether and to what extent the subject institution or program is to be accredited and submits its report to the institution or program. Typically accreditation is awarded for a finite period, such as five years. The accrediting body then updates its publicly available list of accredited institutions or programs. In some cases, provisional accreditation is provided pending corrective actions by the assessed institution or program. A prime accreditation criterion often is that the subject institution or program should operate and use findings from an internal evaluation mechanism.

Why Are Internal Evaluation Mechanisms Needed?

Some large school districts, medical schools, foundations, and government agencies maintain well-funded and adequately staffed evaluation offices, and their evaluators have succeeded in helping their institutions be accountable to constituents, obtain guidance for planning and administering their services, win grants and contracts, and meet requirements of accrediting organizations or other oversight bodies. In order to keep their services up to date and ensure that they are effectively and safely meeting their clients' needs, service institutions and programs should continually obtain pertinent evaluative feedback. This process includes studying the outcome and treatment needs of their clients; evaluating relevant approaches that are being proposed or used elsewhere; evaluating the performance of personnel; closely monitoring and assessing the delivery of services; assessing immediate and long-term outcomes; and searching for ways to make the services more efficient, effective, and safe. Conducting such internal evaluations is a challenging task. The credibility of internal evaluation is enhanced when it is subjected periodically to metaevaluation, in which an independent evaluator evaluates and reports publicly on the quality of internal evaluation work. Such independent metaevaluation also provides direction for strengthening the internal evaluation services. Optimally, metaevaluations are both formative and summative.

Why Is Evaluation a Personal as Well as a Corporate Responsibility?

Even if an institution has a strong evaluation unit, every professional in the institution needs further evaluation. There is no escaping the fact that evaluation is a personal as well as an institutional responsibility. Offices of evaluation and accrediting organizations can help meet an institution's major responsibilities for evaluation and accountability. Offices of evaluation can also provide in-service training and technical support in evaluation to the institution's staff. However, all professionals bear responsibility for formally evaluating their own performance. It is in their interest to do so, because evaluation is an essential means for finding out and acting on what is going right and wrong. Moreover, conducting and acting on sound evaluation is part and parcel of what it means to be a professional: a member of an established profession who continually works to deliver better service. We hope this book will both inspire and assist individual professionals and other service providers as well as evaluation students and specialists to meet their needs for developing competence in and effectively carrying out systematic evaluations.

What Are the Methods of Formal Evaluations?

One aspect that distinguishes formal evaluation from informal evaluation is the area of methodology. When we move our consideration away from evaluations that involve quick, intuitive judgments toward those that entail rigorously gathered findings and effective communications, we must necessarily deal with the complex areas of epistemology, rules of evidence, information sciences, research design, measurement, statistics, communication, and some others. Many principles, tools, and strategies within these areas have pertinence to systematic evaluation. The well-prepared evaluator will have a good command of concepts and techniques in all these areas and will keep informed about potentially useful technological developments. Evaluators who would exert leadership and help advance their profession should contribute to the critique of existing methods and the development of new ones.

Over the years, many evaluators have chosen, even championed, the exclusive use of a few techniques. Some have equated evaluation with their favorite methods—for example, experimental design, standardized testing, questionnaires, or site visits. Other leaders have sharply attacked narrow views of which methods are appropriate and argued for a broader, more eclectic approach, which is where we find ourselves. A key point in the latter position is that use of multiple methods and perspectives enhances the dependability of inferences and conclusions and causes appropriate levels of circumspection.

We believe that evaluators should know about a wide range of pertinent techniques and how well they apply in different evaluative contexts. Then in each evaluative situation, they can assess which techniques are potentially applicable and which most likely would work best and in combination to serve the particular purposes of the given evaluation. Among the technical areas in which we think the professional evaluator should be proficient are proposal writing, research design, budgeting, contracting, scheduling, system analysis, logic models, theorizing, interviewing, focus groups, survey research, case study, content analysis, observation, checklists, goal-free evaluation, advocacy teams, test construction, rating scales, database development and management, statistical analysis, cost analysis, technical writing, and project administration.

What Is the Evaluation Profession, and How Strong Is It?

The formal profession of evaluation emerged only during the last third of the twentieth century. In so short a time period, this young profession has made remarkable progress but still has far to go. The evaluation field now has national and state professional societies of evaluators; annual conventions; a substantial literature, including professional journals and a wide range of theoretical and technical books; specialized Web sites; master's and doctoral programs; institutes and workshops on specialized evaluation topics; client organizations that fund a wide range of evaluations; evaluation companies; guiding principles for evaluators; and standards for program, personnel, and student evaluations. These are substantial gains compared with the field's status in 1964, when it had none of the above.

However, the evaluation field is still immature when compared with established professions, such as medicine, law, engineering, and accounting, and other service areas, such as those of master plumbers, licensed electricians, prosthetists, and dental hygienists. Especially, the evaluation field lacks some of the hallmarks of a mature profession. For example, membership in the American Evaluation Association is open to anyone regardless of training and expertise in evaluation. Furthermore, the field has no mechanisms for certifying competent evaluators. Despite the field's substantial progress, clients of evaluation have no formal means of determining which self-proclaimed evaluators have been certified as competent. And despite institutional, business, and other evaluations being widely recognized as essential to the health of any organization, acceptance of tertiary training to gain qualifications as an evaluator is lagging worldwide.

What Are the Main Historical Milestones in the Development of the Evaluation Field?

The evaluation field evidences only modest efforts to systematically record and analyze its history. Any profession, in order to serve the needs of its clients, must evolve in response to changing societal needs and in consideration of theoretical and technical advancements. Unless the members of a profession develop and maintain a historical perspective on their work, they are likely to persevere in using a stagnant conception of their role, not to remember valuable lessons of the past, not to stimulate and contribute to innovation in their field, and all too frequently to return to deficient methods of the past. It has been said often that those who do not learn from their history are doomed to repeat it.

In this section, we focus on the history of the program evaluation field, especially as evaluation theory and practice evolved in the area of education.[2] We believe this is appropriate and will be instructive, since the profession of evaluation developed earliest and most heavily within the field of education. We provide only a brief historical sketch in order to note the most significant developments in educational program evaluation.

Our historical analysis is grounded in the seminal work of Ralph W. Tyler (described later in this book), who is often spoken of as the father of educational evaluation. Using his initial contributions as the main reference point, we have identified five major periods: (1) the Pre-Tylerian Period, which includes developments before 1930; (2) the Tylerian Age, which spans 1930 to 1945; (3) the Age of Innocence, which runs from 1946 to 1957; (4) the Age of Realism, which covers the years 1958 to 1972; and (5) the Age of Professionalism, which includes developments from 1973 to the present.

The Pre-Tylerian Period: Developments Before 1930

Systematic evaluation was not unknown before 1930, but it was not a recognizable movement. In the mid-1840s in the United States, the common method of assessing student learning and the quality of instruction was an annual oral examination conducted by school committees. Because of a desire for more dependable inspections of schools, in 1845 Boston replaced the oral exams with the first systematic school survey using printed tests. Horace Mann championed this approach and advised Boston to base school policies on factual results from testing the eldest class in each of the city's nineteen schools. The committee running the survey faced problems similar to those seen in today's large testing programs. Especially, teachers felt threatened because they knew that their students' test scores would be viewed as an indicator of their teaching competence.

The initial tests reflected the curriculum of the day, mainly abstract renderings consistent with the prevalent Puritan philosophy. They were chalk-and-slate or quill-and-paper tests, requiring students mainly to recall facts but, in a minor way, also to demonstrate application of what they had learned. Members of the school committees administered the tests during six hours over two days. Test results overall were discouraging. Reports contained a brief, often negative evaluative statement about each school. Mann saw these new methods of inspecting schools as impartial, thorough, and accurate in assessing what pupils had been taught and lauded their use in arriving at independent judgments of schools. In today's language, we could say he judged the new evaluation approach as meeting conditions of objectivity, validity, and reliability. Although the Boston survey spawned similar examination projects elsewhere in the United States, it was not until the end of the nineteenth century that end-of-semester printed tests became a common feature in schools nationwide.

It is generally recognized that Joseph Rice conducted the first formal educational program evaluation in the United States. An education reformer who provided leadership to educational administrators in New York City, in 1895 Rice launched the most ambitious plan ever undertaken to collect data on education. His goal was to confirm that student learning was deficient. Over the next decade, he obtained test scores in spelling and mathematics from about sixteen thousand students. A key finding was that the amount of time spent in spelling each day related little to spelling achievement. The Boston and Rice surveys gave publicity to the survey technique as a means of collecting and analyzing data to help identify and correct deficiencies in the schools and form sound educational policies. Its use in the twentieth century was evident in the 1915 publication of the Cleveland Education Survey. Sponsored by the Survey Committee of the Cleveland Foundation, the twenty-five-volume report assessed every aspect of the school system and was heralded as the most comprehensive study of an entire system ever completed.

The dawning of the twentieth century saw the emergence of yet another approach to evaluation. In applying the concepts of efficiency and standardization to manufacturing, Frederick Taylor had found standardization to contribute to efficiency and assurance of consistent quality in manufactured products. Taylor's success in manufacturing influenced leaders in education to seek standardization and efficiency in schools. Consequently, under the leadership of Edward Thorndike and others, educators launched the now massive enterprise of standardized testing. They believed that standardized tests could check the effectiveness of education and thereby show the way to more efficient student learning. Technology for measuring student achievement and other human characteristics developed strongly in the United States, Great Britain, and some other countries throughout the twentieth century and continues today. Educators and the public have often looked to scores from standardized tests as a basis for judging schools, programs, teachers, and students. Nevertheless, perhaps no other educational practice has generated so much criticism and controversy as standardized testing, especially when high stakes are attached to the results (American Evaluation Association Task Force on High Stakes Testing, 2002).

As a countermovement to rigid testing practices, a progressive education movement developed during the 1920s that espoused the ideas of John Dewey and even earlier writers. Robert Travers (1983) stated the matter extremely well:

> Those engaged in the progressive education movement viewed the new emphasis on standardized achievement testing as a menace to everything they hoped to accomplish. They wanted to make radical changes in the curriculum, but the standardized tests tended to encourage the retention of the established curriculum content. They wanted to emphasize the development of thinking skills, but the tests placed emphasis on the memorization of facts. They wanted to emphasize self-evaluation, with the child's own evaluation of himself as the point from which progress should be measured, but the achievement testers encouraged a competitive system in which a child was judged in terms of his position in a group. The use of criterion-referenced tests was minimal in the 1920s and 1930s, and although such tests would have answered this last criticism of the progressive educators, it would not have resolved even a small fraction of the misgivings that the progressives had about the new achievement testing [p. 144].

Despite a continuing flow of criticisms, the use of objective achievement tests has continued to flourish. The limitations of tests in measuring important educational outcomes, such as abilities to understand, apply, and critique, often are discounted in favor of obtaining quick and easy measures. In the service of educational evaluation, large-scale testing programs have been extremely expensive. We also judge them as grossly inadequate for assessing programs and institutions on merit, worth, probity, feasibility, significance, safety, and equity. Objective testing can play a useful role in educational program evaluations, but it can provide only a small part of the needed information.

While program evaluation only recently has been identified as a field of professional practice, this account illustrates that systematic program evaluation is not a completely recent phenomenon. Some of the modern evaluation work (testing commissions, surveys, accreditation, and experimental comparison of competitors) continues to draw from ideas and techniques that were applied long ago.

The Tylerian Age: 1930 to 1945

In the early 1930s, Ralph Tyler coined the term *educational evaluation* and published a broad and innovative view of both curriculum and evaluation. Over about fifteen years, he developed his views until they constituted an approach that provided a clear-cut alternative to other views (Madaus, 2004; Madaus & Stufflebeam, 1988).

What mainly distinguished his approach was its concentration on clearly stated objectives. In fact, he defined *evaluation* as determining whether objectives had been achieved. As a consequence of this definition, evaluators were supposed to help curriculum developers clarify the student behaviors that were to be produced through the implementation of a curriculum. The resulting behavioral objectives were then to provide the basis for both curriculum and test development. Curriculum design was thus influenced away from the content to be taught and toward the student behaviors to be developed. The technology of test development was to be expanded to provide for tests and other assessment exercises referenced to objectives as well as those referenced to individual differences and national or state norms.

During the 1930s, the United States, as well as the rest of the world, was in the depths of the Great Depression. Schools and other public institutions had stagnated from a lack of resources and optimism. Just as Franklin Roosevelt tried to lead the American economy out of this abyss through his New Deal program, John Dewey and others tried to help education become a dynamic, innovative, and self-renewing system. Called *progressive education*, this movement reflected the philosophy of pragmatism and employed the tools of behavioristic psychology.

Tyler was drawn directly into this movement when he was commissioned to direct the research component of the now famous Eight-Year Study (Smith & Tyler, 1942), which was designed to examine the effectiveness of certain innovative curricula and teaching strategies being employed in thirty schools throughout the United States. The study is noteworthy because it helped Tyler at once expand, test, and demonstrate his conception of educational evaluation.

Through this nationally visible program, Tyler was able to publicize what he saw as clear-cut advantages of his approach over others. Since Tylerian evaluation involves internal comparisons of outcomes with objectives, it does not require costly and disruptive comparisons between experimental and control groups. The approach concentrates on direct measures of achievement, as opposed to indirect approaches that measure such inputs as quality of teaching, number of books in the library, extent of materials, and community involvement. Tylerian evaluations need not be heavily concerned with reliability of differences between the scores of individual students, and they typically cover a wider range of outcome variables than those covered by norm-referenced tests. These arguments were well received throughout American education, and by the mid-1940s, Tyler had set the stage for exerting a heavy influence on how educators and other program evaluators viewed evaluation for the next twenty-five years.

The Age of Innocence: 1946 to 1957

In the ensuing years, Tyler's recommendations were more discussed than applied. Throughout American society, the late 1940s and 1950s were a time to forget the war, leave the depression behind, build and expand capabilities, acquire resources, and engineer and enjoy a good life. We might have called this era the Period of Expansion, except that there was also widespread complacence regarding serious societal problems. As a consequence, we think this time is better referred to as the Age of Innocence, or even as the Age of Social Irresponsibility.

More to the point of educational evaluation, there was expansion of educational offerings, personnel, and facilities. New buildings were erected. New kinds of educational institutions such as community colleges emerged. Small school districts consolidated with others in order to provide the wide range of educational services that were common in larger school systems: mental and physical health services, guidance, food service, music instruction, expanded sports programs, business and technical education, and community education. Enrollments in teacher education programs ballooned, and college enrollments generally increased dramatically.

This general scene in society and education was reflected in educational evaluation. Although there was great expansion of education, society had no particular interest in holding educators accountable, identifying and addressing the needs of the underprivileged, or identifying and solving problems in the education system. While educators wrote about evaluation and collected considerable data, they seem not to have related these efforts to attempts to improve educational services. This lack of a mission carried over into the development of the technical aspects of evaluation as well. There was considerable expansion of tools and strategies for applying the various approaches to evaluation: testing, comparative experimentation, and comparing outcomes and objectives. As a consequence, educators were provided with new tests and test scoring services, algorithms for writing behavioral objectives, taxonomies of objectives, new experimental designs, and new statistical procedures for analyzing educational data.

But these contributions were not derived from any analysis of what information was needed to assess and improve education, and they were not an outgrowth of school-based experience.

During this period, educational evaluations were, as they had been previously, primarily the purview of local school districts. Schools could do evaluation or not, depending on local interest and expertise. Federal and state agencies had not yet become deeply involved in the evaluation of programs. Funds for evaluations came from local coffers, foundations, or professional organizations. This lack of external pressures and support for evaluations at all levels of education would end with the arrival of the next period in the history of evaluation.

The Age of Realism: 1958 to 1972

The Age of Innocence in evaluation came to an abrupt end in the late 1950s and early 1960s with the call for evaluations of large-scale curriculum development projects funded by federal monies. Educators would find during this period that they no longer could do or not do evaluations as they pleased and that further developments of evaluation methodologies would have to be grounded in concerns for accountability, usability, and relevance. Their rude awakenings during this period would mark the end of an era of complacency and help launch profound changes, guided by the public interest and dependent on taxpayer monies for support, that would see evaluation expand as an industry and into a profession.

The federal government responded to the Russian launch of *Sputnik I* in 1957 by enacting the National Defense Education Act of 1958. Among other things, this act provided for new educational programs in mathematics, science, and foreign language and expanded counseling and guidance services and testing programs in school districts. A number of new national curriculum development projects, especially in science and mathematics, were established. Eventually funds were allocated to evaluate these programs.

Four approaches to evaluation were represented in the evaluations done during this period. First, the Tyler approach was used to help define objectives for the new curricula and to assess the degree to which the objectives were later realized. Second, new nationally standardized tests were developed to better reflect the objectives and content of the new curricula and to begin monitoring the educational progress of the nation's youth (Jones, 2003). Third, the professional judgment approach was used to rate proposals and check periodically on the efforts of contractors. Finally, many evaluators undertook to evaluate curriculum development efforts through the use of field experiments.

In the early 1960s, some leaders in educational evaluation realized that their work and their results were not particularly helpful to curriculum developers or responsive to the questions about the programs being raised by those who wanted to assess their effectiveness. The "best and the brightest" of the educational evaluation community were involved in these efforts to evaluate these new curricula; they were adequately financed, and they carefully applied the technology that had been developed during the past decade or more. Despite all this, they began to realize that their efforts were not succeeding.

This negative assessment was well reflected in a landmark article by Cronbach (1963). In looking at the evaluation efforts of the recent past, he sharply criticized the guiding conceptualizations of evaluation for their lack of relevance and utility and advised evaluators to turn away from their penchant for evaluations based on comparisons of the norm-referenced test scores of experimental and control groups. Cronbach counseled evaluators to reconceptualize evaluation not in terms of a horse race between competing programs but instead as a process of gathering and reporting information that could help guide curriculum development. Cronbach argued that analysis and reporting of test item scores would likely prove more useful to teachers than the reporting of average total scores.

Initially, Cronbach's counsel and recommendations went largely unnoticed except by a small circle of evaluation specialists. Nonetheless, his article was seminal, containing hypotheses about the conceptualization and conduct of evaluations that were to be tested and found valid within a few years.

The War on Poverty was launched in 1965. It was grounded in the previous pioneering work of Senator Hubert Humphrey and the charismatic leadership of President John F. Kennedy before his untimely death in 1963. Subsequently, President Lyndon Johnson picked up the reins and used his great political skill to get this landmark legislation passed. Its programs poured billions of dollars into reforms aimed at equalizing and upgrading opportunities for all U.S. citizens across a broad array of health, social, and educational services. The expanding economy enabled the federal government to finance these programs, and there was widespread support throughout the nation for developing what President Johnson termed the Great Society. Accompanying this massive effort to help those in need was a concern in some quarters that the investments might be wasted if appropriate accountability requirements were not imposed.

In response to this concern, Senator Robert Kennedy and some of his colleagues in Congress amended the Elementary and Secondary Education Act of 1965 to include specific evaluation requirements. As a result, Title I of that act (aimed at providing compensatory education to disadvantaged children) specifically required each school district receiving funds under this title to evaluate Title I projects annually using appropriate standardized test data and thereby to assess the extent to which the projects had achieved their objectives.

This requirement, with its specific reference to standardized test data and an assessment of congruence between outcomes and objectives, reflects the state of the art in educational evaluation at that time, based largely on the use of standardized educational achievement tests and superficially on Tyler's objectives-oriented approach. More important, the requirement forced educators to move their concern for educational evaluation from the realm of theory and supposition into the realm of practice and implementation. When school districts began to respond to the evaluation requirements of Title I, they quickly found that the existing concepts, tools, and strategies employed by their evaluators were largely inappropriate for the task.

Available standardized tests had been designed to rank-order students of average ability; they were of little use in diagnosing needs and assessing the gains of disadvantaged children whose educational development lagged far behind that of their middle-class peers. Furthermore, these tests were found to be relatively insensitive to differences between schools and programs, mainly because of their psychometric properties and content coverage. Instead of being measures of outcomes directly relating to the school or a particular program, these tests were at best indirect measures of learning, measuring much the same traits as general ability tests (Kellaghan, Madaus, & Airasian, 1982).

The use of standardized tests entailed another problem. Such an approach to evaluation conflicted with the precepts of the Tylerian approach. Because Tyler recognized and encouraged differences in objectives from locale to locale, this model became difficult to adapt to nationwide standardized testing programs. To be commercially viable, these standardized testing programs had to overlook, to some extent, objectives stressed by particular locales in favor of objectives stressed in the majority of districts.

Also, the Tylerian rationale itself proved inadequate to the evaluation task. There was a dearth of information about the needs and achievement levels of disadvantaged children to guide teachers in developing meaningful behavioral objectives for this population of learners. In retrospect, the enormous investment in training and leading educators to write behavioral objectives was largely unsuccessful and a waste of much time and money. Typically educators learned how to meet the technical requirements of good behavioral objectives, but they did not learn how to derive such objectives from information on the needs and problems of their students. Consequently, once they met the students to be served, the educators soon forgot or set aside as irrelevant the objectives they had written before the start of a project.

Attempts to isolate the effects of Title I projects through the use of experimental and control group designs also failed. Typically such studies showed "no significant differences" in achievement between treated Title I students and comparison groups. This approach was widely tried but was doomed to fail. Title I evaluators could not begin to meet the assumptions required by experimental designs. For example, they usually could not, in a timely manner, obtain valid measures, could not hold treatments constant during the study period, and legally could not randomly assign Title I (disadvantaged) students to control and experimental groups. When the finding of no results was reported, as was generally the case, there was little information on what the treatment was supposed to be and often no data on the degree to which it had in fact been implemented. Also, the emphasis on pre- and posttest scores diverted attention from consideration of the treatment or of treatment implementation. This hugely expensive experiment in testing the utility and feasibility of experimental design evaluations in the Title I program demonstrated rather decisively that this technique is not amenable to highly dynamic, field-based, generalized assistance programs, especially in the course of development.

As a result of the growing disquiet with evaluation efforts and consistently negative findings, Phi Delta Kappa set up a National Study Committee on Evaluation (Stufflebeam et al., 1971). After surveying the scene, this committee concluded that educational evaluation was "seized with a great illness" and called for the development of new theories and methods of evaluation as well as for new training programs for evaluators. This committee's indictment of educational evaluation practice was consistent with a study of government-sponsored evaluations by Guba (1966) and an analysis of the Title I evaluation efforts by Stufflebeam (1966).

At the same time, many new conceptualizations of evaluation began to emerge. Provus (1969), Hammond (1967), Eisner (1975), and Metfessel and Michael (1967) proposed reformulations of the Tyler model. Glaser (1963), Tyler (1967), and Popham (1971) pointed to criterion-referenced testing as an alternative to norm-referenced testing. Cook (1966) called for the use of system analysis techniques to evaluate programs. Scriven (1967, 1974), Stufflebeam (1967, 1971), and Stake (1967) introduced new models for evaluation that departed radically from prior approaches. These conceptualizations recognized the need to evaluate goals, look at inputs, examine implementation and delivery of services, as well as measure intended and unintended outcomes of the program. They also emphasized the need to make (or collect) judgments about the merit or worth of the object being evaluated.

The late 1960s and early 1970s were vibrant with descriptions, discussions, and debates concerning how evaluation should be conceived. The chapters that follow this one deal in depth with the alternative approaches that began to take shape during this period. Lessons had been learned, often by uneasy experience.

The Age of Professionalism: 1973 to the Present

Beginning in about 1973, the field of evaluation began to crystallize and emerge as a distinct profession related to, but quite distinct from, its forerunners of research and testing. The field of evaluation has advanced considerably as a profession, yet it is instructive to consider this development in the context of the field in the previous period.

At that time, evaluators faced an identity crisis. They were uncertain of their role—whether they should be researchers, testers, reformers, administrators, teachers, consultants, or philosophers. What special qualifications, if any, they should possess was unclear. There were no professional organizations dedicated to evaluation as a field or specialized journals through which evaluators could exchange information about their work. Essentially no literature about evaluation existed except for unpublished papers that circulated through an underground network of scholars. There was a paucity of preservice and in-service training opportunities in evaluation. Articulated standards of good practice were confined to educational and psychological tests. The field of evaluation was amorphous and fragmented. Many evaluations had been conducted by untrained personnel or research methodologists who tried unsuccessfully to fit their experimental methods to evaluations (Guba, 1966). Evaluation studies were fraught with confusion, anxiety, and animosity. Evaluation as a field had little stature and no political clout.

Against this backdrop, the progress made by evaluators to professionalize their field beginning in the 1970s is quite remarkable. A number of journals emerged. Many universities now offer at least one course in evaluation methodology (as distinct from research methodology). A few—including the University of Illinois, the University of California at Los Angeles, the University of Minnesota, the University of Virginia, Claremont Graduate University, and Western Michigan University (WMU)—have developed graduate programs in evaluation. The WMU program is the world's only interdisciplinary doctoral program in evaluation.

Increasingly, the field has looked to metaevaluation (Scriven, 1975; Stufflebeam, 1978, 2001) as a means of ensuring and checking the quality of evaluations. A joint committee issued standards for judging evaluations of educational programs, projects, and materials and established a mechanism by which to review and revise the *Standards* and assist the field in their use (Joint Committee on Standards for Educational Evaluation, 1981). This review process has worked effectively, producing the second edition of the *Program Evaluation Standards* in 1994. Moreover, the publication in 1988 of the Joint Committee's *The Personnel Evaluation Standards* signaled an advancement in the methods for assessing systems for evaluating personnel. In addition, the Joint Committee issued *The Student Evaluation*

Standards in 2003. Several other sets of standards with relevance for evaluation also have been published, the most important being AEA's *Guiding Principles for Evaluators* (2004) and the U.S. General Accounting Office's *Government Auditing Standards* (2002, 2003). Many new techniques and methodological approaches have been introduced for evaluating programs, as described in Part Four of this book. The most comprehensive treatment of the state of the art in educational evaluation so far is the *International Handbook of Educational Evaluation* (Kellaghan & Stufflebeam, 2003).

What Are the Main Roles in Evaluation Work?

Thus far, we have given and discussed a basic definition of evaluation, identified a range of evaluative criteria and other evaluation concepts, identified some of the methods involved in evaluation work, and provided a historical overview of the evaluation field. We conclude this chapter by looking at evaluation roles.

Whether one or many persons conduct an evaluation, a number of roles typically have to be implemented, and when one considers the work entailed in supporting and promoting evaluation as a profession, this view of roles becomes even broader. Importantly, those who will be involved as either specialists or generalists in evaluations need a broad view of the pertinent roles to enhance their effective participation and collaboration in the evaluation work. Perhaps nothing is so destructive of the potential contribution of evaluation as the attitude that evaluation is an independent research pursuit of an individual investigator. On the contrary, evaluation at its best involves much collaboration.

In attempting to provide a broad view of the work involved in individual evaluations and in the evaluation profession in general, we have identified twelve basic roles. While other writers might identify a different set and assign different labels, we believe our roles encompass most, if not all, work responsibilities that evaluators might have to implement. Furthermore, in our experience, these twelve roles have been associated with actual job assignments. Of course, there would not always be a one-to-one correspondence between role and job, but we think these twelve roles should be useful for thinking about the broad array of evaluation activities and for considering possible careers in evaluation, designing evaluation training programs, and designing and staffing work of particular evaluations.

Evaluation Client

Most worthwhile evaluations include a client who is integrally involved. This is true whether the study is conducted by one or more evaluators to serve a separate client or by a person to serve his or her own purposes. The client is the person or group that will use the results for some purpose, such as program selection, program improvement, or accountability to a sponsor. The client group encompasses whoever commissioned the evaluation, as well as those who will attend to and use the results. In one way or another, the time and resources required for the evaluation are provided by the client or by one or more persons in the client group. The clients are also crucial sources of the questions to be addressed and of the criteria to be employed in interpreting the results; they also bear primary responsibility for applying the findings. Often an evaluation cannot be done if the client fails to set the stage politically and take steps to ensure full cooperation by those who will be involved.

A variety of key clients are found in educational, social, and health organizations. These include, for example, school district superintendents, hospital administrators, and agency directors; school principals, department chairpersons, and grants administrators; foundation presidents, military leaders, and corporation heads; and teachers, psychologists, and physicians. If evaluation is to contribute maximally to the provision of meritorious and worthy services to people across the wide range of evaluations, this full range of clients should be involved in and served by evaluations. Moreover, we believe they must be actively engaged in commissioning and planning evaluations in order to derive the information they need to do their jobs well.

Therefore, in order to fulfill these expectations, clients should be properly trained, as should all those persons who will be involved in implementing the other eleven roles. Perhaps the most important mission of evaluation training programs, both preservice and in-service, is to prepare clients of evaluation to carry out their evaluation responsibilities. If they do not have a sound concept of evaluation, they will likely avoid it, be passive in their associations with it, not direct it to serve their purposes, or find its products of little interest. But as knowledgeable clients, they can help make evaluation a powerful and useful tool for ensuring the quality and ongoing improvement of professional services. This point is so important that we believe evaluation plans and budgets often should provide for the evaluator to train the client and other stakeholders in the concepts, uses, and proper conduct of evaluation.

Almost without exception, evaluations require review panels during the course of a study. It is essential that clients (and stakeholders) are included in these panels for three main reasons. First, they gain insight into the direction that the evaluation is taking, together with some knowledge of ultimate conclusions. Second, the more knowledge they have about the potential outcomes of the evaluation, the more likely it is that the organization or program will benefit from better-quality services. Finally, by supplying valuable critiques of evaluation plans and draft reports, such panels can contribute to the evaluation's quality, clarity, and relevance.

Evaluation Designer

One of the most fascinating aspects of evaluation work is that it should be viewed as a creative enterprise. Designing an evaluation to respond to a client's information requirements is far from a routine mechanical process. Among other responsibilities, one must conceptualize the questions to be addressed, size up the political scene, lay out a data collection and analysis plan, design the reports and the reporting process, project the staffing and financial requirements, determine how the standards of the evaluation profession will be met, and provide for giving clients and stakeholders a proper measure of evaluation training.

No models of past evaluations or published designs serve as all-purpose solutions to this complex set of planning decisions. On the contrary, evaluation design typically is a continuing conceptual process. To design a good evaluation, one should be a sensitive observer of social settings, a discerning interviewer and listener, and a willing and able learner about the substance of the program to be examined. The evaluator should also be knowledgeable about a wide range of inquiry and communication techniques and be able to draw together diverse pieces of specifications and form them into coherent guiding rationales and practical work plans.

Next to the role of the evaluation client, we see the role of evaluation designer as the most crucial in evaluation work. Those who become proficient in evaluation design are often employed full time as evaluators and are in great demand as consultants to assist evaluation clients in designing and commissioning evaluation studies.

The general evaluation conceptualizations presented in Parts Two and Three of this book provide crucial study material for those who wish to increase their facility in conceptualizing evaluation plans. The chapters in these parts of the book describe the general approaches developed by some of the evaluators who have become widely recognized as experts in designing evaluations. Beyond studying the creative contributions of others, we emphasize that development of one's evaluation design capabilities requires practice—one needs to be involved in designing a wide range of evaluations. This practice, we think, should include some individual work with a client. In addition, students can learn much by serving on evaluation planning teams. Moreover, the study of a wide range of evaluation designs prepared by others provides many good examples and insights into this complex work area. We believe that programs to train evaluators should include practicums and other forms of guided practice in the design of evaluations. And evaluators can increase their evaluation design skills by subjecting their evaluation designs to scrutiny by evaluation experts.

Evaluation Coordinator

Many evaluations draw on the efforts of a number of participants, the use of considerable resources, and services to multiple clients. Hence, a need for considerable coordination of the work effort exists. This need is magnified when an organization has a number of evaluation projects under way. Not surprisingly, the profession includes many evaluation jobs with titles such as assistant superintendent for evaluation, coordinator of evaluation projects, director of the evaluation office, and staff director of the evaluation project.

One implication of this role is that those specializing in evaluation should obtain training in management functions. Another is that those who are assigned to manage evaluation work should possess or acquire basic proficiency in evaluation design. Finally, we believe that major education, health, and social institutions should often organize their evaluation efforts into a well-managed unit of the institution.

Evaluation Caseworkers

Frequently, a crucial, and often separable, role in evaluation is that of evaluation caseworker or fieldworker. This role involves periodic interactions with clients, review of program documents, observation of program activities, interviewing and otherwise gathering information from participants, drafting reports, and assuming primary responsibility for writing up the findings. Sometimes the caseworker is in charge of implementing the complete study design. In other situations, he or she has a narrower responsibility. But this person is vitally involved in interacting with program personnel and helping to carry out the study design. Both technical and human relations skills are required to perform the caseworker role. Moreover, the person assigned to this role should possess or be able to develop credibility with the clients and with those who are carrying out the program.

Evaluation Respondents

A role too often taken for granted is that of the evaluation respondent. Evaluation respondents are the people who fill out the forms, answer the test questions, respond to interview questions, submit their work products, and allow their work to be observed. In many cases, the quality of evaluation information obtained is heavily dependent on the respondents' willingness to cooperate and give their best effort. They are unlikely to do either of these tasks well if they are not informed about their role, promised at least an outline of outcomes, and convinced of the importance of the study. Consequently, those in charge of evaluations should make special efforts to ensure that the study will be of some value to the respondents as well as to other clients. They should also be careful to provide activities by which to motivate and train respondents to respond appropriately.

Technical Support Specialists

Most evaluations involve a certain amount of technical work that requires specialized expertise. For example, there may be a need to conduct and record the results of interviews; develop, administer, and score structured data collection instruments; analyze qualitative and quantitative information; set up and manage databases; and produce audiovisual presentations of the findings. In small-scale evaluations, a single evaluation generalist often has to do all such tasks without specialized assistance. The single evaluation agent is hard-pressed to coordinate and do the necessary fieldwork while also fulfilling all required technical specialties. This evaluation agent needs broad-gauged training in the wide range of relevant specialties. Often he or she must also be able to engage the assistance of qualified consultants.

Inevitably, large-scale studies need to engage specialists to perform these tasks so that the evaluation caseworkers can concentrate their efforts on fieldwork with the evaluation clients and evaluation respondents. This group of experts could include test development specialists, sampling specialists, computer specialists, statisticians, case study specialists, and technical writers.

Information Specialist

One technical role that we have singled out for special attention is the information specialist. This role has an ongoing need for information that pertains to a series of evaluations as opposed to technical problems particular to given studies. The information specialist role is especially important in organizations that maintain evaluation offices. The evaluations conducted by such offices must take into account the institutional setting and its historical context, examine current and past findings to determine trends, and avoid needless duplication of data collection efforts. What is needed, at minimum, is a good system for indexing and storing evaluation reports so that the information they contain can be kept secure and easily accessed in future evaluations. In addition, many organizations would benefit by regularly collecting standardized information to help them track their inputs, processes, and outputs over time, as well as the attitudes of their constituents toward the organization's services.

Fulfillment of the information specialist role requires that the evaluator, or one or more members of the evaluation team, be proficient in information sciences and computer technology. Such proficiency requires knowledge and skills in such areas as communication, computer information systems, database design, computer programming, data processing, financial accounting, and long-range planning. Those who plan to specialize in evaluation should develop a general command of the information specialties, because a certain amount of work in this area is required even in a single-person evaluation. In addition, offices of evaluation often should assign one or more persons to fulfill this important function.

Communication Specialist

All too often effective communication is missing in evaluation work. Evaluators and clients assume that evaluators know their business and somehow will obtain and report the right message; instead, evaluators often address the wrong questions or communicate the findings ineffectively, or both. We wish to make emphatically clear that effective evaluation includes not only collecting and analyzing appropriate information, but also ensuring through effective communication technology that the information will be presented in a useful form and subsequently used. Evaluators should not be held accountable for all misinterpretations and misuses of their reports, but, among other things, they should be held accountable for ensuring that their reports are relevant to the interests of audiences and communicated clearly.

To do so requires that evaluators be skilled in communication technology. They should be able to prepare clearly written reports that are directed to, and understandable by, the intended audience or audiences. Beyond being good writers, they need to be skilled in audience analysis and designing different reports for different audiences. They need facility in communicating findings through means other than printed material; for example, they need skills in public speaking, use of audiovisual techniques, use of public media, managing group processes, and utilizing Web sites. Finally, they need skills of political analysis and conflict management, since evaluations often are involved in controversy.

The communication specialist role has considerable implications for the training of evaluators, their use of consultants, and the staffing of evaluation offices. Clearly, evaluators should obtain training in a broad range of communication techniques. In their practice, they should, at a minimum, submit their draft reports to editors. And evaluation offices often should employ communication specialists or engage relevant consultants to assist in planning evaluations and presenting the findings. Such specialists also have an important role in evaluating and helping to improve an evaluation office's performance over time in communicating its reports to its clients.

We acknowledge that evaluations often have to be done by single evaluators. To do their work well, they need to become proficient in the wide range of roles already identified. Probably the best means of encountering and learning how to address the full range of evaluation roles is by conducting a wide range of single-person evaluations under the tutelage of an evaluation expert. Participation in team evaluation efforts also provides excellent learning opportunities.

We have so far considered only evaluation roles that pertain to an actual evaluation. Now we turn to four others that serve in support roles in developing the evaluation profession.

Evaluation Trainer

Throughout the preceding analysis, we have referred to the training needs of those who participated in evaluation. These needs encompass orientation to specific evaluation plans as well as the development of more generalized understandings and skills, and they include understandings that are acquired through examining one's practice. Moreover, the training needs pertain to the clients and respondents in evaluations, as well as to the evaluation specialists.

Evaluation, like any other profession, should ensure that the participants in evaluation are provided a wide range of sound evaluation learning opportunities. These include specialized training programs leading to graduate degrees in evaluation; service courses that are provided to assist those who are in training for a wide range of professional roles (such as superintendent, social worker, teacher, and physician) to evaluate their professional services; continuing education opportunities in evaluation for both evaluation specialists and generalists; and orientation sessions for the clients and respondents in specific evaluation studies. Such training should present up-to-date content that is relevant to the field problems that the trainees face. Clearly, evaluation training is a crucial role in maintaining and advancing quality evaluation services.

Evaluation Researcher

The mission of any profession is to serve clients as well as possible, and the fulfillment of this commitment is always limited by the current state of knowledge about the field. Therefore, professions need a research ethos. Professionals must study the profession-related needs and problems of their clients, study their services to clients, examine their practices in the light of knowledge and principles from relevant disciplines, examine their work in its historical context, theorize about the professional services, and move knowledge about their field forward through structured examination of the field's guiding assumptions and hypotheses. Chapter Two examines some of these issues.

Vast research programs are evident in mature professions such as medicine and law and in business and industry. In the former case, such research is driven by the professional ethic of delivering the best possible service. In the latter case, the primary motivation is profit and survival in a competitive world. Both areas are strongly aware that improved service and competitiveness depend heavily on a dynamic program of pertinent research.

Although evaluation is as old as civilization, it has existed as a formal field of practice for a very short time. Only since the early 1970s have serious efforts been made to record the history of the field, theorize about evaluation practice, and conduct pertinent descriptive and hypothesis-testing studies. But there is and should be a strong trend toward establishing and maintaining a research base for the field. This trend is especially evident in the exploding literature of the evaluation field, although much of this material does not qualify as research. In any case, we wish to emphasize that research on evaluation is a vital role in ensuring that evaluators progressively improve their services and impacts.

Evaluation Developer

The role of evaluation developer has at its base the function of helping evaluators collectively attain and maintain the status of a profession. What is at issue in this role can be seen in a dictionary definition that characterizes a profession as "a calling requiring specialized knowledge and often long and intensive preparation including instruction in skills and methods as well as in the scientific, historical, or scholarly principles underlying such skills and methods, maintaining by force of organization or concerted opinion high standards of achievement and conduct, and committing its members to continued study and to a kind of work which has as its prime purpose the rendering of a public service" (*Webster's Third New International Dictionary*, 1966, p. 1811).

The evaluation field is beginning to manifest the characteristics of a profession that are contained in this definition. There are now training programs leading to master's and doctoral degrees in evaluation, as well as an extensive and burgeoning literature on evaluation. The evaluation literature prescribes content and experiences to be included in evaluation training programs and analyzes how the programs should draw from related disciplines, such as philosophy, psychology, sociology, and economics. Several professional organizations and sets of guiding principles and professional standards are available to evaluators. And government, the public, and service organizations are continuing to demand evaluations of professional services, as well as provide funds to support evaluations.

Metaevaluator

The final role we wish to emphasize is the overarching and pervasive role of metaevaluator. Involved with evaluating evaluation, the role extends to assessing the worth, merit, and probity of all that the profession is and does, evaluation services, use of evaluations, evaluation training, evaluation research, and organizational development. Metaevaluation invokes the accepted guiding principles and standards of the profession and assesses and tries to ensure that they are met. It also is involved when the standards themselves are examined to identify where they might need to be revised. In one way or another, metaevaluation needs to be incorporated into each activity of the evaluation profession. Sometimes it is a self-assessment activity, as when evaluators, evaluation trainers, evaluation researchers, or officials of evaluation societies scrutinize their plans, work efforts, and products against the standards of the evaluation profession and provide written attestations. In other cases, metaevaluation involves engaging an independent agent to assess professional evaluation services. The aims of metaevaluation are to ensure quality evaluation services, guard against or uncover malpractice or services not in the public interest, provide direction for improving the evaluation profession, and promote increased understanding of the evaluation enterprise. Clearly, all professional evaluators should maintain up-to-date knowledge of the field's standards, incorporate them in their work, be willing to serve as metaevaluator in relation to the work of others in the profession, and be proactive in evaluating and trying to improve the contributions of evaluation to society.

Summing Up the Roles

With this brief discussion of metaevaluation we conclude our overview of evaluation roles. In a sense, we have dissected the role of the professional evaluator and have looked at its constituent parts and support groups. Rightly, we think, this has supported the impression that evaluation is often a team effort. But to conclude that evaluations must involve team efforts would be a misinterpretation. On the contrary, evaluation is necessarily an integral part of every professional's role. Our message is that this role is as difficult as it is important. The obvious fundamental conclusion is that all professionals should develop the capability to meet their evaluation responsibilities well, whether or not they can draw assistance from a team or must perform all of the evaluation functions individually.

One basic step in the right direction is to increase one's facility to conceptualize evaluation problems and approaches in order to facilitate the solution of those problems. The remainder of this book has been prepared to guide this process. It discusses the need for a foundation of evaluation theory and standards, presents and examines in depth a number of alternative evaluation approaches, and provides guidelines for planning and carrying out sound evaluations.

Review Questions

1. Describe an example, drawn from your experience, of how members of society were put at risk or harmed due to a lack of evaluation.
2. Describe an example of how members of society were put at risk or harmed due to a failure to heed and act on the findings of an evaluation.
3. Identify a job in society that should be staffed with an evaluation-oriented decision maker, and note some of the positive benefits associated with the person's possession of evaluation competence.
4. Explain and give examples of evaluation's ubiquitous place in society and its institutions, including its symbiotic relationship to other fields.
5. Cite what you see as the pros and cons of defining evaluation as the comparison of outcomes to objectives.
6. Cite some reasons that evaluators should search for side effects.
7. List the three definitions of evaluation given in the chapter. Then define the intended use of each definition. Subsequently, write an example of how you might use each definition.
8. Define what is meant by *merit* and *worth*. Then, from your experience, write an example of a program or other entity that possessed merit but not worth. Describe how merit and worth were assessed. Explain why assessments of worth are context bounded.
9. Give examples of cases that require comparative evaluations and other cases that require noncomparative evaluations.
10. Compare and contrast the terms *formative evaluation* and *summative evaluation*. What points distinguish informal evaluation from formal evaluation? Is there necessarily any connection between these concepts and formative and summative evaluations?

Group Exercises

This section is particularly relevant to group discussion where problem solving is required. It is designed to extend your insight into some of the issues outlined in this chapter.

Exercise 1. The head of a large state government department found himself under political pressure to commission an evaluation of each of the four divisions of his department. None of these divisions had ever been evaluated except in the most cursory fashion, and then only sporadically. What was evident to stakeholders (the public) was that services were costly but inadequate and that the poor quality of delivery was causing growing frustration.

Realistic financial provision and time lines were made available for this major evaluation, according to the head of the department.

Suppose your group was selected to conduct the evaluation. Outline the important early decisions you would need to make about the form of the evaluation; the kinds of initial understandings you would wish to have with the head of the department and division heads; and the kinds of assurances you would seek and give so that a successful evaluation could eventuate.

Exercise 2. A superintendent of a small school district was beset with problems relating to the introduction of a new state-mandated science program for grades 7 through 9. She had heard of both formative and summative evaluation processes, but had little grasp of their functions and possible benefits if applied to the new science program.

Your services are engaged to give the superintendent a thorough understanding of what constitutes formative and summative evaluations. Outline the relevance to the superintendent's problems of either form of evaluation, suggest a circumstance under which formative evaluation might lead to summative evaluation, and state the kind of cooperation an evaluation team would find essential to complete a successful study.

What advice do you give the superintendent?

Notes

1. The Joint Committee on Standards for Educational Evaluation is a standing committee that was established in 1975. Its approximately eighteen members have been appointed by about fifteen professional societies in the United States and Canada that are concerned with improving evaluations in education. The committee's charge is to develop standards for educational evaluations. So far, it has created standards for evaluations of educational programs, personnel, and students. This book's first author was the committee's founding chair, and the second author assisted in the development of the original set of program evaluation standards.
2. This history of educational evaluation section is based on a previous account by George Madaus and Daniel Stufflebeam (Stufflebeam, Madaus, & Kellaghan, 2000, pp. 3–18).

References

Alkin, M. C., Daillak, R., & White, P. (1979). *Using evaluations: Does evaluation make a difference?* Thousand Oaks, CA: Sage.

American Evaluation Association Ethics Committee. (2004). *Guiding principles for evaluators.* http://www.eval.org/Guiding%20 Principles.htm.

American Evaluation Association Task Force on High Stakes Testing. (2002). *Position statement on high stakes testing in pre-K-12 education.* Louisville, KY: Author.

Cook, D. L. (1966). *Program evaluation and review technique: Applications in education.* Washington, DC: Government Printing Office.

Cronbach, L. J. (1963). Course improvement through evaluation. *Teachers College Record, 64,* 672–683.

Eisner, E. W. (1975, December). *The perceptive eye: Toward the reformation of educational evaluation.* Stanford, CA: Stanford Evaluation Consortium.

Glaser, R. (1963). Instructional technology and the measurement of learning outcomes: Some questions. *American Psychologist, 18,* 519–521.

Government Accountability Office. (2003, June). *Government auditing standards.* Washington, DC: Author. (GAO-03-673G)

Guba, E. G. (1966, October). *A study of title III activities: Report on evaluation.* Paper presented at the National Institute for the Study of Educational Change, Indiana University.

Hammond, R. L. (1967). *Evaluation at the local level.* Address to the Miller Committee for the National Study of ESEA Title III, Washington, DC.

Joint Committee on Standards for Educational Evaluation. (1981). *Standards for evaluations of educational programs, projects, and materials.* New York: McGraw-Hill.

Joint Committee on Standards for Educational Evaluation. (1988). *The personnel evaluation standards.* Thousand Oaks, CA: Corwin Press.

Joint Committee on Standards for Educational Evaluation. (1994). *The program evaluation standards.* Thousand Oaks, CA: Corwin Press.

Joint Committee on Standards for Educational Evaluation. (2003). *The student evaluation standards.* Thousand Oaks, CA: Corwin Press.

Jones, L. V. (2003). National assessment in the United States: The evolution of a nation's report card. In T. Kellaghan & D. Stufflebeam (Eds.), *International handbook of educational evaluation* (pp. 883–904). Norwell, MA: Kluwer.

Kellaghan, T. (1982). Los sistemas escalates coma objecto de evaluacion. In D. Stufflebeam, T. Kellaghan, & B. Alvarez (Eds.), *La evaluacion educativa.* Bogota: Pontificia Universidad Javeriana.

Kellaghan, T., Madaus, G., & Airasian, P. (1982). *The effects of standardized testing.* Norwell, MA: Kluwer.

Kellaghan, T., & Stufflebeam, D. L. (Eds.). (2003). *International handbook of educational evaluation.* Norwell, MA: Kluwer.

Madaus, G. F. (2004). Ralph W. Tyler's contribution to program evaluation. In M. C. Alkin (Ed.), *Evaluation roots: Tracing theorists' views and influences.* Thousand Oaks, CA: Sage.

Madaus, G. F., & Stufflebeam, D. L. (1988). *Educational evaluation: The classical writings of Ralph W. Tyler.* Norwell, MA: Kluwer.

Metfessel, N. S., & Michael, W. B. (1967). A paradigm involving multiple criterion measures for the evaluation of the effectiveness of school programs. *Educational and Psychological Measurement, 27,* 931–943.

Patton, M. Q. (1997). *Utilization-focused evaluation: The new century text* (3rd ed.). Thousand Oaks, CA: Sage.

Popham, W. J. (1971). *Criterion-referenced measurement.* Upper Saddle River, NJ: Educational Technology Publications.

Provus, M. (1969). *Discrepancy evaluation model.* Pittsburgh, PA: Pittsburgh Public Schools.

Sanders, W. L., & Horn, S. (1994). The Tennessee value-added assessment system (TVAAS): Mixed model methodology in educational assessment. *Journal of Personnel Evaluation in Education, 8*(3) 299–311.

Scriven, M. S. (1967). The methodology of evaluation. In *Perspectives of curriculum evaluation.* Skokie, IL: Rand McNally.

Scriven, M. S. (1974). Pros and cons about goal-free evaluation. *Evaluation Comment, 3,* 1–4.

Scriven, M. S. (1975). *Evaluation bias and its control.* Kalamazoo: Western Michigan University, The Evaluation Center.

Scriven, M. (1981). *Evaluation thesaurus* (3rd Ed.). Point Reyes, CA: Edgepress.

Scriven, M. (1991). *Evaluation thesaurus* (4th ed.). Thousand Oaks, CA: Sage.

Smith, E. R., & Tyler, R. W. (1942). *Appraising and recording student progress.* New York: HarperCollins.

Stake, R. E. (1967). The countenance of educational evaluation. *Teachers College Record, 68,* 523–540.

Stake, R. E. (1969). Evaluation design, instrumentation, data collection, and analysis of data. In J. L. Davis (Ed.), *Educational evaluation.* Columbus, OH: State Superintendent of Public Instruction.

Stufflebeam, D. L. (1966). A depth study of the evaluation requirement. *Theory into Practice, 5*(3), 121–133.

Stufflebeam, D. L. (1967). The use and abuse of evaluation in Title III. *Theory into Practice, 6,* 126–133.

Stufflebeam, D. L. (1971). The relevance of the CIPP evaluation model for educational accountability. *Journal of Research and Development in Education, 5*(1), 19–25.

Stufflebeam, D. L. (1978). Metaevaluation: An overview. *Evaluation and the Health Professions, 1*(2), 146–163.

Stufflebeam, D. L. (2001). The metaevaluation imperative. *American Journal of Evaluation, 22*(2), 183–209.

Stufflebeam, D. L., Foley, W. J., Gephart, W. J., Guba, E. G., Hammond, R. L. Merriman, H. O., & Provus, M. M. (1971). *Educational evaluation and decision making in education.* Itasca, IL: Peacock.

Stufflebeam, D. L., Madaus, G. F., & Kellaghan, T. (2000). *Evaluation models: Viewpoints on educational and human services evaluation.* Norwell, MA: Kluwer.

Stufflebeam, D. L., McCormick, C. H., Brinkerhoff, R. O., & Nelson, C. O. (1985). *Conducting educational needs assessment.* Norwell, MA: Kluwer.

Travers, R.M.W. (1983). *How research has changed American schools.* Kalamazoo, MI: Mythos Press.

Tyler, R. W. (1967). Changing concepts of educational evaluation. In R. E. Stake (Ed.), *Perspectives of curriculum evaluation.* Skokie, IL: Rand McNally.

U.S. General Accounting Office. (2002, January). *Government auditing standards: Amendment No. 3 Independence.* Washington, DC: Author.

U.S. General Accounting Office. (2003, June). *Government auditing standards: 2003 revision*. Washington, DC: Author.

Walton, M. (1986). *The Deming management method*. New York: Putnam.

Webster's Third New International Dictionary. (1966). Chicago: Encyclopedia Britannica.

CHAPTER TWO

THE NATURE OF PROGRAM EVALUATION THEORY

This book's central purpose is to present an organized summary of the major contemporary approaches to program evaluation, followed by guidelines for applying the approaches. As background for these tasks, this chapter addresses the fundamental issue of program evaluation theory. In the ongoing development of the program evaluation field, we believe program evaluation approaches should be assessed and improved toward the goal of meeting the requirements of a sound theory.

In this chapter, we look at the topic of program evaluation theory as contrasted with program evaluation approaches because we think program evaluation scholars (and evaluation graduate students) should increase their attention to the rigors of theory development. Why this is so can be seen in a discussion of the functions and requirements of sound theories. We shall proceed in this chapter by outlining general features of program evaluation theory, commenting on the role of theory in the development of the program evaluation discipline, looking specifically at what is meant by the term *program evaluation theory*, and identifying some of the research needed to develop that theory. Following these considerations, we will examine the status of theory development in the program evaluation field; discuss some of the constraints and difficulties attending efforts to develop program evaluation theories; list examples of hypotheses for research on program evaluation; note the potential utility in theory development of grounded theory methods and metaevaluation findings; and reference professional standards for evaluations as a source of research hypotheses. We will use the chapter to identify dimensions for use, later in the book, in characterizing and evaluating the different evaluation approaches.

General Features of Program Evaluation Theories

It is possible to distinguish between general and specific theories of program evaluation. A general theory of program evaluation would characterize the nature of program evaluations, regardless of subject matter, time, and space. Such a general theory would cover a wide range of program evaluations, denote their modal characteristics—including logic and processes of evaluative discourse—and describe in general how program evaluations should be assessed and justified. Specific theories of program evaluation would have many of the same characteristics as a general theory but be delimited to account for program evaluations that are restricted to particular substantive areas, locations, or time periods.

It is important to note that program evaluation theory is only one part of evaluation theory in general. Other parts include, for example, theories concerned with evaluations of personnel, commercial products and services, organizations, manufacturing, governance, policies, and even evaluation theories. Further divisions of evaluation theory are possible when one considers a range of disciplines. One could generate theories of different types of program evaluations—for example, evaluations of educational, social, economic, environmental, missionary, foreign aid, law enforcement, national defense, fundraising, engineering, and business programs. It would therefore be possible to consider general and specific theories of evaluation for the evaluation field as a whole or any of its subareas.

In general, the evaluation profession spans evaluations of all sectors of society. All sectors employ programs, that is, interrelated sets of goal-directed activities. It is in both public and private interests to evaluate programs in order to enhance prospects for success and help ensure accountability to sponsors and constituents. Program evaluation crosses many disciplines and fields of service, is one of the most fully developed and important parts of the broader evaluation field, and is worthy of close study.

Providing a comprehensive view of the development of program evaluation theory is not as challenging as analyzing theory in more mature fields, such as economics, physics, jurisprudence, and psychotherapy. While evaluation theorists have advanced creative and influential models and approaches for conducting program evaluations, these constructions have not been accompanied by a substantial amount of related empirical research. Thus, no substantial body of evidence exists on the functioning of different evaluation approaches. This is so partly because the young evaluation field has been engaged in theory development during a much shorter time period than have the more mature professions. Also, program evaluation scholars tend to be pragmatists. Rather than trying to understand the relationships among variables in program evaluations as they play out in the real world, these scholars have concentrated on putting improved evaluation approaches in the hands of evaluators. Basically, program evaluation scholars have sought to develop approaches that assist evaluators in designing and carrying out useful, defensible program evaluations. For the most part, the program evaluation scholars and other evaluation researchers have not generated and tested propositions from their conceptualizations of program evaluation systematically and used such findings to improve the conceptualizations. Thus, the program evaluation field lacks a sufficient body of research and steadily improving theories flowing from an ongoing process of rigorous, empirically grounded theory development. Nevertheless, the creative, influential constructions of a range of conceptual leaders in evaluation are intriguing, have been influential, and are worthy of examination. They might aptly be termed pretheories or emerging theories. We do most of our analysis of these constructions in Parts Two and Three of this book when we describe and examine twenty-six evaluation approaches.

The Role of Theory in Developing the Program Evaluation Field

Program evaluation, an important field of professional practice, is in its early developmental stages. Only recently has the broader society begun to recognize evaluators as members of an identifiable, creditable profession. Like all other professions, this emergent field's members need to study and continually improve their services. Their aim should be to produce a science of program evaluation—one that is grounded in ongoing conceptualization and rigorous testing of theory-based propositions and continually improves. Theory often has been cited as one of the most useful of all things because it informs practice. Reciprocally, feedback from practice is needed to validate and strengthen theories.

Poor theories mislead practice with serious negative consequences. For example, the theory that defined evaluation as the process of determining whether specific objectives had been achieved misled evaluators for decades as they focused on only intended outcomes, not the crucially important side effects seen in many programs or on context and process. When Ralph Tyler introduced his famous objectives-based approach to evaluation in the 1930s, he provided a valuable service by giving educators a framework for systematically studying and evaluating the effects of educational innovations (Madaus and Stufflebeam, 1988). We see in this paragraph's apparent contradiction about the value of objectives-based evaluation that theories have positive and negative influences, may have differential utilities reflecting the conditions and needs in different eras, should be subjected to ongoing examination and reformulation, and should be recommended for use provided appropriate caveats are observed.

Another example of the ability of theories to mislead is seen in the still shackling position, held by many influential parties, that virtually all program evaluations should employ strict laboratory experimental research methods. This position, often backed by government mandates and funding restrictions, has had a crippling, wasteful influence on the practice of program evaluations. Over the past three decades, evaluation leaders have given compelling arguments against such sweeping requirements (for example, see Guba, 1969; Schwandt, 2004; Stake, 1975, 1988). However, the critics have not dissuaded the government officials, who control purse strings for the bulk of the money available to fund program evaluations, from spending a disproportionate amount of it on field experiments. Here we see that program evaluations are embedded in societal dynamics and highly subject to political forces. It follows that sound program evaluation theories should pay attention to the politics of evaluations and effectively address political issues that bear on the effective conduct of evaluations.

In fact, program evaluation theorists have sometimes played dissident roles in the development of the program evaluation discipline. In their own times, some of the field's creative leaders have been rebels: rebels against a philosophy of a value-free evaluation science, against the philosophy of positivism, against the death grip of laboratory experimental methods on field studies, against the penchant for pursuing scientific adequacy in evaluations to the exclusion of utility, and against the tyranny of standardized testing in evaluating educational programs. Fortunately, the program evaluation field has been blessed with a number of creative theorists who not only attacked what they saw as debilitating traditions in evaluation, but also advanced alternative conceptualizations. Among these are Robert Stake (1976), who called for responsive rather than preordinate evaluations; Michael Scriven (1973), who advocated goal-free evaluation as a countermeasure to the narrowness of goals-based evaluations; and Egon Guba (1978), who proposed a naturalistic approach as opposed to the still in-vogue experimental design approach. These theorists have not turned the tide of government funding away from an exclusive orientation to field experiments, but they have contributed to profession-wide dialogue on the issue.

The Functional and Pragmatic Basis of Extant Program Evaluation Theory

Importantly, these and other evaluation theorists drew their leading ideas from practical experience. They have remained close to field experience data, drawn their creative reconstructions from these experiences, and maintained a functional orientation. The differences among constructions of the program evaluation theorists no doubt stem in part from their different worldviews and philosophies but also from their different evaluation experiences. The historical link between theoretical contributions and practical application has remained evident throughout the development of the program evaluation field. The theorists' conduct of evaluations in widely differing settings no doubt heavily influenced their different constructions of program evaluation. This fact argues strongly that program evaluation theories should direct evaluators to take explicit account of the contextual conditions surrounding their evaluations.

The fact that leading evaluation theorists have never totally embedded their work in the mainstream of empirical research methodology has had several important implications for the program evaluation field. On the one hand, it tended to free program evaluation theory from the stifling grip of conventional modes of thought and preconceptions concerning the conduct of field studies. By being relatively uninvolved in the ongoing institution of formal scientific inquiry, it was easier for program evaluation theorists to question or reject assumptions that were patently accepted by traditional laboratory researchers and to make creative contributions. On the other hand, this lack of involvement also freed them from some of the discipline and responsibility for reasonably systematic and organized formulation and testing of hypotheses, which is the heritage of the well-socialized laboratory researcher. A main reason for writing this chapter is that we believe program evaluation theorists need to continue producing creative, even rebellious conceptualizations of program evaluation approaches but also to proceed with deriving and formally testing theoretical propositions about the proper conduct of program evaluation and then to follow through by reformulating their theories as a consequence.

A Word About Research Related to Program Evaluation Theory

Several studies have looked at the extent to which evaluation practitioners have applied theorists' recommended program evaluation approaches. Christie (2003) addressed this issue by developing a framework to compare reported practices of eight evaluation theorists with reported practices of a group of practitioners who had been evaluating California's Healthy Start Program. Essentially she wanted to learn something about whether evaluation practice mirrors evaluation theory. In response to her survey, a small percentage of the practitioners reported using any of the eight theorists' approaches to evaluation. Datta (2003) reported that this finding is consistent with a few other studies that found that practicing evaluators pay little attention to recommended theoretical approaches to evaluation. Datta warned, however, that the existing evidence on this issue is thin and has noteworthy limitations, especially a lack of generalizability.

Whether Christie's findings hold under further investigation, we think they raise additional fundamental questions. If the finding that evaluators do not apply evaluation theory is generally true, then it is important to ask why they do not. Perhaps the approaches are not sufficiently articulated for practical use, or the practitioners are not competent to carry them out, or the approaches lack convincing evidence that their use produces the needed evaluation results. Or it is possible that evaluators become so accustomed to using only one approach or very few that they become complacent and indifferent to the value of alternative models. Considerations such as determining theory do not feature prominently, if at all.

We think the first three explanations are plausible and should be studied. The third explanation has particular salience for this chapter. It seems understandable that practitioners, however well trained in the discipline of evaluation, would be unlikely to apply, and continue to apply, any evaluation theory unless research had shown that when applied correctly, use of the theory produces sound evaluation results.

An analogy from medicine may help clarify this point. Consider the theory of heart transplant surgery first developed at the Mayo Clinic. It would have been unthinkable to advise the wide body of heart surgeons to transplant hearts before Dr. Michael DeBakey and other prominent heart surgeons had thoroughly tested the procedure and shown it to succeed. Also, dissemination of this practice should have been restricted to surgeons who were properly trained and certified. Indeed, a finding from a study, such as that by Christie (2003), that physicians in general were not employing the new heart transplant approaches would have brought welcome relief.

While application of House's democratic deliberative approach or Patton's utilization-focused evaluation does not portend possible dire outcomes similar to those of heart transplant surgery, the same principles apply. Theoretical approaches in any profession should be carefully researched and validated prior to advocating their widespread use, and those who are to apply the approaches should be specifically trained and certified as competent in their correct application. These principles are hallmarks of any mature profession. From Christie's report (2003), it seems clear that evaluation participants in her sample were not thoroughly trained in the theoretical approaches being researched and maybe not in the logic and methodology of program evaluation in general. Quite possibly the findings from her study are more indicative of the primitive state of training and certifying evaluators and disseminating new evaluation approaches than of the adequacies, inadequacies, and applicability of theoretical approaches to program evaluation.

Nevertheless, we acknowledge that practice of evaluation is and should be pervasive. Informal or amateur evaluation is important, and the evaluation profession should provide conceptual, technical, and training assistance to service providers who have to conduct many of their own evaluations. Even so, the evaluation field should provide practitioners with validated theories and appropriate training.

Program Evaluation Theory Defined

Most of this book deals with program evaluation models or approaches and not the more advanced notion of program evaluation theories. We define a *program evaluation model* as an evaluation theorist's idealized conceptualization for conducting program evaluations. The experience born of trial and error, pragmatism, field practice, ability to develop concepts creatively, and other entities may have been contributing factors to theory underpinning a particular program evaluation model. Whatever the causes, the evaluation field has made substantial progress in developing program evaluation models, and these are valuable. Like theories, evaluation models and approaches also need careful scrutiny and testing. Parts Two and Three of this book are devoted to a critical review and analysis of the major approaches in the field of program evaluation.

Although some writers would characterize those approaches as prescriptive theories, we have reserved the term *theory* for creatively developed yet more rigorously tested conceptualizations of program evaluation. We value the contributions of the evaluation model developers but believe the program evaluation field should seek a higher standard for the meaning of theories of program evaluation. We have thus set more demanding requirements for theories than for evaluation models and approaches.

We find the following dictionary-based definition of a program evaluation theory to be useful (but not sufficient) for considering the scope and rigor required by sound theories of program evaluation: "A program evaluation theory is a coherent set of conceptual, hypothetical, pragmatic, and ethical principles forming a general framework to guide the study and practice of program evaluation." This definition is useful for identifying features by which to classify and examine different theories. Although the definition does not explicitly identify criteria for evaluating a theory, we observe that such criteria become necessary at some stage. According to this definition, a sound program evaluation theory has six main features: overall coherence, core concepts, tested hypotheses on how evaluation procedures produce desired outcomes, workable procedures, ethical requirements, and a general framework for guiding program evaluation practice and conducting research on program evaluation. Effectively addressing this definition's requirements is a worthy goal for developers of program evaluation theories but one that is elusive, far from achievement, and lacking specific criteria for judging theories. We acknowledge that some evaluation approaches rate well on coherence, core concepts, workable procedures, integrity, and guidance for research and practice. However, all of them fall short in producing principles based on empirical research. We will comment briefly on the definition's requirements for conceptual, hypothetical, pragmatic, and ethical principles as related to the general field of program evaluation.

Conceptual Principles

The conceptual nature of program evaluation is evident in the evaluation literature. It contains a wide range of well-developed concepts, such as formative and summative evaluations; constructivist and responsive evaluations; context, input, process, and product evaluations; utilization-focused evaluation; participatory evaluation; utility, feasibility, propriety, and accuracy standards for evaluations; and metaevaluation. Perhaps the most comprehensive listing and definition of such concepts appear in Scriven's *Evaluation Thesaurus* (1991).

Hypothetical Principles

Work in developing research-based principles for conducting program evaluations has been nonexistent. Research efforts to state and confirm hypotheses about what works in program evaluations and under what conditions have been lacking. This is a fertile area for doctoral dissertations and funded research on evaluation. Such hypothesis-testing research should take explicit account of the environmental circumstances surrounding the subject program evaluations. Later in this chapter, we cite some illustrative general hypotheses about evaluation practices that we found in evaluation literature.

Hypothetical principles cover as wide a range of activities as exist under the general rubric of program evaluation. The development of these into definable constructs, based on research, is nonexistent.

Pragmatic Principles

Pragmatic principles denote ways of conducting evaluations that have been shown to work well in evaluation practice. Many valuable evaluation procedures and rules of thumb are available. These have grown from a vast amount of evaluation experience and are evident in such writings as the guidelines contained in the Joint Committee *Program Evaluation Standards* (1994) and the Fitzpatrick, Sanders, and Worthen (2004) *Program Evaluation* textbook, as well as Part Four of this book. Procedural recommendations derived from program evaluation practices are worthy of examination and validation by empirical research.

Ethical Principles

There has been progress in defining ethical principles for program evaluations. This is seen in the American Evaluation Association's *Guiding Principles for Evaluators* (2004), the "Propriety" section of the Joint Committee *Program Evaluation Standards* (1994), and writings of scholars, including Morris (2003).

Application of the preceding definition of a program evaluation theory is not straightforward. Hypothetical principles cover as wide a range of activities as exist under the general rubric of program evaluation. The development of these into definable constructs, based on research, is nonexistent. We cite one (of an endless number) such irksome area (what we cannot nail down is always irksome!). The fine line between intuition and fact has often been discussed and argued by evaluators. Those who give credibility to intuition support the importance of judgments by the evaluator and program stakeholders in program assessment. They contend that experience gives wisdom and insights that have a very real value in making judgments and reaching conclusions. By contrast, those who adopt a strict empiricist approach insist on facts; they want to know what really is happening and have little interest in nonprofessional judgments of the occurrences. To complicate this theoretical issue, an intermediate group happily accedes to both views, depending on pertaining conditions. Is the intuitive adherent right? Is the empiricist right? Is there, in reality, a sharp dichotomy, or can there be a rational and accommodating fusion of the two points of view? There is yet no best answer to these theoretical questions. This is one example where the application of high-quality, systematic research would shed light on unanswered questions. The development of program evaluation, including the theoretical constructs underlying the kinds of approaches we cover in this book, should rely increasingly on strong research.

Criteria for Judging Program Evaluation Theories

Beyond meeting the requirements of the preceding definition of a program evaluation theory, evaluation theorists need to meet certain well-established criteria of a sound theory. Such criteria are seen in various definitions of theory in the professional literature. Scriven (1991) defines theories as "general accounts of a field of phenomena, generating at least explanations and sometimes also predictions and generalizations" (p. 360). Following from this definition (of a general theory), leading criteria for evaluating a program evaluation theory are that it be useful in efficiently generating verifiable predictions or propositions concerning evaluative acts and consequences and provide reliable, valid, actionable direction for ethically conducting effective program evaluations. More specific additional criteria for evaluating the utility of a program evaluation theory, frequently referenced in writings on theory, include clarity and comprehensiveness of assumptions, parsimony, resilience, robustness, generalizability, and heuristic power.

Other criteria for judging program evaluation theories are evident in the Joint Committee *Program Evaluation Standards* (1994) and the American Evaluation Association *Guiding Principles for Evaluators* (2004). The *Program Evaluation Standards* contains thirty specific standards that spell out requirements that program evaluations meet conditions of utility, feasibility, propriety, and accuracy. The *Guiding Principles for Evaluators* require that evaluators practice systematic inquiry, possess the needed competencies, meet conditions of integrity and honesty, steadfastly be respectful of people, and assume responsibility for serving the general and public welfare. It follows that sound theories of program evaluation should at least consider the professional standards and principles of the evaluation field. Exhibit 2.1 provides an organized list of some of the criteria for use in evaluating program evaluation theories.

Theory Development as a Creative Process Subject to Review and Acceptance by Users

While theory development is critically important to advancing program evaluation practice, it is also a creative, complex, difficult enterprise. Typically, sound theory development includes study of practice; taking account of context; making bounded, creative conceptualizations; operationalizing and applying the conceptualizations; rigorously studying applications; and revising conceptualizations. Thus, it is properly conceived as an ongoing, cyclical, practice-linked, research-based, creative process that denotes the appropriate sphere of application.

Theory development basically is an exploratory, even arbitrary process. It is a matter of the free, creative choice of the theorist. Although we can outline the features of a sound theory, characterize a general cycle of ongoing theory development, and suggest criteria for evaluating theories, we will not lay out any one method for the development of program evaluation theories. We should not do so any more than we should tell creative composers, poets, or artists how they must produce their creative contributions. In this sense, a theory of program evaluation is no more or less than an interrelated set of propositions about program

EXHIBIT 2.1. CRITERIA FOR EVALUATING
PROGRAM EVALUATION THEORIES.

Is the theory useful for:

Professionalizing program evaluation
- Generating and testing standards for program evaluations?
- Clarifying roles and goals of program evaluation?
- Developing needed tools and strategies for conducting evaluations?
- Providing structure for program evaluation curricula?

Research
- Generating and testing predictions or propositions concerning evaluative acts and consequences?
- Application to specific classes of program evaluation (the criterion of particularity) or a wide range of program evaluations (the criterion of generalizability)?
- Generating new ideas about evaluation (the criterion of heuristic power)?
- Drawing out lessons from evaluation practice to generate better theory?

Planning evaluations
- Giving evaluators a structure for conceptualizing evaluation problems and approaches?
- Determining and stating comprehensive, clear assumptions for particular evaluations?
- Determining boundaries and taking account of context in particular program evaluations?
- Providing reliable, valid, actionable direction for ethically and systematically conducting effective program evaluations?

Staffing evaluations
- Clarifying roles and responsibilities of evaluators?
- Determining the competencies and other characteristics evaluators need to conduct sound, effective evaluations?
- Determining the areas of needed cooperation and support from evaluation clients and stakeholders?

Guiding evaluations
- Conducting evaluations that are parsimonious, efficient, resilient, robust, and effective?
- Serving clients and the public?
- Promoting evaluations that clients and others can and do use?
- Promoting integrity, honesty, and respect for people in program evaluations?
- Responsibly serving the general and public welfare?

evaluations created by the theorist. It stands on its own as a set of personalized predictions and propositions.

However, the theorist cannot have his theory accepted and applied by just creating it and saying it is good. Like a musical composition, Broadway play, or painting, a program evaluation theory must pass muster with critics and the theorist's broader audience. Program evaluation theories are subject to evaluation by users. Mainly they will judge a theory of program evaluation to be useful or not based primarily on how efficiently and validly the theory generates verifiable predictions about the relation of certain evaluation actions to evaluation outcomes and propositions about how to carry out successful program evaluations that hold up in practice. It is up to the theorists to make and put forward their theories in whatever way they see best. If they want them to count for something and be influential, then the theorists will want to obtain rigorous research on the theories' utility and use the findings to improve the theories.

The Status of Theory Development in the Program Evaluation Field

The relatively young evaluation profession has advanced substantially in conceptualizing the program evaluation enterprise but has far to go in developing overarching, validated theories to guide the study and practice of program evaluation. The program evaluation literature's references to program evaluation theories are numerous, but these references are often pretentious. They usually denote as theories conceptual approaches or evaluation models that lack the comprehensiveness and validation required of sound theories.

Alkin's 2004 book, *Evaluation Roots,* is a case in point. It is valuable in its presentation of various conceptual approaches to program evaluation. However, the book's labeling of these as theories is misleading, since none of them meet the conditions for a fully developed, useful theory. In partial recognition of the primitive state of theory development in program evaluation, Alkin noted that all the theories considered in his book are descriptive, not predictive. Clearly these conceptualizations do not provide validated predictions of the consequences of particular evaluation actions. Moreover, they do not hold up as descriptive theories either. More than characterizing how evaluations actually play out in practice, the conceptualizations Alkin referenced give the particular authors' prescriptions about how evaluations should be done. The presentations are devoid of evidence that evaluations are actually carried out in the ways described, which in itself is not a deficiency. However, the presented conceptualizations are more aptly labeled prescriptive than descriptive.

We will not push this criticism too hard, because the program evaluation field has made substantial progress in conceptualizing approaches to program evaluation, and Alkin's book presents a valuable analysis of this progress. Also, evaluation theorists clearly have reflected on practical program evaluation experiences in conceptualizing their approaches and have sought to make them useful. What we want the reader to consider is that theory development in program evaluation still has far to go. We believe the weakest link in developing program evaluation theories so far is the lack of formulation and rigorous testing of hypotheses about the effects of applying different theoretical approaches in actual program evaluations. We hope sponsors of evaluation research will take note of the critical need to support studies to formulate and test hypotheses about what evaluative actions produce the most beneficial program evaluation outcomes under documented contextual circumstances.

The Importance and Difficulties of Considering Context in Theories of Program Evaluation

Prospects for successful theory development in program evaluation are limited by difficulties of predicting and generalizing in the social sciences. Any sound effort to develop a program evaluation theory needs to take account of the social, political, geographical, and temporal contexts of the program evaluations being studied. Such contexts vary widely in characteristics and influence from evaluation to evaluation. Moreover, the contexts for program evaluations typically are fluid, uncontrolled, and unpredictable. Without considering context, a theorist can hardly posit how a prescribed approach to evaluation will work or not work under any particular set of social, organizational, economic, and other conditions. Moreover, validated predictions, even in the physical sciences, may have a short half-life.

These dilemmas concerning context give a view of the challenge of developing sound theories of program evaluation. We think they also underscore the point that development of program evaluation theories must be ongoing and that theories should regularly be assessed and updated. Furthermore, each program evaluation theory is best based on a wide range of program evaluations, both within particular types of contexts and across different types of contexts. In addition, we think program evaluation theories, if they are to be useful, should advise evaluators to assess and take account of each evaluation's unique context. This requirement is explicitly made in the Context Analysis standard of the Joint Committee's *Program Evaluation Standards* (1994) and the Context Evaluation component of Stufflebeam's CIPP Model for Evaluation (2003).

Need for Multiple Theories of Program Evaluation

We think it noteworthy that evaluation's contradictory persuasions are not resolvable in any single, overall theory. Persuasions labeled positivist, existentialist, constructivist, objectivist, and postmodern include irreconcilable philosophical differences. For example, objectivist approaches posit the existence of an underlying reality and charge evaluators to pursue this. But constructivist evaluators deny the existence of an underlying reality and call on evaluators to collect and report different, likely contradictory, constructions of what is observed. And the existentialist gives particular emphasis to personal experience and responsibility in evaluations, a philosophy often exemplified in case studies. Such opposing conceptualizations of program evaluation can in their own terms be defensible, considering their different underlying precepts, assumptions, and experiences and especially how they work out in practice.

Publications by Alkin (2004), Shadish, Cook, and Leviton (1991), House (1983), Stufflebeam (2001a), Stufflebeam, Madaus, and Kellaghan (2000), and Kellaghan and Stufflebeam (2003) have acknowledged and presented fundamental differences among a wide range of individual conceptualizations of program evaluation. Although none of these conceptualizations meets the requirements for a fully validated theory, together they provide evaluators with a range of different approaches grounded in different philosophical persuasions and a wide range of experiences. We endorse efforts to evolve different, defensible conceptualizations of program evaluation into different validated theories for guiding the study and practice of program evaluation in particular types of settings and according to different philosophical approaches.

The Program Evaluation Field's
Important Theoretical Concepts

In its own right, the practice of program evaluation is heavily a conceptual activity. Conceptualization is an essential ingredient in planning particular evaluations and developing generalized theoretical approaches. For both purposes, evaluators are aided by developing firm knowledge and understanding of the main concepts found in the evaluation literature. Some of these concepts, such as formative and summative evaluations, are held in common by basically all theorists, while others, such as multiple realities and evaluation connoisseurship, are idiosyncratic to particular approaches. Throughout this book, we identify program evaluation concepts that we view as important and present our definitions of these concepts. We suggest that readers incorporate these concepts and definitions into their working vocabularies of evaluation. For the reader's convenience we have compiled these defined concepts in the Glossary at the back of the book.

Hypotheses for Research on Program Evaluation

Efforts to develop program evaluation theory should include rigorous formulation and testing of hypotheses about what works in program evaluations, why, and under what conditions. A search for hypotheses drawn from 2004 Evaluators' Institute courses, our own experiences, and the research literature revealed the following example hypotheses regarding different aspects of program evaluation:

Professional Standards and Principles for Program Evaluations

- Appropriate application of evaluation standards and principles enhances an evaluation's quality and resolution of ethical problems (from Michael Morris's description of his 2004 Evaluators' Institute course).

Involvement of Stakeholders

- Stakeholder involvement enhances use of evaluation findings (Alkin, Daillak, & White, 1979).
- Under certain conditions, stakeholder involvement may lead to studies that are misguided, cost too much, take too long, or never get done (Layzer's description of his 2004 Evaluators' Institute course).

Participatory and Collaborative Evaluations

- Participatory and collaborative approaches used for capacity building enhance program effectiveness and increase evaluation use (Patton's description of his 2004 Evaluators' Institute course).
- Political issues are especially present and influential in participatory evaluations (House, 1993).

Use of Program Theory and Logic Models in Program Evaluations

- Positive effects of the use of program theory and logic models can include conceptual clarity of complex programs, motivation of staff, and better-focused evaluations.
- Negative effects of the use of program theory and logic models can include diversion of time and attention from other critical evaluation activities, provision

of an invalid or misleading picture of a program, and discouragement of critical investigation of causal pathways and unintended outcomes.

- Application of tried-and-true methods of using program theory and logic models helps evaluators and clients identify criteria, develop questions, and identify data sources and bases for comparisons.
- Inappropriate uses of a program theory or a logic model in evaluations include focusing only on intended outcomes, ignoring differential effects for individuals and client subgroups, and seeking only evidence that confirms the theory or model.
- Effective strategies for avoiding use traps include differentiated theory, market segmentation, and competitive elaboration of alternative hypotheses (Patricia Rogers's description of her 2004 Evaluators' Institute course).

Needs Assessment

- Appropriate uses of relevant needs assessments improve the relevance of conclusions about programs (James Altchuld's description of his 2004 Evaluators' Institute course).

Evaluation of Program Implementation

- Effective evaluation of program implementation that provides feedback on critical ingredients of a program helps drive program improvement by fostering understanding of factors affecting implementation and short-term results (Arnold Love's description of his 2004 Evaluators' Institute course).

Surveys

Donald Dillman's description of his 2004 Evaluators' Institute course included the following hypotheses, which have been researched extensively and effectively.

- Particular ways of developing, presenting, and encouraging response to mail and Web survey questions contribute to high response rates and high-quality responses.
- Multiple sources of error must be overcome to produce high-quality survey results.
- Adhering to certain principles for writing questions minimizes measurement error.
- Questions ordered in different ways have different, predictable consequences.
- Self-administered questionnaires and telephone interviews yield different results for particular reasons verified by research.
- Different page layouts influence people to read and answer questions differently for particular reasons.

- Certain survey methods yield high response rates.
- Certain survey methods minimize nonresponse error.

Sampling

- Careful use of sampling methods can save resources and often increase the validity of evaluation findings (Gary Henry's description of his 2004 Evaluators' Institute course).

Applied Measurement

- Proper measurements of a program's feasibility, relevance, and effectiveness—that are systematic, replicable, interpretable, reliable, and valid—are necessary for successful evaluations (Ann Doucette's description of his 2004 Evaluators' Institute course).

Reporting Strategies

- Effective employment of a variety of reporting strategies beyond the written report, applied differentially to audiences, increases their use of findings (Hallie Preskill's description of her 2004 Evaluators' Institute course).

Use of Technology in Evaluation

- Proper use of technology for data collection and analysis, storage and retrieval of information, and dissemination and use of findings contribute to strengthening and reducing the costs of evaluations. (Arnold Love's description of his 2004 Evaluators' Institute course)

Building Organizational Capacity in Evaluation

- Developing and appropriately employing an organization's evaluation capacity leads to more and better learning in organizations (Hallie Preskill's description of her 2004 Evaluators' Institute course).

These hypotheses illustrate the need for empirical research on the evaluation process. Such research should be directed to producing research-based principles for conducting program evaluations akin to those found in the field of survey research. Donald Dillman's research on survey methods provides an excellent exemplar for emulation in other sectors of program evaluation. The grouping of the hypotheses above also illustrates the range and complexity of dimensions to be considered in formulating program evaluation theories.

The Potential Utility of Grounded Theories

In testing hypotheses about evaluation practices, it is important to document and take into account the subject program evaluation's particular circumstances, including pertinent contextual variables. Unlike laboratory experiments in the physical sciences, program evaluations occur in dynamic, uncontrolled settings, their procedures typically unfold in response to evolving stakeholder needs, and they are constrained and affected by complex and changing contextual circumstances. Understanding the functioning of a program evaluation requires extensive, valid description of the evaluation process, the nature of contextual influences, and the evaluation's impacts.

Accordingly, the program evaluation field could benefit by employing the methodology of grounded theories as one theory development tool. By this approach, theorists would generate theories grounded in systematic, rigorous documentation and analysis of actual program evaluations and their particular circumstances. This line of reasoning is consistent with a point made by Leonard Broom in his introduction to Abraham Kaplan's book, *The Conduct of Inquiry* (1964). Broom stated, "The behavioral scientist . . . needs to read from the strengths of his own understanding, insights, expertness, and subject matter and not from the insecurity of a limited familiarity with a remote discipline" (p. xvii). Straus and Corbin (1990) describe and illustrate grounded theory procedures that we see as potentially useful for generating sound theories of program evaluation.

Few, if any, examples of rigorously conducted grounded theories of program evaluation have been published. However, the approaches examined in Parts Two and Three of this book comport with the general notion of grounded theory. They are prescriptions based on their authors' reflections on and critical analyses of a wide range of evaluation experiences. Limitations of these prescriptive theories are that they do not meet requirements for systematic and rigorous testing of theory-based hypotheses and lack documentation of the underlying program evaluation experiences.

The Potential Utility of Metaevaluations in Developing Theories of Program Evaluation

A source of valuable evidence for use in developing program evaluation theories, akin to that from grounded theory work, is found in metaevaluations of program evaluations. These are studies that systematically document and assess program evaluations (a review and analysis of such studies is found in Stufflebeam, 2001b). Program evaluators and their clients need to greatly increase their employment of metaevaluation and should make the results available to evaluation researchers. Fortunately, the *American Journal of Evaluation* encourages submission of metaevaluations. Researchers should use metaevaluation reports systematically to examine the reasons that different evaluation approaches succeeded or failed. We believe theory development efforts can profit by using metaevaluation findings to look at the adequacy and influence of guiding conceptualizations and procedures, implementation of the procedures, propriety considerations, stakeholder involvement, and contextual influences, including political forces and psychological factors.

The Program Evaluation Standards and Theory Development

Chapter Three of this book examines guiding principles and standards for evaluations in depth including, importantly, the Joint Committee *Program Evaluation Standards* (1994), which we refer to frequently. The *Standards* were designed, after intensive literature research and professional activities, to provide principles and guidelines for evaluating educational programs, projects, and materials in many different settings. Although focused on educational evaluation, the *Standards* have applicability and relevance in a wide range of professional and other arenas. This is evident in their four main requirements that evaluations should be useful, feasible, proper, and accurate. Adding to the *Standards'* widespread applicability is the fact that all fields require evaluation of their training and education programs.

The *Standards* book comprises thirty individual standards. Each may be considered as a separate construct, thus open to empirical research. In addition, each includes guidelines to consider and apply as appropriate, plus common errors to avoid. These guidelines and common errors essentially are hypotheses about what actions to take or avoid to produce sound, effective evaluations. Although there is little doubt that the thirty standards individually and collectively have added considerable credibility and direction to the evaluation field, they will remain theoretical constructs until rigorously researched.

Let us consider, as an example, Utility Standard 3, Information Scope and Selection, which states, "Information collected should be broadly selected to address pertinent questions about the program and be responsive to the needs and interests of clients and other specified stakeholders." This standard underlines the importance of gathering information from a broad and relevant scope to meet all clients' decision-making objectives, while also being sufficiently comprehensive to assess an evaluand's merit and worth. Particularly, the standard requires the evaluation to assess a program "in terms of all important variables"; examples include effectiveness, harmful side effects, costs, responses to participants' needs, and relevance of underlying assumptions and values. These elements, taken together with the stakeholder-centered direction of the standard, impose the elements of a theory—but one in need of validation.

There undoubtedly is a potentially rich field for empirical research based on all thirty standards and their associated guidelines and common errors. Directly and indirectly, the effective use of the program evaluation approaches explicated in Part Three of this book depends on satisfying the requirements of *The Program Evaluation Standards*. Clearly, all sound evaluation approaches should meet conditions of utility, feasibility, propriety, and accuracy. Moreover, the general assumption is that these standards provide not only useful guidelines but also, in the opinion of many evaluators, established principles. Only research into these theoretical constructs will confirm their validity as predictors of evaluation outcomes and their standing as validated theories. The stronger the links are between program evaluation approaches and practices, on the one hand, and standards for program evaluation, on the other, the more essential it is that assumptions contained in the latter are confirmed by research.

Summary

Sound theories of program evaluation are needed to advance effective program evaluation practices. The needed theories are coherent sets of conceptual, hypothetical, pragmatic, and ethical principles forming general frameworks to guide the study and practice of program evaluations. They should meet criteria of utility in efficiently generating verifiable predictions or propositions concerning evaluative acts and consequences and provide reliable, valid, actionable direction for ethically conducting effective program evaluations. They should also meet requirements for clarity, comprehensiveness, parsimony, resilience, robustness, generalizability, heuristic power, and ethical public service.

The program evaluation field saw great theoretical progress in the last four decades of the twentieth century. Although much more work is needed, the field's literature developed substantially. It is rich in concepts, standards, guiding principles, practical guidelines, and approaches. It is modestly strong in positing hypotheses. It is strong in testing hypotheses about uses of surveys but otherwise weak in presenting tested hypotheses. Overall, the program evaluation field has far to go in quests to develop and present research-based theories whose predictions hold true.

The program evaluation field would benefit if future program evaluation theory development efforts would convert the best of the current program evaluation approaches to validated theories. In Part Two of this book, we give our assessment of which program evaluation approaches most merit serious theoretical development and practical use. The methods of grounded theories and information from metaevaluations of program evaluations could aid the needed theory development efforts. Moreover, the Joint Committee *Program Evaluation Standards* (1994) provide a framework and hypotheses—in the form of standards, procedural guidelines, and common errors to avoid—to guide empirical research on evaluation. Until sound program evaluation theories are produced, we advise evaluators to retain a healthy amount of circumspection and even skepticism while advisedly using available approaches that match their philosophies and circumstances.

Review Questions

1. Argue the pros and cons of investing time and resources to develop and validate sound theories of evaluation.
2. What are the main differences between general and specific theories of program evaluation and why are both of these needed?
3. Draft a checklist of criteria for use in evaluating evaluation theories.
4. Explain and assess the claim that theory development is a creative, arbitrary process.
5. Explain and assess the claim that multiple theories of program evaluation are needed.
6. Provide examples of conceptual, hypothetical, pragmatic, and ethical principles of program evaluation.
7. Respond to the claim that the program evaluation field has no guiding theories.
8. Describe an example of how failing to consider context in a program evaluation would lead to poor evaluative conclusions.
9. Outline a study you would conduct to test the following hypothesis: Appropriate application of evaluation standards and principles enhances an evaluation's quality and resolution of ethical problems.
10. Provide examples of how use of methods of grounded theory and information from metaevaluations would aid the development of a sound program evaluation theory.

Group Exercises

Work through the following two exercises with your group. It is quite possible that members will reach different conclusions about their best methods of endeavoring to solve the problems. However, members should try to justify their point of view.

Exercise 1. A long-standing difference of opinion exists between two college faculties, Education and Humanities, over the place of theory in evaluation practice, particularly as it applies to program evaluation. The Education faculty contends that a logical start for students to study evaluation is to begin with a solid theoretical basis. The Humanities faculty opposes this view, believing that evaluation is a pragmatic activity and that while a grasp of theory may develop over time, the teaching of approaches and models of evaluation should have paramount importance.

What advice do you give to the staff of these two faculties?

Exercise 2. Let one group member outline a program evaluation that he or she is conversant with. Now refer to the "Hypotheses for Research on Program Evaluation" section in this chapter, and search for hypotheses regarding different aspects of that evaluation. For instance, the hypotheses for testing may apply to the successful aspects of an evaluation (for example, why it works well in its particular context) or could be formulated for future improvement of the evaluation approach or model.

References

Alkin, M. C. (Ed.). (2004). *Evaluation roots: Tracing theorists' views and influences.* Thousand Oaks, CA: Sage.

Alkin, M. C., Daillak, R., & White, B. (1979). *Using evaluations: Does evaluation make a difference?* Thousand Oaks, CA: Sage.

American Evaluation Association. (2004). *Guiding principles for evaluators* [On-line]. Available: http://www.eval.org/Publications/GuidingPrinciples.asp.

Broom, L. (1964). Introduction. In A. Kaplan, *The conduct of inquiry.* San Francisco: Chandler.

Christie, C. (Ed.). (2003, Spring). *The practice-theory relationship in evaluation.* New Directions for Evaluation, no. 97. San Francisco: Jossey-Bass.

Datta, L-E. (2003, Spring). Important questions, intriguing method, incomplete answers. In C. Christie (Ed.), *The practice-theory relationship in evaluation* (pp. 37–46). New Directions for Evaluation, no. 97. San Francisco: Jossey-Bass.

Evaluators' Institute. (2004). *The evaluators' institute program.* Washington, DC: Evaluators' Institute.

Fitzpatrick, J. L., Sanders, J. R., & Worthen, B. R. (2004). *Program evaluation: Alternative approaches and practical guidelines.* Needham Heights, MA: Pearson and Allyn and Bacon.

Guba, E. G. (1969). The failure of educational evaluation. *Educational Technology, 9*(5), 29–38.

Guba, E. G. (1978). *Toward a methodology of naturalistic inquiry in educational evaluation.* Los Angeles: University of California, Center for the Study of Evaluation.

House, E. R. (1983). Assumptions underlying evaluation models. In G. F. Madaus, M. S. Scriven, & D. L. Stufflebeam (Eds.), *Evaluation models: Viewpoints on educational and human services evaluation* (pp. 45–64). Norwell, MA: Kluwer.

House, E. R. (1993). *Professional evaluation–Social impact and political consequences.* Thousand Oaks, CA: Sage.

Joint Committee on Standards for Educational Evaluation. (1994). *The program evaluation standards: How to assess evaluations of educational programs* (2nd ed.). Thousand Oaks, CA: Sage.

Kaplan, A. (1964). *The conduct of inquiry.* San Francisco: Chandler.

Kellaghan, T., & Stufflebeam, D. L. (2003). *International handbook of educational evaluation.* Norwell, MA: Kluwer.

Madaus, G. F., & Stufflebeam, D. L. (1988). *Educational evaluation: The classical writings of Ralph W. Tyler.* Norwell, MA: Kluwer.

Morris, M. (2003). Ethical considerations in evaluation. In T. Kellaghan & D. L. Stufflebeam (Eds.), *International handbook of educational evaluation.* Norwell, MA: Kluwer.

Schwandt, T. (2004). *"Sciencephobia" or legitimate worry? A diagnostic reading of science-based research.* Keynote address at the 2004 Minnesota Evaluation Studies Institute, Minneapolis.

Scriven, M. (1973). Goal-free evaluation. In E. House (Ed.), *School evaluation: The politics and process.* Berkeley, CA: McCutchan.

Scriven, M. (1991). *Evaluation thesaurus* (4th ed.). Thousand Oaks, CA: Sage.

Shadish, W. R., Cook, T. D., & Leviton, L.C.L. (1991). *Foundations of program evaluation.* Thousand Oaks, CA: Sage.

Stake, R. E. (1975). *Program evaluation, particularly responsive evaluation.* Kalamazoo: Western Michigan University Evaluation Center.

Stake, R. E. (1976). A theoretical statement of responsive evaluation. *Studies in Educational Evaluation, 2,* 19–22.

Stake, R. E. (1988). Seeking sweet water. In R. M. Jaeger (Ed.), *Methods for research in education* (pp. 253–300). Washington, DC: American Educational Research Association.

Straus, A., & Corbin, J. (1990). *Basics of qualitative research: Grounded theory of qualitative research.* Thousand Oaks, CA: Sage.

Stufflebeam, D. L. (Ed.). (2001a). *Evaluation models.* New Directions for Evaluation, no. 89. San Francisco: Jossey-Bass.

Stufflebeam, D. L. (2001b). The metaevaluation imperative. *American Journal of Evaluation, 22*(2), 183–209.

Stufflebeam, D. L. (2003). The CIPP model for evaluation. In T. Kellaghan & D. L. Stufflebeam (Eds.), *The international handbook of educational evaluation.* Dordrecht: Kluwer.

Stufflebeam, D. L., Madaus, G. F., & Kellaghan, T. (2000). *Evaluation models: Viewpoints on educational and human services evaluation.* Norwell, MA: Kluwer.

CHAPTER THREE

STANDARDS FOR PROGRAM EVALUATIONS

This chapter is devoted to the standards for guiding and judging evaluations, an essential aspect of any evaluation practice. Standards help ensure that evaluators and their clients communicate effectively and reach a clear, mutual understanding concerning the criteria to be met by an evaluation. Such standards are needed to obviate the possibility that either stakeholders or evaluators might unscrupulously bend evaluation outcomes to suit themselves. Without standards that define acceptable evaluative service, the credibility of evaluation procedures, outcomes, or reporting is left in doubt. To be authoritative and credible, evaluation standards must reflect a general consensus by leading figures in pertinent professional organizations.

Evaluation is an emerging profession, and, following the example of more mature fields, evaluators have established standards and principles by which to guide and assess their work. During the past two decades, the professionalization of evaluation has been considerably strengthened by the development and use of evaluation standards. During this time, professional standards, directed toward sound practice through agreed principles, have become an integral part of the wider community's insistence on criteria and measures to ensure the quality and accountability of evaluations.

In this chapter, we summarize and suggest ways to use the 1994 revision of *The Program Evaluation Standards* developed by the Joint Committee on Standards for Educational Evaluation and accredited by the American National Standards

Institute; the *Guiding Principles for Evaluators*, developed and officially endorsed by the American Evaluation Association (American Evaluation Association 2003 Ethics Committee, 2004); and the 2003 revision of the *Government Auditing Standards* developed by the U.S. Government Accountability Office and required for use in auditing U.S. government programs.

The Joint Committee (1994) defined an evaluation standard as a "principle mutually agreed to by people engaged in a professional practice of evaluation, that, if met, will enhance the quality and fairness of an evaluation" (p. 3). The AEA Task Force noted that an evaluation principle provides evaluators with guidance that is general and conceptual rather than operational. The Government Accountability Office defined auditing standards as broad statements of auditors' responsibilities. Fundamentally, all three documents present general principles, which is the essential meaning of a standard. To aid communication, throughout the chapter, we will use the generic term *standards* to refer to *The Program Evaluation Standards*, the *AEA Guiding Principles for Evaluators*, and the *Government Auditing Standards*.

All three documents provide authoritative direction for guiding and assessing program evaluation studies. *The Program Evaluation Standards* concentrate on evaluations of education and training programs and services in the United States and Canada. They contain considerable specificity about what to do and not do in educational program evaluations and a range of illustrative cases. Although these standards do not directly address evaluations in a wide range of substantive areas—such as engineering, philanthropy, social work, public administration, and community development—it is noteworthy that every field relies heavily on education of its members and that its educational programs should be evaluated regularly. Thus, *The Program Evaluation Standards* have applicability to education enterprises in all fields. The AEA *Guiding Principles* cut across evaluations in many disciplines and service areas but lack the detail and examples found in *The Program Evaluation Standards*. The *Government Auditing Standards* are based on standards of the U.S. accounting and auditing professions, focused on assessing and strengthening the financial accountability of U.S. agencies and federal programs, and contain detailed requirements, recommendations, and prohibitions. It is noteworthy that these standards provide direction for evaluating audit organizations as well as the audits they conduct. This makes the *Government Auditing Standards* potentially useful for assessing both program evaluations and the organizations that conduct these evaluations. While the *Government Auditing Standards* concentrate on financial accounting requirements, this chapter focuses on the parts of these standards that provide direction for evaluating the goals, organization, implementation, and outcomes of federal programs, as well as departments and organizations that conduct program evaluations.

The three sets of standards treated in this chapter are among the most fully developed sets of such professional imperatives for program evaluations. These standards merit serious consideration by professional evaluators and those training to become evaluators in North America and could be generally instructive to such persons in other countries. The standards level the playing field for neophyte and experienced evaluators by providing objective criteria for judging evaluation efforts and evaluation organizations. When armed with a working knowledge of the standards, evaluators can stand on firm ground in crafting and defending their program evaluation plans and assessments of evaluations, helping constituents understand what is required in sound program evaluations, and examining and strengthening an evaluation organization. Use of the standards as planning guides makes the design of evaluations a more certain and efficient process. Their use in evaluations of program evaluations (metaevaluations) is especially important to help users determine how much confidence to place in the evaluations. While the discussion in this chapter is particularly applicable to program evaluations in North America, program evaluators around the world may find these constructions instructive about the pervasive issues in program evaluations that cross national boundaries and alternative formats they might consider when crafting their own standards.

This chapter looks at four topics. First, we discuss the functions of evaluation standards. After that we provide background on why and how the U.S. evaluation standards were developed. Subsequently, we summarize each set of evaluation standards. Finally, we suggest ways of applying the different sets of standards. We hope readers will become allies in disseminating knowledge of and productive use of all three sets of the discussed evaluation standards. A great deal of work needs to be done to help evaluators and their clients learn about and effectively apply the evaluation standards. We need to stress that mastering this chapter's contents is only one important step toward developing a working knowledge of the subject standards. We also urge readers to obtain, study, and apply the actual standards.

The Need for Evaluation Standards

Most professions and many other public service fields have developed and periodically update standards, principles, or codes of performance. They do so in the interest of having their members provide competent, ethical, and safe services. Often the standards, principles, and codes are part of an accrediting, licensing, or certification system intended to ensure high-quality services and protect the interests of the public. Such standards, principles, and codes typically are defined by a standing committee of distinguished members of the service area, in some cases by government licensing or oversight bodies, and occasionally with participation by constituent and client groups. Familiar examples are the standards of practice employed by the fields of law, medicine, dentistry, hospitals, clinical psychology, engineering, educational and psychological testing, auditing, and accounting. Other examples are the codes established for the construction, electrical, plumbing, and food service areas. An important matter in advancing the development and use of standards is that periodically they must be reviewed and revised to keep them up to date, legally viable, and responsive to the field.

We believe that every professional evaluator should know, understand, and faithfully apply appropriate standards of professional evaluation practice. Standards and codes are established and applied in the interest of ensuring and improving quality and protecting the public from shoddy, harmful, fraudulent, or wasteful evaluation services. Standards for program evaluations have several specific functions:

- Provide general principles for addressing a variety of practical issues in evaluation work
- Help ensure that evaluators will employ the evaluation field's best available practices
- Provide direction to make evaluation planning efficient and inclusive of pertinent evaluation questions
- Provide core content for training and educating evaluators and other participants in the evaluation process
- Present evaluators and their constituents with a common language to facilitate communication and collaboration
- Help evaluators achieve and maintain credibility among other professions
- Earn and maintain credibility with public oversight bodies and clients
- Earn and maintain the public's confidence in the evaluation field
- Protect consumers and society from harmful or corrupt practices
- Provide objective criteria for assessing and strengthening evaluation services
- Provide a basis for accountability by evaluators
- Provide a basis for adjudicating claims of malpractice and other disputes
- Provide a conceptual framework and working definitions to help guide research and development in evaluation

Based on these functions, adherence to professional standards for evaluations is at the very heart of professionalism and delivery of sound, useful evaluation services. We believe that current statements of standards for evaluations can serve these functions in the evaluation field.

The standards presented in this chapter were systematically developed, possess strong credibility, and are periodically reviewed and updated. The three sets of standards are distinct but also complementary. Learning and developing the facility to apply the three different sets of standards selectively will enhance one's professionalism and versatility in conducting sound evaluations. Evaluators who are armed with a repertoire of alternative sets of standards are aided in conducting standards-based evaluations in a wide range of disciplines and service areas. Sometimes it will be appropriate to choose one set of standards over the others, because the set is compatible with the particular program area and preferred or mandated by the client group or oversight body. Even then it is often advantageous to derive guidance from two or even all three sets of standards. We can stand behind this position because all three sets of standards are in accord with the same fundamental principles of sound evaluation. We invite readers to study the following material and incorporate what they find as valuable into their working philosophies of program evaluation.

Background of Standards for Program Evaluations

Historically, program evaluators had no need to be concerned about explicit professional standards for program evaluations, because until relatively recently, there was no semblance of an evaluation profession, and there were no standards for evaluations. Such standards came into prominence only during the 1980s and 1990s. Federal agencies had funded thousands of program evaluations as a part of President Lyndon Johnson's War on Poverty and generally found them to be costly and poor in quality and utility. Efforts to reform this embryonic program evaluation movement included establishing authoritative standards and principles for assessing and strengthening evaluation plans and reports. The development of the initial sets of standards and principles signaled both the evaluation field's historic immaturity and weakness and an added step in its movement toward professionalizing evaluation.

With the evolution of evaluation as a profession becoming a reality only during the last quarter of the twentieth century, there was a growing sense among practitioners that acceptable codes of evaluator behavior were needed. The Joint Committee on Standards for Educational Evaluation was established in 1975. Through the years, this standing committee has continued to be sponsored by twelve to fifteen professional societies with a combined membership totaling nearly 3 million. The committee's charge is to perform ongoing development, reviews, and revisions of standards for educational evaluations. This committee issued the

Standards for Evaluations of Educational Programs, Projects, and Materials in 1981 and an updated version in 1994, *The Program Evaluation Standards.* The Joint Committee also published standards for evaluating educational personnel in 1988, and in 2003 it issued a set of standards for evaluations of students. The Joint Committee is accredited by the American National Standards Institute as the only body recognized to set standards for educational evaluations in the United State.

At nearly the same time as the Joint Committee standards were published, the Evaluation Research Society (ERS) produced a second set. The ERS, established in 1976, focused on professionalizing program evaluation as practiced across a wide range of disciplines, government programs, and service areas. This society published a set of standards labeled the *Evaluation Research Society Standards for Program Evaluations* (ERS Standards Committee, 1982). These were fifty-five brief, admonitory statements divided into the following categories: Formulation and Negotiation, Structure and Design, Data Collection and Preparation, Data Analysis and Interpretation, Communication and Disclosure, and Use of Results. In 1986, ERS amalgamated with the Evaluation Network (ENET) to form the American Evaluation Association (AEA), which has a membership of nearly three thousand. AEA subsequently retired the ERS Standards in favor of producing the *AEA Guiding Principles for Program Evaluators* (Shadish, Newman, Scheirer, & Wye, 1995). In July 2004, the AEA membership ratified a revised edition of the *Guiding Principles for Evaluators.*

The U.S. General Accounting Office explicitly included program evaluation in its 1994 and 2003 revisions of the *Government Auditing Standards.* The U.S. federal government's War on Poverty, which began in 1965, spawned many expensive federal programs, which generated a huge need for financial auditing of the programs. In 1972 the General Accounting Office began issuing *Government Auditing Standards.* The initial edition and early revisions of these standards dealt almost exclusively with the financial aspects of federal programs. The 2003 edition includes program audits and evaluations as one of the foci of general standards and presents chapters containing fieldwork standards and reporting standards for performance audits.

Especially noteworthy in the 2003 edition is the new section on independence, which prohibits auditors from simultaneously providing both auditing and consulting services to the same entity. Such commingling of services is seen as an unacceptable conflict of interest. It could lead auditors to evaluate their own work and thus lose their independence and credibility, possibly succumbing to illicit pressures to distort reports. This has been made manifestly clear in the private sector. For example, when Arthur Andersen Company auditors both consulted with and audited the work of the Enron Corporation, Andersen was later charged with covering up and being party to malfeasance in the corporation. Its alleged compromise of its independence contributed to the scandal in which Enron's employees and stockholders lost billions of dollars. Ultimately, this transgression led to the near demise of Andersen, previously one of America's Big Five auditing firms. Clearly, the GAO standard on independence is applicable to program evaluations as well as financial audits, and we think its message probably should be incorporated into future editions of the Joint Committee and AEA standards.

Joint Committee Program Evaluation Standards

The seventeen members of the original Joint Committee on Standards for Educational Evaluation were appointed by twelve professional organizations. The organizations and their appointed members represented a wide range of specialties: school accreditation, counseling and guidance, curriculum, educational administration, higher education, educational measurement, educational research, education governance, program evaluation, psychology, statistics, and teaching. A fundamental requirement of the committee is that it include about equal numbers of members representing client and evaluator perspectives.[1] Over the years, the number of the Joint Committee's sponsoring organizations has increased slightly. (At the publication of the 1994 *The Program Evaluation Standards,* the committee was sponsored by fifteen organizations, including AEA.[2]) Since its inception, the Joint Committee's work has been housed at the Western Michigan University Evaluation Center.

Each edition of *The Program Evaluation Standards* has detailed presentations of the thirty standards. Each standard contains a statement of the standard, an explanation of its requirements, a rationale, guidelines for carrying it out, common errors to be anticipated and avoided, and an illustrative case. The 1994 version covers education and training in such settings as business, government, law, medicine, the military, nursing, professional development, elementary and secondary schools, social service agencies, and colleges and universities.

The thirty standards are grouped according to four essential attributes of a sound evaluation: utility, feasibility, propriety, and accuracy. The Joint Committee advises both evaluators and clients to apply the thirty standards so that their evaluations satisfy all four essential attributes of a sound evaluation. We advise readers to fix firmly in their minds the following four fundamental concepts in *The Program Evaluation Standard:* utility, feasibility, propriety, and accuracy.

Utility

An evaluation should be useful. It should be addressed to those persons and groups that are involved in or responsible for implementing the program being evaluated. The evaluators should ascertain the users' information needs and report to them the relevant evaluative feedback clearly, concisely, and on time. It should help them identify and attend to the program's problems and be aware of important strengths. It should address the users' most important questions while also obtaining the full range of information needed to assess the program's merit and worth. The evaluation should not only report feedback about strengths and weaknesses, but also should assist users in studying and applying the findings. The utility standards reflect the general consensus found in the evaluation literature that program evaluations should effectively address the information needs of clients and other right-to-know audiences and should inform program improvement processes. If there is no prospect that the findings of a contemplated evaluation would be used, the evaluation should not be undertaken.

Feasibility

An evaluation should be feasible. It should employ evaluation procedures that are parsimonious and operable in the program's environment. It should avoid disrupting or otherwise impairing the program. It should control as much as possible the political forces that might otherwise impede or corrupt the evaluation. And it should be conducted as efficiently and cost-effectively as possible. This set of standards emphasizes that evaluation procedures must be workable in real-world settings, not only in experimental laboratories. Overall, the feasibility standards require evaluations to be realistic, prudent, diplomatic, politically viable, frugal, and cost-effective. Despite federal mandates to the contrary, true experiments often are not feasible in field settings, and in such cases, evaluators should employ realistic, naturalistic, multimethod studies.

Propriety

An evaluation should meet conditions of propriety. It should be grounded in clear, written agreements defining the obligations of the evaluator and client for supporting and executing the evaluation. The evaluation should protect all involved parties' rights and dignity. Findings must be honest and not distorted in any way. Reports should be released in accordance with advance disclosure agreements and with applicable freedom of information statutes. Moreover, reports should convey balanced accounts of strengths and weaknesses. These standards reflect the fact that evaluations can affect many people in negative as well as positive ways. The propriety standards are designed to protect the rights of all parties to an evaluation. In general, the propriety standards require that evaluations be conducted legally, ethically, and with due regard for the welfare of those involved in the evaluation as well as those affected by the results.

Accuracy

An evaluation should be accurate. It should clearly describe the program as it was planned and as actually executed. It should describe the program's background and setting. It should report valid and reliable findings. It should identify and substantiate the appropriateness of the evaluation's information sources, measurement methods and devices, analytical procedures, and provisions for bias control and a metaevaluation. It should present the strengths, weaknesses, and limitations of the evaluation's plan, procedures, information, and conclusions. It should describe and assess the extent to which the evaluation provides an independent, unbiased assessment as opposed to a possibly biased self-assessment. In general, this final group of standards requires evaluators to obtain technically sound information, analyze it correctly, report justifiable conclusions, note any pertinent caveats, and obtain or conduct a metaevaluation. The overall rating of an evaluation against the twelve accuracy standards is an index of the evaluation's overall validity.

The Joint Committee's Overall Program and Approach

These four concepts are the foundation stones in each set of standards developed by the Joint Committee. In addition to the 1981 and 1994 editions of *The Program Evaluation Standards,* the committee developed the 1988 *Personnel Evaluation Standards* and the 2003 *Student Evaluation Standards.* In each of its standards-setting projects, the Joint Committee engaged about two hundred persons concerned with the professional practice of evaluation in a systematic process of generating, testing, and clarifying widely shared principles by which to guide, assess, and govern evaluation work in education. In each project, the committee sought widely divergent views on what standards should be adopted and subjected draft standards to field tests and national hearings. The committee subsequently worked through consensus development processes to converge on the final set of standards.

Each set of the Joint Committee *Standards* is a living document. This standing committee encourages users of each set of standards to provide feedback on applications of the standards, along with criticisms and suggestions. From the outset of its work, the Joint Committee has provided for periodic reviews and improvement of the standards. This feature of its work is consistent with requirements for maintaining its accreditation by the American National Standards Institute (ANSI).

The Program Evaluation Standards (Joint Committee, 1994) are summarized in Exhibit 3.1. ANSI approved these *Standards* as an American National Standard on March 15, 1994. Readers are advised to study the full text of *The Program Evaluation Standards,* so that they can internalize them and apply them judiciously at

EXHIBIT 3.1. SUMMARY OF THE
PROGRAM EVALUATION STANDARDS.

Utility

The utility standards are intended to ensure that an evaluation will serve the information needs of intended users.

U1 Stakeholder Identification. Persons involved in or affected by the evaluation should be identified, so that their needs can be addressed.

U2 Evaluator Credibility. The persons conducting the evaluation should be both trustworthy and competent to perform the evaluation, so that the evaluation findings achieve maximum credibility and acceptance.

U3 Information Scope and Selection. Information collected should be broadly selected to address pertinent questions about the program and be responsive to the needs and interests of clients and other specified stakeholders.

U4 Values Identification. The perspectives, procedures, and rationale used to interpret the findings should be carefully described, so that the bases for value judgments are clear.

U5 Report Clarity. The evaluation reports should clearly describe the program being evaluated, including its context and the purposes, procedures, and findings of the evaluation, so that essential information is provided and easily understood.

U6 Report Timeliness and Dissemination. Significant interim findings and evaluation reports should be disseminated to intended users, so that they can be used in a timely fashion.

U7 Evaluation Impact. Evaluations should be planned, conducted, and reported in ways that encourage follow-through by stakeholders, so that the likelihood that the evaluation will be used is increased.

Feasibility

The feasibility standards are intended to ensure that an evaluation will be realistic, prudent, diplomatic, and frugal.

F1 Practical Procedures. The evaluation procedures should be practical, to keep disruption to a minimum while needed information is obtained.

F2 Political Viability. The evaluation should be planned and conducted with anticipation of the different positions of various interest groups, so that their cooperation may be obtained and so that possible attempts by any of these groups to curtail evaluation operations or to bias or misapply the results can be averted or counteracted.

F3 Cost Effectiveness. The evaluation should be efficient and produce information of sufficient value, so that the resources expended can be justified.

Propriety

The propriety standards are intended to ensure that an evaluation will be conducted legally, ethically, and with due regard for the welfare of those involved in the evaluation, as well as those affected by its results.

P1 Service Orientation. Evaluations should be designed to assist organizations to address and effectively serve the needs of the full range of targeted participants.

EXHIBIT 3.1. SUMMARY OF THE
PROGRAM EVALUATION STANDARDS, Cont'd.

P2 Formal Obligations. Obligations of the formal parties to an evaluation (what is to be done, how, by whom, when) should be agreed to in writing, so that these parties are obliged to adhere to all conditions of the agreement or formally to renegotiate it.

P3 Rights of Human Subjects. Evaluations should be designed and conducted to respect and to protect the rights and welfare of human subjects.

P4 Human Interactions. Evaluators should respect human dignity and worth in their inter-actions with other persons associated with an evaluation, so that participants are not threat-ened or harmed.

P5 Complete and Fair Assessment. The evaluation should be complete and fair in its exam-ination and recording of strengths and weaknesses of the program being evaluated, so that strengths can be built upon and problem areas addressed.

P6 Disclosure of Findings. The formal parties to an evaluation should ensure that the full set of evaluation findings along with pertinent limitations are made accessible to the persons af-fected by the evaluation and any others with expressed legal rights to receive the results.

P7 Conflict of Interest. Conflict of interest should be dealt with openly and honestly, so that it does not compromise the evaluation processes and results.

P8 Fiscal Responsibility. The evaluator's allocation and expenditure of resources should reflect sound accountability procedures and otherwise be prudent and ethically responsible, so that expenditures are accounted for and appropriate.

Accuracy

The accuracy standards are intended to ensure that an evaluation will reveal and convey technically adequate information about the features that determine worth or merit of the program being evaluated.

A1 Program Documentation. The program being evaluated should be described and docu-mented clearly and accurately, so that the program is clearly identified.

A2 Context Analysis. The context in which the program exists should be examined in enough detail, so that its likely influences on the program can be identified.

A3 Described Purposes and Procedures. The purposes and procedures of the evaluation should be monitored and described in enough detail, so that they can be identified and assessed.

A4 Defensible Information Sources. The sources of information used in a program evaluation should be described in enough detail, so that the adequacy of the information can be assessed.

A5 Valid Information. The information-gathering procedures should be chosen or developed and then implemented, so that they will ensure that the interpretation arrived at is valid for the intended use.

A6 Reliable Information. The information-gathering procedures should be chosen or de-veloped and then implemented, so that they will ensure that the information obtained is sufficiently reliable for the intended use.

A7 Systematic Information. The information collected, processed, and reported in an evalua-tion should be systematically reviewed, and any errors found should be corrected.

EXHIBIT 3.1. SUMMARY OF THE
PROGRAM EVALUATION STANDARDS, Cont'd.

A8 Analysis of Quantitative Information. Quantitative information in an evaluation should be appropriately and systematically analyzed, so that evaluation questions are effectively answered.

A9 Analysis of Qualitative Information. Qualitative information in an evaluation should be appropriately and systematically analyzed, so that evaluation questions are effectively answered.

A10 Justified Conclusions. The conclusions reached in an evaluation should be explicitly justified, so that stakeholders can assess them.

A11 Impartial Reporting. Reporting procedures should guard against distortion caused by personal feelings and biases of any party to the evaluation, so that evaluation reports fairly reflect the evaluation findings.

A12 Metaevaluation. The evaluation itself should be formatively and summatively evaluated against these and other pertinent standards, so that its conduct is appropriately guided and, on completion, stakeholders can closely examine its strengths and weaknesses.

Source: Reprinted with the permission of the Joint Committee on Standards for Educational Evaluation.

each stage of an evaluation. The summary presented in Exhibit 3.1 is only a starting point and convenient memory aid.

The Joint Committee offered advice on which of the thirty standards are most applicable to each of ten tasks in the evaluation process: deciding whether to evaluate, defining the evaluation problem, designing the evaluation, collecting information, analyzing information, reporting the evaluation, budgeting the evaluation, contracting for evaluation, managing the evaluation, and staffing the evaluation. The committee's judgments of the different standards' applicability to each evaluation task are summarized in Table 3.1. The thirty standards are listed down the side of the matrix, and the ten evaluation tasks are presented across the top. The Xs in the various cells indicate that the committee judged the standard was particularly applicable to the given task. Although the Joint Committee concluded that all of the standards are applicable in all educational program evaluations, the functional analysis is intended to help evaluators quickly identify those standards that are likely to be most relevant to given evaluation tasks.

The committee presented and illustrated five general steps for applying the standards: (1) become acquainted with *The Program Evaluation Standards, (2)* clarify the purposes of the program evaluation, (3) clarify the context of the program evaluation, (4) apply each standard in the light of the purposes and context, and (5) decide what to do with the results. The committee also suggested ways to employ the standards in designing an evaluation training program.

The Program Evaluation Standards are particularly applicable in evaluations of evaluations, that is, metaevaluations. In such studies, the metaevaluator collects information and judgments about the extent to which a program evaluation complied with the requirements for meeting each standard. Then the evaluator judges whether each standard was addressed, partially addressed, not addressed, or not applicable. A profile of these judgments provides bases for judging the evaluation against the considerations of utility, feasibility, propriety, and accuracy and in relation to each standard. When such metaevaluations are carried out early in an evaluation, they provide diagnostic feedback of use in strengthening the evaluation. When completed after a program evaluation, the metaevaluation helps users assess and make prudent use of the evaluation's findings and recommendations or reject them in part or even completely. (Checklists for applying the Joint Committee Standards are available at www.wmich.edu/evalctr/checklists.)

AEA Guiding Principles for Evaluators

In November 1992, AEA created a task force and charged it with developing general guiding principles for evaluation practice. The task force, chaired by William R. Shadish, subsequently drafted the *Guiding Principles for Evaluators*. Following a review process made available to the entire AEA membership, the task force finalized the principles document. After an affirmative vote by the AEA membership, the AEA board adopted the task force's recommended principles as the official AEA evaluation principles. AEA then published the principles in a special issue of its *New Directions for Program Evaluation* periodical (AEA Task Force on Guiding Principles for Evaluators, 1995). During 2002–2003 the *Guiding Principles* were reviewed and revised by the AEA Ethics Committee. In July 2004, the AEA membership ratified the revised *Guiding Principles*. The 2004 AEA *Guiding Principles* comprise five principles and twenty-three underlying normative statements to guide evaluation practice (http://www.eval.org/Publications/GuidingPrinciples.asp). The American Evaluation Association gives blanket permission to reprint the *Guiding Principles* with appropriate attribution. Exhibit 3.2 shows the principles and the associated normative statements as they appear regularly in the inside cover of issues of the *American Journal of Evaluation*.

Significance of the *Guiding Principles*

The AEA *Guiding Principles* provide evaluators with a code of professional behavior. The *Principles* are also applicable to evaluating evaluation designs and reports across a wide array of disciplines. They encourage evaluators to observe systematic inquiry and to respect society by acting honestly and giving priority to public welfare throughout their professional careers.

TABLE 3.1. ANALYSIS OF THE RELATIVE IMPORTANCE OF THE STANDARDS IN PERFORMING THE TASKS IN AN EVALUATION.

	1. Deciding Whether to Evaluate	2. Defining the Evaluation Problem	3. Designing the Evaluation	4. Collecting Information	5. Analyzing Information	6. Reporting the Evaluation	7. Budgeting the Evaluation	8. Contracting the Evaluation	9. Managing the Evaluation	10. Staffing the Evaluation
U1: Stakeholder Identification	X	X	X			X		X	X	
U2: Evaluator Credibility	X			X				X	X	X
U3: Information Scope and Selection			X	X		X	X	X		
U4: Values Identification			X	X	X	X				
U5: Report Clarity						X				
U6: Report Timeliness and Dissemination						X		X	X	
U7: Evaluation Impact	X					X				
F1: Practical Procedures			X	X					X	
F2: Political Viability	X			X				X	X	X
F3: Cost Effectiveness	X				X		X		X	
P1: Service Orientation	X	X				X		X	X	
P2: Formal Agreements	X		X	X			X	X	X	
P3: Rights of Human Subjects				X		X		X	X	
P4: Human Interactions				X						

P5 Complete and Fair Assessment					X		X	
P6 Disclosure of Findings		X	X		X			
P7 Conflict of Interest	X	X	X					X
P8 Fiscal Responsibility			X	X				
A1 Program Documentation			X	X	X	X	X	X
A2 Context Analysis		X			X	X	X	X
A3 Described Purposes and Procedures			X	X	X		X	X
A4 Defensible Information Sources					X		X	
A5 Valid Information							X	
A6 Reliable Information		X					X	
A7 Systematic Information							X	
A8 Analysis of Quantitative Information					X	X	X	
A9 Analysis of Qualitative Information					X	X	X	
A10 Justified Conclusions					X	X	X	
A11 Impartial Reporting	X				X			
A12 Metaevaluation	X	X	X	X	X	X	X	X

EXHIBIT 3.2. AMERICAN EVALUATION
ASSOCIATION GUIDING PRINCIPLES.

A. *Systematic Inquiry. Evaluators conduct systematic, data-based inquiries, and thus should:*

  1. Adhere to the highest technical standards appropriate to the methods they use.

  2. Explore with the client the shortcomings and strengths of evaluation questions and approaches.

  3. Communicate the approaches, methods, and limitations of the evaluation accurately and in sufficient detail to allow others to understand, interpret, and critique their work.

B. *Competence. Evaluators provide competent performance to stakeholders, and thus should:*

  1. Ensure that the evaluation team collectively possesses the education, abilities, skills, and experience appropriate to the evaluation.

  2. Ensure that the evaluation team collectively demonstrates cultural competence and uses appropriate evaluation strategies and skills to work with culturally different groups.

  3. Practice within the limits of their competence, decline to conduct evaluations that fall substantially outside those limits, and make clear any limitations on the evaluation that might result if declining is not feasible.

  4. Seek to maintain and improve their competencies in order to provide the highest level of performance in their evaluations.

C. *Integrity/Honesty. Evaluators display honesty and integrity in their own behavior, and attempt to ensure the honesty and integrity of the entire evaluation process, and thus should:*

  1. Negotiate honestly with clients and relevant stakeholders concerning the costs, tasks, limitations of methodology, scope of results, and uses of data.

  2. Disclose any roles or relationships that might pose a real or apparent conflict of interest prior to accepting an assignment.

  3. Record and report all changes to the original negotiated project plans, and the reasons for them, including any possible impacts that could result.

  4. Be explicit about their own, their clients', and other stakeholders' interests and values related to the evaluation.

  5. Represent accurately their procedures, data, and findings, and attempt to prevent or correct misuse of their work by others.

  6. Work to resolve any concerns related to procedures or activities likely to produce misleading evaluative information, decline to conduct the evaluation if concerns cannot be resolved, and consult colleagues or relevant stakeholders about other ways to proceed if declining is not feasible.

  7. Disclose all sources of financial support for an evaluation, and the source of the request for the evaluation.

D. *Respect for People. Evaluators respect the security, dignity, and self-worth of respondents, program participants, clients, and other evaluation stakeholders, and thus should:*

  1. Seek a comprehensive understanding of the contextual elements of the evaluation.

  2. Abide by current professional ethics, standards, and regulations regarding confidentiality, informed consent, and potential risks or harms to participants.

EXHIBIT 3.2. AMERICAN EVALUATION
ASSOCIATION GUIDING PRINCIPLES, Cont'd.

3. Seek to maximize the benefits and reduce any unnecessary harms that might occur from an evaluation and carefully judge when the benefits from the evaluation or procedure should be foregone because of potential risks.

4. Conduct the evaluation and communicate its results in a way that respects stakeholders' dignity and self-worth.

5. Foster social equity in evaluation, when feasible, so that those who give to the evaluation may benefit in return.

6. Understand, respect, and take into account differences among stakeholders such as culture, religion, disability, age, sexual orientation and ethnicity.

E. *Responsibilities for General and Public Welfare. Evaluators articulate and take into account the diversity of general and public interests and values, and thus should:*

1. Include relevant perspectives and interests of the full range of stakeholders.

2. Consider not only immediate operations and outcomes of the evaluation, but also the broad assumptions, implications and potential side effects.

3. Allow stakeholders' access to, and actively disseminate, evaluative information, and present evaluation results in understandable forms that respect people and honor promises of confidentiality.

4. Maintain a balance between client and other stakeholder needs and interests.

5. Take into account the public interest and good, going beyond analysis of particular stakeholder interests to consider the welfare of society as a whole.

Source: Reprinted with the permission of the American Evaluation Association.

Government Auditing Standards

David M. Walker, comptroller general of the United States, released the 2003 revision of the *Government Auditing Standards* on behalf of the U.S. Government Accountability Office. A U.S. General Accounting Office project team headed by Jeffrey C. Steinhoff had developed the document through a deliberative process including extensive public comments and input from the comptroller general's twenty-one-member Advisory Council on Government Auditing Standards. This revision incorporates the fieldwork and reporting standards issued by the American Institute of Certified Public Accountants. The *Government Auditing Standards* apply to the work of both individual auditors and audit organizations. Here, we provide verbatim statements of standards in the *Government Auditing Standards* document and then paraphrase GAO's narrative concerning the standards.

Auditing of government programs is advanced as vital to fulfilling the government's duty to be accountable to legislative bodies, government officials, and the people. Auditors are seen as responsible for helping interested parties assess and ensure the validity of reported information on the results of programs and the soundness of related systems of internal control. The *Government Auditing Standards* are broad statements of auditors' responsibilities. The standards are intended to represent a floor of acceptable auditing behavior and ensure that auditors manifest competence, integrity, objectivity, and independence in planning, conducting, and reporting on their work. Auditors and audit organizations are expected to follow these standards when required by law, regulation, contract, agreement, or policy. The standards provide a framework to ensure that audits are valid and relevant and also instrumental in improving government management, decision making, oversight, and accountability. A particular thrust of these standards is that auditors should serve their clients and other financial statement users and better protect the public interest by scrutinizing internal controls and reporting on the extent to which the controls deter fraudulent financial reporting, protect assets, and provide an early warning of emerging problems. Auditors who perform work in accordance with the *Government Auditing Standards* are expected to justify any departures from these standards.

The document has eight chapters: (1) Introduction, (2) Types of Government Audits and Attestation Engagements,[3] (3) General Standards, (4) Field Work Standards for Financial Audits, (5) Reporting Standards for Financial Audits, (6) General, Field Work, and Reporting Standards for Attestation Engagements, (7) Field Work Standards for Performance Audits, and (8) Reporting Standards for Performance Audits. Chapters One, Three, Seven, and Eight of the *Government Auditing Standards* are especially applicable to program evaluations.

Several key points from Chapter One of the *Government Auditing Standards* are pertinent to program evaluations. Auditors are charged to serve the public interest and maintain the highest degree of integrity, objectivity, and independence. In carrying out their work, they are to be objective, competent, fact based, intellectually honest, nonpartisan, free of conflicts of interest (in fact or appearance), and nonideological in relationships with evaluatees and users of audit reports. They should honor the public trust, be professional in planning and performing their assessment and reporting functions, and embody the concept of accountability to the public. They should not use obtained information for any personal gain or in any manner that would impede the legitimate and ethical efforts of the audited entity. Auditors are advised to apply the *Government Auditing Standards* to enhance the credibility and reliability of the information that is reported by or obtained from officials of the audited entity. At the outset of an audit, auditors are to inform report users of the audit's goals, schedule, data needs, procedures, and reporting plans. They also are advised to assess relationships with the audited entities continually in order to maintain objectivity and independence and service to the public. When reporting their findings, auditors are to disclose all material or significant facts known to them that, if not disclosed, could misrepresent findings, mislead users, or conceal improper or unlawful practices.

Auditors' organizations are charged to obtain independent peer reviews of compliance with the *Government Auditing Standards*. They are also charged to conduct follow-up investigations to determine whether the audited organization addressed audit findings and recommendations in planning and implementing future engagements.

Chapter One also endorses use of the *Government Auditing Standards* in conjunction with the AEA *Guiding Principles,* the Joint Committee *Program Evaluation Standards,* and other applicable standards. The *Government Auditing Standards* are intended to help ensure that program evaluations provide an independent assessment of the performance and management of programs against objective criteria or best practices. These standards call for program evaluations to provide sound information for program improvement, decision making, and accountability. To address conflicting pressures from various program stakeholders, auditors are charged first and foremost to fulfill their responsibilities to the public.

General Standards

The *Government Auditing Standards* contain four general standards for application to financial audits, attestation engagements, and program evaluations: (1) the independence of the audit organization and its individual auditors; (2) the exercise of sound professional judgment in conducting and reporting audits, exercising quality control, and engaging external peer reviews; (3) the competence and continuing education of audit staff; and (4) provisions for quality control to provide reasonable assurance of complying with applicable auditing standards. These are considered mandatory when performing audits requiring application of the *Government Auditing Standards*. The general standards are targeted to ensure credibility of audit results. The general audit standards follow.

Independence. The general standard related to independence reads as follows: "In all matters relating to the audit work, the audit organization and the individual auditor, whether government or public, should be free both in fact and appearance from personal, external, and organization impairments to independence." This standard is intended to ensure that opinions, conclusions, judgments, and recommendations will be impartial and viewed as impartial by knowledgeable third parties:

• *Personal impairments.* Audit organizations are charged to maintain internal quality control systems to detect whether auditors have any relationships and beliefs that might cause them to be partial or give the appearance of partiality. Individual auditors are charged to notify appropriate officials within their audit organization if they have any personal impairments to independence—for example, friends or family members in the audited entity, financial interest in the entity, previous employment in the audited entity, and seeking employment in the audited organization. To forestall or address personal impairments to independence, audit organizations are charged to establish pertinent independence policies and procedures, communicate these to all auditors in the organization, provide them with appropriate training, monitor compliance with the standard, establish a disciplinary mechanism, promptly resolve personal infringements of independence, and stress that auditors must maintain independence and always act in the public interest.

• *External impairments.* An auditor's independence may be compromised when factors outside the audit organization constrain or interfere with the auditor's ability to render independent and objective opinions and conclusions. Such impairments may occur when managers in the audit organization, oversight body, or funding organization deter needed audit actions; pressure the auditor to distort, excise, or tone down certain judgments; interfere with the selection of information to be examined; unreasonably restrict time allowed to complete the audit; interfere with the selection and appointment of auditors; unduly restrict funding of the audit; or threaten or actually engage in inappropriately modifying the audit report. Audit organizations are charged to identify possible external impairments and ways of addressing them in internal policies and procedures for reporting and resolving external impairments.

• *Organizational impairments.* Audit organizations need to be free from impairments to independence attendant to their place within or relationship to the organization that houses the entity to be audited. Auditors can be presumed to be free of organizational impairments if their audit organization is independent from the audited entity.

The Independence standard spells out a number of ways that audit organizations can meet the requirement of organizational independence. These include assignment to a level of government other than the one housing the audited entity and assignment to a different branch of government within the same level of government as the audited entity. Also, an audit organization may be presumed to be free of organizational impairments to independence if the audit organization's head was directly elected or appointed by a government entity that oversees and has power of removal of the person.

This standard spells out a number of safeguards that may be appropriate for audit organizations that are in structures different from those referenced above. Among these safeguards against organizational impairment to independence are statutory provisions that protect against abolishment of the audit organization by the audited entity; require transparency of reasons for removing the head of the audit agency; prevent the audited entity from interfering in the audit; require the audit organization to report to a governing body that is independent from the audited entity; give the audit organization sole authority over staffing the audit work; or guarantee access to records and documents needed to complete an audit.

Some audit organizations are internal to the organization being audited. To meet the needs of these internal audit organizations, the Independence standard includes provisions and suggestions that may apply to audit units within such organizations as colleges, universities, and hospitals. Main provisions are accountability to the head or deputy head of the organization, reporting results of the audit to the head or deputy head of the organization, and location organizationally outside the staff or line management function of the unit under audit. It is also advised that auditors within an internal audit unit should, if feasible, be under a pay, promotion, and tenure system based on merit. The internal audit organization is charged to document the conditions that make it free from organizational impairments to independence and to subject this documentation to peer review to ensure that all necessary safeguards are met.

Professional Judgment. The second general standard is on professional judgment: "Professional judgment should be used in planning and performing audits and attestation engagements and in reporting results." This standard requires auditors to apply professional judgment to all aspects of their work in order to serve the public interest effectively and maintain utmost integrity, objectivity, and independence. The exercise of professional judgment is intended to help ensure that any material misstatements or significant inaccuracies in data will be detected.

Exercise of professional judgment is required in determining the type of assignment to be performed, pertinent evaluative criteria, the scope of the work, methodological approach, type and amount of needed information, and tests and procedures. Professional judgment is also required in carrying out the study, assessing obtained evidence, evaluating the audit work, and reporting findings.

Auditors are expected to maintain professional skepticism throughout an assignment in judging the sufficiency, competency, and relevance of evidence. They are not to assume that management is dishonest or unquestionably honest. Instead, they are expected to judge evidence on its merits, regardless of beliefs about the honesty and integrity of management.

Competence. The third general standard in the *Government Auditing Standards* concerns auditor and evaluator competence. It is stated as follows: "The staff assigned to perform the audit or attestation engagement should collectively possess adequate professional competence for the tasks required." This standard places responsibility on audit organizations to assign staff members who collectively possess the knowledge, skills, and experience needed to fulfill the particular assignment. Audit organizations are expected to maintain a competent staff by employing a sound process of staff recruitment, hiring, continuous development, and evaluation. To meet the competence requirement, an audit organization may have to employ persons with expertise in a variety of areas, such as accounting, statistics, law, engineering, audit design and methodology, information technology, public administration, economics, social sciences, and actuarial science. Staff members are expected to maintain their professional competence through continuing professional education.

In consideration of work assignments, each staff member is expected to have relevant education, skills, and experience and be knowledgeable of the parts of the *Government Auditing Standards* that pertain to their assignments. An audit team collectively should possess knowledge of the audited entity's environment and the subject matter under review, and should possess good oral and writing communication skills.

Quality Control and Assurance. The fourth general standard, labeled quality control and assurance, states, "Each audit organization performing audits and/or attestation engagements in accordance with (the Government Auditing Standards) should have an appropriate internal quality control system in place and should undergo an external peer review." This standard's intent is to ensure that an audit organization will have and implement a structure, policies, and procedures for internal quality control that will reasonably ensure the organization's compliance with the *Government Auditing Standards.*

The internal quality control mechanism should include procedures for continuous monitoring to assess the appropriateness and effectiveness of the organization's policies and procedures related to the standards. Internal quality control systems are permitted to vary in their sophistication and documentation depending on such factors as the size, nature, and resources of the audit organization and appropriate cost-benefit considerations. Nevertheless, each audit organization is expected to maintain up-to-date documentation that details and demonstrates compliance with its quality control policies and procedures.

Audit organizations are expected to have an independent, external peer review of their auditing and attestation practices at least once every three years. Peer reviews are to focus on the adequacy and effective implementation of internal quality control policies and procedures. Each member of a peer review team is expected to be knowledgeable of the *Government Auditing Standards* and government environment relative to the work being reviewed, a competent peer reviewer, and independent of the audit organization being reviewed. The review team is expected to examine the audit organization's internal quality control policies and procedures and interview various staff of the audit organization to assess their understanding of and compliance with relevant quality control policies and procedures. The team will also sample and assess a reasonable cross-section of the audit organization's performed assignments. The review should be sufficiently comprehensive to conclude whether the audit organization's quality control policies, procedures, and actions were sufficient to provide reasonable assurance that the organization's work conformed to appropriate standards. The peer review team's written report should include at least the scope of the review, caveats, the standards for assessing the peer review system, and an opinion on the adequacy of the structure and implementation of the organization's peer review system.

The importance of peer reviews is seen in the requirement that audit organizations seeking to contract for work in accordance with the *Government Auditing Standards* provide their most recent external peer review report and associated materials to the party contracting for the service. Audit organizations are also expected to transmit their external peer review reports to appropriate oversight bodies. The organizations are advised, on request, to promptly make public their peer review report and associated materials.

The four general standards of the *Government Auditing Standards* are heavily oriented to auditing organizations but also have considerable relevance to program evaluations and the organizations that conduct program evaluations. Clearly, program evaluations can be enhanced by meeting general requirements for independence, professional judgment, competence, and quality control and assurance. We next consider the two chapters on fieldwork and reporting in the *Government Auditing Standards* that directly address the enterprise of program evaluation.

Fieldwork Standards for Performance Audits

The four fieldwork standards for performance audits, within the *Government Auditing Standards* pertain to planning the audit; supervising staff; obtaining sufficient, competent, and relevant evidence; and preparing audit documentation:

Planning. This standard states, "Work is to be adequately planned." Auditors are directed to define audit objectives, scope, and needed methods. These three elements are to be determined together with consideration of their overlap. Moreover, planning of these three elements is to be ongoing throughout the audit.

Essentially, audit objectives denote the questions to be answered. Scope refers to parameters such as the time period to be reviewed, the necessary documentation, and the locations at which the fieldwork will be performed. The methodology comprises the methods and devices for gathering and analyzing needed data.

Staff planning of the audit plan should take into account (1) the nature of the program's significance and the needs of potential users of the audit; (2) the nature of the subject program; (3) the relevance of internal control to the requirements of the audit; (4) methods for detecting significant violations of legal and regulatory requirements, contract provisions, or grant agreements; (5) pertinent evaluative criteria; (6) results of pertinent previous audits; (7) sources of relevant data; (8) need for experts and additional auditors; (9) staff and resources needed to perform the audit; and (10) appropriate means for communicating audit plans to the subject program's managers and others as applicable. The precise requirements for the written audit plan include the program's legal authority, history, objectives, locations, and other relevant background information; standardized audit staff responsibilities; audit procedures for collecting and summarizing information; the bases for assigning work to staff; and the general format and contents of the audit report.

Supervision. The standard states, "Staff are to be properly supervised." In directing the efforts of staff to ensure achievement of audit objectives, supervisors are to provide guidance to staff, keep apprised of significant problems encountered, review work performed, and provide effective on-the-job training. Reviews of audit work are to be documented.

Evidence. The standard states, "Sufficient, competent, and relevant evidence is to be obtained to provide a reasonable basis for the auditors' findings and conclusions." Under this fieldwork standard, auditors should obtain and evaluate sufficient evidence to support their judgments and conclusions pertaining to the audit objectives. Auditors are expected to collect and evaluate evidence relating to internal control or compliance requirements if these are important to complete the audit. Needed evidence may be categorized as physical, documentary, testimonial, and analytical. The evidence should be assessed for its sufficiency (to convince users of the validity of findings), competence (valid, reliable, and consistency with facts), and relevance (logically related to and important to the audit questions) to support the audit findings and conclusions.

Audit Documentation. According to this standard, "Auditors should prepare and maintain audit documentation. Audit documentation related to planning, conducting, and reporting on the audit should contain sufficient information to enable an experienced auditor, who has had no previous connection with the audit, to ascertain from the audit documentation the evidence that supports the auditors' significant judgments and conclusions. Audit documentation should contain support for findings, conclusions, and recommendations before auditors issue their report."

Pursuant to this fourth standard, auditors are advised to exercise professional judgment in documenting their audit work and basically to record their audit work and conclusions related to standards. A continual process of documentation provides the principal support for the auditor's report, aids in conducting and supervising the audit work, and allows for review of audit quality. The documentation should be sufficiently detailed to make clear the audit's purpose, source, and conclusions, and it should be appropriately organized to clearly link the report's findings, conclusions, and recommendations. Audit organizations are expected to establish and implement reasonable policies for the proper storage and control of audit documentation for a time sufficient to satisfy legal and administrative requirements. Another intended use of audit documentation is to facilitate cooperation of government agencies in auditing programs of common interest so that auditors may use each other's work and avoid duplication of effort. Accordingly, auditors should arrange to make their audit documentation readily available to other government auditors or reviewers. At the same time audit organizations need to develop and implement policies to prevent inappropriate release of audit documentation to other than right-to-know audiences.

Reporting Standards for Performance Audits

The four reporting standards for performance audits within the *Government Auditing Standards* pertain to form of reports, report contents, report quality, and report issuance and distribution. For each of these standards we give GAO's definition and then characterize GAO's elaboration of the standard.

Form. The standard states, "Auditors should prepare audit reports communicating the results of each audit." This first standard on reporting results of performance audits requires the report to be written or in some other retrievable form and also to be appropriate for its intended use. Auditors are to consider users' needs, likely demand, and distribution thoughtfully in determining the appropriate form of the report. Depending on users' needs, reports may be in such forms as a chapter report, a letter, briefing slides, videotape, or compact disc. Report forms should be chosen to communicate findings to users at different levels of government, minimize misunderstanding of findings, make results available for public inspection, and facilitate follow-up to identify and assess corrective actions.

Regardless of the form, audit reports are expected to comply with all applicable reporting standards. To promote the use of reports, GAO encourages discussion of report contents with persons having responsibilities in the area being audited. If an audit is aborted, the auditor is expected to communicate the reason for termination in writing—or some other appropriate way—to the managers of the audited entity, the entity requesting the audit, and other appropriate officials.

Report Contents. The standard states, "The audit report should include the objectives, scope, and methodology; the audit results, including findings, conclusions, and recommendations, as appropriate; a reference to compliance with generally accepted government auditing standards; the views of responsible officials; and, if applicable, the nature of any privileged and confidential information omitted."

This standard stipulates the needed contents for performance audit reports. Report users are said to need this information to understand the audit's purpose and nature of work performed, gain a perspective for viewing findings, and identify important limitations of the work.

Audit reports identify the audit objectives in clear, specific, and neutral terms. Typically, this information should be accompanied by explanations of the audit subject and aspect of performance to be examined, why the audit was undertaken, and intended accomplishments. Preferably, the objectives should be measurable and feasible. It may also be necessary to state objectives that were not pursued.

The audit report should also state the audit's scope, that is, the depth and coverage of the audit work. As applicable, auditors are expected to explain the relationship between the population of items sampled and the sample examined; identify organizations, geographical locations, and the period covered; and explain and document problems. Auditors are also expected to report significant constraints on the audit, such as inadequate scope or problems in accessing needed data, records, or individuals. They should identify and justify why any applicable standards were not followed and how this shortcoming could affect the audit results.

In reporting the employed methodology, auditors should clearly explain what was done to achieve audit objectives. The explanation should include the techniques used to gather and analyze evidence, significant assumptions underlying the methods, any comparative techniques employed, evaluative criteria, and, as applicable, the rationale for and inferential power of any sampling design applied.

Findings are to be keyed to the audit objectives and supported by sufficient, competent, and relevant evidence. The findings should be clearly communicated, convincing, and set in proper perspective. Appropriate background information should be provided to help the reader understand the findings and their significance. Pursuant to the audit objectives, audit findings may include criteria, program status, or cause and effect. Auditors are advised to use professional judgment in determining whether or how to report on deficiencies that are clearly inconsequential. They should report the scope of their work on internal control, any significant deficiencies in internal control, all instances of fraud and illegal acts unless they are clearly inconsequential, significant violations of contractual or grant agreements, significant abuse, and appropriate substantiating evidence. If certain pertinent information is prohibited from general disclosure, the audit report should identify the nature of the omitted information and state the requirement that makes the omission necessary. In accordance with applicable law or regulations, auditors should report fraud, illegal acts, violations of contract or grant agreements, or abuse to appropriate outside parties. When called for by the audit objectives, auditors should report conclusions and recommendations, with any recommendations flowing logically from well-established conclusions.

In developing sound reports, it can be helpful to engage members of the audience by having them review a draft of the final report for accuracy and clarity. As feasible, auditors should help report users understand any needs for corrective action and associated recommendations. They should report the reactions by the responsible officials of the audited program to the audit report and any corrective actions they plan to pursue. As appropriate, the auditors should report their agreement or disagreement with the views presented by officials of the audited program. The report should state that the audit was made in accordance with the *Government Auditing Standards* and should acknowledge any deficiencies in this regard. In general, a set of findings is said to be complete to the extent that the audit objectives are met and the report clearly relates the objectives to the findings.

Report Quality Elements. The standard states, "The report should be timely, complete, accurate, objective, convincing, clear, and as concise as the subject permits."

To meet the requirements for timeliness, the auditor is expected to report current, relevant information when the intended users need it. Often it is appropriate to provide interim oral or written reports, which alert officials to matters requiring prompt attention. A final report is required to supply all facts and explanations, the proper context, and appropriate conclusions and recommendations needed to fulfill the audit objectives.

The requirement for accuracy is met by providing evidence that is true, findings that are correctly portrayed, and a report that in all matters is credible and reliable. If data are significant to the audit findings and conclusions but not fully substantiated, the report should clearly indicate limitations of the data and contain no unwarranted conclusions or recommendations based on those data. The report should contain accurate descriptions of the audit's scope and methodology and limit findings and conclusions to the scope of the audit. To ensure that the report is free of errors in logic and reasoning, facts, figures, dates of events, and unsupported conclusions and recommendations, the auditor should consider engaging an independent auditor to investigate and provide assurance of the report's accuracy.

Objectivity is required to ensure that the entire report is balanced in content and tone; that shortcomings are set in an appropriate context; and that evidence is presented in an unbiased, fair manner so that users can be persuaded by the facts. The report's tone should encourage constructive use of findings and recommendations, refrain from negativism, and give credit for the program's positive features.

To be convincing, the audit results have to be responsive to the audit objectives and presented persuasively; conclusions and recommendations must follow logically from the presented facts. Reports are convincing when users judge findings as valid, conclusions as reasonable, and recommendations as potentially beneficial.

All reports should be clear. They should be easy to read and understand and prepared in as simple, straightforward, and nontechnical language as the subject permits. Any needed technical terms, acronyms, and abbreviations should be clearly defined. The report's material should be logically organized. Auditors can make reports easier to read by making effective use of titles, captions, topic sentences, pictures, charts, graphs, and maps. Also, clarity may be enhanced by including a summary of specific answers to the questions in the audit objectives, the most significant findings, the principal conclusions, and reference to recommendations to be found in the full report.

The final element of report quality is conciseness. Reports should not be longer than necessary to convey and support the message. They should be devoid of extraneous detail, and needless repetition should be avoided. Reports that are to the point, fact-based, and concise are seen to be likely to achieve the best results.

Report Issuance and Distribution. This standard states, "Government auditors should submit audit reports to the appropriate officials of the audited entity and to the appropriate officials of the organizations requiring or arranging for the audits, including external funding organizations, such as legislative bodies, unless legal restrictions prevent it. Auditors should also send copies of the reports to other officials who have legal oversight authority or who may be responsible for acting on audit findings and recommendations, and also to others authorized to receive such reports. Unless the report is restricted by law or regulation, or contains privileged or confidential information, auditors should clarify that copies are made available for public inspection. Non-government auditors should clarify report distribution responsibilities with the party contracting for the audit and follow the agreements reached."

Audit reports are to be distributed in a timely manner to officials needing the findings and other interested right-to-know audiences—for example, officials legally authorized to receive the reports, those charged with acting on the report's findings and recommendations, other government personnel who assisted the audited entity, and possibly the public. Audit documentation should specify whether the report is to be available for public inspection. If the audit contains material that is classified or may not be releasable to certain parties or the public for other valid reasons, auditors should limit distribution of the report accordingly.

When a nongovernment auditor is engaged to perform an audit under the *Government Auditing Standards*, the auditor and the engaging organization should reach clear, well-documented agreements on right-to-know audiences; report distribution authority and responsibility; and take steps—as appropriate—to ensure the availability of the report for public inspection. Internal auditors should comply with their organization's arrangements and statutory requirements for distributing reports. The usual practice is to report to a superior who is responsible for distributing the report. The organization's distribution of reports to external audiences should comply with applicable laws, rules, regulations, or policy.

Using Evaluation Standards

Although the three sets of standards examined in this chapter vary in detail and substantive orientation, they are complementary, not contradictory. Fundamentally they are consistent in advocated principles but provide different emphases, cross-checks, and complementary treatments of the requirements for sound evaluations. All three sets of standards are in substantial agreement as to what constitutes sound evaluation practices. Evaluations should be beyond reproach, with evaluators adhering to all relevant laws and ethical codes. Moreover, evaluators should produce valid findings and should be careful not to present unsupportable conclusions and recommendations. In addition, evaluators should carefully sort out their roles as independent inquirers from their social advocacy roles and make sure that their evaluations are not corrupted by conflicts of interest. All three sets are grounded in the proposition that sound auditing and evaluation is vital to the functioning of a healthy society. Service providers and governments must regularly subject their services to evaluation, and evaluators must deliver services that are legal, ethical, effective, accountable, and in the public interest. Standards are a powerful force for bringing about the needed sound evaluation services. Clearly, the three sets of standards comprise a valuable resource of principles, concepts, and procedures for evaluators and their clients.

Depending on particular evaluation assignments, the three sets may be used interchangeably or in concert. Comparisons of the substance of the Joint Committee *Standards* and the 1995 AEA *Guiding Principles* documents revealed key differences and similarities in the standards and principles (Covert, 1995; Sanders, 1995). Essentially everything covered by the AEA principles was also covered by the Joint Committee's standards. However, the latter's coverage is broader, much more detailed, and delves deeper into evaluation issues. No similar comparisons of all three sets of standards have been published. In closing, we present a reprise on each set of standards, discuss priorities for using each set, and outline a general process for applying standards.

The AEA *Guiding Principles* posit that program evaluations should meet requirements for systematic inquiry, competence, integrity and honesty, respect for people, and responsibilities for general and public welfare. Of the three sets of standards, the *Guiding Principles* have the widest applicability and are the most general. They are officially endorsed by the American Evaluation Association and apply to program evaluations across a variety of government and social service sectors. They contain twenty-three important statements to support the five principles, but they lack detailed criteria and guidance. Arguably, these standards should be applied in all U.S. program evaluations, but due to their lack of specificity, they often function best as a secondary set of standards. Their applicability extends beyond the United States to all evaluators who decide to conduct their program evaluations in accordance with AEA's *Guiding Principles.*

The Joint Committee *Program Evaluation Standards* are focused on evaluations of education programs in the United States and Canada; stipulate that evaluations should meet requirements for utility, feasibility, propriety, and accuracy; and provide extensive guidance and an assortment of illustrative cases. Their development was sponsored by more than a dozen professional organizations concerned with improving education. Also, the American National Standards Institute accredited the Joint Committee *Program Evaluation Standards* as the ones to be employed in evaluating education programs in the United States.

The *Government Auditing Standards* are focused on U.S. government-sponsored programs in all areas of government service. They provide general standards on independence, professional judgment, competence, and quality control and assurance. They also provide specific standards for fieldwork and reporting of findings for financial audits, attestation engagements, and performance audits. The general standards and the many specific standards in the chapters on performance audits are relevant to nongovernment as well as government evaluations in a wide range of program areas. Although they are intended for use in evaluating U.S.

government programs, these standards have been used in countries across the world.

Evaluators can use a general nine-step process in applying all three sets of standards:

1. Become thoroughly familiar with each set of standards through systematic orientation and training.
2. Clarify the evaluation's purposes.
3. Clarify the context of the evaluation.
4. Reach agreement with the client on which sets of standards will be applied and, if more than one set, which will be primary, secondary, or tertiary. As a rule of thumb, the *Government Auditing Standards* should be primary in evaluations of U.S. government programs, the Joint Committee *Program Evaluation Standards* should be primary in evaluations of nongovernment education programs in North America, and the AEA *Guiding Principles* should be primary in evaluations of nongovernment programs outside the field of education and secondary in all other program evaluations in the United States.
5. Orient and train stakeholders in the contents of the selected standards and their applicability to ensuring quality in the evaluation and ultimately assessing the program evaluation.
6. Apply the standards proactively through periodic checks on all aspects of the evaluation.
7. Give consideration to engaging an independent party to invoke the standards in conducting formative or summative metaevaluations. Any formative application of the standards should include periodic written reports and feedback sessions aimed at strengthening the ongoing evaluation.
8. Apply the standards to assess the completed program evaluation. Such a summative metaevaluation will have more credibility if conducted by an independent evaluator.
9. Ensure that the summative metaevaluation report is released and effectively communicated to right-to-know audiences.

The primary tool for applying each set of standards is the full-length standards document, not merely a summary of the standards. In addition, checklists are available (at www.wmich.edu/evalctr) to facilitate application of the Joint Committee *Program Evaluation Standards* and the AEA *Guiding Principles*. GAO has issued a series of pamphlets to assist evaluators to learn and apply the *Government Auditing Standards*. A recent one is the GAO-02–870G document titled *Government Auditing Standards: Answers to Independence Standards* (2002). All three sets of standards emphasize that the standards are general guides and that evaluators and their clients should consult and employ much more specific material when dealing with such details as design, measurement, case studies, statistics, reporting, and contracting.

Review Questions

1. State reasons that standards for program evaluation are essential.
2. Why should evaluators feel confident that the three sets of standards presented in this chapter offer authoritative directions for guiding and assessing evaluation studies?
3. Respond to the claim that the introduction of standards with their objective criteria has strengthened the professionalism of all evaluators.
4. Identify eight to ten of the specific functions of program evaluation standards.
5. Outline the most important features of each of the three sets of standards presented in this chapter.
6. Provide a list of dangers inherent in ignoring close reference to standards during the course of an evaluation.
7. Examine and comment on the claim that *The Program Evaluation Standards* are relevant and useful when planning and conducting metaevaluations.
8. Comment: AEA's *Guiding Principles for Evaluators* state general codes of behavior supported by normative statements. Although they do not guide an evaluator in a direct, operational sense, they do have ethical utility.
9. List ten or more significant ways in which the *Government Auditing Standards* ensure the accuracy and credibility of audit results.
10. This chapter has stated that all three sets of standards may be applied to a study in concert, individually, or interchangeably. Briefly outline three evaluation situations where each set of standards appears most appropriate.

Group Exercises

Group discussions arising from the following exercises should give participants a stronger grasp of the purposes and utility of standards. For exercise 2, it would be useful if one group member provided other members with copies of a completed evaluation report (which should not be too extensive) before the discussion session.

Exercise 1. Contrast the evaluation field without published standards (as was the case prior to the 1980s) with the situation today. Discuss the salient differences from the point of view of both evaluator and client. In your discussion, reach conclusions about the enhancement of the evaluation profession with the publication of standards.

Exercise 2. Select an evaluation report. Use the Joint Committee's *Program Evaluation Standards* to evaluate the report (that is, to conduct a metaevaluation). Reach conclusions about the strengths and weaknesses of the evaluation.

Exercise 3. Discuss the kind of situations in which an evaluator would predominantly use, at least as a primary tool, these documents:

- *The Program Evaluation Standards*
- *Guiding Principles for Evaluators*
- *Government Auditing Standards*

Exercise 4. The managing director of a large manufacturing firm has a problem: his section leaders have reported to him that an evaluation of a new program in the firm has caused growing anxiety among the workforce, principally because a whole range of established workers' rights will be abrogated by the evaluation.

She enlists the services of an experienced evaluator to evaluate the program evaluation. Which of the Joint Committee's standards would be especially relevant to this metaevaluation, and why?

Notes

1. The initial committee had the following representatives of user groups: William J. Ellena, Homer O. Elseroad, Philip Hosford, William Mays Jr., Bernard McKenna, James A. Mecklenburger, and James Ward; and the following representatives of methodological specialties: Henry M. Brickell, Donald T. Campbell, Ronald P. Carver, Esther E. Diamond, Egon G. Guba, Robert L. Linn, George F. Madaus, Wendell Rivers, Lorrie Shepard, and Daniel L. Stufflebeam (chair).
2. The sponsors of the Joint Committee on Standards for Educational Evaluation, as of publication of *The Program Evaluation Standards* in 1994, were the American Association of School Administrators, American Educational Research Association, American Evaluation Association, American Federation of Teachers, American Psychological Association, Association for Assessment in Counseling, Association for Supervision and Curriculum Development, Canadian Society for the Study of Education, Council of Chief State School Officers, Council on Postsecondary Accreditation, National Association of Elementary School Principals, National Association of Secondary School Principals, National Council on Measurement in Education, National Education Association, and National School Boards Association.

3. The term *attestation engagement* is not commonly seen in the program evaluation literature. In such an engagement, an auditor issues an examination, a review, or an agreed-on procedures report on a subject matter or an assertion about a subject matter, pursuant to criteria selected by another party. Attestation engagements can cover a broad range of financial or nonfinancial objectives and result in various types of opinion depending on the user's needs.

References

American Evaluation Association Task Force on Guiding Principles for Evaluators. (1995). *Guiding principles for evaluators.* New Directions for Program Evaluation, no. 66. San Francisco: Jossey-Bass.

American Evaluation Association 2003 Ethics Committee. (2004). *Guiding principles for evaluators.* http://www.eval.org/Guiding%20 Principles.htm.

Covert, R. W. (1995). A twenty-year veteran's reflections on the Guiding Principles for Evaluators. In W. R. Shadish, D. L. Newman, M. A. Scheirer, & C. Wye (Eds.), *Guiding principles for evaluators* (pp. 35–45). New Directions for Program Evaluation, no. 66. San Francisco: Jossey-Bass.

ERS Standards Committee (1982). Evaluation Research Society standards for program evaluation. In P. H. Rossi (Ed.), *Standards for evaluation practice.* New Directions for Program Evaluation, no. 15. San Francisco: Jossey-Bass.

Joint Committee on Standards for Educational Evaluation. (1981). *Standards for evaluations of educational programs, projects, and materials.* New York: McGraw-Hill.

Joint Committee on Standards for Educational Evaluation. (1988). *The personnel evaluation standards.* Thousand Oaks, CA: Corwin Press.

Joint Committee on Standards for Educational Evaluation. (1994). *The program evaluation standards: How to assess evaluations of educational programs.* Thousand Oaks, CA: Corwin Press.

Joint Committee on Standards for Educational Evaluation. (2003). *The student evaluation standards.* Thousand Oaks, CA: Corwin Press.

Sanders, J. R. (1995). Standards and principles. In W. R. Shadish, D. L. Newman, M. A. Scheirer, & C. Wye (Eds.), *Guiding principles for evaluators* (pp. 47–53). New Directions for Program Evaluation, no. 66. San Francisco: Jossey-Bass.

Shadish, W. R., Newman, D. L., Scheirer, M. A., & Wye, C. (Eds.). (1995). *Guiding principles for evaluators.* New Directions for Program Evaluation, no. 66. San Francisco: Jossey-Bass.

U.S. General Accounting Office. (1994). *Government auditing standards.* Washington, DC: Author.

U.S. General Accounting Office. (2002, July). *Government auditing standards: Answers to independence standard questions.* Washington, DC: Author.

U.S. General Accounting Office. (2003, June). *Government auditing standards.* Washington, DC: Author.

CHAPTER FOUR

PERSONNEL EVALUATION

The Ghost in Program Evaluations

It is well known that the prospect of a program evaluation makes people nervous. Those who are conducting the program may worry that a low rating would reflect negatively on their competence or performance. The evaluators need information and cooperation from stakeholders and may wonder whether these persons will be reluctant contributors if they believe the evaluation will jeopardize their sense of self-worth, reputation, or jobs. To minimize an evaluation's threat to individuals, evaluators might promise to assess the program, not its personnel. Such an assurance can ease stakeholders' anxiety and encourage their cooperation, but it can also be disingenuous or even a counterproductive cop-out.

Sound program evaluations should consider all relevant factors and not relegate personnel evaluation to what it often is: a ghost set of factors in the program's performance. Key factors in any program's success are assignments, competence, and performance of its personnel. Despite the desire to allay stakeholders' anxiety, evaluators are faced with either conducting a sound evaluation that takes on the challenge of forthrightly looking at a program's personnel or conducting a substandard evaluation that omits or obscures consideration of the program's important personnel component. So what are evaluators to do?

The straightforward answer is that evaluators frankly, sensitively, diplomatically, honestly, and fairly should include the personnel factor in their evaluation contracts, plans, operations, and reports. It would have been easier for us to skip the topic of personnel evaluation in writing this book, as do most textbooks on program evaluation. Had we done so, we would feel guilty of a serious omission.

Nevertheless, we note that assessment of the personnel component should be kept in perspective along with assessments of other program components. We have included this separate chapter on personnel evaluation to underscore the importance of this topic in program evaluations, help correct a long-standing tendency to exclude it from program evaluation discussions, and affirmatively accord it a place among other important components of a sound program evaluation. In this chapter, we offer our perspective on how evaluators can professionally and effectively address the delicate issue of personnel evaluation in their program evaluation assignments. We do so by stating and discussing questions about the personnel matter that program evaluators need to address.

In General, What Is Personnel Evaluation?

Personnel evaluation refers to the systematic assessment of a person's qualifications or performance, or both, in relation to a role and defensible purpose of an institution, profession, program, or other entity. It applies to a wide range of appointments, including the complex of professional, skilled, and unskilled roles in programs, factories, stores, restaurants, airline companies, schools, universities, libraries, hospitals, churches, government agencies, nongovernment service organizations, law firms, military services, sports teams, and many others. Any enterprise's effectiveness and propriety is dependent on the intelligence, special talents, levels of training, values, ethical behavior, attitudes, personal demeanor, social skills, motivation, efforts, collaboration, and achievements of its personnel. Many organizations and specific programs devote much of their budgets to compensate and support their personnel. To make personnel costs pay off, organizations and programs need to address a wide range of personnel matters. We emphasize in this chapter that the degree of personnel effectiveness determines the success or otherwise of a program. For this reason, employers and regulating bodies need valid personnel evaluations to guide personnel decisions and actions, ensure accountability, and foster and assess the ongoing development of human resources. For their part, program evaluators need to conduct program evaluations to help clients and other stakeholders improve programs and diagnose their reasons for success or failure.

What Case Can an Evaluator Make for Assessing a Program's Personnel?

In focusing a program evaluation, the evaluator should stress to the client and other stakeholders that all program components that influence the program's success should be examined. Assessing each of these, and all in combination, is required to identify program aspects that need to be strengthened, as well as those that should be identified as effective and sustained essentially as they are. By attending to areas of deficiency, the program's leaders and staff can improve the program—and improvement is evaluation's most important purpose. If any important program variable is exempted from review, the potential for program improvement is limited accordingly. We also stress that program evaluations help reinforce and sustain a program's success by highlighting and reinforcing its areas of strength. Moreover, assessment of a program's personnel component is needed to help understand why a program succeeded or failed.

Clearly, a program's personnel are one of its most important resources for success. Personnel also are one of the most important variables that can impair a program or cause it to fail. In the spirit of program improvement, it is in the interests of the client and other stakeholders to get feedback on the adequacy of the program's personnel.

Should Program Evaluators Evaluate Individual Program Staff Members?

Program evaluators should never agree or get trapped into evaluating a program's individual administrators or staff members. That is the job of the program's director or other program official. Of course, the program evaluator often should evaluate the extent to which the program has sound provisions for evaluating individual staff members and especially for providing them with helpful feedback. In fact, assessing the adequacy of a program's own personnel evaluation process is one of the most important parts of a program evaluation. To the extent that the program's personnel evaluation system is well designed, well functioning, and effective, the program evaluator will have less to do in gathering new data on the program's personnel. This is so because a well-functioning personnel evaluation system is a powerful force for ensuring the adequacy of personnel selection, assignment, and performance and thereby fostering program improvement and accountability.

How Can a Program Evaluator Appropriately Address a Client's Need for Improved Personnel Evaluation?

While an evaluator should not agree to evaluate a program's individual personnel, sometimes the evaluator can appropriately address the client's needs in this area by advising on the design of a sound personnel evaluation system. Especially, the evaluator can refer the client to the Joint Committee's *Personnel Evaluation Standards* (1988). Fourteen professional societies in the United States and Canada, collectively representing about three million professionals, appointed and sponsored personnel evaluation standards-setting efforts of this eighteen-member committee. Although designed for use in evaluating education personnel, the resulting standards have proved useful for personnel evaluations in other sectors. These include the General Motors Corporation's evaluations of executives and the U.S. Marine Corps' evaluations of officers and enlisted personnel.

The Personnel Evaluation Standards require personnel evaluations to meet four basic requirements:

- The *propriety standards* require evaluations to be ethical and fair to the affected parties, including beneficiaries as well as the service provider.
- The *utility standards* require evaluators to issue results that are credible, informative, timely, and influential. The results should help individuals and groups improve their performance and help superiors make needed personnel decisions and guide staff development and other personnel actions.
- The *feasibility standards* require that evaluation procedures are efficient, politically viable, relatively easy to implement, and adequately funded.
- The *accuracy standards* require that evaluations provide sound information about a person's qualifications and performance. The results should be grounded in an up-to-date position description, take account of the particular work environment and institutional or societal mission, be based on systematic collection and analysis of data, and be validly interpreted and reported.

In explicating these requirements, the committee developed and illustrated detailed standards, with the participation of national and international review panels. Moreover, the committee is a standing body that periodically reviews and, as needed, updates the standards. Users of *The Personnel Evaluation Standards* will find it contains many procedural suggestions for designing, implementing, and using results from sound personnel evaluation systems.

How Can Evaluators Assure Stakeholders That a Program Evaluation Will Be Fair to Individuals?

Evaluators should give clear and documented assurance to stakeholders that they will evaluate the adequacy of a program's personnel complement and the adequacy of their job performance but not the effectiveness of individuals. At first glance, it may be difficult to distinguish between a group of personnel and individuals, but the difference to the program evaluator is significant. Areas of job responsibility include program planning, budgeting, staffing, supervision, staff development, program implementation and evaluation, technical and clerical support, coordination with other entities, collaboration, and dissemination. A program's potential for fulfilling these responsibilities rests heavily on the scope, competence, and performance of its staff. The program's actual fulfillment of its responsibilities depends on the staff's faithful, effective performance of job responsibilities. Effective performance requires appropriately qualified personnel who have clear job assignments and adequate support and successfully carry out their responsibilities. Program evaluators need to assess the extent to which the job responsibilities are being carried out well and, if not, the extent to which the program has appropriately engaged, trained, assigned, encouraged, and supported personnel with the requisite expertise.

Program evaluators should not evaluate and report findings on individual staff members. That evaluation job is important, but it is one for the program leaders or administrators to carry out. Program evaluators should inform stakeholders that evaluation reports will assess whether the program has sufficient qualified personnel to achieve its goals, whether personnel performance is adequate or in need of improvement, whether staff assignments are clear and appropriate, and the extent to which staff are receiving needed encouragement, training, and support. The evaluators should stipulate that they will keep information from and about individual program staff members confidential, that wherever possible they will gather information anonymously, and that they will not report to anyone on the competence or performance of any individual staff member. Moreover, if a program administrator invites the evaluator into a back room and asks for an assessment of a particular staff member, the evaluator should politely but firmly decline to provide information on, or a judgment about, any individual staff member. Our experience has shown the wisdom of providing explicit guidelines to clients from the beginning to obviate the chance of this occurring.

Nevertheless, evaluators should acknowledge to stakeholders that recipients of evaluation reports might infer which staff members were associated with a particular finding. Such inferences are especially likely when only one or a small group of persons were associated with a particular job responsibility, such as program administration.

If evaluators anticipate that particular evaluation findings will damage any individual, they should state the feedback as constructively as they can, consider leaving it out of any report for wide distribution, omit it if it is not consequential to the program's success, or include it in an executive report to the program's director. Making such determinations requires integrity and professional judgment. Whatever the course, the evaluator should report only findings that focus on the program responsibility being performed, not on an individual. The point is to provide right-to-know audiences important evaluative feedback that is clearly in the interest of program improvement, while doing all possible to uphold the dignity and well-being of affected individuals.

We warn again that evaluations for hiring and firing are not appropriate territory for program evaluators. Their territory is assessment of a program's merit and worth, and they should carefully report on all variables that relate to program improvement, including the competence and performance of the program's personnel, in a general or inclusive sense. Evaluators should steadfastly guard against reporting any information that would focus directly on the dignity and worth of any program staff member. In respect to this, it is essential to remember that the performance evaluation of each program staff member is the program's responsibility.

Should Program Evaluators Promise Anonymity or Confidentiality?

In studying a program's personnel component, evaluators often should promise a program's staff members and surveyed beneficiaries a systematic effort to protect confidentiality and typically should use data collection instruments that provide anonymity. The evaluator should strictly control and not share the specific data gathered in interviews and surveys. The evaluation agreement should stipulate that only the evaluator see, and have access to, information collected from or associated with any program staff member. Staff members should be given assurance that this is so during an early information session when the evaluator explains the procedures and protocols.

Of course, evaluators should not make promises they cannot keep and should provide program stakeholders with appropriate caveats. Sometimes laws preclude keeping program evaluation information confidential, especially if a court orders its release. Although this is a rare occurrence, evaluators should forthrightly inform stakeholders that program evaluation records would have to be surrendered in the unlikely event that a court subpoenas them. Also, evaluators should not promise that users of their reports could never associate an individual or group with any particular evaluation findings. In many programs, the nature of an identified deficiency (or strength) will make possible a deduction of what persons were involved. This is especially so when a specific program role is at issue and only one or a small number of persons work in that role.

To mitigate these complications, we advise evaluators to stress to all stakeholders that the evaluation's main orientation is program improvement and that staff or administrator performance, like any other key program component, bears scrutiny as an area whose strengthening might lead to program improvement. Preferably, the program's response to assessed deficiencies in personnel performance will be to institute steps to help the person improve performance, with termination being a possibility only after a period of due process and serious remedial efforts. Program evaluators can and often should counsel program leaders to follow such a fair course of due process in the program's personnel evaluation system.

In What Sense Should a Program Evaluation Evaluate the Program's Personnel?

A program's personnel can be effective to the extent they collectively have the needed competencies to ensure the program's success. Other significant requirements are credibility with program stakeholders; positive motivation, task orientation, good work habits, and integrity; spirit of collaboration and teamwork; clear, relevant assignments; necessary work conditions and resources; appropriate compensation; evaluative feedback on their performance; and responsible, supportive supervision. These factors are clearly relevant and important in the soundness of a program's plans and arrangements and its ultimate success or failure. Assessed deficiencies in any of these areas provide bases for corrective action or points for reference in summing up and interpreting the program's quality. A program's own personnel evaluation system should be able to shed light on these and other factors, all of which may well be included in the evaluation design. However, the program evaluator likely will have to collect additional information on certain factors. In general, the personnel aspects noted could provide the structure for both interviews and surveys focused on the program's personnel component.

How Should a Contract for a Program Evaluation Deal with Personnel Evaluation?

In negotiating agreements for conducting a program evaluation, evaluators are advised to stipulate that they will examine personnel evaluation factors. The focus of the personnel evaluation should be on the overall personnel component, especially on the staff's collective competence and performance of assigned roles and the program's clear direction to personnel and their support and evaluation. The evaluators should make clear to all concerned that they will assess the adequacy of the personnel component overall but will not explicitly evaluate any individual. This is a job, and an important one, for the program's leaders. Even in the case of program supervision, the evaluator should focus on its adequacy and not directly on individual supervisors.

In general, the personnel variables to be examined may be denoted as the sufficiency of the evaluation team, the adequacy of their role definitions, the adequacy of their performance, the adequacy of staff support and supervision, and the adequacy of evaluative feedback to program staff members—that is, the strengths and weaknesses of the personnel evaluation model or procedures adopted by the organization. Desirably, the contract will note that if the evaluator has to report that a program is failing or being hampered by deficient performance of one or more key roles, recipients of the report will be advised to consider why this is so and what could be done to correct the deficiency. Examples for key clients or program directors to consider are role clarification, training, counseling, or, as a last resort, termination. The contract should stress that the program's personnel component will be examined in a manner to denote areas of strength and weakness and in the latter case to identify possible avenues to improvement. For example, if the performance of any staff assignment is weak and detracting from the program's success, the evaluation report would recommend that consideration be given to ensuring that the staff member's assignment is clear and to providing the staff member with pertinent training or other relevant assistance.

The contract also should provide for as much confidentiality and anonymity as possible. For example, most, if not all, surveys should be anonymous. The evaluator should be prohibited from looking at the personnel file of any one member of the program's staff or administration. Also, the evaluator should hold in strict confidence data gathered from interviews and surveys. Only aggregated findings should factor into the evaluator's reported conclusions about the adequacy of the program's personnel.

What Personnel Roles Should a Program Evaluation Examine?

It is advisable to evaluate the performance of the full range of personnel roles in the program. This is important to show both impartiality and fairness in looking at the performance of administrative and staff functions. It is also important to ensure that all personnel contributions that bear on the program's success will be examined. Program roles to be examined appropriately may include governance, administration, day-to-day supervision, technical and clerical support, professional staff, and consultants. It also is important to assess the extent to which individuals' roles are clear and functional in the context of other role assignments, as well as the extent to which collaborators understand and support each other's roles. Such assessments can provide vital feedback for improving a program, especially in its early stages.

In General, What Personnel-Related Questions Should a Program Evaluation Address?

The investigative questions included in program evaluation plans should contain a subset on program personnel. The following is a sample list of such questions intended to help readers think about the scope of questions that might be addressed in particular program evaluations:

1. Considering the program's objectives and projected activities, do the program's personnel possess the full range of needed competencies in such areas as governance, financial management, administration, technical support, clerical support, program content and activities, and consultants?
2. Do the program's personnel collectively enjoy sufficient credibility with constituents regarding technical competence, content knowledge, experience, political savvy, racial and ethnic composition, communication skills, and track record?
3. Are work assignments well documented, up-to-date, clear, functional, and understood and accepted by employees?
4. Do staff members evidence clear understanding, enthusiasm, task orientation, good work habits, and integrity in carrying out their assignments?
5. Do staff members consider their work important and believe they are making important contributions?

6. Do staff members collaborate effectively in a spirit of shared responsibility and teamwork?

7. Are staff members supported with appropriate and sufficient resources to succeed in their assignments?

8. Is the program's work environment conducive to high performance?

9. Are program staff members regularly and validly evaluated and given improvement-oriented feedback?

10. Are all staff members appropriately supervised to assist and ensure their effective performance?

11. Are program staff members appropriately and competitively compensated for their work?

12. Are individual and groups of program staff given appropriate recognition and rewards for stellar performance?

13. Do beginning staff have a satisfactory induction program, and is the program successful in retaining competent staff?

14. To what extent is there high morale among the program's personnel?

15. Is there a priority for particular personnel issues to be addressed?

We hope these questions somewhat reduce any concerns readers might have about incendiary issues involved in looking at personnel in the context of a program evaluation. None of the questions focus directly on an individual. All of them are concerned with possible areas for change that might help staff individually and collectively succeed. That is the constructive spirit in which program evaluators and their clients should approach the matter of personnel evaluation.

In General, What Process Should Be Followed in Assessing a Program's Personnel?

The preceding list of questions can serve as an initial guide to working out the part of the program evaluation that concerns personnel. The following suggestions identify procedures that can be useful in examining a program's personnel. These steps occur as needed and at appropriate times. No particular sequence of steps is intended.

Early on, it is usually propitious to interview the program's director to get her or his take on the adequacy of the program's personnel in terms of qualifications, credibility, assignments, funding, mutual understanding and support of roles, collaboration, and performance. With the program director's assistance, the evaluators typically will obtain and study pertinent documents related to the program's personnel presented in a general fashion. Knowledge about staff qualifications, experience, roles, and the like is essential for evaluation planning purposes.

One of the first documents to review is the program's plan for personnel evaluation. The evaluators should assess such a plan for its adequacy in meeting appropriate standards for personnel evaluations, such as the Joint Committee's *Personnel Evaluation Standards* (1988). These standards require that personnel evaluations satisfy conditions of utility, feasibility, propriety, and accuracy. Especially, they require that evaluations of a person's performance be grounded in a sound job description.

To the extent that the program regularly, systematically, and effectively evaluates its own personnel, program evaluators can limit their collection of new information on the program's personnel. While not looking at any individual's evaluation records, the evaluator should be able to get some of the needed information about the program's personnel by looking at summaries from the program's personnel evaluation system. For example, such summaries might reveal average and dispersion of ratings given to staff members in preceding years, areas of specialization, amounts of relevant experience, degrees and certificates held, job assignments, levels of compensation, staff turnover, and awards received. Evaluators also should consider collecting and reviewing staff, board, and administrator résumés and work assignments. Minutes of staff meetings also can shed light on adequacy of the program's personnel.

In addition, evaluators typically need to obtain information about the program's personnel component by interviewing staff members; possibly administering anonymous surveys to program staff, consultants, and beneficiaries; and possibly conducting focus group meetings.

How Should Evaluators File and Control Information on a Program's Personnel?

Pursuant to contractual provisions, evaluators should carefully file and protect information pertaining to a program's personnel. The information should be kept secure in hard copy or computer files, or both. Only the evaluators and appropriately authorized support staff should be allowed to access the information and only for purposes related to the evaluation. There should be clear procedures for checking out and returning the filed information. A log should be maintained of all instances in which a secretary or other support person accessed the information. The log should document who accessed the file, when he or she removed any information, and when he or she returned it. Computerized information should be similarly protected using restricted files, a list of authorized users of the files, and pertinent passwords. The point of these control measures is to protect individual program staff members from unauthorized or inappropriate use of information about them as individuals. Maintenance of strong controls of such information is also essential to protect the credibility of the program evaluation and promote needed cooperation in the evaluation by program staff.

How Should Program Evaluators Report Information on a Program's Personnel?

The collection and analysis of information about a program's personnel is focused first and foremost on the matter of program improvement. Accordingly, information about personnel matters should be reported at times and to program personnel so as to assist the improvement process. Personnel information also is crucially important in interpreting reasons for a program's level of success, as in a final summative evaluation. Thus, evaluators should report information on personnel in interim, formative evaluation reports (if agreement has been reached that these should be provided) and in the final report.

In the cases of either formative or summative reports, we think information about personnel should be embedded in a broader array of program-related information. This helps keep observations and judgments about personnel in proper context.

In formative reports, it is especially important to identify personnel issues that require attention. For example, innovative programs often experience growing pains due to inadequate role definitions and role confusion among staff, or staff who join a program in midstream may lack needed orientation and training and be confused about what and how they are supposed to perform. Program beneficiaries or other constituents might judge that the program's staff has inadequate ethnic and racial diversity. It may become clear that staff feel frustration due to a lack of supervision or needed resources. It might also be clear that certain program activities are behind schedule or not being performed well. All such issues have implications for personnel-related actions to improve the program. Evaluators should address such issues in their formative reports so as to call attention to areas requiring improvement, but without naming and evaluating any one individual.

In summative reports, evaluators should assess the extent to which the program achieved its goals and effectively addressed the needs of targeted beneficiaries. In general terms, staff should be credited for contributions to the program's success—for example, the program enjoyed strong leadership and administration, line staff effectively carried out their roles and enjoyed strong credibility with stakeholders, consultants provided invaluable technical assistance in specified areas, beneficiaries did their part to make the program succeed, and this list could continue according to the idiosyncratic nature of the program. On the other side, evaluators should note personnel-related deficiencies that likely contributed to a program's lack of success—for example, the program staff lacked expertise in one or more important areas such as computer technology; staff evaluation and supervision were superficial and ineffective; there was counterproductive role confusion among staff that remained uncorrected; line staff received too little orientation, training, or resources to perform their responsibilities well; beneficiaries resisted participation in the program because they believed the staff lacked sufficient diversity; certain personnel declined in their level of effort, possibly due to taking on lame-duck status in the program; there was a serious staff turnover problem due possibly to very low staff salary levels or lack of recognition and reinforcement.

Summary

All of these examples for formative and summative evaluation reports relate to personnel matters. Although none of them references any particular individual, recipients of the reports may make inferences about what parties are responsible for particular program successes or failures. The point of this chapter is that recipients should use the personnel-related information to strengthen a program and contribute to their understanding of what made it succeed or fail. Inescapably, programs work or fail based heavily on the competence and performance of personnel. Again, we stress that program evaluators should evaluate the full range of important variables in a program, including its personnel, but should not specifically evaluate a program's individuals. This remains the professional duty of those directing the program.

Review Questions

1. Why has this chapter called personnel evaluation "the ghost in program evaluation"?
2. If personnel evaluation is such a sensitive matter, why should program evaluators be concerned with it?
3. Comment on this statement: Personnel evaluation is solely the responsibility of the program director.
4. In respect to a program's adopted personnel evaluation policy and procedures, list, with reasons, (1) an appropriate service the program evaluator could provide and (2) an action you would consider inappropriate.

5. A client needs to improve his personnel evaluation system. Suggest, with reasons, two ways the program evaluator could use the Joint Committee's *Personnel Evaluation Standards* (1988) to help improve the system.

6. Program evaluators should assure stakeholders that to the extent possible, evaluations will not evaluate individuals. State actions the evaluator can take to guard against such infringements. Provide an illustrative stated guarantee, complete with any necessary caveat.

7. A program evaluator anticipates that a section of the final report could embarrass or even professionally damage an individual. List the salient steps that the evaluator should take to mitigate any associated possible damage.

8. Respond to the statement that program evaluators should promise stakeholders anonymity.

9. To what extent should program evaluators involve themselves in clients' personnel evaluation systems? Include in your response pertinent contractual arrangements.

10. This chapter has listed fifteen illustrative questions about personnel evaluation that program evaluations can appropriately address. Reread this sample list, and then suggest other questions you consider relevant from your experience.

Group Exercises

Discussions with your fellow students or colleagues should give further insights about the sensitive nexus between program and personnel evaluation.

> *Exercise 1.* The head librarian of a large state library that has serious difficulties affecting its successful operation has been instructed by her governing board to employ a team of evaluators to investigate some of the library's major programs. When her staff hear about the impending evaluation, they are alarmed because they fear that they will be targeted and their personal deficiencies (real or perceived) exposed. They go to the length of threatening strike action. The head librarian states that the evaluation must proceed, but promises that the evaluators will meet with staff to answer questions in an endeavor to allay apprehensions.
>
> Your group wins the contract to carry out the evaluation. Discuss the procedures you will follow before meeting with the staff, the kinds of statements you will make to staff when you meet with them, pertinent written assurances you will arrange with the client, and processes you will adhere to during the course of the study to ensure that emphasis is given to program and not individual personnel evaluation.

Exercise 2. The Joint Committee's *Personnel Evaluation Standards* (1988) offer education and other institutions criteria and guidelines for assessing their systems for evaluating staff. Why is a knowledge of this publication essential for all evaluators, whether they consider themselves predominantly program or personnel evaluators? Discuss this proposition.

Exercise 3. Your group is nearing the end of a lengthy program evaluation. Along the way, you have provided feedback to stakeholders through formative procedures, and you believe you have the confidence of all staff in the program. You have rigorously observed confidentiality and anonymity protocols.

However, as you are planning the final summative report, you realize that it will be impossible to prevent readers from inferring conclusions about individuals. Some of these inferences could prove unpalatable. Discuss ways and means of overcoming, to the extent possible, this incipient problem without compromising the integrity of the study.

Reference

Joint Committee on Standards for Educational Evaluation. (1988). *The personnel evaluation standards.* Thousand Oaks, CA: Corwin Press.

PART TWO

AN EVALUATION OF EVALUATION APPROACHES AND MODELS

The seven chapters in Part Two identify and assess twenty-six approaches often employed to evaluate programs. Chapter Five provides background information for reviewing evaluation approaches. Chapters Six through Ten respectively characterize and assess approaches labeled pseudoevaluation, questions/methods oriented, improvement/accountability, social agenda/advocacy, and eclectic. Chapter Eleven provides a consumer report evaluation of eight of the highest-rated or most used approaches.

CHAPTER FIVE

BACKGROUND FOR ASSESSING EVALUATION APPROACHES AND MODELS

The chapters in Part One provide a firm understanding of the basic concepts and principles of program evaluation. The chapters in Part Two identify and assess twenty-six approaches often employed to evaluate programs. The evaluation approaches and models reviewed here in varying degrees are unique and cover most program evaluation efforts. Our objectives are to help readers decide which of the approaches are most worthy of application and further development and which are best abandoned.

The approaches reviewed here emerged mainly in the United States between 1960 and 1999. Five of the approaches, labeled pseudoevaluations, reflect the political realities of evaluation and are often used illegitimately to falsely characterize (or hide) a program's value. Pseudoevaluations have often arisen from expediency without due consideration to the ethics or professional cogency of their design and implementation. Sadly, repeated use of these approaches has all too often given them a veneer of respectability and legitimacy.

We review these approaches in the hope of helping evaluators and clients identify, avoid, or expose misleading or blatantly corrupt studies offered in the name of evaluation. The remaining twenty-one approaches are typically used legitimately to judge programs. They are divided into quasi-evaluations (approaches narrowly focused on answering one or a few questions or using mainly one method), improvement/accountability approaches (oriented to determining an evaluand's merit and worth), social agenda/advocacy approaches (usually dedicated to righting social injustices), and eclectic approaches (drawing selectively from all available evaluation concepts and methods to serve the needs of a particular user group). We have characterized each approach; assessed its strengths and weaknesses; and considered whether, when, and how it is best applied (if at all). All legitimate approaches are enhanced when keyed to professional standards for evaluations and, accordingly, we assessed the most promising approaches against the Joint Committee (1994) *Program Evaluation Standards*.

The development of many of the reviewed approaches was spurred by a number of seminal writings. These included, in chronological order, publications by Flexner (1910), Tyler (1932, 1942, 1950), Fisher (1951), Lindquist (1953), Campbell and Stanley (1963), Cronbach (1963), Kaplan (1964), Stufflebeam (1966, 1967), Tyler (1966), Glaser and Strauss (1967), Metfessel and Michael (1967), Scriven (1967), Stake (1967), Suchman (1967), Alkin (1969), Guba (1969), Hammond (1972), Lessinger (1970), Provus (1969), Stufflebeam et al. (1971), Parlett and Hamilton (1972), Weiss (1972), House (1973), Rippey (1973), Eisner (1975), Glass (1975), Wolf (1975), Cook and Reichardt (1979), Cronbach and Associates (1980), House (1980), Patton (1980), Joint Committee on Standards for Educational Evaluation (1981), Levin (1983), Stake (1983), Bickman (1990), Chen (1990), Sanders and Horn (1994), Henry, Julnes, and Mark (1998), Cousins (2003), and Brinkerhoff (2003). These and other authors and scholars began to project alternative approaches to program evaluation.

Over the years, a rich literature on a wide variety of alternative program evaluation approaches developed. See, for example, Alkin (2004), Boruch (1994, 2003), Campbell (1988), Chelimsky (1987), Cook and Reichardt (1979), Cousins (2003), Cousins and Earl (1992), Cronbach (1982), Davis and Salasin (1975), Denny (1978), Eisner (1983), Fetterman (1984, 1994), Flinders and Eisner (2000), Greene (1988), Guba (1978), Guba and Lincoln (1981, 1989), Henry et al. (1998), Hofstetter and Alkin (2003), House and Howe (1998, 2000a, 2000b, 2003), Joint Committee on Standards for Educational Evaluation (1994), Karlsson (1998), Kee (1995), Kellaghan and Stufflebeam (2003), Kidder and Fine (1987), Kirst (1990), Koretz (1996), Levin (1983), Levine (1974), Lincoln and Guba (1985), Linn, Baker, and Dunbar (1991), MacDonald (1975), Madaus, Scriven, and Stufflebeam (1983), Madaus and Stufflebeam (1988), Mathison (2005), Mehrens (1972), Messick (1994), National Science Foundation (1997), Nave, Miech, and Mosteller (2000), Nevo (1993), Owens (1973), Patton (1982, 1990, 1994, 1997, 2000, 2003), Platt (1992), Popham (1969), Popham and Carlson (1983), Provus (1971), Rogers (2000), Rossi and Freeman (1993), J. Sanders (1992), W. Sanders (1989), Schwandt (1984, 1989), Scriven (1991, 1993, 1994a, 1994b, 1994c), Shadish, Cook, and Leviton

(1991), M. F. Smith (1986, 1989), N. L. Smith (1987), Stake (1975, 1986, 1988, 1995), Stufflebeam (1997), Stufflebeam, Madaus, and Kellaghan (2000), Stufflebeam and Shinkfield (1985), Torres (1991), Tsang (1997), Tymms (1995), Webster (1975, 1995), Webster, Mendro, and Almaguer (1994), Weiss (1995), Whitmore (1998), Wholey (1995), Worthen and Sanders (1987), Worthen, Sanders, and Fitzpatrick (1997), and Yin (1992).

Following a period of relative inactivity in the 1950s, a succession of international and national forces stimulated the expansion and development of evaluation theory and practice. The main influences were the efforts to vastly strengthen the U.S. defense system spawned by the Soviet Union's 1957 launching of *Sputnik I;* the new U.S. laws in the 1960s to serve minorities and persons with disabilities equitably; federal government evaluation requirements of the Great Society programs initiated in 1965; the movement begun in the 1970s to hold education and social organizations accountable for both prudent use of resources and achievement of objectives; the stress on excellence in the 1980s as a means of increasing U.S. international competitiveness; and the increasing trend in the 1990s and beyond for various organizations, both inside and outside the United States, to employ evaluation to ensure quality, competitiveness, and equity in delivering services. In pursuing reforms, American society has repeatedly pressed schools and colleges, health care organizations, government organizations, and various social welfare enterprises to show through evaluation whether services and improvement efforts were succeeding.

Evaluation Approaches and Models

This book uses the term *evaluation approach* along with *evaluation model* because the former is broad enough to cover illicit as well as laudatory practices. Also, beyond covering both creditable and noncreditable approaches, some authors of evaluation approaches say that the term *model* is too demanding and restrictive to cover their published ideas about how to conduct program evaluations. Moreover, some leading exponents of program evaluation see their work as evolutionary, and therefore some flexibility about aspects of their models is required. But for these two considerations, the term *model* would have been used to encompass most of the evaluation proposals discussed in this book. This is so because most of the presented approaches are idealized or model views for conducting program evaluations according to their authors' beliefs and experiences. For ease of communication, we generally use the terms *evaluation approach* and *evaluation model* interchangeably.

The Importance of Studying Alternative Approaches and Models

The study of alternative evaluation approaches and models is important for professionalizing program evaluation, which will lead to its scientific operation and advancement. Careful, professional study of alternative ways of conducting program evaluations will help evaluators discredit approaches that violate sound principles of evaluation and legitimize and strengthen those that follow the principles. Scientifically, such a review would help evaluation researchers identify, examine, and address conceptual and technical issues pertaining to the development of the evaluation discipline. Operationally, a critical view of alternatives can help evaluators consider, assess, and selectively apply optional and appropriate evaluation frameworks. The review would also provide a sound basis for evaluation training. The main values in studying alternative program evaluation approaches and models are to discover their strengths and weaknesses. Such analysis will help determine which ones merit substantial use, determine when and how they are best applied, obtain direction for improving the approaches and devising better alternatives, and strengthen one's ability to conceptualize hybrid approaches to program evaluation.

The Nature of Program Evaluation

This book employs a broad view of program evaluation. It encompasses assessments of any coordinated set of activities directed at achieving goals. These may be in business enterprises (both large and small), community or state organizations, welfare and voluntary groups—or any other entities where activities have been discernibly planned. More specific examples are assess-ments of ongoing, cyclical programs, such as school curricula, food stamps, housing for the homeless, and annual influenza inoculations; time-bounded projects such as development and dissemination of a fire prevention guide and development of a new instrument for evaluating the performance of factory workers; and national, regional, or state systems of services such as those provided by regional educational service organizations and a state's department of natural resources. Program evaluations overlap with and yet are distinguishable from other forms of evaluation, especially evaluations of students, personnel, materials, and institutions.

Previous Classifications of Alternative Evaluation Approaches

In analyzing the twenty-six evaluation approaches, we considered prior assessments of program evaluation's state of the art. Stake's analysis (1974) of nine program evaluation approaches provided a useful application of advance organizers (the types of variables used to determine information requirements) for ascertaining different types of program evaluations. Hastings's review (1976) of the growth of evaluation theory and practice helped to place the evaluation field in a historical perspective. Guba's book, *The Paradigm Dialog* (1990), and his 1977 presentation and assessment of six major philosophies in evaluation were provocative. House's analysis of approaches (1983) illuminated important philosophical and theoretical distinctions. Scriven's writings on the transdiscipline of evaluation (1991, 1994a) helped sort out different evaluation approaches; they were also invaluable in seeing the approaches in the broader context of evaluations focused on various objects other than programs. The books *Evaluation Models* (Madaus et al., 1983) and *International Handbook of Educational Evaluation* (Kellaghan & Stufflebeam, 2003) provided previous inventories and analyses of evaluation models. All of the assessments helped sharpen the issues addressed.

Definition of Program Evaluation Revisited

In characterizing and assessing evaluation approaches, the various kinds of activities conducted in the name of program evaluation were classified on the basis of their level of conformity to the definition of evaluation given in the Joint Committee's *Program Evaluation Standards* (1994). According to that definition, evaluation is the assessment of something's worth or merit. This definition should be widely acceptable since it is consistent with common dictionary definitions of evaluation; since the Joint Committee (1981, 1988, 1994, 2003) used it in developing professional standards for evaluations of programs, personnel, and students; and since the Joint Committee's standards are accredited by the American National Standards Institute. In Chapter Six, it will become apparent that many studies done in the name of program evaluation either do not conform to the essential meaning of evaluation or directly oppose it.

Classification and Analysis of the Twenty-Six Evaluation Approaches

Using the above definition of evaluation, we classified program evaluation approaches into five categories. The first category includes approaches that promote invalid or incomplete findings (referred to as pseudoevaluations), and the other four include approaches that agree, more or less, with the definition (questions and/or methods-oriented, improvement/accountability, social agenda/advocacy, and eclectic). Of the twenty-six program evaluation approaches that are described, five are classified as pseudoevaluations, fourteen as questions and methods-oriented approaches, three as improvement/accountability-oriented approaches, three as social agenda/advocacy approaches, and one as an eclectic approach.

Each approach is characterized in terms of ten descriptors: (1) advance organizers, that is, the main cues that evaluators use to set up a study; (2) main purposes served; (3) sources of questions addressed; (4) questions that are characteristic of each study type; (5) methods typically employed; (6) those who pioneered in conceptualizing each study type; (7) others who have extended the development and use of each study type; (8) key considerations in determining when to use each approach; (9) strengths of the approach; and (10) weaknesses of the approach. Comments on each of approaches are presented.

Eight approaches that appeared most worthy were then selected for a consumer report analysis. These approaches were evaluated against the requirements of the Joint Committee's *Program Evaluation Standards* (1994) to obtain judgments—of poor, fair, good, very good, or excellent—of each approach's utility, feasibility, propriety, accuracy, and overall merit. The judgments of each of the eight approaches were reached using a specially prepared checklist. For each of the thirty Joint Committee standards, the checklist contained six checkpoints representing the standard's key requirements. We rated each of the eight evaluation approaches on each of the thirty Joint Committee program evaluation standards by judging whether the approach, as defined in the literature and otherwise known to us,—satisfactorily addresses each of the six checkpoints. Regardless of the approach's total score and overall rating, we would have attached a notation of unacceptable to any approach receiving a rating of poor on any one of the vital standards of P1, Service Orientation; A5, Valid Information; A10, Justified Conclusions; and A11, Impartial Reporting. We rated the approaches based on our knowledge of the Joint Committee Program Evaluation Standards, our many years of studying the various evaluation models and approaches, our experience in seeing and assessing how some of these models and approaches worked in practice, and our personal experiences in working with authors of many of the approaches. The first author chaired the Joint Committee on Standards for Educational Evaluation during its first thirteen years and led the development of the first editions of both the program and personnel evaluation standards. The second author served on the staff of the Joint Committee during its development of the first edition of *The Program Evaluation Standards.*

Caveats

We acknowledge, without apology, that the assessments of the approaches and the entries in the summary charts in this part of the book are based on our best judgments. We have taken no poll, and no definitive research exists, to represent a consensus on the characteristics, their strengths and weaknesses, and comparative merits of the different approaches. We also acknowledge a conflict of interest, since the first author developed one of the rated approaches, the CIPP Model. Our analyses reflect a combined total of sixty years of experience in applying and studying different evaluation approaches. In a sense, with our relevant backgrounds and experience, we are the instruments employed in this analysis. Perhaps our assessments fall best under the category of connoisseurship evaluation. We hope our analyses will be useful to evaluators and evaluation students in selecting approaches and also as working hypotheses to be tested to extend and strengthen knowledge of evaluation theory and practice.

We have mainly looked at the approaches as relatively discrete ways to conduct evaluations. In reality, there are many occasions when it is functional to mix and match different approaches, as seen in the mixed methods and eclectic evaluation approaches. A careful analysis of such combinatorial applications no doubt would produce several additional hybrid approaches that might merit examination. That analysis is beyond the scope of this book.

References

Alkin, M. C. (1969). Evaluation theory development. *Evaluation Comment, 2,* 2–7.

Alkin, M. C. (Ed.).(2004). *Evaluation roots.* Thousand Oaks, CA: Sage.

Bickman, L. (1990). Using program theory to describe and measure program quality. In L. Bickman (Ed.), *Advances in program theory.* New Directions for Program Evaluation, no. 47. San Francisco: Jossey-Bass.

Boruch, R. F. (1994). The future of controlled randomized experiments: A briefing. *Evaluation Practice, 15*(3), 265–274.

Boruch, R. F. (2003). Randomized field trials in education. In T. Kellaghan & D. L. Stufflebeam (Eds.), *International handbook of educational evaluation.* Norwell, MA: Kluwer.

Brinkerhoff, R. O. (2003). *The success case method.* San Francisco: Berrett-Koehler.

Campbell, D. T. (1988). *Methodology and epistemology for social science: Selected papers* (E. S. Overman, Ed.). Chicago: University of Chicago Press.

Campbell, D. T., & Stanley, J. C. (1963). Experimental and quasi-experimental designs for research on teaching. In N. L. Gage (Ed.), *Handbook of research on training.* Skokie, IL: Rand McNally.

Chelimsky, E. (1987). What have we learned about the politics of evaluation? *Evaluation Practice, 8*(1), 5–21.

Chen, H. (1990). *Theory driven evaluations.* Thousand Oaks, CA: Sage.

Cook, T. D., & Reichardt, C. S. (Eds.). (1979). *Qualitative and quantitative methods in evaluation research.* Thousand Oaks, CA: Sage.

Cousins, J. B. (2003). Utilization effects of participatory evaluation. In T. Kellaghan & D. L. Stufflebeam (Eds.), *International handbook of educational evaluation* (pp. 245–265). Norwell, MA: Kluwer.

Cousins, J. B., & Earl, L. M. (1992). The case for participatory evaluation. *Educational Evaluation and Policy Analysis, 14*(4), 397–418.

Cronbach, L. J. (1963). Course improvement through evaluation. *Teachers College Record, 64,* 672–683.

Cronbach, L. J. (1982). *Designing evaluations of educational and social programs.* San Francisco: Jossey-Bass.

Cronbach, L. J., & Associates. (1980). *Toward reform of program evaluation.* San Francisco: Jossey-Bass.

Davis, H. R., & Salasin, S. E. (1975). The utilization of evaluation. In E. L. Struening & M. Guttentag (Eds.), *Handbook of evaluation research.* Thousand Oaks, CA: Sage.

Denny, T. (1978, November). *Story telling and educational understanding.* Kalamazoo: Evaluation Center, Western Michigan University.

Eisner, E. W. (1975, March). *The perceptive eye: Toward a reformation of educational evaluation.* Invited address to Division B, Curriculum and Objectives, American Educational Research Association, Washington, DC.

Eisner, E. W. (1983). Educational connoisseurship and criticism: Their form and functions in educational evaluation. In G. F. Madaus, M. Scriven, & D. L. Stufflebeam (Eds.), *Evaluation models.* Norwell, MA: Kluwer.

Fetterman, D. M. (1984). *Ethnography in educational evaluation.* Thousand Oaks, CA: Sage.

Fetterman, D. (1994, February). Empowerment evaluation. *Evaluation Practice, 15*(1), 1–15.

Fisher, R. A. (1951). *The design of experiments* (6th ed.) New York: Hafner.

Flexner, A. (1910). *Medical education in the United States and Canada.* Bethesda, MD: Science and Health Publications.

Flinders, D. J., & Eisner, E. W. (2000). Educational criticism as a form of qualitative inquiry. In D. L. Stufflebeam, G. F. Madaus, & T. Kellaghan (Eds.), *Evaluation models.* Norwell, MA: Kluwer.

Glaser, B. G., & Strauss, A. L. (1967). *The discovery of grounded theory.* Chicago: Aldine.

Glass, G. V (1975). A paradox about excellence of schools and the people in them. *Educational Researcher, 4,* 9–13.

Greene, J. C. (1988). Communication of results and utilization in participatory program evaluation. *Evaluation and Program Planning, 11,* 341–351.

Guba, E. G. (1969). The failure of educational evaluation. *Educational Technology, 9,* 29–38.

Guba, E. G. (1977). *Educational evaluation: The state of the art.* Keynote address at the annual meeting of the Evaluation Network, St. Louis, MO.

Guba, E. G. (1978). *Toward a methodology of naturalistic inquiry in evaluation.* Los Angeles: Center for the Study of Evaluation.

Guba, E. G. (1990). *The paradigm dialog.* Thousand Oaks, CA: Sage.

Guba, E. G., & Lincoln, Y. S. (1981). *Effective evaluation.* San Francisco: Jossey-Bass.

Guba, E. G., & Lincoln, Y. S. (1989). *Fourth generation evaluation.* Thousand Oaks, CA: Sage.

Hammond, R. L. (1972). *Evaluation at the local level.* Tucson, AZ: EPIC Evaluation Center.

Hastings, T. (1976). *A portrayal of the changing evaluation scene.* Keynote speech at the annual meeting of the Evaluation Network, St. Louis, MO.

Henry, G., Julnes, A. & Mark, M. (Eds.). (1998). *Realist evaluation: An emerging theory in support of practice.* New Directions for Evaluation, no. 78. San Francisco: Jossey-Bass.

Hofstetter, C., & Alkin, M. C. (2003). Evaluation use revisited. In T. Kellaghan & D. L. Stufflebeam (Eds.), *International handbook of educational evaluation.* Norwell, MA: Kluwer.

House, E. R. (Ed.). (1973). *School evaluation: The politics and process.* Berkeley, CA: McCutchan.

House, E. R. (1980). *Evaluating with validity.* Thousand Oaks, CA.: Sage.

House, E. R. (1983). Assumptions underlying evaluation models. In G. F. Madaus, M. Scriven, & D. L. Stufflebeam (Eds.), *Evaluation models.* Norwell, MA: Kluwer.

House, E. R., & Howe, K. R. (1998). *Deliberative democratic evaluation in practice.* Boulder: University of Colorado.

House, E. R., & Howe, K. R. (2000a, Spring). Deliberative democratic evaluation. In K. E. Ryan & L. DeStefano (Eds.), *Evaluation as a democratic process: Promoting inclusion, dialogue, and deliberation.* New Directions for Evaluation, no. 85. San Francisco: Jossey-Bass.

House, E. R., & Howe, K. R. (2000b). Deliberative democratic evaluation in practice. In D. L. Stufflebeam, G. F. Madaus, & T. Kellaghan (Eds.), *Evaluation models.* Norwell, MA: Kluwer.

House, E. R., & Howe, K. R. (2003). Deliberative democratic evaluation. In T. Kellaghan & D. L. Stufflebeam (Eds.), *International handbook of educational evaluation.* Norwell, MA: Kluwer.

Joint Committee on Standards for Educational Evaluation. (1981). *Standards for evaluations of educational programs, projects, and materials.* New York: McGraw-Hill.

Joint Committee on Standards for Educational Evaluation. (1988). *The personnel evaluation standards: How to assess systems for evaluating educators.* Thousand Oaks, CA: Corwin Press.

Joint Committee on Standards for Educational Evaluation. (1994). *The program evaluation standards: How to assess evaluations of educational programs.* Thousand Oaks, CA: Corwin Press.

Joint Committee on Standards for Educational Evaluation. (2003). *The student evaluation standards.* Thousand Oaks, CA: Corwin Press.

Kaplan, A. (1964). *The conduct of inquiry.* San Francisco: Chandler.

Karlsson, O. (1998). Socratic dialogue in the Swedish political context. In T. A. Schwandt (Ed.), Scandinavian perspectives on the evaluator's role in informing social policy (pp. 21–38). New Directions for Evaluation, no. 77. San Francisco: Jossey-Bass.

Kee, J. E. (1995). Benefit-cost analysis in program evaluation. In J. S. Wholey, H. P. Hatry, & K. E. Newcomer (Eds.), *Handbook of practical program evaluation* (pp. 456–488). San Francisco: Jossey-Bass.

Kellaghan, T., & Stufflebeam, D. L. (2003). *International handbook of educational evaluation.* Norwell, MA: Kluwer.

Kidder, L., & Fine, M. (1987). Qualitative and quantitative methods: When stories converge. In M. M. Mark & L. Shotland (Eds.), *Multiple methods in program evaluation* (pp. 57–75). New Directions for Program Evaluation, no. 35. San Francisco: Jossey-Bass.

Kirst, M. W. (1990, July). *Accountability: Implications for state and local policymakers.* Washington, DC: Information Services, Office of Educational Research and Improvement, U.S. Department of Education.

Koretz, D. (1996). Using student assessments for educational accountability. In R. Hanushek (Ed.), *Improving the performance of America's schools* (pp. 171–196). Washington, DC: National Academy Press.

Lessinger, L. M. (1970). *Every kid a winner: Accountability in education.* New York: Simon & Schuster.

Levin, H. M. (1983). Cost-effectiveness: A primer. *New Perspectives in Evaluation, 4.* Thousand Oaks, CA: Sage.

Levine, M. (1974, September). Scientific method and the adversary model. *American Psychologist,* 666–677.

Lincoln, Y. S., & Guba, E. G. (1985). *Naturalistic inquiry.* Thousand Oaks, CA: Sage.

Lindquist, E. F. (1953). *Design and analysis of experiments in psychology and education.* Boston: Houghton Mifflin.

Linn, R. L., Baker, E. L., & Dunbar, S. B. (1991). Complex, performance-based assessment: Expectations and validation criteria. *Educational Researcher, 20*(8), 15–21.

MacDonald, B. (1975). Evaluation and the control of education. In D. Tawney (Ed.), *Evaluation: The state of the art.* London: Schools Council.

Madaus, G. F., Scriven, M., & Stufflebeam, D. L. (1983). *Evaluation models.* Norwell, MA: Kluwer.

Madaus, G. F., & Stufflebeam, D. L. (1988). *Educational evaluation: The classical writings of Ralph W. Tyler.* Norwell, MA: Kluwer.

Mathison, S. (2005). *Encyclopedia of evaluation.* Thousand Oaks: Sage.

Mehrens, W. A. (1972). Using performance assessment for accountability purposes. *Educational Measurement: Issues and Practice, 11*(1), 3–10.

Messick, S. (1994). The interplay of evidence and consequences in the validation of performance assessments. *Educational Researcher, 23*(3), 13–23.

Metfessel, N. S., & Michael, W. B. (1967). A paradigm involving multiple criterion measures for the evaluation of the effectiveness of school programs. *Educational and Psychological Measurement, 27*, 931–943.

National Science Foundation. (1997). *User-friendly handbook for mixed method evaluations.* Arlington, VA: Author.

Nave, B., Miech, E. J., & Mosteller, F. (2000). A rare design: The role of field trials in evaluating school practices. In D. L. Stufflebeam, G. F. Madaus, & T. Kellaghan (Eds.), *Evaluation models.* Norwell, MA: Kluwer.

Nevo, D. (1993). The evaluation minded school: An application of perceptions from program evaluation. *Evaluation Practice, 14*(1), 39–47.

Owens, T. (1973). Educational evaluation by adversary proceeding. In E. House (Ed.), *School evaluation: The politics and process.* Berkeley, CA: McCutchan.

Parlett, M., & Hamilton, D. (1972). *Evaluation as illumination: A new approach to the study of innovatory programs.* Edinburgh: Centre for Research in the Educational Sciences, University of Edinburgh.

Patton, M. Q. (1980). *Qualitative evaluation methods.* Thousand Oaks, CA: Sage.

Patton, M. Q. (1982). *Practical evaluation.* Thousand Oaks, CA: Sage.

Patton, M. Q. (1990). *Qualitative evaluation and research methods* (2nd ed.). Thousand Oaks, CA: Sage.

Patton, M. Q. (1994). Developmental evaluation. *Evaluation Practice, 15*(3), 311–319.

Patton, M. Q. (1997). *Utilization-focused evaluation: The new century text* (3rd ed.). Thousand Oaks, CA: Sage.

Patton, M. Q. (2000). Utilization-focused evaluation. In D. L. Stufflebeam, G. F. Madaus, & T. Kellaghan (Eds.), *Evaluation models.* Norwell, MA: Kluwer.

Patton, M. Q. (2003). Utilization-focused evaluation. In T. Kellaghan & D. L. Stufflebeam (Eds.), *International handbook of educational evaluation.* Norwell, MA: Kluwer.

Platt, J. (1992). Case study in American methodological thought. *Current Sociology, 40*(1), 17–48.

Popham, W. J. (1969). Objectives and instruction. In R. Stake (Ed.), *Instructional objectives.* Skokie, IL: Rand McNally.

Popham, W. J., & Carlson, D. (1983). Deep dark deficits of the adversary evaluation model. In G. F. Madaus, M. Scriven, & D. L. Stufflebeam, (Eds.), *Evaluation models.* Norwell, MA: Kluwer.

Provus, M. N. (1969). *Discrepancy evaluation model.* Pittsburgh, PA: Pittsburgh Public Schools.

Provus, M. N. (1971). *Discrepancy evaluation.* Berkeley, CA: McCutcheon.

Rippey, R. M. (Ed.). (1973). *Studies in transactional evaluation.* Berkeley, CA: McCutcheon.

Rogers, P. R. (2000). Program theory: Not whether programs work but how they work. In D. L. Stufflebeam, G. F. Madaus, & T. Kellaghan (Eds.), *Evaluation models.* Norwell, MA: Kluwer.

Rossi, P. H., & Freeman, H. E. (1993). *Evaluation: A systematic approach* (5th ed.). Thousand Oaks, CA: Sage.

Sanders, J. R. (1992). *Evaluating school programs.* Thousand Oaks, CA: Sage.

Sanders, W. L. (1989). *Using customized standardized tests.* Washington, DC: Office of Educational Research and Improvement, U. S. Department of Education. (ERIC Digest No. ED 314429)

Sanders, W. L., & Horn, S. P. (1994). The Tennessee value-added assessment system (TVAAS): Mixed model methodology in educational assessment. *Journal of Personnel Evaluation in Education, 8*(3) 299–311.

Schwandt, T. A. (1984). *An examination of alternative models for socio-behavioral inquiry.* Unpublished doctoral dissertation, Indiana University.

Schwandt, T. A. (1989). Recapturing moral discourse in evaluation. *Educational Researcher, 18*(8), 11–16.

Scriven, M. S. (1967). The methodology of evaluation. In R. E. Stake (Ed.), *Curriculum evaluation.* Skokie, IL: Rand McNally.

Scriven, M. (1991). *Evaluation thesaurus.* Thousand Oaks, CA: Sage.

Scriven, M. (Ed.). (1993, Summer). *Hard-won lessons in program evaluation.* New Directions for Program Evaluation, 58. San Francisco: Jossey-Bass.

Scriven, M. (1994a). Evaluation as a discipline. *Studies in Educational Evaluation, 20*(1), 147–166.

Scriven, M. (1994b). The final synthesis. *Evaluation Practice, 15*(3), 367–382.

Scriven, M. (1994c). Product evaluation: The state of the art. *Evaluation Practice, 15*(1), 45–62.

Shadish, W. R., Cook, T. D., & Leviton, L. C. (1991). *Foundations of program evaluation.* Thousand Oaks, CA: Sage.

Smith, M. F. (1986). The whole is greater: Combining qualitative and quantitative approaches in evaluation studies. In D. Williams (Ed.), *Naturalistic evaluation* (pp. 37–54). New Directions for Program Evaluation, no. 30. San Francisco: Jossey-Bass.

Smith, M. F. (1989). *Evaluability assessment: A practical approach.* Norwell, MA: Kluwer.

Smith, N. L. (1987). Toward the justification of claims in evaluation research. *Evaluation and Program Planning, 10*(4), 309–314.

Stake, R. E. (1967). The countenance of educational evaluation. *Teachers College Record, 68,* 523–540.

Stake, R. E. (1974). *Nine approaches to educational evaluation.* Urbana: University of Illinois, Center for Instructional Research and Curriculum Evaluation. Unpublished chart.

Stake, R. E. (1975, November). *Program evaluation: Particularly responsive evaluation.* Kalamazoo, MI: Western Michigan University Evaluation Center.

Stake, R. E. (1983). Program evaluation, particularly responsive evaluation. In G. F. Madaus, M. Scriven, & D. L. Stufflebeam (Eds.), *Evaluation models* (pp. 287–310). Norwell, MA: Kluwer.

Stake, R. E. (1986). *Quieting reform.* Urbana: University of Illinois Press.

Stake, R. E. (1988). Seeking sweet water. In R. M. Jaeger (Ed.), *Complementary methods for research in education* (pp. 253–300). Washington, DC: American Educational Research Association.

Stake, R. E. (1995). *The art of case study research.* Thousand Oaks, CA: Sage.

Stufflebeam, D. L. (1966, June). A depth study of the evaluation requirement. *Theory into Practice, 5,* 121–134.

Stufflebeam, D. L. (1967, June). The use of and abuse of evaluation in Title III. *Theory into Practice, 6,* 126–133.

Stufflebeam, D. L. (1997). A standards-based perspective on evaluation. In R. L. Stake (Ed.), *Evaluation and the postmodern dilemma: Vol. 3. Advances in program evaluation.* Greenwich, CT: Jai Press.

Stufflebeam, D. L., Foley, W. J., Gephart, W. J., Guba, E. G., Hammond, R. L., Merriman, H. O., & Provus, M. M. (1971). *Educational evaluation and decision making.* Itasca, IL: Peacock.

Stufflebeam, D. L., Madaus, G. F., & Kellaghan, T. (2000). *Evaluation models* (rev. ed.). Norwell, MA: Kluwer.

Stufflebeam, D. L., & Shinkfield, A. J. (1985). *Systematic evaluation.* Norwell, MA: Kluwer.

Suchman, E. A. (1967). *Evaluative research.* New York: Russell Sage Foundation.

Torres, R. T. (1991). Improving the quality of internal evaluation: The evaluator as consultant mediator. *Evaluation and Program Planning, 14*(1), 189–198.

Tsang, M. C. (1997, Winter). Cost analysis for improved educational policymaking and evaluation. *Educational Evaluation and Policy Analysis, 19*(4), 318–324.

Tyler, R. W. (1932). *Service studies in higher education.* Columbus: Bureau of Educational Research, Ohio State University.

Tyler, R. W. (1942). General statement on evaluation. *Journal of Educational Research, 35,* 492–501.

Tyler, R. W. (1950). *Basic principles of curriculum and instruction.* Chicago: University of Chicago Press.

Tyler, R. W. (1966). The objectives and plans for a national assessment of educational progress. *Journal of Educational Measurement, 3,* 1–10.

Tymms, P. (1995). *Setting up a national "value-added" system for primary education in England: Problems and possibilities.* Paper presented at the National Evaluation Institute, Kalamazoo, MI.

Webster, W. J. (1975, March). *The organization and functions of research evaluation in a large urban school district.* Paper presented at the annual meeting of the American Educational Research Association, Washington, DC. (ERIC Clearinghouse on Tests, Measurements, and Evaluation, ED106345)

Webster, W. J. (1995). The connection between personnel evaluation and school evaluation. *Studies in Educational Evaluation, 21,* 227–254.

Webster, W. J., Mendro, R. L., & Almaguer, T. O. (1994). Effectiveness indices: A "value-added" approach to measuring school effect. *Studies in Educational Evaluation, 20,* 113–145.

Weiss, C. H. (1972). *Evaluation.* Upper Saddle River, NJ: Prentice Hall.

Weiss, C. H. (1995). Nothing as practical as good theory: Exploring theory-based evaluation for comprehensive community initiatives for children and families. In J. Connell, A. Kubisch, L. B. Schorr, & C. H. Weiss (Eds.), *New approaches to evaluating community initiatives.* New York: Aspen Institute.

Whitmore, E. (Ed.). (1998). *Understanding and practicing participatory evaluation.* New Directions for Evaluation, no. 80. San Francisco: Jossey-Bass.

Wholey, J. S. (1995). Assessing the feasibility and likely usefulness of evaluation. In J. S. Wholey, H. P. Hatry, & K. E. Newcomer, *Handbook of practical program evaluation* (pp. 15–39). San Francisco: Jossey-Bass.

Wolf, R. L. (1975, November). Trial by jury: A new evaluation method. *Phi Delta Kappan, 3*(57), 185–187.

Worthen, B. R., & Sanders, J. R. (1987). *Educational evaluation: Alternative approaches and practical guidelines.* White Plains, NY: Longman.

Worthen, B. R., Sanders, J. R., & Fitzpatrick, J. L. (1997). *Program evaluation* (2nd ed.). New York: Longman.

Yin, R. K. (1992). The case study as a tool for doing evaluation. *Current Sociology, 40*(1), 121–137.

CHAPTER SIX

PSEUDOEVALUATIONS

Because this book aims at examining and explaining the state of the art in evaluation, it is necessary to discuss bad and questionable practices as well as best efforts. Evaluators and their clients are sometimes tempted to shade, selectively release, overgeneralize, or even falsify findings. In addition, they might falsely characterize constructive efforts—such as providing evaluation training or developing an organization's evaluation capability—as evaluation. Or they might unwittingly conduct an evaluation that serves a hidden, corrupt purpose. Others—lacking true knowledge of evaluation planning, procedures, and standards—may feign evaluation expertise while producing and reporting false outcomes. Although such activities conducted in the name of evaluation might look like sound evaluations, they are aptly termed *pseudoevaluations* if they fail to produce and report valid assessments of merit or worth to all right-to-know audiences.

Pseudoevaluations often are motivated by political objectives. For example, persons holding or seeking authority may present unwarranted claims about their achievements or the faults of their opponents or hide potentially damaging information. Or a "do-gooder" evaluator wanting to pacify, secure acceptance from, or improve the evaluation capabilities of a group of wary, unsophisticated evaluees may compromise an evaluation's independence and water down the results in order to win the confidence of the evaluees or help them gain power. Corrupt evaluations are considered here because they deceive through evaluation and can be used by those in power to mislead constituents or to gain and maintain an unfair advantage over others, especially those with little power. Pseudoevaluations are also considered because they threaten the integrity of the evaluation profession. Conversely, consistent and best practice, widely understood by both evaluator and client, will elevate the profession.

We identified five pseudoevaluation approaches, labeled public relations–inspired studies, politically controlled studies, pandering evaluations, evaluation by pretext, and empowerment under the guise of evaluation. They are primarily distinguished through flaws regarding truth seeking, writing and editing of reports, and dissemination of findings. Public relations studies do not seek truth but instead acquire and broadcast information that provides a favorable, though often false, impression of a program. Politically controlled studies seek the truth but inappropriately control the release of findings to right-to-know audiences. In pandering evaluations, evaluators tell clients what they want to hear rather than what is true; they do so to obtain favors from the client, including future evaluation contracts. Evaluation by pretext begins with a preferred conclusion or decision and rigs data to support the predetermined outcome. In empowerment under the guise of evaluation, an external evaluator pursues the laudable objective of helping clients develop their evaluation expertise and mainstream evaluation in their organization but, in so doing, gives the client the authority to write, rewrite, edit, or selectively release the external evaluator's so-called independent report. In such evaluation work, the desirable end of helping clients increase evaluation capacity does not justify compromising a needed independent evaluation perspective. For this reason, we see empowerment evaluation as false advertising and thus a pseudoevaluation approach. In the remainder of the chapter, we look more closely at each of these false evaluation approaches.

The five kinds of pseudoevaluation we have identified most often occur discreetly—that is, they typify a particular approach. Even more deplorable is that pseudoevaluations may combine two or more elements of these approaches. If this occurs, the procedures move increasingly distant from a true evaluation.

Approach 1: Public Relations–Inspired Studies

The public relations approach begins with an intention to use data to convince constituents that a program is sound and effective. Other labels for the approach are *ideological marketing* (see Ferguson, 1999), *advertising*, and *infomercial*. The public relations approach may meet the standard for addressing all right-to-know audiences, but fails as a legitimate evaluation approach because typically it presents a program's strengths, or an exaggerated view of them, but not its weaknesses.

Clancy and Horner (1999) gave poignant examples of public relations studies that were supposedly but not actually conducted to gain valuable lessons from the 1991 Gulf War:

> In the United States, the Joint Chiefs of Staff and each of the service departments published "Lessons Learned" documents that were in fact advertisements for individual programs, requirements, or services. . . . The so-called "studies" tended to be self-supporting rather than critical of the agency that sponsored the work. And too many of the books, monographs, studies, and official documents misstated the facts, with the aim of salvaging a weapon system, military doctrine, or reputation whose worth could not otherwise be supported. They were public relations documents, not clear-eyed honest appraisals, and they were aimed at influencing the soon-to-come budget reductions and debates over each service's roles and missions [p. 501].

The advance organizer of the public relations study is the propagandist's information needs. The study's purpose is to help a program's leaders or public relations personnel project a convincing, positive public image for a program. The guiding questions are derived from the public relations specialists' and administrators' conceptions of which questions constituents would find most interesting. In general, the public relations study seeks information that would most help an organization confirm its claims of excellence and secure public support. From the start, this type of study seeks not a valid assessment of merit and worth, but information to help the program put its best foot forward. Such studies avoid gathering or releasing negative findings.

Typical methods used in public relations studies are surveys using biased samples; push polls that press respondents to support leading questions designed to garner support for a particular point of view; use of inappropriate norms tables; biased selection of testimonials and anecdotes; massaging of obtained information; selective release of only the positive findings; reporting central tendency but not variation; cover-up of embarrassing incidents; and use of so-called expert advocate consultants. In contrast to the "critical friends" employed in Australian evaluations, public relations studies use "friendly critics." A pervasive characteristic of the public relations evaluator's use of dubious methods is a biased attempt to nurture a good picture for a program. The fatal flaw of built-in bias to report only good things offsets any virtues of this approach. If an organization substitutes biased reporting of only positive findings for balanced evaluations of strengths and weaknesses, it soon will demoralize evaluators who are trying to conduct and report valid evaluations and may discredit the overall practice of evaluation.

By disseminating only positive information on a program's performance while withholding information on shortcomings and problems, evaluators and clients may mislead taxpayers, constituents, and other stakeholders concerning a program's true value and what issues need to be addressed to make it better. The possibility of such positive bias in advocacy evaluations underlies the long-standing policy of Consumers Union not to include advertising by the owners of the products and services being evaluated in its *Consumer Reports* magazine. To maintain credibility with consumers, Consumers Union has, for the most part, maintained an independent perspective and a commitment to identify and report both strengths and weaknesses in the items evaluated and not to supplement this information with biased ads. (An exception is that the magazine advertises its own supplementary publications and services without presenting clear, independent evaluations of them.)

Evaluators need to be cautious about how they relate to the public relations activities of their sponsors, clients, and supervisors. Certainly, public relations documents will reference information from sound evaluations. Evaluators should do what they can to persuade their audiences to make honest use of the evaluation findings. In this book, we emphasize the importance of a clear determination between evaluator and client about a range of issues, including careful rendering of recommendations. Evaluators should not be party to misuses, especially when erroneous reports are issued that predictably will mislead readers to believe that a seriously flawed program is effective. As one safeguard, evaluators can promote and help their clients arrange to have independent metaevaluators examine the organization's production and use of evaluation findings against professional standards for evaluations.

Approach 2: Politically Controlled Studies

The politically controlled study is an approach that can be defensible or indefensible. A politically controlled study is illicit if the evaluator or client (1) withholds the full set of evaluation findings from audiences that have express, legitimate, and legal rights to see the findings; (2) abrogates a prior agreement to fully disclose the evaluation findings; or (3) biases the evaluation message by releasing only part of the findings. It is not legitimate for a client to agree to make the findings of a commissioned evaluation publicly available and then, having previewed the results, to release none or only part of the findings. If and when a client or evaluator violates the formal written agreement on disseminating findings or applicable law, the other party has a right to take appropriate actions or seek an administrative or legal remedy.

An example of a flawed politically controlled evaluation occurred recently when a university's president and provost engaged the institution's faculty to evaluate all of its graduate programs. The objective was to identify programs that should be discontinued for such reasons as low demand, low quality, or poor graduation rates. The study's larger purpose was to help the university cut costs in a period of severe fiscal constraints.

The provost reached an agreement with the faculty on a plan for the evaluation, including a guarantee that the full report would be released. The faculty cooperated fully in presenting the needed information and assessing each program against the agreed-upon evaluation criteria. The provost subsequently collected and reviewed the evidence and released her report, which contained her decisions on programs to discontinue but not the evidentiary basis for the cuts.

The faculty protested that the provost's decisions reflected her biases but not the evidence that they had painstakingly collected. When the demanded information was not released, the faculty voted to censure the provost. She resigned the next day and soon thereafter the university's board of trustees fired the president.

This debacle illustrates the severe costs of corrupt, politically controlled evaluations. Professionals lost their jobs, the incident stimulated much concern in the surrounding community, and many faculty likely became predisposed to mistrust future proposals for evaluations of their work.

Clients sometimes can legitimately commission covert studies and keep the findings private while meeting relevant laws and adhering to an appropriate advance agreement with the evaluator. In the United States, this can be the case for private organizations not governed by public disclosure laws. Furthermore, an evaluator, under legal contractual agreements, can plan, conduct, and report an evaluation for private purposes while not disclosing the findings to any outside party. The key to keeping client-controlled studies in legitimate territory is to reach appropriate, legally defensible, advance written agreements and adhere to the contractual provisions concerning release of the study's findings. Such studies also have to conform to applicable laws on release of information.

The advance organizers for a politically controlled study include implicit or explicit threats faced by the client for a program evaluation or objectives for winning political contests. The client's purpose in commissioning such a study is to secure assistance in acquiring, maintaining, or increasing influence, power, or money. The questions addressed are those of interest to the client and special groups that share the client's interests and aims. Two main questions are of interest to the client: What is the truth, as best can be determined, surrounding a particular dispute or political situation? What information would be advantageous in a potential conflict situation? Typical methods of conducting the politically controlled study include covert investigations, a focus on selected issues, simulation studies, private polls, private information files, and (as a particular downfall) selective release of findings.

Generally the client of the politically controlled study wants information that is as technically sound as possible. However, he or she may also want to withhold findings that do not support his or her position, which would push the covert investigation into pseudoevaluation territory. The strength of the approach is that it stresses the need for accurate information. However, because the client might release information selectively to create or sustain an erroneous picture of a program's merit and worth, might distort or misrepresent the findings, might violate a prior agreement to fully release findings, or might violate a public's right to know law, this type of study can degenerate into a pseudoevaluation.

Inappropriate politically controlled studies undoubtedly contributed to the federal and state sunshine laws in the United States and other countries. Under current U.S. and state freedom of information provisions, most information obtained through the use of public funds must be made available to interested and potentially affected citizens. Thus, there exist legal deterrents to and remedies for illicit, politically controlled evaluations that use public funds. Freedom of information laws are similar in the United States, United Kingdom, Australia, and a number of other countries. Increasingly over the past few years, freedom of information reports relating particularly to politically oriented or politically motivated reviews have disclosed grossly distorted evaluation reports. The consequences have been extremely embarrassing for governments (as investigating clients) and evaluators. They certainly have been damaging for public perceptions of evaluation studies, accounting practices, and independent audits.

Approach 3: Pandering Evaluations

Unfortunately, some evaluators set aside any commitment to integrity of their evaluation services by catering to the client's desires for certain predetermined evaluation conclusions, regardless of a program's actual performance and outcomes. By delivering the desired conclusion, evaluators often position themselves in the good graces of the client. This can put the evaluator in a favored position to conduct additional evaluations for the client in the future.

An example that illustrates the dynamics in pandering evaluations occurred in the context of a federally funded national educational research center. The funding agency required the center to obtain annual external evaluations, and its evaluators would conduct periodic site visits to the center. In those visits, the evaluators would pay special attention to the findings from the center's contracted external evaluations but would also see for themselves what was happening in the funded programs.

Year after year, the federal evaluators were perplexed by the apparent lack of progress by one of the center's programs in spite of the highly favorable reports from the center's external evaluator. The program had developed a psychosocial model of child growth and development and had obtained funds each year to validate the model and then apply it to help schools evaluate and improve their elementary school curriculums. The federal evaluators saw no evidence during the site visits or in the external evaluator's reports of any work to validate the model and apply it to curriculum development. Instead, the external evaluator applauded the program's work in conducting training sessions on the model and publishing articles about it. Increasingly, the federal evaluators came to the conclusion that the external evaluator was only documenting the amount and quality of training sessions on the model and that the applauded journal articles were mainly advertisements for the model and were devoid of validation findings.

Each year the external evaluator had met with the center's director and the program's principal investigator to consider how best to persuade the federal officials that the program was valuable. They had agreed that funding would be placed in jeopardy if the evaluator reported on the program's omissions and failures in validation and curriculum development. The external evaluator was skillful in preparing impressive, laudatory reports on what the program was doing but ducked the question of whether the center was carrying through on its full set of commitments. The center's director and the program's principal investigator were pleased to fund the same external evaluator year after year. In effect, the evaluator each year had bought an evaluation contract for another year by pandering to the client's desires. Eventually the federal agency got wise to this subterfuge; it canceled funding of this program and stipulated that the center find a different, more professional evaluator.

In pandering to the client's desires, the evaluator's advance organizers are the client's preferred evaluation conclusions, often amounting to a favorable report. The evaluator's immediate purpose is to conduct the evaluation in such a way as to curry and maintain favor with the client; the longer-range purpose is to win future evaluation contracts.

The evaluator and client reach agreement on the questions to be addressed by the evaluation. Often these questions are dictated in the funding agreement covering the program to be evaluated and thus may emanate from a federal agency or other sponsor. The client is not overly concerned about the nature of the evaluation questions but is concerned that the "right" answers be given, even if they are not true. The client's aim is to obtain a report of positive program conclusions that will pass muster with the funding agency or perhaps a governing board. If some of the funder's questions cannot be finessed, the client and external evaluator may agree to concentrate on the few that can be answered well and hold the others in abeyance.

To obtain the desired conclusions, the evaluator concentrates on those questions whose answers will place the program in a favorable light. The evaluator then employs methods that on the face appear to be sound but actually may be biased in their applications. The methods are often manipulated in such a way to produce data that appear to support the evaluation's conclusions. Examples are selected anecdotes; push polls; biased samples; biased use of focus groups; carefully selected testimonials; reporting successful cases to the exclusion of failures; argument that certain questions from the sponsor should be considered later; or presenting a narrative, positive statement by the evaluator.

Pandering evaluations aimed at helping evaluators buy future contracts from the client have no redeeming features. They may help the clients hoodwink their sponsors into believing a flawed program is actually sound, but this is a serious disservice to program sponsors and constituents and to the professional practice of evaluation.

Approach 4: Evaluation by Pretext

Evaluation by pretext exists when an evaluator earnestly and honestly proceeds to conduct a sound evaluation to serve a stated purpose that, unknown to the evaluator, is deceptive and false. In such a case, the client is guilty of the indiscretion of misleading the evaluator. The evaluator is guilty of proceeding with the evaluation without confirming that the evaluation's stated purpose is the actual purpose. The nature of this type of pseudoevaluation is seen in the following true example.

A research center's director had recently been appointed and wanted a baseline evaluation of the center's programs. He contracted for an independent evaluation of the programs. When the evaluation team arrived for its three-day site visit, the center director informed them that the evaluation's purpose should be to identify the full range of flaws in the programs as a basis for program improvement.

He had reviewed previous evaluations of the center's programs and found them reassuring regarding the high quality of work in the center. These evaluations had been conducted and reported rigorously and independently. They mainly had found the center's programs to be sound and had lauded them for their importance, rigor, productiveness, and accountability. The director said that while such positive reports had no doubt been good for staff morale, they had not given detailed direction for program improvement. This year he said the evaluators should set aside any search for program strengths; instead, they should concentrate on identifying and cataloging weaknesses.

He said candid reports along these lines would be invaluable to him and the staff for fine-tuning their already good programs and making them truly outstanding. He asked the evaluators to present their findings of program weaknesses at a full staff meeting during the last afternoon of the site visit.

Unfortunately, the evaluators swallowed the director's request and reasoning—hook, line, and sinker. For three days, they delved into each of the center's programs. They were determined to identify and document the full range of weaknesses in each program.

At the end of their visit, the evaluators went to the auditorium where they would orally deliver the findings to the center's staff. To the surprise and consternation of the evaluators, the audience included not only center staff but also officials from the federal agency that was funding the center's work. The evaluators wished they were in a position to present a balanced assessment of each program's strengths and weaknesses because the center's funding undoubtedly was at risk. However, they were prepared only to present what they had searched for and found: program weaknesses. The evaluators' recitations on program weakness placed a pall over the entire meeting and undoubtedly misled the federal officials as to the true merit and worth of the programs being reviewed.

Why would the center's director orchestrate such a disastrous chain of evaluation events? It turned out he had not liked the previous center director, wanted to discredit his leadership, and was seeking to replace center programs with others of his choice. These were the evaluation's real purposes as viewed by the director. In this evaluation by pretext, the evaluators had unwittingly played into the director's hands. With some advance exploration before signing on to do the evaluation, they might have learned of the director's deception and declined the evaluation assignment or insisted on making a valid assessment of strengths and weaknesses.

Before contracting for an evaluation, it is a good idea to obtain information from a wide range of program stakeholders. Especially, it can be enlightening to consider who might be hurt by the evaluation and to invite their reactions. In interacting with stakeholders, the prospective evaluators should outline what they have been asked to do and inquire what concerns they should consider before agreeing to conduct the evaluation. Also, the evaluators probably should not agree to collect and report only strengths or only weaknesses in a program. As the Joint Committee's *Program Evaluation Standards* state (1994), evaluators should fairly appraise both strengths and weaknesses in a program.

The main advance organizer in an evaluation by pretext is the client's directive to evaluators and rationale for the directive, for example, to identify program defects as a basis for program improvement. The client's purpose is not the purpose given to the evaluators. In the example here, the director's purpose was not program improvement, as stated to the evaluators, but program termination and discrediting of the previous director. The client is the source of evaluation questions that guide evaluations by pretext. While the client should be one source of evaluation questions, he or she should not be the only source. Other stakeholders and the evaluators themselves should also contribute evaluation questions. Typical questions in evaluations by pretext focus on negative aspects of a program, but they may be more varied depending on the evaluation's hidden purpose. Evaluations by pretext employ the evaluation questions stated by the client. Thus, methodology is not the source of problems with evaluations by pretext. This approach to evaluation has no redeeming qualities and can be seen as disturbingly Machiavellian.

Approach 5: Empowerment Under the Guise of Evaluation

When an external evaluator's efforts to empower a group to conduct its own evaluations are advanced as external or independent evaluations, they fit our label of empowerment under the guise of evaluation. Such applications give the evaluees the power to write or edit the interim or final reports while claiming or giving the illusion that an independent evaluator prepared and delivered the reports or at least endorsed internal evaluation reports. In such cases, an external evaluator is preoccupied with developing rapport with and assisting a vulnerable or disadvantaged group whose work is to be evaluated. The empowerment evaluator's central objectives are to help the evaluee group maintain and increase resources, train them in evaluation, empower them to conduct and use evaluation to serve their interests, or lend them sufficient credibility to make conducted evaluations influential. The external empowerment evaluator serves as a critical friend (or, more likely, a friendly critic).

Objectives of training and empowering a disadvantaged group to conduct evaluations are laudable in their own right. However, empowering groups to do their own evaluations is not evaluation. It is empowerment by such evaluation capacity development activities as evaluation training, developing an organization's evaluation policies and procedures, or setting up an office of evaluation services. The empowerment activities move into the pseudoevaluation range when an external evaluator credits an internal evaluation as his own, credits a flawed internal evaluation as sound, stands silent when the client attributes the evaluation findings to the external evaluator, or fails to ensure that the evaluation will be subjected to an independent metaevaluation. An actual example of empowerment under the guise of evaluation follows.

A government organization in an African country engaged an American researcher to evaluate an educational improvement program being funded in a remote, primitive area of the country. The evaluator quickly found that the program's funds were mainly going into graft, that there was no discernable effort to implement the agreed-on educational reforms, and that no objectives had been achieved. At this point, the evaluator concluded that the program was a total failure. However, he also realized that the program's target area was poverty stricken and that the situation in the area would only worsen if the government stopped funding the program.

The evaluator decided not to write and submit a report exposing the program's failure. Instead, he chose to redefine his task as empowerment evaluation. Accordingly, he offered evaluation training to area personnel and collaborated with them to produce their own evaluation of the government-sponsored program. The resulting evaluation report was highly positive. The external evaluator acquiesced in the group's submission of the favorable evaluation report to the funding agency and even was supportive by writing a preface to the report. In that preface, he stated that the program's staff were to be congratulated for their development of evaluation capacity and their production of an informative evaluation report. In a private conversation with this external evaluator, he related that the good he had done by helping keep government funding in the poverty-stricken area far outweighed his transgression of endorsing and allowing a faulty evaluation report to go forward.

The claimed short-range benefits of this empowerment evaluation experience were outweighed by the external evaluator's having conveyed very bad lessons to the project staff: (1) biasing an evaluation report is acceptable practice if it helps secure a desirable end, (2) it is acceptable to ask independent evaluators to serve as advocates and give clients control of the evaluation work, (3) project personnel with little or no evaluation expertise should trust their own assessments of their own work, (4) credibility for biased self-evaluations can be bought by selecting the "right" external evaluation expert, and (5) it is unnecessary to subject internal evaluations to credible, independent metaevaluations. All of these lessons orient the clients to continue engaging in corrupt, incompetent evaluation practices.

The advance organizer in studies employing empowerment under the guise of evaluation is an external evaluator's dedication to help a group of evaluees gain power to improve its situation. The purposes of this type of pseudoevaluation are to empower the group to conduct its own evaluations and lend credibility to their evaluations. The questions for such evaluations usually are stipulated by external funding organizations. Typical questions concern whether funded programs are being implemented as promised and whether they are succeeding, most likely from the points of view of staffing strength and positive activities. The external evaluator's method is mainly to provide on-the-job training and technical support to help the evaluees conduct their own evaluations. The external evaluator's efforts become corrupt when the evaluator inappropriately endorses or shares credit for evaluation reports produced by the evaluees or allows the evaluees to falsely attribute evaluation findings to the external evaluator. This type of evaluation has no strengths since it can aid and abet groups to put forth faulty evaluations; reinforces the notion that subterfuge in evaluation is acceptable; teaches corrupt evaluation practices; and is not subjected to credible, independent metaevaluations.

A strict effort to help groups develop evaluation capacity is, of course, commendable. Steps to reduce evaluees' fears of evaluation, train them in evaluation concepts and methods, and involve them in conducting evaluation work are in the interest of mainstreaming evaluation. However, such constructive, capacity-building steps are not evaluation. When evaluation capacity building is labeled empowerment evaluation, it is false advertising because such an effort is not evaluation. Helping staffs develop sound evaluation capacity absolutely requires that they subject their evaluations to credible, independent metaevaluations, a practice that is alien to the precepts of empowerment evaluation. We believe that requiring empowerment evaluations to have an independent metaevaluation would doom the approach's survival or force radical changes in its orientation and application.

An evaluator must not give evaluees power over the external evaluation message, even in the interest of reducing their fear of and antipathy toward the evaluation. The often predictable result of empower ment under the guise of evaluation is essentially a biased self-report that masquerades as an unbiased independent evaluation. Moreover, this is modeling of bad evaluation work; accordingly, evaluees are empowered not to conduct rigorous, creditable evaluations but to make a game of what should be a sound evaluation enterprise.

Summary

While it would be unrealistic to recommend that administrators and other evaluation users not obtain and selectively employ information for maintaining political viability, evaluators should not lend their names and endorsements to evaluations presented by their clients that misrepresent the full set of relevant findings, present falsified reports aimed at winning political contests, or violate applicable laws or prior formal agreements on release of findings. If evaluators acquiesce to and support such pseudoevaluations, they help promote and support injustice, mislead decision making, project an erroneous concept of evaluation, lower confidence in evaluation services, and discredit the evaluation profession.

Even when the evaluator's objective is socially constructive, nothing worthwhile is achieved by empowering groups to conduct their own evaluations if they are essentially taught that biased self-reports, erroneously credited as independent evaluations, are acceptable. We do note that evaluators can give private evaluative feedback to clients legitimately, provided the evaluation is sound and conforms with pertinent laws, statutes, policies, and appropriate contractual agreements on editing and release of findings.

Review Questions

Before addressing these questions, quickly review the chapter for the various types of pseudoevaluation.

1. How do you define pseudoevaluation?
2. Give three examples of politically motivated pseudoevaluation.
3. Name the five pseudoevaluation approaches identified and discussed in this chapter, and give a one-line explanation of each.
4. What is the advance organizer of (a) politically controlled studies, (b) pandering evaluations, and (c) empowerment under guise of evaluation?
5. A distorted, overly positive view of a program is reported, while problematic facts are withheld. Which form of pseudoevaluation applies to this statement?
6. The client is less concerned about the nature of the evaluation questions than answers that conform to desired outcomes—and the evaluator supports this. Which form of pseudoevaluation applies to this statement.
7. An evaluator is commissioned to investigate a program, but is instructed to give emphasis to its positive aspects. What form of pseudoevaluation is this, and why should the "evaluator" be discredited?
8. A company director has her own motives for wishing to empower her employees to do their own evaluation, a situation agreed to by the person commissioned to undertake the evaluation even though he is the purported author of the final report. Identify the flaws in this description.
9. A public school district's superintendent maintains accurate information on each school in her district but withholds from the public all negative information about any school or school staff member. What form of pseudoevaluation is this, and why is the superintendent acting inappropriately and probably illegally?
10. Under what circumstances can evaluators legitimately give private evaluative feedback to clients?

Group Exercises

Exercise 1. What rationale supports the following statement? "Evaluators should not lend their names and endorsements to evaluations presented by their clients that misrepresent the full set of relevant findings."

Exercise 2. Truth is often stranger (and perhaps more disconcerting) than fiction. The following situation is based on fact.

A large mining company in the northwest part of western Australia depended heavily on both federal government subsidies to ensure strong exports as well as an annual report that was received favorably by shareholders. The same firm of evaluators (incorporating auditors) examined the company from 1996 to 2003. Reports to the federal government and shareholders over this time span were produced in glossy format; invariably, the organization was portrayed as flourishing. As a result of questions being asked at the 2003 annual general meeting of shareholders (with government representatives present), a subsequent independent evaluation found a litany of corruption, significantly hiding massive financial losses for the previous six years.

The deceptions of the original firm of evaluators were characterized by

- A tight control of the kinds of information released, influenced strongly by both the senior administrators of the company and federal government officials (who were determined to pursue a favorable balance of trade in mining products with Asian countries)
- A consistent desire to give a glowing annual report, fully knowing that there was legal collusion with mining management and government officials about the questions to be addressed annually and which matters would be omitted
- Data and information manipulated to exaggerate preconceived positive outcomes

In this sorry saga, who was at fault, and why? What advice would you give to the mining company and the federal government for future evaluations?

References

Clancy, T., with Horner, C. (1999). *Every man a tiger.* New York: Putnam, p. 501.
Ferguson, R. (1999, June). Ideological marketing. *The Education Industry Report.*
Joint Committee on Standards for Educational Education. (1994). *The program evaluation standards.* Thousand Oaks, CA: Corwin Press.

CHAPTER SEVEN

QUESTIONS- AND METHODS-ORIENTED EVALUATION APPROACHES (QUASI-EVALUATION STUDIES)

Questions-oriented program evaluation approaches address specified questions (often employing a wide range of methods), and methods-oriented approaches typically use a particular method. Whether the methodology and questions addressed in these approaches are appropriate for assessing a program's merit and worth is a secondary consideration. We have grouped the questions- and methods-oriented approaches together as quasi-evaluation approaches because both tend to narrow an evaluation's scope and often deliver less than a full assessment of merit and worth. The first three approaches discussed (objectives-based studies, accountability studies, and the success case method) are mainly questions-oriented approaches, while the other eleven approaches in this chapter are methods-oriented approaches.

The questions-oriented approaches usually begin with a set of narrowly defined questions. These might be derived from a program's behavioral or operational objectives, a funding agency's pointed accountability requirements, an expert's preferred set of evaluative criteria, or a focused quest to find and delineate cases that evidence unusual success. A methods-oriented approach may employ as its starting point a design for a controlled experiment, a particular standardized test, a cost-analysis procedure, a theory or model of a program, case study procedures, or a management information system. Another kind of methods-oriented approach is the study that starts with an overriding commitment to employ a mixture of qualitative and quantitative methods. The methods-oriented approaches emphasize technical quality. Both the methods-oriented and questions-oriented approaches stress that it is usually better to answer a few pointed questions well than to attempt a broad assessment of a program's merit and worth.

Both the questions-oriented and methods-oriented approaches can be called quasi-evaluation studies because sometimes they happen to provide evidence that fully assesses a program's merit and worth, while in most cases their focus is too narrow or is only tangential to questions of merit and worth. While the approaches are typically labeled as evaluations, they may or may not meet all the requirements of a sound evaluation. Quasi-evaluation studies have legitimate uses apart from their relationship to program evaluation, since they can investigate important though narrow questions. The main caution is that these types of studies not be uncritically equated to evaluation.

Approach 6: Objectives-Based Studies

The objectives-based study is the classic example of a questions-oriented evaluation approach. Madaus and Stufflebeam (1988) provided a comprehensive look at this approach by publishing an edited volume of the classical writings of Ralph W. Tyler. In this approach, some statement of objectives provides the advance organizer. The objectives may be mandated by the client, formulated by the evaluator, or specified by the service providers. Typically the objectives-oriented evaluation is an internal study done by a developer or other program leader. The usual purpose of an objectives-based study is to determine whether the program's objectives have been achieved. Usual audiences are program developers, sponsors, and managers who want to know the extent to which each stated objective was achieved.

The methods used in objectives-based studies essentially involve specifying operational objectives and collecting and analyzing pertinent information to determine how well each objective was achieved. Tyler stressed that a wide range of objective and performance assessment procedures usually should be employed. This sets his approach apart from methods-oriented studies that focus on a particular method, such as an experimental design or a particular standardized test. Criterion-referenced tests and students' work samples are especially relevant to this evaluation approach.

Ralph Tyler is generally acknowledged to be the pioneer in the objectives-based type of study, although Percy Bridgman and E. L. Thorndike should also be credited (Travers, 1977). Several people have developed variations of Tyler's model. They include Bloom, Englehart, Furst, Hill, and Krathwohl (1956), Hammond

(1972), Metfessel and Michael (1967), Popham (1969), Provus (1971), and Steinmetz (1983). Although Tyler developed the objectives-based approach for use in evaluating educational programs, his influence has spread far beyond the confines of education, and objectives-based evaluations can be found in virtually all fields of service.

The objectives-based approach is especially applicable in assessing tightly focused projects that have clear, supportable objectives. Even then, such studies can be strengthened by judging project objectives against the intended beneficiaries' assessed needs, searching for side effects, and studying the process as well as the outcomes.

The objectives-based study has been the most prevalent approach in program evaluation. It has commonsense appeal, program administrators have had a great amount of experience with it, and it makes use of technologies of operational or behavioral objectives, both norm-referenced and criterion-referenced testing, and performance assessments. Common criticisms are that such studies lead to terminal information that is neither timely nor pertinent to improving a program's process, that the information often is far too narrow to constitute a sufficient basis for judging the object's merit and worth, that the studies do not uncover positive and negative side effects, and that they may credit unworthy objectives.

Approach 7: Accountability, Particularly Payment-by-Results Studies

This accountability and payment-by-results approach is a questions-oriented approach and typically narrows the evaluative inquiry to questions about outcomes. In contrast to objectives-based studies, which also focus on outcomes, accountability studies stress the importance of obtaining an external, impartial perspective as contrasted to the internal perspective often preferred in Tylerian, objectives-based studies. Accountability studies became prominent in the early 1970s. They emerged because of widespread disenchantment with the persistent stream of evaluation reports indicating that almost none of the massive state and federal investments in educational and social programs were making any positive, statistically discernable differences. One proposed solution advocated initiating externally administered accountability systems to ensure that service providers would fulfill their responsibilities to develop and apply sound services and that evaluators would find the programs' effects and determine which persons and groups were succeeding and which were not. Key components of many accountability systems are their employment of pass-fail standards, payment for good results, and sanctions for unacceptable performance.

The advance organizers for the accountability study are the persons and groups responsible for producing results, the service providers' work responsibilities, the expected outcomes, pass-fail cut scores, and defined consequences of passing or failing. The study's purposes are to provide constituents with an accurate accounting of results; ensure, through something akin to intimidation, that the results are primarily positive; determine responsibility for good and bad outcomes; administer deserved rewards; and impose appropriate penalties. Accountability questions come from the program's constituents and controllers, such as taxpayers; community groups; policy boards; legislators; and local, state, and national funding organizations. Their main question concerns whether each funded organization charged with responsibility for delivering and improving services is carrying out its assignments and achieving all it should, given the resources invested to support the work.

Typical of other questions-oriented evaluation approaches, accountability studies have employed a wide variety of methods. These include procedures for setting pass-fail standards; payment by results; performance contracting; management by objectives; program input, process, and output databases; program planning and budgeting systems; institutional report cards and profiles; audits of procedural compliance and goal achievement; self-studies; peer reviews focused on established criteria; merit pay for organizations, programs, or individuals; and mandated testing programs. Also included are awards, recognition, sanctions, and takeover or intervention authority by oversight bodies.

Lessinger (1970) is generally acknowledged as a pioneer in the area of accountability. Among those who have extended Lessinger's work are Stenner and Webster (1971), in their development of a handbook for conducting auditing activities, and Kearney, in providing leadership to the Michigan Department of Education in developing the first statewide educational accountability system. Kirst (1990) analyzed the history and diversity of attempts at accountability in education within six broad types of accountability: performance reporting, monitoring and compliance with standards or regulations, incentive systems, reliance on the market, changing locus of authority or control of schools, and changing professional roles. A major attempt at accountability in the 1990s, involving financial rewards and sanctions, was the Kentucky Instructional Results Information System (Koretz & Barron, 1998). This program's failure was clearly associated with fast-paced implementation in advance of validation, reporting and later retraction of flawed results, test results that were not comparable to those in other states, payment by results that fostered teaching to tests and cheating in schools, and heavy expense associated with performance assessments that could not be sustained over time.

Accountability approaches are applicable to organizations and professionals funded and charged to carry out public mandates, deliver public services, and implement specially funded programs. It behooves these program leaders to maintain a dynamic baseline of information needed to demonstrate fulfillment of responsibilities and achievement of positive results. They especially should focus accountability mechanisms on program elements that can be changed with the prospect of improving outcomes. They should also focus accountability to enhance staff cooperation toward achievement of collective goals rather than to intimidate or stimulate counterproductive competition. Moreover, accountability studies that compare programs should fairly consider the programs' contexts, especially beneficiaries' characteristics and needs, local support, available resources, and external forces.

The main advantages of accountability studies are that they are popular among constituent groups and politicians and are aimed at improving public services. They can also provide program personnel with clear expectations against which to plan, execute, and report on their services and contributions. They can be designed to give service providers freedom to innovate on procedures coupled with clear expectations and requirements for producing and reporting on accomplishments. Furthermore, setting up healthy, fair competition between comparable programs can result in better services and products for consumers. Accountability studies typically engage program personnel to record and show their achievements and engage outsiders to provide an independent assessment of accomplishments.

A main disadvantage is that accountability studies often result in invidious comparisons, thereby producing unhealthy competition and much political unrest and acrimony among service providers and between them and their constituents. Also, accountability studies often focus on a too limited set of outcome indicators and can undesirably narrow the range of services. Another disadvantage is that politicians tend to force the implementation of accountability efforts before the needed instruments, scoring rubrics, assessor training, and other items can be planned, developed, field-tested, and validated. Furthermore, prospects for rewards and threats of punishment have often led service providers to cheat in order to ensure positive evaluation reports. In schools, cheating to obtain rewards and avoid penalties has frequently generated bad teaching, bad press, turnover in leadership, and abandonment of the accountability system.

Approach 8: Success Case Method

A recent entry in the lexicon of questions-oriented evaluation approaches is the success case method (SCM), advocated by Robert Brinkerhoff (2003). In this approach, the evaluator deliberately searches for and illuminates instances of success and contrasts these to what is not working in a program. The intent is to discover, analyze, and document any success the program might be having so that, assuming these successes are worthwhile, they can be built on and extended. By comparing least successful instances to most successful instances, and investigating as well the contextual factors that seem to contribute to success or lack of it, the evaluator is often able to make useful suggestions for improving results. Even if a program is marginal or mostly poor in quality and productiveness, it might be possible to find strengths on which the program could build. By identifying and understanding such strengths, the evaluator can discover why a program works and then help program leaders achieve more success. This also may help in deterring program funders from unjustifiably canceling a program that is partially succeeding or could be helped to succeed to a greater extent. Secondarily, discovering and documenting a program's successes can be instrumental in boosting a program staff's morale, giving them reasons to take pride in past accomplishments, contributing concretely and publicly to a foundation of success on which they can build, and deterring funders from unjustifiably canceling a program that is succeeding or could be made to do so.

In responding to a previous draft of this characterization of SCM via an e-mail message, Brinkerhoff stated:

> No program is ever wholly successful or unsuccessful; thus methods that look for "average" or typical outcomes inevitably underestimate strengths and overestimate weaknesses. The SCM helps evaluators capture the successes and then assesses their worth. If the best that a program is doing is not good enough, the SCM evaluation is finished (and so, usually, is the program). But if the good stuff is indeed worthy, then it may make sense to get a greater return on the program investment by leveraging the strengths, which means as well that we have to figure out WHY it works WHEN it works; this is also an aim of the SCM (and is why we always compare the least impactful instances to the most impactful ones).

The orientation of the SCM is not to "throw out the baby with the bath water." As Brinkerhoff (2003) states, "Many evaluation approaches lead to overall 'thumbs up or down' judgments, thus the few successes a program may be having get thrown out in the general bathwater of a larger initiative that is not working well. But, because the SCM looks for success, no matter how small or infrequent, it helps new initiatives grow and become more successful."

The SCM is put forward not as a comprehensive approach to fully assessing an enterprise's merit and worth over time, but as a relatively quick yet defensible means of getting critically important information for use in program improvement. Compared with comprehensive assessments of a program's merit and worth, SCM is narrow in what it assesses and focuses mainly on short-term findings. We think the following example illustrates the intent, spirit, and procedure of the method.

An evaluator had been contracted to evaluate a highly funded vocational education program that was designed for widespread implementation in the secondary schools in Ohio. In accordance with the evaluation contract, the evaluator had conducted a comparative experiment. Schools across Ohio had been randomly assigned to receive the new program or not. Following implementation of the program, the evaluator had compared the two groups on tests of knowledge of vocational education content and other measures of attitude and aspiration. Across all of the outcome measures, the consistent finding was that there were no statistically significant differences between students in the group that had received the program and students in the control schools. The expensive program was thus judged a failure and not worthy of continuation and widespread implementation throughout the schools of Ohio.

Release of these findings brought protests from the schools in the experimental group. Teachers in those schools said the program had made substantial and important impacts on their students, even if the evaluators had been unable to detect the impacts. The teachers said they had seen the impacts with their own eyes. The teachers worried that this less-than-sensitive evaluation would lead to the termination of a meritorious program that had good value for students throughout the state.

These teachers were so persuasive that the evaluator decided to take another look at the data (through what we might today term a success case study). He wanted to ascertain whether he could find convincing evidence that the teachers were correct that the program had made important impacts on their students. Using an item analysis procedure, the evaluator searched for test items that discriminated statistically between experimental and control students. He was surprised at the result of this search. He found a sizable number of items on which students in the experimental schools outperformed the students in the control schools. He found another, small subset of items on which the control students actually outperformed the students in the experimental group. And he found a third set of items that did not differentiate between the two groups. Content analyses of the test items on which the experimental students excelled confirmed what the teachers had been reporting as successes in their classrooms. Moreover, the items that showed superior performance for the experimental group were judged to reflect important impacts. The few items that showed superior responses from students in the control group were deemed important for further investigation, as were the items that showed no differences between the two groups.

The original comparative analysis that combined all of the items in each test had obscured the important underlying statistical interactions among items that differentiated in different directions between the groups and other items that did not discriminate statistically between the groups. The evaluator compiled the new analysis in a supplementary report and sent it to the sponsor, along with the conclusion that the program clearly had succeeded in producing a set of important student outcomes. The evaluator also wrote an important paper reflecting this experience: "Needed: Instruments as Good as Our Eyes" (Brickell, 1976). We think his follow-up evaluation of the Ohio vocational education program was an early example of what Brinkerhoff later came to label the success case method.

The advance organizers in SCM are aspects of a program that, if successful, would be important considerations in sustaining, expanding, or improving the program. The purpose of this approach is to provide change leaders with a simple, dependable, and usually low-cost way of expeditiously finding out how well and in what respects a change effort is working. Sources of questions about where to look for successes (and failures) often are the people who are most directly involved in carrying out the program or receiving its services. Key questions are: What is happening? What is being achieved? What is the importance of the achievements? What is working? What is not? How could the effort be improved?

SCM may draw on the full range of evaluation methods, but typically the methods employed are limited to those required to achieve reasonable rigor while giving low-cost, quick responses to the evaluation questions. The general approach of SCM is to tell a compelling story about the evaluand and to document and corroborate the claims in the story with solid, irrefutable evidence. Brinkerhoff (2003) sees the essence of such evidence as "verifiable and confirmable accounts of the actions and results that real people have experienced using new tools and methods" (p. xi). The evidence may be obtained using such methods as review of records, surveys, interviews, focus groups, post hoc analyses of data, case studies, inferential statistics, and reference to the judicial standards of corroboration and documentation.

Robert Brinkerhoff (2003) is the pioneer in conceptualizing, applying, and publicizing the approach. Scholars whom he credits for influencing his development of SCM include E. G. Guba, B. M. Kibel, A. Simmons, and R. E. Stake. SCM is especially useful in ensuring that a program will be credited for whatever it has done well. When SCM is used as a formative evaluation approach, its principal strength is that it accelerates development by early discovery of what is working and what is not. It is less often used as a summative method, but in this application, the approach's main strength is in ensuring that a program's positive points will be credited. The approach's main limitation is that it does not seek to produce a comprehensive assessment of an evaluand's merit and worth. Accordingly, SCM is best considered as an alternative approach that is especially useful in providing users with quick, reasonably rigorous, and typically low-cost responses to questions related to making an enterprise succeed.

Approach 9: Objective Testing Programs

This approach and the next two are grounded in educational testing. For those outside the field of education, our inclusion of these approaches may seem strange. We have included them for two main reasons. First, program evaluation in its early history drew much of its theory and procedures from experiences in evaluating schools and school programs. Second, educational tests have continued to be a principal means of assessing the merit and worth of schools. This has been patently clear in past presidential election campaigns when candidates from different political parties have called for assessing and rewarding schools based on student scores from national or state tests. In the category of educational testing we look first at Approach 9, the widespread practice of objective testing.

Since the 1930s, American elementary and secondary schools have been inundated with standardized, multiple-choice, norm-referenced testing programs. Probably every school district in the country has some such program. The tests are administered annually by local school districts or state education departments to inform students, parents, educators, and the public at large about the achievements of children and youth. The purposes of testing are to assess the achievements of individual students and groups of students compared with norms, standards, or previous performance. Typically, tests are administered to all students at selected grade levels. Because the test results focus on student outcomes and are conveniently available, many educators have tried to use the results to evaluate the quality of special projects, specific school programs, schools, and even individual educators by inferring that high scores reflect successful efforts and low scores reflect poor efforts. Such inferences can be wrong if the tests were not targeted on particular project or program objectives or the needs of particular target groups of students, if students' background characteristics were not taken into account, if certain students were inappropriately excluded from the testing, if resources and administrative support were not considered, or if students had not been taught the subject matter being tested, for example.

Advance organizers for standardized educational tests include areas of the school curriculum, curricular objectives, content standards, and specified norm groups. The testing programs' main purposes are to compare the test performance scores of individual students and groups of students to those of selected norm groups or to diagnose shortfalls related to particular objectives. Standardized test results also are often used to compare the performance of programs and schools and to examine achievement trends across years. Metrics used to make the comparisons typically are standardized individual scores, mean scores and standard deviations for a group, or the percentage of objectives passed for the total test and subtests. The sources of test questions are usually test publishers and test development and selection committees.

The typical question addressed by testing is whether the test performance of individual students is at or above the average performance of local, state, and national norm or comparison groups. Other questions may concern the percentages of students who surpassed one or more cut-score standards, where the tested group ranks compared with similar groups, and whether achievement is better than in prior years. The main process is to select, administer, score, analyze, interpret, and report the tests.

Lindquist (1951), a major pioneer in this area, was instrumental in developing the Iowa testing programs, the American College Testing Program, the National Merit Scholarship Testing Program, and the General Educational Development Testing Program, as well as the Measurement Research Center at the University of Iowa. Many individuals have contributed substantially to the development of educational testing in the United States, including Ebel (1965), Flanagan (1939), Lord and Novick (1968), and Thorndike (1971). Innovations in testing in the 1980s and 1990s include the development of item response theory (Hambleton & Swaminathan, 1985) and value-added measurement (Sanders & Horn, 1994; Webster, 1995).

If a school's personnel carefully select tests and use them appropriately to assess and improve student learning and report to the public, the expense and effort are highly justified. This is especially so when teachers are assisted to use item analysis results to diagnose and address students' particular learning deficiencies. Student outcome measures for judging specific projects and programs must be validated in terms of the particular objectives and the characteristics and needs of the students served by the program. However, tests should not be relied on exclusively for evaluating specially targeted projects and programs. Results should be interpreted in the light of other information on student characteristics, students' assessed needs, program implementation, student participation, and other measures.

The main advantages of standardized testing programs are that they are efficient in producing valid and reliable information on student performance in many areas of school curricula and that they are a familiar strategy at every level of the school program in virtually all school districts in the United States. The main limitations are that they provide data only about student outcomes; they reinforce students' multiple-choice test-taking behavior rather than their writing and speaking behaviors; they tend to address only lower-order learning objectives; and in many cases, they are perhaps a better indicator of the socioeconomic levels of the students in a given program, school, or school district than of the quality of teaching and learning. Stake (1971) and others have argued effectively that standardized tests often are poor approximations of what teachers actually teach. Moreover, as has been patently clear in evaluations of programs for both disadvantaged and gifted students, norm-referenced tests often do not measure achievements well for low- and high-achieving students. Unfortunately, program evaluators often have made uncritical use of standardized test results to judge a program's outcomes just because the results were conveniently available and had face validity for the public. Often the contents of such tests do not match the program's objectives.

A recent study by the Western Michigan University Evaluation Center illustrates the nature and limitations of an objective testing type of evaluation. The National Education Association contracted the Evaluation Center to evaluate the student achievement results at charter schools operated by a particular school management company. The study's director, Gary Miron, analyzed all the available standardized test data he could obtain for ten schools, which are spread across six states. He examined the scores for each school against pertinent state and national norms and results for the local school district housing the charter school. He looked at achievement trends and compared his findings with those of other test score–based evaluations of the company-managed schools. In many cases, his findings were at odds with those of other evaluators, especially the company's evaluator. In general, his study provided an in-depth look at the available test score evidence and how the charter school students performed in comparison with norms and selected comparison groups. He also assessed whether student test score gains in the charter schools met or exceeded expectations based on state and national norms tables. Miron's study provided important evidence on student achievement in the charter schools, but a number of factors limited his study from being a full evaluation. Because much of the needed test score data were missing, Miron could not determine whether certain students were excluded from the tests or whether the schools' attrition rates were abnormally high. Also, he could not evaluate the merit and worth of the charter schools program because he mainly had student test score data, only one facet of a school program's quality; had too little information on curriculum, teacher quality, materials, parent involvement, and other areas; and looked only at a nonrandom sample of the schools being managed by the company.

Approach 10: Outcome Evaluation as Value-Added Assessment

Systematic, recurrent outcome and value-added assessment, coupled with hierarchical gain score analysis, is a special case of the use of standardized testing to evaluate the effects of programs and policies. The emphasis is often on annual testing at all or a succession of grade levels to assess trends and partial out effects of the different components of an education system, including groups of schools, individual schools, and individual teachers. The intent is to determine what value each entity is adding to the achievements of students served by particular components of the education system and then report the results for policy, accountability, and improvement purposes. The main interest is in aggregates, not performance of individual students.

A state education department may annually collect achievement data from all students (at a succession of grade levels), as is the case in the Tennessee Value-Added Assessment System. The evaluator may analyze the data to look at contrasting gain score trends for different schools. Results may be broken out to make comparisons between curricular areas; teachers; elementary versus middle schools; or size and resource classifications of schools, districts, and areas of a state. What differentiates the approach from the typical standardized achievement testing program is the emphasis on sophisticated gain score and hierarchical analysis of data to delineate effects of system components and identify which ones should be improved and which ones should be commended and reinforced. Otherwise, the two approaches have much in common.

Advance organizers in outcome evaluation employing value-added analysis are systemwide indicators of intended outcomes and a scheme for obtaining, classifying, and analyzing gain scores. The purposes of outcome and value-added assessment systems are to provide direction for policymaking, accountability to constituents, and feedback for improving programs and services. The approach requires standardization of assessment data throughout a system. The questions to be addressed by outcome and value-added evaluations originate from governing bodies, policymakers, the system's professionals, and constituents. In reality, the questions are often limited by the data available from the tests regularly used by the state or school district.

Developers of the outcome and value-added assessment approach include Sanders and Horn (1994), Webster (1995), Webster, Mendro, and Almaguer (1994), and Tymms (1995). Questions that address this form of evaluation follow: To what extent are particular programs adding value to students' achievements? What are the cross-year trends in outcomes? In what sectors of the system is the program working best and poorest? What are key, pervasive shortfalls—in particular, program objectives that require further study and attention? To what extent are program successes and failures associated with the system's groupings of grade levels (for example, primary, middle or junior high, and high school)? To what extent do students sustain their pattern of test score gains as they move from one school building (say, an elementary school building) to another (a middle school building)?

Outcome monitoring involving value-added assessment is probably most appropriate in well-financed state education departments and large school districts having strong support from policy groups, administrators, and service providers. The approach requires systemwide buy-in; politically effective leaders to continually explain and sell the program; annual testing at a succession of grade levels; a smoothly operating, dynamic, computerized baseline of relevant input and output information; highly skilled technicians to make it run efficiently and accurately; a powerful computer system; complicated, large-scale statistical analysis; and high-level commitment to use the results for policy development, accountability, program evaluation, and improvement at all levels of the system.

The central advantage of outcome monitoring involving value-added assessment is in the systematization and institutionalization of a database of outcomes that can be used over time and in a standardized way to study and find means to improve outcomes. This approach makes efficient use of standardized tests; is amenable to analysis of trends at state, district, school, and classroom levels; uses students as their own controls; and emphasizes that students at all ability levels should be helped to grow in knowledge and skills. The approach is conducive to using a standard of continuous progress across years for every student, as opposed to employing static cut scores. The latter, while prevalent in accountability programs, basically fail to take into account meaningful gains by low- or high-achieving students since such gains usually are far removed from the static, cut score standards. Sanders and Horn (1994) have shown that use of static cut scores may produce a "shed pattern," in which students who began below the cut score make the greatest gains, while those who started above the cut score standard make little progress. Like the downward slope, from left to right, of a tool shed, the gains are greatest for previously low-scoring students and progressively lower for the higher achievers. This suggests that teachers may be concentrating mainly on getting students to the cut score standard but not beyond it, thus holding back the high achievers.

A major disadvantage of the outcome and value-added approach is that it is politically volatile since it is used to identify responsibility for successes and failures down to the levels of schools and teachers. It also is heavily reliant on quantitative information such as that coming from standardized, multiple-choice achievement tests. Consequently, the complex and powerful analyses are based on a limited scope of outcome variables. Nevertheless, Sanders (1989) has argued that a strong body of evidence supports the use of well-constructed, standardized, multiple-choice achievement tests. Beyond the issue of outcome measures, the approach does not provide in-depth documentation of program inputs and processes and makes little, if any, use of qualitative methods. Despite advancements in objective measurement and the employment of hierarchical mixed models to determine effects of a system's organizational components and individual staff members, critics of the approach argue that causal factors are so complex that no measurement and analysis system can fairly fix responsibility for the academic progress of individual and collections of students to the level of teachers. Also, personal experience in interviewing educators in all of the schools in a Tennessee school district, subject to the statewide Tennessee value-added student assessment program, showed that none of the teachers, administrators, and counselors interviewed understood or trusted the fairness of this approach.

Approach 11: Performance Testing

In the 1990s, major efforts were made to offset the limitations of typical multiple-choice tests by employing performance or authentic measures. These devices require students to demonstrate their achievements by producing authentic responses to evaluation tasks, such as written or spoken answers, musical or psychomotor presentations, portfolios of work products, or group solutions to defined problems. Arguments for performance tests are that they have high face validity and model and reinforce students' needed life skills. After all, students are not being taught so that they will do well in choosing best answers from a list, but so that they will master underlying understandings and skills and effectively apply them in real-life situations.

The advance organizers in performance assessments are life skill objectives and content-related performance tasks, plus ways that their achievement can be demonstrated in practice. The main purpose of performance tests is to compare the abilities of individual students and groups of students with model performance on given tasks. Grades assigned to each respondent's performance, using set rubrics, enable assessment of the quality of achievements represented and comparisons across groups.

The sources of questions addressed by performance tests are analyses of selected life skill tasks and content specifications in curricular materials. The typical assessment questions concern whether individual students can effectively write, speak, figure, analyze, lead, work cooperatively, and solve given problems up to the level of acceptable standards. The main testing process is to define areas of skills to be assessed; select the type of assessment device; construct the assessment tasks; determine scoring rubrics; define standards for assessing performance; train and calibrate scorers; validate the measures; and administer, score, interpret, and report the results.

In speaking of licensing tests, Flexner (1910) called for tests that ascertain students' practical ability to confront and solve problems in concrete cases. Some of the pioneers in applying performance assessment to state education systems were the state education departments in Vermont and Kentucky (Kentucky Department of Education, 1993; Koretz, 1996a, 1996b; Koretz & Barron, 1998). Other sources of information about the general approach and issues in performance testing include Baker, O'Neil, and Linn (1993), Herman, Gearhart, and Baker (1993), Linn, Baker, and Dunbar (1991), Mehrens (1972), Messick (1994), Stillman et al. (1991), Swanson, Norman, and Linn (1995), Torrance (1993), and Wiggins (1989).

It is often difficult to establish the necessary conditions to employ the performance testing approach. It requires a huge outlay of time and resources for development and application. Typically state education departments and school districts should probably use this approach selectively and only when they can make the investment needed to produce valid results that are worth the large, required investment. Students' writing ability is best assessed and nurtured through obtaining, assessing, and providing critical feedback on their writing.

One advantage of performance tests is minimization of guessing. Requiring students to construct responses to assessment tasks also reinforces writing, computation, scientific experimentation, and other life skills.

Major disadvantages of the approach are the heavy time requirements for administration; the high costs of scoring; the difficulty in achieving reliable scores; the narrow scope of skills that can feasibly be assessed; and lack of norms for comparisons, especially at the national level. In general, performance tests are inefficient, costly, and often of dubious reliability. Moreover, compared with multiple-choice tests, performance tests cover a much narrower range of questions in the same amount of testing time. The nation's largest attempt to install and operate a state accountability system grounded almost totally in performance assessments was the Kentucky Instructional Results Information System. The program failed and was largely replaced with a program of multiple-choice standardized tests.

Approach 12: Experimental Studies

Using controlled experiments, program evaluators randomly assign beneficiaries (such as students or groups of students or patients) or organizations (such as schools or hospitals) to experimental and control groups and then contrast the outcomes after the experimental group received a particular intervention and the control group received no special treatment or some different treatment. This type of study was quite prominent in program evaluations during the late 1960s and early 1970s, when there were federal requirements to assess the effectiveness of federally funded innovations in schools and social service organizations. However, experimental program evaluations subsequently fell into disfavor and disuse. Apparent reasons for this decline are that educators, social workers, and other social service providers rarely can meet the required experimental conditions and assumptions.

This approach is labeled a quasi-evaluation strategy because it starts with questions and a methodology that address only a narrow set of program issues. Experimental methods do not investigate a target population's needs or the particulars of a program's process. Experimental and quasi-experiments are insufficient to address the full range of questions required to assess a program's merit and worth.

In the 1960s, Campbell and Stanley (1963) and others hailed the true experiment as the best and preferred means of evaluating interventions. Many evaluators interpreted this message to mean that they should use only true experiments to evaluate social and education innovations. They often ignored the additional advice that Campbell and Stanley had advanced concerning quasi-experimental designs that could be used acceptably, though not ideally, when a true experiment was not feasible.

This piece of evaluation history is reminiscent of Kaplan's famous warning against the so-called law of the instrument (1964), whereby a given method is equated to a field of inquiry. In such a case, the field of inquiry is restricted to the questions that are answerable by the given method and the conditions required to apply the method. Fisher (1951) specifically warned against equating his experimental methods with science.

In general, experimental design is a method that can contribute importantly to program evaluation, as Nave, Miech, and Mosteller (2000) have demonstrated. However, as they also found, evaluators of education and social programs evaluators rarely have conducted sound and useful experiments.

The advance organizers in experimental studies are problem statements, competing treatments, hypotheses, investigatory questions, and randomized treatment and comparison groups. The usual purpose of the controlled experiment is to determine causal relationships between specified independent and dependent variables, such as between a given instructional method and student standardized-test performance. It is particularly noteworthy that the sources of questions investigated in the experimental study are researchers, program developers, and policy figures and not usually a program's constituents and staff.

The frequent question in the experimental study is, "What are the effects of a given intervention on specified outcome variables?" Typical methods used are experimental and quasi-experimental designs. Pioneers in using experimentation to evaluate programs are Campbell and Stanley (1963), Cronbach and Snow (1969), Lindquist (1953), and Suchman (1967). Others who have developed the methodology of experimentation substantially for program evaluation are Boruch (1994, 2003), Glass and Maguire (1968), and Wiley and Bock (1967).

Evaluators should consider conducting a controlled experiment only when its required conditions and assumptions can be met. Often this requires substantial political influence, substantial funding, and widespread agreement—among the involved funders, service providers, and beneficiaries—to submit to the requirements of the experiment. Such requirements typically include, among others, a stable program that will not have to be studied and modified during the evaluation; the ability to establish and sustain comparable program and control groups; the ability to keep the program and control conditions separate and uncontaminated; and the ability to obtain the needed criterion measures from all or at least representative samples of the members of the program and comparison groups. Evaluability assessment was developed as a particular methodology for determining the feasibility of moving ahead with an experiment (Smith, 1989; Wholey, 1995).

Controlled experiments have a number of advantages. They focus on results and not just intentions or judgments. They provide strong methods for establishing relatively unequivocal causal relationships between treatment and outcome variables, something that can be especially significant when program effects are small but important. Moreover, because of the prevalent use and success of experiments in such fields as medicine and agriculture, the approach has widespread credibility.

These advantages, however, are offset by serious objections to experimenting on school students and other human subjects. It is often considered unethical or even illegal to deprive control group members of the benefits of special funds for improving services. Likewise, many parents do not want schools or other organizations to experiment on their children by applying unproven interventions. Typically schools find it impractical and unreasonable to randomly assign students to treatments and to hold treatments constant throughout the study period. Furthermore, experimental studies provide a much narrower range of information than organizations often need to assess and strengthen their programs. On this point, experimental studies tend to provide terminal information that is not useful for guiding the development and improvement of programs and may in fact thwart ongoing modifications of programs.

An example of a failed field experiment is seen in a personnel experience that occurred in a Great Society era federal program. In the early 1970s, the first author of this book served on a metaevaluation team charged to monitor and evaluate the federally mandated and funded experimental design-based evaluation of the Emergency School Assistance Act program (ESAA). This program provided federal funds to help certain school districts serve a recent dramatic increase of students in the districts. This increase stemmed mainly from a huge Vietnam War–related buildup of military personnel stationed near certain school districts.

In that period of accountability, Congress required federally supported programs to be evaluated. Experimental design advocates had persuaded Congress to mandate, within the ESAA legislation, that ESAA be evaluated by means of a true experiment. With a federal award of about $5 million, a very large sum then, the evaluation contractor designed and proceeded to implement a true experiment in each of several ESAA school districts. The focal question was, "To what extent does an allocation of ESAA funds to certain qualifying schools in each district increase student achievement and other outcomes beyond those seen in equivalent qualifying district schools not receiving ESAA funds?" Members of matched pairs of qualifying schools in each district were randomly assigned to ESAA support or no ESAA support.

Although highly qualified experimental design experts planned and conducted the study and had $5 million at their disposal, they did not satisfactorily answer the study's main question. After the first year, there were no significant differences in the outcome variables of interest. It was found that the experimental and control schools were receiving approximately the same level of expenditures per pupil. Further investigation revealed that as soon as a school district's leaders had learned which of the qualifying schools in the district had been randomly assigned to the ESAA allocation of federal funds, they diverted other local funds to the district's control schools. The district leaders' motivation for doing this clearly seemed aimed at avoiding community controversy over providing unequal support to all the deserving schools. Since there were no significant differences between experimental and control conditions (amount of money per student), there was no prospect for finding a significant difference in student outcomes attributable to the ESAA investment. Ironically, to rescue the evaluation, the evaluators hastily converted it to a set of case studies, a methodological area in which they had limited qualifications.

While some field-based experiments have produced useful information, this case shows that—even with a congressional mandate, much money, and experimental design experts, it can be extremely difficult to meet the requirements of true experiments in field settings. Politics and other unexpected and uncontrollable interferences often impede the success of field experiments in dynamic areas, such as educational innovation. Even if the ESAA experiment had succeeded, it would have provided far less information about what the schools did with the money—the important treatments beyond federal funds—than did the case studies. If the ESAA evaluators had attempted to evaluate the much more complex but relevant treatments—for example, instructional methods and materials, in-service training for teachers, counseling of students, parent involvement, and administrative support—rather than just federal money, they probably would have had little chance of learning much of importance through an experimental approach.

Educators should not presuppose that an experiment is the best or even an acceptable approach in all program evaluation situations. In our experience, experimentally oriented evaluations can be workable and useful under the right circumstances. However, in education and human services, such circumstances are rare.

Approach 13: Management Information Systems

Management information systems are like politically controlled approaches, except that they supply managers with information needed to conduct and report on their programs, as opposed to supplying them with information needed to win a political advantage. The management information approach is also like the decision- and accountability-oriented approach, discussed later in Chapter Eight, except that the decision- and accountability-oriented approach provides information needed to both develop and defend a program's merit and worth, which goes beyond providing information that managers need to implement and report on their management responsibilities. The payment-by-results and accountability approach, described previously, also should not be confused with the management information system approach. Although both approaches maintain a base of information that can be used for accountability, the latter approach includes no scheme for payment by results and sanctions.

The advance organizers in most management information systems include program objectives, specified activities, projected program milestones or events, and a program budget. A management information system's purpose is to continuously supply managers with the information they need to plan, direct, control, and report on their programs or spheres of responsibility.

The sources of questions addressed are the management personnel and their superiors. The main questions they typically want answered are these: Are program activities being implemented according to schedule, according to budget, and with the expected results? To provide ready access to information for addressing such questions, systems regularly store and make accessible up-to-date information on program goals, planned operations, actual operations, staff, program organization, expenditures, threats, problems, publicity, and achievements.

Methods employed in management information systems include system analysis, program evaluation and review technique (PERT), critical path method, program planning and budgeting system, management by objectives, computer-based information systems, periodic staff progress reports, and regular budgetary reporting.

Cook (1966) introduced the use of PERT to education, and Kaufman (1969) wrote about the use of management information systems in education. Business schools and programs in computer information systems regularly provide courses in management information systems, which focus mainly on how to set up and employ computerized information banks for use in organizational decision making.

W. Edwards Deming (1986) argued that managers should pay close attention to process rather than being preoccupied with outcomes. He advanced a systematic approach for monitoring and continuously improving an enterprise's process, arguing that close attention to the process will result in increasingly better outcomes. It is commonly said that in paying attention to this and related advice from Deming, Japanese carmakers and, later, American carmakers greatly increased the quality of automobiles (Aguaro, 1990). Bayless and Massaro (1992) applied Deming's approach to program evaluations in education.

In observing an attempt by a renowned national expert in Deming's methods to apply the approach in some Florida schools, it was concluded that the approach, as applied there, failed. This seemed to be because the industry-based method is not well suited to assessing the complexities of educational processes. Unlike the manufacture of automobiles, educators have no definitive, standardized models for linking exact educational processes to specified outcomes and must address the needs of students possessing a wide range of individual differences.

Nevertheless, given modern database technology, program managers often can and should employ management information systems in multiyear projects and programs. Program databases can provide information not only for keeping programs on track, but also for assisting in the broader study and improvement of program processes and outcomes.

A major advantage of the use of management information systems is in giving managers information they can use to plan, monitor, control, and report on complex operations. A difficulty with the application of this industry-oriented type of system to education and other social services, however, is that the products of many programs are not amenable to a narrow, precise definition, as is the case with a corporation's profit-and-loss statement or its production of standardized products. Moreover, processes in educational and social programs often are complex and evolving rather than straightforward and uniform like those of manufacturing and business. The information gathered in management information systems typically lacks the scope of context, input, process, and outcome information required to assess a program's merit and worth.

Approach 14: Benefit-Cost Analysis

Benefit-cost analysis as applied to program evaluation is a set of largely quantitative procedures used to understand the full costs of a program and to determine and judge what these investments returned in objectives achieved and broader social benefits. The aim is to determine costs associated with program inputs, determine the monetary value of the program outcomes, compute benefit-cost ratios, compare the computed ratios to those of similar programs, and ultimately judge a program's productivity in economic terms.

The benefit-cost analysis approach to program evaluation may be broken down into three levels of procedure: (1) cost analysis of program inputs, (2) cost-effectiveness analysis, and (3) benefit-cost analysis. These may be looked at as a hierarchy. The first type, cost analysis of program inputs, may be done by itself. Such analyses entail an ongoing accumulation of a program's financial history, which is useful in controlling program delivery and expenditures. The program's financial history can be used to compare its actual and projected costs and how costs relate to the costs of similar programs. Cost analyses can also be extremely valuable to outsiders who might be interested in replicating a program.

Cost-effectiveness analysis includes cost analysis of program inputs to determine the cost associated with progress toward achieving each objective. For example, two or more programs' costs and successes in achieving the same objectives might be compared. A program could be judged superior on cost-effectiveness grounds if it had the same costs but superior outcomes as similar programs. Or a program could be judged superior on cost-effectiveness grounds if it achieved the same objectives as more expensive programs. Cost-effectiveness analyses do not require conversion of outcomes to monetary terms but must be keyed to clear, measurable program objectives.

Benefit-cost analyses typically build on a cost analysis of program inputs and a cost-effectiveness analysis. But the benefit-cost analysis goes further. It seeks to identify a broader range of outcomes than just those associated with program objectives. It examines the relationship between the investment in a program and the extent of positive and negative impacts on the program's environment. In doing so, it ascertains and places a monetary value on program inputs and each identified outcome. It identifies a program's benefit-cost ratios and compares these to similar ratios for competing programs. Ultimately benefit-cost studies seek conclusions about the comparative benefits and costs of the examined programs.

Advance organizers for the overall benefit-cost approach are associated with cost breakdowns for both program inputs and outputs. Program input costs may be delineated by line items (for example, personnel, travel, materials, equipment, communications, facilities, contracted services, overhead), program components, and year. In cost-effectiveness analysis, a program's costs are examined in relation to each program objective, and these must be clearly defined and assessed. The more ambitious benefit-cost analyses look at costs associated with main effects and side effects, tangible and intangible outcomes, positive and negative outcomes, and short-term and long-term outcomes—both inside and outside a program. Frequently they also may break down costs by individuals and groups of beneficiaries.

One may also estimate the costs of forgone opportunities and, sometimes, political costs. Even then, the real value of benefits associated with human creativity or self-actualization is nearly impossible to estimate. Consequently, the benefit-cost equation rests on dubious assumptions and uncertain realities.

The purposes of these three levels of benefit-cost analysis are to gain clear knowledge of what resources were invested, how they were invested, and with what effect. In the vernacular, cost-effectiveness and benefit-cost analyses seek to determine the program's bang for the buck. There is great interest in answering this type of question. Policy boards, program planners, and taxpayers are especially interested to know whether program investments are paying off in positive results that exceed or are at least as good as those produced by similar programs. Authoritative information on the benefit-cost approach may be obtained by studying the writings of Kee (1995), Levin (1983), and Tsang (1997).

Benefit-cost analysis is potentially important in most program evaluations. Evaluators are advised to discuss this matter thoroughly with their clients, reach appropriate advance agreements on what should and can be done to obtain the needed cost information, and do as much cost-effectiveness and benefit-cost analysis as can be done well and within reasonable costs.

Benefit-cost analysis is an important but problematic consideration in program evaluations. Most evaluations are amenable to analyzing the costs of program inputs and maintaining a financial history of expenditures. The main impediment is that program authorities often do not want anyone other than the appropriate accountants and auditors looking into their financial books. If cost analysis, even at only the input levels, is to be done, this must be provided for clearly in the initial contractual agreements covering the evaluation work. Performing cost-effectiveness analysis can be feasible if cost analysis of inputs is agreed to; if there are clear, measurable program objectives; and if comparable cost information can be obtained from competing programs. Unfortunately, it is usually hard to meet all these conditions. Even more unfortunate is the fact that it is usually impractical to conduct a thorough benefit-cost analysis. Not only must it meet all the conditions of the analysis of program inputs and cost-effectiveness analysis, it must also place monetary values on identified outcomes, both anticipated and unexpected.

Approach 15: Clarification Hearing

The clarification hearing is one label for the judicial approach to program evaluation. The approach essentially puts a program on trial. Role-playing evaluators competitively implement both a damning prosecution of the program—arguing that it failed—and a defense of the program—arguing that it succeeded. A judge hears arguments within the framework of a jury trial and controls the proceedings according to advance agreements on rules of evidence and trial procedures. The actual proceedings are preceded by the collection of and sharing of evidence by both sides. The prosecuting and defending evaluators may call witnesses and place documents and other exhibits into evidence. A jury hears the proceedings and ultimately makes and issues a ruling on the program's success or failure. Ideally the jury is composed of persons representative of the program's stakeholders. By videotaping the proceedings, after the trial the administering evaluator can produce a condensed videotape as well as printed reports to disseminate what was learned through the process.

The advance organizers for a clarification hearing are criteria of program effectiveness that both the prosecuting and defending sides agree to apply. The main purpose of the judicial approach is to ensure that the evaluation's audience will receive balanced evidence on a program's strengths and weaknesses. The key questions essentially are, Should the program be judged a success or failure? Is it as good as or better than alternative programs that address the same objectives?

Robert Wolf (1975) pioneered the judicial approach to program evaluation. Others who applied, tested, and further developed the approach include Levine (1974), Owens (1973), and Popham and Carlson (1983). Steven Kemis (Stake, 1999, p. 333) conducted a "metaevaluation court" to assess Robert Stake's evaluation of Reader Focused Writing for the Veterans Benefits Administration (1999). Essentially, Kemis sought to identify and investigate issues related to the dependability of the CIRCE study's findings.

Based on the past uses and evaluations of this approach, it can be judged as only marginally relevant to program evaluation. Because of its adversarial nature, the approach encourages evaluators to present biased arguments in order to win their cases. Thus, truth seeking is subordinated to winning. The most effective debaters are likely to convince the jury of their position even when it is poorly founded. The approach is also politically problematic, since it generates considerable acrimony. Despite the attractiveness of using the law, with its attendant rules of evidence, as a metaphor for program evaluation, its promise has not been fulfilled. There are few occasions in which it makes practical sense for evaluators to apply this approach.

Approach 16: Case Study Evaluations

Program evaluation that is based on a case study is a focused, in-depth description, analysis, and synthesis of a particular program or other object. The investigators do not control the program in any way. Rather, they look at it as it is occurring or as it occurred in the past. The study looks at the program in its geographical, cultural, organizational, and historical contexts, closely examining its internal operations and how it uses inputs and processes to produce outcomes. It examines a wide range of intended and unexpected outcomes. It looks at the program's multiple levels and also holistically at the overall program. It characterizes both central dominant themes and variations and aberrations. It defines and describes the program's intended and actual beneficiaries. It examines beneficiaries' needs and the extent to which the program effectively addressed the needs. It employs multiple methods to obtain and integrate multiple sources of information. While it breaks apart and analyzes a program along various dimensions, it also provides an overall characterization of the program.

The main thrust of the case study approach is to delineate and illuminate a program, not necessarily to guide its development or to assess and judge its merit and worth. Hence, this section characterizes the case study approach as a questions- or methods-oriented approach rather than an improvement or accountability approach.

Advance organizers in case studies include the definition of the program, characterization of its geographical and organizational environment, the historical period in which it is to be examined, the program's beneficiaries and their assessed needs, the program's underlying logic of operation and productivity, and the key roles involved in the program. A case study program evaluation's main purpose is to provide stakeholders and their audiences with an authoritative, in-depth, well-documented explication of the program.

The case study should be keyed to the questions of most interest to the evaluation's main audiences. The evaluator must therefore identify and interact with the program's stakeholders. Along the way, stakeholders will be engaged to help plan the study and interpret findings. Ideally, the audiences include the program's oversight body, administrators, staff, financial sponsors, beneficiaries, and potential adopters.

Typical questions posed by some or all of the above audiences are these: What is the program in concept and practice? How has it evolved over time? How does it actually operate to produce outcomes? Who are the players and what do they do? What has it produced? What are the shortfalls and negative side effects? What are the positive side effects? In what ways and to what degrees do various stakeholders value the program? To what extent did the program effectively meet beneficiaries' needs? What were the most important reasons for the program's successes and failures? What are the program's most important unresolved issues? How much has it cost? What are the costs per beneficiary, per component, per line item, and per year? What parts of the program have been successfully transported to other sites? How does this program compare with what might be called critical competitors? These questions illustrate the range of questions that a case study might address; each study will be tempered by the interests of the client, other audiences, and the evaluator.

To conduct effective case studies, evaluators need to employ a wide range of qualitative and quantitative methods. These may include analysis of archives; collection of artifacts such as work samples; content analysis of program documents; independent and participant observations; interviews; logical analysis of operations; focus groups; tests; questionnaires; rating scales; hearings; forums; and maintenance of a program database. Reports may incorporate in-depth descriptions and accounts of key historical trends; focus on critical incidents, photographs, maps, testimony, relevant news clippings, logic models, and cross-break tables; and summarize main conclusions. The case study report may include a description of key dimensions of the case, as determined with the audience, as well as an overall holistic presentation and assessment. Case study reports may involve audio and visual media as well as printed documents.

Case study methods have existed for many years and have been applied in such areas as anthropology, clinical psychology, law, the medical profession, and social work. Pioneers in applying the method to program evaluation include Campbell (1975), Lincoln and Guba (1985), Platt (1992), Smith and Pohland (1974), Stake, Easely, and Anastasiou (1978), Stake (1995), and Yin (1992).

The case study approach is highly appropriate in program evaluation. It requires no controls of treatments and subjects and looks at programs as they naturally occur and evolve. It addresses accuracy issues by employing and triangulating multiple perspectives, methods, and information sources. It employs all relevant methods and information sources. It looks at programs within relevant contexts and describes contextual influences on the program. It looks at programs holistically and in depth. It examines the program's internal workings and how it produces outcomes. It includes systematic procedures for analyzing qualitative information. It can be tailored to focus on the audience's most important questions. It can be done retrospectively or in real time. It can be reported to meet given deadlines and subsequently updated based on further developments. The power of the case study approach is enhanced when multiple case studies are conducted within a programmatic area.

The main limitation of the case study is that some evaluators may mistake its openness and lack of controls as an excuse for approaching it haphazardly and bypassing steps to ensure that findings and interpretations possess rigor as well as relevance. Furthermore, because of a preoccupation with descriptive information, the case study evaluator may not collect sufficient judgmental information to permit a broad-based assessment of a program's merit and worth. Users of the approach might slight quantitative analysis in favor of qualitative analysis. By trying to produce a comprehensive description of a program, the case study evaluator may not produce timely feedback needed to help in program development. To overcome these potential pitfalls, evaluators using the case study approach should fully address the principles of sound evaluation as related to accuracy, utility, feasibility, and propriety.

Approach 17: Criticism and Connoisseurship

The criticism- and connoisseur-based approach grew out of methods used in art criticism and literary criticism. It assumes that certain experts in a given substantive area are capable of in-depth analysis and evaluation that could not be done in other ways. Just as a national survey of wine drinkers could produce information concerning their overall preferences for types of wines and particular vineyards, it would not provide the detailed, creditable judgments of the qualities of particular wines that might be derived from a single connoisseur who has devoted a professional lifetime to the study and grading of wines and whose judgments are highly and widely respected.

The advance organizer for the criticism- and connoisseur-based study is the evaluator's special expertise and sensitivities. The study's purpose is to describe, critically appraise, and illuminate a particular program's merits. The evaluation questions addressed by the criticism and connoisseur-based evaluation are determined by expert evaluators—the critics and authorities who have undertaken the evaluation. Among the major questions they can be expected to ask are these: What are the program's essence and salient characteristics? What merits and demerits distinguish the particular program from others of the same general kind?

The methodology of criticism and connoisseurship includes critics' systematic use of their perceptual sensitivities, past experiences, refined insights, and abilities to communicate their assessments. The evaluator's judgments are conveyed in vivid terms to help the audience appreciate and understand all of the program's nuances. Eisner (1975, 1983) has pioneered this strategy in education. A dozen or more of Eisner's students have conducted research and development on the criticism and connoisseurship approach, including Vallance (1973) and Flinders and Eisner (2000). This approach obviously depends on the chosen expert's qualifications. It also requires an audience that has confidence in, and is willing to accept and use, the critic or connoisseur's report. We would willingly accept and use any evaluation that Elliott Eisner agreed to present, but there are not many Eisners out there.

The main advantage of the criticism- and connoisseur-based study is that it exploits the particular expertise and finely developed insights of persons who have devoted much time and effort to the study of a precise area. Such individuals can provide an array of detailed information that an audience can then use to form a more insightful analysis than otherwise might be possible. The approach's disadvantage is that it is dependent on the expertise and qualifications of the particular expert doing the program evaluation, leaving room for much subjectivity.

Approach 18: Program Theory–Based Evaluation

Program evaluations based on program theory begin with either (1) a well-developed and validated theory of how programs of a certain type within similar settings operate to produce outcomes or (2) an initial stage to approximate such a theory within the context of a particular program evaluation. The former condition is much more reflective of the implicit promises in a theory-based program evaluation, since the existence of a sound theory means that a substantial body of theoretical development has produced and tested a coherent set of conceptual, hypothetical, and pragmatic principles, as well as associated instruments to guide inquiry. The theory can then aid a program evaluator to decide what questions, indicators, and assumed linkages between and among program elements should be used to evaluate a program covered by the theory.

Some theories have been used more or less successfully to evaluate programs, and this gives the approach some measure of viability. For example, health education and behavior change programs are sometimes founded on theoretical frameworks, such as the health belief model (Becker, 1974; Janz & Becker, 1984; Mullen, Hersey, & Iverson, 1987). Other examples are the PRECEDE-PROCEED model for health promotion planning and evaluation (Green & Kreuter, 1991), Bandura's social cognitive theory (1977), the stages-of-change theory of Prochaska and DiClemente (1992), and Peters and Waterman's (1982) theory of successful organizations. When such frameworks exist, their use probably can enhance a program's effectiveness and provide a credible structure for evaluating the program's functioning. Unfortunately, few program areas are buttressed by well-articulated and tested theories.

Thus, most theory-based evaluations begin by setting out to develop a theory that appropriately could be used to guide the particular program evaluation. As will be discussed later in this characterization, such theory development efforts and their linkage to program evaluations are problematic and potentially counterproductive. In any case, let us look at what the theory-based evaluator attempts to achieve.

The point of the theory development or selection effort is to identify advance organizers to guide the evaluation. Essentially these are the mechanisms by which program activities are understood to produce or contribute to program outcomes, along with the appropriate description of context, specification of independent and dependent variables, and portrayal of key linkages. The main purposes of the theory-based program evaluation are to determine the extent to which the program of interest is theoretically sound, understand why it is succeeding or failing, and provide direction for program improvement.

Questions for the program evaluation pertain to and are derived from the guiding theory. Example questions include these: Is the program grounded in an appropriate, well-articulated, and validated theory? Is the employed theory reflective of sound research? Are the program's targeted beneficiaries, design, operation, and intended outcomes consistent with the guiding theory? How well does the program address and serve the targeted beneficiaries' full range of pertinent needs? If the program is consistent with the guiding theory, are the expected results being achieved? Are program inputs and operations producing outcomes in the ways the theory predicts? What changes in the program's design or implementation might produce better outcomes? What elements of the program are essential for successful replication? Overall, was the program theoretically sound, did it operate in accordance with an appropriate theory, did it produce the expected outcomes, were the hypothesized causal linkages confirmed, what program modifications are needed, is the program worthy of continuation or dissemination, and what program features are essential for successful replication?

The nature of these questions suggests that the success of the theory-based approach is dependent on a foundation of sound theory development and validation. This, of course, entails sound conceptualization of at least a context-dependent theory, formulation and rigorous testing of hypotheses derived from the theory, development of guidelines for practical implementation of the theory based on extensive field trials, development of valid instruments for assessing key aspects of the theory, and independent assessment of the theory. Unfortunately, not many program areas in education and the social sciences are grounded in sound theories. Moreover, evaluators wanting to employ a theory-based evaluation do not often find it feasible to conduct the full range of theory development and validation steps and still get the evaluation done effectively and on time. Thus, in claiming to conduct a theory-based evaluation, evaluators often seem to promise much more than they can deliver.

The main procedure typically used in "theory-based program evaluations" is a model of the program's logic. This may be a detailed flowchart of how inputs are thought to produce intended outcomes. It may also be a grounded theory, such as those advocated by Glaser and Strauss (1967). The network analysis of the former approach is typically an armchair theorizing process involving evaluators and persons who are supposed to know how the program is expected to operate and produce results. They discuss, scheme, discuss some more, network, discuss further, and finally produce networks in varying degrees of detail of what is involved in making the program work and how the various elements are linked to produce desired outcomes. The more demanding grounded theory requires a systematic, empirical process of observing events or analyzing materials drawn from operating programs, followed by an extensive modeling process.

Pioneers in applying theory development procedures to program evaluation include Glaser and Strauss (1967) and Weiss (1972, 1995). Other developers of the approach are Bickman (1990), Chen (1990), and Rogers (2000).

In any program evaluation assignment, it is reasonable for the evaluator to examine the extent to which program plans and operations are grounded in an appropriate theory or model. It can also be useful to engage in a modicum of effort to network the program and thereby seek out key variables and linkages. In the enviable but rare situation where a relevant, validated theory exists, the evaluator can beneficially apply it in structuring the evaluation and analyzing findings.

However, if a relevant, defensible theory of the program's logic does not exist, evaluators need not develop one. In fact, if they attempt to do so, they will incur many threats to their evaluation's success. Rather than evaluating a program and its underlying logic, evaluators might usurp the program staff's responsibility for program design. They might do a poor job of theory development, given limitations on time and resources to develop and test an appropriate theory. They might incur the conflict of interest associated with having to evaluate the theory they developed. They might pass off an unvalidated model of the program as a theory, when it meets almost none of the requirements of a sound theory. They might bog down the evaluation in too much effort to develop a theory. They might also focus attention on a theory developed early in a program and later discover that the program has evolved to be a quite different enterprise from what was theorized at the outset. In this case, the initial theory could become a procrustean bed for both the program and the program evaluation.

Overall, there is not much to recommend theory-based program evaluation since doing it right is usually not feasible and failed or misrepresented attempts can be highly counterproductive. Nevertheless, modest attempts to model programs—labeled as such—can be useful for identifying measurement variables, so long as the evaluator does not spend too much time on this and so long as the model is not considered as fixed or as a validated theory. In the rare case where an appropriate theory already exists, the evaluator can make beneficial use of it to help structure and guide the evaluation and interpret the findings.

Approach 19: Mixed-Methods Studies

In an attempt to resolve the long-standing debate about whether program evaluations should employ quantitative or qualitative methods, some authors have proposed that evaluators should regularly combine these methods in given program evaluations (for example, see the National Science Foundation's 1997 *User-Friendly Handbook for Mixed Method Evaluations*). Such recommendations, along with practical guidelines and illustrations, are no doubt useful to many program staff members and to evaluators. But in the main, the recommendation for a mixed-methods approach only highlights a large body of long-standing practice of mixed-methods program evaluation rather than proposing a new approach. All of the approaches discussed in the subsequent chapters of this book employ both qualitative and quantitative methods. What sets them apart from the mixed-methods approach is that their first considerations are not the methods to be employed but the assessment of value or the social mission to be served. The mixed-methods approach is included in this chapter on questions and methods approaches because it is preoccupied with using multiple methods rather than whatever best methods (or, indeed, method) are needed to comprehensively assess a program's merit and worth. As with the other approaches in this section, the mixed-methods approach may or may not fully assess a program's value; thus, it is classified as a quasi-evaluation approach.

The advance organizers of the mixed-methods approach are formative and summative evaluations, qualitative and quantitative methods, and intracase or cross-case analysis. Formative evaluations are employed to examine a program's development and assist in improving its structure and implementation. Summative evaluations basically look at whether objectives were achieved, but may look for a broader array of outcomes. Qualitative and quantitative methods are employed in combination to ensure depth, scope, and dependability of findings. This approach also applies to carefully selected single programs and comparisons of alternative programs.

The basic purposes of the mixed-methods approach are to provide direction for improving programs as they evolve and to assess their effectiveness after they have had time to produce results. Use of both quantitative and qualitative methods is intended to ensure dependable feedback on a wide range of questions; depth of understanding of particular programs; a holistic perspective; and enhancement of the validity, reliability, and usefulness of the full set of findings. Investigators look to quantitative methods for standardized, replicable findings on large data sets. They look to qualitative methods for elucidation of the program's cultural context, dynamics, meaningful patterns and themes, deviant cases, and diverse impacts on individuals as well as groups. Qualitative reporting methods are applied to bring the findings to life and make them clear, persuasive, and interesting. By using both quantitative and qualitative methods, the evaluator secures cross-checks on different subsets of findings and thereby instills greater stakeholder confidence in the overall findings.

The sources of evaluation questions are the program's goals, plans, and stakeholders. The stakeholders often include skeptical as well as supportive audiences. Among the important stakeholders are program administrators and staff, policy boards, financial sponsors, beneficiaries, citizens, and program area experts.

The approach may pursue a wide range of questions. Examples of formative evaluation questions follow: To what extent do program activities follow the program plan, time line, and budget? To what extent is the program achieving its goals? What problems in design or implementation need to be addressed? Examples of summative evaluation questions are: To what extent did the program achieve its goals? Was the program appropriately effective for all beneficiaries? What interesting stories emerged? What are program stakeholders' judgments of program operations, processes, and outcomes? What were the important side effects? Is the program sustainable and transportable?

The approach employs a wide range of methods. Among quantitative methods are surveys using representative samples, both cohort and cross-sectional samples, norm-referenced tests, rating scales, quasi-experiments, significance tests for main effects, and a posteriori statistical tests. The qualitative methods may include ethnography, document analysis, narrative analysis, purposive samples, participant observers, independent observers, key informants, advisory committees, structured and unstructured interviews, focus groups, case studies of individuals and groups, study of outliers, diaries, logic models, grounded theory development, flowcharts, decision trees, matrices, and performance assessments. Reports may include abstracts, executive summaries, full reports, oral briefings, conference presentations, and workshops. They should include a balance of narrative and numerical information.

Considering his book on service studies in higher education, Ralph Tyler (Tyler, 1932) was certainly a pioneer in the mixed-methods approach to program evaluation. Other authors who have written cogently on the approach are Guba and Lincoln (1981, 1989), Kidder and Fine (1987), Lincoln and Guba (1985), Miron (1998), Patton (1990), and Schatzman and Strauss (1973).

It is almost always appropriate to consider using a mixed-methods approach. Certainly, the evaluator should take advantage of opportunities to obtain any and all potentially available information that is relevant to assessing a program's merit and worth. Sometimes a study can be mainly or only qualitative or quantitative. But including both types of information usually strengthens such studies. The key point is to choose methods because they can effectively address the study's questions, not because they are either qualitative or quantitative.

Key advantages of using both qualitative and quantitative methods are that they complement each other in ways that are important to the evaluation's audiences. Information from quantitative methods tends to be standardized, efficient, and amenable to standard tests of reliability, easily summarized and analyzed, and accepted as hard data. Information from qualitative approaches adds depth; can be delivered in interesting, story-like presentations; and provides a means to explore and understand the more superficial quantitative findings. Using both types of method affords important cross-checks on findings.

The main pitfall in pursuing the mixed-methods approach is using multiple methods because this is the popular thing to do rather than because the selected methods best respond to the evaluation questions. Moreover, sometimes evaluators let the combination of methods compensate for a lack of rigor in applying them. Using a mixed methods approach can produce confusing findings if an investigator uncritically mixes positivistic and postmodern paradigms, since quantitative and qualitative methods are derived from different theoretical approaches to inquiry and reflect different conceptions of knowledge. Many evaluators do not possess the requisite foundational knowledge in both the sciences and humanities to effectively combine quantitative and qualitative methods. The approaches in the remainder of this book place proper emphasis on mixed methods, making choice of the methods subservient to the approach's dominant philosophy and to the particular evaluation questions to be addressed.

Summary

The questions and methods approaches to evaluation tend to concentrate on selected questions and methods and thus may or may not fully address an evaluation's fundamental requirement to assess a program's merit and worth. The array of these approaches suggests that the field has advanced considerably since the 1950s, when program evaluations were rare and mainly used approaches grounded in behavioral objectives, standardized tests, or accreditation visits.

Review Questions

1. In what ways do quasi-evaluations narrow the scope of an evaluation?
2. Write a definition for each of the following evaluation approaches:
   a. Objectives-based studies
   b. Objective testing programs

    c. Management information systems

    d. Criticism and connoisseurship studies

Check your definitions against those provided in the Glossary at the back of this book.

3. State the advance organizers for clarification hearings and also for case study evaluations.
4. What methods are typically employed for objectives-based studies and also for accountability (including payment-by-results) studies?
5. What kinds of questions are likely to be asked in respect to the success case method of evaluation?
6. Those subjected to outcome evaluation as value-added assessment have often raised objections to its use. What are the main objections?
7. The main purpose of the performance testing methodologies for assessing respondents' learning is that they have high face validity. Explain the meaning of this contention.
8. Why is it difficult to establish necessary conditions for the performance testing method to be successful?
9. If a program evaluation is to be theoretically based, what are the two (alternative) beginning conditions?
10. We have said that the mixed-method approach is preoccupied with using qualitative and quantitative methods rather than seeking a true assessment of a program's merit and worth. How does this classify the mixed-methods approach as quasi-evaluation?

Group Exercises

This is a lengthy chapter containing considerable information about the nature of fourteen question and methods-oriented evaluation approaches, all of which often fail to fully address a program's merit and worth. Nevertheless, most are commonly used, a situation unlikely to change in the near future. We hope that your discussions will sharpen your views about some of the salient features of these quasi-evaluation approaches.

> *Exercise 1.* Divide your group into two sections, and adjust the following questions and procedures to suit numbers in each section so that as many as possible are able to be involved in discussions.
>
>   Each individual in one group refers to a different quasi-evaluation approach, giving opinions why it is useful to organizations willing to accept

the approach. Members of the other group then outline perceived weaknesses of the approach. (A stern adjudicator will be needed to control this discussion!)

Exercise 2. Discuss this statement: the main weakness in advocating the mixed-methods evaluation approach lies in following the popular path of using mixed methods (that is, both qualitative and quantitative) rather than analyzing those methods that best respond to evaluation questions.

Exercise 3. Increasingly, from the late 1960s to early 1970s, experimental studies, as an evaluation technique or a component of it, lost favor, mainly because this methodology addresses only a restricted view of the evaluand. Discuss whether such a criticism remains in place today for experimental studies as evaluation and under what circumstances.

References

Aguaro, R. (1990). *R. Deming: The American who taught the Japanese about quality.* New York: Fireside.

Baker, E. L., O'Neil, H. R., & Linn, R. L. (1993). Policy and validity prospects for performance-based assessment. *American Psychologist, 48,* 1210–1218.

Bandura, A. (1977). *Social learning theory.* Upper Saddle River, NJ: Prentice Hall.

Bayless, D., & Massaro, G. (1992). *Quality improvement in education today and the future: Adapting W. Edwards Deming's quality improvement principles and methods to education.* Kalamazoo: Center for Research on Educational Accountability and Teacher Evaluation, Evaluation Center, Western Michigan University.

Becker, M. H. (Ed.). (1974). The health belief model and personal health behavior [Whole issue]. *Health Education Monographs, 2,* 324–473.

Bickman, L. (1990). Using program theory to describe and measure program quality. In L. Bickman (Ed.), *Advances in program theory.* New Directions in Program Evaluation, no. 47. San Francisco: Jossey-Bass.

Bloom, B. S., Englehart, M. D., Furst, E. J., Hill, W. H., & Krathwohl, D. R. (1956). *Taxonomy of educational objectives: Handbook I: Cognitive domain.* New York: McKay.

Boruch, R. F. (1994). The future of controlled randomized experiments: A briefing. *Evaluation Practice, 15*(3), 265–274.

Boruch, R. F. (2003). Randomized field trials in education. In T. Kellaghan & D. L. Stufflebeam (Eds.), *International handbook of educational evaluation.* Norwell, MA: Kluwer.

Brickell, M. (1976, July). *Needed: Instruments as good as our eyes.* Kalamazoo: Evaluation Center, Western Michigan University.

Brinkerhoff, R. O. (2003). *The success case method.* San Francisco: Berrett-Koehler.

Campbell, D. T. (1975). Degrees of freedom and the case study. *Comparative Political Studies, 8,* 178–193.

Campbell, D. T., & Stanley, J. C. (1963). Experimental and quasi-experimental designs for research on teaching. In N. L. Gage (Ed.), *Handbook of research on training.* Skokie, IL: Rand McNally.

Chen, H. (1990). *Theory driven evaluations.* Thousand Oaks, CA: Sage.

Clancy, T., with Horner, C. (1999). *Every man a tiger.* New York: Putnam.

Cook, D. L. (1966). *Program evaluation and review techniques, applications in education.* Washington, DC: U.S. Office of Education.

Cronbach, L. J., & Snow, R. E. (1969). *Individual differences in learning ability as a function of instructional variables.* Stanford, CA: Stanford University Press.

Deming, W. E. (1986). *Out of the crisis.* Cambridge, MA: Center for Advanced Engineering Study, Massachusetts Institute of Technology.

Ebel, R. L. (1965). *Measuring educational achievement.* Upper Saddle River, NJ: Prentice-Hall.

Eisner, E. W. (1975, March). *The perceptive eye: Toward a reformation of educational evaluation.* Invited address to Division B, Curriculum and Objectives, American Educational Research Association, Washington, DC.

Eisner, E. W. (1983). Educational connoisseurship and criticism: Their form and functions in educational evaluation. In G. F. Madaus, M. Scriven, & D. L. Stufflebeam (Eds.), *Evaluation models.* Norwell, MA: Kluwer.

Fisher, R. A. (1951). *The design of experiments* (6th ed.) New York: Hafner.

Flanagan, J. C. (1939). General considerations in the selection of test items and a short method of estimating the product-moment coefficient from data at the tails of the disribution. *Journal of Educational Psychology, 30,* 674–680.

Flexner, A. (1910). *Medical education in the United States and Canada.* Bethesda, MD: Science and Health Publications.

Flinders, D. J., & Eisner, E. W. (2000). Educational criticism as a form of qualitative inquiry. In D. L. Stufflebeam, G. F. Madaus, & T. Kellaghan (Eds.). *Evaluation models.* Norwell, MA: Kluwer.

Glaser, B. G., & Strauss, A. L. (1967). *The discovery of grounded theory.* Chicago: Aldine.

Glass, G. V., & Maguire, T. O. (1968). *Analysis of time-series quasi-experiments.* Boulder: Laboratory of Educational Research, University of Colorado.

Green, L. W., & Kreuter, M. W. (1991). *Health promotion planning: An educational and environmental approach* (2nd ed.). Mountain View, CA: Mayfield Publishing.

Guba, E. G., & Lincoln, Y. S. (1981). *Effective evaluation.* San Francisco: Jossey-Bass.

Guba, E. G., & Lincoln, Y. S. (1989). *Fourth generation evaluation.* Thousand Oaks, CA: Sage.

Hambleton, R. K., & Swaminathan, H. (1985). *Item response theory.* Norwell, MA: Kluwer.

Hammond, R. L. (1972). *Evaluation at the local level.* Tucson, AZ: EPIC Evaluation Center.

Herman, J. L., Gearhart, M. G., & Baker, E. L. (1993). Assessing writing portfolios: Issues in the validity and meaning of scores. *Educational Assessment, 1,* 201–224.

Janz, N. K., & Becker, M. H. (1984). The health belief model: A decade later. *Health Education Quarterly, 11,* 1–47.

Kaplan, A. (1964). *The conduct of inquiry.* San Francisco: Chandler.

Kaufman, R. A. (1969, May). Toward educational system planning: Alice in education-land. *Audiovisual Instructor, 14,* 47–48.

Kee, J. E. (1995). Benefit-cost analysis in program evaluation. In J. S. Wholey, H. P. Hatry, & K. E. Newcomer (Eds.), *Handbook of practical program evaluation* (pp. 456–488). San Francisco: Jossey-Bass.

Kentucky Department of Education. (1993). *Kentucky results information system, 1991–92 technical report.* Frankfort, KY: Author.

Kidder, L., & Fine, M. (1987). Qualitative and quantitative methods: When stories converge. In M. Mark & R. Shotland (Eds.), *Multiple methods in program evaluation* (pp. 57–75). New Directions for Program Evaluation, no. 35. San Francisco: Jossey-Bass.

Kirst, M. W. (1990, July). *Accountability: Implications for state and local policymakers.* Washington, DC: Information Services, Office of Educational Research and Improvement, U.S. Department of Education.

Koretz, D. (1996a). *The validity of gains in scores on the Kentucky Instructional Results Information System (KIRIS).* Santa Monica, CA: Rand.

Koretz, D. (1996b). Using student assessments for educational accountability. In R. Hanushek (Ed.), *Improving the performance of America's schools* (pp. 171–196). Washington, DC: National Academy Press.

Koretz, D. M., & Barron, S. I. (1998). *The validity of gains in scores on the Kentucky Instructional Results Information System (KIRIS).* Santa Monica, CA: Rand.

Lessinger, L. M. (1970). *Every kid a winner: Accountability in education.* New York: Simon & Schuster.

Levin, H. M. (1983). *Cost-effectiveness: A primer.* Thousand Oaks, CA: Sage.

Levine, M. (1974, September). Scientific method and the adversary model. *American Psychologist, 666–677.*

Lincoln, Y. S., & Guba, E. G. (1985). *Naturalistic inquiry.* Thousand Oaks, CA: Sage.

Lindquist, E. F. (Ed.). (1951). *Educational measurement.* Washington, DC: American Council on Education.

Lindquist, E. F. (1953). *Design and analysis of experiments in psychology and education.* Boston: Houghton Mifflin.

Linn, R. L., Baker, E. L., & Dunbar, S. B. (1991). Complex, performance-based assessment: Expectations and validation criteria. *Educational Researcher, 20*(8), 15–21.

Lord, F. M., & Novick, M. R. (1968). *Statistical theories of mental test scores.* Reading, MA: Addison-Wesley.

Madaus, G. F., & Stufflebeam, D. L. (1988). *Educational evaluation: The classical writings of Ralph W. Tyler.* Norwell, MA: Kluwer.

Mehrens, W. A. (1972). Using performance assessment for accountability purposes. *Educational Measurement: Issues and Practice, 11*(1), 3–10.

Messick, S. (1994). The interplay of evidence and consequences in the validation of performance assessments. *Educational Researcher, 23*(3), 13–23.

Metfessel, N. S., & Michael, W. B. (1967). A paradigm involving multiple criterion measures for the evaluation of the effectiveness of school programs. *Educational and Psychological Measurement, 27,* 931–943.

Miron, G. (1998). Choosing the right research methods: Qualitative? Quantitative? Or both? In L. Buchert (Ed.), *Education reform in the South in the 1990s.* Paris: UNESCO.

Mullen, P. D., Hersey, J., & Iverson, D. C. (1987). Health behavior models compared. *Social Science and Medicine, 24,* 973–981.

National Science Foundation. (1997). *User-friendly handbook for mixed method evaluations.* Arlington, VA: Author.

Nave, B., Miech, E. J., & Mosteller, F. (2000). A rare design: The role of field trials in evaluating school practices. In D. L. Stufflebeam, G. F. Madaus, & T. Kellaghan (Eds.), *Evaluation models.* Norwell, MA: Kluwer.

Owens, T. (1973). Educational evaluation by adversary proceeding. In E. House (Ed.), *School evaluation: The politics and process*. Berkeley, CA: McCutchan.

Patton, M. Q. (1990). *Qualitative evaluation and research methods* (2nd ed.). Thousand Oaks, CA: Sage.

Peters, T. J., & Waterman, R. H. (1982). *In search of excellence*. New York: Warner Books.

Platt, J. (1992). Case study in American methodological thought. *Current Sociology, 40*(1), 17–48.

Popham, W. J. (1969). Objectives and instruction. In R. Stake (Ed.), *Instructional objectives*. Skokie, IL: Rand McNally.

Popham, W. J., & Carlson, D. (1983). Deep dark deficits of the adversary evaluation model. In G. F. Madaus, M. Scriven, & D. L. Stufflebeam (Eds.), *Evaluation models*. Norwell, MA: Kluwer.

Prochaska, J. O., & DiClemente, C. C. (1992). Stages of change in the modification of problem behaviors. In M. Hersen, R. M. Eisler, & P. M. Miller (Eds.), *Progress in behavior modification, 28*. Sycamore, IL: Sycamore Publishing Company.

Provus, M. N. (1971). *Discrepancy evaluation*. Berkeley, CA: McCutcheon.

Rogers, P. R. (2000). Program theory: Not whether programs work but how they work. In D. L. Stufflebeam, G. F. Madaus, & T. Kellaghan (Eds.), *Evaluation models*. Norwell, MA: Kluwer.

Sanders, W. L. (1989). *Using customized standardized tests*. Washington, DC: Office of Educational Research and Improvement, U. S. Department of Education. (ERIC Digest No. ED 314429)

Sanders, W. L., & Horn, S. P. (1994). The Tennessee value-added assessment system (TVAAS): Mixed model methodology in educational assessment. *Journal of Personnel Evaluation in Education, 8*(3), 299–311.

Schatzman, L., & Strauss, A. L. (1973). *Field research*. Upper Saddle River, NJ: Prentice Hall.

Smith, L. M., & Pohland, P. A. (1974). Educational technology and the rural highlands. In L. M. Smith (Ed.), *Four examples: Economic, anthropological, narrative, and portrayal*. Skokie, IL: Rand McNally.

Smith, M. F. (1989). *Evaluability assessment: A practical approach*. Norwell, MA: Kluwer.

Stake, R. E. (1971). *Measuring what learners learn*. Urbana, IL: Center for Instructional Research and Curriculum Evaluation.

Stake, R. E. (1995). *The art of case study research*. Thousand Oaks, CA: Sage.

Stake, R. E. (1999). Summary of evaluation of reader focused writing for the Veteran's Benefits Administration. *American Journal of Evaluation, 20*(2), 323–343.

Stake, R. E., Easely, J., & Anastasiou, K. (1978). *Case studies in science education*. Washington, DC: National Science Foundation, Directorate for Science Education, Office of Program Integration.

Steinmetz, A. (1983). The discrepancy evaluation model. In G. F. Madaus, M. Scriven, & D. L. Stufflebeam (Eds.), *Evaluation Models* (pp. 79–100). Norwell, MA: Kluwer.

Stenner, A. J., & Webster, W. J. (1971). *Educational program audit handbook*. Arlington, VA: I.D.E.A.

Stillman, P. L., Haley, H. A., Regan, M. B., Philbin, M. M., Smith, S. R., O'Donnell, J., & Pohl, H. (1991). Positive effects of a clinical performance assessment program. *Academic Medicine, 66*, 481–483.

Suchman, E. A. (1967). *Evaluative research*. New York: Russell Sage Foundation.

Swanson, D. B., Norman, R. N., & Linn, R. L. (1995). Performance-based assessment: Lessons from the health professions. *Educational Researcher, 24*(5), 5–11.

Thorndike, R. L. (1971). *Educational measurement* (2nd ed.). Washington, DC: American Council on Education.

Torrance, H. (1993). Combining measurement-driven instruction with authentic assessment: Some initial observations of national assessment in England and Wales. *Educational Evaluation and Policy Analysis, 15,* 81–90.

Travers, R. (1977, October). Presentation in a seminar at the Western Michigan University Evaluation Center, Kalamazoo, MI.

Tsang, M. C. (1997). Cost analysis for improved educational policymaking and evaluation. *Educational Evaluation and Policy Analysis, 19*(4), 318–324.

Tyler, R. W. (1932). *Service studies in higher education.* Columbus: Bureau of Educational Research, Ohio State University.

Tymms, P. (1995). *Setting up a national "value-added" system for primary education in England: Problems and possibilities.* Paper presented at the National Evaluation Institute, Kalamazoo, MI.

Vallance, E. (1973). *Aesthetic criticism and curriculum description.* Unpublished doctoral dissertation, Stanford University.

Webster, W. J. (1995). The connection between personnel evaluation and school evaluation. *Studies in Educational Evaluation, 21,* 227–254.

Webster, W. J., Mendro, R. L., & Almaguer, T. O. (1994). Effectiveness indices: A "value-added" approach to measuring school effect. *Studies in Educational Evaluation, 20,* 113–145.

Weiss, C. H. (1972). *Evaluation.* Upper Saddle River, NJ: Prentice Hall.

Weiss, C. H. (1995). Nothing as practical as good theory: Exploring theory-based evaluation for comprehensive community initiatives for children and families. In J. Connell, A. Kubisch, L. B. Schorr, & C. H. Weiss (Eds.), *New approaches to evaluating community initiatives.* New York: Aspen Institute.

Wholey, J. S. (1995). Assessing the feasibility and likely usefulness of evaluation. In J. S. Wholey, H. P. Hatry, & K. E. Newcomer, *Handbook of practical program evaluation* (pp. 15–39). San Francisco: Jossey-Bass.

Wiggins, G. (1989). A true test: Toward more authentic and equitable assessment. *Phi Delta Kappan, 70,* 703–713.

Wiley, D. E., & Bock, R. D. (1967, Winter). Quasi-experimentation in educational settings: Comment. *School Review,* 353–366.

Wolf, R. L. (1975). Trial by jury: A new evaluation method. *Phi Delta Kappan, 3*(57), 185–187.

Yin, R. K. (1992). The case study as a tool for doing evaluation. *Current Sociology, 40*(1), 121–137.

CHAPTER EIGHT

IMPROVEMENT- AND ACCOUNTABILITY-ORIENTED EVALUATION APPROACHES

This chapter summarizes three approaches that stress the need to fully assess a program's value. These approaches are expansive and seek comprehensiveness in considering the full range of questions and criteria needed to assess a program on such criteria as merit, worth, probity, importance, feasibility, safety, or equity. These approaches often employ the assessed needs of a program's stakeholders as the foundational criteria for assessing the program's worth, based often on democratic principles. In addition, they usually reference all of the pertinent technical and economic criteria for judging the merit or quality of program plans and operations. Improvement- and accountability-oriented evaluations also look for all relevant outcomes, not just those keyed to program objectives. Thus, those evaluations may have an enlightening orientation. Usually such evaluations are objectivist and assume an underlying reality in seeking definitive, unequivocal answers to the evaluation questions. They use multiple qualitative and quantitative assessment methods to provide cross-checks on findings. In general, the approaches conform closely to this book's definition of evaluation because they seek to fully assess a program's value. The approaches are labeled decision and accountability oriented, consumer oriented, and accreditation and certification. The central thrusts of the three approaches, respectively, are to (1) foster improvement and accountability through informing and assessing program decisions, (2) assist consumers to make wise choices among optional programs and services, and (3) help accrediting associations certify meritorious institutions and programs for use by consumers.

Approach 20: Decision- and Accountability-Oriented Studies

The decision- and accountability-oriented approach emphasizes that program evaluation should be used proactively to help improve a program as well as retroactively to judge its value. The approach is distinguished from management information systems and from politically controlled studies mainly because decision and accountability studies emphasize questions of value. The approach's philosophical underpinnings include an objectivist orientation to finding best answers to context-limited questions and subscription to the principles of a well-functioning democratic society, especially human rights, equity, excellence, conservation, probity, and accountability. Practically, the approach serves stakeholders by engaging them in focusing the evaluation; addressing their most important questions plus those required to assess the program's value; providing timely, relevant information to assist decision making and understanding; producing an accountability record; and issuing needed summative evaluation reports. This approach is best represented by the CIPP model for evaluation (Stufflebeam, 2003, 2004, 2005), but elements of the approach are also seen in Cronbach's (1982) general approach to evaluation.

Advance organizers of the decision and accountability approach include decision makers and stakeholders; projected decision situations; program accountability requirements; and the criteria needed to examine a program's value, that is, its merit, worth, probity, feasibility, safety, importance, and equity. Audiences include program decision makers and all other stakeholders, both internal and external to the program: beneficiaries, business and institutional boards, parents and guardians, staff, administrators, program consultants, policymakers, funding authorities, and citizens. The decisions to be informed may include deciding to launch a program; determining the targeted beneficiaries; defining goals and priorities; choosing from competing program strategies; planning procedures; scheduling, staffing, and budgeting the work; monitoring and adjusting operations; and deciding to continue or terminate an effort. Key classes of needed evaluative information are assessments of needs, problems, assets, opportunities, and objectives; identification and assessment of similar programs or alternative program approaches; assessment of procedural plans, budgets, and schedules; assessment of staff qualifications and performance; assessment of program facilities and materials; monitoring and assessment of operations; assessment of intended, unintended, short-range, and long-range outcomes; cost analysis; analyses of relationships between program resources, processes, and outcomes; and comparison of program outcomes and costs with those of similar programs.

The basic purpose of decision- and accountability-oriented studies is to provide a knowledge and value base for making and being accountable for decisions that result in developing, delivering, and making informed use of services that are morally sound and cost-effective. Thus, evaluators must interact with representative members of their audiences; discern their questions; determine appropriate criteria and information requirements (which may extend beyond the audiences' preferences); and report relevant, timely, efficient, and accurate information. Under this approach, an evaluation's most important purpose is not to prove but to improve. The improvement orientation seeks to help a program mature, overcome its early deficiencies, and build on its strengths. However, improvement in a broader sense is sometimes best served by terminating a persistently ineffective program, thus freeing resources for better use. While evaluations following this approach prospectively foster and assist ongoing improvement efforts, they also look retrospectively at what was attempted and accomplished. Thus, the approach is applied both formatively and summatively. Stufflebeam's version of this approach calls for evaluations to adhere to professional standards for evaluations, including utility, feasibility, propriety, and accuracy (Joint Committee, 1994).

The sources of questions addressed by this approach are the concerned and involved stakeholders and the evaluator's view of what questions must be addressed in order to assess a program's value. Stakeholders include all persons and groups involved in making choices related to initiating, planning, funding, staffing, implementing, and using a program's services.

Illustrative questions for the formative evaluation are: Has an appropriate beneficiary population been determined? What beneficiary needs should be addressed? What are the available alternative ways to address these needs, and what are their comparative merits and costs? Are plans for services and participation morally defensible and technically sound? Are there adequate provisions for facilities, materials, staff, and equipment? Are sufficient funds available to complete the program? Are the program's staff members sufficiently qualified and credible? Have appropriate roles been assigned to the different participants, and will they receive sufficient orientation and training? Are the participants effectively carrying out their assignments? Is the program working well? Should it be revised in any way? What are the program's most important strengths? How might the program build on its strengths? Is the program effectively reaching all the targeted beneficiaries? Is the program meeting the participants' needs? Are beneficiaries playing their part to make the program succeed? Is the program designed and functioning at least as well as its counterparts in other settings?

Primary questions in the summative evaluation are: Did the program reach the targeted beneficiaries and meet their pertinent needs? Is the program more cost-effective than competing alternatives? What arrangements, events, and processes contributed to the program's success or failure? Did the program prove to be affordable? Is it beyond reproach? Is there a continued need for the program? Is it sustainable? Is it transportable? Was the program worth the required initial investment?

Answers to the formative and summative questions are to be based on the underlying standard of good programs. They must reach and serve beneficiaries' targeted needs effectively, ethically, and at a reasonable cost and perform as well as or better than reasonably available alternatives.

Many methods may be used in decision- and accountability-oriented program evaluations. These include, among others, surveys, needs assessments, case studies, advocacy teams, carefully recorded and assessed observations, interviews, resident evaluators, participant observers, cost analyses, and quasi-experimental and experimental designs.

To make the approach work, the evaluator must interact regularly with a representative group of stakeholders. In this respect, the approach is compatible with so-called participatory approaches to evaluation. Typically the evaluator at least should establish and engage a representative stakeholder panel to help define evaluation questions, shape evaluation plans, review draft reports, and help disseminate findings. The evaluator's exchanges with stakeholders involve conveying evaluation feedback that may be of use in program improvement, as well as determining what future evaluation reports would be most helpful to program personnel and other stakeholders. Interim reports may assist beneficiaries, program staff, and others to assess program operations and discern problems requiring attention. By maintaining and accessing a dynamic baseline of evaluative information and applications of the information, the evaluator can periodically update the broad group of stakeholders on the program's progress, develop a comprehensive summative evaluation report, and supply program personnel with information for their own accountability reports.

The involvement of stakeholders is consistent with a key principle of the change process: an enterprise—read *evaluation* here—can best effect change in a target group's behavior by involving members in planning, monitoring, and judging the enterprise. By involving stakeholders throughout the evaluation process, decision- and accountability-oriented evaluators lay the groundwork for helping stakeholders understand and value the evaluation process and apply the findings. Stakeholders' active participation in the setting of evaluation questions and procedures is also consistent with a principle of democracy, wherein citizens and stakeholders are given voice in determinations that will affect them.

Cronbach (1963) advised educators to reorient their evaluations from an objectives orientation to a concern for making better program decisions. Although he did not use the terms *formative evaluation* and *summative evaluation,* he essentially identified and defined the underlying concepts before Scriven (1967) attached the now widely used labels to these concepts. In discussing the distinctions between the constructive, proactive orientation, on the one hand, and the retrospective, judgmental orientation, on the other, Cronbach argued for placing more emphasis on the former. He noted the limited functionality of the tradition of stressing retrospective outcomes evaluation. In a later publication (Cronbach and Associates, 1980), Cronbach stressed that evaluations should take a long view and have an illuminating orientation. He saw evaluation's most important services to be enlightening societal groups about the workings of programs over time and informing policy development in key areas of societal need. (This conceptualization was a forerunner of the so-called realist evaluation approach in which Henry, 2005, calls for sustained, long-range study of how a particular program strategy—such as Head Start—works out over decades in various national and international settings.)

Cronbach (1982) operationalized his evaluation approach in the UTOS model. In this model, the evaluator structures the evaluation to identify the units (U) targeted to receive program services, the program treatments (T) to be delivered, the observations (O) to be collected, and the setting (S) to be taken into account.

Following Cronbach's seminal call for evaluations to guide decision making, Stufflebeam (1966, 1967) also argued that evaluations should help program personnel make decisions keyed to meeting beneficiaries' needs. While he advocated an improvement orientation to evaluation, he also stressed that evaluators should both inform decisions and provide information for accountability (Stufflebeam, 1971). He emphasized further that the evaluators should interact with and report to the full range of stakeholders who need to make judgments and choices about a program. Stufflebeam's approach has been encapsulated in the CIPP evaluation model (Stufflebeam, 1967, 2002, 2003, 2004, 2005; Stufflebeam et al., 1971). That model calls for evaluations of context, input, process, and product. Context evaluations assess pertinent needs, assets, opportunities, and problems to assist in formulating or judging goals. Input evaluations identify and assess competing program strategies for meeting beneficiaries' assessed needs. Process evaluations assess the implementation of a selected program strategy. Product evaluations search out, analyze, and judge program results. (A checklist for implementing the CIPP model is available at www.wmich.edu/evalctr/checklists.)

Others who have contributed to the development of a decision and accountability orientation to evaluation are Alkin (1969) and Webster (1975, 1995).

The decision- and accountability-oriented approach is applicable in cases where program staff and other stakeholders require formative evaluation or summative evaluation, or both. It can provide the framework for both internal and external evaluations. When used for internal evaluation, it is often advisable to commission an independent metaevaluation of the inside evaluator's work. Beyond program evaluations, this approach has proved useful in evaluating personnel, students, projects, facilities, and products.

A major advantage of the approach is that it encourages program personnel to use evaluation continuously and systematically to plan and implement programs that meet beneficiaries' targeted needs. Its use aids decision making at all program levels and stresses improvement. It also presents a rationale and framework of information to help program personnel be accountable for their program decisions and actions. Its application involves the full range of stakeholders in the evaluation process to ensure that their evaluation needs are addressed well and to encourage and support them in making effective use of evaluation findings. It is comprehensive in focusing on beneficiaries' needs, program context, program plans and budgets, program operations, and program costs and outcomes. It balances the use of quantitative and qualitative methods. It is keyed to professional standards for evaluations. Finally, the approach emphasizes that evaluations must be grounded in the democratic principles of a free society and themselves be subject to evaluation.

A limitation of the approach is that the collaboration required between an evaluator and stakeholders introduces opportunities for impeding the evaluation or biasing its results, especially when the evaluative situation is politically charged. Furthermore, when evaluators are actively influencing a program's course, they may identify so closely with it that they lose some of the independent, detached perspective needed to provide objective, forthright reports. Moreover, the approach may overemphasize formative evaluation and give too little time and too few resources to summative evaluation. Advance contracting and external metaevaluation have been employed to counteract opportunities for bias and to ensure a proper balance of the formative and summative aspects of evaluation. Although the charge is erroneous, this approach carries the connotation that only top decision makers are served.

Approach 21: Consumer-Oriented Studies

In the consumer-oriented approach, the evaluator is the enlightened surrogate consumer. He or she must draw direct evaluative conclusions about the program being evaluated. Evaluation is viewed as the process of determining something's merit, worth, and significance, with evaluations being the products of that process. The approach regards a consumer's welfare as a program's primary justification and accords that welfare the same primacy in program evaluation. Grounded in a deeply reasoned view of ethics and the common good, together with skills in obtaining and synthesizing pertinent, valid, and reliable information, the evaluator should help developers produce and deliver products and services that are of excellent quality and of great use to consumers (for example, students, their parents, teachers, and taxpayers). More important, the evaluator should help consumers identify and assess the merit, worth, and significance of competing programs, services, and products.

Advance organizers include societal values, consumers' needs, costs, and criteria of goodness in the particular evaluation domain. The purpose of a consumer-oriented program evaluation is to judge the relative merits, worth, and significance of the products and services of alternative programs and thereby to help taxpayers, practitioners, and potential beneficiaries make wise choices. The approach is objectivist in assuming an underlying reality and positing that it is possible, although often extremely difficult, to find best answers. It looks at a program comprehensively in terms of its quality and costs, functionally regarding the assessed needs of the intended beneficiaries, and comparatively considering reasonably available alternative programs. Evaluators are expected to subject their program evaluations to evaluations—what Scriven (1969) termed *metaevaluation*.

The consumer-oriented approach employs a wide range of assessment topics. These include program description, background and context, consumers, resources, function, delivery system, values, standards, process, outcomes, costs, critical competitors, generalizability, statistical significance, bottom-line assessment, practical significance, wide-ranging significance, recommendations, reports, and metaevaluation. The evaluation process begins with consideration of a broad range of such topics, continuously compiles information on all of them, and ultimately culminates in a supercompressed judgment of the program's merit, worth, or significance.

Questions for the consumer-oriented study are derived from society, program constituents, and, especially, the evaluator's frame of reference. One general question is addressed: Which of several alternative programs is the best choice, given their differential costs, merits on a range of criteria, the needs of the consumer group, the values of society at large, and evidence of both positive and negative outcomes?

Methods include checklists, needs assessments, goal-free evaluation, experimental and quasi-experimental designs, modus operandi analysis, applying codes of ethical conduct, and cost analysis (Scriven, 1974). A preferred method is for an external, independent consumer advocate to conduct and report findings of studies of publicly supported programs. The approach is keyed to employing a sound checklist of the program's main aspects. Scriven (1991, 2004a) developed the generic Key Evaluation Checklist for this purpose. (Regular updates of this checklist can be found at www.wmich.edu/evalctr/checklists.) The main evaluative acts in this approach are scoring, grading, ranking, apportioning, and producing the final synthesis (Scriven, 1994a).

Scriven (1967) was a pioneer in applying the consumer-oriented approach to program evaluation, and his work parallels the concurrent work of Ralph Nader and the Consumers Union in the general field of consumerism. Glass (1975) has supported and developed Scriven's approach. Scriven (1967) coined the terms *formative* and *summative evaluation*. He noted that approaches to evaluations can be divergent in early quests for critical competitors and explorations related to clarifying goals and making programs function well. However, he also maintained that evaluations ultimately must converge on summative judgments about a program's merit, worth, or significance. While accepting the importance of formative evaluation, he also argued against Cronbach's position (1963) that formative evaluation should be given the major emphasis. According to Scriven, the fundamental aim of a sound evaluation is to judge a program's merit, comparative value, wide-ranging significance, and overall worth. He sees evaluation as a transdiscipline encompassing all evaluations of various entities across all applied areas and disciplines and comprising a common logic, methodology, and theory that transcends specific evaluation domains, which also have their unique characteristics (Scriven, 1991, 1993, 1994a, 2004b).

The consumer-oriented study requires a highly credible and competent expert, together with either sufficient resources to allow the expert to conduct a thorough study or other means to obtain the needed information. Often a consumer-oriented evaluator is engaged to evaluate a program after its formative stages are over. In these situations, the external consumer-oriented evaluator is often dependent on being able to access a substantial base of information that the program staff had accumulated. If no such base of information exists, the consumer-oriented evaluator will have great difficulty in obtaining enough information to produce a thorough, defensible summative program evaluation.

One of the main advantages of consumer-oriented evaluation is that it is a hard-hitting, independent assessment intended to protect consumers from shoddy programs, services, and products and to guide them to support and use those contributions that best and most cost-effectively address their needs. The approach's stress on independent and objective assessment and its attempt to achieve a comprehensive assessment of merit, worth, and significance yield high credibility with consumer groups. This is aided by Scriven's Key Evaluation Checklist (1994b) and his *Evaluation Thesaurus* (1991), in which he presents and explains the checklist. The approach provides for a summative evaluation to yield a bottom-line judgment of an evaluand's value, preceded by a formative evaluation to help ensure that developers' programs will succeed.

One disadvantage of the consumer-oriented evaluation is that it can be so independent of program staff that it might not assist them in serving consumers better. A summative evaluation that is conducted too early can intimidate developers and stifle their creativity. However, if it is applied only near a program's end, the evaluator may have great difficulty in obtaining sufficient evidence to confidently and credibly judge the program's basic value. This often iconoclastic approach is also heavily dependent on a highly competent, independent, and "bulletproof" evaluator.

Approach 22: Accreditation and Certification

Many educational institutions, hospitals, and other service organizations have been the subject of an accreditation study, and many professionals, at one time or another, have had to meet certification requirements for a given position. Such studies of institutions and personnel are in the realm of accountability-oriented evaluations, as well as having an improvement element. Institutions, institutional programs, and personnel are studied to prove whether they meet requirements of given professions and service authorities and whether they are fit to serve designated functions in society. Typically the feedback reports identify areas for improvement.

The advance organizers used in the accreditation or certification study usually are guidelines and criteria that some accrediting or certifying body has adopted. The evaluation's purpose is to determine whether institutions, institutional programs, or personnel should be approved to deliver specified public services.

The source of questions for accreditation or certification studies is the accrediting or certifying body. Basically, they address these questions: Are institutions and their programs and personnel meeting minimum standards, and how can their performance be improved?

Typical methods used in the accreditation or certification approach are self-study and self-reporting by the individual or institution. In the case of institutions, panels of experts are assigned to visit the institution, verify a self-report, and gather additional information. The basis for the self-studies and the visits by expert panels are usually guidelines and criteria specified by the accrediting or certifying agency.

Accreditation of education was pioneered by the College Entrance Examination Board around 1901. Since then, the accreditation function has been implemented and expanded, especially by the Cooperative Study of Secondary School Standards, dating from around 1933. Subsequently, the accreditation approach has been developed, further expanded, and administered by the North

Central Association of Secondary Schools and Colleges, along with its associated regional accrediting agencies across the United States, and by many other accrediting and certifying bodies. Similar accreditation practices are found in medicine, law, architecture, and many other professions. Hughes and Kushner (2005) provide an up-to-date summary of the general approach to accreditation.

Any area of professional service that potentially could put the public at risk—if services and products are not delivered by highly trained specialists in accordance with standards of good practice and safety—should consider subjecting its programs to accreditation reviews and its personnel to certification processes. Such use of evaluation services is very much in the public interest and is a means of getting feedback that can be used to strengthen capabilities and practices.

The major advantage of the accreditation or certification study is that it aids consumers in making informed judgments about the quality of organizations and programs and the qualifications of individual personnel. Major difficulties are that the guidelines of accrediting and certifying bodies historically have often emphasized inputs and processes and given minimal attention to outcomes. However, a recent trend has been to give more attention to outcomes. Also, the self-study and visitation processes used in accreditation offer many opportunities for corruption and inept assessment. Institutions have been known to present to evaluators only those program components they deem to be successful and to obscure program elements that are failing. Also, institutions have sometimes wined and dined visiting accreditation evaluators in the process of successfully co-opting them to give favorable reports. As is the case for all other evaluation approaches, accreditation and certification processes should be subjected to independent metaevaluations.

Summary

The three improvement- and accountability-oriented approaches emphasize the assessment of value, which is the thrust of the definition of evaluation used to classify the approaches considered in this book. The book turns next to the fourth set of program evaluation approaches: those concerned with using evaluation to further a social agenda.

Review Questions

1. Construct and fill in the cells of a 2-by-3 matrix, summarizing the similarities and differences among the three evaluation approaches reviewed in this chapter.

2. For each of the three evaluation approaches considered in this chapter, give an example to show how the approach has an objectivist orientation.

3. What are the strengths and weaknesses of the consumer-oriented evaluation approach?

4. A company produced a catalogue of information technology equipment that promised to make any business office more efficient and cost-effective and to improve customer relations. What information would you require before placing an order from this catalogue?

5. Construct and fill in the cells of a 2-by-4 matrix to summarize the relationship between the CIPP model's four main types of evaluation and evaluation's formative and summative roles.

6. Obtain a copy of Stufflebeam's CIPP evaluation model checklist (available at www.wmich.edu/evalctr/checklists), and apply it to plan an evaluation of a program with which you are familiar.

7. Explain with examples why Scriven sees the evaluation field as a transdiscipline.

8. Obtain a copy of Scriven's Key Evaluation Checklist (available at www.wmich. edu/evalctr/checklists), and apply it to plan an evaluation of a program with which you are familiar.

9. Explain and give illustrations of the essential services that accreditation studies provide to society.

10. Briefly list the main strengths and weaknesses of the decision- and accountability-oriented approach to evaluation. Now state a situation in which you would find the approach most useful, giving reasons. Then state another situation in which the approach either would not work or would not give satisfactory evaluation outcomes, again giving reasons.

Group Exercises

Work through the following exercises with your group. It is quite possible that members will reach different conclusions about the best responses to the presented assignments. However, members should try to reach a consensus or justify their opposing position.

> *Exercise 1.* A secondary school faces an impending accreditation review that is scheduled to commence about one year from now and is to be completed about eighteen months later. The school is required to complete an institutional self-study during the review's first twelve months. The accrediting organization will then conduct an external evaluation during the review's concluding six months. Weigh the pros and cons of using the CIPP

evaluation model checklist or Scriven's Key Evaluation Checklist to guide the self-study.

Exercise 2. Continuing with the assignment in Exercise 1, develop cases for building metaevaluation into the self-study and the external evaluation. Define the purposes of the metaevaluation of the self-study, and reach and defend a conclusion about whether this metaevaluation should be internal or external, or possibly both. Develop a rationale for a recommendation that the accrediting agency should subject its external evaluation of the school to an independent metaevaluation.

Exercise 3. Cronbach and Scriven disagreed about the emphasis that should be given to formative evaluation and summative evaluation. Develop an evaluation scenario in which Cronbach's position makes more sense. Then develop an evaluation scenario that is more conducive to Scriven's position. Considering the two scenarios, write some guidelines to help evaluators decide when it is better to concentrate more on formative evaluation and when it is preferable to concentrate on summative evaluation.

Exercise 4. Previously we presented rather extensive information about both pseudoevaluation and quasi-evaluation approaches. In this chapter, you have been given an account of improvement and accountability approaches that aim to assess a program's true value. There are significant differences among these three broadly stated approaches.

Working separately within your group, list as many of these differences as you can. Then compare your list with those of the other group members. Finally, make a list of what your group collectively considers the most significant differences among pseudoevaluation, quasi-evaluation, and improvement- and accountability-oriented approaches to program assessment.

References

Alkin, M. C. (1969). Evaluation theory development. *Evaluation Comment, 2,* 2–7.

Cronbach, L. J. (1963). Course improvement through evaluation. *Teachers College Record, 64,* 672–683.

Cronbach, L. J. (1982). *Designing evaluations of educational and social programs.* San Francisco: Jossey-Bass.

Cronbach, L. J., & Associates. (1980). *Toward reform of program evaluation.* San Francisco: Jossey-Bass.

Glass, G. V (1975). A paradox about excellence of schools and the people in them. *Educational Researcher, 4,* 9–13.

Henry, G. T. (2005). Realist evaluation. In S. Mathison (Ed.), *Encyclopedia of evaluation* (pp. 359–362). Thousand Oaks, CA: Sage.

Hughes, M., & Kushner, S. (2005). In S. Mathison (Ed.), *Encyclopedia of evaluation* (pp. 4–7). Thousand Oaks, CA: Sage.

Joint Committee on Standards for Educational Evaluation. (1994). *The program evaluation standards.* Thousand Oaks, CA: Corwin Press.

Scriven, M. S. (1967). The methodology of evaluation. In R. E. Stake (Ed.), *Curriculum evaluation.* Skokie, IL: Rand McNally.

Scriven, M. (1969). An introduction to meta-evaluation. *Educational Product Report, 2,* 36–38.

Scriven, M. (1974). Evaluation perspectives and procedures. In W. J. Popham (Ed.), *Evaluation in education: Current applications.* Berkeley, CA: McCutcheon.

Scriven, M. (1991). *Evaluation thesaurus.* Thousand Oaks, CA: Sage.

Scriven, M. (1993, Summer). *Hard-won lessons in program evaluation.* New Directions for Program Evaluation, no. 58. San Francisco: Jossey-Bass.

Scriven, M. (1994a). Evaluation as a discipline. *Studies in Educational Evaluation, 20*(1), 147–166.

Scriven, M. (1994b). The final synthesis. *Evaluation Practice, 15*(3), 367–382.

Scriven, M. (2004a). *Key evaluation checklist.* http://www.wmich.edu/evalctr/checklists/.

Scriven, M. (2004b). Reflections. In M. C. Alkin (Ed.), *Evaluation roots* (pp. 183–195). Thousand Oaks, CA: Sage.

Stufflebeam, D. L. (1966). A depth study of the evaluation requirement. *Theory into Practice, 5,* 121–134.

Stufflebeam, D. L. (1967). The use of and abuse of evaluation in Title III. *Theory into Practice, 6,* 126–133.

Stufflebeam, D. L. (1971). The relevance of the CIPP evaluation model for educational accountability. *Journal of Research and Development in Education, 5*(1), 19–25.

Stufflebeam, D. L. (2002). *CIPP evaluation model checklist.* http://www.wmich.edu/evalctr/checklists/cippchecklist.htm.

Stufflebeam, D. L. (2003). The CIPP model for evaluation. In T. Kelleghan & D. L. Stufflebeam (Eds.), *International handbook of educational evaluation* (pp. 31–62). Norwell, MA: Kluwer.

Stufflebeam, D. L. (2004). The CIPP model for evaluation. In M. C. Alkin (Ed.), *Evaluation roots.* Thousand Oaks, CA: Sage.

Stufflebeam, D. L. (2005). CIPP model (context, input, process, product). In S. Mathison (Ed.), *International handbook of educational evaluation* (pp. 60–65). Thousand Oaks, CA: Sage.

Stufflebeam, D. L., Foley, W. J., Gephart, W. J., Guba, E. G., Hammond, R. L., Merriman, H. O., & Provus, M. M. (1971). *Educational evaluation and decision making.* Itasca, IL: Peacock.

Webster, W. J. (1975, March). *The organization and functions of research evaluation in a large urban school district.* Paper presented at the annual meeting of the American Educational Research Association, Washington, DC. (ERIC Clearinghouse on Tests, Measurements, and Evaluation, ED106345)

Webster, W. J. (1995). The connection between personnel evaluation and school evaluation. *Studies in Educational Evaluation, 21,* 227–254.

CHAPTER NINE

SOCIAL AGENDA AND ADVOCACY APPROACHES

Social agenda and advocacy approaches are aimed at increasing social justice through program evaluation. These approaches seek to ensure that all segments of society have equal access to educational and social opportunities and services. They advocate affirmative action to give the disadvantaged preferential treatment through program evaluation. If, as many persons have stated, information is power, then these approaches employ program evaluation to empower the disenfranchised.

The three approaches in this set are oriented to employing the perspectives of stakeholders as well as of experts in characterizing, investigating, and judging programs. They favor a constructivist orientation and the use of qualitative methods. For the most part, they eschew the possibility of finding right or best answers and reflect the philosophy of postmodernism, with its attendant stress on cultural pluralism, moral relativity, and multiple realities. They provide for democratic engagement of stakeholders in obtaining and interpreting findings.

There is a concern that these approaches might concentrate so heavily on serving a social mission that they would not meet the standards of a sound evaluation. By giving stakeholders authority for key evaluation decisions, related especially to interpretation and release of findings, evaluators empower these persons to use evaluation to their advantage. Such delegation of authority over important evaluation matters can make the evaluation vulnerable to stakeholders' biases and misuses. Furthermore, if an evaluator is intent on serving the under-privileged, empowering the disenfranchised, or righting educational or social in-justices, he or she might succumb to a conflict of interest and compromise the independent, impartial perspective needed to produce valid findings. For exam-ple, evaluators might be inclined to give a positive report on a program for the disadvantaged if funds allocated to serve these groups would be withdrawn as a consequence of a negative report. In the extreme, an advocacy evaluation could compromise the integrity of the evaluation process to achieve social objectives and thus devolve into a pseudoevaluation.

Nevertheless, there is much to recommend these approaches, since they are strongly oriented to democratic principles of equity and fairness and employ prac-tical procedures for involving the full range of stakeholders. The particular social agenda and advocacy approaches presented in this chapter seem to have sufficient safeguards needed to walk the line between sound evaluation services and politi-cally corrupted evaluations. Worries about bias control in these approaches un-derscore the importance of subjecting advocacy evaluations, as well as all other types of evaluation, to independent metaevaluations grounded in standards for sound evaluations.

Approach 23: Responsive Evaluation or Client-Centered Studies

The classic approach in this set is responsive evaluation (Stake, 1983, 2003, 2004). We also refer to this approach as *client-centered* evaluation, because one pervasive theme is that the evaluator must work with and for the support of a diverse client group, including, for example, teachers, administrators, developers, taxpayers, leg-islators, and financial sponsors. They are the clients in the sense that they support, develop, administer, or directly operate the programs under study and seek or need the evaluator's counsel and advice in understanding, judging, improving, and using programs. The approach charges evaluators to interact continuously with, and re-spond to, the evaluative needs of the various clients, as well as other stakeholders.

This approach contrasts sharply with Scriven's consumer-oriented approach, with its objectivist orientation and stress on reaching supercompressed summative judgments. Stake's evaluators are not the independent, objective assessors advo-cated by Scriven. The responsive/client-centered study embraces local autonomy and helps people who are involved in a program to evaluate it and use the find-ings for program improvement. In a sense, the evaluator is a quite nondirective counselor who uses evaluation to help clients query and gain insights into the workings of relevant projects and services and how these are addressing, or not addressing, targeted needs. Moreover, the responsive approach rejects objectivist evaluation, subscribing to the orientation that there are no best answers and consistently preferable values and that subjective information is preferred. In this approach, the program evaluation may culminate in conflicting findings and conclusions, leaving interpretation to the eyes of the beholders. Responsive evaluation is the leading entry in the relativistic school of evaluation, which calls for a pluralistic, flexible, interactive, holistic, subjective, constructivist, and service-oriented approach. The approach is relativistic because it seeks no final authoritative conclusion, interpreting findings against stakeholders' different and often conflicting values. The approach seeks to examine a program's full countenance and prizes the collection and reporting of multiple, often conflicting perspectives on the value of a program's format, operations, and achievements. Side effects and incidental gains as well as intended outcomes are to be identified and examined.

Robert Stake, the originator of responsive evaluation, is modest in his claims for what evaluations can accomplish. He even has expressed doubts that evaluators can contribute much to improving programs. He has continued to write about evaluation and give advice on the subject because he recognizes that evaluations are going to be done and there is no option to close down the evaluation enterprise. We think he might agree that his contributions are aimed at helping stakeholders make the best of what too often are unhelpful evaluations.

The advance organizers in responsive evaluations are stakeholders' concerns and issues in the program itself, as well as the program's rationale, background, transactions, outcomes, standards, and judgments. The responsive program evaluation may serve many purposes. Some of these are helping people in a local setting gain a perspective on the program's full countenance; understanding the ways that various groups see the program's problems, strengths, and weaknesses; and learning the ways affected people value the program, as well as the ways program experts judge it. The evaluator's process goal is to carry on a continuous search for key questions and standards and effectively communicate useful information to clients as it becomes available.

The responsive/client-centered approach has a strong philosophical base: evaluators should promote equity and fairness, help those with little power, thwart the misuse of power, expose the huckster, unnerve the assured, reassure the insecure, and always help people see things from alternative viewpoints. The approach subscribes to moral relativity and posits that for any given set of findings, there are potentially multiple, conflicting interpretations that are equally plausible. Clients seeking definitive conclusions are unlikely to find them in a responsive evaluation report.

Community, practitioner, and beneficiary groups in the local environment, together with external program area experts, provide the questions addressed by the responsive evaluation study. In general, the groups usually want to know what the program achieved, how it operated, and how it was judged by involved persons and experts in the program area. The more specific evaluation questions emerge as the study unfolds based on the evaluator's continuing interactions with stakeholders and their collaborative assessment of the developing evaluative information.

This approach reflects a formalization of the long-standing practice of informal, intuitive evaluation. It requires a relaxed and continuous exchange between evaluator and clients. It is more divergent than convergent. Basically, the approach calls for continuing communication between evaluator and audience for the purposes of discovering, investigating, and addressing a program's issues. Designs for responsive program evaluations are relatively open-ended and emergent, building to narrative description, rather than aggregating measurements across cases. The evaluator attempts to issue timely responses to clients' concerns and questions by collecting and reporting useful information, even if the needed information was not anticipated at the study's beginning. Concomitant with the ongoing conversation with clients, the evaluator attempts to obtain and present a rich set of information on the program. This includes its philosophical foundation and purposes, history, transactions, dilemmas, and outcomes. Special attention is given to side effects, the standards that various persons hold for the program, and their judgments of the program.

Depending on the evaluation's purpose, the evaluator may legitimately employ a range of methods. Preferred methods are the case study, expressive objectives, purposive sampling, observation, adversary reports, storytelling to convey complexity, sociodrama, and narrative reports. Responsive/client-centered evaluators are charged to check for the existence of stable and consistent findings by employing redundancy in their data-collecting activities and replicating their case studies (Stake, 1995). They are not expected to act as a program's sole or final judges but should collect, process, and report the opinions and judgments of the full range of the program's stakeholders as well as those of pertinent experts. In the end, the evaluator makes a comprehensive statement of what the program is observed to be and references the satisfaction and dissatisfaction that appropriately selected people have toward the program. Overall, the responsive evaluator uses whatever information sources and techniques seem relevant for portraying the program's complexities and multiple realities and communicates the complexity even if the result instills doubt and makes decisions more difficult.

Stake (1967, 1975, 1983, 1999, 2003, 2004) is the pioneer of the responsive type of study, and his approach has been supported and developed by Denny (1978), Greene and Abma (2001), MacDonald (1975), Parlett and Hamilton (1972), Rippey (1973), and Smith and Pohland (1974). Guba's development of constructivist evaluation (1978) was heavily influenced by Stake's writings on responsive evaluation. Stake has expressed skepticism about scientific inquiry as a dependable guide to developing generalizations about human services and pessimism about the potential benefits of formal program evaluations.

The main condition for applying the client-centered approach is a receptive client group and a confident, competent, responsive evaluator. The client must be willing to endorse a quite open, flexible evaluation plan as opposed to a well-developed, detailed, preordinate plan; should expect budgetary requirements to unfold as the study develops; and should be receptive to equitable participation by a representative group of stakeholders. The client must find qualitative methods acceptable and usually be willing to forgo anything like a tightly controlled experimental study, although a controlled field experiment might be employed in exceptional cases. Clients and other involved stakeholders need tolerance, even appreciation for ambiguity, and should hold out only modest hopes of obtaining definitive answers to evaluation questions. Clients must also be receptive to ambiguous findings, multiple interpretations, the employment of competing value perspectives, and the heavy involvement of stakeholders in interpreting and using findings. In this regard, clients should expect to assume responsibility for interpreting and applying findings. Finally, clients must be sufficiently patient to allow the program evaluation to unfold and find its direction based on ongoing interactions between the evaluator and the stakeholders.

A major strength of the responsive/client-centered approach is that it involves action research in which people who are funding, implementing, and using programs are helped to conduct their own evaluations and use the findings to improve their understanding, decisions, and actions. The evaluations look deeply into the stakeholders' main interests and search broadly for relevant information. In general, the evaluator and client study the program's mission and rationale, history, environment, transactions and operations, problems, and outcomes. They make effective use of qualitative methods and triangulate findings from different sources. The approach stresses the importance of searching widely for unintended as well as intended outcomes. It also gives credence to the meaningful participation in the evaluation by the full range of interested stakeholders. Judgments and other inputs from all such persons are respected and incorporated in the evaluations. The approach also provides for effective communication and assessment of findings through a range of techniques, such as focus groups, sociodramas, debates, and stories.

A major weakness is the approach's vulnerability regarding external credibility, since people in the local setting, in effect, have considerable control over the evaluation of their work. Similarly, evaluators working so closely with stakeholders may lose their independent perspectives. As the evaluators advocate for those with little influence, those with authority and responsibility for the subject program may perceive the evaluators as lacking impartiality and evenhandedness. The approach is not amenable to reporting clear findings in time to meet decision or accountability deadlines. Moreover, rather than bringing closure, the approach's adversarial aspects and divergent qualities may generate confusion and contentious relations among stakeholders. Sometimes this cascading, evolving approach may bog down in an unproductive quest for multiple inputs and interpretations. Also, the divergent, open-ended nature of the approach makes for difficulties in budgeting and contracting the evaluation work.

Approach 24: Constructivist Evaluation

Since the mid-1960s, Egon Guba has been developing the tenets of constructivist evaluation under various labels, including experimental design, naturalistic evaluation, effective evaluation, fourth generation evaluation, and constructivist evaluation. Whatever the label, Guba has grounded all renditions in a rejection of the principles and procedures of randomized, controlled, variable-manipulating experimental design. Since the 1970s, when his wife, Yvonna Lincoln, joined him in developing this approach, they regularly have referred to the approach as fourth generation evaluation. With this label they intended to convey the notion that their approach incorporates and goes beyond three earlier generations of evaluation models, which they characterized as focusing respectively on objectives, description, and judgment. To these Guba, and Lincoln added intensive participation of stakeholders in the design, conduct, reporting, and application of evaluations and also the constructions that different stakeholders would bring to bear in judging a program. We see constructivism as the core concept in Guba and Lincoln's approach and thus are referring to their approach in this chapter as constructivist evaluation.

The constructivist approach to program evaluation is heavily philosophical, service oriented, and paradigm driven. The approach rejects the tenets of logical positivism and instead embraces phenomenology and critical theory. Constructivist evaluation rejects the existence of any ultimate reality and employs a subjectivist epistemology. It sees knowledge gained as one or more social-psychological constructions, uncertifiable, often multiple, and constantly problematic and changing. According to Lincoln (2005), the constructions are the "mental meanings, values, beliefs, and sense-making structures in which humans engage to make meaning from events, contexts, activities, and situations in their lives" (p. 162). Obtained constructions are to be treated holistically and analytically in order to reveal and study the underlying values, beliefs, and attitudes. Constructivist evaluation places the evaluators and program stakeholders at the center of the inquiry process, employing all of them as the evaluation's "human instruments." Their focal activities are collecting, analyzing, and evaluating constructions.

Lincoln and Guba proposed constructivist evaluation as a solution to problems they saw in evaluations based on classical experimental design. These problems include nonuse of findings, objectification of human beings, the lack of meaningful involvement of stakeholders in evaluations, and the nonuse of evaluative processes by which people make sense of their worlds and those of others.

Constructivist evaluation insists that evaluators be totally ethical in respecting and advocating for all the participants in an evaluation, especially the disenfranchised. In shaping evaluation questions, evaluators are expected to help stakeholders take into account reasonably stable characteristics of stakeholders, including gender, race, ethnicity, handicaps, socioeconomic status, cultural background, language, and sexual orientation. Values are held to be central in this evaluation approach, and strenuous measures are required both to take account of the full range of stakeholder values and uncover relevant values that may not be apparent to stakeholders. Evaluators are authorized, even expected, to maneuver the evaluation to emancipate and empower involved or affected disenfranchised people in such spheres as civic involvement and democratic participation. Evaluators do this by raising stakeholders' consciousness so that they are energized, informed, and assisted in transforming their world. Through epistemological exchanges, evaluators and stakeholders are expected to arrive at positions that are richly and deeply informed, factual, sophisticated, and nuanced.

The evaluator must respect participants' free will in all aspects of the inquiry and should empower them to help shape and control the evaluation activities in their preferred ways. The evaluation must take account of the varying and often conflicting values of stakeholders. The approach requires explicit dialogue on values, particularly those in conflict. The inquiry process must also be consistent with effective ways of changing and improving society. Thus, stakeholders must play a key role in determining the evaluation questions, variables, and interpretive criteria. Evaluative foci include stakeholders' critical claims, concerns, and issues, as well as the program's objectives. Throughout the study, the evaluator regularly informs and consults stakeholders in all aspects of the study. As findings emerge, they are shared widely with stakeholders. Constructivist evaluators need expertise in mediation, small and large group facilitation, and management.

The approach rescinds any special privilege of scientific evaluators to work in secret and control or manipulate human subjects. In guiding the program evaluation, the evaluator balances verification with a quest for discovery, balances rigor with relevance, and balances the use of quantitative and qualitative methods. The evaluator also provides rich and deep description in preference to precise measurements and statistics. He or she employs a relativist perspective to obtain and analyze findings, stressing locality and specificity over generalizability. The approach requires mixed methods, both quantitative and qualitative. The evaluator posits that there can be no ultimately correct conclusions. He or she exalts openness and the continuing search for more informed and illuminating constructions.

Lincoln and Guba present a set of criteria for judging constructivist evaluations that are analogous to scientific standards of rigor, validity, and value. The constructivist versions are labeled credibility or trustworthiness, transferability beyond the studied context, dependability or reliability, and confirmability of data and data sources. One thrust of these criteria is that the evaluation's trustworthiness and utility be judged from the perspectives of the users of evaluation reports. Also, data are to be traced to their source and verified and conclusions are to be assessed for logic, plausibility, and reasonableness.

In addition to these fairly standard criteria of sound inquiry, Lincoln and Guba present others that are intrinsic to constructivist evaluation. Called authenticity criteria, their labels are *balance/fairness in the evaluation report* (for example, Do evaluation reports present program strengths as well as weaknesses and fairly represent the views of all stakeholders?), *ontological authenticity* (Did the evaluation help stakeholders understand their unconscious or unstated beliefs and values?), *educative authenticity* (Did the evaluation help stakeholders understand each other's perspectives and value positions?), *catalytic authenticity* (Did the evaluation prompt stakeholders to take actions?), and *tactical authenticity* (Did the evaluation effectively advocate for all stakeholders, including especially those with low levels of skill and influence?).

Constructivist evaluation is as much recognizable for what it rejects as for what it proposes. In general, it strongly opposes positivism as a basis for evaluation, with its realist ontology, objectivist epistemology, and experimental method. It rejects any absolutist search for correct answers. It directly opposes the notion of value-free evaluation and attendant efforts to expunge human bias. It rejects positivism's deterministic and reductionist structure and its belief in the possibility of fully explaining studied programs. It also rejects requirements for impartiality that would preclude evaluators from advocating for stakeholders who are seriously disadvantaged and have little or no influence.

Advance organizers of the constructivist approach are basically the philosophical constraints placed on the study, as noted above, including the requirement of collaborative, unfolding inquiry. The main purpose of the approach is to determine and make sense of the variety of constructions that exist or emerge among stakeholders. Inquiry is kept open to ongoing communication and to the gathering, analysis, and synthesis of further constructions. One construction is not considered "truer" than others, but some may be judged as more informed and sophisticated than others. All evaluation conclusions are viewed as indeterminate, with the continuing possibility of finding better answers. All constructions are also context dependent. In this respect, the evaluator defines boundaries on what is being investigated.

The questions addressed in constructivist studies cannot be determined independently of participants' interactions. Evaluator and stakeholders together identify the questions to be addressed. Questions emerge in the process of formulating and discussing the evaluation's purpose, the program's rationale, planning the schedule of discussions, and obtaining various initial persons' views of the program to be evaluated. The questions develop further over the course of the approach's hermeneutic and dialectic processes. Questions may or may not cover the full range of issues involved in assessing something's merit and worth. The set of questions to be studied is never considered fixed.

The constructivist methodology is first divergent, then convergent. Through the use of hermeneutics, the evaluator collects and describes alternative individual constructions on an evaluation question or issue, ensuring that each depiction meets with the respondent's approval. Communication channels are kept open throughout the inquiry, and all respondents are encouraged and facilitated to make their inputs and are kept apprised of all aspects of the study. The evaluator then moves to a dialectical process aimed at achieving as much consensus as possible among different constructions. Respondents are provided with opportunities to review the full range of constructions along with other relevant information. The evaluator engages the respondents in a process of studying and contrasting existing constructions, considering relevant contextual and other information, reasoning out the differences among the constructions, and moving as far as they can toward a consensus. The constructivist evaluation is, in a sense, never-ending. There is always more to learn, and finding ultimately correct answers is considered impossible.

Guba and Lincoln (Guba, 1978; Guba & Lincoln, 1981, 1989; Lincoln & Guba, 1985, 2004; Lincoln, 2003, 2005) are pioneers in applying the constructivist approach to program evaluation. Bhola (1998), a disciple of Guba, has extensive experience in applying the constructivist approach to evaluating programs in Africa. In agreement with Guba, he stresses that evaluations are always a function not only of the evaluator's approach and interactions with stakeholders, but also of his or her personal history and outlook. Schwandt (1984, 1989), another disciple of Guba, has written extensively about the philosophical underpinnings of constructivist evaluation. Fetterman's empowerment evaluation approach (2004, 2005) is closely aligned with constructivist evaluation, since it seeks to engage and serve all stakeholders, especially those with little influence. However, there is a key difference between the constructivist and empowerment evaluation approaches. While the constructivist evaluator retains control of the evaluation and works with stakeholders to develop a consensus, the empowerment evaluator gives away authority for the evaluation to stakeholders, while serving in a technical assistance role. This important distinction is a main reason we classified empowerment evaluation as pseudoevaluation.

The constructivist approach can be applied usefully when evaluator, client, and stakeholders in a program fully agree that the approach is appropriate and that they will cooperate. They should reach agreement based on an understanding of what the approach can and cannot deliver. They need to accept that questions and issues to be studied will unfold throughout the process. They also should be willing to receive ambiguous, possibly contradictory findings, reflecting stakeholders' diverse perspectives. They should know that the shelf life of the findings is likely to be short (not unlike any other evaluation approach, but clearly acknowledged in the constructivist approach). They also need to value qualitative information that largely reflects the variety of stakeholders' perspectives and judgments. However, they should not expect to receive definitive pre-post measures of outcomes or statistical conclusions about causes and effects. While these persons can hope for achieving a consensus in the findings, they should agree that such a consensus might not emerge and that in any case, such a consensus would not necessarily generalize to other settings or time periods.

This approach has a number of advantages. It is exemplary in fully disclosing the whole evaluation process and its findings. It is consistent with the principle of effective change that people are more likely to value and use an evaluation or any other change process if they are consulted and involved in its development. The approach also seeks to directly involve the full range of stakeholders who might be harmed or helped by the evaluation as important, empowered partners in the evaluation enterprise. It is said to be educative for all the participants, whether or not a consensus is reached. It also lowers expectations for what clients can learn about causes and effects. While it does not promise final answers, it moves from a divergent stage, in which it searches widely for insights and judgments, to a convergent stage, in which some unified answers are sought. In addition, it uses participants as instruments in the evaluation, thus taking advantage of their relevant experiences, knowledge, and value perspectives; this greatly reduces the burden of developing, field-testing, and validating information collection instruments before using them. The approach makes effective use of qualitative methods and triangulates findings from different sources.

The approach, however, is limited in its applicability and has some disadvantages. Its openness and exploratory and participatory nature make it difficult to plan and budget for the required extensive and time-consuming process. Because of the need for full involvement and ongoing interaction through both the divergent and convergent stages, it is often difficult to produce the timely reports that funding organizations and decision makers demand. Furthermore, if the approach is to work well, it requires the attention and responsible participation of a wide range of stakeholders. The approach seems to be unrealistically utopian in this regard: widespread, grassroots interest and participation are often hard to obtain and especially to sustain throughout a program evaluation. The situation can be exacerbated by a continuing turnover of stakeholders. While the process emphasizes and promises openness and full disclosure, some participants do not want to tell their private thoughts and judgments to the world. Moreover, stakeholders sometimes are poorly informed about the issues being addressed in an evaluation and thus are poor data sources. While all stakeholders are considered key data collection instruments in constructivist evaluations, it is impractical to calibrate them to ensure they will carefully formulate and report valid observations and judgments. It can be unrealistic to expect that the evaluator can and will take the needed time to inform and then meaningfully involve those who begin as basically ignorant of the program being assessed. Furthermore, constructivist evaluations can be greatly burdened by itinerant evaluation stakeholders who come and go, reopen questions previously addressed, and question consensus previously reached. There is the further issue that some evaluation clients do not take kindly to evaluators who are prone to report competing, perspectivist answers and not take a stand regarding a program's merit and worth. Many clients are not attuned to the constructivist philosophy, and they may value reports that mainly include hard data on outcomes, assessments of statistical significance, and calibrated judgments. They may expect reports to be based on relatively independent perspectives that are free of program participants' conflicts of interest. Since the constructivist approach is a countermeasure to assigning responsibility for successes and failures in a program to certain individuals or groups, many policy boards, administrators, and financial sponsors might see this rejection of accountability as unworkable and unacceptable. It is easy to say that all persons in a program should share the glory or the disgrace; but try to tell this to an exceptionally hard-working and effective teacher in a school program where virtually no one else tries or succeeds.

Approach 25: Deliberative Democratic Evaluation

Perhaps the newest entry in the program evaluation models enterprise is the deliberative democratic approach advanced by House and Howe (2000a, 2000b, 2003) and House (2004, 2005). The approach functions within an explicit democratic framework and charges evaluators to uphold democratic principles in reaching defensible conclusions. It envisions program evaluation as a principled, influential societal institution, contributing to democratization through the issuing of reliable and valid claims.

The advance organizers of deliberative democratic evaluation are seen in its three main dimensions: democratic participation, dialogue to examine and authenticate stakeholders' inputs, and deliberation to arrive at a defensible assessment of a program's merit and worth. House and Howe consider all three dimensions essential in all aspects of a sound program evaluation.

In the democratic dimension, the approach proactively identifies and arranges for the equitable participation of all interested stakeholders throughout the course of the evaluation. Equity is stressed, and power imbalances in which the message of powerful parties would dominate the evaluation message are not tolerated. In the dialogic dimension, the evaluator engages stakeholders and other audiences to assist in compiling preliminary findings. Subsequently, the collaborators seriously discuss and debate the draft findings to ensure that no participant's views are misrepresented. In the culminating deliberative stage, the evaluator honestly considers and discusses with others all inputs obtained but then renders what he or she considers a fully defensible assessment of the program's merit and worth. All interested stakeholders are given voice in the evaluation, and the evaluator acknowledges their views in the final report but may express disagreement with some of them in exercising professional discretion. The deliberative dimension sees the evaluator reaching a reasoned conclusion by reviewing all inputs; debating them with stakeholders and others; reflecting deeply on all the inputs; and then reaching a defensible, well-justified conclusion.

The purpose of the approach is to employ democratic participation in the process of arriving at a defensible assessment of a program. The evaluator determines the evaluation questions to be addressed, but does so through dialogue and deliberation with engaged stakeholders. Presumably, the bottom-line questions concern judgments about the program's merit and its worth to stakeholders.

Methods employed may include discussions with stakeholders, surveys, and debates. Inclusion, dialogue, and deliberation are considered relevant at all stages of an evaluation: inception, design, implementation, analysis, synthesis, write-up, presentation, and discussion. House and Howe present the following ten questions for assessing the adequacy of a democratic deliberative evaluation: Whose interests are represented? Are major stakeholders represented? Are any excluded? Are there serious power imbalances? Are there procedures to control imbalances? How do people participate in the evaluation? How authentic is their participation? How involved is their interaction? Is there reflective deliberation? How considered and extended is the deliberation?

Ernest House originated this approach. He and Kenneth Howe say that many evaluators already implement their proposed principles and point to a monograph by Karlsson (1998) to illustrate their approach. They also refer to a number of authors who have proposed practices that at least in part are compatible with the deliberative democratic approach.

The approach is applicable when a client agrees to fund an evaluation that requires democratic participation of at least a representative group of stakeholders. Thus, the funding agent must be willing to give up sufficient power to allow inputs from a wide range of stakeholders, early disclosure of preliminary findings to all interested parties, and opportunities for the stakeholders to play an influential role in reaching the final conclusions. A representative group of stakeholders must be willing to engage in open and meaningful dialogue and deliberation at all stages of the study.

The approach has many advantages. It is a direct attempt to make evaluations just. It strives for democratic participation of stakeholders at all stages of the evaluation. It seeks to incorporate the views of all interested parties, including insiders and outsiders, disenfranchised persons and groups, as well as those who control the purse strings. Meaningful democratic involvement should direct the evaluation to the issues that people care about and make them inclined to respect and use the evaluation findings. The approach employs dialogue to examine and authenticate stakeholders' inputs. A key advantage over some other advocacy approaches is that the deliberative democratic evaluator expressly reserves the right to rule out inputs that are considered incorrect or unethical. The evaluator is open to all stakeholders' views, carefully considers them, but then renders as defensible a professional judgment of the program as possible. He or she does not leave the responsibility for reaching a defensible final assessment to a majority vote of stakeholders—some of whom are sure to have conflicts of interest and be uninformed or misinformed. In rendering a final judgment, the evaluator ensures closure.

As House and Howe have acknowledged, the deliberative democratic approach is, pending further development and testing, unrealistic and often cannot be fully applied. The approach—in offering and expecting full democratic participation in order to make an evaluation work—reminds us of a colleague who used to despair of ever changing or improving higher education. He would say that changing any aspect of a university would require getting every professor to withhold her or his veto. In view of the ambitious demands of the deliberative democratic approach, House and Howe have proposed it as an ideal to be kept in mind, although evaluators will seldom, if ever, be able to achieve it.

Summary

With the deliberative democratic entry, we close this chapter on social agenda and advocacy evaluation approaches. Although the three approaches summarized here are not exhaustive of these approaches, we think they represent the main themes.

Overall, they provide valuable direction for evaluators and stakeholder groups that seek to meaningfully engage stakeholders in program evaluations while maintaining integrity in the evaluation work.

Space limitations precluded our inclusion of such other social agenda and advocacy entries as participatory evaluation (King, 2005), appreciative inquiry (Preskill, 2005), critical theory evaluation (MacNeil, 2005), feminist evaluation (Seigart, 2005), and illuminative evaluation (Hamilton, 2005). We excluded consideration of the participatory evaluation approach because its main tenet of stakeholder involvement is represented in all three approaches considered in this chapter, as well as a wide range of other evaluation approaches. We also excluded consideration of the empowerment evaluation approach (Fetterman, 2005). Although it clearly is a social agenda and advocacy approach, we think it crosses the line into the pseudoevaluation category discussed in Chapter Six. This is so because empowerment evaluators are advised to give away authority for an evaluation to the client group. This abrogation of evaluation authority and responsibility subjects the study to the possibility that stakeholders will bias or bury findings, release slanted or watered-down reports, or erroneously claim that the evaluation was conducted by an independent evaluator, for example. (See Scriven, 2005, for a detailed account of such problems with empowerment evaluation.)

Review Questions

1. What is the core mission of social agenda and advocacy evaluation approaches to evaluation?
2. What is meant by the claim that social agenda and advocacy approaches to evaluation have an affirmative action orientation?
3. What are two particular threats to the validity of social agenda and advocacy evaluations, and what are the sources of these potential shortcomings?
4. What are two main virtues of social agenda and advocacy evaluation approaches?
5. Why is it essential to subject social agenda and advocacy approaches to independent metaevaluations?
6. What are the similarities and differences among the three social agenda and advocacy approaches on whether an evaluator should reach a bottom-line judgment of a program's value?
7. What reasons are given in this chapter for referring to responsive evaluation as client-centered evaluation?
8. What are two sharp disagreements between Scriven's consumer-oriented evaluation approach and Stake's responsive/client-centered evaluation approach?
9. Constructivist evaluation rejects the principles of any aspect of experimental design. State what Guba and Lincoln emphasize in their approach in place of

randomization and controls of treatments, stated objectives, their exploration, and definitive judgments.

Group Exercises

Exercise 1. Suppose that your group has been approached by a city manager to evaluate a special parks and recreation program. Assume that the city manager knows about responsive evaluation and desires that the evaluation follow this approach. He has asked you to provide orientation to a cross section of community members, including members of the city council. The meeting's purposes are to orient the interested community members to the tenets of responsive evaluation and solicit their support and participation. What main points would you present? Particularly, how would you advance and defend the notion that the evaluation will be pluralistic and relativistic? Also, how would you define the roles of children, parents, program staff, city government officials, and other stakeholders in planning, conducting, reporting, and using findings from this evaluation? How would you explain the specific responsibilities that the various stakeholders will be expected to fulfill?

Exercise 2. Following your presentation in response to exercise 1, suppose that the community's mayor rejects or at least ignores what she has heard and boldly states her preferences for the projected evaluation as follows:

- The evaluators should deliver their report only to the city council.
- The reported conclusions should be grounded in objective information shown to be reliable and valid.
- The evaluation should assess the extent to which the subject program is more effective than similar programs.
- The report should present a clear conclusion on the program's success and its superiority to one or more similar programs.
- The criteria for program success are the program's stated objectives.
- The report should contain clear recommendations for continuing or terminating the program.
- The overall evaluation should be based on a fixed price contract and confined to delivering a single final report within six months.

From the perspective of supporting the city manager's desire for a responsive evaluation, how would you respond to the mayor's hard line on requiring a very different evaluation approach?

References

Bhola, H. S. (1998). Program evaluation for program renewal: A study of the national literacy program in Namibia (NLPN). *Studies in Educational Evaluation, 24*(4), 303–330.

Denny, T. (1978, November). *Story telling and educational understanding.* Kalamazoo: Evaluation Center, Western Michigan University.

Fetterman, D. M. (2004). Branching out or standing on a limb: Looking to our roots for insight. In M. C. Alkin (Ed.), *Evaluation roots: Tracing theorists' views and influences* (pp. 319–330). Thousand Oaks, CA: Sage.

Fetterman, D. M. (2005). Empowerment evaluation. In S. Mathison (Ed.), *Encyclopedia of evaluation* (pp. 125–129). Thousand Oaks, CA: Sage.

Greene, J. C., & Abma, T. A. (Eds.). (2001, Winter). *Responsive evaluation.* New Directions for Evaluation, no. 92. San Francisco: Jossey-Bass.

Guba, E. G. (1978). *Toward a methodology of naturalistic inquiry in evaluation.* Los Angeles: Center for the Study of Evaluation.

Guba, E. G., & Lincoln, Y. S. (1981). *Effective evaluation.* San Francisco: Jossey-Bass.

Guba, E. G., & Lincoln, Y. S. (1989). *Fourth generation evaluation.* Thousand Oaks, CA: Sage.

Hamilton, D. (2005). Illuminative evaluation. In S. Mathison (Ed.), *Encyclopedia of evaluation* (pp. 191–194). Thousand Oaks, CA: Sage.

House, E. R. (2004). Intellectual history in evaluation. In M. C. Alkin (Ed.), *Evaluation roots: Tracing theorists' views and influences* (pp. 218–224). Thousand Oaks, CA: Sage.

House, E. R. (2005). Deliberative democratic evaluation. In S. Mathison (Ed.), *Encyclopedia of evaluation.* (pp. 104–108). Thousand Oaks, CA: Sage.

House, E. R., & Howe, K. R. (1998). *Deliberative democratic evaluation in practice.* Boulder: University of Colorado.

House, E. R., & Howe, K. R. (2000a). Deliberative democratic evaluation In K. E. Ryan & L. DeStefano (Eds.), *Evaluation as a democratic process* (pp. 3–12). New Directions for Evaluation, 85. San Francisco: Jossey-Bass.

House, E. R., & Howe, K. R. (2000b). Deliberative democratic evaluation in practice. In D. L. Stufflebeam, G. F. Madaus, & T. Kellaghan (Eds.), *Evaluation models.* Norwell, MA: Kluwer.

House, E. R., & Howe, K. R. (2003). Deliberative democratic evaluation. In T. Kellaghan & D. L. Stufflebeam (Eds.), *International handbook of educational evaluation* (pp. 79–102). Norwell, MA: Kluwer.

Karlsson, O. (1998). Socratic dialogue in the Swedish political context. In T. A. Schwandt (Ed.), *Scandinavian perspectives on the evaluator's role in informing social policy* (pp. 21–38). New Directions for Evaluation, no. 77. San Francisco: Jossey-Bass.

King, J. A. (2005). Participatory evaluation. In S. Mathison (Ed.), *Encyclopedia of evaluation* (pp. 291–294). Thousand Oaks, CA: Sage.

Lincoln, Y. S. (2003). Constructivist knowing, participatory ethics and responsive evaluation: A model for the 21st century. In T. Kellaghan & D. L. Stufflebeam (Eds.), *International handbook of educational evaluation* (pp. 69–78). Norwell, MA: Kluwer.

Lincoln, Y. S. (2005). Fourth-generation evaluation. In S. Mathison (Ed.), *Encyclopedia of evaluation* (pp. 161–164). Thousand Oaks, CA: Sage.

Lincoln, Y. S., & Guba, E. G. (1985). *Naturalistic inquiry.* Thousand Oaks, CA: Sage.

Lincoln, Y. S., & Guba, E. G. (2004). The roots of fourth generation evaluation. In M. C. Alkin (Ed.), *Evaluation roots: Tracing theorists' views and influences* (pp. 225–242). Thousand Oaks, CA: Sage.

MacDonald, B. (1975). Evaluation and the control of education. In D. Tawney (Ed.), *Evaluation: The state of the art*. London: Schools Council.

MacNeil, C. (2005). Critical theory evaluation. In S. Mathison (Ed.), *Encyclopedia of evaluation*. (pp. 92–94). Thousand Oaks, CA: Sage.

Parlett, M., & Hamilton, D. (1972). *Evaluation as illumination: A new approach to the study of innovatory programs*. Edinburgh: Centre for Research in the Educational Sciences, University of Edinburgh.

Preskill, H. (2005). Appreciative inquiry. In S. Mathison (Ed.), *Encyclopedia of evaluation* (pp. 18–19). Thousand Oaks, CA: Sage.

Rippey, R. M. (Ed.). (1973). *Studies in transactional evaluation*. Berkeley, CA: McCutchan.

Scriven, M. (2005). Review of D. M. Fetterman & A. Wandersman (Eds.), Evaluation principles in practice. *American Journal of Evaluation, 26*(3), 415–147.

Schwandt, T. A. (1984). *An examination of alternative models for socio-behavioral inquiry*. Unpublished doctoral dissertation, Indiana University.

Schwandt, T. A. (1989). Recapturing moral discourse in evaluation. *Educational Researcher, 18*(8), 11–16.

Seigart, D. (2005). Feminist evaluation. In S. Mathison (Ed.), *Encyclopedia of evaluation* (pp. 154–157). Thousand Oaks, CA: Sage.

Smith, L. M., & Pohland, P. A. (1974). Educational technology and the rural highlands. In L. M. Smith (Ed.), *Four examples: Economic, anthropological, narrative, and portrayal*. Skokie, IL: Rand McNally.

Stake, R. E. (1967). The countenance of educational evaluation. *Teachers College Record, 68*, 523–540.

Stake, R. E. (1975, November). *Program evaluation: Particularly responsive evaluation*. Kalamazoo: Western Michigan University Evaluation Center.

Stake, R. E. (1983). Program evaluation, particularly responsive evaluation. In G. F. Madaus, M. Scriven, & D. L. Stufflebeam (Eds.), *Evaluation models* (pp. 287–310). Norwell, MA: Kluwer.

Stake, R. E. (1995). *The art of case study research*. Thousand Oaks, CA: Sage.

Stake, R. E. (1999). Summary of evaluation of reader focused writing for the veterans benefits administration, *American Journal of Evaluation, 20*(2), 323–343.

Stake, R. E. (2003). Responsive evaluation. In T. Kellaghan & D. L. Stufflebeam (Eds.), *International handbook of educational evaluation*, (pp. 63–68). Norwell, MA: Kluwer.

Stake, R. E. (2004). Stake and responsive evaluation. In M. C. Alkin (Ed.), *Evaluation roots: tracing theorists' views and influences* (pp. 203–217). Thousand Oaks, CA: Sage.

CHAPTER TEN

ECLECTIC EVALUATION APPROACHES

Some evaluation theorists have made no commitment to any particular evaluation philosophy, methodological approach, or social mission. Instead, they have advanced pragmatic approaches that draw from and selectively apply ideas and procedures from a wide range of other evaluation approaches. These eclectic evaluation approaches hold no allegiance to any recognized school of evaluation thought and their adherents, but select such doctrines as they wish from various schools and apply them to the study. Eclectic evaluation theorists derive ideas, style, or taste from a broad and diverse range of sources. Their approaches are designed to accommodate needs and preferences of a wide range of evaluation clients and evaluation assignments, often with the express aim of seeking a program's merit and worth unconstrained by the parameters of a single model or approach. Accordingly, evaluators following eclectic approaches employ whatever philosophical base, conceptual framework, and procedures may be conducive to achieving particular evaluation objectives and fulfilling the desires of particular evaluation clients. Evaluators following an eclectic approach on different occasions may conduct a case study, a randomized experiment, a responsive evaluation, an objectives-based study, a decision-oriented evaluation, a connoisseurship study, or something else. More likely, they will selectively employ elements of several evaluation approaches. The eclectic evaluation approaches are distinguished from pseudoevaluations because the former are committed to satisfying criteria of technical soundness, while the latter are not.

Among the eclectic evaluation approaches discussed in the evaluation literature are John Owen's evaluation forms approach (Owen & Rogers, 1999; Owen, 2004), the cluster evaluation approach employed by the W. K. Kellogg Foundation (Millett, 1995; Russon, 2005; Sanders, 1997), and Michael Patton's utilization-focused evaluation approach (1997, 2003, 2004, 2005).

In his evaluation forms approach, Owen drew from the writings of Alkin (1985) on decision uses of evaluation, Scriven (1980) on the logic of evaluation and values clarification, Weiss (1983) and Guba and Lincoln (1989) on stakeholder involvement, Patton (1997) on utilization of findings, Rossi and Freeman (1993) on tailoring of evaluation methods, and Stufflebeam (1983) for an adaptation of the CIPP Model to provide a general classification of evaluation types.

The W. K. Kellogg Foundation spawned its cluster evaluation approach to effect collaborative study of clusters of its funded projects. This approach employs meetings of project evaluators, application of group process techniques, and use of a variety of data collection and synthesis procedures. The aim of cluster evaluation is to help individual projects collaborate with similar projects to select and use common procedures in order to identify outcomes across the projects. Clearly the foundation was seeking an efficient way to evaluate and learn from clusters of projects within its large portfolio of projects.

The most highly developed and widely used of the eclectic evaluation approaches is Michael Patton's utilization-focused evaluation. It draws from the full range of evaluation concepts and methods and uses whatever is deemed relevant to secure meaningful use of findings in particular evaluations. In this chapter, we offer extended discussion of utilization-focused evaluation as a leading exemplar of eclectic evaluation approaches.

Approach 26: Utilization-Focused Evaluation

The utilization-focused approach is explicitly geared to ensure that program evaluations make an impact (Patton, 1997). It is a process for making choices to guide an evaluation study in collaboration with a targeted group of priority users, selected from a broader set of stakeholders, in order to focus effectively on their intended uses of the evaluation. All aspects of a utilization-focused program evaluation are chosen and applied to help the targeted users obtain and apply evaluation findings to their intended uses and maximize the likelihood that they will. Such studies are judged more for the difference they make in improving programs and influencing decisions and actions than for their elegance or technical excellence. Patton argues that no matter how good an evaluation report is, if it only sits on the shelf gathering dust, it will not contribute positively to program improvement and accountability.

In deciding where to place Patton's evaluation approach within the category system used in this book, it became clear that his approach does not fit exclusively in the questions and methods category, the improvement and accountability category, or the social agenda and advocacy category. At first glance, the approach seems to fit quite well in the social agenda and advocacy category. It requires democratic participation of a representative group of stakeholders whom it empowers to determine the evaluation questions and information needs. In this regard, the approach engages the audience to set the agenda for the evaluation to increase the likelihood that the findings will be used. However, utilization-focused evaluations do not necessarily advocate any particular social agenda, such as affirmative action to right injustices and better serve the poor. Although the approach is in agreement with the improvement- and accountability-oriented approaches in guiding decisions, promoting impacts, and invoking the Joint Committee (1994) *Program Evaluation Standards,* it does not quite fit there. It does not, for example, require assessments of merit and worth. In fact, Patton essentially has said that his approach is pragmatic and ubiquitous. In the interest of getting findings used, he will draw on any legitimate approach to evaluation, leaving out any parts that might impede the audience's intended use. For these reasons, we place utilization-focused evaluation in the eclectic category and see it as the prime example of such evaluation approaches.

The advance organizers of utilization-focused program evaluations are, in the abstract, the possible users and uses to be served. Working from this initial conception, the evaluator moves as directly as possible to identify in concrete terms the actual users to be served. Through careful and thorough analysis of stakeholders, the evaluator identifies the multiple and varied perspectives and interests that should be represented in the study. He or she then selects a group that is willing to pay the price of substantial involvement and represents the program's stakeholders. The evaluator then engages this client group to clarify why they need the evaluation, how they intend to apply its findings, how they think it should be conducted, and what types of reports (for example, oral, printed) should be provided. He or she facilitates users' choices by supplying a menu of possible uses, information, and reports for the evaluation. This is done not to supply the choices, but to help the client group thoughtfully focus and shape the study.

The main possible uses of evaluation findings contemplated in this approach are assessment of merit and worth, improvement, and generation of knowledge. The approach also values the evaluation process itself, seeing it as helpful in enhancing shared understandings among stakeholders, bringing support to a program, promoting participation in it, and developing and strengthening organizational capacity. According to Patton, when the evaluation process is sound and functional, a printed final report may not be needed.

In deliberating with intended users, the evaluator emphasizes that the program evaluation's purpose must be to give them the information they need to fulfill their objectives. Such objectives may include socially valuable aims such as combating problems of illiteracy, crime, hunger, homelessness, unemployment, child abuse, spouse or partner abuse, substance abuse, illness, alienation, discrimination, malnourishment, pollution, and bureaucratic waste. However, it is the targeted users who determine the program to be evaluated, what information is required, how and when it must be reported, and how it will be used. Patton explicitly has not sold his approach as one aimed particularly at righting social wrongs, since he leaves evaluation objectives and outcomes to the client and users.

In this approach, the evaluator is no iconoclast, but rather the intended users' technical assistant. Among other roles, he or she is a facilitator of stakeholders' decision making. The process of identifying and aiding relevant decision makers and those who will use information garnered from the evaluation is basic to utilization-focused evaluation. It is very much a participant-oriented approach. Patton states, however, that the evaluation should meet the full range of professional standards for program evaluations, not just utility. It is hard for us to see how this aim is to be achieved, since the evaluator gives so much authority to users of the evaluation. His response is that the evaluator must be an effective negotiator, standing on principles of sound evaluation, but working hard to gear a defensible program evaluation to the targeted users' evolving needs. The utilization-focused evaluation is considered situational and dynamic. Depending on the circumstances, the evaluator may play any of a variety of roles: trainer, planner, negotiator facilitator, measurement expert, internal colleague, external expert, analyst, spokesperson, or mediator.

The evaluator works with the targeted users to determine the evaluation questions. Such questions are to be stipulated locally, may address any of a wide range of concerns, and probably will change over time. Example foci are processes, outcomes, impacts, costs, and cost benefits. The chosen questions are kept in the forefront and provide the basis for information collection and reporting plans and activities, so long as users continue to value and pay attention to the questions. Often, however, the evaluator and client group will adapt, change, or refine the questions as the evaluation unfolds.

All evaluation methods are fair game in a utilization-focused program evaluation. The evaluator will employ whatever methods are relevant creatively (for example, quantitative and qualitative, formative and summative, naturalistic and experimental). As much as possible, the utilization-focused evaluator puts the client group in the driver's seat in determining evaluation methods to ensure that the evaluator focuses on their most important questions; collects the appropriate information; applies the relevant values; answers the key action-oriented questions; uses techniques the users respect; reports the information in a form and at a time to maximize use; convinces stakeholders of the evaluation's integrity and accuracy; and facilitates the users' study, application, and—as appropriate—dissemination of findings. The bases for interpreting evaluation findings are the users' values, and the evaluator will engage in values clarification to ensure that evaluative information and interpretations serve users' purposes. Users are actively involved in interpreting findings. Throughout the evaluation process, the evaluator balances the concern for utility with provisions for validity and cost-effectiveness.

In general, the method of utilization-focused program evaluation is labeled active-reactive-adaptive and situationally responsive, emphasizing that the methodology evolves in response to ongoing deliberations between evaluator and client group and in consideration of contextual dynamics. Patton (1997) says that "evaluators are active in presenting to intended users their own best judgments about appropriate evaluation focus and methods; they are reactive in listening attentively and respectfully to others' concerns; and they are adaptive in finding ways to design evaluations that incorporate diverse interests . . . while meeting high standards of professional practice" (p. 383). Patton (1980, 1982, 1994, 1997, 2004, 2005) is the leading proponent of utilization-based evaluation. Other advocates of the approach are Alkin (1995), Cronbach and Associates (1980), Davis and Salasin (1975), and the Joint Committee on Standards for Educational Evaluation (1994).

As defined by Patton, the approach has virtually universal applicability. It is situational and can be tailored to meet any program evaluation assignment. It carries with it the integrity of sound evaluation principles as defined in the Joint Committee's *Program Evaluation Standards* (1994). Within these general constraints, the evaluator negotiates all aspects of the evaluation to serve specific individuals who need to have a program evaluation performed and intend to make concrete use of the findings. The evaluator selects from the entire range of evaluation techniques those that best suit the particular evaluation. And the evaluator plays any of a wide range of evaluation and improvement-related roles that fit the local needs. The approach requires a substantial outlay of time and resources by all participants, for conducting both the evaluation and the needed follow-through. Nonetheless, the methodological pluralism underlying the approach is aimed directly at reflecting the multiple realities that constitute programs.

The approach is geared to maximizing evaluation impacts. It fits well with a key principle of change: individuals are more likely to understand, value, and use the findings of an evaluation if they were meaningfully involved in the enterprise. As Patton (1997) says, "By actively involving primary intended users, the evaluator is training users in use, preparing the groundwork for use, and reinforcing the intended utility of the evaluation" (p. 22). The approach engages stakeholders to determine the evaluation's purposes and procedures and uses their involvement to promote the use of findings. It takes a more realistic approach to stakeholder involvement than some other evaluation approaches. Rather than trying to reach and work with all stakeholders, Patton's approach works with a select, representative group of users. The approach emphasizes values clarification and attends closely to contextual dynamics. It may selectively use any and all relevant evaluation procedures, whether based on quantitative or qualitative procedures (or both), and triangulates findings from different sources. One significant value of the approach is that a formative rather than a summative emphasis can be initiated, which can shut the gate on program development. Finally, this sophisticated and socially acceptable approach stresses the need to meet all relevant standards for evaluations.

Patton sees the main limitation of the approach as the turnover of involved users. Replacement users may require that the program evaluation be renegotiated, and this may be necessary to sustain or renew the prospects for evaluation impacts. But it can also derail or greatly delay the process. Furthermore, it is easy to say that this approach should meet all of the Joint Committee (1994) standards but hard to see how this can be accomplished with any consistency. The approach seems to be vulnerable to corruption by user groups, since they are given much control over what will be looked at, the questions addressed, the methods employed, and the information to be collected. Moreover, it is often difficult to define and limit the user groups, the reasons for the evaluation, and the audiences for the report (if one eventuates). Stakeholders with conflicts of interest may influence the evaluation inappropriately. For example, they may limit the evaluation to a subset of questions that is too narrow. It may be almost impossible to get a representative users' group to agree on and follow through on a sufficient commitment of time and safeguards to ensure an ethical, valid process of data collection, reporting, and use. Moreover, effective implementation of this approach requires a highly competent, confident evaluator who can approach any situation flexibly without compromising basic professional standards. Strong skills of negotiation are essential, and the evaluator must possess expertise in the full range of quantitative and qualitative evaluation methods, strong communication and political skills, and working knowledge of all applicable standards for evaluations. Unfortunately, not many evaluators are sufficiently trained and experienced to meet these demanding requirements.

Summary

The utilization-focused approach to evaluation concludes our discussion of eclectic evaluation approaches. We have summarized in some detail Patton's excellent contribution in this area. Interested readers may also desire to pursue the referenced readings on Owen's evaluation forms approach (2004) and the W. K. Kellogg approach (Millett, 1995, 1996; Council on Foundations, 1993).

Review Questions

1. What features of Michael Patton's utilization-focused evaluation approach led us to classify the approach as eclectic?
2. Why did we not classify utilization-focused evaluation in (a) the questions and methods category and (b) the social agenda and advocacy category?
3. Why do you think we classified Owen's evaluation forms approach as eclectic, and why do you think we also classified cluster evaluation as an eclectic approach?
4. How does Patton conceive of the users to be served by a utilization-focused evaluation?
5. What are the advance organizers of the utilization-focused approach to evaluation?
6. What are the main elements of the evaluator's role in a utilization-focused evaluation?
7. To what extent does Patton require that a utilization-focused evaluation serve socially valuable aims, such as combating social problems?
8. What is Patton's position regarding the need for utilization-focused evaluations to fulfill the requirements of the Joint Committee *Program Evaluation Standards,* and what do you think Patton would cite as the most important standard or criterion for judging a utilization-focused evaluation?
9. What does Patton mean by the active-reactive-adaptive method of utilization-focused evaluation?
10. What do we cite as main limitations of utilization-focused evaluation?

Group Exercises

You are invited to view the discussion questions that follow in two ways: first, as a review of the available range of credible evaluation models and, second, as placing a sharp focus on eclectic evaluation, particularly Patton's utilization-focused evaluation approach. Prepare for the first objective by looking back at Chapters Seven to Nine (questions- and methods-oriented evaluation models, improvement- and accountability-oriented evaluation approaches, and social agenda and advocacy models) and for the second by reexamining this chapter (eclectic evaluation models).

Exercise 1. The managing director of a chain of sporting goods stores extending throughout Australia has faced a stormy special meeting of shareholders as an outcome of a dismal forecast of annual profits for the ensuring three years. Among other demands from the meeting, he agreed that a "completed survey and assessment [sic]" of the organization's functions will occur forthwith and that a report will be furnished first to the board and then to another special meeting of shareholders within nine months. The meeting also made it abundantly clear that the managing director's job was on the line if the assessment findings indicated that he had been remiss in his leadership, decision making, and vision for the organization.

The managing director pondered his options. He could view the exercise simply from a financial perspective, enlisting the aid of the organization's firm of accountants, supported by the organization's auditors. But he knew that this would inevitably lead to drastic cost cutting, such as further reduction in staff (particularly at the middle management level), a situation difficult to contemplate since a similar ploy three months earlier had led to falling staff morale at all stores. Or he could try to examine the real causes of sales reduction, however revelatory and painful this might be. While economic factors clearly would emerge, he knew that matters like poor and inadequate advertising, diminishing staff morale, suspect staff employment methods and training, and business and associated program planning and execution were organizational weaknesses. These, he knew, would emerge from any examination of the organization.

He wisely decided to employ a reputable group of evaluators who could call on the assistance of financial experts as required.

Imagine that you are this evaluation group. Your initial discussions with the managing director indicate that methodological pluralism will be essential to produce a sound and ethical report with its accompanying recommendations.

As a group, it is your task to discuss ways and means of convincing the managing director of the importance of pursuing the study based on an eclectic approach, such is the wide range of concerns that exist.

Exercise 2. As this chapter has shown, Patton emphasizes the practical implications of alternative (and multiple) evaluation approaches. The user must be given useful information and must be collaboratively involved in program assessment with the evaluator acting as a guide and mentor.

Each member of your group identifies a program evaluation study arising from personal experience or from published material. Each member outlines the purpose of the evaluation and the evaluation method, or methods, used. Then an opinion is given on whether the methodology is appropriate to the study, covering aspects such as these:

- Has the evaluation made a discernible difference, either real or potential, to the program?
- To what extent were stakeholders closely involved in the study and, in particular, relevant decision making?
- Could the approach be used in other program evaluation, or is it site specific?
- Where the approach is eclectic, would a single methodological approach be as effective in defining, examining, and reporting for decision making?

Exercise 3. Discuss to what extent Patton limits the procedures that are appropriate for use in utilization-focused evaluations and the reasons he gives for his rationale.

Exercise 4. Considering that utilization-focused evaluation gives the client group control of the selection of evaluation questions plus significant influence in choosing methods and interpreting findings, how can the evaluator ensure that the evaluation meets the following Joint Committee standards: Utility Standard 3—Information Scope and Selection, Utility Standard 7—Evaluation Impact, Propriety Standard 7—Conflict of Interest, Accuracy Standard 5—Valid Information, and Accuracy Standard 11—Impartial Reporting?

References

Alkin, M. C. (1985). *A guide for evaluation decision makers.* Thousand Oaks, CA: Sage.

Alkin, M. C. (1995, November). *Lessons learned about evaluation use.* Panel presentation at the International Evaluation Conference, American Evaluation Association. Vancouver, British Columbia.

Council on Foundations. (1993). *Evaluation for foundations: Concepts, cases, guidelines, and resources.* San Francisco: Jossey-Bass.

Cronbach, L. J., & Associates (1980). *Toward reform of program evaluation.* San Francisco: Jossey-Bass.

Davis, H. R., & Salasin, S. E. (1975). The utilization of evaluation. In E. L. Struening & M. Guttentag (Eds.), *Handbook of evaluation research.* Thousand Oaks, CA: Sage.

Guba, E. G., & Lincoln, Y. S. (1989). *Fourth generation evaluation.* Thousand Oaks, CA: Sage.

Joint Committee on Standards for Educational Evaluation. (1994). *The program evaluation standards: How to assess evaluations of educational program* (2nd ed.). Thousand Oaks, CA: Corwin Press.

Millett, R. (1995). *W. K. Kellogg Foundation cluster evaluation model of evolving practices.* Battle Creek, MI: W. K. Kellogg Foundation.

Millett, R. (1996). "Empowerment evaluation and the W. K. Kellogg Foundation." In D. M. Fetterman, A. J. Kaftarian, & A. Wandersman (Eds.), *Empowerment evaluation: Knowledge and tools for self-assessment and accountability* (pp. 65-76). Newbury Park, CA: Sage.

Owen, J. M. (2004). Evaluation forms: Toward an inclusive framework for evaluation practice. In M. C. Alkin (Ed.), *Evaluation roots: Tracing theorists' views and influences* (pp. 356–369). Thousand Oaks, CA: Sage.

Owen, J. M., & Rogers, P. (1999). *Program evaluation: Forms and approaches* (2nd ed.). Thousand Oaks: Sage.

Patton, M. Q. (1980). *Qualitative evaluation methods.* Thousand Oaks, CA: Sage.

Patton, M. Q. (1982). *Practical evaluation.* Thousand Oaks, CA: Sage.

Patton, M. Q. (1994). Developmental evaluation. *Evaluation Practice, 15*(3), 311–320.

Patton, M. Q. (1997). *Utilization-focused evaluation: The new century text* (3rd ed.). Thousand Oaks, CA: Sage.

Patton, M. Q. (2003). Utilization-focused evaluation. In T. Kellaghan & D. L. Stufflebeam (Eds.), *International handbook of educational evaluation* (pp. 223–244). Norwell, MA: Kluwer.

Patton, M. Q. (2004). The roots of utilization-focused evaluation. In M. C. Alkin (Ed.), *Evaluation roots: Tracing theorists' views and influences* (pp. 276–292). Thousand Oaks, CA: Sage.

Patton, M. Q. (2005). Utilization-focused evaluation. In S. Mathison (Ed.), *Encyclopedia of evaluation* (pp. 429–432). Thousand Oaks, CA: Sage.

Rossi, P. H., & Freeman H. E. (1993). *Evaluation: A systematic approach.* Thousand Oaks, CA: Sage.

Russon, C. (2005). Cluster evaluation. In S. Mathison (Ed.), *Encyclopedia of evaluation* (pp. 66–67). Thousand Oaks, CA: Sage.

Sanders, J. R. (1997). Cluster evaluation. In E. Chelimsky & W. R. Shadish (Eds.), *Evaluation for the 21st century: A handbook* (pp. 396–404). Thousand Oaks, CA: Sage.

Scriven, M. (1980). *The logic of evaluation.* Point Reyes, CA: Edge Press.

Stufflebeam, D. L. (1983). The CIPP model for program evaluation. In G. F. Madaus, M. S. Scriven, & D. L. Stufflebeam (Eds.), *Evaluation models: Viewpoints on educational and human services evaluation* (pp. 117–141). Norwell, MA: Kluwer.

Weiss, C. (1983). The stakeholder approach to evaluation: Origins and promise. In A. S. Bryk (Ed.), *Stakeholder-based evaluation* (pp. 3–14). New Directions in Program Evaluation, no. 17. San Francisco: Jossey-Bass.

CHAPTER ELEVEN

BEST APPROACHES FOR TWENTY-FIRST-CENTURY EVALUATIONS

Of the variety of evaluation approaches that emerged during the twentieth century, we chose eight for comparative analysis and evaluation. The selected approaches are in the questions and methods category—objectives-based evaluation, experimental design, and case study; in the improvement and accountability category—the CIPP model and consumer-oriented evaluation; in the social agenda and advocacy category, responsive/client-centered evaluation and constructivist evaluation; and in the eclectic category, utilization-focused evaluation. These approaches are more or less applicable to program evaluations, representative of the different categories of evaluation approaches, widely referenced in the professional literature, and seem likely to be used extensively—advisedly or not—beyond 2006. In contrasting and evaluating these approaches, we aimed to help evaluators and their clients critically appraise these approaches before choosing among them. We chose the particular eight approaches, rather than some of the other legitimate evaluation approaches referred to in preceding chapters, because we sought balance in evaluating representative approaches in each category and needed to keep the approaches assessed to a manageable number. Clearly some of the approaches not assessed in this chapter are worthy of consideration by evaluators and their clients. These include especially the benefit-cost analysis, success case method, value-added assessment, connoisseurship evaluation, accreditation, deliberative democratic evaluation, and Owen's evaluation forms approaches. It is not our intention to suggest to readers that our selection of eight leading approaches should be construed as an exclusion of the other legitimate approaches we have discussed or referenced. Indeed, eclectically, it is quite possible to incorporate aspects of these approaches with the selected eight.

The ratings of the selected eight approaches appear in Exhibit 11.1. They are listed in order of judged merit within the categories of questions and methods, improvement and accountability, social agenda and advocacy, and eclectic evaluation approaches. The ratings are based on the Joint Committee's *Program Evaluation Standards* (1994); we derived them using a special checklist keyed to the *Standards.* (The checklist we used is the version with six items per category that appears at www.wmich.edu/evalctr/checklists.) Ratings were computed for each of the utility, feasibility, propriety, and accuracy sections of the Joint Committee standards and overall.

All approaches earned overall ratings of Very Good, except objectives-based evaluation and experimental design, which were judged Good overall. The CIPP model, responsive/client-centered evaluation, and utilization-focused evaluation received ratings of Excellent in the standards area of Utility. The other five approaches received ratings of Good in Utility. The CIPP model was rated Excellent in addressing standards of Feasibility. All other approaches were Very Good in the Feasibility area, except experimental design, which received a rating of Fair. No approach received a rating of Excellent in the Propriety category, with experimental design rated Good and the other seven approaches rated Very Good. In the Accuracy category, the CIPP model was rated Excellent, objectives-based evaluation was rated Good, and the other six approaches were rated Very Good.

The comparatively lower overall rating given to the experimental design approach resulted especially from its rating of Fair for Feasibility. For many evaluation assignments, an experimental design approach would be impractical, vulnerable to political problems, and not cost-effective. The overall rating of Good for the objectives-based approach reflects its narrow focus on the developer's objectives and terminal information plus lack of attention to unanticipated outcomes. The case study approach scored surprisingly well, considering that it is focused on the use of a particular technique. A bonus is that it can be employed on its own or as a component of any of the other approaches. This is also true of Brinkerhoff's commendable approach, the success case method. For most program evaluation assignments, the evaluator is advised to seek a better approach than either experimental design or objectives-based evaluation. Case study is our method of choice in the questions and methods category of evaluation approaches.

The CIPP model scored well on all categories of Joint Committee Standards with all ratings being near the top of the Very Good range or near the bottom of the Excellent range. This approach offers comprehensiveness in assessing all stages of program development and all aspects of a program, serving the full range of stakeholders, providing for formative and summative uses of findings, orientations to both program improvement and accountability, and addressing all thirty Joint Committee standards.

The consumer-oriented approach, with its emphasis on independent assessment of developed products and services, deserves a special place in the lexicon of evaluation approaches. Although the approach is not strongly suited to internal evaluations for improvement, it complements such approaches with an outsider, expert view that becomes important when products and services are put up for dissemination. This approach's relatively lower score in Feasibility, though still in the Very Good category, reflects its dependence on a highly skilled evaluator who strongly guards independence and separation from program personnel. Paradoxically, the approach depends on program personnel for much of the information needed for the evaluation. A high degree of evaluator independence from program personnel can discourage the extensive amount of stakeholder support that the consumer-oriented evaluator requires. This psychological distance can also discourage program personnel from using the external evaluation findings. This approach's relatively high rating on Utility is due not to strong impact on the actions of program personnel but to the high degree of credibility consumers external to a program place on independent evaluations.

The responsive and client-centered approach received stellar ratings across the board and a notably high rating in the Utility category. In contrast to the independence of consumer-oriented evaluation, the responsive approach engenders close collaboration between evaluator and program personnel and other stakeholders. This results in easier access to needed information and stakeholders' better acceptance, support, and use of the evaluation.

The constructivist approach is a well-founded, mainly qualitative approach to evaluation that systematically engages interested parties to help conduct both the divergent and convergent stages of evaluation. It strongly advocates for the least powerful and poorest members of the program stakeholders. Its somewhat depressed rating in Feasibility is due partly to its utopian orientation, which is acknowledged by its creators, and also the difficulty of reaching closure under a framework of multiple values and multiple realities.

Finally, utilization-focused evaluation is a ubiquitous, umbrella approach to evaluation. Its main objective is to get evaluation findings used and accordingly rates high on utility. It also rates high on feasibility, since the stakeholders can strongly influence all aspects of a study, help choose elements with which they are comfortable, and reject those they see as burdensome. Relatively lower but still very good ratings in propriety and accuracy are due to stakeholders' having possibly too much power over elements of evaluation design. This can result in unchecked conflicts of interest and narrow, possibly biased findings.

EXHIBIT 11.1. RATINGS: STRONGEST PROGRAM EVALUATION APPROACHES WITHIN TYPES, LISTED IN ORDER OF COMPLIANCE WITH *THE PROGRAM EVALUATION STANDARDS*.

Evaluation Approach	Graph of Overall Merit					Overall Score and Rating	Utility Rating	Feasibility Rating	Propriety Rating	Accuracy Rating
	P	F	G	VG	E					
Questions and methods										
Case study						81 (VG)	71 (VG)	83 (VG)	81 (VG)	88 (VG)
Objectives based						62 (G)	61 (G)	67 (VG)	50 (G)	69 (VG)
Experimental design						56 (G)	54 (G)	42 (F)	53 (G)	73 (VG)
Improvement and accountability										
CIPP model						92 (VG)	93 (E)	92 (E)	88 (VG)	94 (E)
Consumer oriented						84 (VG)	89 (VG)	75 (VG)	91 (VG)	81 (VG)
Social agenda and advocacy										
Responsive and client centered						84 (VG)	93 (E)	83 (VG)	78 (VG)	81 (VG)
Constructivist						81 (VG)	89 (VG)	67 (VG)	84 (VG)	85 (VG)
Eclectic										
Utilization focused						86 (VG)	93 (E)	92 (E)	78 (VG)	79 (VG)

Note: The first-listed author rated each evaluation approach on each of the thirty Joint Committee program evaluation standards by judging whether the approach endorses each of six key features of the standard. He judged the approach's adequacy on each standard as follows: Excellent, 6; Very Good, 5; Good, 4; Fair, 2–3; Poor, 0–1. The score for the approach on each of the four categories of standards (Utility, Feasibility, Propriety, Accuracy) was then determined by summing the following products: 4 times the number of Excellent ratings, 3 times the number of Very Good ratings, 2 times the number of Good ratings, and 1 times the number of Fair ratings, then dividing the sum by the product of the number of standards in the category by 4. Judgments of the approach's strength in satisfying the Utility, Propriety, and Accuracy standards were then determined according to percentages of the possible quality points for the category of standards as follows: 93–100 percent: Excellent; 68–92 percent: Very Good; 50–67 percent: Good; 25–49 percent: Fair; 0–24 percent: Poor. Judgments of the approach's strength in satisfying the Feasibility standards were determined slightly differently due to the fact the category had only three standards and a score of 11 out of 12 figured to 92 percent rather than 93 percent needed for a judgment of Excellent and a score of 8 out of 12 figured to 67 percent rather than 68 percent for a judgment of Very Good. The percentages used for this category were: 92–100 percent: Excellent; 67–91 percent: Very Good; 50–66 percent: Good; 25–49 percent: Fair; and 0–24 percent: Poor. The final scores were obtained by multiplying the percentage score obtained for each category by 100. The four equalized scores were then summed and divided by 4. The result was judged by comparing it to the total maximum score, 100. Each approach's overall merit was judged as follows: 93–100: Excellent; 68–92: Very Good; 50–67: Good; 25–49: Fair; and 0–24: Poor. Regardless of an approach's total score and overall rating, a notation of unacceptable would have been attached to any approach receiving a poor rating on the vital standards of P1, Service Orientation; A5, Valid Information; A10, Justified Conclusions; and A11, Impartial Reporting. The first author's ratings were based on his knowledge of the Joint Committee Program Evaluation Standards, his many years of studying the various evaluation models and approaches, his personal acquaintance and collaborative evaluation work with authors of almost all of the assessed approaches, and his experience in seeing and assessing how all of these approaches worked in practice. He chaired the Joint Committee on Standards for Educational Evaluation during its first thirteen years and led the development of the first editions of both the program and personnel evaluation standards. Nevertheless, his ratings should be viewed as only his personal set of judgments of these models and approaches. Also, his conflict of interest is acknowledged, since he developed the CIPP model. After he judged the eight evaluation approaches following the method described above, the second author reviewed the judgments and raised questions for discussion. Both authors then deliberated to reach the consensus judgments presented here. The scale ranges in are P = Poor, F = Fair, G = Good, VG = Very Good, E = Excellent.

Summary

All in all, the eight approaches summarized in Exhibit 11.1 bode well for the future application and further development of alternative approaches to program evaluation. The last half of the twentieth century saw considerable development of program evaluation approaches. Based on the ratings presented in this chapter, evaluators and their clients can choose from an array of strong, creditable evaluation approaches.

In this book, twenty-six evaluation approaches were grouped as pseudoevaluations, questions- and methods-oriented evaluations, improvement- and accountability-oriented evaluations, social agenda and advocacy evaluations, and eclectic evaluations. Apart from pseudoevaluations, there is among the approaches an increasingly balanced quest for rigor, relevance, and justice. Clearly the approaches are showing a strong orientation to stakeholder involvement, the use of multiple methods, and impact of evaluation findings.

When compared with professional standards for program evaluations, the best approaches are the CIPP model, utilization focused, responsive and client centered, consumer oriented, case study, and constructivist. All of these approaches are recommended for consideration in program evaluations. Typically, we believe that better alternatives can be found to objectives-based and experimental design approaches.

A critical analysis of evaluation approaches has important implications for evaluators, those who train evaluators, theoreticians concerned with devising better concepts and methods, and those engaged in professionalizing program evaluation. Adherence by these groups to well-constituted and widely accepted principles and standards is relevant and important. A major consideration for the practitioner is that evaluators may encounter considerable difficulties if their perceptions of the study being undertaken differ from those of their clients and audiences. Frequently clients want a politically advantageous study performed, while the evaluator wants to conduct questions- and methods-oriented studies that allow him or her to exploit the methodologies in which he or she was trained. Moreover, audiences usually want values-oriented studies that will help them determine the relative merits and worth of competing programs or advocacy evaluations that will give them voice and control in the issues that affect them.

If evaluators ignore the likely conflicts in purposes, their program evaluations are probably doomed to fail. At an evaluation's outset, evaluators must be keenly sensitive to their own agendas for the study, as well as those that are held by the client and the other right-to-know audiences. The evaluator should advise involved parties of possible conflicts in the evaluation's purposes and should, at the beginning, negotiate a common understanding of the evaluation's purpose and the appropriate approach. Evaluators also should inform participants regularly of the selected approach's logic, rationale, process, and pitfalls. This will enhance stakeholders' cooperation and careful, constructive use of findings. Using negotiation skills, the evaluator should accommodate stakeholder interests and concerns while maintaining the integrity of the evaluation. At the outset of an evaluation, a crucial step in this balancing activity is for the evaluator and client group to reach agreement on the principles and standards that will guide and govern the evaluation. We strongly advise evaluators to advise their clients to adopt the American Evaluation Association's *Guiding Principles* (2004) and Joint Committee's *Program Evaluation Standards* (1994) as the criteria for guiding and judging the projected evaluation.

Evaluation training programs should effectively address the ferment over and development of new program evaluation approaches. Trainers should provide their students with both instruction and field experiences in these approaches. When students fully understand the approaches; see how they are assessed against professional standards and guiding principles; and gain relevant, practical experience in using the approaches, they will be in a position to discern which approaches work best under which sets of circumstances.

For the theoretician, a main point is that all the approaches have inherent strengths and weaknesses. In general, the weaknesses of the politically oriented studies are that they are vulnerable to conflicts of interest and may mislead an audience to develop an unfounded, perhaps erroneous judgment of a program's merit and worth. The main problem with the questions- and methods-oriented studies is that they often address questions that are too narrow to support a full assessment of merit and worth. However, it is also noteworthy that these types of studies compete favorably with improvement- and accountability-oriented evaluation studies, social agenda and advocacy studies, and eclectic studies in the efficiency of methodology employed. Improvement- and accountability-oriented studies, with their concentration on merit and worth, undertake an ambitious task, for it is virtually impossible to fully and unequivocally assess any program's ultimate worth. Such an achievement would require omniscience, infallibility, an unchanging environment, and an unquestioned, singular value base. Nevertheless, the continuing attempt to address questions of merit and worth is essential for the advancement of societal programs. The social agenda and advocacy studies are to be applauded for their quest for equity as well as excellence in programs being studied. They model their mission by attempting to make evaluation a participatory, democratic enterprise. Unfortunately, many pitfalls attend such utopian approaches. These approaches are especially susceptible to bias, and they face practical constraints in involving, informing, and empowering targeted stakeholders and in getting evaluations done on time and within budget. Finally, the eclectic approaches are attractive because of their focus on getting findings used and their resourcefulness in engaging selected stakeholders to pragmatically select and apply conceptual frameworks, criteria, and procedures from all other relevant approaches. Yet any approach that is overly pragmatic and gives away too much authority to program stakeholders can fail to meet standards of ethics and technical rigor.

For the evaluation profession itself, the review of program evaluation approaches underscores the importance of guiding principles, professional standards, and metaevaluations. Guiding principles and standards are needed to maintain a consistently high level of integrity in uses of the various approaches. All legitimate approaches are enhanced when evaluators key their studies to principles and standards for evaluation and obtain independent reviews of their evaluations. Moreover, continuing attention to the requirements of principles and standards will provide valuable direction for developing better approaches.

With this consumer report and analysis of selected evaluation approaches, we conclude Part Two of this book. In Part Three, we describe a program evaluation situation requiring selection and application of an evaluation approach. We then provide in-depth information on six of the approaches just reviewed and consider how each could be applied to address the illustrative evaluation assignment.

Review Questions

The first six review exercises are, in part, preparation for the first group discussion question that follows. Having perused Chapters Seven through Ten, write a brief paragraph identifying the main intentions of each of the evaluation approaches in questions 1 to 6:

1. Case study
2. CIPP model
3. Consumer oriented
4. Responsive and client centered
5. Constructivist
6. Utilization focused
7. Why have the authors rated the objectives-based approach comparatively low on compliance with the Joint Committee Standards with respect to both the Utility and Propriety standards?
8. Are you able to support the Very Good rating of the experimental design approach in respect to compliance with the Accuracy standards but Fair rating in the Feasibility category? Why or why not?

9. In reference to the evaluation approaches discussed in this chapter, we state that "apart from pseudoevaluations, there is among the approaches an increasingly balanced quest for rigor, relevance, and justice." Justify or refute this statement.

10. What are the inherent weaknesses of politically oriented evaluations, and also of improvement- and accountability-oriented studies?

Group Exercises

Exercise 1. This exercise will have greater benefit for the group if members prepare their responses in advance of the meeting. If the exercise is undertaken thoroughly, it should serve two main purposes: first, a further study of the six methods and approaches listed in the Review Questions (questions 1–6) and in-depth study of one of these, and second, a review of Chapter Three (standards for Program Evaluation) and a practical application of the standards.

This exercise focuses on the following approaches to program evaluation: case study, CIPP model, consumer-oriented, responsive and client-centered, constructivist, and utilization focused. Each group member is allocated one of these six. If there are more than six group members, a particular approach will be allocated more than once.

Refer to Exhibit 11.1 and study the procedures underlying the ratings used in it (at first glance, they may appear complicated, but in reality the method is quite straightforward). Using the same methodology, give a rating for your allocated approach on each of the Utility, Feasibility, Propriety, and Accuracy standards and an overall rating. You will need to download and copy the *Program Evaluation Standards Checklist* from www.wmich.edu/evalctr/checklists. Clearly, subjectivity and degree of experience in program development and evaluation will play a part in your ratings. However, a close knowledge of the approach and the exact nature (by definition and example) of each of the thirty standards will provide very useful parameters for your decision making.

As a group discuss:

- The proximity of each member's ratings to the authors'
- Possible reasons for any wide divergences
- The benefits of knowing, and using, the Joint Committee Standards and the associated checklist

Exercise 2. The comment is made in this chapter that "if evaluators ignore the likely conflicts in purposes, their program evaluations are probably doomed to fail." Discuss the ramifications of this statement.

References

American Evaluation Association 2003 Ethics Committee. (2004). *Guiding principles for evaluators.* http://www.eval.org/Guiding%20Principles.htm.

Joint Committee on Standards for Educational Evaluation. (1994). *The program evaluation standards.* Thousand Oaks, CA: Corwin Press.

PART THREE

EXPLICATION AND APPLICATION OF SELECTED EVALUATION APPROACHES

The seven chapters in Part Three are targeted to help readers develop a firm grasp of six approaches to evaluation and their applicability. Chapter Twelve summarizes a completed evaluation of a housing and community development project and a hypothetical request for a follow-up evaluation of the project. The original evaluation showed the project to be of high quality and successful over a seven-year period. The project's sponsor wanted to assess the project's continued success five years later. In Chapters Thirteen through Eighteen, we provide in-depth information about each of six evaluation approaches—experimental design, case study, the CIPP Model, consumer-oriented evaluation, responsive evaluation, and utilization-focused evaluation—and consider how each approach could be applied to the illustrative evaluation assignment.

CHAPTER TWELVE

THE EVALUATION CASE

An Evaluation of an Innovative Housing and Community Development Project

This chapter summarizes a completed project evaluation and presents a request for a plan to conduct a follow-up evaluation of the project. The chapter provides a context for considering how six evaluation approaches could be applied to address the same evaluation assignment. Use of the common case is intended to be instructive in seeing how the approaches are similar and different when applied.

We begin by summarizing a self-help housing project that was funded and conducted by a charitable foundation. We then summarize the process and results of an eight-year evaluation of that project. Finally, we present a request for proposals to conduct a follow-up evaluation of this project five years after the original evaluation.

The case is about a modest-sized, eight-year evaluation of a self-help housing project. The housing focus is useful because the need for housing is common to everybody's experience. The relatively large long-term study enabled us to illustrate the use of a wide range of evaluation techniques. Since evaluators seldom conduct such long-term evaluations, we have balanced our use of the case by focusing the request for a follow-up evaluation at the end of the chapter on a one-year, relatively low-cost evaluation.

Although this case is based in reality, we have modified it to fit the needs of this chapter and have not specifically identified persons and groups involved in the original case or the specific location of the project.

Project Overview

Begun in 1993 and located on a fourteen-acre plot in a depressed agricultural area about fifteen miles from a major city, the self-help housing project was initially targeted to support eighty low-income families in constructing their own houses and together developing a healthy, values-based community. The project was launched by a relatively new charitable foundation, both to address its mission of serving poor families and to learn how to operate housing projects.

The foundation's president decided to build systematic evaluation into this project from its inception, both to maintain accountability and to obtain feedback of use in problem solving, quality assurance, and project improvement. A further indication of this foundation's commitment to evaluation is that its project planners visited and studied other self-help housing projects prior to planning its project. This project also was grounded in and assessed against the foundation's core values of individual worth, caring and nurturing, participation and reciprocity, prevention, self-sufficiency, creativity and innovation, and teamwork and collaboration.

In each project year, the foundation engaged and assisted between six and seventeen families in building their houses together over a period of nine to ten months. The result, after eight years, was eight increments of houses (seventy-five in all) in an attractive, well-maintained, and tranquil community that was home to about 390 people, including approximately 235 children and their parents or guardians. This community, situated near a range of picturesque mountains and magnificent ocean beaches, stands in stark contrast to the economically depressed and crime-ridden community environment immediately outside the project site.

Throughout the project, the foundation sponsored an array of social services for the beneficiaries: counseling, tutoring, field trips, parties, and courses for children and their parents; education grants; leadership training; instruction in community organizing; drug prevention education; a computer room; community meetings and events facilitated by foundation staff; conflict resolution assistance; assistance in obtaining home mortgages; and financial management assistance.

Community covenants included rent-to-own agreements, mortgages, and land-lease contracts. The first of these were provided to enable very low-income families to participate in the project. The three together are designed to help ensure that the community will sustain its adherence to the project's mandated values. By engaging local banks to hold mortgages on sixty-nine of the homes, making rent-to-own agreements on the other six houses, and negotiating a land fee purchase agreement with each home owner, the foundation planned to recoup a large part of its investment in this project while also promoting self-sufficiency among the residents. The foundation deeded the streets to the local government, thus ensuring city services and maintenance of streets and related infrastructure. Overall, this project provides a cogent example of how a charitable organization attempted to employ a fiscally sound and values-based approach to self-help housing in order to address low-income families' needs for affordable housing and help the families help themselves. The project's orientation is to lend a helping hand, not a handout.

The project had these goals:

1. Build a community of low-income working families with children who commit to live in and help sustain a nurturing neighborhood free from violence and substance abuse and devoted to helping others.
2. Increase the geographical area's supply of affordable housing.
3. Develop a sound approach to values-based, self-help housing and community development.

To be selected, the builders were not required to have construction experience, carpentry skills, mechanical aptitude, or top physical condition. Among the entry requirements were not already owning a home, having a family income of not more than 80 percent of the state's median family income, being able to qualify for a mortgage or rent-to-own agreement, having lived positive family values, having at least one child under age eighteen, committing to meet the project's schedule of work, and arranging for child care during the construction period weekends. Applicants were sought by various means, including newspaper and radio advertisements, flyers, letters to area school and social service agency administrators, contacts with churches, and word of mouth.

The foundation assessed applicants and helped those who met the project's admittance criteria to prequalify for mortgages. The induction process included background checks, home visits, credit reports, interviews, group meetings that included role playing with other applicants, sociopsychological assessments, and meetings with bank representatives. Ultimately a team of foundation personnel examined the evidence to screen out unqualified applicants and subsequently choose the builders for each increment. Potentially qualified applicants who were not chosen for a given increment could apply for a later increment. Many did so and were selected later.

At the end of the project's first eight years, sixty-nine families held mortgages and land fee purchase agreements. Six families had agreements to proceed on a rent-to-own basis for two years, after which they must obtain a mortgage. Occupations of the selected builders included warehouse laborer, sanitation worker, construction worker, hospital assistant, security guard, teacher, bus driver, custodian, secretary, mechanic, supermarket clerk, fish processor, and cook. Families' ethnicity included Chinese, Japanese, Native American, Samoan, African American, Hispanic, and Caucasian backgrounds.

The home building was conducted through a combination of self-help construction, supervision by licensed contractors, and contracted construction of certain house features. A builder and cobuilder from each family worked ten hours each Saturday and Sunday over a period of nine to ten months to construct the houses. Usually they were husband and wife, but there were also mother and daughter, brothers, and unmarried couples. The builders were required to purchase their own hand tools. Under the supervision of licensed general contractors, the builders learned home building skills and worked together as a group to construct their houses. The supervising contractors provided the supporting generators, power tools, storage sheds, and vehicles for moving materials. The foundation assigned an on-site project manager to ensure that all aspects of the project moved forward according to plan and that problems were promptly identified and addressed. Each week the manager evaluated and filed reports on the attendance, progress, attitudes, and demeanor of each pair of builders and intervened as needed to address conflicts and other problems.

An especially important practice was the assignment of houses by lottery only after construction was completed. This stimulated the builders to work equally hard and cooperatively on all the houses in their increment. After completion of the first two increments, only four-bedroom houses were built in increment 3 and only three-bedroom houses in increments 4 through 8. The first two increments included both three- and four-bedroom houses, and families knew their category of house from the start. This situation apparently influenced some participants in increment 2 to work hardest on the houses that contained the number of bedrooms they would get. This created some dissension among the builders. Inclusion of all four-bedroom houses in increment 3 eased this problem. Subsequently inclusion of only three-bedroom houses in the remaining four increments reduced costs of the houses and helped ensure that participants would work equally hard on all the houses. These observations are not an indictment of the builders, only a reflection that construction plans need to deal with motivation and human nature as well as architectural and other bricks-and-mortar matters.

The builders' tasks included digging holes for foundation posts; constructing foundations, interior walls, and ceilings; framing; drywalling; siding; roofing; installing tile, cabinets, doors, windows, and fixtures; interior and exterior painting; and some exterior landscaping. Licensed contractors installed carpets and performed the plumbing, electrical, and concrete work. The entire process was subjected to regular inspections and approvals by government inspectors.

The foundation paid the full cost of the general contractors' labor and reimbursable expenses (which included ladders, air hammers, pneumatic nailers, saws, and hauling of refuse). The foundation also provided a community center and other common areas and perimeter fencing.

The families provided sweat equity in lieu of the $7,500 down payment on their homes. Most secured twenty-five-year mortgages, ranging from $48,000 to $59,000. In addition, the project plan called for each family to pay the foundation monthly rent for their home site over thirty years. At that point, the total amount of rent paid—about $52,000—was to be credited against the lot's total value; the $7,500 sweat equity down payment will also be credited against the land's value. The land-lease agreements call for the home owner to make a balloon payment for the remaining cost of the land—about $123,000. Having paid off their home mortgages, the project's leaders expected that home owners would likely take out a new mortgage to pay off the remaining cost of the land. Near the end of the project's eighth year, the foundation's president realized that the requirement for a large balloon payment when the home owners were about to retire would pose a serious hardship. Therefore, she was considering lowering the price of the home owners' lots.

The foundation staffed several key project roles: chief program officer; on-site project manager; construction contractors; subcontractors in various specialty areas; coordinator for recruitment and selection; community development specialist; specialist in services for children, youth, and families; information specialist and secretary; and consultants to address a wide range of administrative and support tasks. The foundation's president exercised leadership, policymaking, and oversight functions throughout the project. Members of the foundation's board were also frequently involved in such activities as visiting the construction site, reviewing plans and progress, and attending formal gatherings to welcome each increment's families and acknowledge completed houses. Project staff regularly delivered or arranged for delivery of key services to families. These included financial and personal counseling and assistance in accessing subsidies such as those associated with installing solar panels.

In the end, seventy-five high-quality, single-family houses were built: fifty-one three-bedroom houses, twelve four-bedroom houses, and twelve duplex homes (six units). The duplex units and three- and four-bedroom houses have two baths and a two-car carport. Most residents installed walls or fences around their homes at their own, considerable expense. Residents are required to plant grass and maintain a neat, well-cared-for lot around their houses. Community covenants strictly prohibit such negative acts as violence and substance abuse. Penalties for violations include possible removal from the community.

The fourteen-acre plot on which these houses sit is in the shape of a triangle and has one entrance from the adjacent main road. It was thought that having only one entrance would make the community more secure from burglaries and other crimes originating outside this housing enclave. Most of the houses are arranged around seven cul-de-sacs. This feature was included in the plan for the community to promote familiarity and positive relations among neighbors and also to provide a safe area for children to play in front of their houses.

When each increment of houses was completed, the foundation held a blessing of the new homes and families. All staff and residents of the housing project plus area clergy and other selected guests were invited to participate in and celebrate this event.

Toward the end of construction of the last increment of houses, the foundation began assisting the residents to think about and plan for taking over and administering the community while sustaining its values. The foundation's coordinator for recruitment and selection had been working with residents for about three years to help them learn about and actually go through the process of forming a home owners' association. Foundation staff members were helping the residents organize and operate covenants, planning, and other committees and assume responsibility for the community's governance, management, and conflict resolution, as well as maintenance of common facilities, including the community center and adjacent playground.

A safeguard against gentrification (a process whereby poor people are displaced as a consequence of affluent persons moving into a neighborhood and upgrading property values) of this project site is that no family can sell its house outright without first offering it for sale to the foundation at the cost of the family's actual investment in the property. If, for whatever reason, a project family left the community, it could take away only its actual dollar investment, including the sweat equity amount. This safeguard provided the foundation with control to ensure that the project would be reserved for service to low-income families for the foreseeable future. A further restriction was that no family could take in renters or long-term visitors and thus overcrowd the community.

The Original Evaluation Plan

At the outset of this project, the foundation engaged a university evaluation center to evaluate the project. The evaluation, which spanned eight years, assessed all eight building increments; examined the project's construction, social support, and community development components; and concluded with a summative evaluation report.

Initial Planning Grant

Upon being invited to conduct a comprehensive, long-term evaluation of the project, the center's director requested and obtained an initial short-term planning grant allowing expenditures up to a limit of twelve thousand dollars. Using about forty-five hundred dollars of the available planning funds, the evaluation team became acquainted with the project, its participants, and the project's environment before designing and contracting for the long-term evaluation. Through the initial planning grant, the evaluators, clients, and other stakeholders developed sound understanding, rapport, and agreements on which to base the ensuing years of evaluation work.

Audiences and Reports

During the project, the center annually presented reports to provide the foundation's leaders and project staff with up-to-date external assessments of the project's progress (three to four reports in the early years of the evaluation and one to two in later years). In accordance with contractual agreements, the interim reports were addressed to the foundation's board and staff for their discretionary use. At the request of the foundation's president, the final report was prepared for the foundation's use for project improvement and accountability, sharing with the project's beneficiaries, and sharing with outside audiences of the foundation's choice.

The reports contained feedback from beneficiaries and foundation staff, plus the evaluators' perspectives. Each report presented findings from a main procedure employed during that year. Every year, one report was based on the interview responses of the builders who had recently completed and moved into their new houses. Depending on the year, other reports could include an environmental analysis, feedback from the traveling observer, case study findings, a goal-free report, or an updated project profile. Together, each year's reports mainly examined the project's environment, documented project operations, identified strengths and weaknesses, and sometimes identified issues requiring the foundation's attention. Each year the evaluators supplemented the main reports with a brief synthesis report, usually in the form of a computer-based visual presentation. This was designed to assist foundation staff in sharing the latest evaluation findings with the board and other audiences. The annual reports were in the vein of project improvement–oriented evaluation, whereas the final report provided an overall summative assessment of the project's significance in respect to merit and worth.

Purposes

The evaluation had four purposes. First, the evaluators provided information to help the project staff take stock of, assess, and improve the ongoing process. Second, they helped the foundation maintain an accountability record, especially for keeping the foundation's board apprised of the project's performance in carrying out planned procedures. Third, they sought to analyze the project's background, process, and outcomes in order to promote better understanding of ways and means of using self-help housing to conduct community development. Finally, the evaluation was keyed to helping the foundation inform developers and other groups about this project's mission, objectives, structure, process, and outcomes and thereby help them consider the project as a possible model for adaptation and use elsewhere. Thus, the evaluation's purposes were improvement, accountability, understanding, and dissemination.

Design

The evaluation design was based on the CIPP evaluation model. The design included a comprehensive approach to assessing context, including the nature, extent, and criticality of beneficiaries' needs and assets and pertinent environmental forces; input, including the responsiveness and strength of project plans and resources; process, involving the appropriateness and adequacy of project operations; and product, meaning the extent, desirability, and significance of intended and unintended outcomes. To gain additional insights into project outcomes, the product evaluation component was divided into four parts: (1) impact, regarding the project's reach to the intended target audience; (2) effectiveness, regarding the quality, desirability, and significance of outcomes; (3) sustainability, concerning the project's institutionalization and long-term viability; and (4) transportability, concerning the utility of the project's meritorious features in other settings.

The CIPP model, as implemented in this project, combined formative and summative evaluation. Formative evaluation presented foundation leaders and staff with periodic feedback keyed to helping them review and strengthen project plans and operations. The composite final report was largely retrospective; it summarized and appraised what was done and accomplished.

Evaluation Questions

The main questions that guided this evaluation were derived from both interactions with project stakeholders and the types of evaluation noted:

- Context: To what extent was the project targeted to important community and beneficiary needs?
- Input: To what extent were the project's structure and procedural and resource plans consistent with foundation values, state-of-the-art standards, feasibility considerations, and sufficient strengths to address the targeted needs?
- Process: To what extent were the project's operations consistent with plans, responsibly conducted, and effective in addressing beneficiaries' needs?
- Impact: What beneficiaries were reached, and to what extent were they the targeted beneficiaries?

- Effectiveness: To what extent did the project meet the needs of the involved beneficiaries?
- Sustainability: To what extent was the project institutionalized in order to sustain its successful implementation?
- Transportability: To what extent could or was the project successfully adapted and applied elsewhere?

Basis for Judging the Project

To the extent that this evaluation would find positive answers to all of the evaluation questions, the evaluators would rate the project high on merit, worth, and significance. Negative assessments regarding any of the questions would point up areas of deficiency that would at least diminish the judgments of soundness and quality or that could discredit the project entirely. The evaluative questions denote a range of important assessment criteria. They include the project's adherence to foundation values, relevance, state-of-the-art character, efficiency, feasibility, responsiveness, quality, viability, adaptability, and significance. It is emphasized that the bottom-line criterion concerns the extent to which the project met the assessed needs of the targeted beneficiaries. If the project failed on this criterion, it would fail overall.

Data Collection Methods

Multiple methods were used to gather data for each component of the evaluation. Table 12.1 lists the primary methods used. The checkmarks in the matrix's cells indicate which parts of the evaluation design were addressed by which evaluation methods. Each part of the evaluation design was addressed by at least three different methods.

Table 12.2 shows the data collection methods in relationship to project years. Not every method was applied every year, but at least three methods were employed during each project year. It is noteworthy that the evaluation's collection of pertinent information was reduced by discontinuation of the environmental analysis and program profile procedures about midway into the study due to the foundation's need to cut the evaluation budget. Each method is characterized below.

Environmental Analysis. Environmental analysis involved gathering contextual information in the forms of available documents and data concerning such matters as area economics, population characteristics, availability of low-income housing, related projects and services, relevant political dynamics, and the housing and related needs and problems of the targeted population. It also involved interviewing persons in various roles in the area and visiting pertinent projects and services.

TABLE 12.1. EVALUATION METHODS RELATED TO EVALUATION TYPES.

	Context	Input	Process	Impact	Effectiveness	Sustainability	Transportability
Environmental analysis	✓		✓				
Project profile		✓					
Traveling observer			✓	✓	✓	✓	
Case study			✓	✓	✓	✓	
Stakeholder interviews	✓		✓	✓	✓	✓	✓
Goal-free evaluation			✓	✓	✓	✓	
Task reports, feedback workshops	✓	✓	✓	✓	✓	✓	✓
Synthesis, final report	✓	✓	✓	✓	✓	✓	✓

TABLE 12.2. EVALUATION METHODS RELATED TO PROJECT YEARS.

	Year 1	Year 2	Year 3	Year 4	Year 5	Year 6	Year 7	Year 8	Year 9
Environmental analysis	✓			✓					
Project profile	✓	✓	✓	✓	✓				
Traveling observer	✓	✓	✓	✓	✓	✓	✓	✓	
Case study		✓	✓	✓			✓		
Stakeholder interviews	✓	✓	✓	✓	✓	✓	✓	✓	
Goal-free evaluation			✓		✓				
Task reports, feedback workshops	✓	✓	✓	✓	✓	✓	✓	✓	✓
Synthesis, final report							✓	✓	

Individuals interviewed for this aspect of the evaluation included area school teachers and administrators, local and state government officials, staff of area charities, officials in the office of public housing, managers of other area housing projects, local social workers, and church officials and service providers.

The foundation viewed the environmental analysis as important and useful early in the project's development when the process of clarifying the target population and examining its needs in the context of the local economy was under way. The procedure was discontinued when the foundation experienced serious financial problems, especially in its stockholdings, and needed to cut back the evaluation as well as other foundation efforts. Foundation staff decided that a continuing environmental analysis was not among their high priorities and asked the evaluators to concentrate on observing and analyzing what was happening at the project site. This change in the evaluation somewhat limited what could be concluded about the relevance of the self-help housing approach to the area's economic and social environment.

Project Profile. Project profiles characterized the project, including its mission, constituents, needs, goals, plan, staff, timetable, resources, progress to date, accomplishments, and recognitions. From the project's beginning, the evaluators wrote and periodically updated a large and growing document that profiled the project as it was established and evolved. While serving the same purpose as a database, the profile was more of an information base with a concentration of qualitative information. Especially included were notations concerning which project features remained stable, which ones changed, and which ones were added. Early in the evaluation, the evaluators prepared the project profile report, submitted the draft to the foundation staff, and then discussed it with them. In following years, as the report grew in size, the staff found that they were reading a lot of what they had read before. For subsequent editions, therefore, they asked the evaluators to highlight the information that had changed or was added and engage them in verifying its accuracy and clarity. Like the environmental analysis, the project profile was also discontinued during the final three years because of the need to cut costs. The project profile reports proved valuable in completing the final report and would have been even more useful had the procedure been continued throughout the evaluation.

Traveling Observers. The traveling observers (also called resident observers) designed and carried out a systematic procedure to monitor and assess project implementation and project outcomes along the way. The observers, who lived near the project site, served as liaisons for the evaluators, who were located in another state and were at the project site only periodically. The employment of a traveling observer according to an explicit protocol is a method in that, as in naturalistic inquiry, the observer is the instrument of inquiry.

Over time, three different traveling observers participated in evaluating the project. These individuals interviewed project participants, maintained a newspaper clippings file pertaining to the project or pertinent issues, and served as advance persons for preparing the way for the university evaluation center's team so that it could be efficient and effective during its periodic visits, collected and reviewed documents pertaining to the project, especially helped identify and assess the project's effects on the children and youth, and conducted interviews pertaining to case studies involving selected families in the community. An invaluable aspect of the traveling observers' work was their briefing of the visiting evaluators on their arrival at the project site to help them become as up-to-date as possible with recent issues and events in the project and its surrounding environment.

In the first year of the evaluation, the traveling observer participated with the lead evaluators in making oral presentations to the project's leader and staff. However, such traveling observer participation in feedback sessions proved dysfunctional and was discontinued. Their presence in the feedback sessions had sometimes spawned defensive exchanges between them and members of the project staff. The lead evaluator became convinced that such dissension would be a continued natural consequence of including the traveling observer in the feedback sessions and that this would likely limit and possibly destroy the traveling observer's effectiveness. Especially, a history of conflict with project staff would make it very difficult for the traveling observer to continue to study the project closely, interact and maintain trust with stakeholders, and provide project leaders with candid reports. Thus, in the final seven years of the evaluation, traveling observers reported only to the lead evaluators, who incorporated traveling observer findings into project evaluation reports.

Case Study. Case studies were conducted as repeated interviews with a panel of project beneficiaries over time, followed by a synthesis of their perspectives on the project. Case studies were undertaken in project years 2, 4, and 7. In the second project year, four families were selected—three from increment 1 and two from increment 2. Four additional families were added in year 4 (one from increment 1, one from increment 2, and two from increment 3), and in year 7, seventeen families were involved (one from increment 1, two from increment 2, three from increment 3, six from increment 4, and five from increment 5). Originally the case studies were intended to track the experiences of individual families over time, with each family being a case. However, it was deemed that anonymity of the families included in the case studies was important but could not be guaranteed in such a small community. Therefore, instead of risking the families' privacy, the case study focus shifted from individual families to the perceptions of the selected families about the project and its impacts on them. Thus, the project was the case.

Case study interview questions focused on the project's impacts on the families' quality of life and relationships, needs of children, the project community and the surrounding community, and the extent that beneficiaries were influenced to help other needy parties. A special protocol was used to guide the case study interviews. The interviews were conducted and written up by the traveling observers. The interviewers especially looked for changes over time in the perceptions of the families interviewed regarding the project's quality and success, particular issues, and how well these issues were being resolved.

Stakeholder Interview. Interviews were conducted with the builders of each increment about three to six months after they moved into their new homes. These interviews provided information about the builders' perceptions of the community, the process they experienced in building the houses, the nature and quality of the construction and community development outcomes, the project's impacts on their lives, and matters related to sustaining and improving their community. The interviews were guided by a protocol that changed only slightly from year to year. The families were highly cooperative and forthcoming in helping the investigators understand the developing project, identify key issues related to project improvement, and assess the project's success in relationship to their family's needs and the broader values-based vision for the community projected by the foundation. Representatives of all but one of the builder pairs participated in the interviews. Usually both builders in each pair participated.

Goal-Free Evaluation. Goal-free evaluations were conducted in years 3 and 5. A goal-free evaluation is one that is conducted by a highly competent evaluator who is not knowledgeable of the project being studied. This technique is especially useful for identifying and assessing unexpected project outcomes. The goal-free evaluators are told that their study of background information pertaining to the project will not include any information concerning the project's goals. The assignment is to enter the project area and the surrounding community and find out what the project actually did and achieved. Questions addressed included, What positive and negative effects flowed from the project? How were these effects judged regarding criteria of merit, such as quality of construction, quality of communication and collaboration within the community, and quality of organization and administration? *Thus, this technique was employed not to determine whether the project achieved what it set out to achieve, but to determine and judge what it actually did and achieved.* The goal-free evaluators interviewed persons both inside and outside the project site, observed project activities, visited other area projects focused on serving low-income families, and collected relevant area statistics and other available information. Observed achievements were credited regardless of project goals and then assessed for their significance. Significance was gauged against the participants' assessed needs and those of the surrounding, broader community.

Task Reports and Feedback Workshops. Throughout the evaluation, the evaluation team held feedback workshops with project staff to go over draft reports. Each report was keyed to one or more techniques and one or more of the evaluation design's components. Draft discussion reports were submitted to project staff well in advance of the time for finalization. Following staff review of draft reports, feedback workshops were conducted involving the evaluation team, project leaders and staff, and other stakeholders that the foundation's leaders invited. After the first year, the traveling observer was excluded from participation in the feedback workshop. These workshops were devoted to discussing the findings, identifying areas of ambiguity and inaccuracy in each report, and updating evaluation plans. Program personnel used the feedback workshops to apply evaluation to their own assessments and decision processes. The evaluators used the feedback both to strengthen and finalize reports and make needed adjustments in evaluation plans. (A checklist for conducting feedback workshops is available at www.wmich/evalctr/checklists.)

Synthesis and Final Report. The final method in this evaluation was that of synthesizing findings and finalizing the evaluation report. The final composite report was compiled by reviewing seven and a half years of previous reports, examining foundation documents, gathering additional information from foundation staff, and reflecting on experiences with the project. A draft of the final report was submitted to the foundation and discussed with foundation leaders and project staff. The evaluators then completed and delivered the report. Later, in their ninth year of involvement, the evaluators presented the findings and conclusions at a retreat of the foundation's board, which included invited interested parties from around the world.

Notably, the final report document is divided into three distinct reports. Report One focuses on the project's antecedents, including the foundation, the project's genesis, and its geographical context. Report Two examines the project's implementation, with an overview of the project and more detailed descriptions of its main operations: recruitment and selection, financing, construction, and social services and community development. Report Three, on the project's results, presents the evaluation design, findings, and overall conclusions. The findings are organized into context, input, process, impact, effectiveness, sustainability, and transportability. The conclusions are divided into merit, worth, and significance. Appendixes provide a list of all evaluation reports; the plan for selecting and interviewing case study families; interview protocols; a list of evaluation roles and participants; the evaluators' metaevaluation, including their attestations of the evaluation's success in meeting the Joint Committee Program Evaluation Standards; and an executive summary. The three reports tell the project's story in both words and photographs, with a photographic account included at the end of each one.

Evaluation Personnel

The evaluation's personnel included a succession of staff members as well as two who served throughout the evaluation. This is not unusual in a longitudinal evaluation. The constants were the lead evaluator and the project editor. For the other members of the team, transition from one to the other was relatively seamless and without difficulties.

Constraints

The evaluation team enjoyed a constructive working relationship with foundation staff and received high levels of cooperation from project beneficiaries. Thus, the evaluation proceeded relatively smoothly over its eight-plus years. The distance of the contracting evaluation center from the project site limited the amount of direct observation that the primary evaluators could do. This was somewhat offset by having an on-site traveling observer and regularly receiving documents from foundation staff. Toward the evaluation's end, funding for the evaluation was reduced, which necessitated discontinuing or reducing certain components of the evaluation, including the project profiles and environmental analyses. These cuts detracted from the evaluation team's ability to examine project outcomes in the context of up-to-date environmental conditions. Also, the evaluators were unable to obtain sufficient information on project costs to analyze and report the project's costs. Partly this was due to the foundation's need to keep its financial information confidential, but also because its accounting system was not set up to partial out all different categories of foundation expenditures to individual projects.

Cost of the Evaluation

A hallmark of the evaluation was its frugality. From the beginning, the evaluators and the sponsor agreed that full cost budgets would be approved, that these would be cost-reimbursable, and that the evaluators would constantly seek ways to cut costs. During one period when the foundation encountered fiscal difficulties with a downturn in the stock market, the evaluation's director charged for only half his time on the evaluation. Also, the evaluation center agreed to cut out some of the evaluation tasks that the foundation considered less important than others. In addition, the evaluation team was able to save the foundation substantial money for the evaluation by such means as sharing travel costs with other center projects being conducted in the self-help housing project's geographical area.

The full cost budget originally projected for this evaluation was $947,815. Due to cuts by the foundation, this amount was reduced to a contracted amount of $731,027. The final cost was $559,980. Thus, the evaluators saved the foundation approximately $171,047, or 23 percent of the contracted amount.

The important points learned from this evaluation's costs are as follows:

- At the outset it is important to budget for all the expected costs of the designed evaluation so that there is potential to carry out all the needed evaluation work.
- It is important for the evaluators and the client to agree on a principle of cost-effectiveness for the evaluation.
- At the outset, it is important for the evaluators and the client to develop an attitude of mutual trust regarding the client's paying what is needed and the evaluator's maintaining frugality.
- To enhance the evaluation's cost-effectiveness, it is desirable to work on a cost-reimbursable basis and charge only for actual costs incurred.
- As feasible, the evaluators should seek ways to save on evaluation costs, for example, by sharing travel costs with other evaluation projects in the project area.
- Sometimes the evaluation's scope should be reduced in the face of unanticipated problems in order to carry through the evaluation's core aspects without canceling it entirely.

We consider these points to be so important that both parties to an evaluation should consider making them a part of the basic working agreements, if not of the formal contract.

Metaevaluation

Although the evaluators advised the client to contract for an independent metaevaluation of this evaluation, this did not occur. As a partial compensation for this lack of an independent metaevaluation, the evaluators reported their attestation of the extent the evaluation satisfied the requirements of each of the thirty Joint Committee *Program Evaluation Standards*. This is good evaluation practice but no substitute for a truly independently funded and conducted metaevaluation. With hindsight, it would have been advisable for a thorough metaevaluation to have been an essential item in contractual arrangements. Such a metaevaluation, had it occurred, would have been of considerable value to both the client and the evaluation team.

Main Evaluation Findings

Ultimately this project substantially addressed the housing and related needs and directly affected the lives of 75 families, or about 390 people (155 adults and 235 children). Through participation in the project, the beneficiaries achieved:

- Vastly improved living circumstances
- A sense of great accomplishment in constructing the houses
- Functional and beautifully landscaped homes
- Affordable mortgages and land-lease purchase agreements (or, in the case of six families, rent-to-own agreements)
- Pride of ownership (for sixty-nine families)
- Community living guided by explicit values, covenants, and rules
- A community of values-oriented neighbors
- A safe, drug-free environment
- Increased knowledge of budgeting
- Skills to maintain their houses
- New friendships with the members of their increment, the program staff, and persons in the larger community
- Access to a wide range of foundation services

The community became a highly supportive environment for children. Family stability was strong, with only one divorce; all children completed their education at the elementary and secondary levels; and only one family left the community. An area of concern was that there were eight teenage pregnancies.

The program made only modest progress toward the goal of giving back to and strengthening the broader community. Also, much work remained in forming a community association and engaging the residents to take over and manage the community.

Turning over the community to the residents was fraught with uncertainties and difficulties. The foundation wanted to retain sufficient control to protect its investment and ensure the community's continued success. Foundation leaders worried that giving authority and responsibility to the residents prematurely could result in the project's deterioration. At the same time, some residents were reluctant to sever ties with the foundation since this might result in the community's receiving greatly reduced support from the foundation. Moreover, political issues and power conflicts within the community made it difficult for residents to establish and employ the needed lines of responsibility and authority. The issue of community self-governance represented perhaps the major threat to the project's long-term success. The foundation deserves credit for its extensive effort to promote community self-governance and sustainability. However, these efforts had yet to succeed. It will be of considerable interest to track further efforts and progress toward this community's sustainability.

On balance, the evaluation found the program to have many more strengths than weaknesses. Especially, it was guided and carried through by a cadre of dedicated, effective foundation officers and staff and hard-working, responsible program beneficiaries.

The evaluation revealed that the program was rich with lessons that can be applied to other community development efforts. Clearly, the foundation demonstrated features and benefits of a learning community guided by systematic evaluation and ongoing efforts to self-improve. The final evaluation report provided the foundation with institutional memory for use in guiding future efforts and informing interested parties about the program's approach, procedures, accomplishments, and problems.

Through this project, the foundation developed substantial expertise and credibility in the area of values-based, self-help housing. Moreover, this project essentially transformed the lives of 390 men, women, and children and significantly enhanced the well-being of the 75 participating families. These families became a powerful potential force for helping to revitalize and improve the community outside the project site. At the end of eight years, there was still little indication that this hope would be realized; nonetheless, this project became a rich example worthy of consideration by other community developers.

A copy of the full evaluation report on which this chapter is based can be found at www.wmich.edu/evalctr/pubs/consuelo. The report's title is *The Spirit of Consuelo* (an evaluation of a values-based, self-help housing and community development project for low-income families).

Request for a Follow-Up Evaluation

Five years following submission of the final report evaluating the project's first eight years, assume the foundation's board has decided to issue a request for proposals to conduct a follow-up evaluation to determine the extent to which the self-help housing project has continued to succeed and overcome its deficiencies and bring to fruition its previously unfinished efforts. Assume that the request for proposal (RFP) includes the description of the project that has been presented in this chapter and also refers potential respondents to the summative evaluation of that project, *The Spirit of Consuelo* (www.wmich.edu/evalctr/pubs/consuelo).

Proposals may apply any of the following evaluation approaches: case study, CIPP model, experimental design, Patton's utilization-focused evaluation, Scriven's consumer-oriented evaluation, or Stake's responsive evaluation. Program records can be reviewed at the foundation. Program beneficiaries can be interviewed, but the interviews cannot be tape-recorded. Program staff will assist the evaluation by collecting and storing some additional information that may not be in its files, provided the evaluators soon identify what information is needed. The evaluation should be completed within a twelve-month period. The foundation will reimburse the evaluators for relevant travel and lodging costs. Additional costs of the evaluation should not exceed fifty thousand dollars. The foundation will be responsible for securing a metaevaluation of this follow-up project evaluation.

The board and staff have identified a list of potential evaluation questions for the follow-up evaluation but do not want to restrict the evaluators to these questions. They want the proposing evaluators to consider the initial list of questions but to amend or add to them as they see best at the beginning of the evaluation or as they determine during its course. The initial list of evaluation questions follows:

- To what extent have the families remained in the community?
- To what extent has the community avoided gentrification?
- To what extent have the families kept up mortgage and land-lease payments?
- To what extent have the families as a whole succeeded in community organizing and self-governance?
- To what extent have the families kept up their property?
- To what extent has the community remained free of violence?
- To what extent has the community remained drug free?
- To what extent has the project made positive impacts on the community's children?
- To what extent has the community helped improve conditions in the outlying environment?
- To what extent have the residents become involved with each other as a collaborative, democratic, supportive community?
- How do residents of the outlying community perceive and judge this self-help housing-based community?
- To what extent has the project helped beneficiaries improve their economic viability?
- To what extent has the community incorporated and lived up to positive family and community values?

- To what extent is the foundation recouping its investment in this project through land-lease and house purchase payments?
- To what extent has the foundation played a limited but appropriate role in supporting the sustained success of this community?
- What should a foundation be prepared to invest to replicate this project?
- To what extent has the design of this project been adapted and applied elsewhere and with what results?
- To what extent has this project achieved results that are superior to those of alternative approaches to housing low-income families?

Summary

This chapter has provided a concrete example of how the CIPP model was used to evaluate a self-help housing project over a period of more than eight years. The chapter also presents a request for a follow-up evaluation of the project. The next six chapters provide in-depth information on six evaluation approaches that were previously summarized in this book. In each of those chapters, we provide commentary on how the approach might be employed to respond to the request for a follow-up evaluation summarized in this chapter.

CHAPTER THIRTEEN

EXPERIMENTAL DESIGN

The experimental design approach to program evaluation is intended to produce unequivocal conclusions about a program's effectiveness. The typical experimental design-based program evaluation involves random assignment of individuals, groups, or institutions to one of two or more study samples; applying a special treatment to one sample and none (or an alternative treatment) to the other sample; holding the treatment conditions constant throughout the evaluation; and ultimately assessing and comparing the samples' posttreatment performances on one or more outcome variables of interest. Random assignment of the experimental subjects to treatment and control (or alternative treatment) conditions is the sine qua non of this approach. It is done to ensure that the samples are equivalent and that posttreatment differences are due only to differences between the treatment and control (or alternative treatment) conditions and to enable the evaluator to estimate the statistical probability that observed differences are not due to chance variation. Assuming there are sufficient numbers of people in each group, an experimental design strengthens the chances that groups may be considered equal on a number of indexes that influence their response to the program's being investigated. Any differences in outcomes that emerge between the study groups following treatment implementation can, with a degree of validity, be attributed to the differences in treatments.

Boruch (2003) documented uses of experimental design for evaluating programs in a wide range of service areas: employment; criminal justice; health care;

cultural enrichment programs for children; preschool, elementary, and secondary
education; distance education; and AIDS reduction. Nave, Miech, and Mosteller
(2000) reviewed seven randomized field trials of education programs. These are
noteworthy for the range of designs employed to apply the principles of experimental design. The study designs demonstrate that randomized experimental design is a fairly large family of related configurations for studying programs' causes
and effects. In general, these applications of experimental design required substantial resources, a high level of methodological expertise, strong political commitment, random assignment of subjects to treatments, sustained cooperation of
experimental subjects, and relatively long periods of control over treatment implementation and data access and collection.

Caveats

Opportunities to meet the requirements of randomized experiments are quite limited. This is especially true in service fields such as education, transportation, and
social services and in innovative, developmental projects where a premium is placed
on creativity, trial and error exploration, and continual feedback for improvement.
The randomized experimental design approach seems to work best when the investigator can muster strong control of experimental variables. Prominent examples are testing seeds, fertilizers, pesticides, and cultivation practices in agriculture;
new drugs in the pharmaceutical industry; innovative procedures in medicine; and
different behavioral stimuli in experimental psychology.

Arguments used against the employment of the true experiments usually are
of two kinds. First, it is thought that a group or groups deprived of the new and
supposedly better treatment are at a decided disadvantage. A stronger argument
is that it is often impossible to keep groups free of a wide range of contaminating
factors. Then there is the logistical difficulty of arranging treatment and control
groups and convincing administrators and a range of stakeholders about the benefits of such procedures. Also, programs that seek continuous improvement and
innovative breakthroughs can be stifled when placed under strict controls required
by a true experimental design.

Boruch (2003) acknowledged that experimental design is not applicable to
many program evaluation situations. Certainly it is not a panacea. We disagree
sharply with the representatives of the U.S. Department of Education who have
often publicly cited randomized, controlled trials as the gold standard of program
evaluation and mandated its exclusive use for federally funded evaluations of educational programs. Sir Ronald Fisher (1951), the experimental design pioneer,

warned that his experimental design approach should not be equated to the method of inquiry, which is what the U.S. Department of Education has done.

While experimental design is valuable in a limited sphere, there are many needs for evaluation for which experimental design is not needed, is inappropriate, or is even counterproductive. These include especially the different stages of formative evaluation—for example, needs assessment, evaluation of program proposals, process evaluation, exception reporting, cost analysis, and monitoring for quality assurance. In such situations, randomization and holding treatments constant likely could constitute undue interference, be irrelevant, and/or be counterproductive. In such cases, preferable options to experimental design could include rigorous applications of many observational and analytical approaches, including especially case study, the success case method, self-reports followed by site visits by visiting teams, connoisseurship, the CIPP model, consumer-oriented evaluation, responsive evaluation, goal-free evaluation, and utilization-focused evaluation.

Even in the sphere of cause-and-effect evaluations, experimental design is only one of a host of applicable methods. Scriven (2005) made this clear when he argued persuasively that causal inferences can be obtained and strongly defended from a range of approaches other than randomized, comparative experiments. He posited that the correct gold standard of cause-and-effect-oriented program evaluations is not mandated randomized experiments but, instead, "conclusions beyond reasonable doubt," whatever the employed method. Such conclusions are obtainable from rigorous application of a wide range of approaches, including, but extending far beyond, experimental design. They include the study of germs and remedies applied to germ-free animals in gnotobiotic laboratories; epidemiological studies to determine causal agents in disease epidemics; diagnostic studies in medicine; diagnostic investigations of failures in buildings, bridges, automobiles, airplanes, and traffic control systems; DNA laboratory tests to determine paternity or criminal involvement; interrupted time-series studies; in-depth case studies; and regression discontinuity studies, among others.

We debated whether to devote a complete chapter to experimental design, thereby possibly giving this approach undue significance, particularly by comparison with the other five widely applicable approaches explored in Part Three. The main reason for our dilemma was that like many others (but not all) in the evaluation field, we hold some reservations about the usefulness and difficulty of implementing randomized, controlled experiments in dynamic worlds of education and social services. The experimental-scientific approach's requirements for randomization, control of treatments, and withholding of ongoing feedback for program improvement can inhibit the study and improvement of a program's merit and worth. On the other hand, it is possible to support the application of randomized, comparative experiments and quasi-experiments to evaluation when they are used appropriately to address cause and effect questions. Thus, despite the strong and often justified criticism of experimental design, we believe that the approach should not be disregarded. In certain well-defined program evaluation circumstances, randomized, controlled experimentation has a place and may elicit valuable information for decision making, especially in the realm of large-scale, highly funded policy evaluation.

Chapter Overview

In this chapter, we present randomized, controlled experimental design as a limited but useful evaluation approach that should be a part of the program evaluator's repertoire. We outline the philosophy and practice of an early, dominant figure in what was termed in the 1960s the scientific approach to evaluation, Edward A. Suchman. We then fast-forward to the early 2000s and discuss contemporary conceptions of randomized field trials and experimental design. We summarize different real-world adaptations of experimental design reviewed by Nave et al. (2000). Then, drawing from ideas of Suchman (1967) and Boruch (2003) and some of our own, we present guidelines for planning experimental design-based evaluations. The chapter concludes with a discussion of the applicability and appropriateness of experimental design to the illustrative evaluation assignment summarized in Chapter Twelve. We show that a true randomized experimental design is not workable in that evaluation situation.

Edward A. Suchman and the Scientific Approach to Evaluation

Edward Suchman set the principles of experimental design within a broad view of policy evaluation and stressed the importance of taking account of the relevant social context. His seminal writings on the topic greatly influenced the publications of other pioneers in experimental design, especially Donald Campbell and Julian Stanley. It is of note that Suchman distinguished between evaluation, which he equated to judgment, and evaluation research, which he denoted as judgment grounded in scientific research. For a time in the 1970s, *evaluation research* was a term much in vogue. It referred to an evaluation (that is, a judgment) based on empirical research and subject to the criteria of sound research, especially reliability and validity. The term *evaluation research* has largely disappeared from the evaluation literature and has been replaced by *evaluation* or *program evaluation*. Nevertheless, Suchman's early writings about evaluation research are highly relevant to the evaluation field as we know it today.

Suchman held that research scientists must base their conclusions primarily on scientific evidence. It follows that he believed that evaluation must be approached with the logic of scientific method. His work and writings during the 1960s, however, emphasized the need to assess programs in relation to their practical setting. For this reason, he suggested specific criteria for assessing program success. His studies in the field of social sciences, particularly public health, made him keenly aware that evaluation research is attended by practical constraints. Moreover, he stated that evaluation researchers, in their attempts to expose desirable and undesirable consequences, must consider relevant values, especially those in conflict.

In a key contribution to the field, *Evaluative Research: Principles and Practice in Public Service and Social Action Programs* (1967), Suchman stressed that evaluators should use whatever research techniques are available and appropriate to the circumstances and needs of a particular evaluation study. While he believed the ideal study would adhere to the classic experimental model, he also stressed that, in reality, evaluation research projects usually use some variation or adaptation of this model. To a large extent, formulation of the objectives and design of an evaluation research study will depend on who conducts the study and the anticipated use of outcomes.

Suchman was not alone in his belief that while evaluators are basically researchers, they must strike a balance between rigorous method and the situation in which they must function. Earlier writers who had advocated a similar approach to evaluation methodology included Klineberg (1955), James (1958), Herzog (1959), and Fleck (1961). Suchman differed from these writers by distinguishing clearly between evaluation and evaluation research. The former he referred to generally as "the process of making judgments of worth," while he considered evaluation research to be "those procedures for collecting and analyzing data which increase the possibility for proving rather than asserting the worth of some social activity" (p. 62). One could deduce that by distinguishing evaluation from evaluation research, Suchman was placing the evaluator in a technical role and reserving the valuational interpretation role for the client, which he often referred to as the administrator.

When he discussed the process of evaluation, he proposed a scientific approach grounded in logical positivism. He saw evaluation as a continuous social process, inherently involving a combination of basic assumptions underlying the activity being evaluated and of the personal values of the study participants as well as of the evaluator. Evaluation, he maintained, must necessarily become a scientific process to take into account this intrinsic subjectivity since it cannot be eliminated. With the development of models and approaches that espouse constructivism and postmodernism and do not want to eliminate subjectivity, many evaluators today would not embrace Suchman's focus on the precepts, standards, and methods of logical positivism and hypothetico-deductive research. It would be a decade after Suchman's untimely death in 1971 that intensive work on broader views of standards for evaluation would be undertaken and some years thereafter before they were being accepted and applied. The development of standards was a watershed in the history of evaluation. These include the standards and guidelines reviewed in Chapter Three and others keyed to experimental studies, including ethical requirements for experiments prescribed by the U.S. Federal Judicial Center and U.S. federal requirements of institutional review boards.

Viewing evaluation as a scientific process, Suchman maintained that the same procedures that we use to discover knowledge could be used to evaluate the degree of success in the application of this knowledge. He held strongly to the concept that by adopting the scientific method, an evaluator will produce findings that are more objective and of ascertainable reliability and validity. He viewed evaluation research as applied research and (with Ralph Tyler) saw its purpose as determining the extent to which a specified program is achieving the desired results. He said the results should be geared to help administrators make sound decisions regarding the program's future. Bearing in mind the dominant role of administrative criteria in determining a study's value, Suchman warned that the evaluator needs to be constantly aware of the potential utility of findings. This emphasis on the necessity for useful findings could give rise, in Suchman's opinion, to a very real problem for the evaluator. Because of strong vested interest, a program administrator will endeavor to control the evaluation, at least to the extent of defining the objectives of the program to be evaluated. To a far greater extent than the basic researcher, the evaluator loses control of the area being investigated. Thus, in Suchman's view it is not the concepts of research per se that make evaluation studies difficult, but rather the practical problems of adhering to these principles in the face of administrative considerations.

When he explored whether evaluation research is ready to play a more significant role, Suchman concluded that it is not. Systematic analysis of the theoretical, methodological, and administrative principles underlying the evaluator's objectives and procedures was needed before positive and meaningful steps forward could be taken confidently. It would not be too far-fetched to assume that almost four decades ago, Suchman was assuming that guidelines were necessary for both evaluator and client. We believe that he would have welcomed the sets of guiding principles and standards that have since been established.

Suchman's Purposes and Principles of Evaluation

Suchman supported the purposes of evaluation listed by Bigman (1961):

1. To discover whether and how well objectives are being fulfilled
2. To determine the reasons for specific successes and failures
3. To uncover the principles underlying a successful program
4. To direct the course of experiments with techniques for increasing effectiveness
5. To lay the basis for further research on the reasons for the relative success of alternative techniques
6. To redefine the means to be used for obtaining objectives and even to redefine subgoals in the light of research findings

These purposes, in Suchman's opinion, suggested an intrinsic relationship between program planning and development, on the one hand, and evaluation, on the other. In effect, the procedures used to achieve these evaluation purposes of evaluation must provide the basic information for designing and, if necessary, redesigning programs. Just as traditional research should lead toward increased understanding of basic processes, so evaluation research should "aim at an increased understanding of applied or administrative processes" (p. 64). This emphasis on the importance of administration and its processes is quite relevant to the evaluative case presented in Chapter Twelve and equally so to any attempt to evaluate the success or otherwise of the program five years after conclusion of the original evaluation.

Importantly, a principle that Suchman strongly espoused is that different situations warrant different evaluation approaches, including different technical methods and criteria for measuring the success in obtaining desired objectives. Based on the assumption that an evaluation study may take several forms and also that the primary function of most studies is to help stakeholders design, develop, and operate programs, Suchman drew the distinction between evaluation and evaluation research. The former designates the process of judging the worth of some activity, regardless of the method employed. Evaluation research, however, designates the specific use of the scientific method for the purpose of making an evaluation. In other words, evaluation can be considered a goal, while evaluation research can be considered a particular means of obtaining that goal.

We strongly stress that while Suchman considered that the use of scientific methodology needed a particular emphasis, he did not rule out the use of nonscientific methods. He acknowledged that in program design and implementation, many evaluation questions can be answered without research. Nevertheless, he maintained that if the basic requirements of evaluation research could be met—that is, underlying assumptions of objectives examined, measurable criteria developed specifically related to objectives, and a controlled situation instituted—then conclusions based on convincing research, and not just subjective judgment, would be the outcome.

Values and the Evaluation Process

A precondition to any evaluation study, Suchman maintained, is the presence of some activity whose objectives are assumed to have value. He defined value as "any aspect of a situation, event, or object that is invested with a preferential interest as being good, bad, desirable, undesirable, or the like "(p. 67). From this, we may construe that values—as modes of organizing human activity based on principles that determine both the goals and implementation of programs, together with the means of obtaining these goals—are a basic precept of any evaluation study. Suchman considered that the evaluation process stems from, and returns to the formation of values, as shown in Figure 13.1.

Despite a gap of decades, Suchman's philosophy that evaluation starts with a particular value (either explicit or implicit) and then proceeds to goal-setting activity—that is, a selection among alternative goals—is in accord with some, but not all, current philosophies of evaluation. Goal-setting forces are necessarily in competition with each other for resources and effort. We cannot argue against criteria being selected to measure goals attainment or that the nature of the goals would determine some of the measures used. However, a number of defensible evaluation approaches are not narrowly focused on goals in their selection of evaluative questions, criteria, and methods. At this stage, Suchman adopts a Tylerian approach when he requires the evaluation to seek the degree to which the operating program has achieved the predetermined objectives. Finally, based on this orientation, he seeks a judgment as to whether goal-directed activity was worthwhile. Elements of this approach will be used in the responses to the request for proposal (RFP) that concludes this chapter.

Figure 13.1 indicates that the act of judgment returns the activity to value formation. Suchman's concept of the cyclical movement of the evaluation process emphasizes the close interrelationship between evaluation and the value-laden nature of program planning and operation. As a result, there is the ever-present possibility of conflict of values between the program administrator and the evaluator. In general terms, it can be said that values play a large role in determining the objectives of social science programs and that the evaluation process that exposes desirable and undesirable consequences of such programs must take into account social values, especially conflicting values.

FIGURE 13.1. EVALUATION PROCESS.

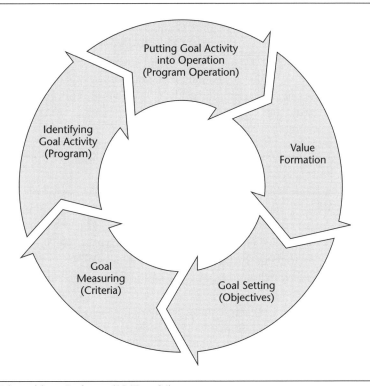

Source: Adapted from Suchman (1967, p. 34).

Assumptions for Evaluation Research Studies

Suchman's main assumption for evaluation studies is that every program has some value for some purpose. It follows that the most identifying feature of evaluation research "is the presence of some goal or objective whose measure of attainment constitutes the main focus of the research problem" (p. 71).

When a clear statement of the program objective to be evaluated has been explicated, the evaluation may be viewed as a study of change. The program to be evaluated constitutes the causal or independent variable, and the desired change is similar to the effect or dependent variable. Characterizing an evaluation study this way, Suchman postulated that the project may be formulated in terms of a series of hypotheses that state that activities A, B, and C will produce results X, Y, and Z.

Objectives and assumptions of an evaluation study are closely tied when the following difficult questions need to be answered before a study commences: What kinds of changes are desired? What means will be used to effect these changes? What signs will enable the change to be recognized? Before these questions can be addressed adequately, the evaluator must be able to diagnose the presence or absence of a social problem and its underlying value system and to define goals indicative of progress in ameliorating that condition.

Suchman outlined six questions that must be answered when formulating the objectives of a program for evaluation purposes and, indeed, the design of the study itself:

1. What is the nature of the content of the objective (for example, change in knowledge, attitudes, or behavior)?
2. Who is the target of the program (for example, large-scale or discrete groups)?
3. When is the desired change to take place (for example, short-term or long-term goals or cyclical, repetitive programs)?
4. Are the objectives unitary or multiple (for example, are the programs similar for all users or different for different groups)?
5. What is the desired magnitude of the effect (for example, widespread or concentrated results)?
6. How is the objective to be attained (for example, voluntary cooperation or mandatory sanctions)?

Many of the answers to these questions will require an examination of the underlying assumptions of the stated objectives. Suchman saw it as the duty of an evaluator to challenge these assumptions if necessary. He stressed that only then can the scientific label truly be applied to the evaluation process.

He classified assumptions into two types: value assumptions and validity assumptions. Value assumptions pertain to the system of beliefs that determines what is good within a society or part of that society. For example, a new education program may be viewed favorably or unfavorably by various groups within a school district. The question the evaluator must answer before investigating the program is, What is success, and from whose point of view?

Validity assumptions are specifically related to program objectives. Such assumptions, for example, underlie the belief of educators that early elementary programs must be consonant with the home influences of each child. Suchman stressed that answers to all validity questions can never be discovered before a program is initiated. The administrator should call on his or her experience and skill to develop practical programs whose assumptions are clearly laid down. The task of the evaluator is then to prove or disprove the significance and defensibility of these assumptions.

It is obvious that with his emphasis on experimental designs, Suchman was well aware of the world around the evaluation researcher and the necessity to deal with a program's constituents with all their strengths, weaknesses, idiosyncrasies, and values.

Suchman's Categories of Evaluation

Suchman spoke of three categories of evaluation studies. *Ultimate evaluation* refers to the determination of the overall success of a program in relation to its statement of objectives. *Preevaluative research* deals with intermediate problems (for example, development of reliable and valid explications of the problem, the definition of goals, and the perfection of techniques) that must be solved before ultimate evaluation may be attempted. *Short-term evaluation* seeks specific information about concrete procedures in terms of immediate utility.

In addition to varying levels of objectives, Suchman considered that evaluation research could be conducted in terms of different categories of effect. These categories represent various criteria of success (or failure) by which a program is judged. He proposed five categories:

1. Effort. Evaluations in this category have as their criterion of success the quantity and quality of program activity that takes place. This is an assessment of input regardless of output. It indicates at least that something is being done to solve a problem.
2. Performance. Criteria in this area measure results of effort rather than the effort itself.
3. Adequacy of performance. This criterion refers to the degree to which effective performance is adequate by comparison with the total amount of need (according to defined objectives).
4. Efficiency. Evaluation in this category addresses the question, Is the capacity of an individual, organization, facility, operation, or activity to produce results in proportion to the effort expended?
5. Process. The purpose of this category is to investigate basic explanations for reasons leading to the findings. Suchman outlined four dimensions of an analysis of process: the attributes of the program, the population exposed to the program, the context within which the program occurred, and the different kinds of effects produced by the program (for example, multiple or unitary effects and duration of effects).

In summary, in discussing types and categories of evaluation, Suchman outlined a basic process to be followed in conducting an evaluation study. This process entails stating objectives in terms of ultimate, intermediate, or immediate goals; examining the underlying assumptions; and instituting criteria of effort, performance, adequacy, efficiency, and process.

The Methodological Aspects of Experimental Designs

Suchman characterized evaluation research as a special kind of applied research whose goal, unlike nonevaluation or basic research, is not to discover knowledge but to test the application of knowledge. With its main emphasis on utility, Suchman posited that evaluation research should provide information for program planning, implementation, and development. Evaluation research, with its various experimental designs, also assumes the particular characteristic of applied research that allows predictions to the outcome of investigation. He said recommendations made in evaluation reports are examples of predictions. Unlike basic, laboratory research, the evaluation study based on experimental design contains an array of variables over which the evaluator has little, if any, control. Suchman stressed that in evaluation research, the observable and measurable variables are the phenomena of interest; the implemented program has as its goal the changing values of these measures. Whereas the underlying concept is of prime importance in basic, theory testing research, such is not the case in applied research, of which evaluation research is a form.

Suchman inadvertently or otherwise struck on the main limitation of the experimental approach in evaluation when he contended that program evaluation may have very little generalizability, because the evaluation is applicable solely to the program being evaluated with its contextual ramifications. In other words, the uncertainty is always present that a program that is effective in one situation very well may not be in another. Moreover, when problem-solving objectives of evaluation research are considered to give strength to administrative decision making for specific needs, further difficulties for external validity always present themselves.

The inherent difference between evaluation research and basic research studies according to Suchman and earlier writers is reflected in the form taken by the statement of the problem. Where pure research (nonevaluation research) questions whether A is related to B and tests this relationship experimentally (under controlled conditions), applied research (evaluation research) questions whether A works effectively to change B and attempts to answer this question empirically by manipulating A and measuring the effect on B. In basic, nonevaluation research, crucial importance is given to an analysis of a process whereby A relates to B; in evaluation research, it is far less important to understand why A produced B. These days, as readers will understand, evaluation emphasis must be given to the process that occurs between program initiation and findings. All five evaluation approaches that follow in Part Three (in Chapters Fourteen to Eighteen) adhere to this concept, as do modern conceptions of experimental design.

The differences between evaluation and nonevaluation research are not absolute, but may be considered to exist on a continuum. Suchman thought that an evaluator therefore should follow as closely as is practical the rules of scientific inquiry, but the evaluator must define and justify where and when these rules have to be adapted to reality.

Principles of Evaluation Research Design

Suchman presented a list of principles to be observed in laying out the design of an evaluation study; the main ones are as follows:

1. A good design is one that is the most suitable for the purpose of the study; whether or not it is scientific is not an issue.
2. There is no such thing as a single correct design; hypotheses can be studied by different methods using different designs.
3. All research design represents a compromise dictated by many practical considerations.
4. An evaluation research design is not a highly specific plan to be followed without deviation, but rather a series of guidelines to ensure that main directions are followed.

In Chapter Six of his 1967 book, Suchman gave details of possible variations in evaluation research design. Interested readers may wish to investigate these designs. Although Suchman believed that the ideal study would adhere to the classic experimental model, he also stressed that in reality, evaluation research projects usually use some variation or adaptation of this model. To a large extent, the formulation of the objectives and design of an evaluation research study will depend on who conducts the study and the anticipated use of the outcomes. He emphasized that while designing a study, an evaluator must be aware that validity considerations are crucial.

According to Suchman, the measurement of the effects of a program requires specification relating to four major categories of variables:

1. Component parts or processes of the program
2. Intended population and actual groups reached
3. Situational conditions within which the program occurred
4. Differential effects of the program

Suchman pointed out that determining both the reliability and validity of the criteria of effectiveness of these variables causes particular problems. For the most part, the evaluator measures not the phenomena being studied directly, but rather indexes of these phenomena. Two obvious problems present themselves. First, how does the evaluator decide on indicators for the criteria of achievement of program objectives? Second, how does the evaluator select from all possible indicators those to be used for a particular purpose?

In presenting ways to solve these problems, Suchman discussed aspects of the methodological concepts of reliability and validity at considerable length. In particular, he emphasized that evaluators should be aware of, and endeavor to control, the main sources of unsystematic variation in evaluation research:

- Subject reliability. Attitudes and behavior are affected by moods, fatigue, and so on.
- Observer reliability. Personal factors influence interpretation of subject's responses.
- Situational reliability. Conditions of measurement produce changes in results, which do not reflect true change in presentation being studied.
- Instrument reliability. All of the above (combined) or specific aspects of the instrument itself (for example, poorly worded questions) affect reliability.
- Processing reliability. Coding errors, occurring randomly, lower reliability.

Validity presents a much broader problem than reliability because it refers not only to specific measures, but also to the significance of the whole evaluation process. The validity of an evaluation study refers to the validity of its specific measures; it also refers to the theory underlying the hypotheses relating the evaluation's activities to its objective. Suchman identified the following sources of bias leading to validity concerns in evaluation studies:

- Propositional validity: the use of incorrect or inappropriate assumptions or theories
- Instrument validity: the use of irrelevant operational indexes
- Sampling validity: lack of population representativeness in the sample
- Observer (evaluator) validity: introduction of a consistent bias based on personal bias or preconceived notions
- Subject validity: habits and predispositions of subjects that introduce invalid biases
- Administration validity: conditions of the study (for example, methods of data collection) that constitute a source of invalidity.
- Analysis validity: deliberate or unintended bias that causes invalidity

The differential effects of a program encompass what Suchman termed *unanticipated* or *unintended effects*. Social phenomena are so complex and interrelated that to change one of its aspects becomes impossible without producing a series of connected changes, which Suchman termed *secondary effects*. These secondary effects of a program can be partially troublesome when the program is intended to be widely disseminated. Federally funded programs in education fall into this category just as much today as in Suchman's time. The evaluator and program administrator must therefore be wary of easy acceptance of secondary positive effects as justification for a program even if its intended objectives are not achieved; decisions concerning generalizability should take into account both intended and unintended effects. However, it is also important to understand that research is a learning process and that the secondary effects (desirable or undesirable), and the analysis of these effects, is an integral part of this process.

Given the preceding account of Suchman's treatment of the foundations of experimental design in the social sciences, we turn next to contemporary treatments of this approach.

Adaptations of Experimental Design

Nave et al. (2000) described seven significant applications of experimental design in education. Their account is valuable because (1) the involved designs are adaptations that had to take account of real-world circumstances; (2) they reveal an array of different ways to apply the principles of experimental design; (3) they demonstrate that under special circumstances, experimental designs can be usefully applied, even in the dynamic world of education; and (4) they illustrate the state-of-the-art of experimental design.

In characterizing such designs, it can be useful to use the following symbols:

P: the defined population to which study findings are to be generalized

R: a random sample of study subjects from a defined population

r: random assignment of study subjects to a treatment or control condition

O: an observation or set of observations made on a criterion variable

T: a treatment

The classic experimental group-control group, posttest only experimental design would be configured using the above symbols as follows:

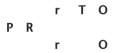

In this design, a specific population of interest (**P**) is defined. The study sample was drawn randomly (**R**) from the defined population. Study subjects were then randomly assigned (**r**) to a special treatment (**T**) or a nonspecial control condition (represented by a blank). Following the experimental group's exposure to the experimental treatment, both groups were assessed on one or more criterion variables of interest (**O**). Subsequently, the evaluator tested the statistical significance of differences between the experimental and control groups on posttreatment measures. It can be assumed further that the evaluator next drew inferences with stated levels of confidence on whether the treatment caused an elevated level of performance on the subject outcome measure and could be expected to do so in the population at large. Such inferences were made possible because subjects were randomly chosen from a known population and because, due to random assignment, there were only chance differences between the members of the treatment and control groups before the treatment was applied to the treatment group.

Next, it is of interest to move beyond this theoretical conception of experimental design and see how the concept has worked out in practice. We will summarize and characterize three of the studies that were reviewed by Nave et al. (2000). These studies illustrate the range of possibilities for applying the principles of experimental design.

Tennessee Class Size Study (1985–1989)

This experiment studied the effects of reduced class size on student achievement in kindergarten and grades 1, 2, and 3 in about eighty diverse public elementary schools throughout Tennessee. The initial study assessed student achievement in math and reading annually for four years. A follow-up study continued to assess the achievement of each group for additional years. We have combined both studies in an overall characterization of the employed experimental design. At the risk of oversimplifying the actual study design, we have represented it as follows:

$$
\begin{array}{cccccccccccccccc}
 & r & T1 & O & T1 & O & T1 & O & T1 & O & O & O & O & O & O \\
P & r & T2 & O & T2 & O & T2 & O & T2 & O & O & O & O & O & O \\
 & r & & O & & O & & O & & O & O & O & O & O & O \\
\end{array}
$$

The population of interest (P) included all the kindergarten and first-, second-, and third grade students and teachers in Tennessee. The study groups were nonrandom samples of sixty-four hundred kindergarten students and three hundred teachers. While the involved schools had accepted invitations to participate, they were from throughout the state and were from inner-city, urban, suburban, and rural areas. Both the students and teachers were randomly divided into and kept in three subgroups for four years. Treatment group 1 students and teachers (T1) were in small classes of thirteen to seventeen students. Treatment group 2 students and teachers (T2) were in regular size classes of from twenty two to twenty five students and also had a teacher's aide. The control group students and teachers (blank) were in regular size classes of from twenty two to twenty five students and had no teacher's aide. Students' reading and arithmetic achievement scores were monitored across the four years of the study and subsequently across additional years. Comparisons between the groups showed that small class sizes had a positive and statistically significant effect lasting at least through the eighth grade. As a consequence, the Tennessee legislature allocated billions of dollars to lower class size in grades K-3 in seventeen impoverished school districts. Subsequent investigation in these seventeen districts showed marked improvement in both math and reading test scores.

The High/Scope Perry Preschool Study (1962–1965 and Beyond)

This experiment studied the effects of a rigorous preschool program for 123 disadvantaged children who were considered to be at risk of failure in school and later life. The treatment was delivered from 1962 through 1965, and treatment and control group participants were followed for more than thirty years. Hypothesized benefits of preschool experience included development of cognitive skills, success in school, graduation from high school, employment, economic self-sufficiency, positive family relationships, social responsibility, and staying out of jail. The design of this study could be configured approximately as follows:

1962—Wave 0

r T1 O O O O O O O O O O O O O O O O O O O O O O O O O O O O O O O O

r   O O O O O O O O O O O O O O O O O O O O O O O O O O O O O O O O

1962—Wave 1

r T2 O T2 O O O O O O O O O O O O O O O O O O O O O O O O O O O O O O O O

r   O   O O O O O O O O O O O O O O O O O O O O O O O O O O O O O O O

1963—Wave 2

r   T2 O T2 O O O O O O O O O O O O O O O O O O O O O O O O O O O O O O O

r   O   O O O O O O O O O O O O O O O O O O O O O O O O O O O O O O

1964—Wave 3

r   T2 O T2 O O O O O O O O O O O O O O O O O O O O O O O O O O O O O O

r   O   O O O O O O O O O O O O O O O O O O O O O O O O O O O O O

1965—Wave 4

r   T2 O T2 O O O O O O O O O O O O O O O O O O O O O O O O O O O O O O O

r   O   O O O O O O O O O O O O O O O O O O O O O O O O O O O O O

This study had five waves of participants, all from Ypsilanti, Michigan—two waves in the first year of the study and one in each of the three subsequent years. Each wave was randomly divided into a treatment group and a control group. The former received daily classroom sessions and home visits, while the latter received no preschool service. During the first year, the Wave 0 group of four-year-olds participated that year in the preschool experience (T1), and the Wave 1 group of three-year-olds (T2) began their two-year stint of preschool. The treatment groups in Waves 2, 3, and 4 (also T2) were three-year-olds who all received two years of preschool experience. As feasible, all experimental and control participants were followed up for more than thirty years. The evaluators applied a wide range of education, social, and economic measures to assess the program's success. Based on these measures, this program yielded many positive short-range and long-range benefits.

The Career Academies Study (1992–2003)

This is a ten-year project to study the effects of career academies on high school students' academic achievement, progress toward graduation, and preparation for postsecondary education and employment. The design of this study can be characterized as follows:

Experimental Group

High-risk students   T   O   T   O   T   O   T   O   O   O   O   O   O   O

r

Low-risk students   T   O   T   O   T   O   T   O   O   O   O   O   O   O

Control Group

High-risk students   O   O   O   O   O   O   O   O   O   O

r

Low-risk students   O   O   O   O   O   O   O   O   O   O

Over a three-year period, about seventeen hundred volunteer eighth- and ninth-grade students across nine schools were randomly divided into a 959-member career academies group and an 805-member control/traditional high school group. For analysis purposes, the experimental and control groups were divided into high-risk and low-risk students. Student outcomes were monitored over a ten-year period using school records and other data on attendance, achievement, course-taking patterns, progress through high school, and post–high school performance. At the end of twelfth grade, high-risk students in the career academy group exceeded their control group counterparts in reduced dropout rates, improved attendance, increased participation in academic courses, and progress toward graduating on time. However, of 490 students who completed twelfth-grade math and reading tests, no significant differences were found between the treatment and control students. Also, when all students' performance was analyzed, there were only minor advantages for the experimental group. This application of experimental design illustrates the increased precision that one can obtain by employing blocking variables on randomized experimental and control groups to look at effects on subgroups, such as males and females, minority and nonminority groups, and low- and high-risk groups.

Contemporary Guidelines for Designing Experiments

As Boruch (2003) noted, experimental design is very much a preordinate approach to evaluation. He advised evaluators to specify basic elements of a contemplated randomized field trial in advance. Below we summarize advice from him as well as Suchman and add some of our own.

Deciding Whether to Proceed with an Experiment

There are many needs for evaluations in which a randomized experiment would be inappropriate, not feasible, or not influential. Before proceeding to conduct an experiment, the evaluator should ascertain the feasibility of the contemplated study (with all its possible social, legal, and ethical issues). As an essential part of planning for the study, the evaluator should conduct an evaluability assessment to determine whether the study would meet the following requirements:

1. There is a well-defined treatment that can be implemented with fidelity.
2. There is confusion about and/or a clear need for information on the treatment's effectiveness.
3. There is (or can be obtained) sufficient clarity and consensus on the program's objectives and the values it should serve to warrant selection of credible and defensible outcome measures.

4. The findings of the projected experimental study would address the study's purpose and effectively address stakeholders' questions.

5. There are a sufficient number of potential experimental subjects to produce stable findings on outcomes.

6. There is assurance that study subjects will consent to be assigned randomly to experimental and control conditions.

7. There is capacity, willingness, and agreement on the part of needed institutions to fully and faithfully play their roles in carrying out a randomized, comparative experiment.

8. There is a strong, documented commitment from authority figures to maintain conditions necessary to faithfully implement the treatment and carry out the study over its full course.

9. Program staff members understand and accept that the evaluation will not provide them with formative evaluation for continual program improvement.

10. Program staff members are on record as agreeing to comply with randomization requirements and retain and hold the program treatment constant during the course of the experiment.

11. Needed approvals from relevant institutional review boards and government organizations are in place to ensure that the needed information can be obtained.

12. Those who are expected to participate in the treatment conditions and provide the needed information have given their written commitment to do so.

13. Any necessary guarantees of anonymity or confidentiality can be fulfilled.

14. The available evaluation staff possesses the technical expertise and availability to competently conduct all aspects of the study.

15. There is reasonable written assurance that the resources required to carry out the full experiment will be provided.

16. There is ample evidence that audiences for the evaluation report trust and have confidence in the evaluation team's integrity and competence.

17. Overall, the contemplated experimental study would be feasible to conduct, be completely ethical, yield valid information on the program's effectiveness, and produce findings that would be used.

If any of the above conditions have not been met or cannot be met, the evaluator should not proceed with an experimental study and possibly should not conduct any other kind of study. Before declining the evaluation assignment, it would be useful to consider whether some other evaluation approach would be feasible and credible and produce valuable information on the subject program. It is possible that persons' unwillingness to meet certain of the above conditions would disappear if the evaluation were not constrained by requirements for randomization and experimental controls. For example, if program staff members knew they would get continual feedback to help improve the program and that using the feedback for program improvement was acceptable, they might be more forthcoming in supplying requested information and cooperating in other ways.

Values, Theory of Change, and Success Variables

As Suchman (1967) stressed, before proceeding with an experiment, the evaluator should determine and examine the values being sought through the program and the theory of how desired changes are to be obtained. These determinations provide the basis for identifying and assessing the needs of intended beneficiaries; defining the desired treatment; clarifying and assessing the ultimate, intermediate, and immediate program goals; determining which intended outcomes are targeted to which parts of the intended beneficiaries; and selecting appropriate outcome measures. It is almost a given that different stakeholders will have different, even contradictory ideas about what the program should do and not do and what it should achieve and not achieve. Also, different intended beneficiaries might have different needs to be served by the program. Some persons are likely to worry that certain of the program's outcomes will be undesirable or harmful to particular program participants or other interested parties.

Before agreeing to conduct the evaluation, the evaluator is advised to meet with representatives of the full range of stakeholders, especially those who might be harmed by implementation of the program. When there are sharp value conflicts relating to the program, the evaluator should consider engaging stakeholders in a values clarification and consensus-building process. The evaluator also should judge whether the determined program goals are ethical and worth achieving.

If clear and defensible program goals have been identified, the evaluator can proceed to design the study based on the program's underlying values. As part of this process, the evaluator should seek to understand the client group's theory of how the program is expected to bring about the desired changes. As Suchman recommended, the evaluator would define the independent and dependent variables, state the hypotheses to be tested, diagnose the social or technical problem underlying the desire for change, clarify the desired changes and whether different changes are being sought for different subsets of beneficiaries, clarify the means to effect the changes, and define the signs of actual change. If serious value conflicts cannot be resolved, if the stakeholders are unable to clarify the value system underlying the program, or if the program treatment and/or goals are unethical, the evaluator should decline to design and conduct the experiment.

Key Evaluation Questions

Having structured a randomized experiment, the evaluator is advised to exploit its power for addressing a wide range of relevant questions. The evaluator should consider addressing questions concerning the program's effects, such as the following:

1. What were the quantity and quality of the effort to carry out the program?
2. What were the program's intended and unintended outcomes?
3. To what extent were program outcomes long range as well as immediate?
4. To what extent did the program target and effectively address the needs of the intended beneficiaries?
5. What were the program's differential effects on different parts of the experimental and control groups?
6. What were the reasons for observed outcomes?
7. How could program administrators make the program more effective or more efficient?
8. Was the investment in the program justified by its outcomes?
9. To what extent did program outcomes lead to changes in policies and practices inside and outside the program's geographical area?
10. What are the program's implications for further research in the program area?

Population, Units of Randomization, and Statistical Power

In many studies, it makes sense to define the population of interest and randomly select the members of the study sample from this group. A random sample drawn from a population of interest enhances the possibility of extrapolating study findings to the larger population. However, in any long-range study, the population of interest at the study's conclusion could be substantially different from the original population. Such forces as gentrification can greatly change the composition and characteristics of a population in a particular area. Also, investigators rarely have sufficient control over sample selection to draw a random sample from a defined population. Usually it is necessary to deal with volunteers or other intact, nonrepresentative groups.

In such cases, about the best an evaluator can do is to randomly assign the members of the convenience group to experimental and control conditions. Random assignment is a powerful technique for ensuring equivalence of the comparison groups. The randomly assigned experimental and control units may be individual persons or intact groups. If the individuals are members of groups such as classrooms, then their interactions with one another make them nonindependent units. In such cases, the need to meet the independence requirements of statistical analysis dictates that the group should be employed as the unit of analysis.

However, this well-established statistical principle can be problematic. If using groups reduces the number of experimental units to only a few, then the power of the analysis to detect treatment differences is low. Violating the assumption of independence by using individuals within groups as the experimental units may add statistical power. Sometimes it can be instructive to perform analyses on both individuals and groups and compare the results. Boruch (2003,) advises that "the main rules of thumb in assuring statistical power are (a) do a statistical power analysis, (b) match on everything possible prior to randomization and then randomize, (c) get as many units as possible, and (d) collect covariate/background data and time series data to increase the trial's power. . ." (p. 113).

Interventions

The heart of any experimental study is one or more well-defined, powerful, and well-implemented treatments whose effects are of practical and often theoretical interest. The evaluator must proceed only on the basis that there is a definite treatment, that it will be faithfully implemented, that it will be held constant, that it will be applied only to the experimental group, and that its implementation can be monitored and verified. On this last point, it is essential that feedback from monitoring the treatment not become part of the treatment. If feasible, it is desirable that treatments be monitored, stabilized, and verified before starting an experiment. In advance of starting an experimental design evaluation, it is prudent to provide program staff with program guidelines and pertinent training. In general, experimental design evaluators should not waste time, resources, and effort in evaluating weak or phantom treatments.

Random Assignment

As noted repeatedly in this chapter, random assignment of subjects to treatments is a core feature of the experimental design approach. Random assignment must be done so that every experimental unit has an independent and equal chance of being assigned to the experimental or control group. It should be done in an unbiased manner and close to the time when the treatment group will be involved in the program. The sample from which subjects will be randomly assigned should be large enough to ensure equivalence between the comparison groups. Boruch (2003) advises that "if it is possible to match or block, prior to randomization, this ought to be done" (p. 115). Prior to random assignment, the evaluator should obtain assurance that all units in the study sample are committed or will be required to participate faithfully in the group to which they are randomly assigned and to do so for the full duration of their intended involvement.

The mechanics of random assignment preferably is done through use of an appropriate software package or a random numbers table. The randomization process should be managed by a person with no vested interest in the program. Boruch (2003) advises against such loose approaches as coin tosses and pulling numbers from a hat because they are prone to bias.

Observation, Measurement, and Theory

The modern concept of experimental design requires a comprehensive approach to data collection. The evaluator should collect both quantitative and qualitative information and should be careful not to collect unneeded information. The required information includes the background characteristics of each person or entity in the treatment and control groups, the program's context, relevant needs-assessment information, intended and actual beneficiaries, field notes on how and how well the experimental treatment was implemented, the activities of persons or entities in the control group, a record of program costs, differential effects, intended and unintended outcomes, and responses to all agreed-on investigatory questions. In choosing measurement variables, the evaluator can be aided by considering the elements of a relevant theory that denote how particular treatments are expected to produce desired outcomes. In assessing the implementation of the treatment, the evaluator should record and keep a count of instances of poor implementation and nonimplementation plus qualitative information on the reasons for noncompliance. The rich array of collected data should be recorded in detailed technical appendixes to the evaluation report.

Management

Evaluations based on experimental design require sustained, competent, and effective management. The study manager must secure the required funding; establish and maintain mutual trust among the involved parties; secure needed cooperation from various individuals, groups, and institutions; appoint and involve advisory panels; involve other interest groups; schedule the needed work; delegate authority and responsibility for different parts of the study; recruit, train, and supervise staff; anticipate and cope with political threats to the study; maintain control of the implementation of the experimental design; take necessary steps to ensure that experimental and control groups are kept separate; maintain communication with all interested parties; foster positive public relations for the study; host visiting dignitaries, researchers, content experts, program stakeholders, and members of the media; maintain fiscal accountability; meet all legal requirements; write and deliver necessary management reports; report on progress to the evaluation's sponsors, client, and professional reference groups; subject the study's plans, process, and reports to independent evaluations; foster dissemination of study findings; and troubleshoot and solve problems as needed. Clearly there is much more to conducting a sound, experimentally-oriented evaluation than just carrying out the technical work. The evaluation management task is essentially the same for all types of evaluation.

In spite of the evaluator's best efforts to effect the needed controls, the conditions required to conduct a successful experiment might break down at any point during the study process. Therefore, it is prudent for the evaluator to prepare contingency plans in case this happens. For example, the evaluator might be prepared, if necessary, to convert the randomized, controlled experiment to a quasi experiment or even a case study.

Analysis

Data from experiments should be thoroughly and systematically analyzed. Appropriate analyses are necessary to determine whether the experiment was carried out as planned, whether the treatment condition of interest produced better results than a control condition or alternative treatment, whether observed differences are practically important, whether the program was more effective for some subgroups of the treatment sample than others, and whether the findings may be extrapolated to other settings. The following are classes of analysis needed to address this range of issues.

Design Implementation Analysis. This analysis is necessary to determine the extent to which treatments were implemented as intended and applied to the intended beneficiaries and to confirm that experimental and control (or alternative treatment) groups did not differ in important ways at the experiment's outset and did not become contaminated with each other along the way. The evaluator should compile and analyze field notes on how and how well the treatment was carried out; the extent to which experimental and control conditions were applied consistently and exclusively to the intended groups; any major deviations from the intended treatment process; and, in general, the fidelity of the implementation of treatments. Most of these analyses will be qualitative in nature. The evaluator should assess the extent to which the comparison groups were equivalent by presenting tables comparing the groups at the experiment's outset on such variables as socioeconomic status, ethnic origin, age, gender, school years completed, aptitude test scores, and grade point average.

Core Analysis. What Boruch (2003) has labeled core analysis addresses the central question in any experiment: Is the observed difference between the comparison groups statistically significant? Such analysis estimates the magnitude of difference between the assessed outcomes for the groups and, based on the theory of randomization, gives a statistical statement of the level of confidence that the difference is not due to chance variation. Determinations of statistical significance follow the rules of *t*-tests, analysis of variance, analysis of covariance, and other relevant tests. Based on the theory of randomization, these tests indicate the number of times (such as less than one or less than five) out of one hundred that the observed difference would be expected based on chance variation. Any observed difference beyond the chosen .05 or .01 significance level is judged to be statistically significant. As Boruch emphasizes, tests of statistical significance must analyze outcome measures for the comparison groups as they were originally randomly assigned. This is required to adhere to the statistical theory and logic associated with comparing equivalent groups. If by some circumstance some members of an experimental group switched to the control group (or vice versa) during the course of the experiment, it is not permissible to switch them from their original assigned group for purposes of analysis. Data on them must be included with the data for the group to which they were originally assigned. This is essential to preserve the validity of the statistical analysis and also ensures conservatism in claiming a statistically significant difference.

Practical Significance. Since policymakers or program stakeholders may not always consider a statistically significant difference important, the investigator often will conduct further analysis (such as an omega square test) to help the interested parties reach a judgment of whether the observed difference has practical significance. More typically, judgments of practical significance will be secured through qualitative means. For example, before findings are obtained, the investigator might engage focus groups to discuss and reach agreement on what level of difference would be sufficiently important to adopt an innovation being compared with current practice. Following a determination of statistically significant findings, the evaluator might reconvene the focus group, confront the participants with their previous conclusions on practical significance and the findings on statistical significance, and engage them to consider whether the statistically significant differences obtained are sufficiently important to warrant adoption of the experimental approach.

    As another approach, the investigator might conduct a cost analysis to help decision makers consider whether the possible improved performance available from adopting a new practice is worth the projected cost of adopting the approach (which could be more or less than the cost of current practice). For example, a school board might not be willing to bear a substantial cost of reduced class size if the statistically significant improvement in test scores is only two or three points on a standardized test.

A Posteriori or Correlational Tests. Often the core analysis will yield a statistically significant interaction between the treatment variable and blocking variables, such as gender or socioeconomic level. In general, such significant interactions indicate that while treatment differences might not be statistically significant overall, there could be significant differences between treatment and control condition results for certain subgroups. For example, reduced class size might not show statistically significant improvement for a total group of students but could reveal significant differences between treatment and nontreatment students from impoverished homes. Probing of such observed subgroup differences through a posteriori or correlational tests may not yield findings that are supportable from the underlying theory of random assignment but can yield hypotheses for further investigation and policy level deliberation.

Literature Review. Still another form of analysis is to conduct a literature review. One would conduct a structured search of the relevant literature to identify studies that were similar to the subject experiment. One's experiment and the relevant similar studies found in the literature would then be compared. They would be contrasted on design, study samples, procedures, and findings. The central question would be whether the subject study produced findings that coincide with those of quite similar studies. Differences in findings would be discussed based on whether they might represent instability in one's findings or possibly be attributable to other factors concerning when the studies were conducted and whether, for example, they differed substantially in study samples, treatments, social context, and criterion measures. The results of such an analysis would be useful in assessing the firmness of one's findings and possibly their generalizability.

Reporting

In accordance with the preordinate nature of randomized experiments, agreements on reporting evaluation findings should be determined at the study's outset and recorded in the study's contract. Key reporting agreements, according to the Joint Committee on Standards for Educational Evaluation (1994), include the following:

- Rightful report recipients. Often these are the client that commissioned the evaluation, those legally responsible for the subject program, those who in some way helped fund the program, those who contributed a substantial amount of information to the evaluation, and other stakeholders who are quoted in or will be affected by the report.

• Use of reports and reporting formats that are appropriate for the different intended users. These may include a main report of study questions, experimental subjects, design, data collection procedures, and findings; an extensive technical report containing instruments, procedures, description of study subjects, analyses, and evaluator qualifications; a report of an independent audit or metaevaluation; a journal article; or a computer-assisted presentation of main points from the study.

• An appropriate schedule of reporting keyed to both the times when different parts of the information will be available for release and the needs of the intended users.

• Specification of authority and responsibility for finalizing and disseminating evaluation findings. The evaluator must retain basic authority for preparing findings and editing reports. Moreover, the evaluation contract should ensure that the evaluator's final report will be provided to an agreed-upon audience. If different reports are to be given to different parts of the audience, this should be specified in the contract along with the proviso that the evaluator will control content and editing. Typically, the evaluator should obtain firm written agreements that the client will assist with getting the appropriate reports to the appropriate subsets of intended users.

Metaevaluation

As with all other approaches to program evaluation, experimental designs should be subjected to formative and summative metaevaluations. Preferably these are conducted by an independent methodologist or a team of methodologists. Formative metaevaluation monitors and provides feedback on the extent to which the evaluation study adheres to the original design. The summative metaevaluation assesses the extent to which the evaluation meets the requirements of utility, feasibility, propriety, and accuracy, as defined in Chapter Three. (For an example, see Finn, Stevens, Stufflebeam, and Walberg, 1997.)

Writers on experimental design have stressed the importance of assessing the validity of an experiment. Earlier in this chapter, we cited Suchman's excellent analysis of the concept of validity. Especially, the experimentally oriented evaluations should assess the following validity questions:

1. Propositional validity. Is the experiment design grounded in correct and appropriate assumptions or theoretical propositions?

2. Instrument validity. Are the measures of process and outcomes relevant to the study's questions and design?
3. Sampling validity. Is the study sample representative of the population of interest?
4. Observer (evaluator) validity. Are study findings free of biases of those engaged in collecting and analyzing information?
5. Subject validity. Are study processes and findings free of biases of the experimental subjects?
6. Administration validity. Are study processes and findings and processes free of biases that might be inherent in the data collection methods employed?
7. Analysis validity. Are study findings free of deliberate or unintended biases in the methods of analysis?

A Few Words About Quasi-Experimental Designs

Because so often it is difficult to implement a true experimental design, evaluators and other researchers may turn to a quasi-experimental design (Campbell & Stanley, 1963; Cook & Campbell, 1979). In certain circumstances, these may be quite feasible because they do not involve random assignment of participants. However, they do require that the treatment be well defined and implemented and, if there is a control group, that it be kept separate from the experimental group. Quasi experiments are claimed to overcome more threats to internal validity—and thus enhance their credibility—than studies that impose no controls on treatments and experimental subjects. Also, quasi-experimental designs have been shown to have better external validity than true experiments (Bracht & Glass, 1968) because the latter often impose controls that would be hard to impose elsewhere. There are two commonly used quasi-experimental designs.

The *pre-post, nonequivalent comparison group design* has elements similar to the randomized experimental and control group pre-post design, but the former's subjects for the study are not randomly assigned to groups. In place of randomization, evaluators endeavor to find a group as similar as possible to the one that will receive the new program through a procedure such as matching experimental and control group subjects. It logically follows that the pretest is a most important part of this design, particularly if it can help demonstrate equivalence of groups. Also, a variety of pretest measures may be used as covariates in order to remove initial differences between the groups.

Another quasi-experimental design that is valuable under prescribed circumstances is the *interrupted time-series design*. It requires that data be collected numerous times prior to the commencement of the program and then many times following its conclusion. This design is particularly useful when the new treatment, in whatever form it might take, must apply widely within a designated area, for example, a school district, a state hospital, a large manufacturing business, or a state's traffic control system. One might analyze the pattern of auto accident–related deaths in years prior to introduction of a mandatory seat belt law compared with such deaths in subsequent years. It is interesting to note that possibly the most frequent application of the interrupted time-series design for evaluation is used in connection with databases that have been regularly updated prior to, through, and following the intervention.

Reprise

Randomized, controlled experimental design was quite prominent in program evaluations during the late 1960s and early 1970s because the U.S. federal government required its use to evaluate federally funded innovations in education and other social services. The approach's consistent widespread failure to produce useful information, especially in education, caused it to lose favor and be replaced by a host of new program evaluation approaches, especially from the mid-1970s through the 1990s. Ironically, the federal government in this century has once more mandated the use of randomized experiments to evaluate federally funded education programs and is holding federal evaluation funds hostage to this requirement. We see this as a serious error in judgment. While there have been some successful experimental design evaluations of education programs, sound experiments that have produced useful information about education programs have been rare. Currently many sound and useful evaluation models and approaches capture the nuances of a program and provide useful formative feedback in ways that experimental design approaches never can. Nevertheless, pioneers using experimentation to evaluate programs, including Boruch (2003), Campbell and Stanley (1963), Cook and Campbell (1979), Cronbach and Snow (1969), Nave et al. (2000), and Suchman (1967), have played a valuable part in program evaluation.

In our effort to be fair and balanced, we devoted most of this chapter to describing the foundations of experimental design and presenting guidelines for deciding when and how to apply the approach. It is quite possible, of course, for an experimental design to be used as a part of a wider evaluation, and we acknowledge that the prevalent use and success of experiments in fields such as medical and agricultural sciences have justifiably gained considerable credibility. It is especially when the units receiving treatments are in social groups, such as schools, that randomized experimental design has severe limitations. We stress that randomized, controlled experimentation must never be construed as the single best methodology in most program evaluation situations. We agree with Scriven (2005) that the appropriate gold standard of cause-and-effect-oriented studies is not a randomized, controlled experiment but conclusions beyond reasonable doubt, whatever evaluation approach is applied. In field situations where true experiments are appropriate and feasible, the practices of randomization and control of treatments can produce sound and useful information on program effectiveness; however, such circumstances are rare.

Applicability of the Experimental Design Method to the Self-Help Housing Project

Chapter Twelve outlined a request for a proposal (RFP) to evaluate the sustained success of a self-help housing project. We must state that we cannot envisage that an experimental design will come close to fitting the bill, as the conversation that follows indicates. This is the setting: Ellen and Bill are two experienced evaluators in a small evaluation firm, headed by Caroline.

We eavesdrop.

Ellen: *The Spirit of Consuelo* Report is about as convincing and complete as any that I have seen. Certainly, it is a good starting point for a subsequent study after five years. My only concern is that Caroline is simply too insistent on an experimental approach to this follow-up study. She apparently is convinced that, like the feds, large programs in the public domain should be reviewed in a semi-scientific fashion. Shades of Suchman!

Bill: I was looking at this RFP with considerable interest until this constraint was landed on us. I know that Caroline wishes to send a response to the foundation as soon as possible—deadline in two weeks, I think—but I don't quite know where to begin. My only suggestion is that you and I work out a response to Caroline, based on what she wants, and hope that we offer sufficient common sense for her to pen a suitable, and perhaps even convincing, proposal to the Consuelo group. But I know it should not be experimental in nature. What do you think?

Ellen: Let's face it: a true experiment is out of the question even as part of this evaluation. Imagine us trying to randomly assign beneficiaries, such as different groups among the self-help housing project, to experimental and control groups and then trying to contrast the outcomes after the experimental group, whatever that might be, receives intervention and the control group receives no special treatment of any kind. Plausibly, this kind of manipulation may have occurred at the start of the program between groups receiving different kinds of financial assistance, but all that's water under the bridge now and, in any case, ethically unsound. Can you think of any kind of quasi-evaluation approach that could be applicable now or even a comparative experimental design? The closest I can get is the posttest-only program and control group design—but here again we would need to assign participants to groups or identify a control group that could be matched to the self-help housing group. In any case, this won't give us any of the kinds of information that the Consuelo clients want. However, practical elements of the posttreatment method could be useful such as surveys, interviews, observations, tests, the success case method, and numerous other ways of exploring the program's success five years on.

Bill: It seems to me that the kinds of procedures you have mentioned will be necessary no matter what approach is used—but random assignment of units, such as different kinds of houses, has no place at all when the clients are looking for a determination of their program's success or otherwise thirteen years after it began.

Ellen: What about field trials? They have gained some traction in recent years.

Bill: Well, this is just another label for randomized experiments that occur in a field setting. Bill Nave and Company specifically refer to this approach as randomized, controlled field trials. Changing the label does not make the approach any more relevant to the outcomes sought by the terms of the RFP.

Ellen: I agree. You and I can think of a host of sound evaluation methods like the improvement and accountability models or the social agenda and advocacy models, which, if planned well, could be used to give us or, rather, the clients, useful and defensible evaluation findings.

Bill: Then again, it seems quite feasible that we could adopt an eclectic approach using the aspects of any of the kinds of models you mentioned to give the best information for the best decisions by the clients of the evaluation.

Ellen: I suggest we reply to Caroline in two ways. First, inform her that it is our considered opinion that any form of randomized experimental approach is inappropriate in this situation, and second, that you and I will meet again shortly to suggest an appropriate method or methods for this proposed evaluation. Perhaps we should also let her know that we would be quite happy to draft the evaluation proposal after we receive her response and also suggest that at least two of our firm's colleagues cast their eyes over it as well.

Bill: Caroline has also asked us for an estimate, at this stage, of a likely time frame for the exercise as well as costs to be included in response to the RFP. The list of questions in the foundation's documents indicates that this will not be a brief evaluation, although I imagine it may not run as long as the stipulated twelve-month period. I see that there was a ceiling of fifty thousand dollars, excluding travel, accommodations, and similar costs, and I imagine that we could complete the task within budget. In any case, we would need to await further developments on both our part and Caroline's before we can do the necessary breakdown of costs.

Ellen: I am still somewhat bemused that Caroline could have put such emphasis on experimental design. It may have its place, but not with this proposed evaluation based on the information we have in the RFP. Is she just trying to make life tough for us?

The preceding conversation illustrates the impossibility of using experimental design methodology in this particular circumstance. The evaluators wisely discarded it immediately as a possibility and began to conjecture alternative ways of planning approaches that could give adequate or better responses to the information sought in the RFP. When Bill and Ellen recover from Caroline's request for an experimental approach, they could also suggest that the client may wish to follow with a metaevaluation for the benefit of the client and other stakeholders.

Review Questions

1. Is it true or false that Suchman's main objective in writing was to make obvious a need for the critical reevaluation of the role and methodology of evaluation research in the area of public service and social action? If true, what were Suchman's conclusions concerning the relationship between evaluation research and the basic tenets of research methodology? If false, what is Suchman's main objective in writing about evaluation research?

2. In what ways did Suchman support his own statement that the primary purpose of an evaluation is to discover program effectiveness when compared with program objectives?

3. Why did Suchman consider that a close relationship should exist between evaluation and program planning and development? In your reply, draw a distinction between pure research and evaluation research.

4. In evaluation, reliability is affected not only by chance errors of the measuring instrument, but also by actual fluctuations of the object being measured. What are some of the major sources of unreliability of measures of change?

5. Nave, Miech, and Mosteller and Boruch concluded that randomized, controlled experiments are rare in education. Considering that the federal government repeatedly has mandated use of this approach, why do you think it is rarely applied successfully in education?

6. Within the realm of statistical power, why does this chapter suggest that sometimes it is instructive to perform and compare analyses on both individuals and groups? How does this suggestion relate to the statistical principles of independence and statistical power?

7. In a true experiment, what are the preferred methods of randomly assigning subjects to treatments? What reasons do you think Boruch would give in advising that the program's director not assign the subjects and that assignment not be based on coin tosses or drawing names from a hat?

8. Based on the modern concept of experimental design, list the main types of information that should be collected before, during, and after a randomized

experiment. Discuss the extent to which this list of information requirements is similar to or different from the information requirements found in other evaluation approaches, such as consumer-oriented evaluation, the CIPP model, and responsive/client-centered evaluation.

9. Define and give an example of each of the following types of analysis employed in experimental studies: design implementation analysis, core analysis, practical significance analysis, a posteriori and correlational tests, and literature review analysis.

10. What is the basis of the claim that quasi experiments rate higher on generalizability or external validity than do randomized, controlled experiments?

Group Exercises

Exercise 1. These discussion questions are based on the evaluation cited in Chapter Twelve and the initial planning by Ellen and Bill in this chapter for a response to the foundation's RFP. In your discussion, cover these questions:

     a. Do you support (and perhaps sympathize with) the stance taken by Ellen and Bill?

     b. Do you see any possibility of a quasi-experimental approach being used, even for a minor segment of the evaluation of the self-help housing project thirteen years after its inception?

     c. What advice on evaluation methods (or, perhaps, a single method) would you give to Caroline to include in her initial (draft) response to the RFP?

Exercise 2. Suchman was one of the first to endeavor to incorporate ideas and knowledge about evaluation into the implementation of new programs, or changes in existing programs, in the public sector. However, his level of interest was directed almost entirely at policy matters rather than education or social service practitioners.

Discuss this statement along these lines:

     a. How does the statement conform with Suchman's somewhat scientific approach to evaluation?

     b. What are some of the main purposes Suchman saw for evaluation?

     c. With significant growth, accomplishments, and comparative sophistication in evaluation methodologies today compared with three or four decades ago, have evaluation emphases changed from policy matters to practitioners? If so, why, and in what directions? If not, why has there been no change?

Exercise 3. Identify and summarize a program with which you are familiar and that you see as potentially amenable to a randomized, controlled experiment.

  a. Write a judgment of "yes" or "no" for this program on each of this chapter's contemporary guidelines for designing experiments.
  b. Present and justify your conclusion on whether a randomized, controlled experiment is appropriate to evaluate the program and, if so, what type of experiment would be appropriate.
  c. If you conclude that a randomized, controlled experiment is not appropriate to evaluate this program, what other approach would you likely use and why?

Exercise 4. Suppose your group is writing a job description to manage the experiment you summarized in question 3. List the main responsibilities for managing the experiment.

Exercise 5. This chapter stressed that experimental design evaluations should be subjected to formative and summative metaevaluations focused on the study's utility, feasibility, propriety, and accuracy. Within the accuracy category, the chapter summarized Suchman's detailed advice on assessing the study's validity. Considering the design you summarized in question 3, state a question that a metaevaluation should address for each of the following: propositional validity, instrument validity, sampling validity, subject validity, administrative validity, and analysis validity.

References

Bigman, S. K. (1961, Winter). Evaluating the effectiveness of religious programs. *Review of Religious Research*, 108–109.

Boruch, R. (2003). Randomized field trials in education. In T. Kellaghan & D. L. Stufflebeam (Eds.), *International handbook of educational evaluation* (pp. 107–124). Norwell, MA: Kluwer.

Bracht, G. H., & Glass, G. V (1968). The external validity of experiments. *American Educational Research Journal, 5*, 437–474.

Campbell, D. T., & Stanley, J. C. (1963). Experimental and quasi-experimental designs for research on teaching. In N. L. Gage (Ed.), *Handbook of research on teaching* (pp. 171–246). Skokie, IL: Rand McNally.

Cook, T. D., & Campbell, D. T. (1979). *Quasi-experimentation: Design and analysis issues for field settings.* Skokie, IL: Rand McNally.

Cronbach, L. J., & Snow, R. (1969). *Individual differences in learning ability as a function of instructional variables.* Stanford, CA: Stanford University Press.

Finn, C. E., Stevens, F. I., Stufflebeam, D. L., & Walberg, H. J. (1997). The New York City Public Schools Integrated Learning Systems Project: A meta-evaluation. *International Journal of Educational Research, 27,* 159–174.

Fisher, R. A. (1951). *Design of experiments* (6th ed). Edinburgh: Oliver and Boyd.

Fleck, A. C. (1961, May). Evaluation as a logical process. *Canadian Journal of Public Health, 52,* 185–191.

Herzog, E. (1959). *Some guidelines for evaluative research.* Washington, DC: U.S. Department of Health, Education, and Welfare.

James, G. (1958). Research by local health departments—Problems, methods, results. *American Journal of Public Health, 48,* 354–379.

Joint Committee on Standards for Educational Evaluation. (1994). *The program evaluation standards* (2nd ed.). Thousand Oaks, CA: Corwin Press.

Klineberg, O. (1955). The problem of evaluation. *International Social Science Bulletin, 7,* 347–362.

Nave, B., Miech, E. J., & Mosteller, F. (2000). The role of field trials in evaluating school practices: A rare design. In D. L. Stufflebeam, G. F. Madaus, & T. Kellaghan (Eds.), *Evaluation models: Viewpoints on educational and human services evaluation* (2nd ed., pp. 145–161). Norwell, MA: Kluwer.

Scriven, M. (2005). Causation. In S. Mathison (Ed.), *Encyclopedia of evaluation* (pp. 43–47). Thousand Oaks, CA: Sage.

Suchman, E. A. (1967). *Evaluative research: Principles and practice in public service and social action programs.* New York: Russell Sage Foundation.

CHAPTER FOURTEEN

CASE STUDY EVALUATIONS

In Chapter Seven, Approach 18 offered a succinct outline of case study evaluations. This approach to the investigation of a naturalistic phenomenon was placed under the general category of questions- and methods-oriented approaches to evaluation, and therefore we considered it to be a form of quasi-evaluation. The dominant reason for this categorization is that some applications of the approach are focused more narrowly than needed to assess a program's merit and worth, while other applications are configured to fully assess a program's value. Accordingly, the case to be evaluated might be a total program, some component of the program (such as its annual budgeting process), or the situation and experiences of one or more individuals being served by the program. In this chapter, we discuss the case study approach mainly as it applies to evaluating a total program.

A case study evaluation's signature feature is an in-depth examination of the case and issuance of a captivating, illuminative report. The evaluator studies, analyzes, and describes the case as fully as possible. He or she examines the case's context, goals or aspirations, plans, resources, unique features, importance, noteworthy actions or operations, achievements, disappointments, needs and problems, and other topics. The evaluator closely observes and meticulously records the case in its natural setting. He or she obtains and reviews pertinent documents, interviews principal parties involved in the case or in a position to share insights about the case, and may collect pertinent photographic evidence. Ultimately the evaluator prepares and issues an in-depth report on the case, with descriptive and judgmental information, perceptions held by different stakeholders and experts, and summary conclusions.

Importantly, the evaluators do not control the program (or program component) in any fashion as they might, for instance, if they were applying an experimental design. Case study investigators closely examine the context, including program beneficiaries' needs, inputs, operations, intended and unintended effects, and any other processes (with all their complexities) that are producing outcomes. Using as many methods as necessary, the evaluators view the program in its different (and possibly opposing) dimensions as part of presenting a general characterization of the case.

Depending on the circumstances, the case study approach may be the optimum way of examining and illuminating a total program. This approach is not confined to a tightly controlled, formalized collection and analysis of data. As emphasis is placed on the ethnographic nature of the program, it is likely that qualitative techniques will be used, with experienced, professional judgment as an ever-present complement to the study. Focus is placed on portrayal of events, testimonials, stored information, and individuals involved in program implementation and direction, so that stakeholders are given information for understanding the program and making needed improvements. This information necessarily will depict the multisided nature of the setting in which the program is in progress. Final reports are usually written for appropriate program decision makers, other stakeholders, and other interested parties. However, preferred courses of action will often be difficult to state with a high level of confidence.

This is not to suggest that the case study method leaves stakeholders languishing in decision-making limbo. Quite the opposite is true. A sound case study provides abundant information for decision making with a clear teasing out of the intricacies that abound in naturalistic settings. The case study evaluators watch, listen, interview, and follow up trails of interest, doubts, and perplexities until they are able to present a full account of the program. They may report only to help a broad audience understand the program and reach their own judgments. Or they may tailor the report to the needs of decision makers by including an array of possible solutions to problems and other ways to improve the program.

One important aspect of case studies is the appropriateness of informant selections, program locations and occasions, and materials for interviews and other modes of data collection. This may be simplified if, for example, there is a single group of program stakeholders or a dominant group representing or participating in a program. Readers will recall that we refer to interviews with all families in the low-cost housing project community outlined in Chapter Twelve. Interviewing members of almost every family (the population of interest) was feasible in that evaluation because all of the families receiving the program were at a single community site, and all agreed to be interviewed. Thus, there was no need for sampling from this population. We acknowledge, however, that this evaluation included interviews of only a small sample of families that applied but were not chosen for the program and that these interviewees were not representative of the unsuccessful applicants. In many case study evaluations, the selection of data sources is difficult and problematic, and the evaluator cannot use the classic approach of random sampling to obtain information representative of a population of interest. There is no simple answer to this ever-present problem for case study evaluators.

To obviate the least credible effects of convenience sampling, evaluators must assess the field of potentially useful respondents to ascertain the representativeness of the overall body of program participants (or decision makers or other stakeholders) and record this information as completely as possible for future reporting. If this is done well, divergences of opinions and approaches to the program will be captured, so that a holistic view of the program and its environment is ultimately possible. Clearly a context evaluation, which includes a needs assessment of program participants and beneficiaries, would be a sound starting point. It would give credibility to decisions made later about selections of individuals, groups, and events for close involvement in a case study. Also, a cardinal principle of case study evaluations is to continue identifying and querying data sources until attaining redundancy of descriptive and judgmental information. On this point, it is essential to note that such redundancy often will include conflicting accounts that might be expected, for example, if one were interviewing Democrats and Republicans about the merits of a proposed piece of legislation.

Case Study Research: Views of Robert Stake

Stake introduces his 1995 book, *The Art of Case Study Research*, in this way:

> A case study is expected to catch the complexity of a single case. A leaf, even a single toothpick, has unique complexities—but rarely will we care to submit it to case study. We study a case when it itself is of very special interest. We look for the detail of interaction with its context. Case study is the study of the particularity and complexity of a single case, coming to understand its activity within important circumstances. In this book, I develop a view of case studies that draws from naturalistic, holistic, ethnographic, phenomenological, and biographic research methods [p. xi].

He goes on to say there are many kinds of case study, all with their place. For example, there are quantitative case studies based on measurement of descriptive variables, an approach often used in medicine, and case studies constructed for instructional purposes, common in colleges of business and law. However, Stake's interest (at least as outlined in his recent writings) is a disciplined, qualitative inquiry: "The qualitative researcher emphasizes episodes of nuances, the sequentiality of happenings in context, the wholeness of the individual" (1995, p. xii). Stake contends that this approach is an effective way of studying educational programs generally, and one particularly useful for program evaluation. He personally organizes the case study around identified issues. However, he advocates that those wishing to pursue case studies be aware that certain other techniques could prove more satisfactory, depending on idiosyncratic style or prevailing circumstances, especially when the object to be studied is a relationship or phenomenon more than an explicit case. In other words, a case study is defined not by a methodology but by choice of object to be studied. As we stated in Approach 16 in Chapter Seven, a case study evaluation's main purpose is to provide stakeholders and their audiences with an authoritative, in-depth, and well-documented interpretation of a program.

Concerning the choice of a name for qualitative studies of single cases, some have preferred *fieldwork* to *case study*. Stake's choice of the latter for evaluative studies resides in the attention it draws to the question of what specifically can be learned about the evaluand: "That epistemological question is the driving question: What can be learned from the single case? I will emphasize designing the study to optimize the understanding of the case rather than generalization beyond" (1994, p. 236).

Stake does not consider that a case study needs to be bound by time. One study may take a few weeks of intensive fieldwork preceded by planning time and followed by close analysis of documentation and writing, entailing some months in all. Another may require even less time—perhaps a week or so—to achieve its aim. And others run for years, depending on the number and magnitude of the issues under focus. Whatever the duration of the study is, the general conceptualization does not differ significantly. An important responsibility is to sharpen identification of the case, whatever it may be, and concentrate on it for as long as it takes to understand its complexities. Moreover, Stake avers that these complexities, such as multiple sponsorship of an innovative program, are subject to the system's boundaries and behavior patterns, which are important in understanding the case (Stake, 1988).

Often there is little choice of case definition allowed the evaluator who bids for an evaluation contract. For instance, Stake himself, in his study of the Harper School in Chicago (1995), focused on aspects of the school as required by the sponsor of the evaluation, the School Finance Authority. This chapter is an excellent example of an investigative case study, showing an idiosyncratic but disciplined approach by the evaluator.

Stake finds it useful to identify three types of case study (1994). The *intrinsic* case study is undertaken to give a better understanding of a particular case for its own worth or interest. In what is termed the *instrumental* case study, examination provides insight into an issue or a theory needing refinement. In this instance, the case takes a back seat, playing a supportive role, and facilitating an understanding of the theory or issue. During the *collective* case study, researchers move further away from the particular case, as they study a number of cases together, so that they can inquire into the phenomenon or population. In advance of the case study, researchers do not know whether the individual cases will manifest common characteristics. Their selection is based on the premise that understanding each individual case will increase knowledge about a larger group of cases. Whether case researchers seek out what is particular about a case or what is common, "the result is likely to be unique" (Stauffer, 1941, cited in Stake, 1994).

Stake considers that uniqueness is likely to be pervasive and encompassing:

- The nature of the case
- Its historical background
- The physical setting
- Other contexts, including economic, political, legal, and aesthetic
- Other cases through which this case is recognized
- Those informants through whom the case can be known

Researchers need to gather data on all six entities (1994).

Although Stake does not entirely disagree with Campbell (1975) that a case study may be a small step toward generalization, his opinion is that the commitment to generalize (or build theory) may be damaging if this commitment draws attention away from an understanding of the case itself. Indeed, these case study researchers deliberately do not seek causal determinations, mainly because their epistemology features coexisting events and conditions more than explanatory links. Perhaps the most unusual claim Stake makes is that not only the values of stakeholders, but also the interpretations to be made by readers (an example of relativistic thinking) should be deliberately honored. Stake sees the evaluator as a unique observer, interacting with a unique evaluand to assist conceptualizing by unique readers. In spite of this small claim to "truth," Stake expresses confidence that a wide range of readers can find such uniqueness useful.

Although some qualitative case study researchers support the case's relating itself, or "telling it as it is," Stake believes it must be the researcher who tells the case's own story while retaining sound empathy with the object of observation. As he says, "More will be pursued than was volunteered. Less will be reported than was learned" (1994, p. 240). When the research transfers knowledge to the reader, difficulties inevitably arise. Stake warns that the case research should provide grounds for validating reported statements, including any generalizations that are made. Use of the concept of a triangulation will prove essential to case study researchers, for their goal is understanding as well as a desire to minimize misinterpretations. Stake sees little place for emphasis on comparison in designing and reporting case studies except where there are multiple cases of intrinsic interest.

The methods of study that Stake supports are the use of the most intelligent observers and observation techniques possible and, underlying this, reflection: "Qualitative case study is characterized by the main researcher spending substantial time *on site* [our emphasis]. Personally, in contact with activities and operations of the case, reflecting, revising meanings of what is going on" (Stake, 1994, p. 242).

We have observed that much of Stake's theory development over the years has been based on field experience. By contrast, some theory developers of the naturalistic or relativistic inclination have given little, if any, indication in their writing that they have experienced more than a modicum of fieldwork. Moreover, as Stake stresses, a selection of a particular case study affords a unique opportunity to learn, and learning from on-site situations is essential for the development of credible theory. Along another line, Stake urges qualitative researchers to be aware of ethical considerations to protect human subjects.

It is not possible in this short account to give more than the briefest outline of the case study research methodology that Stake put forward. The next section explores some of the more frequently used methods. Differing from the mainstream of case study evaluators, Stake emphasizes that the impression that some have that a case study is simply sharp observation is not very useful. A range of disciplines is needed, including designing good questions, conceptual organization, developing a cognitive framework to guide data gathering, and planning structures for appropriate presentation of interpretations to others. (For a clear and cogent description of these and other methodological elements of Stake's approach to case study research, we refer readers to Chapters Two, Four, Five and Seven in *The Art of Case Study Research*.)

Stake (1994, p. 244) summed up what he considered the major conceptual responsibilities of the qualitative case study researcher:

1. Bounding the case and conceptualizing the object of study
2. Selecting phenomena, themes, or issues—that is, the research questions— to emphasize

3. Seeking patterns of data to develop the issues
4. Triangulating key observations and bases for interpretation
5. Selecting alternative interpretations to pursue
6. Developing assertions or generalizations about the case

Stylistic options also play their part. These include the extent to which the report becomes the case's own story, the presentation of generalizations (or, alternatively, assisting readers in their own interpretations), and the extent to which the researcher is described as a participant in the report.

Through his work with case studies, Stake has concluded that this research method can help refine theory, and by the very nature of the complexities it encounters, it can suggest limitations to generalizability. However, understanding of the individual case, not generalization, remains the purpose of the case study. The method is embedded in personal discipline, and its success is determined by this factor.

Case Study Information-Collecting Methods

We have pointed out, as does Stake, that information about a particular phenomenon, using the case study methodology, can be gathered by a wide range of methods, both quantitative and qualitative. Whatever methods are used, the focus of the case study is the case itself. Practitioners have traditionally given particular emphasis to gathering qualitative information, particularly because both the quality and quantity of information are likely to have fewer restrictions than that gathered quantitatively. However, much depends on the method of the investigation, the case itself, the imagination and resourcefulness of the evaluator, and the kind of end information that the client is seeking. Moreover, qualitative approaches that are carried out well should elicit information about both intended and unintended effects. Whatever methods are used, the aim of a case study is always to give as complete a picture as possible of the object being studied so that stakeholders may develop or enrich their understanding of the program and perhaps grasp the report's significance for decision making. The stronger the evaluator's observational and reflective skills are, the greater the understanding of the program will be for those involved in its progress and desired outcomes.

During the course of a study, it is possible that planned methods may change their form or new ones may be introduced according to the nature of the circumstances as they are illuminated. Thus, the evaluator must be flexible, responsive to new or unusual circumstances, and adapt to these as necessary. Record keeping is essential in case studies, even if the information will not be used in the final report. The necessity may not arise for a final report in the traditional sense; results may be conveyed to clients and others in many ways, with the emphasis always on conveying a clear and useful depiction of the program as revealed by the research. Since it is based dominantly on qualitative information about a naturalistic setting, decisions about the reporting format may evolve as the study progresses, with both intermediate and final reporting always being possibilities.

Following is a brief description of some of the more commonly used qualitative methods in case study evaluations.

Documentation

Seeking to understand a program of multiple levels, as well as the holistic nature of the program, evaluators logically should begin with an examination of existing documents, records, and other appropriate materials that give information about the program and characterization about its geographical and organizational environment. Such records will give information about the program's personnel, processes, and progress. Notes should be taken about the key elements of each. While documents should give the perspective of stakeholders at various levels about a program, lack of such important information must be noted for further investigation. Whatever the nature and specificity of records and other documents, the question should arise in evaluators' minds about the kinds of research methods (most likely qualitative) that need to be pursued. The perusal of documents and records has one other advantage: it should clearly delineate aspects of the program and thus save considerable and valuable evaluator time, which can more profitably be spent on salient features of the program.

In assessing documents and records, content analysis procedures could prove to be a valuable tool. Materials are analyzed, described as closely as possible, and processes and trends are noted. Content analysis as a data-analyzing methodology sharpens focus on significant aspects of programs. These points are often exposed on the basis of their repetition within documents or any other useful emphases relevant to the program. Some of this information can be obtained qualitatively or quantitatively, depending on the kind of program knowledge that is presented and what is required. The important point is that the analyzer has in mind the questions to be answered. Quantitative content analysis depends on the development of coding units (such as words, paragraphs, or events), and these are then placed in categories. While either stakeholders or the evaluator may select coding units and categories, the intent of the evaluation in the context of the wider spectrum of the object of the case study must be kept in mind.

Visits to the Program's Naturalistic Setting

We have emphasized the importance of an evaluator's experience and training for sound professional judgments. This is particularly so for site visits involving case studies. While formative emphasis is appropriately given to site visits, this may form the basis of summative conclusions, with judgments usually based on a range of perceptions and evidence about the program. Despite elements of this occurring, the main thrust is toward a qualitative, open-minded inspection of the program. The insightful evaluator will use a whole range of methods during site visits, based on careful advance planning, keen observations, and astute recording for later use. Planning will involve identifying the kinds of information that will be needed (while allowing that other, perhaps unexpected, information may arise); preparing instruments such as checklists to be used on-site; working out the logistics of visits, including timing and personnel involved; and deciding on the kinds of report that will be required in collaboration with the client. If a team is to undertake site visits, planning must extend to group meetings to discuss the allocation of duties and responsibilities and to ensure that the team is working toward the common end.

Observations

Central to the successful completion of any case study is the strength of observations. These may include site visits, a discerning appraisal of interactions among personnel involved in the program, the ways and means that the program is being undertaken and developed (or failing to develop), the strength of program leadership and delegation or otherwise of decision making, and the extent to which key stakeholders (those most affected by the program) are influenced by its evolving outcomes. Observation methods to collect relevant data and information may be quantitative or qualitative, although the latter is more likely to pertain, particularly when the observations are unstructured. Jorgensen (1989) points out the usefulness of unstructured observations during the early stages of a study, as well as the importance of the evaluator's skills to select and delineate critical features. Jorgensen sums up these thoughts:

> The basic goal of these largely unfocused initial observations is to become increasingly familiar with the insiders' world so as to refine and focus subsequent observation and data collection. It is extremely important that you record these observations as soon as possible and with the greatest possible detail because never again will you experience the setting so utterly unfamiliar [p. 82].

As the study progresses, unstructured observations will continue according to the kinds of information that unfolds. If the use of observation is based on meetings with stakeholders (as it often is), increasingly useful depiction of the program is given, with all of its nuances, including the forces that pertain in the program's environment. If the team is carrying out unstructured observations, an ongoing comparison of observations strengthens the understanding of the program's holistic nature.

More structured observations are also essential and worth the time. Unlike unstructured observations that are viewing aspects of the program in a general sense, structured observations focus on the program's idiosyncrasies, events associated with the program, a range of physical aspects, and, in particular, the interactions between leaders and other stakeholders. These interactions have a strong influence on any program and should be carefully noted. Sensitive information may arise from observations. It is therefore most important that observations, particularly pertaining to personnel, be maintained securely and confidentially. The propriety standards developed by the Joint Committee (1994) stress the importance of ethical behavior by evaluators, together with the consequences of dereliction of such standards.

Structured observations must be based on careful planning that will include items such as observation scheduling, the kinds of instruments that will be used, and an appropriate time schedule, to be worked out in collaboration with program administrators. If a team is involved, participant training to ensure reliability among observations will be necessary.

Qualitative observation methods usually focus on the observer's (or observers') viewing the interactions between a group objectively, while collecting information according to a prearranged schedule or checklist. The evaluator also can play a greater participatory role in group discussions, depending on the prevailing circumstances and the kinds of information sought. In such instances, it is usual for the evaluator to ask questions to help elucidate matters that have arisen during the observation period. Again, astute note taking and synthesizing information will help build a more complete picture of the program with all its intricacies.

Interviewing

This is an area where evaluators' true skills are displayed. Preparation for interviews is vital if they are to elicit the kind of information that is sought to illuminate the program. By comparison with a questionnaire, interviews can be a costly exercise, but one that is commonly used to unravel some of the complexities of a program and particularly stakeholders' reactions to these. Stakeholders' concerns about a program and their knowledge of it are perspectives that are essential for accurate and meaningful reporting in whatever form it might take. Much has been written, and will still be written, on successful methods for carrying out interviews. In all of this advice, the essential components are the experience of the interviewer, the degree of preparation, the importance of clear understanding of the program itself and the purpose for the interviewing, and the need to make the respondent feel at ease and useful to the study being undertaken. Once a rapport between the evaluator and respondent is developed, the primary task of the interviewer is to listen and encourage discussion at a professional level.

Focus groups are an extension of interviewing, involving a group of individuals who are closely connected with the program. Focus groups involve interaction between the interviewer and group and between group members themselves. These groups may generate a great deal of useful information about the program, particularly if they have opposing or conflicting views on aspects of the program. The group remains the important aspect of this methodology; the interviewer's task is to make sure that dialogue remains focused on the topic under discussion. The more accurately participants relate to their program reactions and other relevant experiences, the better the focus becomes on sought program changes that may be required. A number of factors come into play. Idiosyncratic beliefs and value systems are never far from the surface during focus groups. Whatever attitudes the participants may hold, these might influence the program's progress and, in many instances, its success or failure. Certainly focus groups, properly conducted, add very useful dimensions to a case study evaluation.

Conclusion

The case study approach is appropriate in program evaluation, particularly since it requires no control of treatments, subjects, and programs in their naturalistic state. In addressing personnel issues, it employs triangulating multiple perspectives using a range of methods (according to the needs of each unique situation) and information sources. From close contextual investigations of influences on the program, the case study evaluator progresses to a holistic, in-depth assessment of the program, with its complexities and human interplays. While it is possible to undertake case studies retrospectively on the basis of recorded data and documents, these are most likely to occur in real time. The case study methodology has become increasingly useful to the evaluator as an investigator and to administrators and other stakeholders seeking accurate depiction of a program.

Applicability of Case Study Evaluation to the Self-Help Housing Project

An evaluation firm that consistently has used the case study methodology over the past two decades shows considerable interest in the foundation's request for a follow-up evaluation of the self-help housing project for low-income families. They decide to respond to the RFP by writing to Dr. Smith, the president of the housing project:

Dear Dr. Smith:

Our firm is very interested in responding to your foundation's request for a follow-up evaluation of your self-help housing project, the details of which were advertised on the Internet. We believe we have the experience, credentials, and public respect necessary to undertake such an evaluation competently.

Bearing in mind the final report and attendant materials relating to the original evaluation as well as the suggested list of questions you have posted, we are confident that in respect to both the time line and financial constraints you have mentioned, we should complete the study and report to your satisfaction. Our aim would be to provide useful information to your foundation for future decision making.

Over the past two decades, our firm has undertaken many evaluations of both small and large projects using a range of evaluation techniques, often with the combination of these within a single study. Our firm emphasizes that the most appropriate method or methods should be used for any particular study. Regarding the subsequent (five-year) evaluation of your project, The Spirit of Consuelo, we have no hesitation in recommending the case study approach. This will provide an overall assessment of the project's development to its present state during the past five years and will place emphasis entirely on the project itself, which thereby becomes "the case" for the case study approach. Obviously individuals as well as events will need to be included in such a study; for this reason, we shall give a brief outline of the procedures we intend to follow if we are successful in gaining this contract.

The case study method will focus on an in-depth examination, description, analysis, and reporting of the housing project. We shall view the program in its natural state (that is, as it actually exists), examining aspects such as historical context and geographical, cultural, and organizational elements. We shall concern ourselves particularly with the internal operation of the project's administration and the many other program aspects that have brought the housing project to its present state. The case study methodology moves a considerable distance from traditional quantitative studies, where the emphases are placed more on measurement procedures, as we shall outline. Moreover, we shall not enter the program with any preconceived ideas, but rather keep our minds open for both intended outcomes (including those in your RFP) and unintended events that have occurred along the way.

We are well aware that your foundation is deeply concerned with the project's beneficiaries and whether their needs have been met during the past five years. To this end, we would wish to carry out what is called a context or needs assessment to form a basis for pursuing that aspect of the study. Again, in this regard, the case study methodology is most apt. So that we may more closely define key questions for the evaluation, we shall need to interact with you, other members of the foundation board, administrators of the program, and, importantly, key stakeholders, particularly the residents themselves (the main beneficiaries, as we understand it, of your project). Our purpose would be to provide these stakeholders and other relevant audiences with a high-quality, in-depth, and fully described exposition of the program.

Clearly, through one means or another, we would need to gather a great deal of confidential information. Please be assured that all such information will be tightly secured and that the rights of individuals and other ethical considerations will be fully respected. In this regard we draw your attention to the propriety standards developed by the Joint Committee on Standards for Educational Evaluation (1994). We are enclosing a copy of the Standards so that we have a mutual understanding of the importance we place on ethical considerations. We shall also adhere to other standards for evaluators outlined in the book.

For its success, the case study approach depends very much on interaction between evaluators and personnel involved in the program, backed by our understanding of salient events. We mention a few relevant matters and procedures to exemplify this point. We will need to view as many documents, records, and other historical or statistical details relevant to the program from the time of its planning to its implementation and now to its progress after five years. We intend to use a process called content analysis to give emphasis and clarification to the most salient issues that have been recorded. We shall need to carry out intensive observations, both structured and unstructured, with the program and its people as they actually exist. Such observations will be undertaken sensitively and professionally so that the perspectives (which will obviously vary with program personnel) are captured and recorded. In addition, early in the evaluation, site visits will be essential. These will allow us to identify specific items of evaluative information to be pursued, develop questions for the evaluation study in consultation with others, and conduct casual or structured interviews with relevant stakeholders.

We consider various kinds of interviews to be an essential, and even basic, component of case studies. These would be both one-on-one and focus groups in nature, with both thoroughly planned before the interviews commence. In all probability, the questions to be asked at interviews will be developed collaboratively with relevant decision makers such as yourself and the administrative and financial leaders of the foundation. Our aim is to develop rapport with respondents, emphasize confidentiality, and gain as many insights into the program from as many perspectives as possible.

As the study progresses, we will wish to gain a deeper knowledge of the program's concepts and practices, what changes have evolved over the previous five-year period, what are actual outcomes, and what areas have failed to meet expectations or even have had a negative influence on the program. We will seek to find out how the various residents have interacted with the administration and, indeed, the extent to which they value your program. Undoubtedly, unresolved issues will need to be examined. We would also need to examine and make an analysis of the cost benefits of the project; in this respect, we have expertise within our firm to give you a sound account of these matters.

Although our depiction of the case study methodology may appear to be subject to excessive openness and perhaps lack of control, let us assure you that this is not the situation. We intend to apply all necessary rigor to the study, including timely feedback during the course of the evaluation and at its conclusion. Our exchanges with you and other stakeholders will be planned on a regular basis. Information provided to you, the client, will provide ample information for judgments that you will wish to make about the project's future. At all stages, our plans for the case study evaluation will be flexible so that we can respond flexibly to circumstances as they arise.

With the strength of our professional evaluation staff, we can guarantee completion of the evaluation project within the stipulated twelve-month period. Our first estimate of costs puts them comfortably under the $50,000 that you are allowing for the evaluation. If our response is viewed favorably by you and the foundation board, we shall provide an itemized breakdown of costs, which primarily will be based on the work of two experienced and highly skilled evaluators. Because they live in your region, it will not be necessary to consider accommodation costs.

We are willing to provide any further information that you require and to meet personally with you or other board members to respond to any questions you may have. We trust that you find our proposal responsive to your RFP for the proposed evaluation.

This brief illustration demonstrates how the case study approach adequately responds to a request for an evaluation study. Necessarily, it does not preempt key questions for the study because these will evolve by careful planning, examination of documents, site visits, and accompanying discussions with stakeholders. The case study justifiably gives promise of illuminating the project in all its complexities and offering sound information for decision makers.

Review Questions

1. What are some of the significant differences between objective testing programs (Approach 11) and the case study methodology of evaluation?
2. There are marked differences between Brinkerhoff's success case method (Approach 10) and the case study approach. State these differences.
3. What do you understand by structured observations and unstructured observations?

4. How would you use content analysis to delineate salient issues in an examination of documents and records?
5. What qualities should evaluators possess, and what main procedures should they follow to carry out interviews successfully?
6. You have been commissioned to carry out a case study of a grade 4 music and arts program. Which of the following two questions is the more appropriate (following Stake's advice)?

   a. What can I learn from this single case?
   b. What qualitative research methods must I use to generate unequivocal representation of such programs?

   Give reasons for your choice of question and why you rejected the alternative.
7. Why is the quantitative approach to a case study more appropriate (for example) in medicine than in the situation outlined in question 6?
8. What does Stake mean by *intrinsic, instrumental,* and *collective case studies?*
9. Stake gives six ways in which a program is unique (and researchers are required, he maintains, to gather data on all six). Identify these six unique entities.
10. Stake tightens the disciplines needed for an effective case study beyond sharp observation only. What are these disciplines, and why do you consider them important?

Group Exercises

Exercise 1. Stake maintains that a case study is defined not by a methodology but by choice of object to be studied. Discuss this statement along these lines:

- Stake's view on what should be the base intent of a case study
- The general types of evaluation methodologies (if any) he views as appropriate to a particular study
- How a choice of object is to be defined

Exercise 2. Is Stake unrealistic in stating that a case study does not need to be bound by time? In your discussion, refer to the time constraint given in the low-cost housing foundation's RFP.

Exercise 3. In Chapter Seven, for Approach 18, we stated (perhaps controversially) that "case study investigators do not control the program in any way." On your understanding of case study methodology in this book and elsewhere, do you agree or disagree with this statement? Why or why not?

References

Campbell, D. (1975). Reforms as experiments. In E. Struening & M. Guttentag (Eds.), *Handbook of evaluation research*. Thousand Oaks, CA: Sage.

Joint Committee on Standards for Educational Evaluation. (1994). *The program evaluation standards*. Thousand Oaks, CA: Corwin Press.

Jorgensen, D. L. (1989). *Participant observation: A methodology for human studies*. Thousand Oaks, CA: Sage.

Stake, R. E. (1988). Seeking sweet water. In R. Jaeger (Ed.), *Complementary methods for research in education* (pp. 253–300). Washington, DC: American Educational Research Association.

Stake, R. E. (1994). Case studies. In N. K. Denzin & Y. S. Lincoln (Eds.), *Handbook of qualitative research* (pp. 236–247). Thousand Oaks, CA: Sage.

Stake, R. E. (1995). *The art of case study research*. Thousand Oaks, CA: Sage.

Stauffer, S. (1941). Notes on the case study and the unique case. *Sociometry, 4*, 349–357.

CHAPTER FIFTEEN

DANIEL STUFFLEBEAM'S CIPP MODEL FOR EVALUATION

An Improvement/Accountability Approach

This chapter describes and illustrates the use of the CIPP model for evaluation. It is a comprehensive framework for conducting formative and summative evaluations of programs, projects, personnel, products, organizations, and evaluation systems. This model was originated in the late 1960s to help improve and achieve accountability for U.S. school projects, especially those keyed to improving teaching and learning in inner-city school districts. Over the years, the model has been further developed. It has been adapted and applied in the United States and many other countries and inside and outside education. Areas of application include government, philanthropy, international development, the military, distance education; productivity of private colleges and Historically Black Colleges; community programming for youth; community and economic development; house construction and rehabilitation; organized religion; and systems for evaluating teachers, administrators, and military personnel. The model has been used extensively in Australia for evaluating university departments and private schools.

Pertinent references to development and application of the model include Adams (1971), Candoli, Cullen, and Stufflebeam (1997), Gally (1984), Granger, Grierson, Quirino, and Romano (1965), Guba and Stufflebeam (1968), Nevo (1974), Stufflebeam (1966, 1967, 1969, 1971, 1983, 1985, 1997, 2000, 2002, 2003a, 2003b, 2004, 2005), Stufflebeam et al. (1971), Stufflebeam and Webster (1988), and Webster (1975). A detailed checklist for applying the CIPP Model is available at www.wmich.edu/evalctr.

Three key definitions undergird the CIPP model. An *evaluation* is a systematic investigation of some object's value. Operationally, evaluation is the process of delineating, obtaining, reporting, and applying descriptive and judgmental information about some object's merit, worth, significance, and probity in order to guide decision making, support accountability, disseminate effective practices, and increase understanding of the involved phenomena. Professional *standards* for evaluations are principles commonly agreed to by specialists in the conduct and use of evaluations for the measure of an evaluation's utility, feasibility, propriety, and accuracy. Basically, the CIPP model is an organized approach to meeting the evaluation profession's standards as defined by the Joint Committee on Standards for Educational Evaluation (1988, 1994, 2003).

This chapter summarizes context, input, process, and product evaluations; analyzes their formative and summative roles; summarizes the model's roots; presents the model's philosophical stance and code of ethics; looks at its values component; delineates the CIPP categories and identifies relevant procedures for each one; explains and illustrates the model's systems orientation to improvement; and applies the model to the request for an evaluation of the housing project presented in Chapter Twelve.

Overview of the CIPP Categories

The CIPP model's core concepts are denoted by the acronym CIPP, which stands for evaluations of an entity's context, inputs, processes, and products. *Context evaluations* assess needs, problems, assets, and opportunities to help decision makers define goals and priorities and to help the relevant users judge goals, priorities, and outcomes. *Input evaluations* assess alternative approaches, competing action plans, staffing plans, and budgets for their feasibility and potential cost-effectiveness to meet targeted needs and achieve goals. Decision makers use input evaluations in choosing among competing plans, writing funding proposals, allocating resources, assigning staff, scheduling work, and ultimately helping others judge an effort's plans and budget. *Process evaluations* assess the implementation of plans to help staff carry out activities and, later, to help the broad group of users judge program implementation and interpret outcomes. *Product evaluations* identify and assess outcomes—intended and unintended, short term and long term—to help a staff keep an enterprise focused on achieving important outcomes and ultimately to help the broader group of users gauge the effort's success in meeting targeted needs. In summing up long-term evaluations, the product evaluation (Did it succeed?) component may be divided into assessments of impact, effectiveness, sustainability, and transportability. These product evaluation subparts ask, Were the right beneficiaries reached? Were their targeted needs met? Were the gains for beneficiaries and mechanisms to achieve the gains sustained? Did the processes that produced the gains prove transportable and adaptable for effective use elsewhere?

Formative and Summative Roles of Context, Input, Process, and Product Evaluations

Consistent with its improvement focus, the CIPP model places priority on guiding planning and implementation of development efforts. In the model's formative role, context, input, process, and product evaluations respectively ask, What needs to be done? How should it be done? Is it being done? Is it succeeding? The evaluator submits interim reports addressing these questions to keep stakeholders informed about findings, help guide and strengthen decision making, and help staff work toward achieving a successful outcome. In this vein, the model's intent is to supply evaluation users—such as policy boards, administrators, and project staffs—with timely, valid information of use in identifying an appropriate area for development; formulating sound goals, activity plans, and budgets (often associated with change efforts); successfully carrying out work plans; strengthening existing programs or services; periodically deciding whether and, if so, how to repeat or expand an effort; disseminating effective practices; contributing to knowledge in the area of service; and meeting a financial sponsor's accountability requirements.

The model also advocates and provides direction for conducting retrospective, summative evaluations to serve a broad range of stakeholders. They include, among others, funding organizations, persons receiving or considering using the sponsored services, policy groups and program specialists outside the program being evaluated, and researchers. In the summative report, the evaluator refers to the store of formative context, input, process, and product information and obtains other needed information. The evaluator uses this information to address the following retrospective questions: Were important needs addressed? Was the effort guided by a defensible design and budget? Was the service design executed competently and modified as needed? Did the effort succeed, and why or why not? Potential consumers need answers to such summative questions to help assess the quality, cost, utility, and competitiveness of products and services they might acquire and use. Other stakeholders might want evidence on the extent to which their tax dollars or other types of support yielded responsible actions and worthwhile outcomes. If evaluators effectively conduct, document, and report formative evaluations, they will have much of the information needed to produce a defensible summative evaluation report. Such information will prove invaluable to insiders and outsiders engaged to summatively evaluate a project, program, service, or other entity.

Table 15.1 summarizes uses of the CIPP model for both formative and summative evaluations. The matrix's eight cells encompass much of the evaluative information required to guide enterprises and produce credible, and therefore defensible, summative evaluation reports.

Roots of the CIPP Model

The CIPP model is based on learning by doing and an ongoing effort to identify and correct mistakes made in evaluation practice. The history of the model's development parallels and is a main part of the development of evaluation models and procedures since the mid-1960s. Like other new approaches to evaluation, it was created because the classic evaluation approaches of experimental design, objectives-based evaluation, and standardized achievement testing proved to be of limited use and often unworkable and even counterproductive for evaluating emergent programs in dynamic social contexts. (A detailed account of the development of the model is given in Alkin, 2004.)

The early work in developing the model is documented in *Educational Evaluation and Decision Making* (Stufflebeam et al., 1971), a book produced by a national study committee on evaluation that Phi Delta Kappa International (PDK) appointed in 1969. The book sharply criticized the traditional views of evaluation, analyzed the evaluative information needs in decision making, elaborated the CIPP model, closely examined the problems of multilevel evaluation, addressed the issue of institutionalizing the CIPP model, discussed needs for evaluation training, and suggested that criteria for judging evaluations should include utility and feasibility as well as technical adequacy.

An important lesson regarding criteria for assessing evaluations was that evaluations can go very wrong if they are keyed exclusively to criteria of technical adequacy, such as the requirements for internal and external validity then being promulgated for judging experiments (Campbell & Stanley, 1963). The PDK book's breakout of utility criteria into relevance, importance, timeliness, clarity, and credibility was a precursor of work the Joint Committee on Standards for Educational Evaluation would do in defining standards for evaluations of utility, feasibility, propriety, and accuracy (Joint Committee, 1981, 1988, 1994, 2003).

TABLE 15.1. THE RELEVANCE OF FOUR EVALUATION TYPES TO FORMATIVE AND SUMMATIVE EVALUATION ROLES.

Evaluation Roles	Context	Input	Process	Product
Formative evaluation: Prospective application of CIPP information to assist decision making and quality assurance	Guidance for identifying needed interventions and choosing and ranking goals (based on assessing needs, problems, assets, and opportunities).	Guidance for choosing a program or other strategy (based on assessing alternative strategies and resource allocation plans), also for examining the work plan	Guidance for implementing the operational plan (based on monitoring and judging program activities)	Guidance for continuing, modifying, adopting, or terminating the effort (based on assessing outcomes and side effects)
Summative evaluation: Retrospective use of CIPP information to sum up the program's merit, worth, probity, and significance	Comparison of goals and priorities to assessed needs, problems, assets, and opportunities	Comparison of the program's strategy, design, and budget to those of critical competitors and the targeted needs of beneficiaries	Full description of the actual process and costs, plus comparison of the designed and actual processes and costs	Comparison of outcomes and side effects to targeted needs and, as feasible, to results of competitive programs; interpretation of results against the effort's assessed context, inputs, and processes

The Philosophy and Code of Ethics Underlying the CIPP Model

The CIPP model has a strong orientation to service and the principles of a free society. It calls for evaluators and clients to identify and involve rightful beneficiaries, clarify their needs for services, obtain information of use in designing responsive programs and other services, assess and help guide effective implementation of services, and ultimately assess the services' merit, worth, significance, and probity. The thrust of CIPP evaluations is to provide sound information that will help service providers regularly assess and improve services and make effective and efficient use of resources, time, and technology in order to serve the well-being and targeted needs of rightful beneficiaries appropriately and equitably.

Involving and Serving Stakeholders

CIPP evaluations must be grounded in the democratic principles of equity and fairness. A key concept used in the model is that of stakeholders: those who are intended to use the findings, those who may otherwise be affected by the evaluation, and those expected to contribute to the evaluation. Consistent with the Joint Committee's *Program Evaluation Standards* (1994), evaluators should search out all relevant stakeholder groups and engage at least their representatives in hermeneutic and consensus-building processes to help affirm foundational values, define evaluation questions, clarify evaluative criteria, contribute needed information, help interpret findings, and assess evaluation reports.

Since information empowers those who hold the information, the CIPP model emphasizes the importance of even-handedness in involving and informing all of a program's stakeholders. Moreover, evaluators should strive to reach and involve those most in need and with little access to and influence over services. While evaluators should control the evaluation process to ensure its integrity, CIPP evaluations accord beneficiaries and other stakeholders more than a passive recipient's role. Evaluators are charged to keep stakeholders informed and provide them appropriate opportunities to contribute. Involving all levels of stakeholders is considered ethically responsible because it equitably empowers the disadvantaged as well as the advantaged to help define the appropriate evaluation questions and criteria, provide evaluative input, critique draft reports, and receive, review, and use evaluation findings. Involving all stakeholder groups is also wise because sustained, consequential involvement positions stakeholders to contribute information and valuable insights and inclines them to study, accept, value, and act on evaluation reports.

Improvement Orientation

A fundamental tenet of the CIPP model is that the most important purpose of evaluation is not to prove, but to improve. This idea was originally put forth by Egon Guba when serving on the Phi Delta Kappa National Study Committee on Evaluation (Stufflebeam et al., 1971). Evaluation is thus conceived primarily as a functional activity oriented in the long run to stimulating, aiding, and abetting efforts to strengthen and improve enterprises. The model also posits that some programs or other services will prove unworthy of attempts to improve them and should be discredited or terminated. By helping stop unneeded, corrupt, or hopelessly flawed efforts, evaluations serve an advisory improvement function through assisting organizations to free resources and time for worthy efforts. Also, the model charges evaluators to identify and report valuable lessons from both failed and successful efforts.

Objectivist Orientation

The CIPP model's epistemological orientation is objectivist, not relativist. Objectivist evaluations are based on the theory that moral good is objective and independent of personal or merely human feelings. Such evaluations are firmly grounded in ethical principles, such as the United Nations's Universal Declaration of Human Rights and the U.S. Bill of Rights; strive to control bias, prejudice, and conflicts of interest in conducting assessments and reaching conclusions; invoke and justify appropriate and (where they exist) established technical standards of merit; obtain and validate findings from multiple sources; search for best answers, although these may be difficult to find; set forth and justify best available conclusions about the evaluand; report findings honestly, fairly, and as circumspectly as necessary to all right-to-know audiences; subject the evaluation process and findings to independent assessments against pertinent standards; and identify needs for further investigation. Fundamentally, objectivist evaluations are intended over time to lead to conclusions that are correct—not correct or incorrect relative to an evaluator's or other party's predilections, position, preferences, or point of view. The model contends that when different objectivist evaluations are focused on the same object in a given setting, when they are keyed to fundamental principles of a free society and to agreed-on criteria of merit, when they meaningfully engage all stakeholder groups in the quest for answers, and when they conform to the evaluation field's standards, different, competent evaluators will arrive at fundamentally equivalent, defensible conclusions.

Standards and Metaevaluation

The model calls for evaluators to meet the professional standards of evaluation and subject their evaluations to both formative and summative metaevaluations. The main standards invoked in the model require evaluations to meet professionally defined requirements for utility, feasibility, propriety, and accuracy. At a minimum, evaluators should conduct their own formative and summative metaevaluations. They should use the formative metaevaluation to guide the evaluation work and correct deficiencies along the way. In the final evaluation report, the evaluators should state and explain their judgments of the extent to which the evaluation met each of the relevant Joint Committee (1988, 1994, 2003) standards. As feasible, the evaluation should be subjected to an external, independent metaevaluation. Preferably, a party other than the evaluators, such as the client or a private foundation, should choose and fund the external metaevaluator. This helps avoid any appearance or fact of a conflict of interest having influenced the content of the external metaevaluation report. The external metaevaluator's report should be made available to all members of the right-to-know audience. (Further information on these points appears in Chapter Three and this book's concluding chapter.)

The Model's Values Component

Figure 15.1 summarizes the basic elements of the CIPP Model in three concentric circles and portrays the central importance of defined values. The inner circle denotes the core values that should be defined and used to undergird a given evaluation. The wheel surrounding the values is divided into four evaluative foci associated with any program or other endeavor: goals, plans, actions, and outcomes. The outer wheel indicates the type of evaluation that serves each of the four evaluative foci: context, input, process, and product evaluation. Each two-directional arrow represents a reciprocal relationship between a particular evaluative focus and a type of evaluation.

The goal-setting task raises questions for a context evaluation, which in turn provides information for validating or improving goals. Planning improvement efforts generates questions for an input evaluation, which correspondingly provides judgments of plans and direction for strengthening plans. Program actions bring up questions for a process evaluation, which provides judgments of activities plus feedback for strengthening staff performance. Accomplishments, lack of accomplishments, and side effects command the attention of product evaluations, which ultimately issue judgments of outcomes and identify needs for achieving better results.

FIGURE 15.1. KEY COMPONENTS OF THE CIPP EVALUATION MODEL AND ASSOCIATED RELATIONSHIPS WITH PROGRAMS.

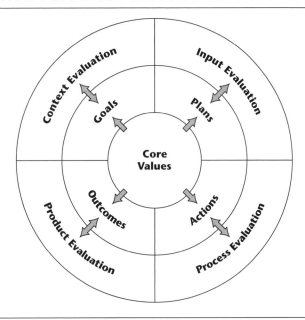

These relationships are made functional by grounding evaluations in core values, referenced in the scheme's inner circle. Evaluation's root term is *value*. This term refers to any of a range of ideals held by a society, group, or individual. The CIPP model calls for the evaluator and client to identify and clarify the values that will undergird particular evaluations. Examples of educational values—applied in evaluations of U.S. public school programs—are success in helping all students meet a state's mandated academic standards; helping all children develop basic academic skills; helping each child fulfill her or his potential for educational development; assisting and reinforcing the development of students' special gifts and talents; upholding human rights; meeting the needs of disabled and underprivileged children; developing students as good citizens; ensuring equality of opportunity; effectively engaging parents in the healthy development of their children; nurturing and developing the school's primary resource, its teachers; attaining excellence in all aspects of schooling; conserving and using resources efficiently; ensuring safety of products and procedures; maintaining separation of church and state; employing research and innovation to strengthen teaching and learning; and maintaining accountability. Essentially evaluators should take into account a set of pertinent societal, institutional, program, and professional and technical values when assessing programs or other entities.

The values provide the foundation for deriving or validating particular evaluative criteria. Selected criteria, along with stakeholders' questions, help clarify an evaluation's information needs. These in turn provide the basis for selecting and constructing the evaluation instruments and procedures, accessing existing information, and defining interpretive standards.

Also, a values framework provides a well-knit point of reference for detecting unexpected defects and strengths. For example, through broad values-oriented surveillance, an evaluator might discover that a program excels in meeting students' targeted academic needs but has serious deficiencies, such as racist practices, unsafe equipment, teacher burnouts, or graft. On the positive side, examination of a program against a backdrop of appropriate values might uncover unexpected positive outcomes, such as strengthened community support of schools, invention of better teaching practices, or more engaged and supportive parents.

Delineation of the CIPP Categories and Relevant Procedures

This section provides a more specific discussion of each type of evaluation. Table 15.2 provides a convenient overview of the essential meanings of context, input, process, and product evaluation. It defines these four types of studies according to their objectives, methods, and uses. This section also describes certain techniques that evaluators have found useful for conducting each type of evaluation. No one evaluation would likely use all of the techniques referred to here. They are presented to give an idea of the range of qualitative and quantitative methods that are potentially applicable in CIPP evaluations.

Context Evaluation

Context evaluation assesses needs, problems, assets, and opportunities within a defined environment. *Needs* include those things that are necessary or useful for fulfilling a defensible purpose. *Problems* are impediments to overcome in meeting and continuing to meet targeted needs. *Assets* include accessible expertise and services, usually in the local area, that could be used to help fulfill the targeted purpose. *Opportunities* especially include funding programs that might be tapped to support efforts to meet needs and solve associated problems. *Defensible purposes* define what is to be achieved related to the institution's mission while adhering to ethical and legal standards.

While context evaluation is often referred to as needs assessment, the latter term is too narrow since it focuses on needs and omits concerns about problems,

TABLE 15.2. FOUR TYPES OF EVALUATION.

	Context Evaluation	Input Evaluation	Process Evaluation	Product Evaluation
Objective	To define the relevant context, identify the target population and assess its needs, identify opportunities for addressing the needs, diagnose problems underlying the needs, and judge whether program goals are sufficiently responsive to the assessed needs	To identify and assess system capabilities, alternative program strategies, procedural designs for implementing the strategies, budgets, and schedules	To identify or predict defects in the procedural design or its implementation, provide information for the preprogrammed decisions, and record and judge procedural events and activities	To collect descriptions and judgments of outcomes and relate them to objectives and to context, input, and process information; and to interpret their merit, worth, significance, and probity
Method	Using such methods as system analysis, survey, document review, secondary data analysis, hearings, interviews, diagnostic tests, and the Delphi technique	Inventorying and analyzing available human and material resources, solution strategies, and procedural designs for relevance, feasibility, cost, and economy; using such methods as literature search, visits to exemplary programs, advocate teams, and pilot trials	Monitoring the activity's potential procedural barriers and remaining alert to unanticipated ones, obtaining specified information for programmed decisions, describing the actual process, and continually interacting with and observing the activities of project staff and other stakeholders	By defining operationally and measuring outcome criteria, collecting judgments of outcomes from stakeholders, performing both qualitative and quantitative analyses, and comparing outcomes with assessed needs
Relation to decision making in the change process	For deciding on the setting to be served; the goals associated with meeting needs or using opportunities; the priorities for budgeting time and resources; the objectives associated with solving problems, that is, for planning needed changes; and providing a basis for judging outcomes	For selecting sources of support, solution strategies, and procedural designs, that is, for structuring change activities and budgeting and scheduling the program activities; and providing a basis for judging implementation	For implementing and refining the program design and procedure, that is, for effecting process control and providing a log of the actual process for later use in interpreting outcomes	For deciding to continue, terminate, modify, or refocus a change activity; and for presenting a clear record of effects (intended and unintended, positive and negative), compared with assessed needs and targeted objectives

assets, and opportunities. All four elements are critically important in designing sound programs, projects, and services and should be considered in context evaluations. A context evaluation's main objectives are to:

- Set boundaries on and describe the setting for the intended service
- Identify intended beneficiaries and assess their needs
- Identify problems or barriers to meeting the assessed needs
- Identify relevant, accessible assets and funding opportunities that could be used to address the targeted needs
- Provide a basis for setting improvement-oriented goals
- Assess the clarity and appropriateness of improvement-oriented goals
- Provide a basis for judging outcomes of a targeted improvement or service effort

Context evaluations may be initiated before, during, or even after a project, program, or other intervention. In the before case, organizations may carry out context evaluations as narrowly bounded studies to help set goals and priorities in a particular area. When an evaluation is started during or after a project or other intervention, institutions often conduct and report context evaluations in combination with input, process, and product evaluations. Here, context evaluations are useful for judging established goals and helping the audience assess the effort's worth in meeting beneficiaries' needs.

A context evaluation's methodology may involve collecting a variety of information about members of the target population and their surrounding environment and conducting various types of analysis. A usual starting point is to ask the clients and other stakeholders to help define the study's boundaries. Subsequently evaluators may employ a variety of techniques to generate and test hypotheses about needed services or changes in existing services. These might include reviewing documents, analyzing demographic and performance data, conducting hearings and community forums, and interviewing beneficiaries and other stakeholders.

The evaluators might construct a survey instrument to investigate identified hypotheses concerning the existence of beneficiaries' needs. Then they could administer it to a carefully defined sample of stakeholders. The evaluators could also make the survey instrument available more generally to anyone who wishes to provide input. They would analyze the two sets of responses separately.

Evaluators should examine existing records to identify performance patterns and background information on the target population. In education, these might include immunization records; enrollment in different levels of courses; attendance; school grades; test scores; honors; graduation rates; participation in extracurricular activities; participation in special education; participation in free and reduced-fee meal programs; participation in further education; housing situations; employment and health histories; or feedback from teachers, parents, former students, counselors, coaches, health personnel, librarians, custodians, administrators, or employers.

The evaluators might administer special diagnostic tests to members of the target population. They might engage an expert review panel to visit, closely observe, and identify needs, problems, assets, and opportunities in the targeted environment. The evaluators might conduct focus group meetings to review the gathered information. They might use a consensus-building technique such as Delphi to solidify agreements about priority needs and goals. These procedures contribute to an in-depth perspective on the system's functioning and highest-priority needs.

Often audiences need to view an effort within both its present setting and its historical context. Considering the relevant history helps decision makers avoid past mistakes. Thus, the methodology of context evaluation includes historical analysis and literature review as well as methods aimed at characterizing and understanding current environmental conditions. After the initial context evaluation, organizations often need to continue collecting, organizing, filing, and reporting context evaluation data, since needs, problems, assets, and opportunities are subject to change.

In some situations, the evaluator should look beyond the local context to ascertain whether a program has widespread relevance. For example, a successful early childhood program might produce a ripple effect that eventually improves early childhood programming far beyond the program's setting. In such cases, the evaluator would judge the program not only on its worth in addressing the needs of targeted beneficiaries, but also its significance in serving beneficiaries outside the program's area of operation. To the extent a context evaluation shows that a proposed program has widespread significance, the program developer can make an especially strong case for external financial support.

Context evaluations have a wide range of possible constructive uses. A context evaluation might provide a means by which an administrator communicates with constituents to gain a shared conception of the organization's strengths and weaknesses, needs, assets, opportunities, and priority problems. A program developer could use context evaluation information to support a request for external grants or contracts. A university might use a context evaluation to convince a funding agency that it directed a proposed project at an urgent need or to convince a state legislature to increase the institution's funding. A social service organization might use context evaluation information to formulate objectives for staff development or to identify target populations for priority assistance. A school would use a context evaluation to help students and their parents or advisers focus their attention on developmental areas requiring more progress. An institution also could use context evaluation information to help decide how to make the institution stronger by cutting marginally important or ineffective programs.

Context evaluation information is particularly useful when an organization needs to assess the worth and significance of what an intervention accomplished. Here the organization assesses whether the investment in improvement effectively addressed the targeted needs of intended beneficiaries. The evaluator also refers to context evaluation findings to assess the appropriateness of goals and relevance of project plans. Similarly, the evaluator uses context evaluation findings to examine how the intervention's process is affecting improvements outside the local setting. Considering such uses, an organization can benefit greatly by establishing, keeping up to date, and using information from a context evaluation database.

Input Evaluation

An input evaluation's main orientation is to help prescribe a program by which to make needed changes. It does this by searching out and critically examining potentially relevant approaches, including the one already being used. Input evaluation is a precursor of the success or failure and efficiency of a change effort. Initial decisions to allocate resources constrain change projects. A potentially effective solution to a problem will have no possibility of impact if a planning group does not at least identify it and assess its merits. A secondary orientation of an input evaluation is to inform interested parties about what programmatic approach was chosen, over what alternatives, and why. In this sense, input evaluation information is an important source of a developer's accountability for its design and budgeting of an improvement effort.

Essentially, an input evaluation should identify and rate relevant approaches and assist decision makers to prepare the chosen approach for execution. It should also search the clients' environment for political barriers, financial or legal constraints, and potentially available resources. An input evaluation's overall intent is to help decision makers examine alternative strategies for addressing assessed needs of targeted beneficiaries, evolve a workable plan and appropriate budget, and develop an accountability record for defending its procedural and resource plans. Another important function is to help program leaders avoid the wasteful practice of pursuing proposed innovations that predictably would fail or at least waste resources.

Evaluators conduct input evaluations in several stages. These occur in no set sequence. An evaluator might first review the state of practice in meeting the specified needs and objectives. This could include a number of possible components:

- Reviewing relevant literature
- Visiting exemplary programs
- Consulting experts and representatives of government
- Querying pertinent information services (for example, those on the World Wide Web)
- Reviewing a pertinent article in *Consumer Reports* or similar publications that critically review available products and services
- Inviting proposals from involved staff

Evaluators might organize this information in a special planning room. They might engage a special study group to investigate it or conduct a special planning seminar to analyze the material. The evaluators would use the information to assess whether potentially acceptable solution strategies exist. They would rate promising approaches on relevant criteria. Examples are listed below:

- Responsiveness to assessed needs of targeted beneficiaries
- Responsiveness to targeted organizational problems
- Potential effectiveness
- Cost
- Political viability
- Administrative feasibility
- Potential for important impacts outside the local area

Next, the evaluators could advise the decision makers about whether they should seek a novel solution. In seeking an innovation, the client and evaluators might document criteria the innovation should meet, structure a request for proposal, obtain competing proposals, and rate them on the chosen criteria. Subsequently the evaluators might rank the potentially acceptable proposals and suggest how the institution could combine their best features. They might conduct a hearing to obtain additional information. They could ask staff and administrators to express concerns. They would appraise resources and barriers that the institution should consider when installing the intervention. The planning group could then use the accumulated information to design and budget for what they see as the best combination strategy and action plan.

Input evaluations have several applications. A chief one is in preparing a proposal for submission to a funding organization or policy board. Another is to assess one's existing practice, whether or not it seems satisfactory, against what is being done elsewhere and proposed in the literature. Input evaluation has been used in the Dallas Independent School District; the Des Moines, Iowa, Public

Schools; and the Shaker Heights, Ohio, School District. They used it to decide whether locally generated proposals for innovation would likely be cost-effective. The public school district for Detroit also used input evaluation to generate and assess alternative architectural designs for new school buildings. In addition to informing and facilitating decisions, input evaluation records help authorities defend their choice of one course of action above other possibilities. Administrators and policy boards can find input evaluation records useful when they must publicly defend sizable expenditures for new programs.

The advocacy teams technique is a procedure designed specifically for conducting input evaluations. This technique is especially applicable in situations where institutions lack effective means to meet targeted needs and stakeholders hold opposing views on what strategy the institution should adopt. The evaluators convene two or more teams of experts and stakeholders. They give the teams the objectives, background data on needs, specifications for a solution strategy, and criteria for evaluating the teams' proposed strategies. They may staff these teams to match members' preferences and expertise to the nature of proposed alternative strategies. Evaluators should do so, especially if stakeholders severely disagree about what type of approach they would accept. The advocacy teams then compete, preferably in isolation from one another, to develop a winning solution strategy. A panel of experts and stakeholders rates the advocacy team reports. The institution might also field-test the teams' proposed strategies. Subsequently the institution would operationalize the winning strategy. Alternatively, it might combine and operationalize the best features of the two or more competing strategies.

The advocacy team technique's advantages are that it provides a systematic approach for:

- Designing interventions to meet assessed needs
- Generating and assessing competing strategies
- Exploiting bias and competition in a constructive search for effective alternatives
- Addressing controversy and breaking down stalemates that stand in the way of progress
- Involving personnel from the adopting system in devising, assessing, and operationalizing improvement programs
- Documenting why a particular solution strategy was selected

Additional information, including a technical manual and the results of five field tests of the technique, is available in Reinhard (1972).

Process Evaluation

A process evaluation is an ongoing check on a plan's implementation and documentation of the process. One objective is to provide staff and managers feedback about the extent to which they are carrying out planned activities on schedule, as planned and budgeted, and efficiently. Another is to guide staff to improve the procedural and budgetary plans appropriately. Typically staff cannot determine all aspects of such plans when a project starts. Also, they must alter the plans if some initial decisions are unsound or not feasible. Still another objective is to periodically assess the extent to which participants accept and can carry out their roles. A process evaluation should contrast activities and expenditures with the plan and budget, describe implementation problems, and assess how well the staff addressed them. It should document and analyze the efforts' costs. Finally, it should report how observers and participants judged the process' quality.

The linchpin of a sound process evaluation is the process evaluator. More often than not, staff failure to obtain guidance for implementation and document their activities and expenditures is due to a failure to assign anyone to do this work. Sponsors and institutions too often assume erroneously that the managers and staff will adequately evaluate process as a normal part of their assignments. They can routinely do some review and documentation through activities such as staff meetings, minutes of the meetings, and periodic accounting reports. However, these do not fulfill the requirements of a sound process evaluation. Experience has shown that project staffs can usually meet these requirements well only by assigning an evaluator to provide ongoing review, feedback, and documentation.

A process evaluator has much work to do in monitoring and documenting an intervention's activities and expenditures. Initially, the process evaluator could review the relevant strategy, work plans, budget, and any prior background evaluation to identify what planned activities they should monitor. Possible examples are delivering services to beneficiaries, hiring and training staff, supervising staff, conducting staff meetings, monitoring and inspecting work flow, securing and maintaining equipment, ordering and distributing materials, controlling finances, documenting expenditures, managing project information, and keeping constituents informed.

With process evaluation issues such as those mentioned above in mind, the process evaluator could develop a general schedule of data collection activities and begin carrying them out. Initially these probably should be as unobtrusive as possible so as not to threaten staff, get in their way, or constrain or interfere with the process. As rapport develops, the process evaluator can use a more structured approach. At the outset, the process evaluator should obtain an overview of how the work is going. He or she could visit and observe centers of activity, review pertinent documents (especially the work plans, budgets, accounting reports, and minutes of meetings), attend staff meetings, and interview key participants. The evaluator then could prepare a brief report that summarizes the data collection plan, findings, and observed issues. He or she should highlight existing or impending process problems that the staff should address. The evaluator could then deliver this report at a staff meeting.

He or she might invite the staff's director to lead a discussion of the report. The project team could then use the report for decision making as it sees fit. Also, the process evaluator could review plans for further data collection and the subsequent report with the staff and ask them to react to the plan. They could identify what information they would find most useful at the next meeting. They could also suggest how the evaluator could best collect certain items of information. These might include observations, staff-kept diaries, interviews, or questionnaires. The evaluator should ask the staff when they could best use the next evaluation report.

Using this feedback, the evaluator would schedule future feedback sessions. He or she would modify the data collection plan as appropriate and proceed accordingly. The evaluator should continually show that process evaluation helps staff carry out its work through a kind of quality assurance and ongoing problem-solving process. He or she should also sustain the effort to document the process and lessons learned.

The evaluator should periodically report on how well the staff carried out the work plan and integrated it into the surrounding environment. He or she should describe main deviations from the plan and should note variations concerning how different persons, groups, or sites are carrying out the plan. He or she should also characterize and assess the ongoing planning activity and record of expenditures.

Staff members use process evaluation to guide activities, correct faulty plans, and maintain accountability records. Some managers use regularly scheduled process evaluation feedback sessions to keep staff on their toes and abreast of their responsibilities. Process evaluation records are useful for accountability, since funding agencies, policy boards, and constituents typically want objective and substantive confirmation of whether grantees did what they had proposed and expended allocated funds appropriately. Process evaluations can also help external audiences learn what was done in an enterprise and at what cost in case they want to conduct a similar effort. Such information is useful to new staff as part of their orientation to what has gone before. Moreover, process evaluation information is vital for interpreting product evaluation results. One needs to learn what was done in a project before deciding why program outcomes turned out as they did.

Over the years, the Evaluation Center at Western Michigan University has developed and employed a procedure labeled the traveling observer technique

(Evers, 1980, Reed, 1991; Thompson, 1986). This technique most heavily addresses process evaluation data requirements but, like other techniques, also provides data of use in context, input, and product evaluation. The technique involves sending a preprogrammed investigator to a program's field sites. This evaluator investigates and characterizes how the staff members are carrying out the project at the different sites and then reports the findings to the other evaluation team members.

The traveling observer follows a set schedule of data collection and writes and delivers reports according to preestablished formats and reporting specifications. Before entering the field, the traveling observer develops a traveling observer handbook (Alexander, 1974; Nowakowski, 1974; Reed, 1989; Sandberg, 1986; Sumida, 1994). With the principal evaluator, he or she tailors this evaluation tool to the evaluation's questions. This handbook includes the following parts:

- Traveling observer's credentials
- Evaluation questions
- Description of the study sites and program activities
- Contact personnel and telephone numbers
- Maps showing project locations
- Data sources suggested, including interviewees and pertinent documents
- Protocols for contacting field personnel and obtaining needed permissions and cooperation
- Rules concerning professional behavior expected
- Safeguards to help the traveling observer avoid co-optation by program staff
- Sampling plans, including both preset samples and exploratory grapevine sampling
- Recommended data collection procedures
- Data collection instruments
- Data collection schedule
- Daily log or diary format
- Rules for processing information and keeping it secure
- The audience for the traveling observer feedback
- Reporting specifications and schedule, including interim progress reports, briefing sessions, and expense reports
- Criteria for judging traveling observer reports
- Rules about communicating and disseminating findings, including provisions for reporting to those who supplied data for the traveling observer study
- Any responsibilities for scheduling and facilitating follow-up investigations, for example, by a site visit team of experts
- Issues that may arise and what to do about them

- Form for the traveling observer's periodic self-assessment
- Budget to support the traveling observer's work, including spending limitations and reporting requirements

In an early application of this technique, the Evaluation Center sent out traveling observers as advance persons to do initial investigation on two $5 million statewide National Science Foundation programs. The center assigned the traveling observers to prepare the way for follow-up site visits by high-level teams composed of national experts in science, mathematics, technology, evaluation, and education. Each program included many projects at many sites across the state. The evaluation budget was insufficient to send the five-member teams of high-priced experts to all the potentially important sites, so the center programmed and sent a traveling observer to study the program in each state. Each traveling observer spent two weeks investigating the program and prepared a report that contained findings and a tentative site visit agenda for the follow-up teams of experts. The traveling observers also contacted program personnel to prepare them for the follow-up visits and to gain their understanding and support for the evaluation. On the first day of the team site visits, each traveling observer distributed her or his report and explained the results. The traveling observers also oriented the teams to the geography, politics, personalities, and other characteristics of the program. They presented the teams with a tentative site visit agenda and answered their questions. The traveling observer's recommended plans for the site visit team included sending different members of the team to different project sites and some total team meetings with key program personnel.

During the week-long team visits, the traveling observers remained accessible by telephone so they could help the site team members. At the end of this study, the center engaged Michael Scriven to evaluate the evaluation. He reported that the traveling observer reports were so informative that except for the credibility added by the national experts, the traveling observers could have evaluated the programs successfully without the experts. Overall, the Evaluation Center has found that the traveling observer technique is a powerful evaluation tool; it is systematic, flexible, efficient, and inexpensive. Its focal use is to conduct process evaluation, but it sets the process in the context of assessed needs, program structure, and outcomes. It also is useful in preparing for follow-up, in-depth site visits.

Product Evaluation

The purpose of a product evaluation is to measure, interpret, and judge an enterprise's achievements. Its main objective is to ascertain the extent to which the evaluand met the needs of all the rightful beneficiaries. Feedback about achievements is important both during an activity cycle and at its conclusion. A product evaluation should assess intended and unintended outcomes and positive and negative outcomes. Moreover, evaluators often should extend product evaluation to assess long-term outcomes.

A product evaluation should gather and analyze stakeholders' judgments of the enterprise. Sometimes it should compare the effort's outcomes with those of similar enterprises. Frequently the client wants to know whether the enterprise achieved its objectives and was worth the investment. If appropriate, evaluators should interpret whether poor implementation of the work plan caused poor outcomes. Finally, a product evaluation should usually view outcomes from several vantage points: in the aggregate, for subgroups, and sometimes for individuals.

Product evaluations follow no set algorithm, but many methods are applicable. Evaluators should use a combination of techniques. This aids them in making a comprehensive search for outcomes. It also helps them cross-check the various findings.

To assess performance beyond objectives, evaluators need to search for unanticipated outcomes, both positive and negative. They might conduct hearings or group interviews to generate hypotheses about the full range of outcomes and follow these up with clinical investigations intended to confirm or disconfirm the hypotheses. They might conduct case studies of the experiences of a carefully selected sample of participants to obtain an in-depth view of the program's effects. They might survey, by telephone or mail, a sample of participants to obtain their judgments of the service and their views of both positive and negative findings. They might ask participants to submit concrete examples of how the project or other service influenced their work or well-being. These could be written pieces, other work products, or new job status. They might engage observers to identify program and comparison groups' achievements. They might also compare identified program achievements with a comprehensive checklist of outcomes of similar programs or services.

Evaluators might conduct a goal-free evaluation (Scriven, 1991). Accordingly the evaluator engages an investigator to find whatever effects an intervention produced. The evaluator purposely does not inform the goal-free investigator about the intervention's goals. The point is to prevent the investigator from developing tunnel vision focused on stated goals. The evaluator then contrasts identified effects with the program beneficiaries' assessed needs. This provides a unique approach to assessing the intervention's value, whatever its goals.

Reporting of product evaluation findings may occur at different stages. Evaluators may submit interim reports during each project cycle. These should show the extent to which the intervention is addressing and meeting targeted needs. End-of-cycle reports may sum up the results achieved. Such reports should interpret the results in the light of assessed needs, costs incurred, and execution of the plan. Evaluators may also submit follow-up reports to assess long-term outcomes. In such reports, evaluators might analyze the results in the aggregate, for subgroups, and for individuals.

People use product evaluations to decide whether a given program, project, service, or other enterprise is worth continuing, repeating, or extending to other settings. It also should provide direction for modifying the enterprise or replacing it so that the institution will more cost-effectively serve the needs of all members of the target audience. Of course, it should help potential adopters decide whether the approach merits their serious consideration. Product evaluations have psychological implications, since by showing signs of growth or superiority to competing approaches, they reinforce the efforts of both staff and program recipients; or they may dampen enthusiasm and reduce motivation when the results are poor.

Regarding the latter point, evaluators should not publicly release product evaluation findings too soon. A project requires time to achieve results for which it should be held accountable. Premature release of a product evaluation report might unjustly discourage continuation of the project because no results were found. If public reports of product evaluation are delayed for a reasonable amount of time, the evaluator might discover late-blooming, important outcomes that would support continuation of the project. Also, an evaluator can stifle project staff members' creativity by being overzealous in conducting and reporting product evaluations during a project's exploratory stage. Of course, the evaluator can respond appropriately to staff requests for ongoing formative product evaluation findings; usually such early interim results should be shared only with the project's staff members as an aid to their quest for success. Rules of thumb are that evaluators should be low key in conducting product evaluations early in a project and should not report product evaluation findings beyond the project staff until they have had ample time to install and stabilize procedural plans. The evaluator should distribute product evaluation findings to right-to-know audiences after the project has had a fair chance to mature and produce its outcomes. Clearly, evaluators need to exercise professional judgment and discretion in deciding matters of conducting and reporting product evaluation findings.

Product evaluation information is an essential component of an accountability report. When authorities document significant achievements, they can better convince community and funding organizations to provide additional financial and political support. If authorities learn that the intervention made no important gains, they can cancel the investment. This frees funds for worthier interventions. Moreover, other developers can use the product evaluation report to help decide whether it is appropriate to pursue a similar course of action.

CIPP as a Systems Strategy for Improvement

The CIPP model is a social systems approach to evaluation. A social system is an interrelated set of activities that function together to fulfill a mission and achieve defined goals within a certain context. Within this view, evaluation appropriately promotes and assists goal achievement and ongoing improvement. The model opposes the views that evaluations should be one-shot investigations, activities solely conducted by evaluators, or only instruments of accountability for externally funded projects. Instead, it treats evaluation as a tool by which evaluators, in concert with stakeholders, help programs, projects, and other services, work better for the beneficiaries. Fundamentally the model is designed to promote growth. Applied correctly, it is a sustained, ongoing effort to help an organization's leaders and staff obtain, organize, and use feedback systematically to validate goals, meet targeted beneficiary needs, and pass accountability examinations.

The flowchart in Figure 15.2 displays the CIPP model's systems orientation. To explain and illustrate this flowchart, we will consider evaluation in the context of a social ministries committee's efforts to meet the needs of foster care youths in its geographical area. The committee includes representatives from area churches and has a long-standing, positive record of providing support to foster care children and families. Recently, however, this committee conducted a context evaluation to determine whether certain needs of foster care are being met. This context evaluation activity is represented in the upper left-hand corner of Figure 15.2.

Upon reviewing a published national report on older foster care children, the committee became concerned that area eighteen- and nineteen-year-old youths probably were vulnerable to serious culture shock when they left the area's foster care system. Study of such youths in the local area uncovered startling facts. Over the five years after leaving their foster care families, about 40 percent of the area's foster teenagers soon became homeless, suffered emotional breakdowns, or committed crimes and were incarcerated. The committee found further that these older youths often needed, but did not receive, assistance in securing shelter, clothing, food, employment, further education, health care, and psychological and emotional support. A main reason for such unmet needs was that once a foster youth turns eighteen, foster parents receive no further financial assistance. Consequently, many of them are unable or unwilling to continue housing the youths. Subsequently, many eighteen-year-old foster care youths are abruptly turned out of their foster care home. They are not ready to fend for themselves and encounter serious difficulties. Regrettably, they have nowhere to belong. Based on these context

FIGURE 15.2. THE FLOW OF A CIPP EVALUATION IN FOSTERING AND ASSESSING SYSTEM IMPROVEMENT.

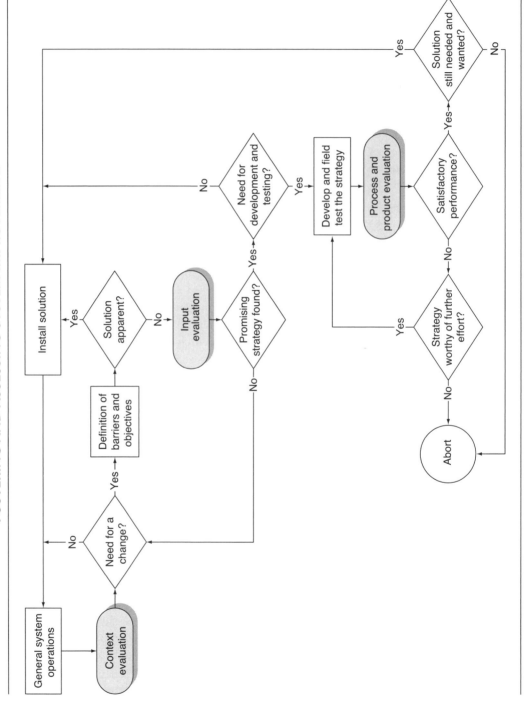

evaluation findings, the committee decided to mount a program for the area's older foster youths called Transition from Foster Care to Productive Adult Life.

In planning the program, the committee consulted local community agencies and service groups to ascertain whether they already possessed some appropriate and available comprehensive support strategy that the church group could get funded and then immediately install. They found no such strategy. Therefore, with the assistance of a volunteer evaluation specialist, the church committee proceeded to plan and conduct an input evaluation aimed at identifying and rating the relevance and feasibility of alternative ways to serve youths who are exiting the foster care system. The evaluator emphasized that development of competing proposals would stimulate creativity and identify an appropriately broad range of problem solution strategies.

This evaluation began with a review of the relevant literature and queries to state and local support organizations with some experience in managing or assisting foster care. The committee conducted focus groups, meetings in area organizations, interviews with a wide range of community personnel, and a communitywide conference to investigate the issue. Those providing information and deliberating were from the local foster care agency, Habitat for Humanity, area courts, law enforcement, city management, churches, a community foundation, the Salvation Army, a local hospital, and a university. These sources also included former foster care parents and children and military recruiters. The respondents were asked to give their perceptions of the needs and problems of this group of youths and identify ways they thought area groups could respond effectively.

The volunteer evaluator next organized the social ministries committee into two proposal writing groups and supplemented each group with additional volunteers from the community. Each group was assigned to use the information obtained so far to write a plan for addressing the identified needs of the subject foster care youth. Criteria for developing and evaluating the proposals were drawn from the needs and problems identified in the context evaluation and criteria for funding proposals from prospective funding organizations. In general, these criteria were responsiveness to the defined needs and problems of older foster care youths; goals for the foster care intervention; consistency with relevant research on children and youth; compatibility with the community's existing foster care support system; availability of committed volunteers; cost of development; long-term affordability; acceptability to foster care youths; potential benefits to the local community and economy of helping foster care youth become productive, self-actualized citizens; inclusion of formative and summative evaluation plans; and responsiveness to any unique proposal requirements of prospective funding organizations. Each team was also given an outline of points to be included in its proposal.

Upon completion of the proposals, the evaluator convened and chaired a group of area persons concerned and knowledgeable about the foster care issue. This group evaluated the alternative funding proposals against the prescribed criteria, identified the strongest parts of each proposal, and recommended how these might be merged into an overall plan. The group made recommendations about how the merged plan could be used to develop different proposals for different funding organizations.

Using the results of this input evaluation, the committee developed the overall program plan. It included a resource center where youths could obtain clothing, bedding, kitchen utensils, and other housewares; a program to recruit, train, and engage community members to serve as mentors to the youths; a committee of local business representatives to help youths find jobs; a committee of local health care professionals to help youths receive needed health care; a scholarship program to help qualified youths pursue further education; a support group with regular meetings where youths could share and address their problems and develop life skills; screened and approved host families to rent rooms to youth; and the development and ongoing support of several supervised independent-living group homes.

Subsequently the committee contacted area churches, community service groups, colleges and universities, Habitat for Humanity, Big Brothers–Big Sisters, hospitals, local media, and several prospective funding organizations for financial and other kinds of assistance. The committee informed these parties about the context evaluation and input evaluation findings and summarized the resulting program plan. Following discussions with these groups, the committee wrote and submitted specific funding proposals and requests for assistance in keeping with the overall plan and the parts of the work that the different funding and other groups found to be within their targeted areas of support or involvement. Subsequently, the social ministries committee received several grants and other kinds of support and proceeded to oversee and help implement the overall program and each of its parts.

Fortunately, the volunteer evaluator had convinced the committee to build continuing evaluation into their plans. Accordingly, the evaluator continued to support the committee's work by coordinating and assisting both process and product evaluations. The legwork in these evaluations was done by community volunteers and university graduate students. At monthly meetings, the evaluators presented the committee with process evaluation reports focused on how well each part of the Transition from Foster Care to Productive Adult Life program was being carried out. Periodically they presented product evaluation findings that focused on the overall program's successes and failures with individual youths and groups of youths and on the success and cost-effectiveness of each part of the program. Especially they compared the identified outcomes to the needs and problems found in the original context evaluation. The committee used the feedback to gauge the success of the program and each component, solve emergent problems, adjust plans, carry on with the work, write new proposals, and seek additional funding and other forms of support.

At appropriate intervals, the committee compiled and presented evaluation results to its support groups. Key issues addressed were whether the program and its individual components were succeeding and whether the needed funding was warranted and sustainable. The results proved to be highly positive and cost-effective. All the support organizations were convinced of the value of the program and helped the committee establish an ongoing, stable base of monetary and nonmonetary support. Based on the valuable contribution of evaluation to this effort, the committee wisely decided to continue its context evaluation surveillance of the needs of older foster care youth and also to continue the proposal writing and the process and product evaluations of the installed interventions.

Summary

The CIPP model treats evaluation as an essential concomitant of improvement and accountability within a framework of appropriate values and a quest for clear, unambiguous answers. It responds to the reality that evaluations of innovative, evolving efforts typically cannot employ controlled, randomized experiments or work from published evaluation instruments, both of which yield far too little information by focusing narrowly on particular aspects of the program being evaluated. The CIPP Model is configured especially to enable and guide comprehensive, systematic examination of social and education programs that occur in the dynamic, septic conditions of the real world, not the controlled conditions of experimental psychology, double-blind experiments in medicine, and split-plot crop studies in agriculture.

The model sees evaluation as essential to societal progress and the well-being of individuals and groups. It contends that societal groups cannot make their programs, services, and products better unless they learn where they are weak and strong. Developers and service providers cannot be sure their goals are worthy unless they validate the goals' consistency with sound values and responsiveness to beneficiaries' assessed needs. Developers and service providers cannot plan effectively and invest their time and resources wisely if they do not identify and assess options. They cannot earn continued respect and support if they cannot show that they have responsibly carried out their plans and produced beneficial results. They cannot build on past experiences if they do not preserve, study, and act on lessons from failed and successful efforts. They cannot convince consumers to buy or support their services and products unless their claims for the value of these services are valid and honestly reported. Institutional personnel cannot meet all of their evaluation needs if they do not both contract for external evaluations and also build and apply capacity to conduct internal evaluations. Evaluators cannot defend their evaluative conclusions unless they key them to both sound information and clear, defensible values. Moreover, internal and external evaluators cannot maintain credibility for their evaluations if they do not subject them to metaevaluations against appropriate standards. The model employs multiple methods, is based on a wide range of applications, and is supported by an extensive theoretical and pragmatic literature.

Application of the CIPP Model to the Self-Help Housing Project

The original evaluation of the self-help housing project for low-income families described in Chapter Twelve was based on the CIPP model. Here we use that model to respond to the request for a follow-up evaluation of the project. We do so in the following letter proposal:

Dear President X:

I appreciate your letter requesting a plan by which Western Michigan University would conduct a follow-up evaluation of your foundation's Spirit of Consuelo self-help housing project for low-income families. As you will recall, I previously led the eight-year evaluation of the project and did so by employing the CIPP model for evaluation. I believe selected components of the CIPP model are appropriate for building on the past evaluation and addressing your questions concerning the project's longer term success. I would be willing to lead the follow-up evaluation and engage needed personnel from Western Michigan University. Indeed, my Western Michigan University colleagues and I continue to be keenly interested in how well the Consuelo project's original successes have been sustained. Clearly, important lessons can be gained from that innovative, values-based approach to addressing the housing and community development needs of the working poor. Such lessons should be of interest to many persons and groups in the areas of housing, community development, and social services in general.

We have reviewed the evaluation questions you sent and also information from the original eight-year evaluation. These provide a substantial foundation for planning and conducting the needed follow-up evaluation. We are also mindful of the stipulations that the evaluation should be completed within a twelve-month period and within a $50,000 budget, plus funds needed for travel. We agree to the first of these limitations, but based on careful analysis of the minimum level of work required to assess the project, we will need $62,590. We have prepared an evaluation plan that responds directly to your request for a proposal and is ready for implementation. Nevertheless, we want to make sure you understand the plan and see it as appropriately responsive to your needs. Therefore, during our first visit, we recommend that we meet with your group to review the evaluation plan, refine it as needed, and prepare it for implementation.

Due to the budgetary restrictions—even at the $62,590 level—we will not attempt to conduct a full-scale follow-up evaluation but will concentrate on your most important questions and a level of data collection within the funding limit. The follow-up evaluation will have two main components: *effectiveness* and *sustainability evaluations.* The main questions for these components, respectively, are, What is the current level of the project's success? and To what extent have the successes attained during the project's first eight years and the mechanisms for producing the successes been sustained?

Beyond addressing these questions, we will also be vigilant and opportunistic in gathering and reporting readily available information relating to the project's context, reach, service to the area's working poor, and its transportability. We will look at the efforts and successes of both the foundation and the self-help housing community. Touchstones for interpreting evaluation findings will be the foundation's values. In 1999, the foundation listed these as spirituality, individual worth, caring and nurturing, participation and reciprocity, prevention, creativity and innovation, and teamwork and collaboration. We agree it is important for the foundation to consider the extent to which the self-help housing community fully manifests these values.

In general, the evaluation plan calls for three visits to the project site and the foundation. Although not included in our budget for this evaluation, the evaluators also would be willing to participate in any follow-up conferences dedicated to discussing and disseminating evaluation findings. The key information sources are project beneficiaries, foundation staff and records, and other interested parties. The main methods will be interviews, observation, document analysis, and photography. Priority will be given to interviewing samples of the members of the rent-to-own and owner project families. The evaluation's main product will be a summative evaluation report. We plan to submit fifteen copies of the report, plus an electronic copy so that you can make additional copies. We recommend that the foundation disseminate and discuss the report with the full range of interested parties, including the foundation board; the project families; and area housing, community development, and social service groups. This might occur in a conference focused on the project and the follow-up evaluation report.

As with our previous evaluation, we plan to key this evaluation to meet the Joint Committee (1994) Program Evaluation Standards requirements for utility, feasibility, propriety, and accuracy. We will report our assessment of the extent to which the evaluation satisfies each of the thirty standards. Also, we recommend that the foundation secure and fund an independent evaluation of our evaluation plan and final report.

Site Visit One

Our first visit will be for fourteen person-days (two persons for seven days each). We will concentrate on interviewing foundation staff; engaging them to review and help refine the evaluation plan; developing an outline for the final report; securing foundation assistance in accessing project records and scheduling interviews of project family members; arranging for office space to conduct interviews and review project records; studying project records; visiting the project site; having informal exchanges there and in the surrounding community; photographing the project site and surrounding community; drawing samples of rent-to-own and owner family members to be interviewed; drafting interview protocols; reviewing the samples, protocols, and outline for the final report with foundation staff; asking the foundation to appoint a sounding board or review panel for engagement in reviewing the draft evaluation materials; briefing foundation staff on the results of the site visit; and scheduling and arranging for future interviews and other project activities.

The project budget will allow interviewing approximately 25 percent (about twenty) of the project families. We propose drawing randomly about one-fourth of the families in each increment for interviews. We will review the drawn sample with foundation staff to ensure that an appropriate range of different families has been drawn. If the original sample does not include at least two of the rent-to-own families, we will randomly draw the needed number of additional rent-to-own families.

Between our first and second site visits, we will finalize the work planned and begun during the first visit. Especially we will finalize the protocol for interviewing project family members. We will confirm the schedule and arrangements for the interviews. We will also update our outline for the final evaluation report and send it to the foundation for review and distribution to the evaluation review panel. We plan to devote eight person-days to this work.

Recommendation for a Review Panel

We recommend that the foundation recruit and appoint approximately ten members for an evaluation review panel. The foundation would ask this group to serve as the evaluation's sounding board. Members would read draft evaluation materials in advance of attending meetings, participate in two meetings, and provide their critical reactions to evaluation plans and materials. Following the evaluators' first site visit, the foundation would send panel members a copy of the evaluation plan. The panel would meet during the evaluators' second site visit for learning the evaluation plan and reviewing and reacting to the outline for the final evaluation report. Following the evaluators' second visit, the foundation would send panelists a copy of the draft evaluation report. The foundation would convene the panel during the evaluators' third visit. The panel would provide critical reactions to the draft evaluation report and suggestions for effective dissemination of findings. The evaluators would use the panel's feedback to finalize the report.

We think the foundation would find panel inputs useful for disseminating evaluation findings. The foundation might also want to bring this panel together at a post-evaluation conference to discuss and help disseminate evaluation findings. We suggest that members of this approximately ten-member sounding board include a staff member who was involved in the project, two members of project families, the foundation's president and accountant, one member of the foundation's board, an area leader of housing the poor, a representative of the project area's local elementary school, a social worker in the project area, a government official in the project area, and others as determined by the foundation's president.

Site Visit Two

Our second visit will be for sixteen person-days (two persons for eight days each). It will be devoted almost exclusively to interviewing members of the project families. Upon arrival, we will check in briefly at the foundation office. Subsequently, we will travel to the project site to conduct interviews. Generally we plan to interview four families during each of five days but will be available to conduct interviews during three additional days as needed. Our plan calls for conducting two interviews each morning and two each afternoon. If needed, we will conduct some of the interviews during the evening. We propose to interview both adults in each family, if both can be available. Based on their preference, we will conduct the interview at the project's community center or the family's home. Each interview will require about seventy-five minutes. Experience has shown that interviews tend to require more time when conducted in the homes. To make sure each interview can be fully implemented, we plan to start each interview such that we will have an hour and forty-five minutes before starting the next interview. In general, we would like to schedule the first morning interview to start at 8:30 A.M. and the second one at 10:15 A.M. Similarly, we would like to start the first afternoon interview at 1:30 P.M. and the second one at 3:15 P.M. We will exercise flexibility in applying this framework.

Two evaluators will conduct each interview. At the outset of each interview, we will inform the interviewees that we consider them the most important experts in reporting on the project's success and any of its shortcomings. We will ask them to keep their responses candid, and we will commit to keep their individual responses confidential. We will give each interviewee a copy of the interview questions to keep in front of them and peruse as we ask the questions. We will ensure that all questions on the protocol are addressed or at least asked, although not necessarily in a strictly linear order. We will also invite interviewees to contribute information they consider important that is not covered by the printed interview questions. One evaluator will state the interview questions and ask follow-up questions as appropriate. The other evaluator will keep detailed notes from the interview. We will not tape-record the interviews.

Following interviews conducted in the morning, the evaluators will review, discuss, and start summarizing the interview results. They will do so as well following the afternoon interviews and any evening interviews.

Prior to completing this site visit, we will stop at the foundation and present an oral progress report. We will also meet with the evaluation review panel to go over the evaluation plan and hear their reactions and suggestions regarding the outline for the final report and the foundation's needs to disseminate evaluation findings.

First Draft of the Evaluation Report

Following the second site visit, the evaluators will summarize and analyze the interview findings. The evaluators will then compile all information and photographs gathered to date and produce the first draft of the evaluation report. In advance of the evaluators' third visit to the foundation, the evaluators will send fifteen copies of the draft report to the foundation for review and distribution to the evaluation review panel. We plan to devote fifteen person-days to these efforts.

A tentative outline for the evaluation report is as follows:

- Executive Summary
- Introduction
- Part I: Antecedents of This Evaluation
    The Foundation
    The Project
    The Context
    Results Achieved During the First Eight Years
    Photographs from the Original Evaluation
- Part II: Findings of the Follow-up Evaluation
    Evaluation Design
    Effectiveness and Sustainability Findings
    Comparison of the Findings with the Foundation's Values
    Conclusions Concerning the Project's Merit, Worth, Probity, and Significance
    Key Lessons Learned
    Photographs of the Current Scene
- Appendix
    Protocols for Each Evaluation Method
    Internal Metaevaluation
    About the Evaluators

Site Visit Three

The third site visit will consume four person-days (two days for each evaluator). We will conduct a feedback workshop with the foundation's staff and the evaluation review panel focused on the draft final report. We will also tie up any loose ends of the evaluation as needed.

Following the third visit, we will finalize the evaluation report and send fifteen copies to the foundation. We plan to devote six person-days to this effort.

Evaluation Methods

We are not ready to finalize protocols for interviews and other evaluation methods. However, we have compiled the following lists of potential questions to assist in creating the evaluation instruments.

Interviews of Project Family Members

A tentative list of pertinent questions that residents of the self-help housing community should be able to address appears below:

1. What are the project's most important areas of success? What benefits have been most important to you?
2. What are the project's most important shortcomings?
3. What impacts has the project made on the community's children? What are the main successes? Are there any problems or negative impacts on children? What would you cite as the most important needs of the community's children?
4. Has the community emerged as a collaborative, democratic, supportive community? Why or why not?
5. What is the community's progress in community organizing and self-governance?
6. What is the status of the effort to establish and operate a community association?
7. Has the community remained peaceful and free of violence? Are there problems in this area?
8. Has the community remained free of substance abuse? Are there problems in this area?
9. Has the community remained free of crime? Please elaborate.
10. To what extent have residents reached out to and addressed needs of persons in the outlying community?
11. What is the quality of the local elementary school?
12. To what extent have project residents helped strengthen the local elementary school?
13. What needs and problems in the self-help housing community require attention?
14. What are the needs of the community's children for educational services and support in transitioning to adult life?
15. What is the status of the outlying community regarding employment, violence, substance abuse, crime, and quality of housing?
16. How has the foundation continued to relate to the community? What is the nature and quality of that relationship?
17. How well have the community covenants worked out? Are there any issues regarding the covenants?

18. How and how well are the community center and common areas being maintained?
19. To what extent has the community remained free of overcrowding?
20. How well have the project's arrangements for mortgages and land-lease payments worked?
21. Has the community incorporated and lived up to positive family and community values?

As I list the project's values, please comment about the community's adherence to each one: prizing each individual's worth, caring and nurturing of others, participation and giving back to the larger community, prevention of problems, creativity and innovation, teamwork and collaboration, and spirituality.

22. If you were advising a foundation on planning a project such as yours, what advice would you offer?
23. Are there other questions we should have asked? Please do not hesitate to provide any additional input you view as relevant.

Following the open-ended questions, we plan to ask the respondents to provide a joint rating of outstanding, good, poor, or very poor on each of the following basic questions:

• Overall, how do you rate the foundation's initial eight years of work in developing a safe, healthy, viable community?
• Overall, how do you rate the residents' accomplishments during the last five years in sustaining and strengthening the community?

Summaries of the respondents' ratings on these two questions will assist interpretation of the qualitative responses to interview questions. It will be particularly interesting to see the extent of agreement across families in the ratings and to compare ratings on the two questions.

Interviews of Foundation Personnel and Review of Records

Possible questions for interviewing foundation personnel and reviewing project records are as follows:

1. What does the foundation see as the project's most important successes?
2. What does the foundation see as the project's most important weaknesses?
3. To what extent have community residents adhered to the project's covenants?
4. Has the city adequately maintained the project's streets and continued other city services?
5. To what extent have the original families remained in the community?
6. What, if any, steps has the foundation taken to ease the burden on residents of the projected balloon payment for land-lease purchase?
7. To what extent has the community avoided gentrification?
8. To what extent have the families kept up mortgage and land-lease payments?

9. To what extent is the foundation recouping its investment in this project—through land-lease and house purchase payments?
10. If the foundation were to develop a balance sheet for the project, what would be the costs of the project compared with the financial returns received so far?
11. To what extent have the families kept up their property?
12. What have been the project's most important impacts on children?
13. What should a foundation be prepared to invest to replicate this project?
14. To what extent has the design of this project been adapted and applied elsewhere, and with what results?
15. What do foundation officials see as the most important lessons learned from this project?
16. To what extent has the foundation built on this project to conduct other projects and with what results?

Interviews with Persons Residing Outside the Project

Possible questions for interviewing residents of the community outside the project are as follows:

1. How do residents of the community perceive and judge the value of the self-help housing community?
2. What are the benefits of having this self-help housing project in the area?
3. How has the project affected the children that live in the self-help housing community?
4. Are there any problems relating to the project?
5. What is the status of the area regarding employment, violence, substance abuse, crime, and quality of housing?

Evaluation Staff

Two senior evaluators will conduct this evaluation: the evaluator who led the original evaluation and the evaluator who collaborated with him in completing the final report of that evaluation. Together they have seventy years of experience in the evaluation field, much experience in helping develop the evaluation profession, and many evaluation publications. Résumés for both evaluators are available at www.wmich.edu/evalctr, as is a résumé for the Western Michigan University Evaluation Center. The center will also provide the needed editing and clerical support.

Proposed Contractual Agreements

Key contractual agreements needed to carry out this evaluation are as follows:

- The foundation will make available to the evaluators pertinent documents and files related to the project.

- The evaluators will treat all materials as confidential and not attribute obtained and reported information to any individual.
- The evaluators will strictly control all obtained information in a secure location at Western Michigan University, with access given only to members of the evaluation team.
- The foundation will assist the evaluators in scheduling interviews with project beneficiaries.
- The evaluators will not tape-record interviews with project beneficiaries.
- The final report will be delivered to the foundation within twelve months of starting the project. The evaluators will provide fifteen copies of the report plus an electronic file containing the report.
- The evaluator will provide the foundation with a prerelease draft of the evaluation report and will correct factual errors and address any issues of ambiguity.
- The evaluator will key the evaluation work to the Joint Committee (1994) Program Evaluation Standards.
- The evaluator will have authority for editing and finalizing the evaluation report.
- The foundation will provide the evaluation report to specified audiences in accordance with advance agreements on dissemination.
- The foundation will pay a fixed-price amount of $62,590 for the evaluation work and will also reimburse the evaluator's organization for associated travel costs.
- The contract will be with Western Michigan University, which will control and account for proper expenditure of funds for the evaluation.
- The evaluator will conduct an internal metaevaluation of the evaluation.
- It is proposed that the foundation commission and fund an external metaevaluation, but this would be at the discretion of the foundation.

Budget

Projections for expending the $62,590 needed to complete the evaluation are as follows:

Lead evaluators (63 days @ $800—fringe loaded)	$50,400
Clerical and editorial support	$3,500
Communications, materials, reports, etc.	$3,000
Indirect costs (10%)	$5,690
Total	$62,590

Final Remarks

The preceding is offered as an initial but not necessarily final response to the foundation's request for a follow-up evaluation of the self-help housing project. Within boundaries of feasibility, we have responded directly to your specifications for the study.

Implementation of this plan would provide you, your foundation colleagues, and other interested parties with an independent, credible, timely assessment of the project's continued level of success and at a reasonable cost.

As noted above, our request for $62,590, plus funds for travel expenses exceeds the $50,000 you stipulated in the request for proposals. If our price precludes our participation, there is a possibility for reducing the budget by changing the staffing plan. If we replaced one senior evaluator with a university graduate research associate, the budget could be reduced to approximately $46,000. The Evaluation Center has a number of highly competent graduate associates, and I am confident we could select one who would provide excellent evaluation service. The trade-off is that you and we would not have the benefit of engaging one of the nationally credible evaluators who developed great insight into the project during the original evaluation. In any case, we are willing to discuss and address any reservations you might have about our proposed budget.

On the other side, because of the financial restriction, we excluded three evaluation procedures that are highly relevant to and would enhance a follow-up evaluation of the project. These are updates of the goal-free evaluation and environmental analysis employed in the previous evaluation. Also, we think an in-depth cost analysis of the project would be highly instructive to both the foundation and potential adopters of the self-help housing project approach. We mention these in case the foundation could afford and would now or in the future desire to obtain such assessments. If so, we would be glad to prepare and submit the needed study plans and budgets.

Overall, I believe the above evaluation plan is sufficient to meet the Joint Committee Program Evaluation Standards. Regarding the study's *utility,* the plan directly addresses your prescribed questions, recommends engaging a stakeholder panel to promote utilization of findings, engages the two senior evaluators who successfully conducted the previous evaluation, focuses on the foundation's values, schedules the work within the prescribed twelve-month period, provides for prerelease reviews of reports to help ensure accuracy and clarity, recommends a conference for sharing evaluation findings, and notes that the evaluators would be available to assist with follow-up activities. On the matter of the evaluation's *feasibility,* we will use the relatively uncomplicated procedures of interviews, document review, observation, and photography. We will interview persons from a relatively small but representative sample of families, will secure the foundation's help in meeting with families, and will keep costs low without compromising the quality of the study. Regarding *propriety,* we will not tape-record interviews and will protect the identities of data sources; also, we propose contractual agreements on the important matters of editing and releasing reports, maintaining security of obtained information, and ensuring fiscal accountability. The plan is also sufficiently strong in the area of *accuracy.* We will photograph and collect information on the project's environment. We will obtain information from the key data sources of community families, foundation personnel, previous project staff members, other knowledgeable parties, and project records. We will use random sampling to ensure representativeness of the families to be interviewed. We will carefully develop and employ data collection protocols keyed directly to the study's questions, secure critical reviews of drafts of the protocols, present both qualitative and quantitative findings, key our conclusions to obtained data, engage stakeholders to critically review our draft report, give our attestation of the extent to which the final report meets each of the thirty Joint Committee Program Evaluation Standards, and have recommended that the foundation arrange and fund an independent evaluation of our follow-up evaluation.

Again, thank you for inviting us to submit a plan to conduct the needed follow-up evaluation of your important, innovative self-help housing project. I hope we will be chosen to conduct this study. If you have questions or need additional information, please let me know. I look forward to hearing from you.

This example shows that an application of the CIPP model need not always include context, input, process, and product evaluations. Based on the client's needs, this plan included only context and product evaluations. Although the evaluator presented a fairly extensive plan, he emphasized its flexibility and openness to modification during the study. Strong provision for stakeholder involvement should strengthen the evaluation and promote use of findings. The evaluator's risk in proposing a budget in excess of the prescribed $50,000 was somewhat mitigated by his offer to replace a senior evaluator with a less expensive graduate student evaluator if necessary. The plan's provision for stakeholder inputs was matched with a contractual provision guaranteeing that the evaluator would have authority for editing reports. The lists of potential interview questions should foster immediate stakeholder assistance in better focusing the evaluation. The plan is keyed to professional standards but contains no contractual provision to ensure that the foundation would contract for an independent metaevaluation.

Review Questions

1. Why and how was the CIPP model developed?
2. What are the similarities and differences between the concepts of needs assessment and context evaluation?
3. What is the essential meaning of input evaluation, and what are at least two illustrations of its use?
4. What is the relationship between the concepts of context, input, process, and product evaluations and the concepts of formative and summative evaluations?
5. What are examples of the use of process evaluations for formative and summative purposes?
6. What is the traveling observer technique, how is it applied within the framework of the CIPP model, and what are advantages of using the approach?

7. What is meant by the CIPP model's objectivist orientation?
8. What is the role of values in the CIPP model, and how are these identified and applied?
9. What is the advocacy teams technique, and what is an illustration of its use in an input evaluation?
10. What is meant by the claim that the CIPP model is a social systems approach to evaluation, and what is the value of this orientation?

Group Exercises

Exercise 1. The CIPP Model's operational definition of evaluation is "the process of delineating, obtaining, reporting, and applying descriptive and judgmental information about some object's merit, worth, significance, and probity in order to guide decision making, support accountability, disseminate effective practices, and increase understanding of the involved phenomena." How does implementation of this definition satisfy the Joint Committee Standards requirements that evaluations should meet conditions of utility, feasibility, propriety, and accuracy?

Exercise 2. Suppose you were asked to conduct a product evaluation of a state's long-standing policy to prohibit smoking in public buildings. What might you look at within the product evaluation's subparts of impact, effectiveness, sustainability, and transportability? How might the goal-free evaluation technique be useful in this evaluation?

Exercise 3. This chapter's response to Chapter Twelve's request for an evaluation proposal rejected the stipulation that the evaluation be conducted within a limit of $50,000, plus costs needed for travel. Was this a bad or a reasonable decision? How adequately did the evaluation proposal rationalize this decision? If you were responding to the request for proposal within the context of the CIPP model, how would you have addressed the issue of funds needed to conduct the evaluation?

Exercise 4. Drawing on the principles and standards presented in Chapter Three, how would you judge the adequacy of the plan in this chapter for evaluating the self-help housing project reviewed in Chapter Twelve? How would you improve this plan?

References

Adams, J. A. (1971). *A study of the status, scope and nature of educational evaluation in Michigan's public K-12 school districts.* Unpublished doctoral dissertation, Ohio State University.

Alexander, D. (1974). *Handbook for traveling observers.* Kalamazoo: Western Michigan University Evaluation Center.

Alkin, M. C. (2004). *Evaluation roots: Tracing theorists' views and influences.* Thousand Oaks, CA: Sage.

Campbell, D. T., & Stanley, J. C. (1963). Experimental and quasi-experimental designs for research on teaching. In N. L. Gage (Ed.), *Handbook of research on teaching* (pp. 171–246). Skokie, IL: Rand McNally.

Candoli, I. C., Cullen, K., & Stufflebeam, D. L. (1997). *Superintendent performance evaluation: Current practice and directions for improvement.* Norwell, MA: Kluwer.

Evers, J. (1980). *A field study of goal-based and goal-free evaluation techniques.* Unpublished doctoral dissertation, Western Michigan University.

Gally, J. (1984, April). *The evaluation component.* Paper presented at the annual meeting of the American Educational Research Association, New Orleans.

Granger, A., Grierson, J., Quirino, T. R., & Romano, B. (1965). *Training in planning, monitoring, and evaluation for agricultural research management: Manual 4–evaluation.* The Hague: International Service for National Agricultural Research.

Guba, E. G., & Stufflebeam, D. L. (1968). Evaluation: The process of stimulating, aiding, and abetting insightful action. In R. Ingle & W. Gephart (Eds.), *Problems in the training of educational researchers.* Bloomington, IN: Phi Delta Kappa.

Joint Committee on Standards for Educational Evaluation. (1981). *Standards for evaluations of educational programs, projects, and materials.* New York: McGraw-Hill.

Joint Committee on Standards for Educational Evaluation. (1988). *The personnel evaluation standards.* Thousand Oaks, CA: Corwin Press.

Joint Committee on Standards for Educational Evaluation. (1994). *The program evaluation standards.* Thousand Oaks, CA: Corwin Press.

Joint Committee on Standards for Educational Evaluation. (2003). *The student evaluation standards.* Thousand Oaks, CA: Corwin Press.

Nevo, D. (1974). *Evaluation priorities of students, teachers, and principals.* Unpublished doctoral dissertation, Ohio State University.

Nowakowski, J. A. (1974). *Handbook for traveling observers.* Kalamazoo, MI: Western Michigan University Evaluation Center.

Reed, M. (1989). *WMU traveling observer handbook* (5th ed.). Kalamazoo: Western Michigan University Evaluation Center.

Reed, M. (1991). *The evolution of the traveling observer (TO) role.* Paper presented at the annual meeting of the American Educational Research Association, Chicago.

Reinhard, D. (1972). *Methodology development for input evaluation using advocate and design teams.* Unpublished doctoral dissertation, Ohio State University.

Sandberg, J. (1986). *Alabama educator inservice traveling observer handbook.* Kalamazoo: Western Michigan University Evaluation Center.

Scriven, M. (1991). *Evaluation thesaurus* (4th ed.). Thousand Oaks, CA: Sage.

Stufflebeam, D. L. (1966, January). *Evaluation under Title I of the Elementary and Secondary Education Act of 1967.* Address delivered at the Title I Evaluation Conference sponsored by the Michigan State Department of Education, Lansing, MI.

Stufflebeam, D. L. (1967). The use and abuse of evaluation in Title III. *Theory into Practice, 6,* 126–133.

Stufflebeam, D. L. (1969). Evaluation as enlightenment for decision making. In A. Walcott (Ed.), *Improving educational assessment and an inventory of measures of affective behavior.* Washington, DC: Association for Supervision and Curriculum Development.

Stufflebeam, D. L. (1971). The use of experimental design in educational evaluation. *Journal of Educational Measurement, 8*(4), 267–274.

Stufflebeam, D. L. (1983). The CIPP model for program evaluation. In G. F. Madaus, M. Scriven, & D. L. Stufflebeam (Eds.), *Evaluation models* (pp. 117–141). Norwell, MA: Kluwer.

Stufflebeam, D. L. (1985). Stufflebeam's improvement-oriented evaluation. In D. L. Stufflebeam & A. J. Shinkfield, *Systematic evaluation* (pp. 151–207). Norwell, MA: Kluwer.

Stufflebeam, D. L. (1997). *Strategies for institutionalizing evaluation: Revisited.* Kalamazoo: Western Michigan University Evaluation Center.

Stufflebeam, D. L. (2000). The CIPP model for evaluation. In D. L. Stufflebeam, G. F. Madaus, & T. Kellaghan (Eds.), *Evaluation models* (2nd ed., pp. 279–317). Norwell, MA: Kluwer.

Stufflebeam, D. L. (2002). *CIPP evaluation model checklist.* www.wmich.edu/evalctr/checklists.

Stufflebeam, D. L. (2003a). The CIPP model for evaluation. In T. Kellaghan & D. L. Stufflebeam (Eds.), *The international handbook of educational evaluation.* Norwell, MA: Kluwer.

Stufflebeam, D. L. (2003b). Institutionalizing evaluation in schools. In T. Kellaghan & D. L. Stufflebeam (Eds.), *The international handbook of educational evaluation.* Norwell, MA: Kluwer.

Stufflebeam, D. L. (2004). The 21st-century CIPP Model: Origins, development, and use. In M. C. Alkin (Ed.), *Evaluation roots.* Thousand Oaks, CA: Sage.

Stufflebeam, D. L. (2005). CIPP model (context, input, process, product). In S. Mathison (Ed.), *Encyclopedia of evaluation.* Thousand Oaks, CA: Sage.

Stufflebeam, D. L., Foley, W. J., Gephart, W. J., Guba, E. G., Hammond, R. L., Merriman, H. O., & Provus, M. M. (1971). *Educational evaluation and decision making.* Itasca, IL: Peacock.

Stufflebeam, D. L., & Webster, W. J. (1988). Evaluation as an administrative function. In N. Boyan (Ed.), *Handbook of research on educational administration* (pp. 569–601). White Plains, NY: Longman.

Sumida, J. (1994). *The Waianae self-help housing initiative: Ke Aka Ho 'ona: Traveling observer handbook.* Kalamazoo: Western Michigan University Evaluation Center.

Thompson, T. L. (1986). *Final synthesis report of the life services project traveling observer procedure.* Kalamazoo: Western Michigan University Evaluation Center.

Webster, W. J. (1975, March). *The organization and functions of research and evaluation in large urban school districts.* Paper presented at the annual meeting of the American Educational Research Association, Washington, DC.

CHAPTER SIXTEEN

MICHAEL SCRIVEN'S CONSUMER-ORIENTED APPROACH TO EVALUATION

Michael Scriven has sharply criticized evaluation ideologies that focus on achieving the developer's objectives rather than meeting consumers' needs. He has proposed a rich array of concepts and methods that are designed to move evaluation from its objectives orientation to one keyed to assessed needs and societal ideals. Moreover, he has characterized evaluation as a vital transdiscipline that inheres in all disciplined intellectual and practical endeavors and one that needs to be developed and maintained as a discipline in its own right. He has called on evaluation theorists and practitioners to take necessary steps to advance their field in all of its important dimensions so that it can be applied meaningfully across the full range of societal enterprises.

Consistent with this interest, Scriven currently is directing the Western Michigan University interdisciplinary doctoral program in evaluation. It is a joint effort of the Colleges of Arts and Sciences, Education, Engineering and Applied Sciences, Health and Human Services, and the Evaluation Center to engage professors and recruit students from the full range of disciplinary backgrounds. The program prepares students to apply evaluation across diverse disciplinary and service areas and to help develop evaluation as a transdiscipline.

Scriven has many conceptual contributions to his credit (Scriven, 1991a, 1993). The most prominent of these are formative evaluation and summative evaluation. Summative evaluation enables consumers to decide whether a developed product or service—refined by the use of the evaluation process in its first, formative role—represents a sufficiently significant advance on the available alternatives to justify its purchase and use. Scriven has identified the key methods of evaluation as scoring, ranking, grading, and apportioning and has noted that the logic of evaluation involves gathering and summarizing facts; collecting, clarifying, and verifying relevant values and standards; and synthesizing evidence and values into evaluative conclusions. While he sees experimental design as a valuable evaluation tool, he notes that this is only one of a range of methods for reaching defensible conclusions about cause and effect. He has developed and continues to refine a practical tool for applying his evaluation approach labeled the Key Evaluation Checklist.

Chapter Overview

In this chapter, we summarize Scriven's background and trace and discuss his theoretical, methodological, and professional contributions. We characterize his basic orientation to and definition of evaluation. We reference his critical appraisal of Tyler's objectives-based and Cronbach's formative approaches to evaluation. We discuss his formative-summative conceptualization and identify a range of concepts he has introduced in the literature. We highlight his key methodological tool, the Key Evaluation Checklist. We summarize his 1983 attack on prevailing evaluation ideologies and a few of his methodological suggestions. Particularly, we present his case that randomized, controlled experiments are not the only way to address questions about cause and effect effectively. We describe his breakout of basic evaluation methods into scoring, ranking, grading, and apportioning and illustrate the application of these methods. We discuss his views on product evaluation. We note his argument that evaluation is a self-referent discipline requiring every evaluator and the evaluation profession to obtain evaluations of their work. We conclude by considering how an evaluator might apply his approach to respond to the request, presented in Chapter Twelve, for an evaluation of a self-help housing project.

Scriven's Background

Michael Scriven is a philosopher of science and an expert in critical thinking who has contributed extensively to the growth of evaluation theory and the evaluation profession. He has sharply criticized both classical and more recent conceptualizations of evaluation. He has grounded his consumerist view of evaluation in basic philosophical propositions of objectivism and pragmatism and has evolved concepts and methods to help articulate and apply his approach. He has also been one of the foremost leaders in the effort to professionalize evaluation work and develop the evaluation discipline.

Scriven was born in England and raised in Australia. He earned his bachelors degree in mathematics and his masters degree in applied mathematics and symbolic logic at the University of Melbourne. Subsequently, he completed his Ph.D. in philosophy of science at Oxford University. He has served in ten universities in the U.S., Australia, and New Zealand. Since 2004, he has been professor of philosophy and associate director of the Evaluation Center at Western Michigan University. The foundations of Scriven's evaluation approach are described in Alkin (2004).

Scriven's Basic Orientation to Evaluation

We chose to label Scriven's approach "consumer-oriented evaluation" in order to characterize his basic pragmatic orientation to addressing consumers' needs. In an audiotape prepared for the American Educational Research Association (1969), he stated that the proper role of the evaluator is that of "an enlightened surrogate consumer." In this role, the evaluator serves as informed social conscience. Such service, he said, is the "foundation stone of professional ethics in evaluation work." Accordingly, evaluators armed with skills in obtaining pertinent and accurate information and with a deeply reasoned view of ethics and the common good should help professionals produce products and services that are of high quality, of best buys for consumers, and in service to humankind. They also should help consumers identify and assess the merit, worth, and wide-range significance of alternative goods and services.

According to Scriven (1991a), "Evaluation is the process of determining the merit, worth and value of things, and evaluations are the products of that process" (p. 1). He has emphasized that evaluators must be able to arrive at defensible value judgments rather than simply to measure things or determine whether goals have been achieved. Instead of accepting a developer's goals as given, an evaluator, according to Scriven, must judge whether achievement of the goals would contribute to the welfare of the consumers. Regardless of the goals, the evaluator must identify outcomes and assess their value from the perspective of consumers' needs. He advanced this position when he introduced the concept of goal-free evaluation (1974).

Scriven's practical approach to evaluation in general calls for identifying and ranking the optional programs and products that are available to consumers, based on the options' relative costs and effects and in consideration of the assessed needs of consumers and the broader society. He has often identified the magazine *Consumer Reports* as exemplary of what professional evaluation should contribute, although in his piece on product evaluation discussed later in this chapter, he criticized Consumers Union (publisher of *Consumer Reports*) for what he saw as lowering its technical standards and relaxing its independence from commercial interests.

Scriven's Definition of Evaluation

Over the years, Scriven's suggested definition of evaluation has evolved, but its basic message has remained the same. In a classic article (1967), he defined evaluation as a methodological activity that "consists simply in the gathering and combining of performance data with a weighted set of goal scales to yield either comparative or numerical ratings, and in the justification of (1) the data-gathering instruments, (2) the weighting, and (3) the selection of goals" (p. 40). While Scriven has charged evaluators to evaluate the worth or merit of something, more recently he has added *significance* to these bottom-line criteria. His concept of significance is evident: "One of the most important questions professional evaluators should regularly consider is the extent to which evaluation has made a contribution to the welfare of humankind, more generally, to the welfare of the planet we inhabit" (2004, p. 183).

In discussing the thrust of his intended meaning of evaluation, we often have heard him say that evaluations are best executed by engaging an independent evaluator to render a judgment of some object based on the accumulated evidence about how it compares with competing objects in meeting the assessed needs of consumers. According to this view, evaluation is preferably comparative; by implication, it looks at comparative costs as well as benefits; it concerns how best to meet the needs of consumers; optimally, it is a professional activity involving systematic procedures; it should be conducted as objectively as possible and often by an independent evaluator; and it must culminate in judgments. However, we also note that Scriven sees evaluation as a self-referent activity in which evaluators must evaluate their own work as well as obtain independent assessments of their evaluations.

Critique of Other Persuasions

Scriven has sharply criticized other views of evaluation and has used his critical analysis to extend his own position. He has charged that the Tylerian tradition, which sees evaluation as determining whether objectives have been achieved, is fundamentally flawed, since it is essentially value free (meaning that the evaluator rather uncritically accepts the developer's values as reflected in stated goals). He sees evaluations based on this approach as potentially invalid, since the developer's goals may be immoral, unrealistic, unrepresentative of the assessed needs of consumers, mainly in the developer's interest, or too narrow to encompass possibly crucial side effects. Instead of using goals to guide and judge effects, Scriven argued that evaluators should judge the goals and not be constrained by them in the search for outcomes. Whether the program was guided by meritorious goals, he believes, evaluators should search out all of the results of a program, assess the needs of consumers, and use both sets of assessments to arrive at conclusions about the merit, worth, and significance of programs.

Scriven also took issue with the advice offered by Cronbach (1963). Cronbach had criticized the prevalent practice of evaluating educational programs by using norm-referenced tests to compare the performance of experimental and control groups and had counseled the use of a more developmentally oriented approach. Cronbach advised against exclusive use of comparative experimental designs and suggested that a variety of measures should be used to study a particular program in depth while it is being developed and that the results should be used to help guide the development. In analyzing achievement test data, Cronbach preferred item analysis to help diagnose teaching and learning deficiencies to the more customary norms-based analysis of total test scores. Scriven said that this advice by Cronbach clouded the important distinction between the goal and roles of evaluation and in fact tended to equate evaluation to only one of its roles, or what Scriven labeled *formative evaluation*. Building on this critique, Scriven extended his view of evaluation in his classic article, "The Methodology of Evaluation" (1967), where he introduced the terms *formative* and *summative evaluation*. Cronbach clearly played an important part in identifying the concepts of formative and summative evaluation, to which Scriven applied labels that have stood the test of time.

Formative and Summative Evaluations

In his 1967 article, Scriven argued that the evaluator's main responsibility is to make informed judgments. He emphasized that the goal of evaluation is always the same: to judge value. But, he continued, the roles of evaluation are enormously varied. They may "form part of a teacher-training activity, of the process of curriculum development, of a field experiment connected with the improvement of learning theory, of an investigation preliminary to a decision about the purchase or rejection of materials" (pp. 40–41). He reasoned that the failure to distinguish between the goal of evaluation (to judge the value of something) and its roles (constructive uses of evaluative data) has led to the dilution of what is called *evaluation* so that it no longer achieves its goal of assessing value. In other words, he said, evaluators, in trying to help educators improve their programs, too often become co-opted and fail to judge the programs. For Scriven, evaluation must provide an objective assessment of value.

With the paramount importance of the goal of evaluation firmly established, Scriven proceeded to analyze the roles of evaluation. He cited two main roles: formative, to assist in developing programs and other objects, and summative, to assess the value of the object once it has been developed. We note that it is not the nature of collected information that determines whether an evaluation is formative or summative but how it is used. If the information is used to guide development, the evaluation is formative. If it is used to sum up the value of something, the evaluation is summative. In these respects, the same data may be used for either formative or summative evaluations.

Evaluation in its formative application is an integral part of the development process. It provides continual feedback to assist in planning, developing, and delivering a program or service. In curriculum development, it addresses questions about content validity, vocabulary level, usability, appropriateness of media, durability of materials, efficiency, staffing, and other matters. In classrooms, it may entail close and continuing assessment of teaching acts and each student's progress, with feedback used to strengthen both teaching and learning. In general, formative evaluation is done to help persons improve whatever they are developing, operating, or delivering.

In the summative role, evaluation "may serve to enable administrators to decide whether the entire finished curriculum, refined by the use of the evaluation process in its first (formative) role, represents a sufficiently significant advance on the available alternatives to justify the expense of adoption by a school system" (Scriven, 1967, pp. 41–42). Usually an external evaluator should perform a summative evaluation in order to enhance objectivity, and the findings should be made public. This type of evaluation searches for all effects of the object and examines them against the assessed needs of the relevant consumers. It compares the costs and effects of the object to those of what Scriven has called critical competitors, especially less expensive but equally effective alternatives. In case the audience might be predisposed to judge only outcomes against the developer's goals, the summative evaluation provides judgments about the extent to which the goals validly reflect assessed needs. Overall, summative evaluation serves consumers by providing them with independent assessments that compare the costs, merits, worth, and significance of competing programs or products.

Recently Scriven (2004) added a third major role of evaluations, labeled *ascriptive evaluation*. He identified such evaluations as not connected to a developmental process. An example that occurs to us is that a historian might conduct a retrospective evaluation of Henry Kaiser's use of competitions between his California and Oregon factories, which miraculously speeded up the production of warships during World War II. This historian's evaluation would not be usable for improving Kaiser's employment of competition in the shipbuilding process (the formative role) or advising anyone about whether to purchase ships that Kaiser developed (a summative role). However, the historian's evaluation could yield an interesting analysis and judgment of Kaiser's use of competition in shipbuilding.

While we have strained to illustrate Scriven's definition of ascriptive evaluation through this example, we think *summative evaluation* adequately covers this and other such examples. This is especially so if one uses Scriven's original definitions of formative and summative evaluations as denoting uses of information rather than what information was collected and why, how, where, and when it was collected. We think the label *ascriptive evaluation* might prove to be superfluous and disappear from the lexicon of evaluation concepts and terms.

Amateur Versus Professional Evaluation

In the early stages of development, Scriven prefers what he refers to as "amateur evaluation" (self-evaluation by persons with minimal evaluation expertise) to "professional evaluation." Developers, when they serve as their own evaluators, may be somewhat unsystematic and subjective; but they are also supportive, nonthreatening, dedicated to producing a success, and tolerant of vague objectives and exploratory development procedures. Hence, they are unlikely to stifle creativity in the early stages of development. Professional evaluators, if involved too early, may "dampen the creative fires of a productive group" (Scriven, 1967, p. 45), slow the development process by urging that objectives be clarified, or lose their objective perspective by becoming too closely aligned with the production effort, among other considerations. Professional evaluators are needed, however, to perform both formative and summative evaluation during the later stages of development.

Both types of evaluation require high-level technical skills and objectivity seldom possessed by persons on the development staff who are not specially trained in the theory and methodology of evaluation. Scriven recommends that a professional evaluator be included on the development staff to perform formative evaluation, and he has often advised that external professional evaluators be commissioned to conduct and report summative evaluations.

Intrinsic and Payoff Evaluation

Scriven distinguishes between intrinsic and payoff evaluations. Intrinsic evaluation appraises the qualities of an instrumentality, regardless of its effects on clients, by assessing such features as goals, structure, methodology, qualifications and attitudes of staff, facilities, public credibility, and past record. Payoff evaluation is concerned not with the nature of the program, textbook, theory, or other object but rather with its effects on clients. Such effects might include test scores, job performance, or health status. Scriven acknowledges the importance of intrinsic evaluation, but emphasizes that one must also determine and judge outcomes, since causal links between process and outcome variables are rarely, if ever, known for certain. He explains that both types can contribute to either formative or summative roles. He has often criticized accrediting boards for their preference for intrinsic criteria, such as number of books in an institution's library; upkeep of facilities; staff credentials and reputation; and, on the other side, their relative inattention to outcome variables, such as performance of graduates.

Goal-Free Evaluation

In yet another move against the widespread preoccupation with goal-based evaluation, Scriven introduced a counterproposal labeled *goal-free evaluation* (Scriven, 1974). According to this approach, the evaluator purposely remains ignorant of a program's printed goals and searches for all effects of a program regardless of its developer's objectives. There are no side effects to examine, since data about all effects, whatever the program's intent, are equally admissible. If a program is doing what it was supposed to do, then the evaluation should confirm this, but the evaluator will also be more likely to uncover unanticipated effects that the goal-based evaluators would miss because of their preoccupation with stated goals. Scriven says that goal-free evaluation is reversible and complementary: one can start out goal free in order to search for all effects and then shift to the goal-based approach to ensure the evaluation will determine whether goals were achieved, or both types of evaluation can be conducted simultaneously by different evaluators. Advantages of goal-free evaluation, according to Scriven, are that it is less intrusive than goal-based evaluation; more adaptable to midstream goal shifts; better at finding side effects; less prone to social, perceptual, and cognitive bias; more professionally challenging; and more equitable in considering a wide range of values.

Goal-free evaluation is an innovative approach that is helpful in implementing the consumer-oriented approach to evaluation. In our evaluation practice, we have found that goal-free evaluation provides important supplementary information, expands the sources of evaluative information, is especially good in turning up unexpected findings, is a relatively low-cost procedure, and is welcomed and appreciated by clients.

Needs Assessment

One challenge in using goal-free evaluation concerns how to assign value meaning to findings. If outcomes are identified without regard for what one is trying to accomplish, then how can one sort out the desirable from the undesirable consequences? Scriven's answer is that one must compare the observed outcomes to the assessed needs of the consumers. But if a need is a discrepancy between something real and something ideal, and if an ideal is a goal, then aren't needs assessments goal based and, therefore, aren't goal-free evaluations also goal based? Scriven says no. First, a developer's goals are not necessarily consistent with some set of ideals such as those embedded in democracy. In any case, he maintains that the classic conception of need as a discrepancy between something real and something ideal is wrong, since ideals are often unrealistic. Because the needs of consumers are a fundamental concept in his approach, he and his students extensively conceptualized and researched this concept.

For Scriven (Scriven and Roth, 1977), a need is anything essential for a satisfactory mode of existence, anything without which that mode of existence or level of performance would fall below a satisfactory level (1977, p. 25). Some examples he has used are vitamin C and functional literacy. In the absence of these things, a person would be physically ill or socially and intellectually debilitated; hence, the person needs them. For Scriven, needs assessment is a process for discovering facts about what things if not provided or if withdrawn would result in perverse consequences by any reasonable standards of good and bad. Given the results of such a needs assessment, an evaluator can determine the criteria and standards to be used in obtaining evidence, profiling critical competitors, and ranking or grading them. Through this process, the evaluator essentially finally judges evaluation objects as good, bad, or indifferent (or first, second, third) depending on how well each contributes to meeting the identified needs. Scriven (1991a) presented logical arguments for employing a needs-based approach to defining criteria and indicators and reaching evaluative conclusions and gave some leads on how to make this work in practice. However, much technical development will be required before needs assessment will offer a feasible means of defining evaluative criteria and standards and judging outcomes in a timely manner.

Scoring, Ranking, Grading, and Apportioning

Scriven (1991a) has identified four main methods that are potentially relevant to all types of evaluation: scoring, ranking, grading, and apportioning. *Scoring* involves assigning numbers to an evaluand or some aspect of an evaluand. These numbers represent a sum of quality points, of which the points usually are assumed to be equal in value and additive. The range of possible scores usually is taken to represent lowest measure of merit to highest measure of merit. However, the value meaning of any single score is unclear without additional information.

Evaluands may be *ranked* based on their scores on a particular evaluative procedure. The relative ranks then indicate the merits of the evaluands compared with one another, but not to particular levels of merit. Depending on whether the involved scale is ordinal, interval, or ratio, the distances between the scores of the different evaluands may or may not be considered equal.

To obtain absolute judgments of merit, *grades* must be assigned to each possible score. For example, on a 10-point scale, grades might be assigned as follows: 0–2: F; 3 or 4: D; 5 or 6: C; 7–9: B; and 10: A. Determining appropriate ranges of scores for each potential grade requires examination of relevant information about the evaluand and similar evaluands; careful, systematic analysis of relevant evidence and logical arguments; and analysis of the nature and difficulty levels of items in the measurement device.

The fourth main method, *apportionment,* involves allocation of a finite set of resources to alternative evaluands; this typically involves scoring, ranking, and grading, which contribute to the final synthesis step. An example of a university that had to reconsider the doctoral programs it would support provides an example of apportionment evaluation.

The university had insufficient funds to support all of its doctoral programs and needed to determine which programs should be discontinued and how the available funds should be allocated to the remaining programs. The board of trustees stipulated that no tenured or tenure-track faculty in discontinued programs would be dismissed; instead, they would be given opportunities to fill other open positions in the university or replace nontenure-track staff. Given the evaluation's political nature, the university contracted with a highly credible external evaluator to coordinate and control this evaluation. The evaluation also included meaningful involvement and input from stakeholders, especially doctoral students and their professors. The evaluation used the procedures of scoring, ranking, and grading as predicates to the final synthesis and apportionment step.

The board contracted with an external panel to conduct a metaevaluation of this apportionment evaluation. The metaevaluation panel included a university president, a provost, a graduate dean, a college dean, a Nobel laureate professor, a doctoral student, and an evaluation expert. This team was charged to evaluate the apportionment evaluation plan, the draft of the final report, and the final report.

At the outset, the evaluator, the university's leaders, and a representative group of stakeholders compiled a set of criteria for evaluating and contrasting the programs fairly:

1. *Need for the program's graduates* as indicated by a record of more than a 70 percent rate of graduates finding employment in the subject discipline within one year of graduation
2. *Selection criteria and decision rules* judged by external experts in the discipline to ensure acceptance of only high-quality students
3. *Rigorous application of the selection criteria,* as evidenced by students' entry-level credentials, test scores, and previous grade point averages, plus judgments by external experts
4. An acceptable *number of students,* defined as more than ten active students for each year of the program's existence (following the first year), up to and including the last three years
5. *High-quality students,* with no more than 20 percent having a cumulative grade point average below 3.5 during the previous year
6. Acceptable *graduation rate,* defined as at least 80 percent of students graduating within four years of entry to the program (with programs existing less than four years to be given a provisional pass on this criterion)
7. *Qualified faculty,* including at least three tenured faculty who have been actively engaged with the program's students
8. A duly approved *curriculum* and one that is judged positively by pertinent experts from outside the university
9. *High-quality courses,* as judged by the program's students and graduates and external experts
10. *Timely courses* that students can take when they need them, to be judged based on interviews with students and examination of their records of courses compared with their approved courses of study
11. Pertinent *and rigorously conducted internships,* as judged by the program's students, graduates, and external experts
12. A noteworthy flow of *grants and contracts* providing students with meaningful practical and research experiences, as indicated by funded projects and students' positive judgments of their associated experiences
13. High-quality *dissertations* as judged by external experts and as further indicated by spin-off publications
14. An outstanding record of *research* by the program's faculty as evidenced by grants and at least two noteworthy publications per year per faculty member
15. Positive *reputation of the program* in the discipline, as judged by external experts in the discipline
16. *Cost-effectiveness* of the program, judged as acceptable or not based on subtracting the program's annual amount of grant and contract funds from its annual cost to the university, dividing the difference by the number of program graduates and comparing the per-graduate net cost with those of all the university's

other doctoral programs. The program's rank in this distribution is to be considered when decisions are reached to retain or not retain the program.

Working from these criteria, the external evaluator and the university's provost divided the criteria into essential criteria (numbers 1–7, 11, and 13) and important criteria (the remainder). The evaluator developed pertinent scoring rubrics. The evaluator and provost then defined rules for deciding whether a program met or failed each criterion, and the evaluator constructed a pertinent rating scale. The evaluator and provost also developed specifications and a schedule for each program to follow in preparing a portfolio of relevant evidence. Furthermore, they determined a plan and budget for commissioning panels of external experts to evaluate each program. The evaluator and provost reviewed this plan, including a budget, with a group of university stakeholders appointed by the university's president. After making some modifications, the provost presented the plan to the president. She reviewed the plan with the external metaevaluation panel and, after securing some further clarifications and improvements from the evaluator and provost, approved the plan. Subsequently the evaluator and provost conducted orientation and training sessions for all groups that would participate in the evaluation.

In due course, the external evaluator obtained and reviewed the programs' portfolios and the assessments by external teams. He then scored and rated each program. He did so first in relation to the essential criteria. All programs that failed to meet one or more of these criteria were designated for termination. In these determinations, the ranking was implicit in the partitioning of programs as acceptable and unacceptable. Next, the evaluator scored each remaining program on the remaining important criteria. Using preestablished decision rules, he subsequently converted the scores into ratings of excellent, good, or marginal. For each program, he prepared a profile of ratings on the important criteria and then computed an overall weighted average grade of excellent, good, or marginal. In addition, for each program, he appended an explanation of the rationale, information, and procedures used to arrive at the profile of ratings and the final grade.

Programs with an overall grade of excellent were assessed to determine their bottom-line needs for funds. Basically these included costs of faculty and support positions, research associateships, materials and equipment, travel, research, and communications. The total of these funds was subtracted from the available funds. This process was repeated with the programs graded as good and subsequently with the programs graded as marginal.

Under this analysis, funds were not available to support continuation of any of the programs designated for termination pursuant to the first round of analysis keyed to the essential criteria or any of the programs graded as marginal in the subsequent analyses keyed to the important criteria. Following these assessments, the evaluator presented a draft of the results to the university's leaders, a representative group of stakeholders, and the external metaevaluation panel. After receiving criticisms of the draft report, the evaluator corrected factual errors, clarified areas of ambiguity, and submitted the final report to the university's provost and president. The provost then aired the report at a universitywide meeting, which stimulated heated exchange. Subsequently the provost considered the issues raised and prepared and submitted his recommendations to the university's president. The president approved the report and submitted it to the board for action.

The board reviewed the report with the metaevaluation panel and concluded it was sufficient and defensible. It subsequently approved the elimination of all but one of the programs identified for discontinuation. It mandated the reform of one marginal program because it was in an area of high need and had many students. The board also decided to eliminate three programs that had been graded as good because they all had marginal ratings on criteria 8, 12, and 16 and because the board judged that the funds being spent on these programs could be deployed more effectively elsewhere. The board directed the president to allocate the recovered funds to reform the one marginal program and strengthen two programs that had been rated excellent. The board also instructed the president to place the marginal program on probation; to direct that it dramatically improve on criteria 8, 9, 12, and 14; and to put it under close scrutiny. Finally, the board directed the president to work out a process for phasing out the programs slated for elimination such that the university would meet commitments to existing students.

This simplified example of an apportionment evaluation illustrates the differences and the complemental nature of the acts of scoring, ranking, grading, and apportioning and their functioning within a politically charged setting.

Checklists

Checklists, central to Scriven's methodological approach (2005a), contain relevant criteria for evaluating a particular object or making comparative evaluations of competing objects. Scriven constructs such checklists to guide the collection of relevant evidence and to grade or rank the objects of the evaluation. He employs both generic and particularized checklists. The former include only the defined criteria for evaluating a class of objects. The particularized checklists include the defined criteria, rating levels, weights, and threshold standards of acceptability, all determined in consideration of an evaluation's context. His basis for constructing generic checklists is the understanding of the nature and intended function of the object. In developing the particularized checklists, he requires close consideration of the operating context and the needs of both the client and the intended beneficiaries. (His definition of and rationale for evaluation checklists appear at www.wmich.edu/evalctr/checklists.)

Scriven (1994a) noted that constructing evaluation checklists is difficult due to the necessity to meet conditions such as the following:

1. Comprehensiveness in addressing all important criteria
2. Non-overlapping checkpoints to avoid double-weighting of an area of overlap
3. Focus on direct measures of merit rather than statistical correlates of merit, although empirically validated indicators may be employed if direct measures are not feasible
4. Consistent level of description for all checkpoints
5. Amenable to operational definition and application to allow determining whether and how well an entity meets a checkpoint

Key Evaluation Checklist

As a means to both plan and evaluate evaluations, Scriven developed, and has continually refined, his Key Evaluation Checklist (available for downloading at www.wmich.edu/evalctr). It is generic but can be adapted for use in particular evaluations, including evaluations of evaluations.[1] The checklist reflects Scriven's view that evaluation has multiple dimensions, must address pertinent values, should employ multiple perspectives, involves multiple levels of measurement, should use multiple methods, and usually should culminate in a bottom-line evaluative conclusion. He has sometimes referred to the Key Evaluation Checklist as the multimodel of evaluation.

The checklist is divided into four major parts. Part A: Preliminaries contains an executive summary, a preface (examining the source and nature of the request or need for the evaluation), and methodology (for example, comparative or non-comparative; scoring, ranking, grading, or apportioning; or some combination of these). Part B: Foundations provides background and context, descriptions and definitions of the program and its components, consumers of the program, program resources, and values (minimum standards and weights). Part C: Subevaluations offers evaluations of process, outcomes, costs, comparisons (alternatives), and generalizability. Part D: Conclusions comprises an evaluation of overall significance, possible recommendations and explanations, responsibility for the evaluation and justification, a report for distribution, needed support, and metaevaluation.

These parts of the evaluation checklist need not be performed in any particular sequence, but all must be addressed or at least considered before the checklist has been implemented correctly. Also, an evaluator may cycle through the checklist several times during the evaluation of a program. Early cycles are formative evaluation; the last cycle is what Scriven terms summative evaluation.

The rationale of the Key Evaluation Checklist is that evaluation is essentially a data-reduction process, whereby large amounts of data are obtained and assessed and then synthesized into an overall judgment of value. In describing this data-reduction process, Scriven suggests that the early steps help characterize a program or product and the later ones help assess its validity. Since Scriven has frequently revised the checklist, readers are advised to periodically check on its current content (www.wmich.edu/evalctr/checklists).

The Final Synthesis

Scriven (1994b) presented extensive philosophical, theoretical, and methodological analysis of the synthesis step in an evaluation. He noted that many evaluations that are impeccably conducted through the planning and data collection and analysis stages fail because the evaluator makes a leap from the data to a high-inference judgment, which often is only an idiosyncratic non sequitur. Such judgments may reflect the evaluator's (or client's) biases more than the relevant background information and may stimulate mistrust of the evaluation rather than insightful action. Scriven says:

> Sometimes . . . there is no way to avoid relying on judgment at this point. But, whether we call the last step clinical inference, intuition, professional judgment, connoisseurship, or impressionism, the solid body of the clinical vs. statistical research makes it clear that we rely on it at considerable peril. That research shows how a very simple rule, if it is empirically-based, can beat expert judgment—including the combined judgment of a panel of experts—in almost all cases [p. 367].

What are needed, according to Scriven, are clear—but not simplistic—rules for deciding whether and how to reach justified conclusions. He adds that often these are not to be found.

One needs to pursue the final synthesis step under the assumption that it may be desirable and feasible to carry it out and proceed as far down this course as makes sense. The steps in the process are searching for an appropriate decision rule; deriving criteria admissible in probative judgments; deriving criteria of goodness inherent in the classical definition of the evaluative object; assessing the needs and preferences of the client and beneficiaries; obtaining evidence of each object's status on the criteria of merit, worth, and significance; weighing the criteria;

profiling the results; deciding whether to try for a final synthesis; and, if warranted, combining the results to reach an overall conclusion.

To decide whether to make a final synthesis, Scriven advises evaluators to consider three factors:

- Determine what the evaluation client needs. Must he or she have a final synthesis that compares critical competitors—all of which pass minimally acceptable standards on all significant criteria—on appropriately weighted criteria of merit? Or, for example, does the client need only a report card or profile on how each object rates on each criterion?
- Consider the limitations of the available data. If the available data are complete on each object for each criterion and the evaluator and client have been able to determine defensible weights and standards, the evaluator can both rank and grade the evaluation objects. Otherwise he or she should stop at the point of displaying each object's profile, taking into account the fact that the profiles may be incomplete.
- Examine the configuration of available facts. If the facts reveal a tie between one or more objects, report this and do not try to pick a winner. Instead, advise the client to pick randomly or apply some additional, defensible criterion.

In launching the final synthesis step, Scriven advises evaluators that whenever possible, they should get a valid rule in place by which different evaluators using the same data set would reach the same evaluative conclusion. If this is possible, the final synthesis stage presumably is a fairly straightforward process. However, if such a rule is not to be found, which will often be the case, then Scriven advises evaluators to try for heuristics and rubrics and, failing that, to train and calibrate judges. If all these steps fail or are seen in advance to be not feasible, then the evaluator should stop short of reporting a final synthesized judgment of value and instead should deliver, for each evaluation object, a properly circumspect profile of performance levels on the significant criteria that guided the evaluation.

Scriven recommends several general procedures for reaching the final synthesis. One is what he calls "probative inference." According to Scriven (1994b), "It is inference that makes a prima facie case for a conclusion: the kind of inference . . . which is highly contextual" (p. 371). This involves deriving values from facts. Scriven (1994b) refers to evaluative claims as facts if they are extremely reliable judgments made by experienced judges against simple valid standards—judgments that are scrutinized, consciously or unconsciously, by a trained evaluator for errors of fact, standards, judgment, or inference.

As another procedure, he notes that one legitimate type of factual claim in deciding on criteria and ultimately reaching an evaluative conclusion is quasi definitional. For example, maintaining discipline in the classroom is generally regarded as an essential component of the definition of good teaching, which makes effective classroom management an essential criterion for evaluating teaching. Examples Scriven gives are "Good watches . . . keep good time" and "Good judges . . . do not take bribes" (p. 372). Since these definitional claims can be supported by factual and analytical evidence about use and the way watches and judges work, they are significant, not arbitrary, criteria for evaluating watches and judges. Under this approach, the evaluator defines and defends the criteria of merit by determining the factual claims inherent in a concept of interest and identifying known, relevant facts about objects covered by this concept. These functional analysis steps provide a foundation for comparing evaluation objects on the selected criteria and for judging each object in absolute terms against standards of what should be expected of the objects.

Another frequent step in the synthesis process involves assessments of the beneficiaries' needs and wants. Scriven (1994b) notes:

> Assuming that the client's problem calls for a ranking, then you must turn to the needs and—to a lesser extent—the preferences of the targeted recipients to provide the . . . relevant criteria and their weights. . . . Typically, the procedure would require you to try for a comprehensive list of criteria and tentative weights based on the concept, the experience of the service providers, and the literature, and take that to the consumers for additions [p. 377].

As a last point about the final synthesis step, Scriven (1994b) warns against the fallacy of the numerical weight and sum (NWS) approach to reaching an evaluative conclusion. This relatively common approach involves computing an overall score on an evaluation object by summing across all criteria the products of each criterion's weight times the object's score on the criterion. This procedure could erroneously give a passing grade to an object that failed or did poorly on the most important criteria but scored high on less important or even trivial criteria. To replace this faulty synthesis procedure, Scriven (1994b) offers what he calls the qualitative weight and sum approach (QWS). This approach begins by rating the evaluative criteria on their significance as essential, very important, important, just significant, and not significant. The not significant criteria are dropped. Then the evaluator immediately drops from further consideration any object that fails to pass the essential criteria. Scriven says the essential criteria then become a moot point because the remaining evaluative objects meet them. (We see this conclusion as not always the case, as explained below.) Subsequently the evaluator develops for each remaining object three scores: the number of criteria passed in each remaining significance group—very important, important, and just significant. Keeping the three scores separate means "that no number of points scored in the currency of lower-weighted criteria can overpower points picked up on a higher-weighted criterion" (1994b, p. 376).

We see Scriven's QWS procedure as creative and useful but too restrictive. Sometimes a simple sum of criteria met in a category will be sufficient to judge an object's merit in the category and sometimes not. We would not necessarily drop consideration of the essential criteria following the discarding of objects that failed on these (although according to Scriven's procedure, we recognize that the remaining objects would all have a score equal to the category's number of criteria). Nor would we categorically reject a weight and sum approach to arrive at scores of merit. If a rating scale is applied to each criterion in a category, some objects would surely score higher than others on given criteria and on the total of criteria in the category. We think such variations often will be of interest to decision makers. Although Scriven does not provide for rating each object's relative level of satisfaction of each criterion, we think this possibility should be preserved, although not required. If each object is rated, say, on a three-point scale on each criterion (1: pass; 2: pass with distinction; and 3: exemplary), then a total category score could be obtained for each object by summing the ratings and dividing by the number of criteria in the category. Keeping each set of category scores separate would preserve Scriven's objective of ensuring that points on lower-weighted criteria would not overpower points earned on higher-weighted criteria. Rating each object on criteria within a category would also reveal each object's relative rated merit within the category.

A weight and sum approach could be employed next to obtain an overall score for each object. For example, one could compute an object's overall score by first weighting each category of criteria (say, 4 for the essential criteria, 3 for the very important criteria, 2 for the important criteria, and 1 for the just significant criteria). Then for each object and category of criteria, one would multiply the category's weight by the object's normalized category score. Next, the evaluator would sum each object's four weighted category scores and divide by 4. Subsequently the evaluator could rank all objects still under review on their derived total scores. A report showing ranks of objects within and across categories of criteria would prove useful for drawing conclusions and making decisions about the different objects. We believe that decision makers often would want to see how objects that made the initial cut ranked within the categories of essential, very important, important, just significant criteria, and overall. We suggest the procedure we have outlined as a perhaps useful extension of Scriven's QWS approach. This extension might be labeled the qualitative and numerical weight and sum approach (QNWS).

Metaevaluation

The final item in the Key Evaluation Checklist calls for the evaluation of evaluation. Scriven introduced this concept in 1968, when he published an article responding to questions about how to evaluate evaluation instruments. He cited this as one of many concerns in metaevaluation and emphasized that evaluators have a professional obligation to ensure that their proposed or completed evaluations are subjected to competent evaluation. His rationale is that evaluation is a particularly self-referent subject since . . . evaluation applies to the process and products of all serious human endeavor and hence to evaluation" (p. 36). He notes that metaevaluation can be formative, in assisting the evaluator to design and conduct a sound evaluation, or summative, in giving the client independent evidence about the technical competence of the primary evaluator and the soundness of his or her reports. Scriven's methodological suggestions for conducting metaevaluations include the use of his Key Evaluation Checklist to assess an evaluation as a product, the use of some other checklists, or the use of professional evaluation standards. (Also see Scriven, 1975, on evaluation bias and its control.)

Evaluation Ideologies

Scriven has been one of the most thoughtful and vocal critics of prevailing views of evaluation. Consistent with this critical stance, he has emphasized that evaluation is a particularly self-referent subject, which adheres to his advocacy of metaevaluation. He has classified the prevailing views of evaluation into four groups and critiqued each extensively in the hope of convincing evaluators to recognize and shed certain biases, which he said have debilitated evaluation work. Then he used his analysis of strengths and weaknesses of each approach to strengthen his rationale for the Key Evaluation Checklist. He has described this checklist model as one that encompasses the best features of all other serious proposals about how to do evaluation and one that avoids the flaws that he identified in the other proposals. Further insight can be gained into Scriven's philosophy of evaluation in general and the Key Evaluation Checklist in particular by carefully considering his analysis of alternative ideologies (Scriven, 1983). Therefore, we next capture his most salient points regarding each of the four ideologies: the separatist, positivist, managerial, and relativist ideologies.

Separatist Ideology

Scriven sees the separatist ideology as rooted in the denial or rejection of the proposition that evaluation is a self-referent activity. This ideology is best reflected in evaluation proposals that require the appointment of evaluators who are totally independent of what is to be evaluated. Establishing and maintaining this independence of evaluator from the evaluand is often seen as essential for ensuring that evaluation reports are unbiased. In addition, evaluators who practice this ideology, according to Scriven, often fail to recognize or address the need to have their own work evaluated. Quite possibly many of them see such metaevaluation as a concern for somebody else, since evaluators, according to their separatist view, could not be objective in evaluating their own work. Hence, Scriven pointed to the paradox of an evaluator who earns a living by evaluating the work of others but fails to see, or may even resist, evaluation of his or her own services.

Underlying this kind of professional parasitism, Scriven sees a basic human flaw: "valuephobia, a pervasive fear of being evaluated" (p. 230). It is manifest when evaluators, who are in close contact with the person whose work they evaluate, become co-opted, lose their critical perspective, and praise what they might have criticized had they maintained greater distance from the evaluand. Valuephobia may also be present when evaluators resist, or at least avoid, having their evaluations evaluated. It is present when evaluators, in assessing programs, are careful not to evaluate the program's personnel.

In opposition to the separatist position, Scriven argued that professionals, including professional evaluators, need to acknowledge and deal straightforwardly with the self-referent nature of evaluation. The hallmark of a professional is subjecting one's work to evaluation. The fact that all evaluations are prone to bias should not deter one from evaluating one's own work or commissioning someone else to do so. Instead, one should respond by conducting the evaluation in as unbiased a manner as possible and subjecting the evaluation to scrutiny against recognized standards of sound evaluation. In program evaluations, one should look realistically at the staff as well as the other aspects of the program since success and failure invariably are inseparable from the work of the staff and there will be little prospect for improvement through evaluation if guidance for improving the performance of staff is not provided (see Chapter Four).

Positivist Ideology

Scriven saw a second ideology, that of logical positivism, as another overreaction to valuephobia. In the positivists' attempts to remove bias from scientific works, Scriven thought they overreacted to the point of trying to render twentieth-century science in general and evaluation in particular as value free. Whereas the separatists reject the self-referent nature of science or evaluation, the positivists reject the evaluative nature of science. Scriven pointed to a number of contradictory cases—for example, educational psychologists who assert that no evaluative judgments can be made with objectivity yet easily produce evaluative judgments about the performance of their students. Scriven's response to the flaws of positivism is to give central importance to the practice of assigning value meanings to the findings obtained in evaluation studies.

Managerial Ideology

For Scriven, "well-managed evaluation" often means much more than one that is guided by a competent administrator. It can instead involve "a very self-serving indulgence in valuephobia" (p. 238) by both program managers and evaluators. Program managers may impose rigid controls over the evaluation they commission so that there will be no surprises. They may want only their program evaluated, not the personnel who operate it and especially not its administrator. And they might insist that the evaluation be limited to determining whether their stated goals for the program have been achieved and that it be restricted from judging their work based on somebody else's wishes for the program.

From the manager's perspective, this managerial ideology clearly includes a bias toward producing favorable reports. According to Scriven, many evaluators are willing to fulfill the manager's wishes for favorable, predictable reports because of a parallel set of self-serving reasons. They want future contracts or to retain their evaluation position in the institution; giving a favorable report, or at least one that does not make their client and sponsor nervous, is in the best interest of obtaining future work. They are often willing to partial out any concern for personnel evaluation because this helps make the evaluation more independent of the different and often conflicting value positions that different persons involved in the program might hold. The manager's request for limiting the assessment to what had been intended is especially congenial since the evaluators not only will avoid having to assess the implementation of the program and especially the performance of staff members in it, but also will avoid having to deal with values, since they are presumed to be given in the program manager's goals.

In the managerial ideology, then, we can see the possibility of a confluence of the separatist, positivist, and managerial ideologies—all with bad effect. By avoiding evaluation of the manager and staff (consistent with the separatist ideology), keeping the evaluation as a technical service devoid of value determinations (the positivist approach), and helping the managers get the good report they need on the accomplishment of their goals (the managerial ideology), the evaluator has effectively rendered evaluation as a disservice and not a contribution to society.

With the bent outlined above, the study, according to Scriven, would exclude many vital aspects of a sound evaluation. It would deter rather than assist clients to examine their goals and services critically. By concentrating on the developer's goals, it would fail to ensure that the service had value for addressing the consumers' needs. It likely would be myopic and not consider whether the service or program or product is a "best buy," when it could serve the client better by exposing and comparing alternatives. And it would likely skirt issues concerned with ethics and prudent use of scarce resources. For Scriven, the widely seen adherence to the managerial ideology and its connections to other bad evaluation practices is a travesty for society and for the evaluation profession. He has used his critical analysis of this stance as a platform from which to advocate a series of reforms, which are seen in his Key Evaluation Checklist:

- Performing needs assessments as a basis for judging whether a program has produced beneficial outcomes
- Evaluating "goal free" so as not to become preoccupied with the developer's goals and thereby miss finding important but unanticipated outcomes, good and bad
- Comparing what is being evaluated to viable alternatives
- Examining services for their cost-effectiveness
- Combining personnel and program evaluation

Relativist Ideology

Another ideology that Scriven has seen as flawed and debilitating in its influence on evaluation work is the relativist ideology. Scriven sees it as an overreaction to problems associated with the positivist ideology. Whereas the positivists often have put forth the view that there is an objective reality that can be known by anyone who can and will use unbiased assessment procedures, the relativists have charged that this construction is overly simplistic and can only lead to narrow assessments that give exclusive and undue prominence to the perspective of some group in power under the mistaken view that their perspective and assessments are objective. In response to the hazards of positivism, the relativists assert that all is relative, that there is no objective truth. Therefore, they call for multiple perspectives, criteria, measures, and answers.

Scriven has seen much of this movement in the evaluation field as an overreaction that sometimes denies the possibility of objective determinations of merit or even objectively correct descriptions of programs. While he also rejects the existence of a single correct description, he counsels us not to abandon the idea that there is an objective reality. While it may be a complex reality beyond our existing capabilities to comprehend and describe thoroughly, we only delude ourselves if we pretend it does not exist. He counsels instead that we may need to relativize our descriptions to different audiences. But he cautions us not to accept all conflicting descriptions as correct as, we think, some of the more pedantic relativists seem prone to do. Instead, we are advised, as evaluators, to seek out the "best," the "better," the "ideal."

Avenues to Causal Inference

The past forty years have seen substantial controversy in the evaluation field related to the concept of causal conclusions in evaluations. Campbell and Stanley (1963) argued that researchers and evaluators should assess the extent to which a project had caused observed outcomes and that the best way to obtain valid findings about cause and effect is through rigorous application of randomized, controlled experiments. Since then, the U.S. federal government has repeatedly designated randomized, controlled experimental design as the gold standard for evaluations and often has mandated this approach for use in federally funded evaluations. Such requirements have held hostage much of the federal funding available for evaluations, with government officials releasing these funds only to evaluators who agree to conduct a randomized, controlled experiment. This practice directly opposes the advice of Fisher (1951), the father of experimental design. He expressly directed inquirers not to equate his experimental methods with science. Consistent with Fisher's position, many evaluation and research methodologists have sharply criticized the U.S. government's requirements for experiments, arguing that nonexperimental methods often are superior to a controlled, randomized experiment in detecting causal relationships and creating deep understanding of programs. Nevertheless, a number of leading researchers have continued to convince federal government officials that only sound randomized, controlled experiments can provide defensible conclusions about causes and effects in the programs of education, health, and human services.

Scriven (2005b) has strongly criticized the near monopoly that experimental design holds over federally funded evaluation. He posited that the gold standard for evaluations should not be experimentally determined conclusions but conclusions beyond reasonable doubt. Arguing that experiments often are inadequate and not even the best way to address questions of cause and effect, he stated, "We must agree that cause is an epistemological primitive, well understood by humans but not entirely reducible to other logical notions such as necessity and sufficiency"

(p. 44). In apparent causal linkages of the execution of a program to observed outcomes, Scriven says equal or better outcomes might have been produced by another program not under review or that, apart from the study's controlled conditions, the experimental program might not produce the same outcomes when applied in a naturalistic setting. The latter point gives credence to those who argue for in-depth case studies of programs in their natural settings. Scriven concluded that the claim that randomized, controlled experiments are consistently superior in identifying necessary and sufficient conditions that caused observed outcomes is a fallacy whose exposure should clearly make room for a range of methodological approaches to studies of cause and effect.

In advancing the range of methodological approaches that can meet his gold standard of conclusions beyond reasonable doubt, Scriven looked to both quantitative and qualitative designs. When they were suitably applied, he credited the following quantitative designs as meeting his gold standard: double-blind studies; single-blind studies; randomized, controlled experiments; regression discontinuity studies; strong interrupted time-series studies; and identical-twin studies. Looking beyond these quantitative designs, Scriven also identified designs in the broader sphere of scientific inquiry: laboratory investigations used in forensic studies of the cause of a death; engineering studies of the cause of a structural failure in, for example, a bridge, a building, or a jet airliner; astrophysicists' conclusions drawn from systematic applications of astronomy methods and anthropological methods such as those applied by Darwin; and historical analysis. (We would add epidemiological studies and studies of the effects of specified agents on germ-free animals.) After identifying this range of designs that can meet the standard of conclusions beyond reasonable doubt, Scriven cited randomized, controlled experimentation as only one of at least eight scientifically acceptable approaches to studying and reaching conclusions on causes and effects.

Subsequently Scriven presented his final synthesis regarding an appropriate general methodology for identifying and crediting a program's effects. Fundamentally he sees observation as the most important and reliable source of causal claims. He stated, "The basic kind of causal data, vast quantities of highly reliable and checkable causal data, comes from observation, not from elaborate experiments" (p. 46). He said this conclusion liberates such field sciences as biology and anthropology from second-class citizenship in reaching and defending claims based on observed causal connections. Moreover, he said, rigorous applications of case study methodology can produce defensible causal claims. However, he stressed that all studies of cause and effect should be subjected to strong methods of verification. Among others, these methods are independent confirmation, valid triangulation, detailed documentation, systematic elimination of alternative possible causes, and systematic qualitative analysis of causal chains and patterns. In the end, Scriven acknowledges that development of valid causal claims is complex and difficult. Accordingly, he calls for an approach to studying causal connections that is grounded in systematic observation, applies multiple methods for determining cause, and meets demanding standards of scientific explanation.

Product Evaluation

In 1994, Scriven (1994a) presented what he considered to be the state of the art in product evaluation. Essentially, this article either encapsulates or alludes to some of the important concepts that Scriven had developed over the years and that have been reported in this chapter: needs assessment, goal-free evaluation, standards of various kinds (particularly those that refer to ethical, legal, or political considerations), metaevaluation, and the managerial ideology (particularly in respect to aspects of the Key Evaluation Checklist).

We have extracted and summarized key aspects of Scriven's (1994a) article on product evaluation.

The Place and Importance of Product Evaluation

Scriven began his article (1994a) in this way:

> Product evaluation is important for several reasons. The obvious one, which makes it sometimes a life-saving matter for the consumer, arises because our lives, and the quality of those lives, depend on the evaluation of products by external agencies—for example, on the evaluation of drugs and of automobile safety systems. The second, a (metaphorically) life-saving matter for inventors, manufacturers, and service providers, is the role of product evaluation in the improvement of products and services, a role which has, for example, driven the computer field to an unmatched rate of improvement, although the quality of its product evaluation leaves much room for further improvement. The third reason for its importance is its involvement *within* other applied fields of evaluation, particularly within program evaluation.
>
> The extent of this involvement is only now beginning to be appreciated, just as the extent of the involvement of personnel evaluation within program evaluation is only now emerging. An important example comes from the evaluation of programs using educational technology to improve instruction. . . . It is rare that these programs can be evaluated without serious evaluation of the technology itself; yet it is also rare that the evaluation or the technology manages to avoid falling into the trap of using expert reviewers with shared

bias or using independents who make invalid commentary from ignorance. The fourth consideration is that product evaluation has long served as an exemplar *for* other applied fields in evaluation, an effect which has been considerable and could still be extended with profit. . . . The goal-free approach to program evaluation is an example [p. 45].

The article offers general remarks about the field, followed by analysis of strengths and weaknesses of product evaluation by leading practitioners in consumer products, the automobile industry, and computers. Particular emphasis is given to Consumers Union.

Despite the fact that product evaluation has long been practiced—perhaps longer than any other type of evaluation—its methodology has not received the same attention as program evaluation. However, in the past fifty years, product evaluation has become considerably more developed and certainly more public. Scriven commented that the increase in extent is exemplified by the development of technology assessment and an emerging literature on evaluating medical tests. The most obvious indication of the growing sophistication of product evaluation is the extensive array of magazines and newsletters devoting space to product testing outcomes. Moreover, as Scriven pointed out, the burgeoning of the field is also exemplified by growing emphasis on comparative rather than stand-alone tests. The consumer benefits by these activities; both utility and validity of choice improve. The overall outcome is an extremely useful, although often complex set of resources—"if you know how to get to them and how to use them" (p. 46).

However, these improvements in product evaluation for the consumer do not necessarily reflect better product evaluation by manufacturers and vendors. Poor product evaluations have often resulted in poor-quality products and services. Scriven gave a prime example where the U.S. automobile industry steadfastly refused to improve the quality of products, despite adverse criticism by external product assessors. He pointed out that as a result, there was a steady decline until the industry itself took stock of its position in relation to the price, reliability, and performance of foreign vehicles.

Basic Methodology

In answer to the question of how product evaluation should be done, Scriven advised that the same general formula should be followed as for all other evaluations. This entails identifying and validating criteria of merit, determining performance on those criteria of judgment, and integrating the two on the basis of some valid principle. "All the skill lies in the application of that formula"

(1994a, p. 47). Specific details of a product evaluation will vary according to the field of the product being tested and an exact knowledge of specific consumer needs. Scriven stated that as a methodology, evaluation is a transdiscipline,[2] and developing this methodology poses a dilemma faced by the pursuit of logic (another transdiscipline) over two millennia. One can attempt to provide a general model, but this often turns out to be too difficult to apply reliably to other cases. Or one can focus on weaknesses, or "traps," known in logic as the "fallacies approach." Scriven sees the fallacies approach as possibly the most convincing to use in establishing a methodology for product evaluation. It forms the framework and focus of what is to follow.

How well is product evaluation done? Scriven noted that most of the tributes had already been given, so his article focused on the shortcomings (in line with the fallacies approach). The shortcomings, which are serious, are most often seen in the faulty use of the formula for good evaluation, particularly in the incorrect application of widely validated principles to specific cases. In that respect, the problems are like those in most applied fields in evaluation; for example in ethics, it is usually not the Ten Commandments (or their equivalent) that are in dispute, but how to apply them to specific cases.

Consumers Union

Scriven (1994a, p. 48) noted the importance of *Consumer Reports*, the official organ of Consumers Union (CU), and acknowledged its status of a standard bearer, albeit de facto, for product evaluation. However, he also presented a litany of shortcomings in the magazine's approach to product evaluation. He observed that it is no surprise that in the course of becoming extremely powerful, wealthy, and the principal institution of its kind, CU has also become almost immune to serious criticism. As a result, he said, its earned respect as a "near flawless paradigm of the state of the art" (p. 48). has slipped. For example, while CU has steadfastly excluded advertisements of the objects evaluated in its magazine, it began advertising its own products in its own magazine. Scriven saw this as "a change which surely tends to shift its value system near to that of the advertiser rather than the consumer or evaluator" (p. 48). Another cited mistake was frequent use of the fallacious numerical weight and sum model for the synthesis of subevaluations. Scriven stressed that this is a serious error in any evaluation, including product evaluation, when failure in a single component could override success in all the others. On the other side of such criticisms, Scriven noted that *Consumer Reports* generally remains an invaluable resource for consumers, since most of its findings are based on good work.

Professionalization of Evaluation

The description of Scriven's 1994 article gives some indication of the extent to which he has been a main force for developing evaluation theory and methodology and professionalizing the evaluation field. His interests and contributions have covered virtually all aspects of evaluation, and his development of them has been influential. As its first president, he helped to establish and develop the Evaluation Network, a professional organization for evaluators from education, health, government, and social programs and one of the two organizations that merged to become the American Evaluation Association (AEA). He developed the Evaluation Network newsletter into the highly respected publication *Evaluation News*, which evolved into the *American Journal of Evaluation*, and recently he developed an online evaluation journal. He was the 1999 president of AEA. We judge his 1991 *Evaluation Thesaurus* to be the most important compilation of theoretical and philosophical ideas about evaluation. He has supported the Joint Committee's production of professional standards for evaluations (see Chapter Three), but criticized it for generating standards only for evaluations of programs, personnel, and students. He notes that given evaluation's ubiquitous nature, such standards are needed for evaluations in every discipline and area of service. Accordingly, we wonder if he would judge that the American National Standards Institute (ANSI) is making a sufficient response to this need for evaluation standards, since ANSI has approved more than ten thousand such national standards, including those of the Joint Committee. As noted previously, Scriven is directing the Western Michigan University interdisciplinary doctoral program in evaluation, thereby carrying out his position that evaluation has wide applications across disciplines and service areas. Scriven is the well-deserved recipient of many awards and prizes.

Application of Scriven's Consumerist Approach Project

In this illustration of how Scriven's consumer-oriented evaluation approach applies in practice, assume that a university professor residing in the locale of the self-help housing project described in Chapter Twelve engaged some of his doctoral students to collaborate in preparing and submitting a proposal to conduct the needed follow-up evaluation. The following memorandum to the Consuelo Foundation conveys the proposed evaluation plan:

I am pleased to respond to your request for a follow-up evaluation of the self-help housing project. The evaluation will be conducted under the auspices of X University and completed within the prescribed twelve-month time period and $50,000 limit. Additional costs for travel and accommodations will be minimal, because all the proposed evaluation staff reside in the project's immediate geographical area. I have more than forty years of evaluation experience and will lead this study. A copy of my résumé is attached. In addition, I plan to engage three of my advanced evaluation graduate students to assist in conducting the evaluation. This will keep costs low; allow for wide-ranging, in-depth inquiry; and also guarantee, under my supervision, highly competent evaluation service. Clerical support will be provided by the Evaluation Research Center, which I direct.

Our basic approach involves applying Dr. Michael Scriven's Key Evaluation Checklist. A copy is attached. By systematically applying this checklist, we will compile, sort through, and synthesize the great deal of information needed to understand and judge the project's merit, worth, and wide-ranging significance. Especially, we will closely examine and report the extent to which the project's achievements in the developmental years have been sustained. Following is an outline for the projected final evaluation report as broken out by the different components of the Key Evaluation Checklist. This outline shows both the methods we will employ and the information we will report.

Part A: Preliminaries

Executive Summary

First, the report will provide a concise executive summary, geared especially for your use and that of the board. In this summary we will identify the key evaluation questions, the evidence we obtained, and our conclusions. These will focus on the project's technical merit, worth to the targeted beneficiaries, strengths and weaknesses compared with other approaches to housing low-income families, significance to the service areas of community development and housing, and record of sustained quality and impact.

Preface

In our preface to the main report, we will note the key focus of this evaluation. It will include your initial request for the evaluation, the main questions that are of interest to you and the board, and additional questions that should be of interest to foundation personnel and other stakeholders. We will also explain our basic methodological approach. In general, it will include a review of relevant project records; visits to the project site; interviews with key stakeholders; compilation of data on the area's needs for low-income housing; collection and review of information on similar housing projects; a functional analysis of the project's governance, operations, and resources; a goal-free evaluation to identify the project's full range of outcomes; and a synthesis of the obtained information into bottom-line judgments.

Part B: Foundations

Background and Context

Your foundation, the project beneficiaries, and other parties made substantial efforts over an eight-year period to ensure this project's success. Considering the broad range of potential readers of our evaluation report, we will reprise the project's origins, rationale, target audience, goals and targeted needs, and area characteristics.

Needs Assessment

We will also conduct a needs assessment. At one level, this assessment will identify needs for housing among the area's low-income families and will also take account of and report on pertinent problems and assets in the local environment. The second level of the needs assessment will look particularly at the needs of the individual and collectivity of families in the self-help housing community. The survey of these needs will look at such areas as finances, employment and employability, education, health, safety, community governance, and community upkeep. These needs assessment results will be used to interpret the importance of project outcomes in affecting the needs of individual families, the self-help housing community, and the surrounding area.

Descriptions and Definitions

We will provide needed definitions and descriptions to help a broad range of readers grasp the nature of this project and its components. Especially, we will characterize the project's beneficiaries, governance, structure, key players, developmental process, and resources. In addition, we will document the foundation's values for this project and, based on deliberations with foundation leaders, identify minimum standards and weights on key dimensions related to the project's sustainability.

PART C: Subevaluations

Process Evaluation

We will carefully investigate the process involved in making this project work, especially in the postdevelopment period. Initially, we will study the foundation's recorded history of this project to ascertain how residents, supported by others, have continued to sustain community functioning. In addition, we will make site visits to observe activities within the community and interview a sample of residents. We will evaluate the project's ongoing process by drawing conclusions about residents' collaboration in sustaining the project's purposes and values, activities that have worked especially well, and issues and problems in the process.

Outcome Evaluation

While the process evaluation is in progress, we will also make a systematic search for project outcomes. We will look for and report on outcomes that are positive and negative and unexpected as well as intended. Our basic method of outcome evaluation will be a goal-free evaluation. One of the three graduate students selected to participate in this study will be insulated from knowing the project's goals. The intent here is to prevent this evaluator from becoming preoccupied with a search for intended outcomes. Instead, the evaluator will be charged to search far and wide for all outcomes of the project. To guide the search for project outcomes, the goal-free evaluator will be acquainted with the area of self-help housing and community development efforts targeted to the working poor. She will then develop a checklist of possible outcomes of such projects and a goal-free evaluation handbook to guide the search for relevant evidence. The evaluator will then collect the goal-free information on outcomes using relevant procedures—including document analysis and interviews with persons both inside and outside the self-help housing community. Selection of interviewees will follow a snowball sampling approach, with each interviewee being asked to identify other persons with important knowledge of the project. Ultimately the goal-free evaluator will compile a goal-free evaluation report. Conclusions in that report will be based on the evaluator's comparison of identified outcomes to the needs assessment findings referenced earlier.

Costs
The lead evaluator will identify and analyze costs and sources of revenue involved in sustaining the self-help housing community. Categories of cost will include maintenance of common areas and upkeep of family homes and properties. Estimates of such costs will be obtained by interviewing community leaders and heads of individual households. We will also interview foundation personnel and representatives of involved lending institutions to obtain relevant data on payments of mortgage and landlease bills. Wherever possible, we will obtain and analyze actual financial reports and records. From this subevaluation, we intend to estimate the costs and needed sources of revenue for sustaining the self-help housing community.

Comparisons
We understand that the Self-Help Housing Project is innovative and unique and that it has influenced other housing projects. To help gauge its significance, it is appropriate to contrast its approach, costs, outcomes, and benefits to other similar projects. One of the three involved graduate students will make a systematic review of relevant alternative approaches to meeting the housing and community development needs of low-income families. This work will involve a literature review, search of relevant Web sites, visits to housing authorities and projects in the local area, and profiling of identified projects and the Consuelo project on a relevant checklist. We will make sure to report any evidence of your project's influence on other housing and community development projects. The graduate student will write a report on the relative characteristics and merits of the identified projects and on the influences the project has had on other related efforts. This report will culminate in a judgment of the project's stature compared with the identified similar efforts.

Part D: Conclusions

Evaluation of Overall Significance

Given the rich array of information gathered by the aforementioned procedures, we will determine and provide our bottom-line judgments of the project's current status. We will judge it on seven categories of criteria: (1) overall technical merit, (2) value to the involved families and their children, (3) impact on the broader community, (4) sustained level of success, (5) superiority (or not) to alternative housing and community development approaches, (6) influence on other housing and community development projects, and (7) overall cost-effectiveness. Basically, we intend to present a grade of outstanding, good, poor, or very poor on each of the seven areas for judgment. For each rendered judgment, we will present narrative and references to relevant data so that readers will see a clear rationale for each judgment. Finally, we will provide an inventory of any issues and problems that we see as needing attention.

Responsibility for the Evaluation

As noted earlier, the X University Evaluation Research Center will be responsible for this evaluation. A copy of the center's vita is attached. The evaluation will be led by Dr. X, the author of this proposal. He will team with the following three advanced evaluation graduate students: Mr. A, Ms. B, and Ms. C. Copies of their résumés are attached.

Report

The final evaluation report will follow the structure of this proposal. We will append the noted subreports. For all reports, we will submit to the foundation a precompletion draft and subsequently correct identified factual errors and ambiguities. We will then finalize and submit each report. In addition, we are willing to meet with foundation leaders to discuss findings as they may desire.

Support

Pursuant to the RFP, we request a fixed-price contract of $50,000 and agreement that our costs for any travel and accommodations will be covered by the foundation. We also request assistance in accessing documents and personnel required to conduct the evaluation. Our needs for working space at the foundation will be minimal, since the team can work in the offices of X University's Evaluation Research Center. It is also understood that we will control the editing of our final report and that the foundation will make the report public.

Metaevaluation

We believe it is very important that the foundation obtain an independent evaluation of our evaluation of the self-help housing project. The $50,000 set aside for our work is not sufficient to fund an independent metaevaluation. Moreover, to prevent the appearance or fact of undue influence by us in selecting the metaevaluator, it is important that the foundation make this selection and provide the needed funds, The cost of the needed metaevaluation should be modest. The Key Evaluation Checklist would provide an appropriate framework for the needed metaevaluation. In using the checklist, the metaevaluator would help you and your foundation colleagues judge every aspect of our evaluation and the justification of our conclusions. However, the structure of the metaevaluation should be determined by your staff and the selected metaevaluator.

This completes our response to your RFP. We hope to be selected to conduct this important evaluation and look forward to providing your foundation with a highly informative report and aid to your programming in the self-help housing and community development areas. Please let me know if you require any additional information about our plan or capabilities. I look forward to hearing from you.

This chapter provides an overview of Michael Scriven's many conceptual and methodological contributions to evaluation. Typically, his philosophically based recommendations are countermeasures to what he sees as wrong and dysfunctional in traditional views of evaluation, especially a focus on developers' goals. By following his philosophy, an evaluator seeks to find those approaches that best address the assessed needs of consumers. His main approaches are formative evaluations keyed to helping develop sound programs and products and summative evaluations that assess the merit, worth, and significance of developed products and services. He developed the Key Evaluation Checklist for applying his approach, as was illustrated above. He sees evaluation as a vital transdiscipline that is inherent in all disciplined intellectual and practical endeavors and one that needs to be developed and maintained as a discipline in its own right.

Review Questions

1. Without trying to make a verbatim response, how would you characterize Scriven's definition of *evaluation*? How is it similar to or different from Ralph Tyler's objectives-based definition of evaluation? What is the role of judgment in Scriven's approach to evaluation?
2. What is Scriven's definition of *needs assessment*? What is its role in Scriven's evaluation approach?
3. Why did Scriven distinguish between the goal and roles of evaluation? What are formative and summative evaluations? How are they related to the goal and role distinction? How would Scriven and Cronbach differ in their rating of the relative importance of formative evaluation and summative evaluation?
4. What is the distinction between goals-based and goal-free evaluation? Why did Scriven say that goal-free evaluation is reversible? What general process is involved in conducting a goal-free evaluation? What is the role of needs assessment in a goal-free evaluation?

5. What are the essential meanings of the basic evaluation methods of scoring, ranking, grading, and apportioning? How are they different? How are they complementary?

6. What is the function of the Key Evaluation Checklist? What are its main sections? How would it be used in both designing and reporting an evaluation?

7. What is metaevaluation? What roles are served by metaevaluation? Who should conduct metaevaluations? What does Scriven see as the relevance of the Key Evaluation Checklist to conducting a metaevaluation?

8. What is involved in the synthesis step in an evaluation? What does Scriven identify as flaws in evaluators' typical practices in reaching bottom-line evaluative conclusions? How has he addressed these flaws in his recommended approach to synthesizing evaluation findings?

9. Why is Scriven critical of evaluators' use of the numerical weight and sum (NWS) approach to reaching evaluative conclusions? What does he see as the most grievous mistakes in using this procedure? What is his qualitative weight and sum (QWS) approach? What reasons does he give for using the latter procedure to overcome the mistakes involved in applying the NWS approach?

10. Why does Scriven reject the position that randomized controlled experimental design is the gold standard for reaching cause-and-effect conclusions? What general methodology does he advocate for assessing a program's causal connections to outcomes?

Group Exercises

Exercise 1. Is all evaluation comparative? Why or why not?

Exercise 2. Are formative evaluation and summative evaluation conceptually and operationally distinct concepts? Why or why not? What illustrations support your group's responses to these questions?

Exercise 3. If an evaluator judges a program at one point in time, does she lose her independence and objectivity regarding her future evaluations of the program? Why or why not? If yes, must an evaluator terminate her relationship to a program once she has submitted her judgment of it? If not, how can the evaluator avoid being co-opted by a program staff that acquiesces to her initial judgments and recommendations? Does metaevaluation have a role in addressing difficulties in this area? Why or why not?

Exercise 4. What are the key distinctions between relativist and objectivist philosophies of evaluation? What are the implications of each of these philosophies regarding the collection and synthesis of evaluative information?

Exercise 5. If your group were designing a course on appropriate methodologies for evaluating cause and effect, what would be the main topics in this course?

Notes

1. In expanding the checklist to conduct a particular metaevaluation, presumably one would need to respond to the questions in the checklist, assess the needs (of the client and consumers) for the evaluation, use this information to determine weights for each criterion in the checklist, and define judgment levels. Then one could use the checklist to collect information about the completed evaluation on each defined criterion, grade it on each criterion, profile it on the criteria, consider its strengths and weaknesses in consideration of the preassigned weights, and reach an overall conclusion about the merit and worth of the evaluation.
2. Scriven has promoted this concept strongly since about 1991. Transdiscipline comprises a number of autonomous applied fields, together with a core discipline whose principal mission is developing tools for the use of the applied fields and other disciplines. Statistics, measurement, logic, and now evaluation are perhaps the most important examples.

References

Alkin, M. C. (2004). *Evaluation roots: Tracing theorists' views and influences.* Thousand Oaks, CA: Sage.

Campbell, D. T., & Stanley, J. C. (1963). Experimental and quasi-experimental designs for research on teaching. In N. L. Gage (Ed.), *Handbook of research on teaching.* Skokie, IL: Rand McNally.

Cronbach, L. J. (1963). Course improvement through evaluation. *Teachers College Record, 64,* 672–683.

Fisher, R. A. (1951). *Design of experiments* (6th ed.). Edinburgh: Oliver and Boyd.

Joint Committee on Standards for Educational Evaluation. (1981). *Standards for evaluations of educational programs, projects, and materials.* New York: McGraw-Hill.

Scriven, M. (1967). The methodology of evaluation. In R. Tyler, R. Gagne, & M. Scriven (Eds.), *Perspectives on curriculum evaluation* (pp. 39-83). AERA Monograph Series on Curriculum Evaluation, No. 1. Skokie, IL: Rand McNally.

Scriven, M. (1968). An introduction to metaevaluation. *Educational Products Report, 2*(5), 36–38.

Scriven, M. (1969). *Evaluation skills* (Audiotape No. 6B). Washington, DC: American Educational Research Association.

Scriven, M. (1974). Prose and cons about goal-free evaluation. *Evaluation Comment, 3,* 1–4.

Scriven, M. (1975). *Evaluation bias and its control.* Kalamazoo: Western Michigan University, The Evaluation Center.

Scriven, M. (1983). Evaluation ideologies. In G. F. Madaus, M. Scriven, & D. L. Stufflebeam (Eds.), *Evaluation models.* Norwell, MA: Kluwer.

Scriven, M. (1991a). *Evaluation thesaurus* (4th ed.). Thousand Oaks, CA: Sage.

Scriven, M. (1991b). Key evaluation checklist [On-line]. Available: www.wmich.edu/evalctr/checklists.

Scriven, M. (1993). *Hard-won lessons in program evaluation.* New Directions for Program Evaluation, no. 58. San Francisco: Jossey-Bass.

Scriven, M. (1994a, February). Product evaluation–the state of the art. *Evaluation Practice, 15*(1), 45–62.

Scriven, M. (1994b). The final synthesis. *Evaluation Practice, 15*(3), 367–382.

Scriven, M. (2004). Reflections. In M. C. Alkin (Ed.), *Evaluation roots: Tracing theorists' views and influences.* Thousand Oaks, CA: Sage.

Scriven, M. (2005a). Checklists. In S. Mathison (Ed.), *Encyclopedia of evaluation.* Thousand Oaks, CA: Sage.

Scriven, M. (2005b). Causation. In S. Mathison (Ed.), *Encyclopedia of evaluation.* Thousand Oaks, CA: Sage.

Scriven, M., & Roth, J. E. (1977). Needs assessment. *Evaluation News, 2,* 25–28.

CHAPTER SEVENTEEN

ROBERT STAKE'S RESPONSIVE/CLIENT-CENTERED EVALUATION APPROACH

R obert Stake has contributed uniquely to the philosophical and theoretical development of evaluation. In response to the sweeping federal requirements for evaluation that were imposed on American education in the 1960s, Stake (1967) introduced a new approach that became known as the countenance model for evaluation. This approach built on Ralph Tyler's notion that evaluators should compare intended and observed outcomes, but it broadened the concept of evaluation by calling for examination of background, process, standards, and judgments as well as outcomes. Stake developed his philosophy of evaluation during the late 1960s and early 1970s and in 1975 presented his extended view under the label of "responsive evaluation." This presentation retained the countenance approach's emphasis on examining the full countenance of a program, but it broke sharply from the Tylerian tradition of gathering data to discuss whether intentions had been realized. Instead, responsive evaluation assumed that intentions would change and called for continuing communication between evaluator and audience for the purposes of discovering, investigating, and addressing issues. According to Stake, rational judgment in evaluation is a decision as to how much attention to pay to the standards of each reference group in deciding whether to take some administrative action. We have labeled Stake's responsive approach responsive/client-centered evaluation because Stake stressed the importance of involving and serving the full range of a program's stakeholders.

We see Stake as the leader of the social agenda/advocacy school of evaluation, which calls for a pluralistic, flexible, interactive, holistic, subjective, constructivist, and service-oriented approach. Stake's approach is relativistic since it seeks no final authoritative conclusion, but instead interprets findings against the different and often conflicting values of stakeholders. Moreover, Stake emphasizes that the evaluator's judgment, not only in design but also in the expression of the quality of the evaluand, is one of the most important judgments in his approach to gathering and analyzing a wide range of other judgments. It is noteworthy that Stake's writings on evaluation initially focused on education and later were expanded to assist evaluations in additional disciplines and service areas.

This chapter begins by reviewing Stake's background. We then describe his initial countenance approach to evaluation. Subsequently, we look in detail at the responsive/client-centered approach and also identify some of his methodological contributions. The chapter concludes by considering how an evaluator might apply the responsive/client-centered approach to evaluate the self-help housing project described in Chapter Twelve.

Stake's Professional Background

In the 1950s Stake taught mathematics at the U.S. Naval Academy Preparatory School and later completed his Ph.D. program in psychometrics at Princeton University. In 1963, he joined the faculty at the University of Illinois, where he taught in the educational psychology department and served as associate director of the Center for Instructional Research and Curriculum Evaluation (CIRCE) under Thomas Hastings. Hastings had brought him to Illinois to do research on instruction, but Stake's interest was soon captured by the new work Hastings and Lee Cronbach were doing in curriculum evaluation. When Hastings retired in 1978, Stake became director of CIRCE and held that position until he retired in the early 2000s.

His thinking seems to have been influenced by several noteworthy factors. His early training and experiences in mathematics, statistics, and measurement made him conversant about the application of concepts and methods in these areas to the practice of educational evaluation. As he became increasingly skeptical about the classical conception of measurement and its employment in evaluation, his status as a trained expert in these areas gave credibility to his attacks and counterproposals and influenced his audiences to consider his views seriously.

In the mid-1960s, he attacked the classical view of evaluation as narrow, mechanistic, and not helpful (Stake, 1967). His disenchantment seems to have been aided and abetted by Cronbach, who until 1964 was a professor at the University of Illinois. Cronbach (1963) had argued that evaluation's basic function in education should be to guide curriculum improvement, not to judge completed, packaged curricula; he had argued further that comparative evaluations of curriculum alternatives based on posttest average test scores were neither informative nor helpful. Stake later built on these claims when he argued against comparative experiments, called for full descriptions of programs, and emphasized the importance of subjective information.

The influence of Ralph Tyler, who had defined evaluation as determining the extent to which valued objectives had been achieved, was also evident in Stake's early writing. In his "countenance" paper, he advocated comparing intended and actual outcomes, but also recommended that evaluators assess antecedent conditions and ongoing transactions, intended and actual. In other words, he expanded on Tyler's thinking. This link between Stake's and Tyler's work seems understandable, since Tyler's conceptualization (1942) had been the dominant view of evaluation since the 1940s. Also, both Cronbach and Hastings, who were highly influential to Stake's professional development, had studied under Tyler. Particularly, Hastings's research demonstrated to Stake that teachers had little use for the measurements and measurement concepts championed by professional education testers.

Stake also was obviously influenced by Michael Scriven's argument (1967) that evaluators must judge. Stake agreed that judgments must be included in evaluations, but he argued, for a number of reasons, that evaluators should collect, process, and report other persons' judgments and consider these along with their own judgments.

Another main factor that obviously influenced Stake's views about evaluation was CIRCE's involvement with projects in the late 1960s, most of them housed at universities. The projects were developmental in nature; although they were open to study, observation, and feedback for improvement by evaluators, they were neither stabilized nor available for controlled, variable-manipulating investigation by researchers. Many of these projects were education for the gifted or curriculum development institutes for teachers. The federal evaluation requirements were in essence Tylerian, calling for evidence that sponsored projects had achieved their objectives as measured by appropriate achievement tests. Stake and his colleagues judged that available published achievement tests were largely inappropriate for evaluating the federal education projects.

Stake's 1967 "Countenance of Educational Evaluation" Article

Stake's 1967 article, "The Countenance of Educational Evaluation," was offered not as a specific guide for designing an evaluation, but as general background reading for those facing such a task. In this article, Stake wanted to help projects meet the federal evaluation requirements in a manner both acceptable to the government and useful to staff and other constituencies. In presenting this article, Stake did not intend to offer a model. (However, many readers perceived his recommendations to constitute one; hence, the frequently used label "countenance model.") Instead, he intended to provide an overview of evaluation. By countenance, he meant the face of evaluation, the whole picture, an overview. He thought that different models (or persuasions) would fit here or there, and the countenance was a grid or map on which to locate them. Stake's approach reflects an attempt to adapt and expand on Tylerian evaluation to meet needs current at that time, and it presents a broad view of the many data that can be used to answer the questions of various clients. Its main purpose was to help readers see the wide range of data that might be used in an evaluation. Following its publication, the article was widely referenced in discussions of educational evaluation.

Stake chose the title of his article to convey a particular message to evaluation specialists and educators in general. He said that few educators see education "in the round." In particular, he noted that formal evaluations often focus narrowly on a few variables in a program (such as outcomes associated with objectives) and that informal evaluations often reflect a few people's opinions (but not carefully collected empirical data). He urged educators and evaluators alike to recognize the shortcomings of their usual evaluation practices and forthwith to pay attention to the full countenance of evaluation.

This countenance, he said, includes (1) description and judgment of a program; (2) a variety of data sources; (3) analyses of congruence and contingencies; (4) identification of pertinent, often conflicting standards; and (5) multiple uses of evaluation. Fundamentally, he noted that evaluating a program requires that it be fully described and judged, and he dealt in some detail with these concepts before presenting his overall approach.

Description

In considering description as a basic act of evaluation, Stake referenced the prior works of Tyler and Cronbach. The proponents of Tyler's approach had focused their descriptive efforts on discerning the extent that objectives are achieved. Against the advice of Tyler, who advocated using a wide range of data, they had narrowed their purview by focusing on specific behavioral objectives and employing mainly standardized achievement tests. Stake criticized this narrowness and supported Cronbach's suggestions that educators should broaden their concept of achievements and ways of measuring them. Stake (1967) advised educators to "implore measurement specialists to develop a methodology that reflects the fullness, the complexity, and the importance of their programs" (p. 84). More specifically, he stated, "The traditional concern of educational measurement specialists for reliability of individual student scores and predictive validity is a questionable resource. For evaluation of curricula, attention to the individual differences among students should give way to attention to the contingencies among background conditions, classroom activities, and scholastic outcomes" (p. 85). As discussed later in this chapter, Stake charged educators to fully describe intended and actual antecedent conditions, instructional transactions, and outcomes and to examine the congruences and contingencies among them.

Judgment

Stake agreed with Scriven's position (1967) that an evaluation has not taken place until a judgment has been made. But he questioned the wisdom of assigning the responsibility of judgment solely (or sometimes even partially) to evaluation specialists.

Such a practice, he said, would be unrealistic for three main reasons. Educators, perceiving that evaluators would be the sole judges of their programs, would be unlikely to cooperate with their data collection efforts. Moreover, evaluators might be censored or criticized by those among their colleagues who believe that evaluators, acting as judges—as opposed to objective inquirers—will make social science and behavioral research suspect. Also, Stake suggested that few evaluators would feel qualified to discuss what is best for a briefly known school and community.

To respond to this dilemma, Stake suggested a compromise position. Although he doubted that evaluators could or should act as sole or final judges of most programs they evaluate, he thought they were uniquely qualified to collect and objectively process the opinions and judgments of other people. He recommended that evaluations of school programs should portray the merit and fault perceived by well-identified groups, and he mentioned five groups as having important opinions about education: spokespersons for society at large, subject matter experts, teachers, parents, and students.

This compromise recommendation satisfied Stake's worry about Scriven's advice that evaluators must render the final judgments. Especially, Stake claimed that his recommendation obviated what he believed to be two questionable assumptions underlying Scriven's advice: (1) that a program judged best would be best for all students and (2) that local option is invalid if it is at odds with the common good. Evaluators would not have to make either assumption if they gathered, processed, and reported judgments from a wide range of reference groups.

Format for Data Collection

Of central importance to Stake's overall approach are the concepts of antecedents, transactions, and outcomes. Stake commented that if evaluators would gather, analyze, and report information about all of these from a variety of sources, they would more successfully approach the objective of dealing with the full countenance of evaluation than they would by persisting in their attempts to determine whether objectives had been achieved. Each of these three concepts is complex and requires explanation.

Antecedents refer to relevant background information. In particular, Stake saw this type of information as including any condition existing prior to teaching and learning that may relate to outcomes—for example, whether a student had eaten a good breakfast before coming to school, whether he had completed his homework assignment, or whether he had had a good night's sleep; or whether the teachers' union opposed required in-service training participation. In order to fully describe and judge a program or learning episode, Stake argued that evaluators must identify and analyze the pertinent antecedent conditions.

Stake's second class of information, the *instructional transactions,* includes the countless encounters of students with other persons, such as teachers, parents, counselors, tutors, and other students. Stake advised evaluators to conduct a kind of ongoing process evaluation in order to discern the actual workings of the program.

Outcomes pertain to what results from a program. These include abilities, achievement, attitudes, and aspirations. They also include impacts on all participants: teachers, parents, administrators, custodians, students, and others. They include results that are evident and obscure, intended and unintended, short range and long range.

Stake used antecedents, transactions, and outcomes as core concepts to structure his view of what should be done in describing and judging a program. For that he focused on intents and observations. By *intents,* Stake referred to all that is planned for, including antecedent conditions, teaching and learning activities, and desired outcomes; he advised evaluators to study what educators exclude as well as what they include under the rubric "intents" and to express educators' intents in language that is meaningful to them (not necessarily in the form of behavioral objectives).

Observations refers to antecedents, transactions, and outcomes that are observed and recorded. Consistent with Tyler's approach, observations may be collected from a variety of sources and data collection instruments. Stake advised evaluators to search broadly for the existence of both intended and unintended occurrences.

The following list illustrates the kinds of descriptive information that an evaluator might collect as viewed from Stake's perspective:

1. The teacher said that students would enroll in the music appreciation class because they wanted to be there (*intended antecedent*).
2. However, 40 percent of the students complained that their parents had coerced them to enroll (*observed antecedent*).

3. The music appreciation curriculum guide specified that students were to spend forty minutes a week listening to music and twenty minutes discussing it (*intended transactions*).

4. On the average, the students were observed to spend nineteen minutes a week listening to music, three minutes discussing it, twenty minutes in a study hall activity, and the remainder of the time doing a variety of other things (*observed transactions*).

5. At the end of the course, the students were expected, among other things, to be able to name the composers of selected musical pieces played for them (*intended outcome*).

6. On average, the students correctly named the composers of two out of ten pieces that were played for them; also, unexpectedly, a parent of one of the students contributed a sizable sum of money to help expand the school's music library (*observed outcomes*).

Although the preceding example is simplistic, it illustrates one basic message Stake was conveying: through studying intended and actual antecedents, transactions, and outcomes, evaluators should be stimulated to describe programs more fully than if they zeroed in on outcomes related to objectives. Stake acknowledged that the boundaries between the cells in his description matrix are vague. But, he said, this situation is unimportant, since the main intent is to stimulate evaluators to think broadly and to give them a heuristic for doing so.

In addition to describing the program of interest in relation to the description matrix, Stake directed evaluators to investigate the program's rationale carefully. In effect, what is the program's philosophical background and purposes? Once informed of the program's rationale, the evaluator can use it as a basis for judging program intents. For example, does the planned program constitute a logical step in implementing basic purposes? Stake also observed that the rationale is of use in choosing reference groups that later would be called on to identify standards and pass judgment.

In concluding his discussion of rationale, Stake cautioned evaluators not to overrationalize a program. They should avoid imposing their philosophy and logic on the program. Evaluators should characterize whatever rationale is found in the language of the program staff, not necessarily their own. Although he did not say so, we presume further that Stake would advise evaluators to call attention to problems they perceive in a program's rationale, such as ambiguity, inconsistency, illegality, or immorality.

Following his explanations of the description and rationale, Stake turned to a discussion of ways descriptive information is analyzed. He identified congruence analysis and contingency analysis as the two basic classes of analysis.

Congruence analysis asks whether what was intended occurred. Were the observed antecedent conditions congruent with those that were expected? Did teachers carry out the directions of the curriculum guide? Were the intended outcomes achieved, and were there additional outcomes? Congruence analysis essentially is identical to Malcolm Provus's recommendation (1971) that evaluators should search for discrepancies between what was intended and what occurred.

In citing contingency analysis, Stake argued that "since evaluation is the search for relationships that permit improvement of education, the evaluator's task is one of identifying outcomes that are contingent upon particular antecedent conditions and instructional transactions" (p. 94). He explained further that it is important to investigate contingencies among both intentions and observations. Contingency analysis was Stake's approach to addressing clients' frequent demands for information on a program's causes and effects.

The appropriate criterion for identifying and assessing contingencies between intended antecedents and transactions and intended transactions and outcomes is logic. Is it reasonable to assume that the expected background circumstances would permit exercise of the intended instruction and that the latter would lead to the intended outcomes? Stake observed that in conducting logical analyses, evaluators must rely on their previous experience with similar populations and programs and that they might obtain useful insights by studying relevant research literature and, we infer, reports of evaluations of similar programs. Logical analysis of contingencies among intentions is important, as Provus (1971) observed, in guiding judgments about a program's theoretical soundness and structural adequacy.

Contingency analyses of observed conditions, according to Stake, are to be based on the criterion of empirical evidence. Are there correlations between actual background circumstances and observed instructional activities and between the latter and certain outcomes (unintended and undesired as well as intended and desired)? Can any of the correlations be defended as causal? Stake noted that contingency analyses require data from within the program under investigation and might involve review of data reported in relevant research reports.

Stake also concluded that the requirements associated with contingency analysis imply special qualifications for the evaluators of given programs. These include familiarity with the relevant theoretical and research literature and prior experience in studying similar programs. Since a single evaluator is unlikely to have these specific qualifications, as well as all the analytical, technical, communication, political, and administrative skills required in evaluation, Stake argued that sound evaluation usually requires a team approach.

The collection and analysis of descriptive information and the description of the program's rationale provide the basis for the third major feature of the countenance approach: identifying standards and formulating judgments about the program's merit. Basically, Stake advised evaluators to determine both standards and judgments for the three core concepts of antecedents, transactions, and outcomes.

Stake defined *standards* as explicit criteria for assessing the excellence of an educational offering. He observed that school grades, standardized test scores, and opinions of teachers are not good indicators of the excellence of students; in general, he said that the evaluations then in vogue did not have wide reference value. He cautioned that in a healthy society, different parties should be expected to have different standards. He also cited and supported the claim by Clark and Guba (1965) that different stages in curriculum development involve different criteria. In regard to the complexity of the criterion problem, he advised evaluators to make known, with as much scope and clarity as possible, which standards are held by whom and to take into account both general, pervasive standards and the judgments made by individuals and groups about a particular program.

Stake's concept of judgments is inextricably tied to his view of standards. He said, "Rational judgment in educational evaluation is a decision as to how much attention to pay to the standards of each reference group (point of view) in deciding whether or not to take some administrative action" (p. 99). Moreover, he identified two types of standards to serve as bases for judgments: absolute standards (personal convictions about what is good and desirable in a program) and relative standards (characteristics of alternative programs that are deemed to be satisfactory).

Although Stake has not seen evaluation as any kind of orderly process, the following tasks are more or less inherent in the process he recommended:

1. The evaluator collects and analyzes the descriptive information and describes the program's rationale.
2. The evaluator identifies the absolute standards—those formal and informal convictions held by relevant reference groups of what standards of excellence should obtain.
3. The evaluator gathers descriptive data from other programs and derives relative standards against which to compare the program of interest.
4. The evaluator assesses the extent to which the programs of interest meet the absolute and relative standards.
5. Singly or in collaboration with others, the evaluator judges the program, that is, decides which standards to heed. More specifically, he assigns a weight, an importance, to each set of standards.

In contrasting relative and absolute standards, Stake cited a pertinent disagreement between Scriven and Cronbach. Cronbach (1963) had charged that curriculum-comparing studies are poor investments because they do not generalize well to the local situation and because alternate programs have evolved to serve the needs of different groups and have different purposes. In general, he had advised evaluators not to conduct comparative studies but instead to perform in-depth process studies aimed at helping to improve individual programs. Scriven (1967), in contrast, had called for direct comparison of a program with its "critical competitors" as the best basis for judging the program's merit. Whereas Scriven's favored frame of reference was *Consumer Reports* magazine, which evaluates competing consumer products and services, Cronbach recognized that the educators of the 1960s needed evaluations not of completed educational products and services but of the processes involved in developing the products and services. Scriven acknowledged the need for process studies of the type called for by Cronbach (Scriven labeled these "formative evaluations") but said they were (at least then) of secondary importance compared with the comparative studies aimed at judging a program's relative merit (he called these summative evaluations).

Stake saw a need for both types of studies and observed that their relative importance would vary according to the purpose of the evaluation to be undertaken. That is, he argued that the full countenance of evaluation involves different uses of evaluation reports. He saw comparative summative evaluations as needed by an educator faced with a decision of which program to adopt, but not by the curriculum specialist faced with the task of designing and developing a new program or with responsibility for improving an existing program. The latter's need for evaluation service would be served better by the formative type of study advocated by Cronbach.

In concluding the countenance article, Stake acknowledged the difficulty of using it literally. He said that a team approach would usually be required. Specializations to be reflected by the team might include instructional technology, psychometric testing and scaling, research design and analysis, dissemination of information, social anthropology, economics, and philosophy. He also called for the development of new and better ways of processing judgments and for ways of making evaluations less intrusive. In regard to the last point, he said that the countenance of evaluation should be one of data gathering that leads to decision making, not to troublemaking.

In spite of the difficulties of implementing this approach, Stake urged educators to make their evaluations more deliberate and formal. He suggested they clarify their responsibilities regarding individual evaluations by answering five questions:

1. Is the evaluation to be descriptive, judgmental, or both?
2. Is the evaluation to emphasize antecedents, transactions, outcomes, or their functional contingencies?
3. Is the evaluation to emphasize congruence?

4. Is the evaluation to focus on a single program or to be comparative?
5. Is the evaluation intended to guide development or to choose among available curricula?

Finally, Stake looked to the future and urged that evaluations be used to develop the knowledge base about education. He urged educators to develop data banks that document causes and effects, congruence of intent and accomplishment, and a panorama of judgments of those concerned with the programs evaluated.

The following major points are drawn from the countenance of evaluation article:

- Evaluations should help audiences see and improve what they are doing.
- Evaluators should describe programs in relation to antecedents and transactions as well as outcomes.
- Side effects and incidental gains as well as intended outcomes should be studied.
- Evaluators should avoid rendering final summative conclusions and instead collect, analyze, and reflect the judgments of a wide range of people having interest in the object of the evaluation.
- Experiments and standardized tests are often inappropriate or insufficient to meet the purposes of an evaluation and should frequently be replaced or supplemented with a variety of methods, including soft, subjective approaches.

Responsive Evaluation Approach

We turn now to Stake's extension of his philosophy of evaluation under the label "responsive evaluation." This extension appeared in "Program Evaluation: Particularly Responsive Evaluation," which Stake (1975a, 1975b) presented at the Conference on New Trends in Evaluation in Gotenborg, Sweden, and subsequently published in the Occasional Papers series of the Western Michigan University Evaluation Center. With the issuance of this paper, "responsive evaluation" replaced "countenance evaluation" as the popular label for Stake's approach. However, this new formulation retained much of what he had included in his countenance article. The major departure was that he turned sharply away from Tyler's objectives orientation. In fact, he presented responsive evaluation as much in terms of its differences from Tylerian evaluation as in terms of its own unity, wholeness, and integrity. In essence, then, the countenance paper served as a bridge between Tylerian, or preordinate, evaluation and a new and relatively distinct view of evaluation called responsive evaluation. Stake (1976) said that in fact, the responsive view reflects the long-standing practice of informal, intuitive evaluation, somewhat formalized.

In introducing responsive evaluation, he noted that his attention was on evaluation of programs, which might be strictly or loosely defined, big or small and, we infer, ongoing or ad hoc. In considering his approach, he asked his audience to assume that someone had been commissioned to evaluate a program and that the program most likely was under way. He noted that there would be specific clients or audiences to be served and that usually they would include those responsible for carrying out the program. The evaluator, Stake observed, would be responsible for communicating with these specific audiences. These guiding assumptions clearly are consistent with tenets of the countenance paper: that the evaluator's point of entry usually comes sometime after a program has started and that the evaluator's main role usually will be to provide useful evaluative information to those persons who are operating the programs.

Stake identified responsive evaluation as an alternative to eight other evaluation approaches: (1) the pretest-posttest model (preferred by most researchers); (2) the accreditation model involving a self-study and visit by outside experts (liked by educators, according to Stake, if they can choose the visitors, but disliked by researchers, since it relies on secondhand information); (3) the applied research on instruction model (advocated by Cronbach, 1963, 1980); (4) consumer-oriented evaluation (recommended by Scriven, 1967, 1974, 1993); (5) decision-oriented evaluation (proposed by Stufflebeam, 1966; Stufflebeam et al., 1971); (6) metaevaluation (introduced by Scriven, 1976): (7) goal-free evaluation (conceptualized by Scriven, 1973); and (8) adversarial evaluation (advocated by Owens, 1973, and Wolf, 1973). Stake saw the first two of these as the primary models of program evaluation and chose specifically to present responsive evaluation as a clear-cut alternative to the pretest-posttest model, which he labeled preordinate evaluation.

Stake identified responsive evaluation as an approach being advocated by Parlett and Hamilton (1972), MacDonald (1975), Smith and Pahland (1974), and Rippey (1973). Fundamentally, he said, the approach emphasizes settings where learning occurs, teaching transactions, judgment data, holistic reporting, and giving assistance to educators.

In grounding the responsive approach, Stake subscribed to a generalized definition of evaluation that he attributed to Scriven. According to this definition, evaluation is an observed value compared to some standard. Stake characterized this definition in the following ratio:

$$\text{Evaluation} = \frac{\text{Whole constellation of values held for a program}}{\text{Complex of expectations and criteria that different people have for the program}}$$

Stake noted that the evaluator's basic task is neither to solve the equation numerically nor, as he said Scriven had advocated, to obtain a descriptive summary grade for the program. Instead, Stake advised the evaluator to make a comprehensive statement of what the program is observed to be and to reference the satisfaction and dissatisfaction that appropriately selected people feel toward the program. In discussing responsive evaluation, Stake did not see the evaluator as formally gathering standards, rating them for importance, and reducing the ratings to an overall judgment. Instead, the evaluator would merely reference—not adjudicate, rank, or synthesize—people's feelings about a program.

Responsive Versus Preordinate Evaluation

Throughout his presentation, Stake repeatedly contrasted responsive evaluation with preordinate evaluation. Stake's eleven key distinctions are summarized in Table 17.1.

The first and perhaps most telling distinction concerns the purpose of the inquiry. The purpose of a preordinate evaluation usually is seen to be focused narrowly on answering a standard question: To what extent were the preestablished objectives achieved? On the other side, a responsive evaluation is aimed at helping the client understand problems and uncover strengths and weaknesses in the program (as seen by various groups).

The second distinction concerns the scope of services that the evaluator provides. In a preordinate evaluation, the evaluator collects, analyzes, and reports findings in accordance with a strict, prespecified plan. The responsive evaluator, in contrast, searches for pertinent issues and questions throughout the study and attempts to respond in a timely manner by collecting and reporting useful information, even if the need for such information had not been anticipated at the start of the study. In general, the scope of preordinate evaluations is narrow compared with the broad range of issues that might be considered in a responsive evaluation.

Another distinction is in the formality and specificity of the written agreements to govern the evaluation. Often formal obligations of the main parties to the evaluation are agreed to in writing at the outset of the study in either type of evaluation. However, contracts for preordinate evaluation are likely to be formal, specific, comprehensive, and binding, whereas those for responsive evaluations are likely to be general, flexible, and open-ended.

A fourth difference between the two types of evaluations is in their orientations. Preordinate evaluators examine program intents, including especially the objectives, procedures, and time line laid out in the program proposal, in order to decide what information to gather. In effect, they are predisposed to gather those data required

TABLE 17.1. MAIN DISTINCTIONS BETWEEN PREORDINATE AND RESPONSIVE EVALUATION.

Distinction	Preordinate Evaluation	Responsive Evaluation
Purpose	To determine the extent that goals and objectives were achieved	To help the client discern and address strengths and weaknesses
Scope of services	Meets information requirements as agreed on at the outset of the study	Responds to audience requirements for information throughout the study
Contracts	Obligations of the formal parties to the evaluation are negotiated and defined as specifically as possible at the beginning of the study	Purpose and procedures are outlined very generally from the outset and evolved during the study
Main orientation	Program intents, indicator variables	Program issues, events
Designs	Prespecified	Emergent
Methodology	Reflective of the research model: intervene and observe	Reflective of what people do naturally: observe and interpret, particularize
Preferred techniques	Experimental design, behavioral objectives, hypotheses, random sampling, objective tests, summary statistics, and research type reports	Case study, expressive objectives, purposive sampling, observation, adversarial hearings, and expressive reports
Communications between evaluator and client	Formal and infrequent	Informal and continuous
Bases for valuational interpretation	Refers to the prestated objectives, a norm group, or a competitive program	Refers to different value perspectives of people at hand
Key trade-offs	Sacrifices direct service to those in the program in order to produce objective research reports	Sacrifices some precision in measurement in order to increase usefulness
Provisions for reducing bias	Use of objective procedures and independent perspective	Replications and operational definition of ambiguous terms

to ascertain whether the program's objectives had been achieved and sometimes whether the program had been carried out as designed. Responsive evaluators do not let the rhetoric of the proposal be so determining. Guided by certain expectations of what will be important, they examine program activities and problems but remain free to settle on certain events or questions as most important. They see preoccupation with program proposals akin to putting on blinders.

The two types of studies are guided by designs of considerably different types. Designs for preordinate evaluations are prespecified as much as possible, since the objectives of the study are given and since the controls, interventions, and definition of constructs common to this type of study need to be arranged at the outset. Designs for responsive evaluations are more open-ended and emergent, building to narrative description, rather than aggregating measurement over cases. Controls and program interventions are seldom planned. The evaluator intends, throughout the study, to discover and respond to those questions deemed important by various clients.

Coinciding with the difference in types of design is a marked difference in the methodological approaches used by the two types of evaluation. Preordinate evaluations in general employ the research model. Here the evaluator usually intervenes with two or more treatments, assigns them to two different but comparable groups, observes their relative impact on students or clients as measured by a few criterion variables, and tests hypotheses about their differential effects. According to Stake, preordinate evaluation reflects more a stimulus-response model and responsive evaluation reverses the sequence. Responsive evaluation is response-stimulus evaluation in the sense that the evaluator responds first, that is, observes a naturally occurring program. The responsive evaluator does not assign subjects to treatments or control the program's delivery. However, the evaluator stimulates actions in the program by reporting what has been observed to the client group. In general, the methodologies of preordinate evaluation and responsive evaluation are experimental and naturalistic, respectively.

Accordingly, different techniques are preferred in the two approaches. In preordinate evaluation, the techniques of choice are experimental designs, behavioral objectives, hypotheses, random sampling, standardized tests, inferential statistics, and research-type reports. Techniques preferred by responsive evaluators are case study (Stake, 1988, 1994, 1995; Stake & Easley, 1978; Stauffer, 1941), expressive objectives, purposive sampling, observation, adversarial hearings, narrative reports, and storytelling to provide stakeholders with vicarious experiences related to the program.

Communications between evaluator and client in the two types of studies play different roles. In preordinate studies, communication is employed to reach advance agreements about how and why the study will be conducted, to check periodically during the study to ensure that participants are fulfilling their responsibilities, and to present the final report. In general, the preordinate evaluator tries to communicate formally and infrequently with the client. Conversely, the communications between the responsive evaluator and client are intended to be informal and frequent. As opposed to being prearranged, communication in responsive evaluation should occur more naturally. Stake views a more relaxed and continuous exchange between evaluator and client as essential, since the intent is to carry on a continuous search for key questions and provide the client with useful information as it becomes available.

The two types of evaluation also differ in their approach to valuational interpretation. In attaching value meaning to observed outcomes, the preordinate evaluator refers to prestated objectives or to the performance level of a norm group or students in a competitive program. The responsive evaluator does not necessarily exclude these sources, but is sure to refer to the different value perspectives of those people actually involved in the specific program under study. Moreover, the responsive evaluator does not seek a single conclusion about the goodness or badness of the program, but instead tries to reflect all the interpretations obtained from the reference groups.

Stake consistently acknowledged in his writings that evaluations serve a wide range of purposes and legitimately may follow different approaches. While he explained why he usually preferred responsive evaluation, he also noted that there are always trade-offs with any approach. Specifically, he said that preordinate evaluations sacrifice direct service to those in the program in order to produce more rigorous, objective research reports. Responsive evaluations sacrifice some precision in measurement in order to increase the usefulness of the reports for those involved in the particular program.

The eleventh and final distinction between preordinate evaluation and responsive evaluation concerns provisions for reducing bias, a dominant theme in preordinate evaluation. Objective procedures and independent perspectives are employed to ensure that the obtained information will stand certain tests of technical adequacy. Responsive evaluation also has tests of technical adequacy, but they are less easily verified. Responsive evaluation emphasizes the importance of subjective information and deemphasizes the use of standardized, objective techniques, allowing some greater bias. Stake maintained that there are other ways to reduce bias. Especially, he charged responsive evaluators to check for the existence of stable and consistent findings by employing redundancy in their data-gathering activities and replicating their case studies. He also advised them to promote understanding of their reports by presenting operational definitions of ambiguous terms. But, all in all, Stake has been more willing to leave bias for the reader to identify and interpret.

Table 17.1 presents our perception of the main distinctions between preordinate and responsive evaluation. Table 17.2 contains a different kind of comparison. In this one, Stake estimated the percentages of time the preordinate and responsive evaluators would devote to different evaluation activities in a typical case. Stake's estimates reflect, so far as we know, only his opinion and may be considerably at odds with other views of reality.

In discussing his comparison of a preordinate evaluation and responsive evaluation, Stake emphasized that a main thematic difference is in the purposes, amounts, and kinds of communications with the client. The preordinate evaluator communicates with the client before the study to establish the conditions necessary to carry it through, little or not at all during the study because such communications then might bias the way the program operates, and formally at the conclusion of the study through a printed report conveying a detailed description of evaluation design, activities, and findings. In contrast to this characterization of stilted, mainly one-way communication, Stake depicted the responsive evaluator as engaging continuously in two-way communications in order to learn of important issues that the client wants investigated and, as information becomes available, to provide useful feedback to the client.

TABLE 17.2. STAKE'S ESTIMATES OF HOW PREORDINATE AND RESPONSIVE EVALUATORS ALLOCATE THEIR TIME.

Tasks	Preordinate Evaluation	Responsive Evaluation
Identifying issues, goals	10%	10%
Preparing instruments	30	15
Observing program	5	30
Administering tests	10	—
Gathering judgments	—	15
Learning client needs	—	5
Processing formal data	25	5
Preparing informal reports	—	10
Preparing formal reports	20	10

Source: Stake (1975a).

Stake charged that reporting by preordinate evaluators is too focused and limited. He said its formal and technically sophisticated appearance causes clients to mistake its message for truth too easily. He said that because of its dependence on mathematical equations and formalistic prose, it is also unlikely to tell the client what the program was like.

To avoid the pitfalls of preordinate reporting, Stake advised responsive evaluators to develop their powers of communication. He said they should use whatever techniques are effective in helping their audiences gain vicarious feelings of the nature of the program. He suggested using storytelling (see Denny, 1978) to portray complexity and said that more ambiguity rather than less might be needed in their reports. In general, he said, evaluation reports should reveal the multiple realities of an educational experience, that is, the different views and understandings that different participants and observers have regarding the experience.

In rounding out his comparison of the two approaches, Stake said that responsive evaluation will be criticized for sampling error, but that the size of the error may be small compared with the gains through improved communications with the audience. He acknowledged, however, that the preordinate approach is needed and sometimes does a more effective job.

Substantive Structure of Responsive Evaluation

Beyond contrasting preordinate evaluation and responsive evaluation, Stake expanded on his concept of responsive evaluation. He especially did so by describing its substantive and functional structures.

Stake identified advance organizers as the first part of the substantive structure. In responsive evaluation, he saw these as issues. We infer that he meant areas of disagreement, uncertainty, and concern. He said an issue is a useful advance organizer because it reflects a sense of complexity, immediacy, and valuing. While it provides direction for investigation, it militates against the narrowly focused gathering of quantitative data. In order to identify and address issues, Stake advised the evaluator to become familiar with the program by talking with people, to reach a mutual understanding of the existence of certain issues, and then to use the issues as a structure for further discussions and for developing data collection plans. He emphasized that the evaluator should identify and respond to issues throughout the evaluation.

Stake identified the second part of the substantive structure of responsive evaluation as consisting of the data collection format in his countenance paper. In addition to issues, he saw this format as providing additional structure for data gathering. Through the use of the data-gathering format of the countenance model, the evaluator would seek to identify multiple, even contradictory perspectives and to check on congruences and contingencies. The relevant observations include the program's rationale; its intended and observed antecedents, transactions, and outcomes; various standards that different groups believe it should meet; and their different judgments of it.

Stake identified human observers as the third part of the substantive structure of responsive evaluation. He underscored their importance and claimed that they are the best instruments for investigating many evaluation issues.

The fourth and final part of the substantive structure of responsive evaluation is validation. Stake charged the responsive evaluator to get sufficient information from numerous independent and credible sources so that it effectively represents perceived status of the program, however complex.

Functional Structure of Evaluations

Stake next considered the functional structure of the responsive evaluation approach. In discussing how to evaluate responsively, he said that the approach requires a large expenditure on observation. He said that there are no linear phases: observation and feedback are important throughout the evaluation.

Given these provisos, Stake presented the functional structure of responsive evaluation in the form of twelve tasks that might be represented as the hours on a clock. He emphasized this is not a standard clock; it moves clockwise, counterclockwise, and cross-clockwise in whatever way is required to best meet the client's needs. We presume that he intended the notion of a clock only as a heuristic, not a set of technical guidelines, since in the article, he neither explained nor illustrated its use. We offer the following interpretation of how an evaluator might address the twelve tasks:

Twelve o'clock: The evaluator talks with clients, program staff, and audiences. These exchanges occur often during the evaluation and touch on a wide range of topics. These might include whether the clients want an evaluation and, if so, why; what they see as the important questions; what they think of the evaluator's representations of value questions, activities, curriculum content, student products; and the like.

One o'clock: The evaluator, in collaboration with the client, examines the scope of the program to be evaluated. Often what is inside and outside a program is perceived variously and ambiguously.

Two o'clock: The evaluator overviews program activities. This is a rather unstructured, exploratory, characterizing activity, since the step at seven o'clock calls for structured observations using some of the data collection constructs provided by the countenance article.

Three o'clock: The evaluator seeks to discover purposes for the evaluation and concerns that various people have about the program.

Four o'clock: The evaluator analyzes the issues and concerns and synthesizes them to provide a basis for determining data needs. To accomplish this conceptualization, the evaluator might gather different viewpoints of what is and is not currently worthwhile in the program and what should be added.

Five o'clock: The evaluator identifies data needs with respect to investigating the issues. This would be a rather interactive derivation from the issues' conceptualization, working back and forth between data potentials and problem contexts.

Six o'clock: The evaluator plans the data collection activities: makes a plan of observations, selects observers and instruments (if any), identifies records to be examined, selects samples (perhaps), and arranges for observations and other data collection activities.

*Seven o'clo*ck: The evaluator observes antecedents, transactions, and outcomes. We presume the evaluator would also examine the program rationale and collect standards and judgments pertinent to the program's antecedents, transactions, and outcomes.

Eight o'clock: The evaluator analyzes the obtained information by developing themes seen in the information, using it to prepare portrayals of the program and perhaps doing case studies. With the help of observers, the evaluator might develop brief narratives, product displays, graphs, photographic displays, sketches, a sociodrama, taped presentations, and the like.

Nine o'clock: The evaluator checks the validity of findings and analyses. Various tests of record quality are conducted. Program personnel then react to the quality of portrayals.

Ten o'clock: The evaluator winnows and formats information in order to make it maximally useful to audiences. Audiences should be informed of the assembled data and queried on what information would be of most value to them. Reactions should be collected from authority figures and other members of the audience. The evaluator should then design communications so as to maximize available information in order to respond to the different needs of the difference audiences.

Eleven o'clock: The evaluator prepares formal reports if they are required. Depending on prior agreements with the client and audience needs, a printed report may not be necessary.

We suspect that the main message of the evaluation clock is to be found not in its twelve tasks, but in the general strategy it implies. Stake elaborated on this strategy in terms of its utility and legitimacy compared with that of preordinate evaluation. He observed that explicitness is not essential in order to indicate worth and that the type of explicitness advocated in preordinate evaluation increased the danger of misstatement. In deciding how much and in what form to communicate, Stake saw the audiences' purposes as paramount. He said that different styles of evaluation will serve different purposes and noted that the evaluator may need to discover what legitimacies the audiences honor. But he claimed that responsive evaluation can be useful in both formative evaluation (when the staff needs help in monitoring its program) and summative evaluation (when audiences want to understand program activities, strengths, and shortcomings, and when the evaluator feels a vicarious experience should be provided). He acknowledged that preordinate evaluation is the preferred approach when assessments of goal achievement, the keeping of promises, and tests of hypotheses are sought. He also agreed that the measures in preordinate evaluation are more objective and reliable. Nevertheless, Stake concluded that all evaluation should be adaptive; obviously, he saw responsive evaluation as clearly superior in meeting this standard.

Application of Responsive Evaluation

Recall that the request for an evaluation proposal included in Chapter Twelve seeks a follow-up evaluation of the self-help housing project for low-income families that is described in that chapter. We see Stake's responsive evaluation approach as applicable to that assignment. A responsive evaluator making an initial response to the RFP might write a letter of interest to the foundation, such as the following:

Dear President X:

Thank you for inviting my organization to consider responding to your request for a follow-up evaluation of your foundation's self-help housing project for low-income families. I am pleased to submit this initial response on behalf of X Evaluation Company.

The description of the original project is helpful, as is the board's list of tentative evaluation questions. We have also reviewed and found useful the summative evaluation report of this project, titled The Spirit of Consuelo. These provide excellent starting points from which to launch the follow-up investigation. I am pleased to provide a general sketch of how we would approach the assignment.

Our proposed evaluation approach is labeled *responsive evaluation.* The chief tenets of this approach are that an evaluation should address issues and questions that are of interest to the full range of project stakeholders and should do so from their different perspectives, as well as the evaluator's. Moreover, all the evaluation questions and issues need not be identified at the evaluation's outset. Instead, under this approach, evaluators and stakeholders interact throughout the course of the evaluation to identify issues worthy of investigation, review findings as they emerge, and raise other questions and issues for further study. In general, procedures of responsive evaluation include snowball sampling to continually search out and query stakeholders, extensive interviewing of stakeholders plus observation of project activities, collection and study of relevant documents, collection and analysis of stakeholders' judgments, and ongoing interactions with stakeholders to identify project issues and evaluation questions, review findings as they emerge, and update evaluation plans. Evaluation procedures are never considered fixed. They are determined and applied flexibly pursuant to the flow of project issues and evaluation questions and also in consideration of the client's preferences. In the approach's search for a project's outcomes, it is considered essential to search out positive and negative side effects in addition to whether the project achieved its objectives. Communication of findings is considered as ongoing and natural, with heavy emphasis on oral communication as well as the expected printed, largely narrative reports. In the end, the responsive evaluation helps the client and other stakeholders see how the full range of parties concerned with a project judge its history, process, successes, shortcomings, and standards.

Clearly, the questions you have listed in the RFP are a good starting point for this evaluation. We would review these with project stakeholders, get their understanding of them, and include what we learn in our reports. I am sure you agree that it will also be important to you and the board for the evaluator to identify evaluative questions and issues that may be on the minds of other stakeholders, especially the residents of the self-help housing community, their neighbors outside the project boundaries, and other interested parties in the area. Also, you and members of the board might find it useful for us to identify questions that other community developers might raise about these projects, especially related to how this project compares with others and possibly regarding the national significance and transportability of your project.

In our approach to evaluation, we would thus plan to interact with and identify the questions and issues seen by representatives of the full range of interested parties. Thus, the initial stage of our evaluation would entail a good deal of contact and informal exchange with stakeholders. These would include residents of the community, staff who worked on the project, past and present members of the foundation board, social servants and businesspersons in the area of the project site, past and present foundation administrators, and persons from the outside who have visited the project. This is a partial list. We would ask each person contacted to identify other persons we should interview and to identify the questions and issues that they see as especially important for this follow-up investigation.

We would undertake a good deal of document analysis. We would plan to spend considerable time at the foundation studying documents related to the project and reviewing the individual reports associated with the original summative evaluation.

Following a stage of identification and informal exchange with stakeholders, we would employ some more structured procedures. These could include structured interviews, focus groups, case studies of selected families and individual children, and independent goal-free evaluations. Protocols for our procedures would be structured based on the earlier preliminary investigations.

As the projected inquiry process unfolds, we would plan to have regular exchanges with you and other stakeholders. We suggest that the foundation form a stakeholder panel to hear and discuss reports. The composition of this panel could include, for example, the foundation president, one or more representatives of the foundation board, members of the foundation staff, three or four members of the self-help housing community, and two or three representatives of the neighborhood outside the project community. In the end, we might not issue a final summative proclamation about the project's success, but instead help you and others see the full set of judgments that the full range of stakeholders have submitted about all aspects of the project that interest them, including your key question about the project's long-term viability.

We believe that a meaningful follow-up evaluation of this project can be completed within the stipulated twelve-month period and $50,000, excluding travel and lodging costs. We would plan to allocate the $50,000 approximately as follows:

Principal evaluator—30 days @ $500	$15,000
Associate evaluator—24 days @ $500	$12,000
Clerical assistant/editor—25 days @ $200	$ 5,000
Research associate—30 days @ 150	$ 4,500
Materials, supplies, communications, and amenities for meetings with stakeholders	$ 2,800
Reports	$ 4,000
Indirect costs—15%	$ 6,495
Total	$49,795

The X Evaluation Company has had substantial experience in applying the responsive evaluation approach. We and our clients have found our collaborative/stakeholder-oriented approach to be useful in addressing stakeholders' questions and interests. Nevertheless, we acknowledge that different parties can see and judge complex projects very differently and that usually there are no easy answers to difficult questions. It is very much in the interest of fair judgments and project improvement to identify and seriously consider all relevant points of view fairly. A copy of our institutional vita is attached.

We are interested in conducting this evaluation because we think that providing housing for low-income families is a critical and widespread area of need. Based on the original summative evaluation of this project, it appears that your foundation has produced and applied a quite innovative approach to this issue. The project's grounding in values, its service to families representing diverse ethnic groups, its focus on supporting the healthy development of children, and its early success make this endeavor especially worthy of study. We commend you and your colleagues for seeking a follow-up evaluation to determine the extent of the project's continued success. Clearly, you have raised a key question related to all challenging innovative efforts: Can their success be sustained?

The primary sources of information needed for the follow-up evaluation are project-related documents and the people who are involved in and interested in this community. We assume the foundation will give the evaluators access to its documents concerning this project. We hope we can examine financial information needed to perform a modest cost analysis of the project if this is of interest to you and other stakeholders and has not been done. We would appreciate assistance from foundation personnel in being introduced to the project community's residents. Perhaps a meeting could be held at the project site's community center to introduce us and afford an opportunity for us to explain to residents our evaluation plan, request their participation, and hear their suggestions.

Following our initial contact with the residents, we would plan to stay at a motel near the project community during our site visits and devote considerable time to moving around the community and talking with residents. In later visits, we would like to organize and conduct more structured interviews and focus groups. Our central focus will be on learning as much as we can from the community's residents. In addition, using our snowball sampling approach, we will interview persons outside the project site, including members of the surrounding neighborhood and the foundation. Following each substantial contact, we will write what we have learned in our field notebook.

During the course of this evaluation, we expect to make approximately nine visits to the project site. During each visit, we would like to meet with the foundation president or her or his designee and other parties that you may deem appropriate. During every other visit, we would also like to meet with a broader stakeholder panel. We suggest that this occur at either the project site's community center or foundation offices. We have budgeted a modest amount of funds for providing coffee and snacks at such meetings as may occur at the community center.

All field notes and data obtained through this evaluation will be kept in confidence and maintained in locked files in our offices at X Evaluation Company. Only authorized members of the evaluation team will be given access to these files, and the information in these files will be used only for this evaluation's purposes.

Reporting would be an ongoing process. As mentioned above, we propose to meet at least with the foundation president or her or his designee each time we visit the project site. We invite her or him to include other stakeholders in the meetings as she or he deems appropriate. We would offer oral reports and such printed materials as are available and relevant and report findings as they emerge. We propose to develop a semifinal report to be submitted for review and discussion during approximately the eighth month of the evaluation. We propose to review and discuss this with the stakeholder panel referenced above. Subsequently, we would finalize the report and submit it to the foundation. We propose that the foundation make the report widely available to stakeholders. We also suggest that the foundation hold a conference where interested parties would learn about and discuss the details of the evaluation findings. Funds for such a conference are not included in our budget for this evaluation. We propose that the foundation explicitly grant the evaluators the right to write and publish articles based on the findings of this study. We would review prepublication drafts of such articles with personnel of the foundation to ensure that they contain no erroneous or misleading information.

We stress that our plan for the evaluation should be considered flexible, so that we can be as responsive as practicable to stakeholders' questions and interests. Key occasions for reviewing and adjusting evaluation plans and, as needed, the evaluation budget would be the frequent meetings between the evaluators and foundation personnel.

Finally, we recommend that the foundation arrange for and fund an independent metaevaluation of our evaluation. Feedback from such an independent assessment of our work and reports would help us maintain utmost quality and relevance in our work and help you and your colleagues judge the validity of our findings and conclusions.

Again, thank you for the invitation to bid on the follow-up evaluation of your foundation's self-help housing project. I hope this letter proposal is responsive to your needs. Please do not hesitate to contact me if you have additional questions about this plan or need further information about our organization. My colleagues and I look forward to hearing from you.

The illustration shows how the responsive/client-centered evaluation approach could be applied to a typical request for an evaluation. The plan is quite general and open to change and refinement over the course of the study. It gives the client and other stakeholders a strong hand in adapting the evaluation questions, procedures, and reporting plans. And it promises no definitive answers. It projects no particular use of rigorous techniques and allocates most of its funds to on-site work by two evaluators. It proposes to open findings to all interested parties and recommends that the client fund an independent metaevaluation of the proposed evaluation. The illustration is based on the contents of this chapter and Stake's Checklist for Negotiating an Agreement to Evaluate an Educational Programme, which is available at www.wmich.edu/evalctr. Also, as will be seen in the group discussion questions at the end of this chapter, the letter proposal is not necessarily sufficient.

Review Questions

1. What did Robert Stake have in mind when he titled his 1967 article "The Countenance of Educational Evaluation"? Why might he object to people characterizing the contents of this article as "the countenance of evaluation model"?

2. How did Stake's countenance approach build on and also depart from Tyler's objectives-oriented approach to evaluation?

3. Using a project with which you are familiar, give examples of Stake's concepts of intended and actual antecedents, transactions, and outcomes. Based on your responses, give examples of contingencies among actual transactions and outcomes.

4. What is the importance of side effects in Stake's writings on evaluation?

5. What is Stake's position concerning the role of judgment in evaluation?

6. Why did we characterize the approach as responsive/client-centered evaluation? In your reply, mention the main tenets of responsive evaluation.

7. What are the distinctions between preordinate evaluation and responsive/client-centered evaluation?

8. What are the main points of agreement and disagreement between the evaluation philosophies of Stake and Scriven?

9. According to Stake, a preordinate evaluator and a responsive evaluator would each allocate about 10 percent of the evaluation's effort to identifying issues and goals in responding to the same evaluation assignment. Using his estimates, the two evaluators would allocate strikingly different amounts of time to preparing instruments and gathering judgments. Characterize these differences.

10. What procedures are most useful and appropriate in conducting responsive/client-centered evaluations?

Group Exercises

Reread the request for a proposal in Chapter Twelve to evaluate a self-help housing project and the hypothetical response in the form of a letter proposal. Then discuss how your group would respond to the following questions:

Exercise 1. The foundation's representative has responded that to be funded, the letter proposal must be expanded to include a time line of evaluation tasks. How would your group respond to this requirement?

Exercise 2. The foundation has requested clarification on what types of information will be collected and reported. Respond within the provisos of responsive/client-centered evaluation.

Exercise 3. Further to the foundation's response to the letter proposal, it was indicated that the foundation's board expects the evaluators to provide a judgment of the project's sustainability. How would your group respond?

Indicate the extent to which you would present the required judgment and the procedures you would employ to do so.

Exercise 4. In response to the evaluators' expressed desires to perform a cost analysis of the project, the foundation responded that obtaining the needed cost data would be too difficult and that the foundation has no interest in obtaining an analysis of the project's costs. How would your group respond?

References

Clark, D. L., & Guba, E. G. (1965, October). *An examination of potential change roles in education.* Paper presented at the Seminar on Innovation in Planning School Curricular, Airlie-house, VA.

Cronbach, L. J. (1963). Course improvement through evaluation. *Teachers College Record, 64,* 672–683.

Cronbach, L. J. (1980). *Toward reform of program evaluation.* San Francisco: Jossey-Bass.

Denny, T. (1978, November). *Story telling and educational understanding.* Kalamazoo: Evaluation Center, Western Michigan University.

MacDonald, B. (1975). Evaluation and the control of education. In D. Tawney (Ed.), *Evaluation: The state of the art.* London: Schools Council.

Owens, T. (1973). Educational evaluation by adversary proceedings. In E. House (Ed.), *School evaluation: The politics and process.* Berkeley, CA: McCutchan.

Parlett, M., & Hamilton, D. (1972). *Evaluation as illumination: A new approach to the study on innovatory programs.* Edinburgh: Centre for Research in the Educational Sciences, University of Edinburgh.

Provus, M. N. (1971). *Discrepancy evaluation.* Berkeley, CA: McCutchan.

Rippey, R. M. (Ed.). (1973). *Studies in transactional evaluation.* Berkeley, CA: McCutchan.

Scriven, M. S. (1967). The methodology of evaluation. In *Perspectives of curriculum evaluation.* Skokie, IL: Rand McNally.

Scriven, M. S. (1973). Goal-free evaluation. In E. House (Ed.), *School evaluation: The politics and process.* Berkeley, CA: McCutchan.

Scriven, M. S. (1974). Evaluation perspectives and procedures. In W. J. Popham (Ed.), *Evaluation in education: Current applications.* Berkeley, CA: McCutcheon.

Scriven, M. S. (1976). *Evaluation bias and its control.* Kalamazoo: Evaluation Center, Western Michigan University.

Scriven, M. S. (1993). *Hard-won lessons in program evaluation.* New Directions for Program Evaluation, no. 58. San Francisco: Jossey-Bass

Smith, L. M., & Pahland, P. A. (1974). *Educational technology and the rural highlands.* In L. M. Smith (Ed.), *Four examples: Economic, anthropological, narrative, and portrayal.* Skokie, IL: Rand McNally.

Stake, R. E. (1967). The countenance of educational evaluation. *Teachers College Record, 68,* 523–540.

Stake, R. E. (1975a). *Program evaluation, particularly responsive evaluation.* Kalamazoo: Evaluation Center, Western Michigan University.

Stake, R. E. (1975b). *Evaluating the arts in education: A responsive approach.* Columbus, OH: Merrill.

Stake, R. E. (1976). A theoretical statement of responsive evaluation. *Studies in Educational Evaluation, 2,* 19–22.

Stake, R. E. (1988). Seeking sweet water. In R. M. Jaeger (Ed.), *Complementary methods for research in education* (pp. 253–300). Washington, DC: American Educational Research Association.

Stake, R. E. (1994). Case studies. In N. K. Denzin & Y. S. Lincoln (Eds.), *Handbook of qualitative research* (pp. 236–247). Thousand Oaks, CA: Sage.

Stake, R. E. (1995). *The art of case study research.* Thousand Oaks, CA: Sage.

Stake, R. E., & Easley, J. A., Jr. (Eds.). (1978). *Case studies in science education, 1*(2). Urbana: CIRCE, University of Illinois College of Education.

Stauffer, S. (1941). Notes on the case study and the unique case. *Sociometry, 4,* 349–357.

Stufflebeam, D. L. (1966). A depth study of the evaluation requirement. *Theory into Practice, 5,* 121–134.

Stufflebeam, D. L., Foley, W. J., Gephart, W. J., Guba, E. G., Hammond, R. L., Merriman, H. O., & Provus, M. M. (1971). *Educational evaluation and decision making in education.* Itasca, IL: Peacock.

Tyler, R. W. (1942). General statement on evaluation. *Journal of Educational Research, 35,* 492–501.

Wolf, R. L. (1973). *The application of select legal concepts to educational evaluation.* Unpublished doctoral dissertation, University of Illinois.

CHAPTER EIGHTEEN

MICHAEL PATTON'S UTILIZATION-FOCUSED EVALUATION

In Chapter Ten, emphasis was given to utilization-focused evaluation (UFE), and in particular, the contributions made to this approach by Michael Patton. However, the concept of usefulness of an evaluation has been present in numerous evaluation approaches and models from the early 1970s. Grounded in empirical knowledge, utilization theorists were closely allied to decision-oriented theorists. As Alkin (2004) points out, "This class of theories is concerned with designing evaluations that are intended to inform decision-making, but it is not their *only* function to ensure that evaluation results have a direct impact on program decision-making and organizational change" (p. 44). He also states that "Stufflebeam's evaluation approach engages stakeholders (usually in decision-making positions) in focusing the evaluation and making sure the evaluation addresses their most important questions, providing timely, relevant information to assist decision-making and producing an accountability record" (p. 45). Alkin goes on to say that "Stufflebeam is positioned as the first name on the use branch of the theory tree" (p. 45). In effect, some evaluation theorists realized early that one vital aspect of the success of any evaluation is the extent to which it can bring about discernible change and how this can be achieved. While this chapter will center on Patton's work in UFE, acknowledgment will be given to others who have developed this approach or aspects of it. Because adherents of this approach, and Patton in particular, generally subscribe to the underlying importance of widely accepted standards for evaluation, we have included UFE as the sixth approach to evaluation that we commend to readers for close consideration.

Those who follow the UFE pattern are disinclined to be concerned primarily with the needs of decision makers; rather, they stress procedures and processes that enhance the usefulness of the evaluation to an identified group of stakeholders. In this way, and only in this way, UFE evaluators believe that the study will have an impact. The pathway of evaluations, as all experienced practitioners well know, is strewn with neglected reports, even though their formulation has been painstakingly correct. An approach such as UFE places a heavy professional imposition on evaluators because they must ensure that the study conforms to utility standards (Joint Committee on Standards for Educational Evaluation, 1994) and also that evaluators make studies clearly usable. How this may be achieved is the challenge to UFE evaluators. The crucial point is that focus must be placed on identified potential users of the program being investigated so that user-oriented evaluation will give the opportunity for practical, effective outcomes. UFE is a process for developing an evaluation study in collaboration and negotiation with a targeted group of priority users, selected from a wider set of stakeholders, to focus on and effectively serve useful outcomes for the intended users of the evaluation.

Some outstanding figures in evaluation have suggested the value of UFE. These include, for example, Weiss (1972), Alkin (numerous references in the 1970s), Patton (1980), Cronbach and Associates (1980), and the Joint Committee (1981, 1994), where the utility of evaluation outcomes is given one of four major imperatives for a credible evaluation. From the early 1970s onward, Alkin showed a preference for working with primary users from the start of an evaluation in an endeavor to understand the value system of users of a program so that outcome data could be related to users' values and not to any others' values. Now, Alkin presents a variety of possible outcomes in interactive sessions, seeking views of participants on their judgments, which are based on their value systems. Alkin offers one personally applicable caveat: "He acknowledges that there are conditions under which it is not tenable to engage intended primary users in this prejudgment process. Under such circumstances, he prefers to present evaluation data as factually as possible without imposing value judgment, unless there are extreme cases that demand that valuing takes place" (Alkin, 2004, p. 50).

We also acknowledge the implied emphasis Eisner gives to valuing and judging the culture and opinions of evaluation users rather than decision makers. He asked, "What is the value of what is happening?" (Eisner, 1991, p. 171) and answered by stating that valuing is a critical element in the evaluation process. Again, this shows a divergence from the decision-making emphasis as he underlined procedures that are in sympathy with the ultimate use of the evaluation appealing to a broad spectrum of identified primary users and other stakeholders. Eisner, like Alkin, views evaluation's purpose as not necessarily to serve decision making but primarily to ensure that the evaluation occurs expeditiously and with the aim that utilization actually occurs. Between such a claim and reality lies a need for considerable evaluator expertise, sustained consultative work, trust building, and mutual desire by the evaluator and a selected client group to make certain that outcomes will be positive, acceptably operational, and useful. Positivity, it should be noted, is based very much on emphasis given to a strong improvement orientation.

All theorists of UFE agree that the chance of an evaluation being proven useful is raised by the identification and involvement of those who have an immediate stake in the findings of the evaluation, are influenced by its outcomes, and therefore individually care about ultimate recommendations (if these occur, as mostly they will). Thus, the identification of such people must be given a powerful focus. If these committed stakeholders are missed, the whole exercise may prove futile. As discussion on Patton's approach to UFE shows later, the evaluator must be closely involved in the process for selecting a committed group of program users and aiding, if possible, their total commitment to the evaluation planning, process, outcomes, and associated improvement and developmental commitment to their own program. Clearly, emphasis is given at all stages to the ownership of users and to improving the program with which they are closely associated.

Some General Aspects of Michael Patton's UFE

It is generally acknowledged that the prominent developer of the utilization-focused approach to evaluation is Michael Patton (1980, 1982, 1984, 1997, 2003). A former professor of sociology at the University of Minnesota and a former president of the American Evaluation Association, Patton currently is an independent evaluator. Since the early 1970s, he has conducted numerous evaluations, taught many evaluation workshops and courses, and published widely on the theory and practice of evaluation. His passion has been to develop methodology and teach its application so that evaluators will conduct useful evaluations and get the findings used. He steadfastly attempts to show how evaluators, and specifically targeted audiences, can secure and apply evaluation findings that will make a positive difference in combating such problems as crime, disease, ignorance, inequality, malnutrition, mental anguish, poverty, and unemployment. His writings and teachings have strongly influenced many evaluators and clients first and foremost to gear evaluations to utilization, even above such other crucial criteria as technical adequacy and efficiency.

In his textbook *Utilization-Focused Evaluation*, Patton (1997) stated his developed views about UFE. He offered these definitions of program evaluation in general and of UFE: "Program evaluation is the systematic collection of information about the activities, characteristics, and outcomes of programs to make judgments about the program, improve program effectiveness and/or inform decisions about future programming. Utilization-focused program evaluation (as opposed to program evaluation in general) is evaluation done for and with specific intended primary users for specific, intended uses" (p. 23). He considers UFE to be a process for making decisions about a wide range of idiosyncratic issues in collaboration with an identified group of primary users focusing on their intended uses of the evaluation.

Like all other followers of UFE, Patton begins with a firm belief that an evaluation must be judged by its use. This places the onus of responsibility on the evaluator to design and process a study such that all activities, from start to finish, will give predominant emphasis to its utility. Therefore, the evaluator must focus on intended use by those who will use the outcomes of the evaluation. This entails a defined assessment of those who are primary users of the program and their commitment to its utilization. Such specificity is essential.

Significantly, the evaluator is not a distant judge in this process but a facilitator of judgments that are needed at each stage of the study. A group of primary intended users is identified, representative as far as possible of the total cohort of stakeholders, whose values (and not those of the evaluator) will determine the nature of recommendations arising from the evaluation. This selected group will apply evaluation findings and implement any recommendations that are made. It should not be assumed that Patton gives the responsibility for the planning and process of this evaluation to this selected group. To the contrary, the evaluator is expected to be fully in control of both the planning and facilitation of the study (a matter further explained in this chapter).

Patton stresses that the review and reporting of evaluation should permeate all stages of the study and should encompass the steps of description and analysis, interpretation, judgment, and recommendations. Along the way, UFE evaluations should draw from the full range of inquiry and communication methods that are appropriate to the information needs of the users.

The Personal Aspect of UFE

Patton maintains that the group selected to represent the wider cohort of stakeholders should be the actual users of the evaluation. He nominates them as the "intended primary users." In a list of fourteen UFE premises (later outlined in this chapter), he accords them first place on this list.

If an evaluation of a program is to be used, the personal factor, according to Patton, is primary. The identification of people who clearly have a stake in programs is essential, as is their concern about the outcomes generated by the study and their commitment to its use. Here there is a deviation from the five approaches and models of evaluation presented in the other chapters in Part Three. The evaluation must also be dedicated to the enhancement of the study's outcomes and thus must involve the culture and values of the group selected to represent all stakeholders. Moreover, the UFE evaluator must be strongly involved in persuading intended users to commit to the developed outcomes of the (by now) shared evaluation enterprise. It is no small task to involve intended users in an evaluation study at every stage, from beginning to end, to the extent that they see and believe that potential changes are to their benefit and that they should willingly contribute to these proposed changes.

UFE therefore focuses on individuals who are users of the program while also acknowledging other users to be served. This entails careful analysis of the total cohort of stakeholders and identifying which users could best represent the interests of all stakeholders. This selection process is vital to the success of the consequent study. As we stated in Chapter Ten, the evaluation must identify representatives of the multiple and varied perspectives of those involved in the program.

Having selected this special client group, the evaluator engages them to clarify why they need the evaluation, what they hope outcomes might be, how the exercise should be conducted, what part they see themselves playing, what type of reports they envisage, and, finally, how they think the findings should be used to improve the program. During this process, the evaluator acts as a guide or mentor, not an authoritarian figure or dominating expert. Users' choices are aided by the evaluator's supplying a menu of possible evaluation approaches, methodologies, user-participation activities, and types of reports (perhaps both formative and summative, depending on the user group's decisions). Patton does not consider a final written report as always necessary. Adherents of UFE are adamant that the more closely program users are involved in the planning and execution of evaluation, the greater their focus will be on the study and the greater their feeling of ownership will be.

The highly personal, dynamic, and situational nature of UFE underlies Patton's (2003) summary of the working relationship between evaluator and client group that encapsulates the approach he has so strongly developed and espouses. He states: "In considering the rich and varied menu of evaluation, utilization-focused evaluation can include any evaluative purpose (formative, summative, developmental), any kind of data (quantitative, qualitative, mixed), any kind of design (e.g., naturalistic, experimental) and any kind of focus (processes, outcomes, impacts, costs, and cost-benefit, among many possibilities)" (p. 2).

From the evaluator's perspective, the personal factor involves leadership, enthusiasm, sound advice, listening skills, and respecting all members of the selected representative group. These people will need good information, guidance in decision making, allaying of concerns about aspects of the study, and a strengthening of the many roles they must play if the evaluation is to be seen to be successful to them, the primary users of the evaluation. Patton's emphasis on the personal factor is supported by other writers and practitioners. For instance, Cronbach and Associates (1980) stated, "Nothing makes a larger difference in the use of evaluations than the personal factor—the interest of officials in learning from the evaluation and desire of the evaluator to get attention for what he knows" (p. 6).

There is no doubt that the personal factor directs evaluators to specific people, their problems, and their interests. In this way, evaluation use is enhanced.

The Evaluator's Roles

With emphasis on the primacy of the personal factor, Patton dismisses the idea of addressing evaluation reports (if they are produced) to audiences other than immediate users. In line with this approach, he deliberately narrows the list of potential users to a manageable number, and they alone will determine the nature of reports and negotiate other aspects of the study, with the evaluator acting more as a consultant than in a traditional evaluative role as we have described in the preceding chapters. Thus, the evaluator's role as negotiator is paramount. Depending on the circumstances and concurrence of the primary users, the evaluator might play any of a variety of other roles: trainer, group facilitator, problem solver, diplomat, change agent, measurement expert, experimental design expert, qualitative inquiry expert, content expert, creative consultant, internal colleague, independent auditor, policy analyst, and mediator. However, the evaluator will always negotiate with the primary intended users what roles beyond that of negotiator they will play. Moreover, the evaluator will conduct and act on the negotiations within appropriate ethical bounds and in accordance with the evaluation field's standards and principles.

UFE and Values and Judgments

Patton and other UFE practitioners have found that the exploration and development of questions for the evaluation cannot be undertaken in isolation from the values of the selected client group. It is their program, and their values must undergird any program examination jointly undertaken by the evaluator and themselves. Since the purpose of UFE is to effect findings that must be used, the evaluator must facilitate intended users' selection of values and judgments and the decisions that arise from these. Utilization-focused evaluators agree with many other evaluation approaches that, by definition, evaluations are grounded in values. However, instead of imposing external values, the utilization-focused evaluator works with particular intended users (clients, service providers, support staff, and beneficiaries) to determine which values should substantiate and validate the collection and interpretation of the needed information.

Patton has observed that evaluation use is too important to allow evaluators to choose the questions and render the judgments, particularly since the users have the responsibility to make and implement program decisions. The key principle here is that those with responsibility to use evaluations in program processes should have the authority to decide what values are most appropriate, what questions should be addressed (because these are always value laden), what information is most needed, how the information is best acquired, and what interpretations and decisions should be made. Because of its stress on impact, this position gives preference to decision makers' values and questions over those of the program's wider beneficiaries and other stakeholders.

Theoretically, UFE is aligned with relativist and constructivist evaluation approaches on the selection and application of values. Generally UFE is consistent with Stake's responsive evaluation approach (1983), which assesses a program relative to the stakeholders' values and judgments rather than independently determined merit and worth criteria. However, whereas Stake follows the postmodern line that dismisses the possibility and desirability of unifying values and judgments, UFE seeks consensus on both values and judgments in order to support and expedite the decision process. In this latter respect, UFE accords with a constructivist approach advocated by Guba and Lincoln (1989). This is true when UFE engages a truly representative—though select—group of stakeholders, accords equal influence to each member, assists the group in considering alternative values, and subsequently aids them to reach consensus on and apply their preferred values. Under these circumstances, UFE departs from the divergent emphasis in Stake's approach and invokes the consensus development as well as the hermeneutic processes advocated by Guba and Lincoln.

Negotiating: Active–Reactive–Adaptive Processes

Patton emphasizes that the negotiation process between the evaluator and the client group should progress from the planning stage to completion of the study. Much depends on the situation of any particular evaluation: its people, its culture, and its idiosyncrasies. While accepted standards must always prevail, these must be applied to the specific program users in a specific situation. Negotiating at every turn strengthens the chances of final outcomes that program users value and therefore have a high probability of being accepted and acted on. From the utilization-focused perspective, there is not one right way to conduct an evaluation; rather, a design should be developed by negotiation that appeals to users and potential users of the program. Patton (2003) reinforces this concept: "The right way . . . is the way that will be meaningful and useful to the specific evaluators and intended users involved, and finding that way requires interaction, negotiation, and situational analysis" (p. 228).

Patton underlines the full meaning of negotiation with his active–reactive–adaptive description of interactive discussion, advice, and general consultation that continues throughout the study between the utilization-focused evaluator and the select client group, the intended users. It has both descriptive elements centered on decision making and prescriptive elements in respect to the evaluator who must act and react with advice that adheres to standards, such as the Joint Committee standards.

Patton goes on to state that utilization-focused evaluators must be *active* in purposefully identifying intended program users and in formulating with these users questions that will shape the study. Evaluators are *reactive* in focusing on the thinking of users and responding to their ideas. This process continues until the completion of the evaluation, with the evaluator always showing the flexibility required to accommodate situational changes. This leads to the *adaptive* element that again incorporates flexibility, particularly with respect to evaluation questions and designs as the understanding of the study situations and developments by both evaluators and users increases. Patton insists that utilization-focused evaluators must immerse themselves in the challenges as they arise and become patently responsive to users' wishes and views. As users' reactions and thinking will vary and change in any particular evaluation, the evaluator must be aware that approaches will change with every study. Accordingly, the roles and methodologies of the evaluation will change, as all phases of the action–reaction–adaptation pattern will adjust to the consideration of options.

As the evaluator plays the roles of both external expert and creative consultant, the evaluator's skills, knowledge, and ethical values are of paramount importance. Just as the utilization-focused evaluator must be wary not to impose a focus on a predisposed methodological approach, so too must the selected user group not seek to impose its views dogmatically on the way the evaluation should unfold. Negotiation compromises are made, with the stress always placed on the utility of outcomes. The process of negotiation and consequent decision making and action are valuable experiences for the user group, particularly if these processes reinforce the values of change leading to outcomes that will actually be employed by those who claim increasing ownership of the evaluation and knowledge of its purposes.

Patton's Eclectic Approach

Chapter Ten gave prominence to Patton's strongly held eclectic evaluation proclivities. As a pragmatic approach, UFE advocates no particular evaluation model, theory, values, system of criteria and indicators, methods, or procedures. Instead, it is a process designed to help specific users examine the evaluation methods cornucopia and the local situation, then choose the model, methods, values, criteria, indicators, and intended users that best fit the local situation. The utilization-focused evaluator needs a broad repertoire of evaluation ideas and resources and should follow a flexible, responsive, and creative approach to designing and conducting evaluations. The main point in designing the evaluation is to ensure that the intended users' questions are answered in such a way that they will respect, understand, and apply the findings.

To summarize, utilization-focused evaluators and their specific clients may conduct evaluations that are formative and/or summative, qualitative and/or quantitative, preordinate and/or responsive, and naturalistic and/or experimental. They may choose to investigate and report on any of a wide range of indicators: costs (and cost benefits), needs, attitudes, processes, outputs, outcomes, and impacts. They may also issue written interim and final reports or engage only in verbal exchanges. Although the approach is open to using any evaluation method that applies to the local need, it tends to be more responsive and interactive than preordinate and independent. It calls for problem solving and a creative process of adapting evaluation procedures to meet the local and specific evaluation needs as they emerge.

Discovering the most functional structure and most appropriate methods for the given circumstance requires the technical skill of the evaluator and an incorporation of the wishes of the selected group as they come to a deeper understanding of the study's direction.

Clarifying and Focusing the Program's Goals

In the early focusing meetings, the UFE evaluator engages the client group in clarifying why they need the evaluation, how they intend to apply its findings, how they think it should be conducted, and what values should be invoked. In deliberating with the intended users, the evaluator emphasizes that the program's purpose must be to give them the information they need to fulfill their objectives. UFEs are not explicitly intended to address social problems. They have that appearance because UFE client groups often desire to combat certain social problems. Although this approach is not unique in helping users address social problems, it explicitly justifies investments in the evaluation because of its potential utility to help client groups address problems that they judge important.

The evaluator facilitates the users' choices by advice about possible purposes, uses, questions, and possibly reports for the evaluation. This is done not to supply the choices but to help the client group thoughtfully focus and shape the study based largely on its culture. The study is targeted at users who determine the evaluation's focus, required information, how and when findings must be reported, and how they will be used.

Patton advocates goals-based evaluation and extensive efforts to clarify the goals and keep them up-to-date. He sees this as one useful way to focus evaluations, though not the only way. He suggests a six-part framework for clarifying program goals and using them in the evaluation:

1. A specific target group of beneficiaries
2. Desired outcomes of the group
3. Indicators of each outcome
4. Targeted performance levels on each indicator (if judged appropriate and desired)
5. Detailed data collection plan keyed to the indicators
6. Specification of how findings will be used

Of these steps, Patton (1997) noted, "While these are listed in the order in which intended users and staff typically conceptualize them, the conceptualization process is not linear. . . . The point is to end up with all elements specified, consistent with each other, and mutually reinforcing" (p. 163).

Patton (1997) has identified and advocated consideration of several alternative bases for focusing evaluations. One is Michael Scriven's recommendation that evaluators not consider goals but instead gather information on a broad range of outcomes and judge whether they meet the assessed needs of targeted beneficiaries. Other named foci are future decisions, critical issues or concerns, stakeholder perspectives, and evaluative questions. Beyond these, Patton presents an extensive list of about fifty ways of focusing evaluations (1997). He argues for careful, resourceful focusing of evaluations because he sees studying the wrong issues as a waste of both intellect and emotion. The message is that putting aside the time to carefully focus an evaluation for maximum utility is most beneficial.

Collecting and Analyzing Information and Reporting Findings

Any data collection and analysis methods are acceptable in the utilization-focus program evaluation. UFE's active–reactive–adaptive and situationally responsive approach ensures that the methodology evolves in response to ongoing deliberations and negotiations between the evaluator and client group and in consideration of contextual dynamics. Different information sources and methods are used to address questions from different perspectives and to cross-check findings. As much as possible, the utilization-focused evaluator puts the client group in a primary position to determine evaluation methods so that they will make sure that the evaluator addresses their most important questions, places the correct emphasis on collecting the right information, uses techniques they respect, and reports information in a form that is both understandable and timely. The UFE evaluator must convince stakeholders of the evaluation's integrity and accuracy as well as facilitate the users' knowledge of the findings and the appropriate dissemination of these.

The bases for interpreting the evaluation findings are the users' values, with the evaluator engaging in as much value clarification as needed to ensure that the evaluative information and interpretation serve the users' purposes. The users are actively involved in interpreting findings. Throughout the evaluation process, the evaluator balances the concern for utility with provisions for validity and cost-effectiveness.

Patton (1997) stated that "evaluators are active in presenting to intended users their own best judgments and knowledge about appropriate evaluation focus and methods; they are reactive in listening attentively and respectively to others' concerns; and they are adaptive in finding ways to design evaluations that incorporate diverse interests while meeting high standards of professional practice" (p. 299).

UFE evaluators generally concur that they should help their audiences stand outside the program and gain a better perspective on what is occurring. In addressing this purpose, Patton notes that the preparation for review and use should start early in the evaluation. For example, one can engage the users' group to examine a set of simulated findings or give them findings and make predictions about their outcomes. Such activities increase the users' interest and help build readiness to examine and use the ensuing evaluation reports. Such discussions can be invaluable in considering what questions, types of data, analyses, and data displays will be most important toward the evaluation's end. Such simulations can also be instrumental in training the client group in how to view, assess, and use findings and in making their expectations of the evaluation more realistic. Simulations also provide the evaluator with the means of testing the client group's commitment to use the evaluation findings.

Patton's (1997, p. 307) framework for reviewing findings has four steps:

1. Description and analysis
2. Interpretation
3. Judgment
4. Recommendations

He emphasizes that the primary intended users should be involved in all four stages. In addition, he stresses that the evaluator must make the findings interesting and easy to grasp. When the utilization-focused evaluator finally produces a report, it should be focused on the most important questions. It should be ". . . arranged, ordered, and organized in some reasonable format that permits decision-makers to detect patterns" (Patton, 1997, p. 307). And the evaluator is told to keep the message simple.

Summary of Premises of Utilization-Focused Evaluation

Patton (2003) gives a succinct fourteen-point summary of the premises he considers as underlying his version of UFE. Following is a brief account of the premises, which in many ways are unequivocal statements of what convinces Patton about the worth of UFE and how such a study should progress:

1. Commitment to intended users should be the driving force in an evaluation.
2. Strategizing about use is ongoing and continues from the very beginning of the evaluation.
3. The personal factor contributes significantly to use; it is a psychological imperative.
4. Careful and thoughtful stakeholder analysis should inform identification of primary intended users, taking into account the varied and multiple interests that surround any program, and therefore any evaluation.
5. Evaluations must be focused in some way. Focusing on intended use by intended users is the most useful way.
6. Focusing on an intended use requires making deliberate and thoughtful choices, including judging merit or worth (summative evaluation), improving programs (instrumental use), and generating knowledge (conceptual).
7. Useful evaluations must be designed and adapted situationally. Standardized recipe approaches will not work.
8. Intended users' commitment to use can be nurtured and enhanced by actively engaging them in making significant decisions about the evaluation.
9. High-quality, not high-quantity, participation is the goal. The quantity of group interaction time can be adversely related to the quality of the process.
10. High-quality involvement of intended users will result in high-quality, useful evaluations.
11. Evaluators have a rightful stake in an evaluation in that their credibility and integrity are always at risk; this is the mandate for evaluators to be active–reactive–adaptive.

12. Evaluators committed to enhancing use have a responsibility to train users in evaluation processes and the uses of the information.
13. Use is different from reporting and dissemination. Reporting and dissemination may be means to facilitate use, but they should not be confused with such intended uses as making decisions, improving programs, changing thinking, and generating knowledge.
14. Serious attention to use involves financial and time costs that are far from trivial. The benefits of these costs are manifested in greater use.

Limitations of the UFE Approach

Patton sees the main limitation of UFE to be turnover of involved users. Replacement users may require that the program evaluation be renegotiated in order to sustain or renew the prospects for evaluation impacts. But replacements can also derail or greatly delay the process. Furthermore, it is easy to say that this approach should meet all the Joint Committee's standards (1994) but hard to see how this can be accomplished with any consistency. The approach seems to be vulnerable to bias and corruption by the users' group. After all, those involved are only a subset of the program's stakeholders. The intended users' group may not represent all the stakeholders' interests if the evaluator has not been successful in recruiting their representative group and keeping all of them involved. Nevertheless, this possibly biased group is given much control over what would be looked at, what questions are addressed, and what information is employed. Moreover, whatever the group's representativeness, stakeholders with conflicts of interest may inappropriately influence the evaluation, especially if the evaluator is inexperienced and vulnerable to manipulation. The involved and empowered stakeholders may inappropriately limit the evaluation to only a subset of the important questions and pertinent bases for interpretation. It may also be close to impossible to have the users' group agree on a sufficient commitment of time, resources, and safeguards to ensure an ethical, valid process of data collection, reporting, and use.

UFE evaluators face a dilemma. If they fully empower the select stakeholder group to control the evaluation, that group may better accept and use the findings. However, as we have argued, the interests of other important stakeholders may not be addressed. If the UFE evaluator insists on compliance to professional standards of evaluation, then the stakeholder group may be less willing to incur the required political risks, including costs and time. As with all other dilemmas, there seems to be no easy out for UFE evaluators to give users their way and also meet the full range of standards of the evaluation field.

Clearly, effective implementation of this approach requires a highly competent, confident evaluator who can approach any situation flexibly, resourcefully, and creatively without compromising basic professional standards and principles. Strong negotiation skills are essential, and the evaluator must possess expertise in the full range of quantitative and qualitative evaluation methods, strong communication and political skills, working knowledge of all applicable standards for evaluation, and commitment to uphold the standards.

None of the above is to deny that the UFE approach to evaluation has important value since its strong requirement for competence places a premium on rigorous, selective, and effective evaluation training programs.

Summary

UFE is a process through which the evaluator works with primary and intended users to make decisions in designing and conducting evaluations that will best serve the evaluation's intended users. Such decisions involve the full range of evaluation tasks, including identification of primary users and specific users, selection of data collection methods, analysis of findings, and formatting and reporting of findings, together with follow-up support to ensure that findings are used.

The approach is geared to a psychology of use. Systematic involvement of the intended users in the entire evaluation process helps ensure that they will develop ownership of the evaluation process and findings, develop the necessary understanding of the information, and consequently act intelligently based on the evaluation findings. The evaluator essentially lays the groundwork for use by engaging the users as partners in all stages of the evaluation process. In the most positive sense of the word, the evaluator co-opts the users to participate fully in the evaluation process and its application to program decision making. The selected group is encouraged throughout the evaluation to accept the study as their own. Another positive aspect is that UFE helps the users ensure that the evaluator will fit the evaluation services appropriately to their needs, priorities, and agendas. UFE strives for a symbiosis between evaluator and user.

Applicability of Utilization-Focused Evaluation to the Self-Help Housing Project

The request for an evaluation proposal outlined in Chapter Twelve called for a further evaluation of the self-help housing project for low-income families. With some reservations, we envisage utilization-focused evaluation, especially as formulated and promoted by Michael Patton, as potentially useful for the assignment, provided (and only provided) that the foundation's board is willing to transfer at least some decision-making authority to project users. A UFE evaluator would likely write a letter to the foundation president something along these lines:

Dear Dr. Jones:

The firm of which I am head partner is very interested in responding to your recent e-mail request for a follow-up evaluation of your self-help housing project. We note that it is five years since the completion of the original evaluation and support your contention that a further, thorough review would be beneficial to the ongoing health of this important project.

Having perused the final evaluation report and the various informative attachments, we are confident that we will satisfactorily address the various questions you have posed. We are also confident that we can meet suggested time lines (at least for interim reports and a final assessment), together with the financial limits you have set.

From the start, I must state that the methodology my staff and I use may very well differ from other submissions you receive. Our approach, called *utilization-focused evaluation,* gives prime emphasis to the usefulness of evaluation findings. In numerous successful studies in past years, we have empowered intended users of evaluation findings—including program beneficiaries—to help guide and control the evaluation. Consequently, these persons have acquired an interest in and respect for the evaluation's questions and findings. Moreover, they have developed a sense of ownership of the study and acted in accordance with its findings. If a study's intended users are not meaningfully involved in planning and guiding a study and in reviewing findings, we firmly believe from our experience that valuable resources of time, money, and expertise for an evaluation can be wasted all too easily.

Perhaps more than most other evaluation approaches, utilization-focused evaluation (UFE) faces social problems squarely. From our reading of your proposal document, it is clear that your project is facing numerous, challenging social issues. We are confident that our approach goes a considerable distance toward developing recommendations to ameliorate these.

In a somewhat academic vein (and apologies if you are conversant with our methodology), utilization-focused evaluation is generally understood to mean a process for making decisions about a range of relevant issues in collaboration with an identified group of primary evaluation users focusing on their intended uses of evaluation. Let me offer further explanation. Utilization-focused evaluation follows these main steps, which we practice:

1. We identify and organize intended users of the outcomes of the study.
2. We develop joint agreements between ourselves as evaluators and the selected users (a group representative of those associated with the program) to (a) determine the evaluation's focus and (b) define intended uses of the findings.
3. Working in close concert with a selected group of users, we will choose an evaluation design and methods that are responsive to users' stated needs and methods appropriate to the evaluation. These choices will be developed in practical,

sensible, and understandable terms, arising from flexible, feasible, and ethical considerations on our part and from deliberations with the intended users.
4. We will collect and analyze needed information by working in collaboration with the selected group of intended users and thus gain reactions from them.
5. We will actively engage the intended users in interpreting results, making judgments based on the findings, forming recommendations, and making decisions.
6. Finally, we shall make decisions with the intended users on dissemination of the findings.

These six steps appear logically sequential and linear, but in reality they include many substeps that are both interacting and looping. What is important, we have found, is that each main step and significant substeps are performed effectively by negotiating and collaborating with intended users. The study is complete when there is a strong desire by program users to implement recommendations based on their intimate knowledge of the evaluation from start to finish. We consider that an evaluation is successful when it is actually used for program or project improvement.

Because UFE is focused on a particular situation with its idiosyncratic population, we think that we can meet the requirements of your proposed assignment. Please be assured that our evaluations conform to sound standards and principles. As outlined above, we would need your assurance that we could select a representative group to negotiate with our evaluation team from start to finish of the evaluation. Such selection would necessarily take into consideration the diversity of the low-cost housing population, together with administrative, maintenance, and other support staff. Moreover, we would welcome at least one board member of your foundation in the selected group. In passing, we acknowledge the fruitful information you have posted on the Net under Project Profiles developed during the previous evaluation. This information is invaluable for a UFE approach because it helps to structure what would be our initial goal: to select a representative group to work closely and in conjunction with our consultative evaluation team.

UFE professionals—and our record indicates that we are this—are not bound by any particular evaluation technique. To the contrary, we select from the entire range of techniques and approaches those that best suit the evaluation of a project. We would present to the selected group, with advice, a menu of evaluation approaches, techniques, and roles for their consideration. We feel that unless primary intended users are comfortable with aspects of the evaluation as it develops, it is unlikely that the findings will have maximum impact. We firmly believe that we take a more realistic approach to the stakeholder (primarily the representative group) involvement than some other advocacy approaches.

Bearing in mind the likely span of cultural differences in your low-cost housing population, we would give particular attention to values clarification early in the study; in fact, such procedures would be part of a selection of a primary intended users group. This would constitute a vital part of elucidating the contextual dynamics and of laying the foundation for the collaborative work between the evaluation team and representatives of those associated with a low-cost housing project.

In advance, we must state that turnover of the representative stakeholder group could derail this evaluation or any others that follow the UFE approach. To the extent possible, therefore, we would seek organizational assurance that such changeover could be kept to a minimum and that the replacement of users would be easily negotiated.

The evaluation team would work closely with the selected user group whose views will not only be fully respected, but indeed would direct the nature of the study. As it progresses, both evaluator and group members would gain deep insights into the program, how it has evolved during the past five years, and what improvements should occur. The evaluation must have an impact, and it must be put to use by the users themselves. This is our aim; our record proves that we can achieve it.

At this stage, we would need to analyze the costs involved more closely. In this regard, we have expertise within our organization to give advice on financial matters. What we can state unequivocally is that costs will fall within the limits you have set. Our early estimate of costs puts them safely under the $50,000 you are allowing for the evaluation. If our response to your RFP is viewed favorably, we shall forward an itemized breakdown of costs. These will be based on the work of one lead evaluator, supported by two experienced evaluators. All are skilled in the performance of utilization-focused evaluation.

You may be assured that we would meet other requirements of your RFP, in particular, the time lines you have set for the completion of the study and for both interim and final reporting.

We acknowledge that the UFE approach to your proposed study may be different from what you may have expected in response to your RFP. Nonetheless, there is a growing emphasis on the importance of utility in evaluations, strengthened by the recognition of the work of the Joint Committee on Standards for Educational Evaluation's publications of program evaluation standards. The enclosed copy of these standards (1994) shows that one of four sections focuses on the need to make evaluation useful (see Utility Standards, pp. 23–59).

If you need further information, we are willing to supply it, together with responses to any questions your foundation board may have.

This illustration poses one obvious difficulty: the usual nexus between evaluator and client (in this case, the foundation's board) does not exist. Instead, the board must be willing to surrender decision making to a group of users of the low-cost housing project rather than assuming this as their right. Certainly, a board member has been invited to join the selected group, but this appears to be a token gesture to authority to help secure a contract.

It does appear that this response to the RFP may not be successful. The UFE firm, obviously convinced of the worthwhileness of its approach, will live to fight another day.

Review Questions

1. What distinctions does Patton draw between program evaluation and utilization-focused program evaluation?
2. What is the prime intention of utilization-focused evaluators, and what is the initial procedure to ensure that this aim succeeds?
3. In what particular aspect does Elliot Eisner support UFE rather than more traditional approaches to evaluation?
4. Why are the following sets of knowledge basic to an effective utilization-focused evaluation: group process, values analysis, professional standards for evaluation, content analysis, and negotiation?
5. The psychology of use undergirding UFE is based on what premise?
6. Why does Patton insist that users must be involved in goals clarification?
7. In conducting UFE studies, what level of consideration should be given to assessing the program's implementation, and why is this so?
8. Describe the three terms in Patton's active–reactive–adaptive approach, and explain how they are linked.
9. According to Patton, what is the main limitation of UFE?
10. Give reasons why the word *focused* is such a vital component of UFE.

Group Exercises

Exercise 1. Following UFE doctrine, what bases should be used to judge an evaluation?

Exercise 2. How would a UFE evaluator address the values issue in an evaluation? In discussing this question, explore possible difficulties that could arise for the evaluator.

Exercise 3. To what extent is UFE compatible with the other five evaluation approaches described in Part Three (Chapters Thirteen to Seventeen)?

Exercise 4. Suppose your group has been commissioned to assess the adequacy of a UFE evaluator's proposed primary intended users' panel. Bearing in mind the requirements of UFE, what factors would you examine to decide on the efficacy or otherwise of the evaluator's selection?

Exercise 5. UFE claims to follow and adhere to all Joint Committee (1994) standards of utility, feasibility, propriety, and accuracy. Yet how can UFE evaluators meet these standards while acceding to the intended users' desires? For example, the targeted group may want to avoid collecting relevant but potentially embarrassing information—contrary to standards U2, A4, and A5—and there are numerous other potential conflicts.

Peruse the Joint Committee standards, and you will find other possible discrepancies between the UFE approach to evaluation and the stated demands of the standards. Discuss the ramifications of these potential divergencies.

References

Alkin, M. C. (2004). *Evaluation roots: Tracing theorists' views and influences.* Thousand Oaks, CA: Sage.

Cronbach, L. J., & Associates. (1980). *Toward reform of program evaluation.* San Francisco: Jossey-Bass.

Eisner, E. (1991). Taking a second look: Educational connoisseurship revisited. In M. W. McLaughlin & D. C. Phillips (Eds.), *Evaluation and education: At quarter-century: Ninetieth yearbook of the National Society for the Study of Education, Part 11* (pp. 169–187). Chicago: University of Chicago Press.

Guba, E. G., & Lincoln, Y. S. (1989). *Fourth generation evaluation.* Thousand Oaks, CA: Sage.

Joint Committee on Standards for Educational Evaluation. (1981). *Standards for evaluations of educational programs, projects, and materials.* New York: McGraw-Hill.

Joint Committee on Standards for Educational Evaluation. (1994). *The program evaluation standards: How to assess evaluations of educational programs.* Thousand Oaks, CA: Corwin Press.

Patton, M. Q. (1980). *Qualitative evaluation methods.* Thousand Oaks, CA: Sage.

Patton, M. Q. (1982). *Practical evaluation.* Thousand Oaks, CA: Sage.

Patton, M. Q. (1984). An alternative evaluation approach for the problem-solving training program: A utilization-focused evaluation program. *Evaluation and Program Planning, 7,* 189–92.

Patton, M. Q. (1997). *Utilization-focused evaluation: The new century text* (3rd ed.). Thousand Oaks, CA: Sage.

Patton, M. Q. (2003). Utilization-focused evaluation. In T. Kellaghan & D. L. Stufflebeam (Eds.), *International handbook of educational evaluation* (pp. 223–244). Norwell, MA: Kluwer.

Stake, R. E. (1983). Program evaluation, particularly responsive evaluation. In G. F. Madaus, M. Scriven, & D. L. Stufflebeam (Eds.), *Evaluation models* (pp. 287–310). *Boston*: Kluwer.

Weiss, C. (1972). *Evaluating action programs: Readings in social action and education.* Needham Heights, MA: Allyn & Bacon.

PART FOUR

EVALUATION TASKS, PROCEDURES, AND TOOLS AND THE METAEVALUATION IMPERATIVE

This final part of the book addresses the practical, procedural, and self-referent aspects of sound evaluations. We have projected a methodology for general application to all sound evaluation approaches. The discussion includes practical procedures and tools plus many illustrations of their use. In Chapters Nineteen through Twenty-Six, we delve into the methodology of evaluation in a sequence that proceeds through an evaluation's start-up, design, budgeting, contracting, information collection, analysis, synthesis, reporting, and follow-up. We bring the book to a close in Chapter Twenty-Seven by discussing the metaevaluation imperative. This final message is that evaluators, like any other group of professionals, must subject their services to formative and summative evaluations for purposes of both improvement and accountability.

CHAPTER NINETEEN

IDENTIFYING AND ASSESSING EVALUATION OPPORTUNITIES

A key question on the mind of evaluators, especially beginners, is, How do I find opportunities to apply my evaluation skills? Evaluators need to distinguish between evaluation opportunities that are or are not worth pursuing. An internal evaluator sometimes will need to determine how to ameliorate the negative aspects of an evaluation assignment that cannot be declined.

In this chapter, we draw from our many years of experience to share lessons we have learned related to identifying and assessing evaluation opportunities. On completing the chapter, readers should have a good notion of how to identify and examine evaluation opportunities. Especially, they should be helped to decide judiciously whether an evaluation opportunity is worth pursuing or should be avoided if possible. In cases where the evaluator cannot reject an evaluation assignment, we offer advice on how to proceed carefully and professionally. We also offer our perspectives on how to derive benefits from attending bidders' conferences.

Sources of Evaluation Opportunities

Opportunities for conducting evaluations derive from five major sources: a published or direct mail request for an evaluation (request for proposal, RFP), a published request for a quotation (RFQ) to implement an evaluation whose design is given, an assignment given to an internal evaluator to conduct a particular evaluation, a solicitation to a particular (usually well-known) evaluator to conduct a study, or an evaluator-initiated proposal to conduct an evaluation that the evaluator sees as important.

Evaluation RFPs

It is quite common for funding organizations to publish or mail out requests for evaluations (RFPs). The issuing organization may be a branch of federal, state, or local government; a charitable foundation; or some other organization. The request may be announced in a publication such as *Commerce Business Daily*, in which the particulars of the requested study are summarized and information is given on how to obtain the RFP. Alternatively, the requester may mail the full RFP or information on how to get it to preselected groups or individuals that are seen as qualified and potential bidders.

Contents of evaluation RFPs may be highly variable. Some contain extremely detailed information on the evaluand and any previous evaluations of it, plus the particulars of the needed evaluation. Other RFPs may be quite general, with an indication that the organization wants the bidders to suggest the needed details and to exercise creativity. Both highly specific and more general evaluation RFPs usually indicate the evaluation's time line, main questions to be answered, needed information, the required reports, a recommended structure for proposals, the criteria for evaluating proposals, the deadline for submitting a proposal, references to relevant background materials, and the persons who can answer potential bidders' questions. Many RFPs give no indication of the amount of money available to support the evaluation or only a general indication of available funds. Some RFPs stipulate that the agreement will be on a cost-reimbursable basis, while others call for a fixed-price agreement. Often a published RFP will note the time and place of a bidders' conference where potential bidders will receive orientation from the sponsor and be able to ask questions pertaining to the competition.

Some RFPs require a fully developed and detailed proposal for the entire evaluation. Others call for initial proposals to develop an evaluation plan. In the former case, the sponsor will likely choose one contractor to proceed with the entire evaluation on a preordinate basis. In the latter situation, the sponsor may fund several bidders to produce competitive evaluation plans. The sponsor would then assess the different plans produced under the initial planning contracts and select one or a combination of plans to guide the long-term evaluation.

Another variable in evaluation RFPs concerns the nature of the award. Typically, the award is a contract that specifies the agreements on how the selected bidder will conduct and report the evaluation. However, the award may be a grant rather than a contract. Under the terms of a grant, the evaluator is given a sum of money under which he or she will have discretion on what questions to address and how to carry out the evaluation. Here, the evaluator is given maximum flexibility and professional discretion and needs to account only for how the money was spent. Still another type of award is the cooperative agreement. This arrangement requires that the evaluator and the sponsor collaborate in conducting and reporting the evaluation, with the evaluator needing to consult the sponsor on decisions during the course of the evaluation. Clearly, a grant or contract is the preferred type of award. They are less prone to conflicts of interest between the evaluator and sponsor and undue influence by the sponsor. They are more in keeping with the evaluators' needs to maintain an independent perspective and edit their own report.

In order to learn about evaluation RFPs, evaluators should monitor the *Commerce Business Daily* and other publications that announce evaluation opportunities. They should also make their evaluation qualifications and interests known to potential sponsors by visiting the organizations and submitting relevant printed materials. Depending on the level of rapport developed with an organization, it can be a good idea to make frequent visits to the organization in order to keep apprised of evaluation RFPs that are being developed. Regarding the development of relationships with funding organizations, it can be highly advantageous to consult with an organization or provide volunteer services. Such services may include evaluating evaluation proposals, critiquing draft RFPs, or even helping to develop evaluation RFPs. While participation in developing an evaluation RFP likely will preclude one from responding, there are side benefits of such service. Particularly, one often becomes privy to other evaluation RFPs that are in the pipeline. Also, such participation is an opportunity to demonstrate both interest in and competence to contribute to the organization's evaluation needs.

Over time, the best way to gain early awareness of evaluation RFPs consistently is to develop and make known a track record of outstanding evaluation work. As in any other walk of life, nothing succeeds like success. Frequently, RFP issuers will find evaluators who are known for their extensive and consistently high level of evaluation service rather than vice versa.

We also note from our experience that if one learns about an evaluation RFP only after it has been published, it may be a waste of time and effort to write a proposal. In such situations, the time to respond may be very short. Also, other respondents may have been privy to the RFP during its development and have a long head start in developing their proposal. For many of the evaluation contracts we have won, we have been in the latter position. Although such situations do not constitute a level playing field, they are a part of the real world of RFP competitions. Nevertheless, many evaluation RFPs attracted no or only a few evaluation proposals. Thus, it is not always a bad idea to bid on evaluation RFPs that one only learned about in a publication.

We also note that there have been RFP cases where the subject evaluation was "wired" to a particular respondent. Thus, many respondents to a fictitious RFP wasted their time in writing an evaluation proposal because the preferred evaluator always had odds stacked in his or her favor. Possibly this evaluator had excelled in conducting previous evaluations of the subject program, had established a valuable database on the program, had acquired and maintained a staff with just the right qualifications to proceed with subsequent evaluations, and had earned the confidence of the program sponsor and other stakeholders. Understandably, the client organization wanted to sustain and build on its past investment in this evaluation contractor. While the organization was compelled by statutory or other reasons to seek bids, it was always predictable that they would hire the evaluator of record again. To address this dilemma, the sponsor might well have written the RFP so that the evaluator of record would be the obvious choice, for example, because it exceeded any other party's experience in evaluating the subject program and possessed just the right combination of staff qualifications. We cite this type of dubious practice as a part of the real world of evaluation RFPs. We advise evaluators to be alert to such situations so as not to waste time bidding on wired evaluation "opportunities."

In looking at any evaluation RFP, potential bidders should carefully scrutinize the opportunity. Questions to ask include the following:

- Does this program's evaluation history reveal that the sponsor has had a sustained, successful relationship with a particular evaluator who is likely or at least eligible to bid on this evaluation?
- Is the time line for responding unusually short?
- Does the RFP spell out criteria for selecting a bidder that almost excludes any party other than the evaluator of record?
- Is the content of the RFP built largely on evaluation plans and reports that were authored by the evaluator of record?
- Does the RFP essentially require the precise methodology that the evaluator of record employed in previous evaluations of this program?

If the answers to these questions are all or mainly yes, then it might be prudent to forgo responding to the particular evaluation RFP.

Evaluation RFQs

An evaluation RFQ is similar to an RFP in all matters except for the openness of elements of evaluation design. Whereas an evaluation RFP asks the respondent to propose a plan for conducting the subject evaluation, the RFQ stipulates the method to be employed and asks the respondent to quote a price for conducting the specified study. The prescribed elements of design in an RFQ almost always are highly specific and leave the successful bidder little room for creativity and discretion. From our vantage point, RFQs are not attractive options for applying one's evaluation skills. They place the evaluator essentially in a technical role and may prevent explorations that are necessary to assess a program's merit and worth. We acknowledge that the given evaluation design might have been developed carefully and appropriately, that the sponsor appropriately can seek out an evaluator to faithfully execute the design, and that providing such evaluation service is legitimate, if not creative.

Before pursuing an RFQ, an evaluator might want to address the following questions:

- Is the prescribed methodology appropriately responsive to the full range of important questions concerning the program's merit?
- Will implementation of the stipulated methods assuredly expose a failed program as well as hail one that succeeded?
- Does the prescribed methodology include an appropriate range of qualitative as well as quantitative methods?
- Is the prescribed methodology unbiased in looking at both strengths and weaknesses?
- Will implementation of the stipulated reporting plan ensure that findings are accessible to all right-to-know audiences?
- Does the prescribed methodology allow access to all relevant sources of information about the program?
- Will the prescribed methodology allow the evaluator to conduct an evaluation in which he or she can take pride?
- Will implementation of the prescribed methodology meet the standards of the evaluation field?

To the extent that an evaluator has to answer these questions in the negative, he or she might want to find better opportunities for applying his or her evaluation skills.

Internal Evaluation Assignments

Many evaluators are not independent contractors but instead are internal evaluators. They work within their organization and address its evaluation needs. Often those needs entail conducting evaluations of the organization's externally funded projects. Other times, internal evaluators assess certain programs or divisions within their organization.

Internal evaluations are vital to an organization's health and accountability. They are especially important for guiding program planning and improvement. In addition to the internal evaluations, the organization often has to bring in outside evaluators, who are more independent than the insiders. However, it is the internal evaluators who by and large provide the information that the outside evaluators use to reach their conclusions and judgments. Thus, internal evaluators have an important role in helping the organization maintain its accountability, even when outsiders conduct and report the evaluations.

In an organization of any size, there are more needs for evaluation than the internal evaluators can address. Therefore, it is crucial that the organization has a process for assigning evaluation priorities, allocating evaluation resources, and scheduling the work. We think the internal evaluation team should annually assess the organization's needs for evaluation, work with the organization's hierarchy to set evaluation priorities, and develop and carry out an annual program of internal evaluations. In addition to planned and scheduled internal evaluations, it is also important to maintain an evaluation contingency fund by which to address those emergent and important needs for evaluation that were not predicted.

One way to set the priorities and also foster use of evaluation findings is to establish an evaluation stakeholder panel. The members should be representative of the organization's structure both horizontally and vertically. Such a panel's responsibilities could be to review annual assessments of needs for evaluation, help set annual priorities for allocating evaluation resources, review evaluation plans and reports, help promote use of evaluation findings, and help develop the organization's evaluation policies and procedures.

Clearly, internal evaluators face a difficult obstacle regarding their natural conflicts of interest. As professional inquirers, they need to issue valid assessments of merit and worth. Yet they also have to contribute to their organization's welfare and not cause it to fail or experience undue embarrassment, as might be the case in issuing and disseminating negative reports. To walk the fine line between valid, forthright evaluation and advocacy of their organization's welfare, we think the organization should adopt and follow the standards of the evaluation field. This implies that all decision makers within the organization, at all levels, must become as conversant with adopted standards as the evaluator. The internal evaluators should faithfully follow these standards in conducting their evaluations. If it is clear that they cannot do so in a particular evaluation case, then they should use the standards to convince their organization to contract with an outside evaluator or at least an outside metaevaluator. If it is not feasible to bring in an outside party, the internal evaluators should make clear in their report the problems they faced, how they addressed these, and what they see as limitations of their findings together with the reasons.

Sole-Source Requests for Evaluation

Experienced evaluators often have the experience of being pursued on a sole-source basis to conduct evaluations. This can be a fortunate situation for the evaluator for a number of reasons. First, there is a good prospect that the evaluation findings will be used, since the sponsor wants the evaluation done. Second, the evaluator usually will be given discretion in matters of evaluation design. Third, on rare occasions, the sponsor may inform the evaluator that he or she, within reasonable limits, has a blank check to fund all appropriate evaluation tasks. Fourth, the evaluator often will be allowed to set a reasonable time line in order to accomplish the needed work. Clearly, an evaluator who is pursued by a sponsor and given an exclusive evaluation opportunity will want to seriously consider the opportunity before turning it aside.

Nevertheless, there can be good reasons to reject such opportunities. Possibly the sponsor is seeking a good report, not in terms of quality, but in terms of a positive judgment of the evaluand and is willing to pay a high price for the desired positive report. Conversely, the sponsor may be seeking and willing to pay handsomely for an unmitigated indictment of a program. Or more subtly, the sponsor may open the way for a professionally sound evaluation but plan to use any indication of a program's weakness to fire the director or cancel the program. We have seen examples of each of these in our evaluation work. As we argued in Chapter Six, evaluators should not be in the business of conducting pseudoevaluations.

Accordingly, we advise evaluators who are sought out by a sponsor to undertake a background investigation before signing on to do the evaluation. It is especially important to identify and have an exchange with persons and groups that might experience harm as a consequence of the evaluation. Often they can shed insights into any hidden agenda for the evaluation. In general, it is important to learn as much as possible about the political climate surrounding the evaluation request before signing on. If red flags appear, the prospective evaluator can decide not to proceed or to proceed only under contractual terms that protect the evaluation's integrity and safeguard the legitimate interests of program stakeholders.

An evaluator can increase the prospects of being sought out for evaluation assignments in a number of ways. Most important is to develop a track record of conducting technically competent and useful evaluations. It is also a good idea to publish lessons learned and conduct training sessions based on one's evaluations. Evaluators are wise to render service to potential client organizations, for example, by helping to evaluate evaluation proposals and develop evaluation RFPs. The evaluator can prepare and disseminate a brochure describing his or her qualifications, experience, and availability for evaluation work. In addition, the evaluator might study the annual reports of prospective evaluation clients and send them a letter indicating his or her availability and interest in evaluating their programs. It is prudent to schedule visits to prospective funding organizations and provide them with information that has relevance to their evaluation needs. Also, evaluation organizations can maintain a Web site that includes evaluation exemplars and information about the organization and its staff. (An excellent example is www. wmich.edu/evalctr.) To the degree that qualified evaluators or evaluation organizations conduct activities such as those identified, they are likely to have many evaluation opportunities essentially walk through their doorway. However, we emphasize that before signing on, the prospective evaluator should carefully scrutinize all such opportunities for the possibility of inappropriate hidden agendas.

Evaluator-Initiated Evaluation Opportunities

Experienced evaluators often develop a track record of conducting evaluations within a given domain, such as charter schools, computer technology, community development, best business practice, employment, science education, or digital imaging technology. As they proceed from evaluation to evaluation, they will see needs for important studies that could help advance the area or perhaps help turn it in a new direction. Accordingly, such evaluators likely will not wait for a relevant RFP or other evaluation opportunity to emerge. Instead, they will act proactively to help generate an appropriate evaluation opportunity. The following scenario, based on many actual evaluator-generated evaluations that we are aware of, illustrates how the proactive evaluator might proceed.

An evaluator might schedule a visit to an organization that has funded evaluations in the particular area and that may have discretionary funds for field-initiated evaluations. Examples of such organizations are foundations or government agencies with a history of work in the evaluator's area of interest. In the course of scheduling the visit, the prospective evaluator might send a brief letter noting the need for evaluation in the substantive field and his or her desire to explore that need and how it could be addressed. (The initial contact could also be an informal encounter between the evaluator and a representative of the funding organization at a professional meeting.) The evaluator might take along to the scheduled meeting some brief written material, such as a list of talking points. However, he or she would be smart not to present, during this initial meeting, anything like a full-blown evaluation plan. Instead, it is better to establish rapport with the funding organization's staff and engage in a give-and-take exchange about the need for evaluation and how it could be addressed best. At the meeting's conclusion, the evaluator likely would suggest and secure agreement on appropriate next steps. Typically the evaluator would send the funding organization a summary of the initial meeting, including any consensus that was reached, plus a draft evaluation plan. Subsequently the evaluator might engage in one or more follow-up meetings so that he or she and personnel of the funding organization could go over and strengthen the evaluation plan. If all goes well in the process of exchange and collaborative planning, the funding organization may ask the evaluator to submit a formal proposal for sole source funding.

In summary, the evaluator should pursue a process of interaction and development of mutual understanding prior to detailing the evaluation plan, a process that could require months. Throughout the process of dialogue and deliberation, the evaluator should document the exchanges and after each meeting should send a record of what was discussed, including any key agreements on next steps.

Cultivation of funding organizations followed by a collaborative development of evaluation plans is a close to ideal way for evaluators to pursue a line of evaluation work. Of course, the evaluator must protect the integrity of the evaluation plan and process and not allow the sponsor inappropriate control over the evaluation procedures or reports. The evaluator should ground the evaluation in standards of the evaluation field, attest at appropriate points in the evaluation process to the extent that the evaluation met the standards, and do everything possible to ensure that the evaluation is subjected to an independent metaevaluation. By pursuing such safeguards, the evaluator should be able to retain an appropriate level of independence in the evaluation work while deriving the benefits of a functional working relationship with the funding organization. If at all possible, the evaluator should obtain a grant rather than a contract or a cooperative agreement. However, given the institution of appropriate safeguards, a defensible evaluator-initiated evaluation can be conducted under any of these arrangements.

Bidders' Conferences

In the case of relatively high-cost evaluations, the sponsor often announces and conducts a bidders' conference. Its purpose is to provide all potential bidders an equal opportunity to receive background information about the needed evaluation and address questions to the sponsor's representatives. The conference typically is conducted in an auditorium and run for one to two hours. Conference leaders will be closely scripted in terms of the questions they can and cannot answer. The conference begins with an overview of the needed evaluation and the bidding requirements. Often the presenters distribute materials to supplement the evaluation RFP. The bulk of the meeting follows a question-and-answer format. Usually this segment is tape-recorded, with a transcription sent to all those in attendance and others if they request it. In addition, the sponsor will distribute a list of all conference attendees.

Attendance at the conference is not a condition for entering or winning the proposal writing competition. However, there are several advantages to attending.

First, an evaluator can make sure that his or her most important questions are asked. Second, it is always of interest to see who is in attendance. Observing who asks which questions and how different attendees interact before and after the session may help the evaluator size up the competition. Also, by attending and interacting with some of the participants, an evaluator can consider possible advantages of partnering with other attendees to make a collaborative proposal.

In attending the conference, it is important to remember that the attendees are potential competitors. Before, during, and following the conference, they are likely to seek information from or about you and your organization that could help them win the proposal competition. Thus, attendees must be wary of disclosing proprietary information that would help a competitor. Such information could include whether one has decided to bid, who likely would lead the effort, what other staff members will be involved, what consultants are being sought, what one's history is regarding the particular RFP, what one considers a probable dollar cost for the evaluation, whether one would collaborate with another organization, what background planning has already been done, and what political support has been lined up. It is wise never to volunteer information to others on any such matters and not to ask questions in the public meeting that would reveal information that could advantage the competitors. During the meeting, an evaluator usually is wise to wait before posing questions to see if other attendees ask those questions. This is because posing questions can expose one's plans for responding to the RFP. Also, one should be careful not to volunteer proprietary information when interacting with attendees before and after the session. On the other side, one should listen intently during the meeting and before and after it for information helpful in writing a winning proposal. Also, it is important to take good notes based on attendance at the meeting, since the transcripts might or not be complete and forthcoming in a timely fashion.

The preceding discussion of gamesmanship in responding to evaluation RFPs may seem distasteful. In fact, we found it distasteful to have to write about it. However, evaluations occur in a political context. It would be naive not to consider and effectively address the political realities of competitions for evaluation projects. To make this error would consistently put one on the losing side. It would also be wasteful of the invested time and funds.

Summary

In this chapter, we have offered leads about how best to find, assess, and address evaluation opportunities. Evaluators may uncover and pursue a wide range of evaluation opportunities. These include RFPs, RFQs, internal evaluation assignments, sole-source evaluations, and evaluator-initiated opportunities. In responding to or generating such opportunities, we have stressed that evaluators should carefully assess whether potential opportunities are worth pursuing on both feasibility and ethical grounds. We have emphasized that evaluators should always hold their evaluations to the standards of the evaluation field and that they should seek to have their evaluations subjected to independent metaevaluations. We have also given our perspective on how best to participate in bidding conferences.

Review Questions

1. What is an evaluation RFP, and what are the sources of such RFPs?
2. What are signs that you would have a poor shot at winning an evaluation RFP competition?
3. What is meant by the observation that an evaluation RFP is "wired," and what are the signs that this is the case?
4. Why is it important to consider whether an RFP calls for a grant, contract, or cooperative agreement, and why would an evaluator usually prefer a grant?
5. What are the hazards of entering into a cooperative agreement, and what steps can an evaluator take to protect the integrity of such an evaluation?
6. What is an RFQ, and why does one not appeal to an evaluator's creativity?
7. What are evaluation review panels, what should be the membership of such panels, and what is their role in internal evaluation systems?
8. What is a sole-source opportunity for an evaluation, and what are possible reasons to reject such an opportunity?
9. What is an evaluator-initiated evaluation opportunity, and what steps could an evaluator follow to effectively generate such an opportunity?
10. What is a bidders' conference, what are the advantages of attending one, and what are some cautions associated with one's behavior at the conference?

Group Exercises

Exercise 1. Outline a strategy that a neophyte evaluator could follow to consistently learn about evaluation opportunities.

Exercise 2. Suppose you were outlining a policy to address conflict-of-interest issues in an internal evaluation system. Define the potential conflict-of-interest issues, and list safeguards an organization could institute to address the issues effectively.

Exercise 3. What are the advantages of responding to a sole-source request for an evaluation, what are potential threats to such an evaluation's integrity, and what can the evaluator do to protect the evaluation's integrity?

Exercise 4. What are some of the basic precautions an evaluator should observe when considering responding to any form of requests for evaluation proposals?

CHAPTER TWENTY

FIRST STEPS IN ADDRESSING EVALUATION OPPORTUNITIES

After deciding to pursue a program evaluation opportunity, one must engage in an array of start-up activities: recruiting team members and collaborators, establishing an institutional base of support for the projected work, developing thorough familiarity with the need for the evaluation, stipulating the standards for guiding and assessing the evaluation, obtaining such appendix materials as letters of support and vita, and planning for a stakeholder review panel. These are preliminary to the detailed work in developing the technical evaluation design, creating an appropriate budget, drafting a contract to cover the evaluation work, and packaging and submitting the evaluation proposal materials.

Often the prospective evaluator will need to pursue the initial start-up tasks expeditiously, especially in responding to a competitive evaluation RFP. Three main reasons underlie the need to move ahead proactively and promptly. First, the evaluator needs to recruit the most qualified staff, consultants, and (as appropriate) collaborating organizations before the competition lines them up. Second, he or she needs to draft evaluation proposal materials early, so that successive drafts can be prepared and critically reviewed, and so that ultimately a highly competitive final proposal is prepared. Third, he or she needs to provide ample time to channel the proposal materials through the human subjects institutional review board and to acquire all the needed support and signatures from one's institution.

In this chapter, we define some of the initial start-up activities and offer our advice. In ensuing chapters, we address other evaluation start-up activities, particularly evaluation design, evaluation budgeting, and evaluation contracting. We recognize that the contents of this chapter (and the other Part Four chapters) are especially applicable to relatively large-scale evaluations that require a team of participants. Nonetheless, many of the lessons apply to small studies conducted by a single-evaluator.

Developing the Evaluation Team

One of the highest-priority start-up activities is to begin determining and obtaining commitments from prospective evaluation participants. Having decided to proceed with the evaluation, the initiator should have a firm idea of the needed evaluation expertise. The evaluation roles listed at the end of Chapter One provide a kind of checklist of potentially relevant evaluation roles. Example roles for a particular evaluation could be evaluation designer and manager, subject matter specialist, field data collector, measurement and analysis specialist, communications specialist, editor, and secretary. Full-time staff members might fill certain roles, and part-time consultants could carry out other roles. A large-scale evaluation might also require collaborating with one or more other organizations.

After identifying the needed evaluation roles, the evaluator should proceed with all due haste to recruit participants for the evaluation team. Experienced evaluators often have in mind a range of highly qualified persons with the needed expertise. However, even experienced evaluators often contact trusted colleagues for recommendations and look into the literature for persons who have published in the relevant substantive and technical areas. These are useful moves.

After listing potential evaluation participants, it is time to start contacting them in person or by telephone. In the ensuing exchanges, the initiator should identify the evaluand, the sponsor, the purpose of the evaluation, the main evaluation questions, the projected evaluation approach, the time line, the role and amount of time envisioned for the person (or organization), and the expected level of compensation for the needed service once the evaluation is funded. Moreover, the context of the evaluation, and in particular any abnormal political climate, should be clearly explicated. The initiator should respond to the potential recruits' questions and be open to hearing and using their ideas. For recruits who are willing to commit, the initiator should request a copy of their résumé and a letter stating their willingness to participate once the evaluation is funded. These materials will be placed in the proposal's appendix. Also, the initiator should keep all the recruits informed as the evaluation planning proceeds.

Establishing Institutional Support for the Projected Evaluation

An early task for an evaluation initiator in preparing to submit a proposal is to gain support from his or her own organization. The initiator should inform his or her relevant superiors and colleagues of the plan to write and submit a proposal, the time line for completing and delivering the proposal, and the needed institutional resources, sign-offs, and assistance. At this early stage, institutional staff leaders should be informed of the amount of money believed to be available for the evaluation work. The initiators should also be frank in discussing the feasibility of submitting a winning proposal, given the institution's likely requirements for indirect cost reimbursement. In some cases, it may be feasible for the institution to provide some type of matching support, such as a reduction in the indirect cost rate or contributed time of one or more evaluation staff members. Discussions of institutional support should also include matters such as needed release time for certain of the institution's staff members and possible subcontracts to other organizations whose services will be needed. In the latter case, it will be important to talk early with the organization's attorneys who would be involved in writing and approving any needed subcontracts.

A point often overlooked is the need for the parent organization to give due credit for evaluation contributions to their staff members who participate in the evaluation. Staff members' excellent performance on a contracted evaluation should count toward their salary increases, promotions, and, as relevant, tenure. It is wise to work out in advance how the organization will provide evaluation participants just recognitions and rewards.

Many organizations have human subjects institutional review boards that typically have authority to prevent a proposal from going forward if it does not satisfy the board's standards. The boards have forms to fill out and often have a time-consuming review process that can be onerous. Clearly, the initiator of an evaluation proposal should contact the review board early and make sure the members understand the intention to submit a proposal plus the time frame. The initiator should fill out and submit review board forms as soon as possible. More than one excellent evaluation proposal has been rejected or has not been pursued because it failed to meet review board requirements in a timely fashion.

Developing Thorough Familiarity with the Need for the Evaluation

Prior to deciding to pursue the evaluation opportunity, the initiator will have learned a good deal about the evaluand and the need for the evaluation by studying the RFP (if there is one) and possibly attending a bidders' conference. However, such activities are only the beginning of what needs to be done. In addition, the initiator should search out relevant materials and people who know a good deal about the situation. Relevant materials might include past evaluations of the evaluand, journal articles, newspaper clippings, and a Web site. Key informants could include persons who previously evaluated the evaluand, experts in the subject matter area, and persons who have conducted and published research in the program area. As relevant materials are identified, the initiator and collaborators should study and discuss them and place them in an evaluation project library. Similarly, they should hold discussions with the identified key informants. In general, the initiator and colleagues should learn all they can relevant to the evaluation assignment.

Stipulating Standards for Guiding and Assessing the Evaluation

In Chapter Three we presented three sets of evaluation standards: the Joint Committee's *Program Evaluation Standards*, the American Evaluation Association's *Guiding Principles for Evaluators*, and the Government Accountability Office's *Government Auditing Standards*. We also explained the fundamental importance of standards for guiding and assessing evaluation work. Depending on the particular evaluation situation and the initiator's preference, we think any of these three sets of standards provides an appropriate foundation for a program evaluation. In planning an evaluation, we advise the initiator to select one or more of these sets of standards and present them to the evaluation team as the guiding policy for the contemplated evaluation. The initiator should require all participants in the evaluation to learn and apply the selected standards. These standards should be made an explicit part of the funding proposal.

Developing the Evaluation Proposal's Appendix

Unfortunately, many evaluation planners wait until the last moment to compile an appendix of essential background information to the evaluation proposal. Consequently, some needed materials may not be included, and the included materials may be superficial or poorly prepared.

From the start of preparing to submit a proposal, the initiator should begin soliciting and compiling the appendix materials. These may include, among others, a summary of the adopted evaluation standards, an institutional vita, personal résumés, a list of members of an evaluation review panel, and letters of commitment.

It is important to scrutinize and be selective in what goes in the appendix. For key staff members, full-length résumés may be important, while summaries may suffice for less crucial participants. In obtaining letters of commitment, it can be useful to provide the letter writers with a model letter of commitment. This needs to be done as early as possible, so that one can follow up to obtain letters from late respondents. As one further develops the evaluation design, it may also be possible and important to include sample evaluation instruments.

Planning for a Stakeholder Review Panel

In many evaluations, it can be important to arrange for the involvement of a stakeholder review panel. The role of this panel should include reviewing and critiquing draft evaluation materials, helping to disseminate evaluation findings, and, as appropriate, facilitating data collection. The panel's membership could include staff members of the program being evaluated, constituents of the program, relevant policymakers, evaluation experts, and persons from the organization that funds the subject program. Effective employment of such a review panel can help ensure that all evaluation instruments and reports are of high quality and that evaluation findings are heeded and used by the intended audience.

Summary

In this chapter, we have noted some of the key early steps in developing a winning evaluation proposal. These steps are essential in establishing a strong foundation for the projected evaluation. Evaluation planners who give short shrift to such start-up tasks do so at the peril of their evaluation planning efforts.

Review Questions

1. Give your own definition of *evaluation sponsor*, and then compare it with the definition in the Glossary at the back of this book.
2. Give your own definition of *evaluation stakeholders*, and then compare it with the definition in the Glossary at the back of this book.

3. In general terms, give five essential start-up activities for large-scale program evaluation.

4. Identify some of the roles needed for an evaluation when a team effort is required.

5. On what basis, and with what procedures, would an evaluation initiator recruit participants for an evaluation team?

6. Why must an evaluation organization be frank with its staff during the preparation stage of submitting a proposal?

7. Many organizations have a human subjects review board. Why is it important to involve such a group from the early work of submitting an evaluation proposal?

8. Name some of the kinds of relevant materials that an evaluation leader (and colleagues) should investigate about the evaluand before an evaluation proposal is submitted.

9. Give reasons that an evaluation leader should require all participants in a study to be conversant with selected evaluation standards.

10. When should an appendix of essential background information to the evaluation proposal be compiled? What are some of the items that could be included?

Group Exercises

Exercise 1. Your group are principals in a large evaluation organization. You have responded strongly and confidently to a competitive RFP, and you have been encouraged by the evaluation sponsor to continue planning toward a final submission. Your initial delight is somewhat tempered by the realization that a considerable amount of work and compromises will need to be made with your own staff, and also external consultants, so that a convincing final submission may be presented. You realize that action toward this final stage must not be delayed, particularly because you are aware of another evaluation group similarly placed to you, and also that an imaginative, thorough, and proactive plan must stand the best chance with the sponsor. What are some of the steps you would take to:

- Convince your own staff to become involved (include relevant rewards if you wish)?
- Get a head start on your competitor in recruiting the most qualified (external) consultants?
- Organize a review of pertinent materials?

- Draft early proposals, and arrange their immediate critiquing?
- Time these early proposals so that they may be considered by the sponsor's human subjects institutional review board, and assuming no impediments are presented?
- Present your final proposal, in electronic and printed form, to the evaluation-sponsoring organization?

In discussing these points, consider problems that could occur at any stage, and suggest ways of overcoming them.

Exercise 2. One section of this chapter deals with the significance of the evaluation leader's (and colleagues', by inference) becoming very familiar with a need for an evaluation (as outlined, for instance, in an RFP). Expand on the suggestions and statements presented, and build a convincing argument for the evaluand to be thoroughly identified so that the case for the final proposal's being accepted is strengthened.

CHAPTER TWENTY-ONE

DESIGNING EVALUATIONS

Having decided to conduct a study, the evaluator needs to prepare an appropriate design. An evaluation design is the set of decisions required to carry out the needed evaluation. These focus especially on determining the evaluand, questions to be addressed, criteria to be applied, information to be collected, information collection and analysis tools and procedures, data control provisions, synthesis procedure, reports and reporting methods, and steps to promote and support use of findings. Practically, the evaluator needs to project design decisions before the evaluation work begins because they provide the basis for budgeting, contracting, staffing, and scheduling the needed work. In randomized experiments, the initial core design decisions are considered fixed because the evaluator seeks to hold treatment and control conditions separate and constant in order to identify their differential effects on assigned treatment and control groups of subjects. In the more general case of program evaluations, initial design decisions often must be reconsidered or fleshed out as the evaluation unfolds. This is especially so in formative and responsive evaluations. In such evaluations, the evaluator expects information needs to evolve as interim reports surface new issues, the subject program matures (or falters), and the client and other stakeholders raise new questions. Even in field experiments, contextual dynamics and needs and actions of experimental subjects may erode the evaluator's control over treatment and control conditions and cause the evaluator to modify the experimental design, or even replace it with a nonexperimental approach. In general, evaluators should periodically revisit, update, and delineate evaluation design decisions in consideration of evolving study conditions and client or other stakeholder needs. We advise readers to fix firmly in their minds that evaluation design is both process and product: initial design decisions appropriately are often general and tentative and become increasingly specific as the evaluation unfolds.

Over the course of an evaluation, the evaluator must exercise excellent communication and negotiation skills, responsiveness, and technical expertise in reaching and evolving sound design decisions. Overall, the evaluation design should address the audience's information needs, provide for judging the evaluand's merit and worth, be true to the evaluator's chosen evaluation model or approach, be capable of execution in the evaluand's setting, and in general meet the standards of the evaluation field. To address such challenges effectively, an evaluator requires an appropriate repertoire of qualitative and quantitative methods, planning and administrative competence, ability to meet evaluation standards, political skills, and a good measure of creativity.

In addressing the topic of evaluation design, first we present and discuss a fictionalized example of an evaluation design that is based on an actual evaluation. We have focused on a fairly complex evaluation because it provides a basis for looking at a wide range of evaluation tasks and methods, in both this and subsequent chapters, and because it illustrates the frequent situation in which an evaluation design starts out as a general plan and takes on specificity after the study is funded and launched. The evaluation was keyed to professional standards for evaluations and had profound effects on the client's decisions, and in those respects, it was exemplary. A bonus is that the example is an evaluation of a military personnel evaluation system that has the structural characteristics of a program evaluation (assessment of an interrelated set of goal-directed activities) and the content of personnel evaluation.

Second, we present and discuss a generic checklist for use in making evaluation design decisions or checking the adequacy of a completed evaluation design. This checklist is applicable to any of the wide range of defensible evaluation models and approaches and may be used in conjunction with the design recommendations included with a chosen evaluation model or approach. It is a tool for use in constructing an initial design, fleshing it out as the evaluation proceeds, and checking the adequacy of a proposed design. The checklist is useful to both evaluators and clients. We also reference particular checkpoints in order to apprise the reader of the additional design decisions that the evaluation team had to make during its evaluation of the military personnel evaluation system.

A Design Used for Evaluating the Performance Review System of a Military Organization

The evaluation design reviewed in this chapter focuses on an evaluation of The U.S. Marine Corps' (USMC) system for evaluating the job performance of its officers, staff noncommissioned officers, and sergeants. The corps's commanding general was dissatisfied with his organization's performance review system (PRS); had ordered the organization's personnel department to obtain an independent evaluation of that system; and required completion of the evaluation and subsequent reform of PRS by the end of his term as commanding general, which would occur soon. An official of this organization invited a particular evaluator to lead the needed evaluation. The evaluator subsequently prepared and submitted the general evaluation design described below. The corps took two months to process the proposal and ultimately approved it, along with a fixed-price award of about $440,000, leaving six months to complete the work. The evaluator and his team fleshed out this design in the course of conducting the evaluation, as will be discussed in subsequent chapters.

Task Order for the Evaluation

This example began when the commanding general's representative provided the evaluator with a task order and offered a sole-source contract. The key tasks were to (1) assess the strengths and weaknesses of the existing PRS, (2) identify and assess alternative personnel evaluation systems, (3) design a preferred system, and (4) develop a comprehensive plan for implementing the recommended system. The corps required the contractor to complete all four tasks within eight months, which, due to a lengthy award process and a fixed deadline for the final report, became a six-month period. Deliverables were monthly progress reports, a scheduled interim report for each task, and a final report. USMC also directed the contractor to brief the corps's sponsoring committee and its study advisory committee on each task report and the final report. Sitting on the sponsoring committee were eleven general officers, two sergeant majors, five colonels, four majors, and two captains. The members of the study advisory committee were a brigadier general, two lieutenant colonels, three majors, two captains, one sergeant major, and two civilian employees of the PRS. Separate sessions were scheduled to brief each committee on each report; these were to be conducted at USMC headquarters in Washington, D.C. Each printed report was to be delivered to the corps a minimum of ten working days prior to the scheduled briefing sessions. Given the extensive amount of needed work, the short time line, and the significance of the problem, the sponsor set no limit on the funds to be allocated to this project. The evaluator could request whatever amount of funding was required to do the job well and on time. The corps would make available to the contractor all relevant information concerning its PRS, assign staff officers to support and provide liaison to the evaluation project, provide meeting space and equipment at USMC headquarters, provide access to enlisted personnel and officers for interviews at USMC-Quantico headquarters base, and provide the needed funds.

Especially noteworthy in the task order was the corps's appointment of two panels to read and react to all evaluation reports, a requirement that the evaluators brief the panels on the reports, an explicit schedule of briefing sessions, and the fact that each panel was chaired by a high-ranking general officer. These highly responsible provisions by the study's sponsor did much to ensure that the client would critically review and use findings as appropriate. While it was also helpful that the corps allowed the evaluator and his team to interview marines, it was a decided limitation that this had to occur at the Quantico, Va. headquarters base, where the marines were under the close scrutiny of military leaders and might be expected to be less than candid about strengths and weaknesses of PRS procedures and leadership. As evident in subsequent chapters, the evaluator later sought and secured approval to observe PRS operations and interview marines at other bases, which yielded more candid responses than those obtained at the Quantico, Va. post. It is also noteworthy that the task order required the contractor to conduct evaluations of PRS and alternative personnel evaluation systems and also to produce plans for responding to the evaluation findings. While evaluators often prefer only to evaluate and not to recommend solutions, in this case combining the two types of tasks proved functional and in the interest of helping the corps improve its personnel evaluation system.

Need for the Evaluation Project

The corps had used the subject evaluation system for many years as the basis for retention, promotion, assignment, and mustering out decisions. Congress periodically allocates finite numbers of positions at each rank in each military service. The distribution of positions, in each service, from lower to higher ranks approximates a pyramid for both enlisted and officer ranks. For example, in the corps slots could be about nine thousand at the sergeant (E5) level but fewer than two hundred at the sergeant major (E9) level and, analogously, second lieutenants (O1) could number about three thousand compared with approximately four hundred colonels (O6). From the bottom to the top levels of ranks, there is increasing pressure to make room for new marines at each higher level. Of necessity, the corps (and all other military services) employs an up-or-out promotion system. Since each higher-level rank has fewer slots than the immediately lower rank, not all meritorious marines can be promoted. This is especially so at higher ranks. After a certain number of years in their rank, theoretically each marine has to make room for a newcomer. (An exception is when enlistments in the service are not fully meeting the requirements of a certain military specialty. In such cases, a marine with the high-need specialty could be retained even if he or she failed a promotion review.) Depending on the needs of the service, after a defined period of time in a rank, a marine typically must be promoted or mustered out.

The corps has a promotion board for each rank, and the boards must make the crucially important decisions of which marines to promote. They do so based largely on fitness reports prepared by the marine's immediate superior. The fitness report documents a senior's observations and assessment of the marine's performance, potential, and quality and is intended to be an accurate assessment of what is accomplished compared against job requirements. The supervisor is supposed to rate the marine against missions, tasks, and standards that previously were communicated to the marine and also against the marine's potential to serve at more senior levels and to accept ever-increasing responsibility. In making the ratings, the superior is expected to focus on known USMC values and the best of marine virtues and not on his or her personal preferences. At the lower ranks, almost all marines are promoted; for example, 95 percent of second lieutenants are promoted to first lieutenant, 88 percent of first lieutenants to captain, 75 percent of captains to major, 55 percent of majors to lieutenant colonel, and 48 percent of lieutenant colonels to colonel. Such percentages change from year to year depending on the needs of the service and the availability of marines at each rank for consideration to be promoted.

Over the years, the commanding officers' ratings of marines had become highly suspect, and the PRS had fallen into disrepute. Criticisms of the system included unrealistic performance standards for promotion, a rating scale that yielded unreliable assessments, subjective ratings that were subject to bias, rampant inflation in grading and reporting performance ratings, and the lack of a mechanism to audit ratings and correct invalid ratings. It had become common to rate marines who did not perform well down from "Outstanding" to "Excellent." The lower levels of the scale were rarely, if ever, used. Thus, there was little differentiation in the ratings. The rampant grade inflation made it hard for the corps's promotion boards to discern which marines most merited promotions. The PRS had lost credibility with many marines, including some who had been promoted by the system to the level of a general officer. Marines throughout the corps worried that promotion boards were using faulty evaluative information and making many poor or unjust promotions and mustering-out decisions. The suspected culprits were a faulty fitness report form and unreliable procedures for applying the form. Organizationwide concerns about the PRS were seen as impairing morale among the troops and possibly weakening the corps's ability to fight and help win wars.

The Evaluation Design

To investigate and address the problems in the PRS, the evaluator designed a project grounded in the Joint Committee's *The Personnel Evaluation Standards* (1988) and the CIPP evaluation model. The objectives listed below were identified as fully responsive to the evaluation needs underlying this project, but extending beyond the constraints of the corps's task order. Because the requested work was required to be completed within six months following contract approval, the project plan and budget realistically could be keyed only to completing the first four objectives and starting work on the fifth. The evaluator noted that based on the outcomes of the Phase 1 objectives, he and his group would be willing to undertake a follow-on project to assist the corps in fully achieving objective 5 and addressing objectives 6 through 14. He considered it important to apprise the corps of the full scope of needed work, but not to promise more than could be accomplished within six months.

Objectives

Following is the full set of fourteen recommended objectives, with the first five providing the basis for the contracted evaluation work:

Foundation for the Project

1. Adapt and adopt the Joint Committee's *Personnel Evaluation Standards* (1988) as the official standards of quality for the PRS.

Context Evaluation

2. Evaluate the current PRS against the adapted *Personnel Evaluation Standards* in order to identify strengths to be built on and problems to be solved or avoided.
3. Use the Objective 2 results and relevant research and development literature to determine with appropriate corps leadership the specifications for the new PRS.

Input Evaluation

4. Identify and develop alternative personnel evaluation systems and evaluate them against the *Personnel Evaluation Standards* and against the specifications for the new PRS.
5. Assist corps leaders to converge the best features of the alternative personnel evaluation systems into a sound design for the new PRS—including versions for evaluating the performance of officers, staff noncommissioned officers, and sergeants and provisions for auditing and correcting mistakes in individual personnel evaluations.

Process and Product Evaluations

6. Prepare a plan for testing and validating each version of the new PRS.
7. Train designated USMC personnel to field-test each version of the new PRS.
8. Conduct field tests, to include process and product evaluations.
9. Evaluate the implementation and results of the field tests.
10. Assist appropriate USMC leaders in making needed corrections to the new PRS.

Institutionalization of the New PRS

11. Prepare the implementation resources for each version of the PRS: manuals, instruments, report formats, funding plans, training materials, appeals mechanism, and so on.
12. Design procedures for the transition of current marines' performance assessment records into the new system.
13. Assist appropriate corps leaders to set up and install an ongoing process for monitoring each version of the new PRS and improving it as needed.
14. Assist appropriate corps leaders to set up and install an ongoing program for training USMC personnel to implement each version of the new PRS.

Required Features of the New PRS

In general, it is wise to restate or characterize a potential sponsor's criteria for evaluating the evaluand, as stated in the task order or RFP. Such a recapitulation can reassure the potential sponsor that you are giving appropriate consideration to the criteria they see as important. Summarizing the sponsor's stated evaluative criteria also helps the proposal writer conduct and communicate assessments in terms that the client values and understands. Of course, the evaluator must not acquiesce to inappropriate criteria or necessarily limit the evaluation to only the client's criteria. Given these provisos, the following is a characterization of USMC's criteria for a new PRS:

1. A clear framework for identifying marine duties to be assessed at several levels of experience and responsibility: supervisory, managerial, company and field grade officers, and executive
2. A sound, workable procedure for articulating appropriate performance expectations for promotion and other personnel actions for each evaluee
3. Sound, workable procedures to ensure validity, reliability, objectivity, and creditability in appraising how well an individual meets performance expectations
4. Clear rules and procedures for identifying the authorized users and uses of appraisal results
5. Specifications to ensure that performance records are appropriate for the intended uses
6. Effective means for clear communications of the appraisal results to the evaluee and authorized users
7. Appropriate measures to make the transition into the new PRS and fairly consider records of personnel whose performance was reported using the current system
8. An effective mechanism to hear appeals, audit the ratings, and correct invalid findings
9. Safeguards against ratings inflation
10. A mechanism for regularly assessing and improving each version of the PRS

The evaluator saw these criteria for a new PRS as entirely appropriate although not sufficient.

Standards of Sound Performance Evaluation

Beyond the sponsor-generated criteria, the evaluator recommended that the corps adopt a comprehensive set of professional standards of sound performance evaluation for use in evaluating the existing PRS and alternative personnel evaluation systems, designing the new PRS, and periodically reviewing and improving the new PRS. The set recommended was adapted from *The Personnel Evaluation Standards* (Joint Committee, 1988). The proposed standards require that performance evaluation systems be designed, implemented, and used to meet requirements of utility, propriety, feasibility, and accuracy. The specific standards recommended for each of these attributes are summarized below. As shown below, the evaluation contractor provided parenthesized commentary to help explain some of the standards.

Utility. The recommended utility standards are intended to guide evaluations so that they will be informative, timely, and influential for use in strengthening personnel performance and making personnel decisions:

> U1—Constructive Orientation. Performance evaluations should be constructive, so that they help USMC develop human resources and encourage and assist those evaluated to provide excellent service.

> U2—Defined Uses. The users and the intended uses of a performance evaluation should be defined, so that the evaluation can address appropriate questions and supply the needed information.

> (This standard requires the development of clear rules and procedures for identifying the authorized users and uses of appraisal results.)

> U3—Evaluator Credibility. The performance evaluation system should be managed and executed by persons with the necessary qualifications, skills, training, and authority; and evaluators should conduct themselves in a professional, even-handed manner, so that evaluation reports are respected and used.

> U4—Functional Reporting. Reports should be clear, timely, accurate, and germane, so that they are of practical value to the evaluee, supervisor, and other appropriate users.

> (This standard requires development of clear specifications to ensure that performance records are appropriate for the intended uses and that effective means are used to clearly communicate the appraisal results to the evaluee and authorized users.)

> U5 Follow-Up and Impact. Performance evaluations should be followed up, so that users and evaluees are aided to understand the results and take appropriate actions.

> (This standard requires development and application of appropriate procedures for the transition to the new system and fair consideration of performance evaluation records of personnel whose performance was reported using the current system.)

Propriety. The recommended propriety standards require that evaluations be conducted legally, ethically, and with due regard for fairness to evaluees, users of evaluation results, and persons supervised and served by the evaluees:

P1—Service Orientation. Evaluations of marines should promote sound principles of democracy, fulfillment of the corps's mission and objectives, and effective performance of duties, so that the corps faithfully and effectively fulfills its constitutional obligations to the United States.

(According to this standard, performance evaluations should be planned, conducted, and used so that each marine is required and supported to effectively serve her or his country by carrying out assigned, appropriate duties and so that, where indicated, sanctions that are in the best interest of the United States are enforced.)

P2—Formal Evaluation Guidelines. Guidelines for performance evaluations should be recorded in statements of policy and performance evaluation manuals, so that evaluations are consistent, equitable, in accordance with pertinent laws and military codes, and effectively carried out.

P3—Conflict of Interest. Conflicts of interest should be identified and dealt with openly and honestly, so that they do not compromise the evaluation process and results.

(This standard reflects the fact that conflicts of interest are inherent in any system where the supervisor evaluates the subordinate and must be controlled through effective mechanisms such as the use of independent evaluators; complete, factual service records; self-reports; appeals mechanisms; and regular monitoring and assessment of the evaluation system.)

P4—Access to Performance Evaluation Reports. Access to reports of performance evaluation should be limited to individuals with a legitimate need to review and use the reports, so that appropriate use of information is ensured.

(In accordance with this standard, there must be clear rules and procedures for limiting access to performance evaluation records to appropriately authorized persons.)

P5—Interaction with Evaluees. The evaluation should address evaluees in a professional, fair manner, so that their motivation, service reputations, self-esteem, and attitude toward performance appraisal are enhanced, or at least not needlessly and unfairly damaged.

(In keeping with this standard, performance evaluation should be conveyed and employed as a mechanism to enhance performance and pride in excellent service and to provide a fair basis for personnel decisions, not as a tool to intimidate, discourage, or mete out punishment.)

Feasibility. The recommended feasibility standards call for evaluation systems that are as easy to implement as possible, efficient in their use of time and resources, adequately funded to effectively maintain and improve evaluations, and viable within the context of the environment:

> F1—Practical Procedures. Performance evaluation procedures should be planned and conducted, so that they produce needed information while minimizing disruption and cost.
>
> (Wherever possible, the data collection activities for performance evaluation should be integrated into the ongoing process of supervision, personnel records, and personnel decision making.)
>
> F2—Political Viability. Performance evaluation procedures should be planned and conducted, so that representatives of all concerned parties are constructively involved in designing the system, testing it, and making it work.
>
> (In keeping with this standard, it will be important to keep interested parties informed about the professional nature of the development process through an effective communication process.)
>
> F3—Fiscal Viability. Adequate time and resources should be provided for performance evaluation activities, so that evaluation plans can be effectively and efficiently implemented.
>
> (To meet this standard it will be especially important to provide for the ongoing training, calibrating, and monitoring of evaluators.)

Accuracy. The accuracy standards require that the obtained information be technically accurate and that conclusions be linked logically to the data:

> A1—Defined Role. The role, responsibilities, performance objectives, and needed qualifications of the evaluee should be clearly defined, so that the evaluator can determine valid assessment data.
>
> (In accordance with this standard, these definitions should be derived from a clear, official framework for identifying marine duties at several levels of experience and responsibility: supervisory, managerial, company and field grade officers, and executive. There also should be a sound, workable procedure for articulating appropriate performance expectations for promotion and other personnel actions for each evaluee. There should be procedures for reviewing and updating performance criteria as appropriate.)

A2—Work Environment. The context in which the evaluee works should be identified, described, and recorded, so that environmental influences and constraints on performance can be considered in the evaluation.

A3—Documentation of Procedures. The evaluation procedures followed should be documented, so that the evaluees and other users can assess the actual, in relation to intended, procedures.

(In keeping with this standard it is especially important that evaluators should be required to cite the duties evaluated, the evidence used to reach judgments and recommendations, how the evidence was obtained, and why it is considered sufficient and credible.)

A4—Valid Measurement. The data collection and rating procedures should be chosen or developed and implemented on the basis of the described role and the intended use, so that the inferences concerning the evaluee are valid.

(To meet this standard, these procedures should be a matter of record well before the performance evaluation is completed.)

A5—Reliable Measurement. Data collection and rating procedures should be chosen or developed to ensure reliability, so that the information obtained will provide consistent indications of the performance of the evaluee.

A6—Systematic Data Control. The information used in the evaluation should be kept secure and should be carefully processed and maintained, so as to ensure that the data maintained and analyzed are the same as the data collected.

A7—Bias Control. The evaluation process should provide safeguards against bias, so that the evaluee's performance is assessed fairly.

(To meet this standard requires an effective mechanism to review evaluations, hear appeals, audit ratings, and correct invalid findings. Explicit safeguards against ratings inflation must be built into the system.)

A8—Monitoring Evaluation Systems. The personnel evaluation system should be reviewed periodically and systematically against the above twenty standards, so that appropriate revisions can be made.

(Meeting this standard requires a mechanism for regularly assessing and improving the PRS and for explicitly protecting against grade inflation.)

At the outset of the evaluation, the corps readily embraced the recommended standards and the associated parenthesized comments. It is noteworthy that it asked for only two changes in the standards, both in the area of Feasibility. One change was to rename the Political Viability standard "Consensus Development." (USMC leaders did not want anyone to think they were trying to be politically correct.) The other change was to add a standard called "Transition to the New PRS." This added standard required provision for systematic adoption and installation of the new evaluation system. The evaluator and his team judged both changes to be sound and appropriate to the situation. The adapted standards then became the official USMC standards for assessing and improving the personnel evaluation system.

The General Study Plan

The evaluator next presented a general plan for the evaluation. It stated that the evaluation project would be divided into five main tasks: (1) project organization and background analysis (weeks 1 through 6), (2) a context evaluation of the current PRS (weeks 3 through 10), (3) an input evaluation to identify and analyze alternative performance evaluation systems and literature review (weeks 7 though 18), (4) preparation and reporting of conclusions and recommendations for a new PRS (weeks 19 through 26), and (5) beginning efforts to plan for development and implementation of the proposed new PRS (weeks 27 through 34).

Correlated with the above tasks, the evaluator projected that the evaluation project would provide five main reports to the study sponsor, at a pace of about one per month. Evaluation team members were designated as E for the principal investigator and E1, E2, E3, E4, and E5 for other team members. The projected reports were as follows:

Finalized Project Plan

- Including preliminary background analysis of PRS and proposed PRS standards
- Principal authors: E and E2
- For delivery during week 6

Evaluation of the Current PRS (Context Evaluation)

- Including comparison of the current PRS to the PRS standards and proposed specifications for the new PRS
- Principal authors: E3 and E4
- For delivery during week 10

Evaluation of Alternative PRS's (Input Evaluation)

- Including descriptions of promising systems used in other branches of the military and in business and industry; comparison of these systems to designated standards; and literature review

- Principal authors: E5, E6, and E1
- For delivery during week 18

Conclusions and Recommendations

- Including conclusions about the reasons for the failure of the present PRS, the merits of alternative PRSs, and a general design for the new PRS
- Principal authors: E, E1, E2, and E4
- For delivery during week 26

*Plan for Development and Implementation of the Proposed New PRS
(including Process and Product Evaluation plans)*

- Draft plans for operationalizing, field-testing, correcting, and installing the proposed new PRS
- Principal authors: E, E1, and E6
- For delivery during week 34

Project Personnel

The evaluation project tasks were to be performed by a central project team and three associated task groups, with the evaluator serving as project director. The team members, their project assignments, and their most pertinent areas of expertise were as follows:

E: Project director—Personnel evaluation standards

E1: Project manager—Project management

E2: Context evaluation task group chair—Performance measurement

E3: Context evaluation task group member—Statistics and computer technology

E4: Input evaluation/PRS alternatives task group chair—Personnel psychology

E5: Input evaluation/PRS alternative task group member—Military evaluation systems

The proposal included résumés for all proposed key project personnel. All members arguably were among the nation's top professionals in their specialties, and three of them had relevant military experience.

The central project team was designated to review and finalize reports from the three project task groups and ultimately to be responsible for reporting project conclusions and recommendations. This team was configured to include experts in personnel evaluation standards (E), personnel psychology (E4), performance measurement (E2), military personnel evaluation systems (E5), and project management (E1). The team's core responsibility was to serve as the project's working board. In addition to participating in team decision making, each member was given a major project task assignment.

The project management task group members were E, E1, a secretary, and two research assistants. The evaluator (E) would oversee the work and ensure that it was consistent with the project's policies. Serving as project manager, E1 would hire the needed staff, provide them with necessary orientation and training, coordinate the work of the involved personnel, provide staff support to the central project team, keep the project on schedule and within budget, and ensure that reports were prepared and delivered in a timely manner. The secretary would have charge of report production, final technical editing of reports, and control of project information. E1's assistant would conduct the literature review and be in charge of drafting the task 5 report on planning and implementing the new PRS.

The context evaluation task group members were E2 as chair, E3, and two research associates. This group was slated to analyze the corps's existing PRS against the adopted personnel evaluation standards and the requirements of the task order. It would report its findings to the central project team and assist the team in finalizing its report on the evaluation of the current PRS.

The input evaluation/PRS alternatives task group members were E4 as chair, E5, and a research associate. This group was assigned to search out, describe, and evaluate the alternative PRSs against the selected standards and the task order requirements. It would report its findings on the state of the art reflected in alternative personnel evaluation systems to the central project team.

This proposal acknowledged that the corps's sponsoring committee and study advisory committee and their designated representatives would provide ongoing oversight of the team's project work. Also, the proposal projected that the evaluator would deliver reports and provide in-person briefings to these committees approximately as follows:

During week 6: Final project plan

During week 10: Context evaluation of the current PRS

During week 18: Input evaluation of alternative PRSs and literature review

During week 26: Conclusions and recommendations

During week 34: Plan for developing, implementing, and evaluating through process and product evaluations each version of the new PRS

Project Performance Plan

Building on the general plan, the proposal provided a schedule of work. The project's tasks and subtasks are listed below, followed by the scheduled period for the work. Project personnel slated to carry out each subtask are noted in parentheses after each subtask.

Task 1: Organization and Background Analysis (weeks 1 through 6)

1. Prepare the project plan, obtain USMC and university approval, and choose project personnel—weeks 1 and 2: E, four days; E1, five days; secretary, two days
2. Hire project staff—weeks 1 through 3: E1, ten days
3. Plan for, conduct, and follow up a meeting with USMC's Manpower Analysis, Evaluation, and Coordination Branch (MA) to establish protocols, clarify roles and responsibilities, and present initial documentation and data requirements—during week 2: E, two days; E1, three days; secretary, one day
4. Obtain and analyze pertinent documentation of the present PRS—weeks 2 and 3: E, two days; E1, four days; research associate, ten days; secretary, three days
5. Prepare for, conduct, and follow up three-day organizational team meeting; review project plan and PRS materials; make assignments; update the project schedule; and agree on a set of evaluation standards to recommend—weeks 3 and 4: E, five days; secretary, nine days; E1, six days; research associate, five days; E2, three days; E3, three days; E4, three days; E5, three days
6. Prepare first report to include an updated project plan, a recommended set of standards for judging personnel evaluation systems, and procedures and instrumentation for applying the standards—weeks 5 and 6: E, two days; E1, three days; secretary, 3 days
7. Deliver first report to the corps's Evaluation Office (EO) in Washington, D.C., during week 6: E, one day; E1, one day

Task 2: Context Evaluation of the Existing System (weeks 3 through 10)

1. Reach agreement with EO's commanding general by conference telephone call on the professional standards to be applied to the evaluation system—about week 7: E, one day; E1, one day; E2, one day; E4, one day; E1's assistant, one day; EO representatives
2. Follow up the conference telephone call in task 2.1 by compiling and distributing the agreed-on standards to all participants in the project—during week 8: E, one day; E1, two days; E1's assistant, one day; secretary, one day

3. Develop a descriptive report on how the current PRS and fitness report systems are intended to operate and how they actually operate—during weeks 3 and 4: E1, three days; research associate, eight days; secretary, three days

4. Develop a report reviewing and analyzing completed studies of PRS and the relevant literature—during weeks 3, 4, and 5: E1, three days; research associate, four days; secretary, three days

5. Develop a report proposing a preliminary list of performance qualities that should be measured by a corps unique evaluation system—during weeks 3 and 4: E1, two days; research associate, four days; secretary, two days

6. Plan, conduct, and follow up a two-day meeting to provide orientation to the context evaluation task group and launch their evaluation of the current PRS—during week 7: E, four days; E1, four days; E2, three days; E3, four days; research associate, three days; secretary, five days

7. Augment the literature review, prepare an updated report focused on the strengths and weaknesses of alternative personnel evaluation systems, and distribute the report—during weeks 7 and 8: E, one day; E1, two days; research associate, four days; secretary, three days

8. Plan, conduct, and follow up a meeting for two days to evaluate the current PRS by applying the adapted and adopted *Personnel Evaluation Standards* and USMC's requirements for the new system—during week 8: E, three days; E1, four days; E2, three days; E3, six days; research associate, three days

9. Prepare a context evaluation report on the evaluation of the current PRS, proposing requirements to be met by the new system, and submit the report to E1—during week 10: E2, one day; E3, four days; research associate, two days

10. Deliver finalized context evaluation report—during week 11: E, one day; E1, one day

Task 3: Input Evaluation to Identify and Evaluate Alternative Personnel Evaluation Systems (weeks 9 through 20)

1. Plan, conduct, and follow up a two-day meeting to provide orientation to the Input Evaluation/PRS Alternatives Task Group, familiarizing them with the Task 2 report—during weeks 10 or 11: E, three days; E1, four days; E4, three days; E5, two days; research associate, three days

2. Prepare a report identifying, reviewing, and analyzing alternative performance evaluation systems used by other U.S. armed services, federal agencies, or appropriate civilian organizations, and submit the report to E1. Assess the appropriateness and validity of the identified systems as a tool for retaining, promoting, and assigning the career force by assessing them against the adapted and adopted *Personnel Evaluation Standards* and task order requirements for the

new PRS—weeks 7 through 16: E1, one day; E4, four days; E5, three days; research associate, six days; secretary, four days

3. Plan, conduct, and follow up a two-day meeting of the central project team to review and reach agreements for finalizing the input evaluation report identifying and assessing alternative personnel evaluation systems and to update the plan for the remainder of the project—approximately week 12: E, three days; E1, four days; E2, two days; E3, two days; E4, two days; E5, two days; research associate, four days

4. Finalize the Input Evaluation/Task 3 Report—during weeks 17 and 18: E, one day; secretary, one day

5. Deliver Input Evaluation/Task 3 Report—during week 19: E, one day; E1, one day

A unique aspect of the corps's task order for this project is its requirement that the contractor evaluate PRS to identify its flaws and also propose a solution. Many evaluators would resist taking responsibility to recommend solutions to identified problems. They might argue correctly that an evaluation of an evaluand can identify its strengths and weaknesses but that such findings do not point to the best corrective actions. In this case, the evaluation team successfully addressed the issue of providing recommendations by conducting a context evaluation to diagnose problems in the corps's personnel evaluation system and subsequently conducting an input evaluation to identify and assess alternative personnel evaluation systems that might replace the corps's PRS. Conducting distinct but related context and input evaluations is an apt and defensible way for evaluators to address a client's request for evaluations that both identify problems and recommend solutions.

Task 4: Conclusions and Recommendations (weeks 19 through 27)

1. Plan, conduct, and follow up a three-day meeting of the central project team to draft recommendations, including a preferred evaluation system, a field-test and validation plan (including process and product evaluation designs), and a timetable for installation—during weeks 19 through 21: E, five days; E1, seven days; E2, three days; E3, three days; E4, three days; E5, three days; research associate, five days

2. Finalize the Conclusions and Recommendations Report, including conclusions about the reasons for the failure of the existing PRS, the merits of alternative personnel evaluation systems, and a design for a new PRS that builds on the Context Evaluation/Task 2 and Input Evaluation/Task 3 reports and meets the requirements of the task order and the adapted and adopted personnel evaluation standards—during weeks 22 through 26: E, two days; E1, two days]; research associate, three days; secretary, two days

3. Deliver the Conclusions and Recommendations Report—during week 27: E, one day; E1, two days; E2, one day], E4, one day

Task 5: Planning for Development, Evaluation, and Implementation of the Proposed New PRS (weeks 27 through 34)

1. Meet in Washington, D.C., with USMC representatives to reach agreement on steps to follow up the Conclusions and Recommendations Report—approximately week 27: E, one day; E1, two days
2. Draft a plan for development, evaluation, and implementation of the new PRS—during weeks 18 through 30: E, two days; E1, seven days; research associate, ten days; secretary, three days
3. Plan, conduct, and follow up a two-day meeting to critique and improve the implementation plan—weeks 31 and 32: E, three days; E1, four days; E2, two days; E3, two days; E4, two days; E5, two days; secretary, four days
4. Finalize the implementation plan for submission to USMC—weeks 29 through 33: E, two days; E1, four days; research associate, eight days; secretary, six days
5. Deliver plan for development, evaluation, and implementation of the new PRS—week 34: E, two days; E1, two days

The initial design for this evaluation project was general. It did not specify the data collection, analysis, and reporting procedures. Instead, the evaluator's proposal stated that, once funded, the project's first task would be to produce the needed specific procedures. The project staff would develop such items as interview protocols, specifications for sampling interviewees, a plan for sampling and analyzing fitness reports, and scales and procedures for rating personnel evaluation systems against the personnel evaluation standards. Given the short time line to design and carry out the project and the evaluation team members' needs to become acquainted with the corps, it was both realistic and prudent to delay specific design decisions until the project got under way. Even in other situations where the time line is not short, evaluators can benefit by conducting a small planning project before committing to specific evaluation procedures. An initial "get acquainted" planning project can help the evaluators develop rapport with program stakeholders, acquire insights of use in planning the evaluation, and agree on criteria for judging the evaluand. Once the PRS evaluation project got started, the evaluator and USMC's leaders agreed that the entire improvement project should be grounded in an officially adopted set of professional standards for sound personnel evaluations. This plan was based on the assumption that the project team would have approximately eight months to complete the work; thus, the thirty-four-week schedule of work. However, the corps took two months to process the contract and the thirty-four-week plan had to be compressed into about twenty-five weeks. Later, when the evaluator and corps agreed that some additional work should be done, USMC issued a supplementary contract for about seven additional weeks of work. These developments illustrate that evaluation design often needs to be an ongoing process.

Principal Features of the Case

The evaluation design explored here was general in nature and therefore incomplete. However, it was sufficiently specific to win a $440,000 contract. The CIPP model formed the structure for this problem-solving project. The context, input, process, and product components, respectively, would investigate the following major questions: What deficiencies in the existing PRS need to be corrected? What alternative approach would meet the need for improvement best? Is the chosen new approach being carried out as intended? Is it promoting the most deserving marines? The sponsor had not sought competitive bids but had chosen the evaluator for this assignment. No doubt the sponsor had found the chosen evaluator's track record and reputation to be relevant and strong and had judged that he and his team would conduct the project competently and on time and would design the details for the project. We acknowledge these idiosyncratic characteristics of the evaluation because evaluators often have to provide much more detail in their evaluation proposals than set out in the example. Clearly, each evaluation opportunity has its unique characteristics, and the evaluator should consider these when deciding how much specificity to include in the initial evaluation design. At a minimum, the prospective contractor must put forth a general methodological approach, such as this case's employment of the CIPP model, and show its relevance to the particular evaluation. Usually, however, the evaluator must flesh out the evaluation design as the study unfolds.

A Generic Checklist for Designing Evaluations

We now offer a generic evaluation design checklist that evaluators and their clients can use to plan the full range of relevant evaluation operations in the needed level of detail. The evaluation design checklist appears in Exhibit 21.1. The checklist is intended as both an advance organizer and a reminder of key matters to be considered before and during an evaluation. We will illustrate the latter application of the checklist by noting how the evaluation team delineated key aspects of their evaluation of the USMC PRS. This checklist is based on the first named author's Evaluation Design Checklist available at www.wmich.edu/evalctr/checklists.

EXHIBIT 21.1. EVALUATION DESIGN CHECKLIST.

A. Focusing the Evaluation

1. Determine and clarify the evaluand and client.

2. Identify the major levels of evaluation audiences, for example, program leaders, staff, and recipients.

3. Identify each audience's questions, information needs, and concerns about the evaluation.

4. Identify parties who might be harmed by the evaluation, and obtain their input.

5. Examine the background of the request for the evaluation and its social and political contexts.

6. Identify and address potential barriers to the evaluation, for example, the need to gather sensitive information, access to all the relevant information, human subject review requirements, requirements for confidentiality or anonymity, opponents of the evaluation, conflicts of interest, issues of race and language, indirect cost rate, and availability of needed funds.

7. Identify and review relevant information, for example, previous evaluations of the evaluand, evaluations of similar evaluands, pertinent literature, and relevant needs assessments.

8. Agree with the client on standards for guiding and assessing the evaluation.

9. Agree with the client on the evaluation model or approach to be applied.

10. Agree with the client on the time frame, the evaluators, key evaluation questions, required reports, client and stakeholder responsibilities, and allowable cost for the evaluation.

11. Advise the client to fund an independent metaevaluation.

12. Decide whether to proceed with the assignment.

B. Collecting Information

1. Consider collecting a wide range of information about the evaluand: context, history, beneficiaries, benefactors, goals and structure, contrast to similar evaluands, schedule, resources, costs, staff, implementation, main effects, side effects, reputation, judgments by stakeholders and experts, sustainability, and transportability, for example.

2. Choose the framework for collecting information: case study, sample survey, field experiment, or a multimethod study, for example.

3. Determine the information sources: documents, files, databases, financial records, beneficiaries, staff, funders, experts, government officials, or community interest groups.

4. Determine the information collection instruments and methods, for example, interviews, participant observers, focus groups, literature review, search of archives, Delphi, survey, rating scales, knowledge tests, debates, site visits, photography, video records, log diaries, goal-free study, or case study.

5. Specify the sampling procedures for each source: purposive, probability, or convenience.

6. Seek to address each main question with multiple methods and data points.

7. Schedule information collection, denoting times when each information source and each method will be engaged.

EXHIBIT 21.1. EVALUATION DESIGN CHECKLIST, Cont'd.

8. Assign responsibilities for information collection.

9. Give the client and other interested parties a rationale for the information collection plan.

10. Review the information collection plan's feasibility with the client, and consider making prudent reductions.

C. Organizing Information

1. Develop plans and assignments for coding, verifying, filing, controlling, and retrieving information.

2. Design a database for the obtained information, including appropriate software.

3. Specify the equipment, facilities, materials, and personnel required to process and control the evaluation's information.

D. Analyzing Information

1. Identify bases for interpreting findings, such as beneficiaries' needs, objectives, standards, norms, the evaluand's previous costs and performance, costs and performance of similar evaluands, and judgments by experts and program stakeholders.

2. Specify qualitative analysis procedures, for example, thematic analysis, content analysis, summaries, scenarios, or contrasts of photographs.

3. Specify quantitative analysis procedures; examples are descriptive statistics; trend analysis; cost analysis; significance tests for main effects, interactions, and simple effects; effect parameter analysis; meta-analysis; item analysis; factor analysis; regression analysis; and charts, tables, and graphs.

4. Select appropriate computer programs to facilitate quantitative and qualitative analyses.

5. Plan to search for trends, patterns, and themes in the qualitative information.

6. Plan to contrast different subsets of qualitative and quantitative information to identify both corroborative and contradictory findings.

7. Plan to address each evaluative question by referencing and citing the relevant qualitative and quantitative information.

8. Plan to use qualitative information to elaborate and explain quantitative findings.

9. Plan to state caveats as appropriate in consideration of any inconclusive or contradictory findings.

10. Plan to synthesize quantitative and qualitative information, for example, by embedding quantitative information within a qualitative narrative or by embedding interview responses and other qualitative findings in the discussion of quantitative findings.

11. Anticipate that the client or other stakeholders may require recommendations to correct problems identified in the findings, and be prepared to explain that the same data that uncovered the problems are unlikely to provide valid direction for solving the problems

12. Consider planning a follow-up project to generate and validly assess alternative courses of action for solving identified problems; such procedures might include an input evaluation of available alternative solution strategies, creation and evaluation of new solution strategies, engagement of relevant experts, review of relevant literature, or a working conference to chart and assess possible courses of action.

EXHIBIT 21.1. EVALUATION DESIGN CHECKLIST, Cont'd.

E. Reporting Information

1. Clarify the audiences for evaluation reports, for example, the program's client, staff, policy board, and beneficiaries.

2. Identify reports needed by different audiences, such as interim, final, or component-specific reports; context, input, process, and product evaluation reports; technical appendixes; executive summary; and an internal metaevaluation report.

3. For each report, determine the appropriate formats, such as printed, oral, electronic, multimedia, storytelling, or sociodrama.

4. Outline the contents of at least the main reports, showing how findings from different sources and methods will be synthesized to answer the main evaluation questions.

5. Consider dividing the final report into three subreports: Program Antecedents (for those who need background information), Program Implementation (for those who would replicate the program), and Program Results (for the entire audience).

6. In technical appendixes, plan to include résumés of evaluation staff and consultants, information collection instruments and protocols, reports of findings for particular data collection procedures, data tables, a log of data collection activities, a list of interim reports, the evaluation contract, a summary of evaluation costs, and an internal account of how well the evaluation met the standards of the evaluation profession.

7. Develop a plan and schedule for delivering reports to the right-to-know audiences

8. As appropriate, obtain prerelease reviews of draft reports.

9. Conduct feedback workshops to assist the client group in reviewing and discussing draft evaluation reports.

F. Administering the Evaluation

1. Delineate the evaluation schedule.

2. Define and plan to meet staff and resource requirements.

3. Ensure that the evaluation plan is sufficient to meet pertinent standards of the evaluation field.

4. Provide for at least internal formative and summative metaevaluations.

5. Delineate a budget for the evaluation.

6. Negotiate an evaluation contract, specifying audiences, evaluator responsibilities and protocols, and editorial and dissemination responsibility and authority.

7. Provide for reviewing and updating the evaluation plan and contract as needed.

Source: Daniel L. Stufflebeam.

As evident in Exhibit 21.1, the logical structure of evaluation design includes elements that commonly apply to a wide range of evaluation assignments and alternative evaluation approaches. The checklist is intended as a generic guide to decisions that typically need to be considered when planning and conducting an evaluation. The checkpoints are especially relevant when responding to a potential client's request for a demanding, complex evaluation. However, the checklist is intended for use across a broad range of evaluation assignments, both small and large, and for use with a number of approaches to evaluation. It may be used alone or in combination with other checklists. For example, it could be used with the checklists we present in subsequent chapters concerned with budgeting and contracting for evaluations, reporting evaluation findings, and conducting metaevaluations. When the contemplated evaluation is small and will have only a modest budget, evaluators and their clients can find it useful to consider the full range of evaluation design issues before setting aside those that are not feasible, not particularly relevant to the situation, and not especially important. Since this checklist is intended for evaluators who work under very different circumstances and constraints, the user will need to exercise wise judgment and discretion in determining and applying its most applicable parts pursuant to the needs of particular evaluations.

Although the checklist is an ordered list of elements commonly included in evaluation designs, these elements should not necessarily be treated in a strict linear sequence. Often evaluators cycle through the elements repeatedly while planning for and negotiating an evaluation and also during the course of the evaluation. In each such cycle, some elements are addressed, and others typically are set aside for attention later or abandoned because they do not apply to the particular situation. As noted in the example in this chapter, evaluation design is as much process as product. In using this checklist, the objective should be to develop an evaluation plan for a sound, responsive, and effective evaluation over time. We will look briefly at each section of the checklist, paying particular attention to how it applies to the evaluation of the USMC personnel evaluation system.

Focusing the Evaluation

When first considering an opportunity to conduct an evaluation, the evaluator should carefully focus the projected work in order to lay a sound foundation for the contemplated study. A careful preliminary investigation is also important for ensuring that it would be wise to proceed. Sometimes an evaluator will learn through early investigation and deliberations with interested parties that it is not in the cards to conduct a professionally responsible evaluation. For example, the client may want to use the evaluation to kill a program, whatever the evaluation findings. Or the client may insist on editing the final report. The evaluator should smoke out such illicit reasons for an evaluation, obtain the needed remedies, or reject the assignment. More positively, the twelve checkpoints provide a valuable guide for putting a defensible evaluation assignment on solid ground.

Essentially, the task order and evaluation design presented in the first part of this chapter satisfactorily addressed the focusing checkpoints and incorporated the up-front agreements in the originally approved evaluation plan. Two exceptions can be mentioned. First, regarding checkpoint A.6, it was not clear at the evaluation's outset that USMC would restrict the evaluators to interviewing only marines who were present at the Quantico, Virginia, headquarters base. During the evaluation, it became evident that the evaluators should interview marines on other bases, who more likely would give candid assessments of the PRS. At first, the corps's leadership denied access to marines on other bases. Ultimately, however, this decision was reversed; the corps issued a supplementary contract, and the evaluators obtained the needed interviews. This example illustrates the importance of negotiating matters that are vital to the evaluation's success before signing a contract. It also illustrates that design issues sometimes need to be renegotiated during a study.

A second exception to the evaluation example on meeting all focusing checkpoints concerns checkpoint A.11. For whatever reason, the evaluators did not advise USMC leaders to fund an independent metaevaluation. Essentially, the two USMC panels provided this function by reviewing all of the evaluation reports. Ultimately, the corps commandant provided the evaluators with a unit citation for outstanding service to the corps. The evaluators were proud to accept this judgment as one kind of important independent metaevaluation. Nevertheless, one could fault the evaluation of PRS because it did not specifically recommend that USMC fund an independent evaluation of the evaluation team's work and reports.

Collecting Information

The second category of checkpoints in Exhibit 21.1 deals with the core issue of collecting information from which to judge an evaluand. Checkpoint B.1 advises the evaluator to consider collecting a wide range of information, such as the evaluand's background, structure, activities, costs, other resources, and outcomes. To obtain the selected information, checkpoint B.2 calls for choice of an appropriate information collection framework, which often will entail a combination of methods. Checkpoints B.3 through B.7 ask for details concerning information sources, instruments and methods, and sampling procedures and how information will be combined to answer each evaluative question. Checkpoints B.7 and

B.8 require developing an information collection schedule and assigning responsibilities for collecting the information. The final two checkpoints in this category involve justifying the information collection plan and considering whether it should be reduced. The information collection checkpoints can all be considered when first planning an evaluation. Realistically, however, decisions on many of these matters often are made as an evaluation proceeds, and even then may have to be revised later.

The military evaluation example initially addressed the information collection checkpoints by employing the CIPP model, which calls for collecting a wide range of information under the labels of context, input, process, and product evaluation. Once the evaluation was funded, the context and input evaluation task groups developed and implemented specific data collection plans.

The context evaluation task group pursued a multimethod approach. Among the methods employed were the following:

- Content analysis of past evaluations of PRS
- Examination of recorded problems, recommended improvements, and subsequent actions drawn from previous evaluations of PRS and from a succession of action reports
- Content analysis of PRS regulations, procedures, and forms
- Content analysis of the stock and code phrases in an unofficial guide, commonly known to and used by marine corps supervisors for writing fitness reports
- Preparation and use of interview guides to obtain information from a cross-section of marines and members of promotion boards
- Mailed survey to a representative sample of sergeants being reviewed for promotion
- Obtaining and analyzing promotion records in terms of ranks, military specialties, gender, race, and venues of service
- Computer-based content analysis of a sample of seventy-five thousand fitness reports and promotion results
- Observation of sessions to train supervisors in evaluating subordinates
- Construction and application of a scale for rating the PRS against the corps's adapted and adopted personnel evaluation standards and for listing strengths and weaknesses for each standard

The input evaluation team implemented a two-stage study. First, it conducted case studies of the personnel evaluation systems of four U.S. military services, two foreign country military services, and two U.S. private corporations. It subsequently rated and listed strengths and weaknesses of each system against the corps's adopted personnel evaluation standards. Since none of the systems re-

viewed satisfactorily met the twenty-one applicable standards, the input evaluation team next conducted an advocate teams study. This first entailed engaging
three teams to study the information so far amassed and using it to create three
competitive proposals for a new PRS. Once these proposals were generated, the
evaluation's central project team rated each one, listed its strengths and weaknesses
against each of the twenty-one applicable standards, and reported the findings to
corps's sponsoring committee.

Organizing Information

Evaluations require an effective approach to information management. For each
set of information, the evaluator needs to follow systematic steps to ensure its accuracy and security. Some data must be coded for later summary and analysis,
and some will need to be keyed into a computer. In all such operations, the evaluator should train those who will carry out the work, supervise them, regularly
check their work for accuracy, and ensure that only authorized personnel access
and use the stored information. As seen in checkpoint C.3, after developing an
information management plan, the evaluator should arrange for the needed
equipment, facilities, materials, and personnel needed to process and control the
evaluation's information.

Early in an evaluation, the evaluator needs to establish a functional system to
file, control, and retrieve information that directly reflects the evaluation's structure. Although no one system of categories would apply to all evaluations, general examples can be offered. Materials involved in focusing the evaluation could
include the task order or RFP; proposal; contract; budget; human subjects review
records; staff; consultants; evaluative standards and criteria; correspondence fold-
ers for key participants; pertinent background reports and literature; the evaluation
schedule; and rules for accessing, using, and returning filed information. Information collection files could be divided into each method or instrument, sampling
plans, information sources and their protocols, information collection assignments,
plans and materials for training information collection personnel, news clippings,
and specific data collection schedules. Information analysis materials could include analysis plans for all sets of information, plans for synthesizing findings from
different sets of information, information analysis assignments, and pertinent computer programs. The section on reporting could include draft and final versions
of all reports, records of stakeholder critiques of draft reports, technical appendixes, multimedia materials to support presentations of findings, and plans for
presenting findings.

A functional evaluation project filing system should have clear rules and
arrangements for keeping the information secure, while giving evaluation team

members ready access to pertinent information. The lead evaluator should establish a list of personnel who can access and use the information. In many evaluations, the evaluator should remove or have removed the identities of individuals associated with given evaluation records before making them available to evaluation team members for review and analysis. Evaluation project files should be maintained in locked filing cabinets in lockable offices and be controlled by an evaluation team member such as the project secretary. It is also a good idea to have a system for signing a log sheet before checking out a piece of information. In general, the rules and procedures of any good library apply to the control and use of evaluation project records.

In some evaluations, it is appropriate to establish and maintain a database, especially if one is to track and record the performance of an evaluand over time. The establishment and use of such a database requires selection of appropriate computer software and a process and assignments for checking, coding, verifying, and recording data. The evaluator needs to ensure that those who are charged to carry out the database functions are appropriately trained and supervised. Provisions should be made to keep such information secure and accessible only to authorized persons.

Analyzing Information

This section of the checklist provides a detailed list of suggestions for analyzing evaluative information. These suggestions basically are self-explanatory, and we will make only some supporting general observations about analysis issues. Further discussion and specific examples are provided in Chapter Twenty-Five.

In general, analyses in evaluations should be keyed to answering the basic evaluation questions and judging the evaluand. As seen in checkpoint D.1, optional bases for judging a program's merit and worth include assessed needs of beneficiaries, program objectives, professional standards (such as were employed in this chapter's military evaluation case), national or state norms, a previous level of performance, performance by similar evaluands, and judgments of the evaluand rendered by pertinent experts or beneficiaries. Together the evaluator and client should determine the bases that will be most appropriate in the particular study.

To develop and support judgments of an evaluand against the selected bases, the evaluator needs to employ systematic analyses of both qualitative and quantitative information. The technical literature of research and evaluation contains a rich cornucopia of pertinent methods, as is evident in checkpoints D.2 and D.3, plus a wide range of relevant computer programs. The evaluator needs to choose methods and software that address the key evaluation questions and whose assumptions can be met by the available information. Often it will not be possible to meet a procedure's required assumptions perfectly concerning such matters as the nature of the measurement scale, randomization of subjects, and independence of observations. In such cases, it can be especially useful to employ multiple analysis procedures to a given data set in order to provide checks and balances on findings from the different analysis techniques. In general, it is good analysis practice to contrast different subsets of qualitative and quantitative information to identify both corroborative and contradictory findings.

Ultimately the evaluator needs to synthesize results from analyses of the different sets of information. The objectives of the synthesis are to combine findings to answer each evaluation question and reach bottom-line judgments of the evaluand. In presenting these judgments, we think it is useful to organize conclusions regarding the evaluand's merit or quality, its worth in addressing beneficiaries' needs, its superiority to other objects based on cost-effectiveness, its significance for use in other settings, and its probity as an ethical response to the beneficiaries' needs.

Some final words are in order regarding recommendations. In typical evaluations, the resultant information and analyses do not provide justifiable bases for making recommendations on how to improve or, especially, replace the evaluand. The reason is that the evaluator has not gathered and analyzed information about such matters as the merit, worth, and cost-effectiveness of the contemplated recommendations. Typically, the latter are conceptualized or identified through group deliberations, but are not grounded in empirical study. It can be misleading and professionally irresponsible to advance recommendations that rest on flimsy grounds. An exception is seen in the input evaluation component of the CIPP model. In a follow-up input evaluation, an evaluator would systematically generate and validly assess alternative courses of action for solving problems that were identified by the original evaluation or for replacing the evaluand. Under such circumstances, the evaluator stands on solid ground when presenting recommendations, because they are based on systematic, empirical inquiry. Of course, in order to generate such empirically grounded recommendations, the evaluator and client need to agree that such a follow-up investigation is needed and will be appropriately scheduled and funded.

Reporting Information

A fundamental goal of any evaluation is to communicate findings to members of the audience effectively and secure their appropriate use of the reported information. Steps to promote and secure use of findings are critical parts of the evaluation design and need to be addressed at the outset of planning the evaluation and throughout the study. Initially the identity of the main client will be clear. For example, in the USMC personnel evaluation case, the key client was the corps' commandant. However, an influential evaluation should address the questions and information needs of a much broader group than the client. It must reach those who will make decisions based on the findings, those who will have operational responsibility for applying the findings to improve the evaluand, and those who are paying for or using the assessed services.

It is vital to study all segments of the intended audience in order to identify their different needs for information and prepare and schedule delivery of appropriate reports. In general, the different reports might include component-specific reports such as context, input, process, and product reports; reports keyed to particular methods, such as surveys, ratings, case studies, or content analysis; interim progress reports; the final report; and technical appendixes. Depending on the needs of the audience for each report, the evaluator might plan to employ a variety of formats beyond the printed report. Presentation modes could be oral, electronic, multimedia, or sociodrama.

The evaluator should most often arrange to have appropriate interactions with the client and others throughout the evaluation. This is important to discern their most important information needs, motivate them to receive and use the findings, deliver evaluation findings when they can be used best, obtain their assistance in gathering data, and receive stakeholders' critiques of previous reports. In order to promote use of findings, the evaluator should seize appropriate opportunities to engage members of the audience in exchanges about evaluation plans and findings. In advance of data collection, it can be useful to outline the contents of a projected report, complete with "dummy tables," and to go over this with the client or other members of the audience. In later exchanges, the evaluator should seek explicit feedback from the audience about the strengths and weaknesses of previous reports and what information would be most useful in future reports. A cautionary note is that the evaluator should take care to maintain the evaluation's independence and receive and assess stakeholders' feedback for whatever it is worth. The evaluator should not empower stakeholders to make or strongly influence evaluation design decisions and must not pander to any illegitimate stakeholder desires and interests.

Often interim reports are as influential as, or even more influential than, the final report. This is especially so in formative, decision-oriented, and responsive evaluations. In such studies, the evaluator should plan carefully and carry out the interim evaluation reporting effectively. It can be very useful to establish a review panel representing the different levels of the audience, periodically deliver findings to this group, interact with the group about the relevance of the reported information, obtain the group's critical reactions to each report, and obtain their views about what information would be most useful in future reports.

Beyond the interim reports, clients typically require a comprehensive final report. We have found it useful to divide such reports into three main parts. A program antecedents part can be useful to persons who need background information on the program, including when, why, and how it was started and by whom; its location and environment; and its institutional home. The program implementation part can be of special interest to groups that might want to replicate the subject program. This part should be highly descriptive rather than evaluative. It should identify the program's objectives, beneficiaries, governance, staff, organization, operations, and funding. The program results report should be addressed to the entire need-to-know audience. It should summarize the evaluation design and process; present the findings for each main question; and synthesize the findings to present conclusions regarding the program's merit, worth, significance, cost-effectiveness, and probity. In addition to these three main parts, a final evaluation report should include a set of technical appendixes. As seen in checkpoint E.6, these could include résumés for each member of the evaluation team, information collection instruments and protocols, reports of findings for particular evaluation procedures, data tables, a log of evaluation activities, a list of evaluation reports, a summary of evaluation costs, a copy of the evaluation contract, and an internal account of how well the evaluation met the standards of the evaluation profession.

Lessons learned from the USMC personnel evaluation suggest that the utility of interim reports is enhanced by conducting review sessions and carrying out steps such as the following:

1. Engage the client to appoint a review panel that is representative of program stakeholders.
2. Secure the client's agreement to chair the review panel and make panelist responsibilities clear.
3. Schedule each feedback session with the panel well in advance.
4. Distribute the most recent draft report along with an agenda to the review panel members about ten days prior to the feedback session.
6. Have the client start the session by going over the session's objectives and agenda.
7. Use a multimedia approach to brief the review panel on key aspects of the report, including questions, methodology, obtained findings, and key issues for discussion.
8. Engage the review panel's chair to lead a discussion of findings and their implications for action.

9. Assist the panel's discussion of findings as appropriate, but do not dominate or become defensive.
10. Following the chair's discussion of findings with the panel, ask the panel members to voice their reactions to the report; identify their most important needs for information in future reports; and, as appropriate, assist future data collection efforts.
11. Have the chair ask each panel member to cite the meeting's most important outcomes and then summarize the meeting from his or her perspective.
12. Schedule the next review session, summarize pertinent next steps, and thank all present for their participation.
13. Following the meeting, prepare and distribute the minutes to all participants.

Administering the Evaluation

All evaluations require effective administration, a key responsibility of the lead evaluator. The initial evaluation plan should include a schedule of evaluation activities and staff assignments, and these should be updated as appropriate during the evaluation. The schedule should be worked out with the client to ensure stakeholder availability in data collection as well as reporting. In consideration of the scheduled evaluation tasks, the plan should include an appropriate budget. Among the key cost items are evaluation staff, consultants, materials and equipment, facilities, communication and other services, travel, and indirect costs. Building on the evaluation schedule and budget, the evaluator also should negotiate a contract that guarantees the evaluation's viability and integrity. The evaluation plan should provide for reviewing and updating the evaluation design and contract as needed. Later chapters address the budgeting and contracting tasks in considerable detail.

A most important administrative task is staffing the evaluation. Here the evaluator should recruit, assign, train, and coordinate staff members such that they effectively carry out all aspects of the evaluation and earn the confidence of the client and other stakeholders. Required competencies often include high-level measurement, statistics, and computer skills; qualitative methods; the ability to establish rapport and working relationships with personnel in the field; knowledge of the evaluand's content; facility with multimedia presentation methods; and excellent writing, editing, and oral communication skills. In developing an evaluation team, the lead evaluator should take into account the ethnic and other characteristics of stakeholders and ensure that the assembled evaluation team can earn the trust and confidence of all segments of the audience. It is often desirable for the evaluator and client to arrange for the involvement of a review panel whose members are representative of the program's stakeholders.

The evaluator should take steps to ensure that the evaluation will meet the standards of the evaluation field. The evaluation design should be grounded in appropriate standards, and the evaluator needs to obtain the client's endorsement of the standards. In addition, the evaluator should provide internal formative and summative metaevaluations of the evaluation work against the adopted standards and advise the client to contract for an independent metaevaluation of the completed study. We address this topic in depth in this book's final chapter.

Summary

In this chapter we provided a perspective on the crucial topic of evaluation design. We began by summarizing and discussing an actual design based on the CIPP model. Although this design was quite general, it was funded at a level of $440,000, and its implementation led to a highly influential and well-received evaluation. This case illustrates that evaluation design is as much process as product, as the design for evaluating the USMC personnel evaluation system had to evolve and broaden along the way.

We then presented a generic evaluation design checklist. It is configured to work not only with the CIPP model but with any other defensible evaluation approach. Moreover, it is intended to be useful in generating an initial design and periodically reviewing and updating the design. It is not intended as a cookie-cutter approach to design but as a flexible tool that allows evaluators ample room for creativity. Once the evaluator has worked out a design that is responsive to and properly reflective of a client's need for an evaluation, we think the evaluator would find the checklist useful for ensuring that all aspects of a sound and functional evaluation have been addressed.

Review Questions

1. From reading this chapter, how would you define evaluation design? In general, what main topics should be included in an initial evaluation design? Why must the evaluator make design decisions before the evaluation commences?
2. "Evaluation design is both process and product." Place this statement in the context of designs for preordinate evaluations and responsive or formative evaluations.
3. Give reasons that it is essential to train personnel who are field-testing a new personnel evaluation system.

4. It is important to restate a potential client's criteria for evaluating the evalu-and. Such a summary serves several useful purposes. What are some of these?

5. In the project discussed in this chapter, the military organization agreed to the evaluator's recommended set of standards for the new performance review system but added a standard, labeled Transition to the New PRS. Give reasons that this was an important addition.

6. When developing a large-scale personnel evaluation system such as the one depicted in this chapter, the evaluation team should carry out a succession of tasks for producing and validating the new system. Within the context of the CIPP model, list and provide rationales for at least five such tasks.

7. Conducting distinct but related context and input evaluations, as we have stated, is an apt way for evaluators to address a client's request for evaluations that both identify problems and recommend solutions. Give reasons that this approach is defensible, bearing in mind that it is usually inappropriate for an evaluator to offer the best corrective actions. Also, explain why typically it is problematic for evaluators to present recommendations.

8. The importance of negotiating features of the evaluation before signing a contract based on an agreed design cannot be overestimated. Why is this so?

9. If it is to be influential, why should an evaluation address the questions and information needs of a considerably broader group than the client? How does consideration of this matter have a bearing on the design of the evaluation?

Group Exercises

Exercise 1. The board of a nationwide retailer whose sales have slumped for the past five years decided to have the company evaluated. In brief, the RFP states that the focus will be on national and state administrations, management of individual stores, and communication among these entities. The RFP gives the green light for peripheral issues such as quality control and deployment of stock to be examined by the evaluation. Moreover, if other major deficiencies in the system become apparent during the evaluation, these also will become part of the study following consultation with the board chairperson, managing director, and other persons on the review committee. Initially, a project performance plan is required from respondents to the RFP to indicate the quality of a schedule of work that the board could expect from the respondents.

    Imagine that your study group constitutes a sizable evaluation firm. Realizing that the requested undertaking would be a huge task, requiring detailed planning and a considerably expanded and skilled workforce, you nevertheless decide to respond to the RFP.

Using the five tasks as outlined in this chapter as a guide, develop a possible schedule of work (omitting any consideration at this early stage of time allotments).

One member of your group could act as a recorder of points developed under each of the five tasks.

Exercise 2. This chapter has emphasized that planning an evaluation design is an ongoing process. Thus, your initial plan developed in exercise 1 will necessarily be general. Describe the process your group would follow to make the design more specific, concrete, and actionable.

Exercise 3. Return to your performance (tasks) plan, and discuss possible ways in which this could change or be embellished as the evaluation study develops and planning becomes more specific.

Reference

Joint Committee on Standards for Educational Evaluation (1988). *The personnel evaluation standards.* Thousand Oaks, CA: Corwin Press.

CHAPTER TWENTY-TWO

BUDGETING EVALUATIONS

While developing an evaluation design, the evaluator cannot escape bearing in mind costs associated with the planned study. These need not be explicated in any detail initially, but inevitably cost will become an integral part of planning an evaluation. Evaluation design and budgeting are two early basics of planning an evaluation. A budget should provide a best estimate of the funds required to successfully carry out the full range of planned evaluation tasks. The design will have indicated the tasks to be performed; an analysis of these will give an indication of predictable costs. However, the structure and specificity of initial evaluation budgets will vary depending on the nature of the evaluation project and the type of financial award.

In 1980, Cronbach et al. stated that "deciding on a suitable level of expenditure is . . . one of the subtlest aspects of evaluation planning" (p. 265). This advice could suggest that ideally, a budget could be developed and agreed to by consultation between evaluator and client (or sponsor, depending on the nature of the evaluation). The ideal situation, unfortunately, is not the norm. Collaborative planning may not be possible from the beginning if the client sets budgetary limitations for the study. Such a situation can be frustrating for an evaluator, particularly an experienced one, whose ability to assess budgetary requirements is set aside. However, more frequently, the client does not have a definite sum of money (initially at least) in mind, and the development of a budget is left in the evaluator's hands. Whether this budget is accepted by the client depends strongly on how it is stated, developed, and justified. In this chapter, we present ways in which a convincing, ethical, and defensible budget may be formulated.

While a good evaluation design provides a solid grounding for budgetary discussions and possible decisions, clients nevertheless may be quite unaware of the extent of information an evaluation may produce and also of attendant costs. If evaluator-client discussions clarify such issues, including budgetary limitations, at an early stage of the evaluation design, the chances of effective decisions at later stages of the study are enhanced. As we pointed out in Chapter Twenty-One, evaluation designs must remain sensibly flexible. Similarly, if at all possible, budgets must retain a degree of flexibility, particularly if new opportunities, which could be exploited, arise as the study progresses. We offer advice on this matter later in this chapter when discussing budgetary cushioning.

The budgeting process should be sensitive to whether the evaluation design will be preordinate or responsive and formative. Under the former condition, the evaluation tasks are delineated in advance, and an up-front budget can be specified in detail and considered relatively fixed. Nevertheless, budgets for formative or responsive evaluations necessarily are general and in need of periodic updating as clients respond to interim reports and update their information requirements. Sponsors will differ in the amount of specificity they require depending on the type of award: grant, fixed price, cost reimbursable, cost plus, or cooperative. Under grants and fixed-price agreements, the sponsor is mainly concerned that the evaluation will produce informative, high-quality outcomes and usually will not ask for extensive detail on how funds will be allocated and expended to achieve the result. Under cost-reimbursable, cost-plus, and cooperative agreements, the sponsor is more likely to require detailed breakouts of projected charges. Another consideration in the budgeting process is that the sponsor may be uncertain of which evaluation components it is able and willing to support. Accordingly, the sponsor might ask for a modular budget, allowing for funding only part of the evaluation or withholding decisions about certain components until later. A final consideration is one's institution, which will require a certain level of detail for internal accounting and auditing purposes, regardless of the sponsor's requirements for specificity.

We begin by providing an overall perspective on the ethics of building and implementing evaluation budgets. Then we report and discuss the budget for the military personnel evaluation presented in Chapter Twenty-One. Since that evaluation employed a fixed-price contract and was quite general, we examine budgeting under other types of agreements. Finally, we present and explain a generic checklist for building an evaluation budget.

Ethical Imperatives in Budgeting Evaluations

Basically, an evaluation budget should enable the evaluator to implement the full range of proposed tasks at such a high level of quality and professionalism that the sponsor is convinced about the potential and defensible strength of the study. If the sponsor's funding constraints preclude successfully carrying out the requested evaluation tasks, the evaluator should consider pursuing the following actions. The first is to justify and request the additionally needed funds. If the client cannot agree to increase funding, the evaluator should consider seeking a reduction in the study's scope in order to do well whatever is done with the available funds. Failing such a scope-reduction effort, the evaluator should consider respectfully declining the assignment to avoid doing a marginal- or low-quality piece of work. If an underfunded assignment cannot be declined, the evaluator should consider stating in the final evaluation report that funding restrictions may have negatively affected the reliability and validity of reported findings.

The main point here is to emphasize that before proceeding with a planned evaluation, the evaluator should take all reasonable steps to ensure that he or she will have the resources necessary to conduct a professionally responsible study. Such assurances are obtained through up-front agreements on the evaluation tasks and funds. Alternatively, the evaluator might get the client to agree in writing to clarify information needs along the way and allocate additional funds as appropriate. Successful evaluation budgeting is not simply about winning evaluation grants and contracts; it is about establishing and maintaining financial viability for a professionally defensible evaluation.

We cannot overemphasize that it is wise and professionally responsible to ground a designed evaluation in an up-front, honest, and competently prepared estimate of the needed funds. To the extent the evaluation assignment is fully designed in advance, the evaluator should provide his or her best estimate of a full-cost budget. If the evaluation assignment is general and expected to evolve, the evaluator should offer a tentative budget aligned with what is known of the assignment and include provisions for periodically updating the budget as the evaluation assignment develops. The general principle is that evaluators should build budgets that fairly and accurately present the level of funds needed to professionally carry out the designed evaluation activities.

The evaluator should not act dishonestly or incompetently in budgeting a designed evaluation. Unfortunately, it is not uncommon for evaluation contractors to submit highly inflated budgets or gross underestimates of the needed funds. Overestimates of needed funds occur especially in sole-source situations where an evaluator initiated a proposal to conduct an evaluation or where the client sought services from a particular evaluator. In either case, an evaluator who is bidding on a noncompetitive award might intentionally grossly overbid a job in order to make a sizable profit or do so out of inexperience and incompetence. We see opportunistic, client-gouging practice as unprofessional. Any possibilities for inflating evaluation budgets provide a prime reason that clients should seek independent assessments of a prospective evaluator's evaluation design and budget.

A fringe area of overbudgeting has caused some clients to be cynical about hiring university professors to conduct evaluations. We have seen all too many cases where the evaluator surreptitiously inflated an evaluation budget in order to support activities with no relationship to the evaluation. The excess funds were used for such unauthorized purposes as supporting graduate students, conducting research, hiring outside speakers, paying employees who do not work on the evaluation, buying equipment or furniture not related to the evaluation, or funding trips to conventions. The evaluator can justify such expenditures of contracted evaluation funds only if the client previously agreed that the expenditures are an acceptable part of the contracted budget. Otherwise, we believe the evaluator would be misappropriating the evaluation funds and engaging in professional misconduct by using contracted evaluation funds for unauthorized uses. Under an up-front negotiation, the sponsor might agree to a cost-plus contract to allow support of functions not related to the evaluation. The sponsor could see such overinvestment as part of the price to obtain the evaluator's service. A cost-plus budget is appropriate so long as the evaluator clearly discloses the elements that are unrelated to the evaluation and the sponsor agrees to fund them.

In the case of underbidding a job, a naive, do-gooder, neophyte evaluator might unintentionally request far less than the needed funds and later fail in the assignment or face the embarrassment of admitting poor budgetary planning and requesting additional funds. In a competitive bidding process, an experienced but unscrupulous evaluator might intentionally submit a low-ball budget in order to win the competition and thus essentially buy the contract. In such cases, the contractor knows beforehand that he or she will have to return to the sponsor lamenting that the original budget unfortunately was an underestimate and that additional funds are needed. In cases where the evaluator grossly underbid the evaluation job, intentionally or unintentionally, and got funded, the sponsor faces three undesirable options: give in to the evaluator's request for more money, let the evaluation proceed with insufficient funds and produce a poor outcome, or cancel the contract and incur the loss of expended funds without receiving the needed report.

We advise evaluators to act professionally and prudently in preparing their budgets. When possible, evaluators should develop their best estimate of a full-cost evaluation budget. In this way, they deal honestly with clients and also ensure that the evaluation will have the necessary funds to succeed. However, there is bound to be error in all budget projections for an evaluation. Accordingly, evaluators sometimes need to err on the side of requesting slightly more funds than might be needed. Such padding of the budget is in the interest of ensuring that the evaluator can cover unexpected costs and produce a high quality evaluation.

A full-cost budget with no inflation factor for contingencies might still prove to be larger than necessary. This can occur for a variety of reasons. For example, not all needed staff may be hired as soon as was projected, thus saving on personnel costs. Or some projected participants in evaluation meetings might not make all the needed trips, thus saving personnel and travel money. It might prove possible to institute cost-saving measures and thus expend less for the evaluation than was originally projected. For example, conference telephone calls might be substituted for originally projected face-to-face meetings. Or if the evaluator is conducting other work in the study's field site, travel costs might be split between the two projects and thus save money for each of them.

Given the imperatives to conduct a sound evaluation and also to ask only for fair financial compensation, the evaluator should take appropriate steps not to overcharge the sponsor. While an initial full-cost budget (or one that is modestly padded) provides insurance that an evaluation can succeed and is thus sound evaluation practice, we also advise the evaluator to be frugal toward making the evaluation cost-effective. If allowed or required by the contract, the evaluator should consider returning unused funds to the sponsor or possibly agree to use the surplus to conduct additional relevant work. In our experience, however, clients do not always want or have authority to accept returned funds or additional service. Nevertheless, it is ethical for the evaluator to discuss these possibilities with the client.

We have sought to project a strong ethical position pertaining to evaluation budgeting. However, some caveats should be reiterated. The advice to prepare an up-front, full-cost budget is particularly appropriate to preordinate, extensively planned evaluation studies. In such cases, one knows essentially what will occur in the evaluation and can make quite reliable cost estimates. However, costing out evaluation work is less tractable in responsive and formative evaluations where information needs will continually unfold. In such cases, we advise the evaluator to provide best estimates of evaluation costs in the original budget, along with stipulations that the cost estimates will be revisited and updated to keep pace with evolving evaluation requirements. Alternatively, the evaluator might request a small planning grant to allow development of a sound evaluation design and budget prior to contracting for the entire evaluation. In all efforts to build an evaluation budget, the evaluator should strive to budget what is required to produce a professionally responsible evaluation, exercise utmost fiscal integrity, and disclose any requests for funds beyond those necessary to conduct the study.

A Fixed-Price Budget for Evaluating a Personnel Evaluation System

The evaluation of the military personnel evaluation system presented in Chapter Twenty-One was grounded in a fixed-price, sole-source contract. The contractor stipulated that the evaluator had to complete the project within eight months and could request whatever money would be necessary to complete the job well and on time. Moreover, the sponsor stressed that the contractor should be sure to request all the needed funds since there would be no opportunity to renegotiate this amount. An evaluation plan and budget were needed almost immediately. With all due haste, the evaluator prepared and submitted the following budget.

Considering the relatively large amount of requested funds, the budget in Exhibit 22.1 includes little detail. Under a fixed-price agreement, the sponsor found the level of specificity sufficient, since the evaluators were contractually obligated to complete the stipulated tasks to the satisfaction of the military organi-

EXHIBIT 22.1. BUDGET FOR THE UNITED STATES MARINE CORPS PERSONNEL EVALUATION PROJECT.

Budget Line	Item Cost	Total
A. Personnel		
1. Salaries	$98,284	
2. Fringe benefits	38,331	
Total personnel		$136,615
B. Travel		20,439
C. Consultants		
1. Honoraria	82,000	
2. Travel plus support services for consultant team leaders	65,526	
Total consultants		147,526
D. Supplies		1,760
E. Services (phone, photocopying, computer use, and postage)		27,444
F. Total direct costs		333,784
G. Total indirect costs		97,979
H. Total project costs		431,763

zation by the mandated deadline and since cost was not an issue of importance to the sponsor.

However, the detail in this budget was not sufficient for the evaluation team's parent organization. Its administrators needed considerably more specific information in order to ensure that resources would be sufficient to do the job, charge project expenses to the proper line items, account for expenditures, and audit the effort. The evaluators were able to meet institutional budgeting requirements because of the way the evaluation design was constructed. Accordingly, they provided their budget office with budget notes that explained projected costs for personnel, fringe benefits, travel, consultants, supplies, services, and indirect costs.

Personnel costs were derived and delineated from the work plan in the evaluation design. That plan was explicit in noting the number of days each staff member would work on the project. A basic personnel cost was determined for each staff member by multiplying his or her daily rate by the number of days to be worked in the project. This provided the institution with the basic line item estimated cost for each staff member who would work on the evaluation. In preparing the budget for the sponsor, the evaluator had summed the cost for each staff member to obtain the salary total of $98,284. The fringe benefit amount of $38,331 was determined by multiplying the institution's 39 percent fringe rate by the total salary amount ($98,284). The total estimated personnel *cost* then came to $136,615.

The estimated travel cost for the institution's staff was also built from the evaluation plan. It was estimated that costs for each trip by a staff member would average $650 for plane tickets and rental cars and $160 per day for lodging, meal, and associated expenses. Since the staff members were projected to make twenty-one trips involving thirty-seven days, the total travel cost for staff amounted to $19,570 plus a (padded) amount of $869 for incidental and unexpected meeting expenses. These amounts were within the institution's guidelines for travel expenses in expensive venues. The amounts summed to the staff travel total of $20,439.

Consultant honoraria were determined by summing the number of consultant days in the evaluation design document (76), adding 6 to allow hiring additional consultants if needed, and multiplying the total of 82 times a daily consultant rate of $1,000. This yielded the total consultant honoraria figure of $82,000.

The consultant travel plus support services for consultant team leaders figure was determined by totaling the number of consultant trips found in the evaluation design (25), identifying, from the design, the total number of days the consultants would be engaged in the trips (67), multiplying 25 times $750, multiplying 67 times $200, and summing the two products. To this result of $32,150, the evaluator added $33,376. Each context and input evaluation consultant team leader was allotted $15,000 for support services and their discretionary use. In addition, $3,376 was allocated to a contingency fund for paying the travel costs of additional consultants that likely would need to be hired. These budgetary provisions accounted for the consultant travel plus support services line item of $65,526.

It is noteworthy that the travel cost rates used for staff were lower than those for the evaluation's consultants. This was due to such circumstances as all staff members being located at one site relatively close to the location of most of the projected off-campus work and using the same airline and car rental companies. Also, the institution could negotiate airplane and rental car costs for staff in advance. The more varied and less predictable travel cost circumstances for consultants led the evaluator to employ the higher cost estimates for consultants.

The supplies line item estimate of $1,760 was included to cover paper and related materials for producing the updated evaluation plan, materials for each meeting, and draft and final reports for the five contracted tasks.

The services line item of $27,444 assumed that on average, the project would expend $3,430 during each of eight months on such items as communications, photocopying, computer use, and postage. This rather large amount reflected the fact that the project would involve intensive collaboration and numerous teleconferences among a nationwide network of project personnel.

The total direct costs item of $333,784 is the sum of the line items already enumerated, and the indirect costs figure was derived by multiplying $333,784 times the institution's indirect cost rate of 29 percent, which was a blended on-campus and off-campus rate. Adding the resulting $97,979 indirect costs amount to the total direct cost yielded the bottom-line amount of $431,763.

In many evaluation contracts, budget details such as those presented above would be appended to the budget summary as budget notes for each cost item. In the military evaluation example, such notes were presented to the contractor's budget office but were not included in the budget submitted to the sponsor.

In the end, the evaluation team used about $50,000 less than the fixed price amount of $431,763. This was largely due to the fact that the originally projected eight-month project became a six-month project. The military organization took two months to process the contract, and the commandant's deadline for the final report remained fixed. Also, the evaluator no doubt somewhat overestimated the cost for the work.

When it became clear that the project would end with about a 13 percent surplus over what was expended, the evaluator informed the sponsor that his team would be willing to use the excess funds to perform additional service or return the unused funds. By this time, the evaluator had convinced the sponsor to allow site visits to bases other than those included in the original evaluation contract and noted that the original award had sufficient funds to cover the cost for that added work. In addition, the evaluator suggested that part of the excess funds be used later to support the field-testing and institutionalization of the new evaluation system. The military organization's response was that it had no ability to accept a return of unused funds or authorize its use beyond the originally negotiated tasks. Ironically, the military organization issued an additional contract and associated award of $15,000 to support the evaluation team's added site visits. The evaluator's institution ended up with a windfall surplus of about $50,000. Such can be the nature of fixed-price evaluation agreements. But an institution could lose money on a fixed-price evaluation if the work had been underbid.

Other Types of Evaluation Budgets

Although the evaluation project discussed above was conducted under a fixed-price contract, it might have been pursued under some other type of agreement. In this section, we define and discuss evaluation budgeting under grants, cost-reimbursable contracts, cost-plus agreements, cooperative agreements, and modular budgets.

Evaluation Budgeting Under Grants

An evaluation grant is a financial award to support a qualified evaluator to conduct a study of interest to the evaluator, contains social value, lies within the sponsor's mission, and is seen to be at a fundable level. For example, a charitable foundation concerned with improving public schools might approve and fund a field-initiated proposal to conduct a comparative evaluation of nineteenth- and twentieth-century school governance policies in a selected number of states. Here the evaluator focused and issued the request for funds. The sponsor saw the proposed study as worthy, related to its mission, competently planned and staffed, and financially supportable. Consequently it awarded a grant to support the proposed evaluation. Similar to a fixed-price contract, the sponsor typically would expect the evaluator to use the funds wisely but not return unused funds.

Depending on the policies of the granting organization, the budget for a grant often may be quite general, as was the case with the example military evaluation. The main difference between a grant and a fixed-price contract is related not to the funding, but to the sponsor's control over the study's tasks and reporting of findings. In the military evaluation example, the sponsor stipulated the tasks to be completed and required that findings be reported only to the sponsor. Under a grant, the sponsor generally would not specify the study's tasks or control release of findings. The granting organization's main interests would be to ensure that the proposed study has social value and is related to the sponsor's mission, that the evaluator has the needed competence and record of professional responsibility, and that the requested amount of funds is available and appropriate to achieve the grant's objectives.

Another difference between a grant and a fixed-price contract concerns indirect costs. In the military example, the budget included a 29 percent indirect costs charge to cover such unspecified items as heat, light, custodial service, security, facilities, and fiscal accounting. Often granting organizations will pay little or no money for indirect costs. The rationale is that the award is a charitable contribution to support the recipient's goals and program and is not a particular service to the granting organization. Furthermore, the position often is advanced that if the funded study is central to the work of the recipient organization, it should make an in-kind contribution, for example, by covering the associated overhead costs.

Budgeting under a grant has minimal risks to the sponsor and the evaluator. The sponsor typically requires only that level of accounting to ensure that funds were expended to achieve the project's approved purposes. If grant funds were used inappropriately, the granting organization could require that the funds be returned. The grantee's main risk in grant-related budgeting is that the evaluator might promise more than can be achieved with the granted amount of money. When this occurs, the evaluator's efforts might fail and be judged negatively, or the grantee organization might have to acquire additional funds internally or externally to get the job done.

Both clients and contractors derive important benefits from engaging in grants for evaluations. Usually organizations that award such grants have substantial funds to expend on pursuing a clear and socially important mission. What they usually lack are the creative ideas, technical capabilities, field researchers, and supervisors to plan, carry out, and oversee important studies. Granting organizations meet these needs by attracting and issuing grants for high-quality, field-initiated evaluation projects. These organizations also benefit because grants require minimal oversight of the grantee's operations and expenditures. Evaluators benefit from grants because they usually are flexible and leave much room for creativity and evolution in the supported project. Moreover, if the evaluator inadvertently overestimated the needed funds despite careful planning, the evaluator's organization usually stands to retain the surplus.

Evaluation Budgeting Under Cost-Reimbursable Contracts

A cost-reimbursable evaluation contract is an agreement that the evaluator will account for, report, and be reimbursed for actual evaluation project expenditures. In the case of the military evaluation, under a cost-reimbursable contract, the evaluator would have billed the sponsor for only those funds actually expended. As long as the cumulative total did not exceed the original agreed-on total funding amount and the evaluator had performed competently and responsibly, the sponsor would have paid the submitted bills. In the end, the sponsor would have kept any unused funds.

Typically a cost-reimbursable budget should break out cost estimates in considerably more specificity than was seen in the fixed-price military evaluation example. Also, the sponsor usually will require budget notes that explain each budget item. Reporting evaluation expenditures against a detailed line-item budget usually will provide a sufficient basis for reimbursement. A detailed work plan in the evaluation design provides a foundation for working out a detailed line-item budget and associated budget notes.

A cost-reimbursable budget decidedly is in the interest of funding organizations. Under such an arrangement, their risks are minimal. They pay only for completion of agreed-on work and do not have to pay any amount above the agreed-on ceiling price for the work. If the original budget was insufficient to complete the project, the sponsor has the discretion to award additional funds or terminate its support of the effort. Risks to the evaluator in this type of budget can, but need not, be considerable. The main pitfall occurs when the work was underbid. In such a situation, the evaluator might have to incur the additional costs of completing the grant's scope of work. To the extent the evaluator has made a valid estimate of costs or has obtained provisions for periodic updating of the budget, a cost-reimbursement arrangement usually provides a sound financial basis for conducting a defensible evaluation. Of course, under this type of budget, the contracting organization does not stand to reap a financial profit from the project.

Evaluation Budgeting Under Cost-Plus Agreements

A cost-plus agreement includes the funds needed to conduct an evaluation assignment plus an additional agreed-on charge for the evaluator's services outside the sphere of the contracted evaluation. Cost-plus budgets are of three types: cost plus a fee, cost plus a grant, and cost plus a profit.

Under a cost-plus-a-fee budget, the additional funds would be used to help sustain the contracting organization. Here the budget would specify an institutional sustainability fee, such as 1 percent of the direct costs. Under a cost-plus-a-grant budget, the additional funds could be used to support program functions, such as supporting graduate students, research on evaluation, or an evaluation conference. In preparing this part of the budget, the evaluator likely would provide a separate line item for the project components that are outside the contracted evaluation tasks. This might simply be a specified charge or a line-item budget for the projected activities. Usually the sponsor would be asked to pay the requested cost-plus amount as a grant rather than a cost-reimbursement charge. For-profit evaluation organizations typically employ some type of cost-plus-profit budgets in order to make financial gain from contracted evaluations. The profit margin might be hidden, as when it is incorporated into inflated personnel hourly charges or overhead. Or it might be explicitly included as a percentage of direct costs. In either case, we advise the contractor to be up front in disclosing how it budgeted for its profit margin.

A cost-plus budget can be built into a grant, a fixed-price agreement, or a cost-reimbursable agreement. In the last case, the agreement might call for the evaluator to charge only the actual costs of the evaluation plus the agreed-on added amount for the evaluator's organization. We see a cost-plus budget as ethical and appropriate so long as the evaluator and sponsor explicitly settle on such a provision in the original agreement. We discourage evaluators from surreptitiously inflating their budgets in order to reap a sizable surplus or fund unauthorized activities.

Neither the sponsor nor the evaluator incurs remarkable risks in cost-plus budgets as long as there is appropriate disclosure of the basis for the funding request. By buying into such an arrangement, the sponsor will purchase the desired evaluation work and willingly provide additional funds to the contracting organization for its other uses. The contracting organization will get the funds it needs to carry out the evaluation assignment plus additional funding to further its organizational viability and accomplishments. The risks and benefits related to the cost of the evaluation portion of the budget are the same as those defined above, depending on whether that part of the budget is a grant, a fixed-price agreement, or a cost-reimbursable agreement.

Evaluation Budgeting Under Cooperative Agreements

A cooperative evaluation agreement is an arrangement for the evaluator and sponsor to collaborate in conducting the evaluation. Under such an agreement, the evaluator and sponsor share responsibility and authority for carrying out the evaluation work. They also share the resources needed to discharge their joint and individual responsibilities.

Cooperative agreements can be beneficial when there is an appropriate differentiation of sponsor and evaluator roles. For example, the sponsor can facilitate the evaluator's work by such contributions as providing office space, clerical support, assistance in gathering data, and support for stakeholder involvement and cooperation. However, cooperative agreements also have the potential to thwart the conduct of an effective and professionally defensible evaluation.

The basic issue is that such agreements set aside the evaluator's independence. Unless evaluator and sponsor roles are differentiated and delineated clearly, appropriately, and in enforceable ways, the evaluator can be put in the unfortunate position of having responsibility for the study's success and integrity but lacking authority to do what is needed. In such instances, the sponsor may be positioned to act on its conflicts of interests. For example, it might censor, inappropriately edit, or withhold release of embarrassing reports. It might insist on hiring persons for the evaluation team who are not the most qualified for the work. Or it might not discharge its responsibilities in a timely fashion. Also, the sponsor might inappropriately control the use of evaluation funds. As in empowerment evaluations, an evaluation under a cooperative agreement can place the evaluator in the position of lending technical assistance and undeserved credibility to a client who is in the evaluation's driver's seat. In general, a cooperative evaluation agreement is a threat to the evaluator's ability to carry out and report an independent study.

Of course, part of the cooperative agreement should focus on the budget. Often the allocated funds will be divided between the evaluator and sponsor. The evaluator should delineate his or her funding requirements and stipulate in the contract that he or she will have appropriate control over use of the necessary funds. The agreement should also be clear about funds and related resources that the sponsor will expend in carrying out its part of the evaluation work.

The client benefits from a cooperative agreement by being in a position to strongly influence the evaluation. The evaluator especially benefits when the client organization facilitates the evaluation.

Nevertheless, we think cooperative agreements are the weakest and most problematic type of evaluation arrangement. Considering the potential for problems in such arrangements, it is difficult to include a sufficient set of safeguards. If an evaluator must enter into a cooperative agreement, it is essential to negotiate a clear and appropriate contract according to the guidelines set out in Chapter Twenty-Three. The agreement should stipulate that the evaluator will have appropriate authority over expending necessary funds. Also, it is a good idea to secure an agreement that an independent metaevaluator will oversee and report on the effort.

Modular Evaluation Budgets

Modular evaluation budgets delineate the funding requirement for each part of a designed evaluation project or for each project year. It can be important to modularize an evaluation budget for three main reasons: a sponsor might be uncertain about how much of a proposed evaluation it can or would want to fund, several prospective sponsors might want to share the funding of the evaluation work, or the evaluator might be able to be explicit about certain modules of the project but only tentative about others. In such cases, there is a need to provide a budget for each task of the designed evaluation project or for each year of work. A modularized presentation is appropriate with all the other budget types discussed in this chapter.

We can see how modularized budgets work for evaluations with several tasks by revisiting the military evaluation example. That evaluation had five main tasks. Since the sponsor chose to fund all five tasks, it required only a bottom-line amount for the total job. To arrive at this amount, the evaluator developed and submitted the line-item budget shown in Exhibit 22.1. Had the sponsor required a modularized budget, the evaluator could have constructed one based on the evaluation design's delineation of evaluation activities. Exhibit 22.2 is an illustrative framework for constructing such a modularized budget that breaks out evaluation tasks. Use of such a framework generates line-item costs for each project task and the total project. Exhibit 22.3 shows how a budget would be broken out by line item and year. Exhibit 22.4 shows how a budget could be summarized by task and year.

EXHIBIT 22.2. AN ILLUSTRATIVE FRAMEWORK FOR CONSTRUCTING A MODULARIZED EVALUATION BUDGET SHOWING LINE ITEMS AND TASKS.

Line Item	Task 1	Task 2	Task 3	Task 4	Task 5	Total

A. Personnel
   1. Salaries
   2. Fringe benefits
     Total personnel						

B. Travel						

C. Consultants
   1. Honoraria
   2. Travel plus
     support services
     for consultant
     team leaders
     Total consultants						

D. Supplies						

E. Services (telephone,
   photocopying,
   computer use,
   and postage)						

F. Total direct costs						
G. Total indirect costs						
H. Total project costs						

EXHIBIT 22.3. AN ILLUSTRATIVE FRAMEWORK FOR CONSTRUCTING A MODULARIZED EVALUATION BUDGET SHOWING LINE ITEMS AND YEARS.

Line Item	Year 1	Year 2	Year 3	Year 4	Year 5	Total

A. Personnel
   1. Salaries
   2. Fringe benefits
     Total personnel						

B. Travel						

C. Consultants
   1. Honoraria
   2. Travel plus
     support services
     for consultant
     team leaders
     Total consultants						

D. Supplies						

E. Services (telephone,
   photocopying,
   computer use,
   and postage)						

F. Total direct costs						
G. Total indirect costs						
H. Total project costs						

EXHIBIT 22.4. AN ILLUSTRATIVE FRAMEWORK FOR CONSTRUCTING A MODULARIZED EVALUATION BUDGET SUMMARIZING COSTS BY TASK AND YEAR.

Task	Year 1	Year 2	Year 3	Year 4	Year 5	Total
Task 1						
Task 2						
Task 3						
Task 4						
Task 5						
Total						

Summary of Budget Types

Table 22.1 summarizes the budget types discussed in this chapter. Often evaluators will not have a choice of the type of budget to use because the dispenser of funds usually dictates the type of budget it will accept. However, there are occasions when the evaluator can propose a type of budget to be followed. In these situations, we suggest that the evaluator carefully consider what type of budget would best serve the purposes of the evaluation and the interests of the involved parties. Key considerations are risks and benefits to the sponsor and contractor. In general, we advise against employing a cooperative agreement. However, under appropriate safeguards, it can be advantageous for the evaluator to secure the sponsor's assistance in involving stakeholders, housing evaluation operations, providing access to pertinent files, clearing the way for data collection, and so forth. The key pitfalls to avoid in cooperative agreements are compromising the evaluators' independence and denying them the authority required to fulfill their evaluation responsibilities. No matter what type of budget is employed, it can be appropriate to break it out not only by line item but also by task and year.

A Generic Checklist for Developing Evaluation Budgets

We conclude this chapter by presenting and discussing the generic checklist for budgeting evaluations displayed in Exhibit 22.5. The checklist is intended for use in both constructing and reviewing a budget and proposed set of financial agreements. This checklist lists ten major tasks to carry out in establishing a sound financial basis for a projected evaluation. Each task is divided into specific items to consider during the budget development process. In general, the checklist is best applied by considering the ten tasks in the given order. However, one often will skip and later return to some of the specific items. We advise users of the checklist to cycle through it repeatedly during the budget development process. Below we provide commentary on each of the checklist's ten tasks.

Task 1: Ensure That the Evaluation Design Is Sufficiently Detailed

A sound evaluation design is a precondition for developing a functional, complete, and defensible evaluation budget. When starting the budget development process, the evaluator should ensure that the evaluation design is as fully developed as the situation warrants. The checklist sets out the essential design components: the major tasks, activities, staff and consultants, nonpersonnel resources, funding period and schedule, and any subcontracts. Such design elements should be clearly defined in order for the evaluator to confidently assign costs for carrying out the evaluation. If any essential design elements are missing or unclear, the evaluator should, as feasible, improve the design as needed. In the case of a responsive or formative evaluation where all details cannot be specified in advance, the evaluator should seek agreements that the evaluation budget will be updated periodically as the evaluation design and activities evolve.

Task 2: Determine the Types of Budget Agreement

There are several types of budget agreements, each entailing different costing approaches and levels of detail. The evaluator should clearly determine the type of budget to be employed. If the budget is subject to periodic updates, as in the case of a formative or responsive evaluation, the evaluator should confirm this with the sponsor in writing.

Task 3: Determine the Needed Level of Budget Detail

The evaluator should next determine how much budget detail to provide. Partly this will depend on the type of budget being employed. For example, the sponsor of a grant or fixed-price contract may require only a total cost figure or a general breakout of estimated costs and charges. Other sponsors and the evaluator's home institution typically require much more detail. Task 3 shows that the more detailed presentations include a detailed line-item budget. It can be appropriate to divide any type of budget by task, year, or local contribution. Even when there are no requirements for delineating costs, the evaluator often can benefit by preparing and using the budget breakouts as management tools. Whether the sponsor requires a detailed budget, the evaluator typically should prepare notes that explain each budget item. Normally the evaluator's budget office will require such detailed budget information.

Task 4: Determine Pertinent Cost Factors

Task 4 contains an extensive list of potential cost factors. Evaluators should carefully consider the full range of these factors and possibly others. Doing so helps ensure that the evaluator will have at hand the rates needed to compute costs for the full range of projected cost items.

The first item in this task concerns a possible budget ceiling and is especially noteworthy. We advise evaluators to investigate whether the sponsor has in mind a limit for the amount of funding for the evaluation and, if so, to at least attempt

TABLE 22.1. SUMMARY OF BUDGET TYPES.

Budget Type	Key Points	Risks to Client	Risks to Evaluator	Benefits for Client	Benefits for Evaluator
Fixed price	Firm amount to be paid for performing the sponsor's defined scope of work	Might pay much more than the actual cost if the needed funds were overestimated	Might incur a financial loss if needed funds were underestimated	Likely will obtain the needed service at an acceptable price	Might gain a profit if needed funds were overestimated
Grant	Award for an approved study with minimal oversight and control by the sponsor and often without reimbursement for indirect costs	Minimal if proper accounting ensures proper expenditure of funds	Minimal if the evaluator receives sufficient internal and external resources to meet study objectives	A means of pursuing its mission that requires minimal oversight	A flexible source of funds to creatively pursue the evaluator's study objectives
Cost-reimbursable	Payment is restricted to actual expenditures up to a given limit	Minimal because payments are for successful completion of tasks up to a specified limit	Success is jeopardized if the evaluator underbid the job; otherwise minimal	Funds achievement of the client's objectives at cost and not above a limit	Usually provides a sound financial basis for completing a defensible study

Cost plus a fee, grant, or profit margin	Funds cover the evaluation's needs plus a portion to support other contractor functions	Minimal, because the funds will purchase the desired study and cover an additionally approved award to the contractor	Minimal as long as the evaluator accurately estimated costs for the evaluation and properly disclosed the additional charge	Will purchase the desired evaluation and knowingly provide additional financial assistance to the contractor	Receipt of funds needed to conduct the evaluation plus additional money to support organizational sustainability and accomplishments
Cooperative agreement	Contractor and client share responsibility and authority for conducting the evaluation	Moderate; while the client retains much control over program and financial decisions, there is potential for conflict with the contractor concerning responsibility and authority	Substantial because the evaluator loses independence and the client can exert strong, even inappropriate influence on the work	Can strongly influence the contractor's decisions and actions	The client might perform important evaluation tasks related, for example, to stakeholder cooperation, clerical support, and data collection
Modular	Budget is broken out by major task or project year	None, because cost estimates are delineated and better justified	Moderate; while the breakout strengthens mutual understanding of the budget, it also might tempt the client to drop certain important parts of the evaluation	Assists the client to decide what components to fund or to delay decisions about some of them	Provides a basis for allocating funds to tasks or years, for giving general estimates for some of the work, and for delaying firm estimates until later

EXHIBIT 22.5. A GENERIC CHECKLIST
FOR DEVELOPING EVALUATION BUDGETS.

1. Ensure that the evaluation design includes sufficient detail for building a sound budget.
   ____ Tasks
   ____ Activities
   ____ Personnel and consultants
   ____ Nonpersonnel resources
   ____ Funding period and schedule
   ____ Subcontracts
   ____ Provisions for updating the budget as appropriate

2. Determine the appropriate types of budget agreement. (Check all that apply.)
   ____ Grant
   ____ Fixed-price contract
   ____ Cost-reimbursable contract
   ____ Cost plus fee
   ____ Cost plus grant
   ____ Cost plus profit
   ____ Cooperative agreement
   ____ Subject to updates

3. Determine the required level of budget detail. (Check all that apply.)
   ____ Line-item budget
   ____ Line item by task
   ____ Line item by year
   ____ Task by year
   ____ Total budget only
   ____ Breakout of local contribution
   ____ Budget notes

4. Determine pertinent cost factors. (Check all that apply.)
   ____ Budget ceiling
   ____ Allowance for preaward costs
   ____ Hiring costs
   ____ Name and daily salary rate for each staff member
   ____ Name and hourly salary rate for each staff member
   ____ Fringe rates for each category of staff
   ____ Number of workdays for each staff member
   ____ Number of work hours for each staff member
   ____ Daily rate for staff per diem

EXHIBIT 22.5. A GENERIC CHECKLIST
FOR DEVELOPING EVALUATION BUDGETS, Cont'd.

____ Projected number of staff trips

____ Projected average travel cost per staff trip

____ Name and daily rate for each consultant

____ Number of workdays for each consultant

____ Name and hourly rate for each consultant

____ Number of work hours for each consultant

____ Projected number of consultant trips

____ Projected total travel days for consultants

____ Daily rate for consultant per diem

____ Projected average travel cost per consultant trip

____ Indirect cost rate

____ Factor for annual staff salary increments

____ Factor for annual level of inflation

____ Institutional sustainability fee factor

____ Profit factor

____ Other

5. Determine line items. (Check all that apply.)

____ Personnel salaries

____ Personnel fringe benefits

____ Total personnel

____ Travel

____ Consultant honoraria

____ Consultant travel

____ Consultant materials and other support

____ Total consultant costs

____ Supplies

____ Telephone

____ Photocopying and printing

____ Computers

____ Postage

____ Total direct costs

____ Indirect costs

____ Institutional sustainability fee

____ Supplemental grant

____ Contractor profit

____ Subcontracts

____ Other costs

EXHIBIT 22.5. A GENERIC CHECKLIST
FOR DEVELOPING EVALUATION BUDGETS, Cont'd.

6. Group line items for convenience.
   ____ Personnel
   ____ Travel
   ____ Consultants
   ____ Supplies
   ____ Services
   ____ Subcontracts
   ____ Total direct costs
   ____ Total indirect costs
   ____ Total project costs
   ____ Budget notes

7. Determine local contribution, if any. (Check all that apply.)
   ____ Reduction or elimination of indirect cost charges
   ____ Contributed time of staff members
   ____ Institutional funding of certain direct expenses
   ____ Other

8. Compute costs and charges. (Check all that apply.)
   ____ By year
   ____ By project tasks
   ____ By subcontract
   ____ Overall
   ____ Local contribution
   ____ Add the budget notes
   ____ Obtain a budget review and finalize

9. Provide for institutional fiscal accountability.
   ____ Responsibility for internal accounting
   ____ Responsibility for financial reporting
   ____ Provision for internal audit of project finances

10. Clarify requirements for payment.
   ____ Funding source and contact persons
   ____ Financial reporting requirements
   ____ Schedule of financial reports
   ____ Amounts and schedule of payments

Source: Daniel L. Stufflebeam.

to determine what it is. Often the sponsor will have established such a limit. Sometimes the limit will be published. In other cases, the sponsor might reveal it if asked. Information on an evaluation's funding limit can be very useful in building an evaluation budget. It helps the evaluator consider whether the evaluation is feasible given funding restrictions. It also helps the evaluator determine how much of a local contribution might be necessary to supplement the sponsor's funds in order to conduct a sound evaluation. For example, the contracting organization might decide to reduce its indirect cost rate in order to have the full complement of needed funds.

Not all factors in this task need or should be incorporated in an evaluation budget. For example, the budget should be based on either daily rates or hourly rates for staff and consultants—not both. Employing both of these in a given budget is likely to confuse the sponsor and other reviewers. Moreover, some evaluations might not involve travel or employment of consultants, and many will not include an institutional sustainability fee or a profit factor. In addition, only multiyear projects need to include increases to cover inflation and salary increments.

Notice that there are separate tasks for estimated travel costs for staff and consultants. This reflects the possibility that staff travel cost rates may differ substantially from those for consultants. The evaluator may be able to bargain for lower travel rates for staff because of the projected high volume of their travel. Or consultant travel costs could be lower than those of staff if the consultants live close to the evaluation site and staff are located farther away.

Staff and consultant pay rates in this task assume that the evaluation design has identified those who will carry out the evaluation. In such a case, it is possible to specify exact pay rates. However, some evaluation designs may identify only the categories of personnel to be involved, with some staff selections to occur following funding. In such a case the evaluator should identify and provide costs for categories of staff.

Exhibit 22.6 is a worksheet for estimating personnel costs by category. The daily rates are only examples, because these should be determined according to circumstances. Separate estimates are given for core staff, graduate students (assuming that the evaluation is university associated), and consultants. One reason for this is that universities do not charge for or provide fringe benefits to graduate students and consultants. Another reason for separating out consultants is that government authorities in the United States consider consultants exempt from unemployment compensation charges to the contractor only if they are treated as independent contractors and not as regular staff.

In evaluations that span multiple years, the evaluator can complete a useful separate worksheet for each project year. In these cases, the evaluator should project and provide for annual increments related to inflation and salary increases.

EXHIBIT 22.6. WORKSHEET FOR DETERMINING COSTS FOR CATEGORIES OF PERSONNEL.

Personnel Categories	Task 1		Task 2		Task 3		Total	
	Days	Cost	Days	Cost	Days	Cost	Days	Cost
Core evaluation staff								
Principal investigator: $800/day								
High-level methodologists: $600/day								
Field researchers: $300/day								
Technical support: $250/day								
Clerical: $110/day								
Total core staff without fringe								
Fringe rate: 40 percent								
Total senior staff: fringe loaded								
Graduate students								
Advanced: $175/day								
Entry level $125/day								
Total graduate students								
Consultants								
High level: $800/day								
Medium level: $400/day								
Total consultants								
Total personnel								

Depending on recent economic trends, such increments might range between 0 and 5 percent.

Another item in this task that merits special mention concerns the basis and rate for indirect costs. Most contracting organizations have an established indirect rate for inclusion in proposals, and usually sponsors agree to pay that rate. However, some sponsors agree to pay indirect costs on only part of the direct costs (or not at all). For example, the sponsor might decide to pay travel costs directly rather than have them included in the evaluation budget. This arrangement has the effect of lowering the indirect cost charges to the sponsor. In such a case, the evaluator would provide the sponsor an estimate of travel costs, but not include the estimate in the evaluation budget. By agreement, evaluation team members would submit travel bills to the sponsor, who would then reimburse the team members. In general, the evaluator should be alert to the prospective sponsor's policies and practices regarding direct and indirect costs.

Task 5: Determine Line Items

Task 5 is to determine all items to be covered by the evaluation budget. We have included items that commonly appear in evaluation budgets. We suggest that evaluators check all items that apply to their particular evaluations. Subsequently, they should consider whether other items should be added to the list. Task 5 is highly important in the budget development process. Its purpose is to ensure that evaluators do not fail to project all of the evaluation's costs.

Task 6: Group Line Items for Convenience

In task 6 the evaluator groups the items identified in task 5 into typical budget categories. The intent is to provide the sponsor with an efficient presentation of budget information. The items in task 6 are fairly standard in evaluation budgets, but can be modified according to the preferences of a sponsor and evaluator.

Task 7: Determine Local Contribution, If Any

Task 7 advises the evaluator to consider whether her or his parent organization should make a contribution to the evaluation. In certain agreements, such as grants, the sponsor may require a contribution from the contractor, for example, elimination or reduction of indirect cost charges. Or the evaluator might know the approximate limit of available funds from the sponsor and discern that charging the full indirect cost rate would preclude receiving funds needed for a fully responsive and technically sound evaluation. In such cases, the contractor might agree to lower or waive its indirect cost rate. Other contractor contributions might be in sharing the cost of personnel and directly funding certain evaluation tasks. Whatever the contractor's local contribution, it is wise to report it along with the submitted budget. Accordingly, the evaluator should consider including a local contributions column in each project year's line item budget.

Task 8: Compute the Evaluation's Costs and Charges

Provided that the preceding tasks have been accomplished, the evaluator can accurately compute the evaluation's costs and charges. The evaluation design, sponsor's needs, and requirements of one's home institution will determine the nature of the required budget displays. A basic rule is to develop the budget first at its most detailed level, then aggregate as appropriate. For example, if the evaluation has multiple tasks and will be conducted across multiple years, the evaluator should begin by developing a line-item budget, broken out by tasks for each year. At this stage, the evaluator should consider padding certain budget items, to a modest level, to make sure the evaluation is not underbid. Each year's budget display should be backed up with an appropriate set of explanatory budget notes. Subsequently the master set of figures can be aggregated in various ways to serve the interests of different audiences. Also, a summary set of budget notes can be prepared and appended to the proposal. When the budget charts and notes have been completed, the evaluator should obtain critiques of the budget and use them to correct and finalize the budget.

Task 9: Provide for Institutional Fiscal Accountability

In evaluation proposals, it is appropriate to provide the sponsor with assurances that the evaluation's finances will be appropriately and professionally monitored, controlled, and reported. Even in small, single-evaluator studies, the evaluator will need to keep track of expenditures and carry out some type of internal accounting. In sizable evaluations that are conducted in universities or other contracting organizations, the evaluator should inform the sponsor of the agents who will control and make internal audits of the use of funds. In addition, the evaluator needs to inform the sponsor of the office and employees who will be making financial reports and answering queries from the sponsor. All such arrangements are in the interest of effecting sound fiscal accountability and professional relationships with the sponsor. In many cases, the sponsor will explicitly require the submission of such information as part of the evaluation proposal. Even if the sponsor makes no such requirements, the evaluator is wise to provide for and report plans for maintaining fiscal accountability.

Task 10: Clarify Requirements for Payment

As a final budget preparation task, the evaluator should reach agreements on sponsor and contractor responsibilities regarding payment for the evaluation. Agreement between evaluator and sponsor, particularly in the case of large or longitudinal studies, may require legal advice before contracts are completed. The evaluator needs to identify the office and contact person charged to make the payments on behalf of the sponsor. Also, the evaluator will want to clarify the sponsor's requirements for financial reports and when they should be submitted. On the other side, the evaluator should clarify the amounts and schedule of payments to be received from the sponsor. While it is not done often, the evaluator is advised to summarize her or his understanding regarding the above matters in a budget note.

This concludes our discussion of Exhibit 22.5. We have seen that budgeting for evaluation studies is a complex process, because different types of budgets are involved in serving a wide range of different evaluation assignments. Nevertheless, one can follow a systematic, step-by-step process to arrive at the needed budget. The Generic Checklist for Developing Evaluation Budgets is recommended as a tool for making the budgeting process efficient and sound.

Summary

In this chapter we undertook to present a wide-ranging yet practical discussion of budgeting for evaluations. We stressed that budgeting should be a fully ethical process and discussed some of the ethical pitfalls in evaluation budgeting. We referred to Chapter Twenty-One's military evaluation case as an example of a fixed-price, line-item budget. Subsequently, we defined budgets keyed to grants, cost-reimbursable and cost-plus agreements, and cooperative agreements. We also noted that any of these types of budgets can and often should be broken out by year and task. Finally, we presented and explained a checklist for use in systematically developing evaluation budgets.

Budgeting is a key part of evaluation work, and it should be done ethically and well. Additional valuable sources of information on evaluation budgeting are *The Contract and Fee-Setting Guide for Consultants and Professionals* by Howard L. Shenson (1990) and *A Checklist for Developing and Evaluating Evaluation Budgets* by Jerry Horn (2001).

Review Questions

1. Why is it possible to give a specified budget for a preordinate evaluation but not for a responsive or formative evaluation?
2. There are connections between evaluation design and budgetary considerations. Referring to Chapter Twenty-One, state at least three such connections, together with the part that evaluator-client collaboration might play in strengthening budgetary decisions.
3. Why are ethical considerations so important in the formative stages of composing an evaluation budget, and why should an evaluator seek only fair financial compensation?
4. What are the attractions of a fixed-price agreement for both evaluator and sponsor?
5. List, with a brief comment for each, five dominant budget areas that need to be considered when planning an evaluation budget.
6. List at least ten cost factors to be determined in the budget development process, and explain the importance of such factors in completing the budget.
7. What do you understand by a cost-reimbursable evaluation contract and also by a cost-plus agreement?
8. Why is it that neither the evaluator nor sponsor is likely to incur remarkable risks in a cost-plus budget, provided appropriate disclosures are made by both parties?
9. Why is independence a serious issue in cooperative agreements? On the other side, what does an evaluator stand to gain from a cooperative evaluation agreement?
10. What are modular evaluation budgets, and under what circumstances can they prove useful?

Group Exercises

Exercise 1. Cooperative agreements are the weakest and most problematic type of evaluation arrangement. Discuss this statement from the budgetary point of view, and reach conclusions about its validity (or otherwise).

Exercise 2. This chapter has provided a budget checklist of ten tasks that we advise evaluators to draw on during any budget development process. As a group, reread this section of the chapter, memorizing salient features of each of the ten tasks. Then appoint a leader whose charge is to ask a group member to describe reasons for a particular task in some detail and comment on its importance from the viewpoint of both evaluator and sponsor. After all ten tasks have been tackled, the group leader will open the discussion to encompass any other evaluation budgetary matters.

References

Cronbach, L. J., Ambron, S. R., Dornbusch, S. M., Hess, R. D., Hornik, R. C., Phillips, D. C., Walker, D. F., & Weiner, S. S. (1980). *Toward reform of program evaluation*. San Francisco: Jossey-Bass.

Horn, J. (2001, December). *A checklist for developing and evaluating evaluation budgets.* www.wmich.edu/evalctr/checklists.

Shenson, H. L. (1990). *The contract and fee-setting guide for consultants and professionals.* Hoboken, NJ: Wiley.

CHAPTER TWENTY-THREE

CONTRACTING EVALUATIONS

Trust, but verify.

Closely allied to designing an evaluation (Chapter Twenty-One) and evaluation budgeting (Chapter Twenty-Two) is evaluation contracting. Although we presented these chapters as somewhat separate entities, in fact aspects of them are closely intertwined. Let us imagine that an evaluation design has been agreed to by both evaluator and sponsor or client and also that budgetary arrangements have been accepted. There now remains the significant step of ensuring that a contract satisfactory to both parties is formulated following negotiations. Such a contract must provide ample evidence that the evaluation study will be conducted in a positive, useful, legal, ethical, and professional fashion, based on mutual trust between evaluator and client.

Negotiating an evaluation contract or memorandum of understanding is one of the most important steps to ensure an evaluation's success. This process, which we label evaluation contracting, establishes a trusting relationship between an evaluator and a client and grounds their agreements in a written instrument for holding each party accountable and resolving disputes. In this chapter, we define terms associated with advance evaluation agreements, explain the role and importance of such agreements, discuss the process of negotiating agreements, and present a checklist for developing and assessing evaluation agreements.

Definitions of Evaluation Contracts and Memorandums of Understanding

Evaluation agreements may take the form of a formal contract or a less formal memorandum of understanding. Both forms of agreement should provide a framework of mutual understandings for proceeding with the evaluation work. The formal contract is most applicable in external evaluations, and memorandums of agreement are best suited to internal evaluations.

Evaluation Contracts

We define *evaluation contract* as a legally enforceable, written agreement between the evaluator and the client regarding the evaluation's specifications and both parties' responsibilities. An evaluation agreement could be only oral and still be legally enforceable, but for practical reasons, we recommend that the contract be written. The written words provide concrete information to review. Written agreements help reduce later possibilities for misunderstandings and disputes far better than do oral agreements that each party may remember differently. It is desirable that the client and evaluator define, at least in general terms, what would constitute a breach of the agreement by either party and what consequent actions may be taken. The contract should be consistent with pertinent federal and state laws and local regulations. Also, it should stipulate bases and procedures for canceling or amending the agreement during the evaluation. Before finalizing the contract, it is often appropriate to have it reviewed by an attorney.

Evaluation Memorandums of Understanding

A *memorandum of understanding* is similar to an evaluation contract except that the former is less formal. It is an evaluator's write-up of her or his understanding of the agreements reached with the client for proceeding with an evaluation. At a minimum, it should denote what is to be done, by whom, how, where, and when (including completion date). The memorandum could even be drawn from the minutes of an evaluation planning meeting.

An evaluator writes and submits the memorandum of agreement to the client, typically an official of the evaluator's organization. The client then reviews and approves, amends, or rejects the proposed agreement. Such memorandums are especially applicable in cases of internal evaluations where a formal written contract would be atypical and awkward. For example, having met with the school district superintendent and discussed a particular evaluation assignment, the district's evaluator would prepare a memorandum reporting their agreements and submit it for the superintendent's approval or amendment. Beyond stating the agreements reached in the previous meeting, the memorandum often would set out the evaluation's details. In this memorandum, the evaluator would ask the superintendent to approve the contents of the memo in writing or engage in further deliberation.

Common Requirements of Evaluation Contracts and Memorandums of Agreement

According to the Joint Committee on Standards for Educational Evaluation (1994), evaluators should write evaluation agreements that contain ". . .mutual understandings of the specified expectations and responsibilities of both the client and the evaluator" (p. 87). The committee continues, "Having entered into such an agreement, both parties have an obligation to carry it out in a forthright manner or to renegotiate it. Neither party is obligated to honor decisions made unilaterally by the other" (p. 87). It would be a mistake for the client or evaluator to act unilaterally in any matter where the evaluation agreement required joint decision making. Moreover, neither the client nor the evaluator should change the evaluation's design, scope, time line, or cost without revisiting and amending the agreement. It is essential that the agreement be professionally grounded and keyed to the evaluation assignment, design, and budget. It should be as comprehensive as past evaluation planning allows. It should be stated clearly, recorded in writing, and signed by both parties. Usually it is prudent to cite the evaluation design and budget as clear parts of the agreement.

An evaluation agreement should be negotiated and completed before starting the study. It should cover as fully as possible the full range of issues that might impede or cause an evaluation to fail. Often many of these issues are not covered in the evaluation design, and it would be a mistake to consider the evaluation proposal as the complete written agreement. Among the matters for agreement are the evaluation design, data collection and reporting schedule, access to needed information, protection of evaluation participants, individual and joint responsibilities for conducting the evaluation, security of the obtained information, evaluation reports and other deliverables, right-to-know audiences, agreements by certain stakeholders to cooperate with the evaluation, editorial responsibility and authority, dissemination of reports, arrangements to foster use of findings, and funding. Other agreements should define the standards for judging the evaluation, the study's objectives and scope of work, safeguards against the possible corruption of the evaluation, deliverables and their due dates, protocols to be observed in collecting and reporting information, provisions for keeping and reporting financial records, and the terms of compensation for the work. Both the evaluator and client will have important responsibilities for achieving a professionally defensible and effective evaluation. These responsibilities should be clearly defined and differentiated. Moreover, areas of authority for each party should be defined pursuant to the party's responsibilities for the study.

Although written evaluation agreements should be as explicit as possible, they also should allow for appropriate, mutually agreeable adjustments during the evaluation. The agreements will be more tentative in formative than summative evaluations. However, even in tightly designed, preordinate evaluations, it would be a mistake to make the contract so detailed that it impedes the evaluator's creativity. Also, the evaluator and client should keep their perspective on the study's purposes when applying the evaluation agreement. They should not adhere so rigidly to the contract that they cannot make or unduly delay changes dictated by common sense.

Rationale for Evaluation Contracting

Evaluators need to be skillful in negotiating advance written evaluation agreements for a number of reasons. In general, such agreements clarify understandings, build rapport and trust in the process of reaching the agreements, help prevent disputes between the client and evaluators, and provide a basis for resolving any future evaluation-related disagreements. Advance agreements can mean the difference between an evaluation's success and failure. They can help reduce and resolve a wide range of possible day-to-day misunderstandings or lapses in memory. Without advance agreements, the evaluation process is subject to misunderstanding, disputes, efforts to compromise the findings, attack, or even the client's withdrawal of cooperation and funds. In one high-stakes study, reference to the advance agreements on editorial authority and release of findings helped prevent the client from burying the report or rewriting it. It helped the evaluators give assurance to members of the evaluation audience that the study had provided for and maintained its independence and objectivity. Clients may also reference sound contracts to convince their policy boards or constituents that the institution contracted for sound, clearly defined evaluation services and can hold the evaluators to the agreements.

We stress the importance of consulting with stakeholders prior to finalizing an evaluation agreement. This will not always be feasible, especially in national competitions for awards to conduct a large-scale evaluation. The basic principle is that evaluators should take all feasible steps to consult, or at least take into account, the interests of stakeholders prior to finalizing an evaluation agreement. Moreover, it is wise to provide for their inputs during the study.

The Need to Meet Organizational Contracting Requirements

Of necessity, evaluators need to be familiar and involved with the contracting practices of their organization and those of particular sponsors. Federal agencies, foundations, and other sponsoring organizations often require that they and the evaluator's organization enter into a formal contract prior to launching a study. In such cases, it is typical for attorneys in both the sponsoring organization and the contracting organization to become involved. We suggest that evaluators become acquainted with the contracting practices of their own organization and with those of potential sponsors. In our experience, attorneys can be useful in protecting their organization's interests and those of stakeholders, especially related to equal opportunity employment of evaluation team members, rights of human subjects, deliverables, dissemination, and payments. However, evaluators should not leave all the contracting to the lawyers, who typically will not be sensitive to the full range of relevant methodological issues.

Political Reasons for Evaluation Agreements

Another reason for negotiating advance evaluation agreements concerns the politics of evaluation. Evaluations can be intensely political, and political influences can impede or even cause an evaluation to fail or be a party to unethical use of findings. Unchecked political forces can cause an evaluation to be unfair in its effects on program stakeholders. For example, in one of our evaluations, after completing the study, we learned that the client originally had no interest in obtaining information on the subject program's merit and worth. Instead, he had contracted for and used the evaluation report as a pretext for discharging the program's director, with whom he had a personality conflict. Although the report was decidedly positive, the client referenced the few indications of slight program inadequacy as the basis for firing the director. In another instance of our experience, from the start the CEO had no intention of divulging to stakeholders any but favorable evaluation outcomes. Had we previously uncovered these clients' illicit reasons for requesting an evaluation, we would not have contracted to do the studies. These examples illustrate that an evaluator should, as feasibly possible, examine carefully the politics surrounding a request for an evaluation before signing on to do the job.

Evaluators often need to make a wide search for the political forces that could have a negative influence on the evaluation. They should then institute relevant safeguards or, if appropriate and possible, decline the assignment. When possible, evaluators should interview persons who might be harmed by the evaluation and give them every opportunity to express any concerns they have about the projected evaluation. Stakeholders who are vulnerable and in a position to be hurt by an evaluation often can clue an evaluator to possibilities for illicit political influence.

Political threats can emanate from interest groups that want to bias, censor, or edit the evaluator's findings or even prevent its release to rightful audiences. Unfortunately, a client might have sought the evaluation as a cat's-paw for attacking an adversary or otherwise taking unfair advantage of stakeholders. Evaluators must be exceptionally careful not to become a tool of one side in a political dispute. Therefore, before finalizing an evaluation agreement and accepting the evaluation assignment, good practice is to search out and get input from a representative range of stakeholders. This sort of investigation can prove invaluable in deciding what to include in a proposed evaluation agreement and subsequently deciding whether to proceed with the assignment. Evaluators should take all feasible steps to institute effective measures to ensure that political pressures will not interfere with or corrupt the evaluation. If sufficient safeguards cannot be instituted, the evaluator is wise to decline the assignment, if that is possible.

We understand that evaluators who conduct studies in their own institution often cannot opt out of an evaluation assignment. However, they can do relevant background work before formulating a recommended evaluation agreement. Moreover, by keying the agreement to professional standards for evaluations, they are in a strong position to argue their case for a sound evaluation agreement. Reaching clear and professionally defensible understandings and written agreements with the client—about such matters as access to data, editing and release of reports, and use of findings—before starting a study is an important way to head off political threats to the study. Also, the internal evaluator faced with a problematic assignment can provide the client with a printed presentation of the caveats under which the evaluation has to be conducted. In addition, he or she could ask the client to arrange for an independent metaevaluation based on appropriate professional standards.

Not all political influences are undesirable in evaluation work, however. By interacting with a representative group of stakeholders, the evaluator can build interest in and support for the evaluation. Stakeholders' involvement in the evaluation also can motivate them to consider and use evaluation findings. On this point, it can be useful to appoint a stakeholder review panel and engage it throughout the evaluation to review and react to data collection plans and draft evaluation instruments and reports. Such a group can provide the evaluator with feedback of value in strengthening evaluation plans and materials. In the process of doing the reviews, members of the panel may increase their interest in and knowledge of evaluation procedures and therefore become more enthusiastic about using the evaluation's findings. Also, the panelists can become important opinion leaders for encouraging and assisting other stakeholders to take stock of and use the evaluation's reports.

Practical and Technical Reasons for Evaluation Contracts

Among the many practical and technical reasons for negotiating advance evaluation agreements are establishing clarity on deadlines; protocols for entering program facilities and collecting information from files and contacting human subjects; cooperation and support from personnel in the client's organization; and responsibility and authority for disseminating findings. The evaluation design will have treated many of these items in detail. In contracting, it is important to make all such design items a matter of contractual agreement so that the evaluator can efficiently and effectively carry out the work with the approval and support of the client and other stakeholders. The evaluator should also include in the contract any important items that are not encompassed in the evaluation design and budget.

Negotiating Evaluation Agreements

The process of negotiating evaluation agreements affords the evaluator and client an opportunity to base the evaluation effort on a constructive working relationship. It is in the interests of both the client and evaluator to start their relationship in an atmosphere of mutual respect, confidence, and effective communication. Such a positive atmosphere is conducive to successfully addressing the many sensitive negotiation issues. In addition, the process of developing the evaluation agreement affords the client and evaluator a valuable opportunity to review the evaluation design and budget and to clarify their individual and joint expectations, responsibilities, and rights in the evaluation.

In addition to negotiating with the client, the evaluator should, as feasible, consult others who will be involved in, affected by, or interested in the evaluation but are not parties to the written agreement. It would be a mistake to expect participation in the evaluation by persons who had not previously agreed to cooperate. When possible, such agreements for cooperation should be obtained in advance because they can be much harder to arrange later. When this is not feasible, the evaluator should explicitly include in the evaluation design and contract provisions for consulting stakeholders and obtaining their inputs and agreements to participate during the study. Among the stakeholders to be contacted are those whose work will be assessed, those who will contribute information, administrators and staff in buildings where the evaluation will take place, members of the media, leaders of pertinent community organizations, and interested community members. The evaluator should, as feasible, seek out anyone who might be harmed by the evaluation so they can air any concerns they might have. If possible, all such consultations should occur before the evaluation agreement is signed. When this is not possible, the evaluator should ensure that these stakeholders have opportunities to present their views during the evaluation. Moreover, it is a good idea to have the draft agreement reviewed by a lawyer before it is finalized and signed.

Prior to contracting, the evaluator will already have developed an evaluation design and budget. Whether in a formal request for proposal situation or a more informal sole-source case, the evaluator will present these items for the client's review and approval. Assuming that the evaluator's proposal is not rejected outright, the client typically will ask for some clarifications or changes.

Often this is where the negotiation process begins. Typically the client and evaluator communicate about needs to revise the evaluation design and budget, and the evaluator makes mutually acceptable changes. Subsequently either the client or the evaluator will prepare the first draft of the evaluation agreement for review and agreement by both sides. If the evaluator does this work, he or she should have obtained stakeholder inputs if possible and composed an appropriate draft agreement. If the sponsor prepared the first draft agreement, the evaluator would gather stakeholder input, possibly consult with an attorney, and desirably have an outside party review the draft for clarity and soundness. Ultimately this process should lead to a sound evaluation agreement—one that is keyed to professional standards, the evaluation design, and budget; protects participants and other affected parties; and ensures that the evaluation can be conducted efficiently and effectively.

An Evaluation Contracting Checklist

Exhibit 23.1 is a checklist designed to help evaluators and clients identify key contractual issues and make and record their agreements for conducting an evaluation. Not all checklist items apply in every evaluation agreement. However, it is prudent to consider all of them when starting the negotiation and when reviewing a draft agreement. Then the parties to the agreement can select those items that should be incorporated in the agreement or revise the draft agreement as appropriate. The evaluator can code each item as important and incorporated or

EXHIBIT 23.1. EVALUATION CONTRACTS CHECKLIST.

This checklist was designed to help evaluators and clients identify key contractual issues and make and record their agreements for conducting an evaluation. Advance agreements on these matters can mean the difference between an evaluation's success and failure. Without such agreements, the evaluation process is constantly subject to misunderstanding, disputes, efforts to compromise the findings, attack, or withdrawal—by the client—of cooperation and funds. On the other side, sound agreements enhance shared understandings and cooperation.

Check each item that is important and incorporated. Write NA for each item that is not applicable (NA). Leave blank any item that is important but not agreed to.

Basic Considerations

____ Object of the evaluation, for example, a program

____ Purpose of the evaluation

____ Client

____ Other right-to-know audiences

____ Authorized evaluators

____ Guiding values and criteria

____ Standards for judging the evaluation

____ Contractual questions

Information

____ Required information

____ Data collection procedures

____ Information sources

____ Respondent selection criteria and process

____ Provisions to obtain needed permissions to collect data

____ Follow-up procedures to ensure adequate information

____ Provisions for ensuring the quality of obtained information

____ Provisions to store and maintain security of collected information

Analysis

____ Procedures for analyzing quantitative information

____ Procedures for analyzing qualitative information

Synthesis

____ Participants in the process to reach conclusions

____ Procedures and guidelines for synthesizing findings and reaching conclusions

____ Decisions on whether evaluation reports should include recommendations

EXHIBIT 23.1. EVALUATION CONTRACTS CHECKLIST, Cont'd.

Reports

____ Deliverables and due dates

____ Interim report formats, content, length, audiences, and methods of delivery

____ Final report format, content, length, audiences, and methods of delivery

____ Restrictions and permissions to publish information from or based on the evaluation

Reporting Safeguards

____ Anonymity, confidentiality

____ Prerelease review of reports

____ Conditions for participating in prerelease reviews

____ Rebuttal by evaluees

____ Editorial authority

____ Final authority to release reports

Protocol

____ Contact persons

____ Rules for contacting program personnel

____ Communication channels and assistance

Evaluation Management

____ Time line for evaluation work of client and evaluators

____ Assignment of evaluation responsibilities

Client Responsibilities

____ Access to information

____ Services

____ Personnel

____ Information

____ Facilities

____ Equipment

____ Materials

____ Transportation assistance

____ Work space

Evaluation Budget

____ Fixed price, cost reimbursement, cost plus

____ Payment amounts and dates

____ Conditions for payment, including delivery of required reports

EXHIBIT 23.1. EVALUATION CONTRACTS CHECKLIST, Cont'd.

____ Budget limits or restrictions
____ Agreed-on indirect and overhead rates
____ Contacts for budgetary matters

Review and Control of the Evaluation

____ Contract amendment and cancellation provisions
____ Provisions for periodic review, modification, and renegotiation of the design as needed
____ Provision for evaluating the evaluation against professional standards of sound evaluation

Preparer _____   Date _____

Source: Daniel L. Stufflebeam (2006).

not applicable, or leave it blank, indicating no agreement, although the item may be viewed as important. Mainly the checklist is a tool for evaluators to use in detailing and negotiating evaluation agreements; they can also sign, date, and retain the completed checklist as a convenient summary of what they intended the agreement to cover. We will not elaborate and comment on the checklist items because we see them as self-explanatory.

Summary

This chapter has addressed the pivotal issue of evaluation contracting. An evaluation agreement may be in the form of a formal, legally enforceable contract or a less formal memorandum of agreement. In either case, the agreement should be professionally grounded, keyed to the evaluation design and budget, eminently fair to all parties to the evaluation, oriented to ensuring the evaluation's feasibility, open to later amendment, and negotiated and signed in advance of starting the study. Evaluators should negotiate sound advance agreements for their studies because these help to prevent failure or abuses of the evaluation and also aid in securing stakeholder interest and cooperation. Sound contracting for evaluations is a process that begins with an evaluation design and budget and culminates in an agreement signed by the client and the evaluator. During the negotiation process, the evaluator is advised to obtain and take into account as much input as possible from the full range of stakeholders. We concluded the chapter by presenting a checklist of the full range of issues to consider when either developing or assessing an evaluation agreement.

Evaluations occur in the real world where everything that can go wrong is likely to do so if unchecked. Sound evaluation contracting provides a systematic approach to making an evaluation as failproof as possible.

Review Questions

1. What do you understand by the terms *evaluation agreements* and *evaluation contract*?
2. Identify two ways in which evaluation agreements help reduce the possibility of later misunderstandings and disputes between evaluator and client.
3. What is the main difference between a memorandum of understanding and an evaluation contract?
4. There are inherent dangers in situations where either evaluator or client acts unilaterally in aspects of an evaluation agreement. What are the likely consequences of such actions?
5. When should an evaluation agreement be negotiated, and why?
6. Give reasons for the importance of consulting stakeholders prior to finalizing an evaluation agreement whenever possible.
7. Give reasons that evaluators should be thoroughly conversant with the contracting practices of their own organization before progressing to contractual arrangements with clients.
8. Why should evaluators take all feasible precautions to ensure that political pressures do not interfere with or corrupt the evaluation?
9. How can discussions with representative stakeholders in advance of contractual arrangements being made with the client help an evaluator decide whether to pursue the assignment?
10. Identify as many practical reasons for negotiating advance evaluation agreements as you can.

Group Exercises

Exercise 1. Considerable emphasis is given in this chapter to the importance of a constructive working relationship being established between evaluator and client. Discuss the following topics:

     a. What factors make this relationship so vital
     b. How you would go about building such a relationship

c. Who should be involved before an evaluation agreement is concluded

d. What some of the factors are that could preclude a contract's being made

Exercise 2. We have maintained that evaluation designing, budgeting, and contracting are closely linked.

Discuss this contention in general terms, and then select an actual evaluation known to a group member and find whether the three listed procedures were interrelated.

Reference

Joint Committee on Standards for Educational Evaluation. (1994). *The program evaluation standards* (2nd ed.). Thousand Oaks, CA: Corwin Press.

CHAPTER TWENTY-FOUR

COLLECTING EVALUATIVE INFORMATION

After negotiating an evaluation agreement, the evaluator turns to the central task of collecting the needed information. Responses to the study's questions can be only as good and defensible as the supporting information. That information should address the full scope of questions developed by evaluator-client collaboration and possess sufficient depth. It should be reliable, appropriate, and credible. It also should be combinable into a coherent whole for reaching valid conclusions about the evaluand's merit and worth. The contract must reflect these intended outcomes. Collecting the needed information requires responsiveness to audience interests, technical competence, legal and ethical actions, human relations skills, meticulous management of information, and good measures of creativity and resourcefulness.

In this chapter, we present a perspective and practical advice on the information collection task. We begin with a reminder of those professional standards that are most relevant to collecting information. We then present a framework within which to plan information collection activities; it is intended to ensure sufficient scope of obtained information and to encompass the evaluand's background, structure, operations, costs, and accomplishments. We end by summarizing selected information collection techniques that have proved especially useful in our evaluations.

Key Standards for Information Collection

The evaluation discipline includes clear standards, a vast literature, and strong procedures for developing, validating, and employing tools for collecting information. The Joint Committee on Standards for Educational Evaluation (1994) defined a range of standards to be met by an evaluation's information collection devices and activities: Information Scope and Selection, Rights of Human Subjects, Program Documentation, Context Analysis, Defensible Information Sources, Valid Information, Reliable Information, and Systematic Information. Moreover, the literature pertinent to meeting these standards is extensive. It includes guidelines and procedures for developing instrument blueprints, constructing response items, drafting and pilot-testing instruments, performing item analysis, finalizing instruments, developing norms, performing reliability and validity studies, selecting appropriate samples of respondents, controlling information collection conditions, verifying obtained data, keeping collected information secure, a range of ethical considerations, and many more. To the extent evaluators can find or develop instruments—both quantitative and qualitative—that pass muster within the canons of valid assessment, they are in a strong position to collect and defend the information needed to evaluate a program or other evaluand. By using a sufficiently broad range of pertinent and defensible information, evaluators can answer evaluative questions confidently, reach conclusions about an evaluand's quality and accomplishments, and persuasively advocate use of the evaluation's findings.

Therefore, evaluators need a firm grasp of standards for collecting sound evaluative information and should attend as carefully and systematically as they can to meeting the standards. In this section, we review what we consider to be the most important Joint Committee (1994) standards related to collecting evaluative information. For each standard, we present the Joint Committee's summary statement of the standard, explain it, add our comments, and note its relevance to the collection of evaluative information. We advise readers to consult the full text of each standard (Joint Committee, 1994).

Before proceeding, a caveat is needed. The practical constraints of many evaluation assignments preclude or make it extremely difficult to fully meet the standards associated with sound information collection. Evaluators often cannot pick instruments off the shelf that are fully valid for collecting information needed to draw inferences in the particular evaluation. In addition, they rarely have sufficient time and resources to carry out a full sequence of developing, pilot testing, reformulating, norming, and validating new instruments, a process that could require years of painstaking and expensive work. Typically, competent evaluators construct new instruments as systematically as they can, use other available instruments that may have only marginal validity for the particular study, gather existing relevant extant information, and repeatedly recycle the information collection process until findings are stable and defendable. In proceeding in this manner, evaluators need to take reasonably feasible steps to meet the standards related to information collection. However, they should not expect users of the evaluation to be comfortable or completely satisfied with information collection procedures and tools that fall short of fully meeting the laws of sound inquiry. Especially, evaluators should report to users any deficiencies in their collected information. Among the steps an evaluator should take to overcome weaknesses in information collection instruments is to build in cross-checks on findings. The main way to do this is to employ multiple sources of information and multiple methods, look for consensus in findings, and report both discrepancies and agreements in the findings. In sum, evaluators should take the standards seriously and do all they can to meet them, and they must forthrightly report limitations in the presented information. From this perspective, evaluators' modest aims are to help their audience at least increase the rationality and defensibility of their conclusions, judgments, and decisions.

Information Scope and Selection

The standard states, "Information collected should be broadly selected to address pertinent questions about the program and be responsive to the needs and interests of clients and other specified stakeholders" (Joint Committee, 1994, p. 37). It thus has two parts: scope and selectivity. To meet the spirit of the standard, evaluators often provide both more and less information than the client requests.

The evaluators should collect information that has sufficient scope to address the audience's most important information needs and support a judgment of merit and worth. Typically the evaluators should obtain information on all the important variables (for example, beneficiaries' needs and participation, program goals and assumptions, program design and implementation, program costs and outcomes, and positive and negative side effects). They should collect information on all the essential questions, whether the client and stakeholders specifically request the information. This is in keeping with the dictum that an evaluation is not just an information service, but essentially an assessment of merit and worth. As the Joint Committee (1994) states, "Evaluators should determine what the client considers significant but should also suggest significant areas the client may have overlooked, including areas identified by other stakeholders" (p. 37). Later in the chapter, we present a framework to help evaluators and clients ensure that they at least consider a comprehensive set of possible assessment variables.

The second important aspect of this standard is that evaluators necessarily have to be selective in deciding what information to collect. Typically it is not feasible to satisfy all the information interests of all the stakeholders. However, not all of the contemplated information will be equally important to stakeholders or essential for reaching evaluative conclusions. Initially the evaluators should identify the potential body of relevant information, including the information that the client and stakeholders desire and also what is needed to render a judgment of merit and worth. Subsequently the evaluators should work with the client and stakeholders to separate the most important items of information from those that are only desirable or of minor importance. Then in consideration of available funds and time, the evaluators should select the information to be collected judiciously.

Rights of Human Subjects

The standard states, "Evaluations should be designed and conducted to respect and protect the rights and welfare of human subjects" (Joint Committee, 1994, p. 93).

Most program evaluations gather information from and pertaining to a wide range of persons associated with the subject program: program beneficiaries, staff, administrators, policymakers, community members, and others. Without due process and care, evaluators might unwittingly or otherwise violate such persons' rights. Such violations can embarrass and otherwise harm the affected persons, evoke legal prosecution or professional sanctions, stir up dissension, and discredit and render the evaluation ineffective. Thus, evaluators systematically should identify and make provisions for adhering to all applicable rights of those who are party to the evaluation. Among the human rights to uphold are those concerned directly with the persons' roles in the evaluation and a wide range of more pervasive rights. Some rights are based in law, while others derive from ethics and common courtesy. The Joint Committee (1994) notes, "Legal provisions bearing on rights of persons include those dealing with consent for participation, privilege of withdrawal without prejudice and without withdrawal of treatment or services, privacy of certain opinions and information, confidentiality of information, and health and safety protections" (p. 93). In addition, ethical, commonsense, and courtesy considerations require evaluators to honor evaluation participants' rights to place limits on the extent and timing of their involvement in information collection, decline experiences they consider to be detrimental or uncomfortable, and respect the cultural and social values of all participants.

One important way to uphold rights of human subjects is to vet one's evaluation design through the appropriate institutional review board. Another is to follow the advice in the full text of the Joint Committee's Rights of Human Subjects standard assiduously. In following that advice, the evaluator should consider developing and sharing with human subjects the procedures that the evaluator and client will follow to ensure that participants' rights are protected. The evaluators should inform prospective information providers how the information they provide will be used. They should secure written permission from duly authorized parties for access to individual records and should make every effort to protect the identity of those who respond to evaluation instruments or otherwise supply information. They should obtain permission from respondents and the client to tape-record interviews (if the evaluators desire to do so). While it is often desirable to provide confidentiality or anonymity in gathering information, the evaluator should not promise either one when it cannot be guaranteed. In some evaluations, it is also desirable to make special provisions for language-minority participants to supply information for the evaluation, even if this means translating instruments into their first language. Certainly, when minors are involved in program evaluation (as occurs, for instance, with school-based studies), parental permission must be sought and given, and often an appropriate adult should be present during an interview session.

Program Documentation

The standard states, "The program being evaluated should be described and documented clearly and accurately, so that the program is clearly identified" (Joint Committee, 1994, p. 127).

When a final evaluation report is issued, readers need to know what was evaluated. It is insufficient to describe the program only as it was originally conceived, because its implementation may have been quite different. Also, it is not enough to characterize the program only in general terms, because many readers need detail. Readers who are interested in replicating the program require sufficient particulars to compare the program with critical competitors. If they decide to adopt the program, they need specific information to help decide how to organize their version of the program, launch it, and make it work. When a program fails, program funders and administrators need information on program expenditures, staffing, and operations in order to diagnose the reasons for failure. Moreover, researchers who want to understand a program's effects need detailed information about the program's actual operations so they can relate parts of the program to its outcomes.

Evaluators should collect sufficient information to help members of the audience understand both the program's original plan and its actual implementation. Clearly evaluators should collect information on how the program was structured, governed, staffed, financed, and carried out; where it was conducted; what facilities were used; how participants were oriented and trained; how much community involvement took place in the program (if any); and how program funds were budgeted and spent. Relevant sources of extant information about the program include generalized program descriptions, proposals, public relations reports, minutes of staff meetings, media presentations, newspaper accounts, expenditure reports, and progress and final reports. Additional information might need to be collected from participant observers, independent observers, interviews with various program participants, focus groups, and direct observation by the evaluators. Photographic records can also prove enlightening. In collecting information, it is wise to obtain both holistic descriptions and descriptions of program components. Over time, it can be useful to record time-specific descriptions in order to document and contrast changes in the program and identify trends. It is especially important to search out discrepancies between intended and actual program operations. Program documentation is a major and highly important information collection task.

Context Analysis

The standard states, "The context in which the program exists should be examined in enough detail, so that its likely influences on the program can be identified" (Joint Committee, 1994, p. 133).

We have seen repeatedly that a program's context can heavily influence how the program is designed and operated and what it achieves. Two or more programs with the same design often differ considerably in process and outcomes due to influences of their background and environmental circumstances. In order to understand how a program acquired its particular characteristics and its success or failure, evaluators need to collect considerable contextual information. Important contextual variables include the program's geographical location, the relevant political and social milieu, the economic health of the surrounding community, program-related needs and problems in the area, pertinent legislation, availability of special funds for work in the program area, highly influential persons, highly influential environmental events, how and why the program got started, its organizational home, its timing, its potential contributions to the locale, actual beneficiaries and their program-related needs, competing programs in the area, and pertinent state and national influences.

Formative evaluations require contextual information to help a program take account of local circumstances and identify and address beneficiaries' needs and problems. Summative evaluations require contextual information to help audiences understand why a program succeeded or failed and to prevent erroneous interpretations that the findings have wider applicability than the context justifies.

To consider how a program might work elsewhere, audiences need to know what highly influential contextual dynamics would have to be present in another setting. For example, an audience might want to know whether a program's success had been aided heavily by a strongly supportive community, a charismatic and unusually effective political leader, a sizable subsidy from a local foundation, or a history of social service agency cooperation. From another point of interest, an audience still might want to consider replicating an unsuccessful program if its failure clearly was due to environmental circumstances beyond the program's control. Examples of such negative influence could be local unrest, weak leadership and direction, a fiscal crisis in the program's organization, high staff turnover, or area devastation by a hurricane or tornado.

In describing a program's context, evaluators should draw information from multiple sources. Examples are minutes of board meetings, news accounts, area demographic statistics, area economic data, and pertinent legislation. Also, evaluators are advised to maintain a log of unusual circumstances. Negative forces might include a destructive flood, a strike in the program's organization, departure of a major area corporation, embezzlement of program funds, civil unrest, unanticipated changed legislation, unexpected opposition from area interest groups, or a health epidemic. Unexpected positive influences could be a major corporation's move to the area, an unanticipated grant from a national philanthropic foundation, or a scientific discovery. Relevant contextual information can be obtained from a wide range of individuals and groups, including school district officials and administrators, the local chamber of commerce, members of fraternal organizations, local clergy, real estate agents, newspaper reporters, corporation officials, local charitable foundation officials, social service organizations, law enforcement officials, court officials, and area business persons.

Defensible Information Sources

The standard states, "The sources of information used in a program evaluation should be described in enough detail, so that the adequacy of the information can be assessed" (Joint Committee, 1994, p. 141).

Because evaluation is mainly a time-constrained enterprise that functions under real-world complexities, evaluators typically should employ a variety of techniques to collect information from multiple sources. Sources may include program staff and beneficiaries, administrators and policy board members, newspapers and public records, program proposals and reports, data tapes, and program files. Evaluators employ a variety of techniques to tap these sources. Persons may be surveyed, tested, interviewed, engaged in focus groups or hearings, or asked to complete a rating scale. Documents and data files may be coded and subjected to content analysis. Program activities may be observed or photographed. Typically evaluators should employ both qualitative and quantitative methods. By using a variety of techniques to obtain information from multiple sources, the evaluators provide cross-checks and perspective for addressing each major evaluation question and help ameliorate limitations of individual sources and methods.

For each source of information, evaluators often cannot collect all of the potentially relevant information. For example, they cannot observe, test, and interview every beneficiary during every day of a program. No one would expect or tolerate such an extreme quest for information. In selecting information sources and methods, evaluators should avoid overloading respondents with unreasonable requests for providing information. Evaluators often collect information from only a sample of beneficiaries and only on a few days in the program. Moreover, they may have time to examine only a sample of records and other documents. Consequently, they need to be selective in collecting information.

Such selectivity introduces possibilities for both skewed and missing information. If the information is not representative of what occurred in the program or of responses that might have been obtained from all members of a particular respondent group, the evaluators may draw wrong conclusions and mislead the audience. Therefore, they need to introduce appropriate safeguards to enhance representativeness and transparency in their findings. They should be forthright in reporting limitations of their information sources. The Joint Committee (1994) advises evaluators to "document, justify, and report their sources of information, the criteria and methods used to select them, the means used to obtain information from them, and any unique and biasing features of the obtained information." The committee notes further that "poor documentation and description of information sources can reduce an evaluation's credibility" (p. 141). The evaluation's technical appendix should include documentation of information sources, the information collection process, and the instruments used to collect the information.

In most studies, evaluators draw samples from pertinent reference groups and document sets according to a wide range of sampling techniques. In some cases, evaluators employ simple random or stratified random sampling in order to estimate population parameters, such as the proportions of males and females in the population and the average and standard deviation of each group's postprogram achievement test scores. In general, a random sample is a subset of the members of a population such that each member has an equal, unbiased chance of being selected for the sample. A stratified random sample is one in which the population of interest is partitioned—for example, into males and females—followed by random selection of members from each part of the population.

The technology of random sampling allows an evaluator to set acceptable confidence intervals and draw a sample of sufficient size to achieve the desired level of precision. If the requirements of random sampling are met (and valid measures are obtained), the evaluators can reach defensible inferences about certain features of the population of interest. Unfortunately, it is often difficult in evaluation studies to meet the requirements of random sampling. Sampled subjects may agree to participate and later leave the program or opt out, subjects selected for a control group might switch to the experimental group, or subjects selected for interviews might not appear for the interview. The evaluator should document and report such deviations from their sampling plan. (For detailed and useful information on sampling techniques, see Henry, 1990; Kish, 1965; and Dillman & Tarnai, 1978.)

Although random samples generally are advocated in the evaluation literature, in the real world of evaluation, evaluators employ a variety of other sampling approaches with beneficial results. They may employ purposive sampling to obtain information from key informants such as the policy board's chairperson, the program's director, each program task leader, and the program's internal evaluator. In many evaluations, it is essential to obtain information from such stakeholders, and random sampling would not be applicable. Another especially useful technique is snowball sampling: interviewing one or a few individuals at the outset and asking each to identify others who should be interviewed. The evaluators then follow these leads and ask each successive interviewee to suggest other interviewees. Within limits of time and resources, the evaluators continue this process until they achieve redundancy in the collected information. An advantage of this approach is that it can guide evaluators to contact key informants who otherwise might not have been interviewed.

Despite an evaluation's sampling plan, interested stakeholders who were not sampled may desire to provide their input. There are good reasons for the evaluator to accept their information and incorporate it in the evaluation. Doing so lends credibility to the study and can influence the volunteers to take study findings seriously. Also, the evaluator may learn unique and valuable lessons from the volunteers. The main caveat here is that the evaluator should keep the volunteered information separate from the other obtained information, analyze the different sets separately, and inform readers of the limitations of such volunteer samples.

Not all evaluations have to employ sampling of respondents. Some studies obtain information from all of a program's beneficiaries, each staff member, and each member of the policy board. That was essentially the case in the example presented in Chapter Twelve. When data are gathered from all members of a population, one can report the results directly. In such cases, there is no need to make inferences from a sample to the population because information has been drawn from the total population. When evaluators can do this, they simplify their tasks of analyzing and reporting findings considerably. In planning data collection activities, we think it often is appropriate to consider the feasibility and desirability of taking measures from all members of the populations of interest. If this can and should be done, the evaluator proceeds to take population measures and sets aside concerns about sampling. Otherwise the evaluator can select and apply appropriate sampling techniques.

Whether they employ sampling or a population assessment approach, evaluators should report the information selection experience forthrightly, including its nature and its strengths and weaknesses. They should describe the sources of information, document the techniques and processes by which information was collected from each source, and document changes and difficulties that occurred along the way. When information was gathered through a cascading or iterative process, evaluators should report and justify the rules they followed to decide when to cease collecting information, for example, because of redundancy, new information that was only of marginal importance, or lack of additional time or resources. In regard to information that was collected according to a prespecified plan, the evaluators should report the original plan, any deviations from the plan, and the import of the deviations for interpreting findings.

Evaluators typically obtain both qualitative and quantitative information. They should not preordinately value one type of information more than the other, but should report the strengths and weaknesses of each and also their complementary nature. Again, we stress that evaluators should document and report both strengths and deficiencies in their information sources and, as appropriate, caution the audience not to place undue confidence in the obtained information.

Valid Information

The standard states, "The information gathering procedures should be chosen or developed and then implemented, so that they will assure that the interpretation arrived at is valid for the intended use" (Joint Committee, 1994, p. 145).

Validity concerns the soundness and defensibility of inferences or conclusions that are drawn from the information-gathering processes and products. Among the possible information-gathering products and associated processes are results of interviews, observations, document reviews, hearings, forums, focus groups, testimony, administration of rating scales, and administration of performance tests or objective tests. The processes should be chosen and employed to produce information that is relevant to study questions, reliable, and sufficient in scope and depth to answer all the evaluation's questions.

Validation of instruments and procedures is required to test and ensure the soundness of the obtained information for answering the study's questions. According to the Joint Committee on Standards for Educational Evaluation (1994), "Validation is the process of compiling evidence that supports the interpretations and uses of the data and information collected using one or more . . . instruments and procedures" (p. 145).

Following are the tasks in a sound process to validate use of a given information collection tool or procedure:

- Provide a detailed description of the program attribute about which information will be required; examples are program context, design, implementation, and outcomes.
- Determine the type of information a particular information collection tool or procedure is intended to acquire, for example, a description or judgment.
- Determine the type of information the tool or procedure provides.
- Describe in detail how the tool or procedure was applied and how well its application was monitored and controlled.
- Describe in detail and assess the credibility of the persons who collected or supplied the study's information.
- Determine the appropriate unit of analysis.
- Analyze the reliability of the obtained information, that is, its consistency and reproducibility, and judge whether reliability is sufficient for the intended use.
- Describe in detail and assess the procedures used to score, code, analyze, and interpret the obtained information.
- Compile qualitative and quantitative evidence that justifies or refutes the evaluation's intended use of the obtained information.
- Make an overall assessment of the inferences or conclusions drawn from the obtained information.

Validity resides not in any instrument or procedure but in its use in generating inferences and conclusions in a particular study. It is incorrect to generalize that an instrument or tool is valid or not valid. Instead, the evaluator should judge as valid or not valid the inferences or conclusions emanating from a particular use of an instrument or procedure. The key determinant of validity depends on how fully and dependably the obtained information answers the study's questions.

Evaluators should avoid the common mistake of assuming that their intended use of a procedure or instrument is justified because an investigator reported high validity in another study. Instead, evaluators need to validate their inferences or conclusions pursuant to the study's particular questions and based on assessments of that study's procedures and obtained information.

Due to feasibility constraints, evaluators often have to employ tools and procedures whose uses in the particular study do not evidence optimal validity. To counter this, they should employ multiple information collection methods to provide checks and balances on possibly weak measures and ensure that the combination of methods effectively addresses all of the study's questions. They should validate the inferences and conclusions resulting from multiple measures individually and in combination to ensure that the obtained information is pertinent, sufficient, and defensible. They should also report weaknesses in the obtained information and, as appropriate, warn readers to be cautious in using the findings. Especially, they should document their validation procedures and claims in a detailed technical appendix.

Following are practical tasks to assist evaluators in meeting validity requirements:

- Engage program personnel and other stakeholders to check proposed information collection tools and procedures against the evaluation questions.
- In choosing or developing information collection tools, pay close attention to the characteristics of the intended respondents (for example, their reading ability, physical disabilities, conflicts of interest, or native language) that might affect the validity of their responses.
- Obtain and report validity evidence from other similar studies that used the same evaluation tools.
- Follow sound instrument development procedures to minimize biased or confused answers from respondents; for example, in each item of a rating scale, include only a single point to be rated.
- Select appropriately qualified information collection personnel; provide them with orientation, training, support, and supervision; and document their qualifications and performance in the evaluation report's technical appendix.
- Carefully plan, monitor, supervise, and document information collection processes.
- Document and report significant contextual influences on information collection in the evaluation report's technical appendix.
- Report the validity claims and evidence for each evaluation tool and procedure and for all of them in combination in the evaluation report's methods section or technical appendix.

Reliable Information

The standard states, "The information gathering procedures should be chosen or developed and then implemented, so that they will assure that the information obtained is sufficiently reliable for the intended use" (Joint Committee, 1994, p. 153).

An evaluative conclusion cannot be valid if it is based on unreliable information. Information is unreliable to the extent that it contains unexplained contradictions and inconsistencies or if different answers would be obtained under subsequent but similar information collection conditions, absent a known intervention. Information is reliable when its consistency is evident: it is free of internal contradictions and, when repeated, information collection episodes would, as expected, yield the same answers.

One gauges the reliability of information by examining its amount and types of variation, including desired or explainable variation and unwanted variation. Most information-gathering procedures give information with some amount of internal disagreement, or if applied repeatedly, give at least slightly different answers between settings, groups, and different times of collection. Some of the variation could be due to random error in the procedure, such as traffic noise that may have caused some interviewees to misunderstand some of the questions or, as another example, poor motivation by some examinees to try their best to give correct answers to questions on a state achievement test. Other parts of the variation could be due to systematic, explainable sources. Examples are respondents who experience different parts of a program, males and females who might have different needs and respond to the same program experiences quite differently, and new program experiences that occur between times of information collection. Reliability should be judged negatively to the extent that there are wide variations in accounts or judgments of program operations or outcomes that could not be explained by systematic sources of variation.

Depending on the nature of the evaluation, evaluators can be concerned about different forms of reliability: stability, equivalence, and internal consistency. In some instances, the evaluator will expect information to be stable from one occasion to the next. For example, in a time-series study of the effects of a new vaccine, the evaluator might expect a succession of premeasures of morbidity in a population to be about the same and a succession of posttreatment measures of morbidity to be reduced but stable. The investigator is quite pleased to see an improvement from premeasures to postmeasures and would not count this as unreliability. However, he or she might be dissatisfied with substantial variations within the succession of pretreatment measures or the succession of posttreatment measures. Either of these could indicate low reliability regarding stability.

Another form of reliability concerns equivalence. Sometimes information is gathered at multiple sites, where essentially equivalent groups experienced the same program, and the evaluator expects findings to vary only as a function of differences in group composition and variations in how the program was delivered. Variation due to how the information was collected would be a mark against the equivalence of findings. Another example of equivalence reliability occurs in education, when alternate forms of a test are expected to yield equivalent scores for equivalent groups. One determines the level of equivalence unreliability in this circumstance by first separating out variance due to differences among the groups of examinees (for example, socioeconomic or private education levels) and then identifying and assessing the remaining unexplained variation.

One of the most common forms of reliability concerns internal consistency. This form looks at the extent of agreement between multiple assessments of a program and aspects of a program or other object. An example is an index of interjudge reliability that assesses the extent of agreement among ratings by independent judges. Other examples are the extent to which all items in an achievement test or attitude scale correlate positively with one another and with the total score, the consistency of characterizations provided by different observers, and the consistency of assessed needs identified by different analysts who examined the same set of materials.

Evaluators should determine which forms of reliability are most applicable to their study and make appropriate assessments. For all forms of reliability, they should strive to reduce or document the amount and impact of unwanted variation on the evaluation's information and conclusions. Following are actions evaluators can take to ensure that their evaluation conclusions are based on reliable information:

- When choosing from extant instruments, select ones that previously yielded information with acceptable reliability for answering questions like those in the projected evaluation.
- Clearly determine the unit of analysis for each information collection device, and assess reliability at that level of discourse.
- Carefully develop and follow a blueprint in constructing each information collection device, to include its rationale, target questions, sources of information, means of administration, and appropriate form of reliability assessment.
- Draft, pilot-test, and refine all new instruments.
- Engage stakeholders to review draft instruments and draft sets of findings, and carefully consider and address their assessments.
- Depending on the size of the evaluation, engage multiple data collectors, and examine their findings for consistency.
- Systematically train data collectors and those who will code, score, and analyze obtained information.

- Document reliability procedures and results in the evaluation report's methods section or technical appendix.

Systematic Information

The standard states, "The information collected, processed, and reported in an evaluation should be systematically reviewed, and any errors found should be corrected" (Joint Committee, 1994, p. 159).

Systematic information control is an information management process to ensure that an evaluation's information is regularly and carefully checked, made as error free as possible, and kept secure. There are numerous errors to avoid that include mistakes in collecting, scoring, coding, recording, organizing, filing, releasing, analyzing, and reporting information. Information might be collected from the wrong respondents. Interviewers might not adhere to the interview protocol. Information coders may not apply coding guidelines correctly. Data tapes or files may be misplaced. Unauthorized persons might be able to access filed information. Data might be analyzed inappropriately or incorrectly. There may be clerical errors in the preparation of reports. Results might be reported without needed caveats concerning errors that were discovered but not corrected. Erroneous data might be included in reports. Report findings might be leaked. These are only some of the things that can go wrong in the course of obtaining, processing, and reporting information.

Evaluators should institute safeguards to prevent all such mistakes. Otherwise members of the audience may be misled to place unwarranted confidence in erroneous information, or the evaluation might become the center of controversy. When mistakes are uncovered belatedly, the evaluation is likely to be discredited and rendered useless. A sound information management process includes systematic orientation and training of evaluation personnel, close supervision of all aspects of the evaluation, and checks for accuracy. It also includes a secure filing system including rules and systematic procedures for accessing, reviewing, and replacing files. Evaluators should maintain control of original information and results and, as appropriate, make copies for the use of coders and analysts. Often they should engage persons who supplied information to review it for accuracy. It is especially important to verify data entry for accuracy and to proofread data tables and other renderings of the evaluative information.

The Standards' Key Themes Concerning Information Collection

As seen in this section (and Chapter Three), the evaluation field has developed a set of strong standards to help evaluators obtain defensible information. We advise evaluators to master and regularly apply professional standards for evaluations. The Joint Committee's *Program Evaluation Standards* (1994) provides many helpful references accompanying each standard. The eight standards highlighted and elaborated on here are especially helpful in fostering the collection of sound information. A theme that runs through these standards is the necessity of employing multiple information sources and multiple procedures. These are needed to cover the scope of needed information and to provide checks and balances on individual procedures that, for practical reasons, often cannot be fully validated. Moreover, most evaluations should be based on obtaining, analyzing, and synthesizing qualitative and quantitative information. Another important theme in the section is that evaluators should document and report in detail their information collection procedures and the strengths and weaknesses of the obtained information. We recommend that evaluators include such information in a technical appendix.

An Information Collection Framework

Table 24.1 offers a framework for planning an evaluation's information collection component. It is intended to help evaluators consider a comprehensive set of potential information needs and a wide range of possibly relevant information collection procedures and subsequently to relate the two. At the top of the table are seven areas of information needs drawn from the CIPP model, which was presented in Chapter Fifteen. Arrayed down the vertical dimension are fifteen techniques that we and other evaluators have found particularly useful in a wide range of evaluations. The Xs in the cells illustrate how an overall information collection plan might be charted and summarized. Such a summary is especially useful to assess the extent to which the plan provides for multiple measures of each area of information and to communicate the overall scheme to the client. The rows with blanks illustrate that not all procedures are necessarily relevant or needed in particular studies.

Table 24.1 is intended for use in conceptualizing an overall master plan of information collection. Subsequently, additional tables can be constructed to elaborate the information collection plan. Evaluators can adapt the table by replacing its horizontal dimension with a time line to show which procedures will be applied at which times. This analysis helps avoid collecting too much information at any one time and also is an aid to scheduling information collection activities. Table 24.2 is an illustration of this adaptation of Table 24.1.

Tables 24.1 and 24.2 summarize macrolevel plans and are useful especially for communicating with clients. In addition, evaluators require plans at the microlevel to guide the specific work of information collection. Each information area should be broken out in terms of specific information needs. Table 24.3 illustrates how this is done in relation to the information area of program outcomes. In this table, the information area has been divided into intended effects, side effects, and cost-effectiveness. Similar derivative tables can be constructed for

TABLE 24.1. A FRAMEWORK FOR PLANNING AN EVALUATION'S INFORMATION COLLECTION.

Areas of Information

Information Collection Procedures	Program Context and Beneficiaries' Needs	Program Plan and Competing Approaches	Program Activities and Costs	Program Reach to Targeted Beneficiaries	Program Outcomes	Program Sustainability	Program Transportability
Document, files, and data tape retrieval and review	X	X	X	X	X	X	
Literature review		X					
Interviews	X		X	X	X	X	X
Traveling observer or resident researcher			X				
Site visits		X	X			X	
Surveys							
Rating scales							
Focus groups				X		X	X
Hearing							
Public forum							
Observations			X				
Case studies					X		
Goal-free studies					X		X
Knowledge tests							
Self-assessment devices							

Note: This table illustrates how different procedures might be designated to obtain different types of information.

TABLE 24.2. ILLUSTRATIVE TIME LINE FOR APPLYING AN EVALUATION'S DIFFERENT INFORMATION COLLECTION PROCEDURES.

Time Periods in the Evaluation

Information Collection Procedures	Period 1 (Start-Up and Context Evaluation)	Period 2 (Input Evaluation)	Period 3 (Process Evaluation and Cost Analysis)	Period 4 (Process and Impact Evaluations)	Period 5 (Outcome Evaluation)	Period 6 (Sustainability and Transportability Evaluation)	Period 7 (Final Report Preparation and Delivery)
Document, files, and data tape retrieval and review	X	X	X	X	X	X	
Literature review		X					
Interviews	X		X	X	X	X	
Traveling observer or resident researcher			X	X			
Site visits		X	X			X	
Surveys							
Rating scales							
Focus groups				X		X	
Hearing							
Public forum							
Observations			X	X			
Mini-case studies					X		
Goal-free studies					X	X	
Knowledge tests							
Self-assessment devices							

TABLE 24.3. FRAMEWORK FOR PLANNING AN EVALUATION'S INFORMATION COLLECTION COMPONENT.

Information Collection Procedures	Aspects of Program Outcomes		
	Intended Effects	Side Effects	Cost-Effectiveness
Document, files, and data tape retrieval and review	X		X
Literature review			
Interviews	X	X	
Traveling observer or resident researcher			
Site visits			
Surveys			
Rating scales			
Focus groups			
Hearing			
Public forum			
Observations			
Mini–case studies	X	X	
Goal-free studies	X	X	
Knowledge tests			
Self-assessment devices			

Note: The table illustrates how different procedures might be designated to obtain information for assessing different aspects of program outcomes.

each area of information. (See Chapter Fifteen for breakouts of each of the seven areas of information.)

Useful Methods for Collecting Information

We have recommended that evaluators consider and selectively apply a variety of information collection methods. These include qualitative and quantitative methods, and they are used to obtain information from a wide range of sources. Such sources include existing records and other printed material, data tapes, relevant publications, and the full range of program stakeholders, including especially the beneficiaries and program personnel, other interested parties, experts with relevant expertise, and the investigators. In this section, we describe and comment on some methods that we have found especially useful in evaluations and are not widely discussed in the evaluation literature.

Document, File, and Data Tape Retrieval and Review

As a general practice, it is wise to start the information collection process by identifying and collecting relevant existing information for analysis. Collecting and using such information enhances both the scope of obtained information and efficiency in the information collection process. Working from existing information can produce cost savings for the evaluation.

This practice may also enhance accuracy, since much of the information will have already been assessed systematically and edited. Using existing information is considerate of respondents, since the investigator will not need to ask them to supply information that is already collected, sound, and accessible. However, the use of existing information does not entirely limit evaluators' questioning of stakeholders about that information. Evaluators often need stakeholders to verify the accuracy of the information, cross-check areas that may be in conflict, and clear up ambiguities. In selecting and using existing information, evaluators should remember that it was obtained for purposes other than answering their evaluation's questions. Therefore, they should ensure that the information is valid for its intended use in the particular evaluation. As Table 24.2 shows, the collection and analysis of existing documents, files, and data tapes continues throughout the evaluation process.

Existing information of potential use in an evaluation may be of many types. Exhibit 24.1 provides a checklist of some of the files and documents that may be relevant in particular studies. For convenience, we have grouped the items of information according to where they likely will be found. The left-hand column contains information that typically exists outside the program and its home institution, and the right-hand column presents information more likely to be present in the program or its home institution. However, in the case of an evaluation of a national or state-level program, some of the information in the left-hand column might be considered internal information. The main points of the exhibit are that evaluators should consider a broad range of documents and files that may be responsive to evaluative questions of interest and then should use those that are found to be relevant and valid for the intended use.

The most pertinent existing information is likely to be available at the program site. In identifying and accessing this information, the evaluator should consult the client, and together they should institute safeguards against violating the rights of

EXHIBIT 24.1. CHECKLIST OF DOCUMENTS
AND FILES OF POTENTIAL USE IN EVALUATIONS.

Often External to the Program	Often Internal to the Program
____ Community demographic information	____ Statistics on targeted beneficiaries
____ Census reports	____ Needs assessment reports
____ Consumer reports	____ Institutional mission
____ Journal articles	____ Strategic plan
____ Almanac	____ Curriculum
____ Encyclopedias	____ Collective bargaining agreement
____ Magazines	____ Institutional policies handbook
____ Laws and statutes	____ Program proposal
____ Court records	____ Program progress reports
____ Police reports	____ Program evaluation reports
____ Real estate records	____ Minutes of meetings
____ Chamber of commerce records	____ Staff résumés
____ Accreditation standards	____ Program budget
____ State standards	____ Program financial records
____ State achievement test reports	____ Accounting reports
____ National achievement test reports	____ Audit reports
____ Polls	____ Log of visitors to the program
____ National survey reports	____ Correspondence
____ State survey reports	____ Local achievement test reports
____ Local survey reports	____ School district attendance records
____ Newspaper articles	____ School district graduation records
____ National data tapes	____ School district discipline records
____ State data tapes	____ Local survey reports
____ *Congressional Record*	____ Hospital charts
____ White House reports	____ Immunization records
____ Government department reports	____ College admission records
____ Professional society reports	____ College graduation records
____ Health department reports	____ Local data tapes
____ Stock market indexes	____ Accident reports
____ Internet sites	____ Insurance records
____ Information clearinghouses	____ Publicity releases
____ Other	____ Other

anyone associated with the information. Other relevant information may be found by conducting searches on the Internet and visiting the local library, newspaper offices, government agencies, social service organizations, and other organizations. The evaluator should plan and budget as required for retrieving and assessing relevant existing information.

Literature Reviews

A special case of retrieving and analyzing existing information is the standard literature review, as typically employed in doctoral dissertation research. Such reviews have two particular uses in evaluations. When planning an evaluation, the evaluators may obtain ideas and instruments usefully by identifying and examining the methods and tools used in similar evaluations. In its second use, the evaluators can conduct a literature review of evaluation and research reports to assist in answering one or more of the evaluation's substantive questions. Conducting, reporting, and otherwise using literature reviews lends scholarly credibility to an evaluation and also can save time and resources that would otherwise be devoted to devising instruments or collecting information that only duplicates previous efforts. Obviously the Internet is a valuable source of information.

Each of the two types of literature review starts with a specific question. For example, in the case of planning an evaluation, one might focus the literature review to determine what procedures and instruments have been used to assess preschool children's needs for immunization. In the case of answering a substantive question, one might seek national statistics on the incidence of Attention Deficit Disorder Syndrome among first- and second-grade students. This could be a part of the evaluation's needs assessment.

To investigate either question, the evaluators might begin by doing an informal exploratory search of the applicable literature, perhaps with the assistance of an expert consultant or a librarian. Subsequently, the evaluators would need to define their search parameters. These could include (1) a set time period within which documents were published; (2) reports only from doctoral dissertations, specified refereed journals, and externally funded evaluations; and (3) key words from the question being addressed. The evaluators would next use an appropriate computer search engine to identify documents that meet the search criteria. Subsequently they would screen these to cull documents that do not address the question of interest. Next, they would systematically review the remaining documents to identify pertinent responses to the question of interest and evaluate the quality of those responses. The results from this review would be studied to identify areas of agreement and contradictions. In addition, the evaluators would scrutinize references in the documents carefully and obtain and study additional relevant documents that were not in the original set. They could then analyze and synthesize the obtained information and incorporate it with other information to answer the question of interest.

In the case of the first example given above, the evaluators would use the information to choose or develop methods and instruments for conducting the projected evaluation. They would pay special attention to validity and reliability evidence related to identified tools and methods. Regarding the second example, the evaluators would use the literature review results to assist in reporting the national incidence of attention deficit disorder syndrome in first- and second-grade children. Such information could provide a valuable baseline against which to examine and interpret local statistics on the disorder.

Interviews

Among the most useful evaluation methods is the interview. This procedure enables the evaluator to obtain descriptive and judgmental information from a wide range of persons who have important perspectives on a program, its setting, or its beneficiaries. Interviews may be highly structured and inflexible, as in the case of many telephone interviews; relatively unstructured and exploratory; or quite structured but flexible in their administration. They may be conducted with individuals or groups or face to face or over a telephone. All of these variations of interviews can be highly informative. What they have in common is a quest to obtain valuable information for use in understanding and judging a program or other evaluand or to obtain leads for pursuing additional information sources.

Whatever the type of interview, its effectiveness and fairness depend on a number of common factors. The interview should be thought through in advance and well planned in terms of the information being sought. The interview protocol should be drafted as clearly as possible, critiqued by others, pilot-tested, and refined. Interviewees should be selected carefully, though not necessarily to represent a population. Depending on the purpose of the interviews, interviewees may be chosen based on random, purposive, or snowball sampling. When possible, they should be contacted in advance to request their agreement to participate. They should be informed of the evaluation's purpose and the roles of interviewee and interviewer. They should also be informed of the amount of time for the interview. In our experience, most interviews should consume fifty minutes or less. Interviewees should be informed whether their responses will be anonymous or kept in confidence. If not, the evaluator should obtain written permission to associate responses with the particular respondent or not proceed further with that interviewee. If the interviewer desires to tape-record the interview, the evaluator should so inform the interviewee and obtain permission. If the interviewee declines this condition, the evaluator should agree to use paper and pencil to document interviewee responses. As appropriate, the evaluators also should consult prospective interviewees about when and where the interview should be conducted. In some of our evaluations, interviewees preferred to be interviewed in their homes. This can have the advantage of observing the interviewee in his or her home environment, but is also subject to distractions. We have sometimes experienced children running about, telephone interruptions, a television playing in an adjoining room, visitors arriving to observe, and a chain saw roaring just outside the house. In general, we prefer a neutral, quiet site for conducting face-to-face interviews; nevertheless, there can be good reasons to conduct interviews in an interviewee's home or other setting.

When the interviewee agrees to participate, the interview should be scheduled at a time that is convenient for him or her, which in some cases could be immediately. Prior to an interview scheduled for a future time, it is prudent to telephone interviewees or send them a note with a reminder of the approaching interview, as do many doctors and dentists to help prevent no-shows.

It is important to establish rapport with the interviewee at the outset. The interviewer might review the interview's purpose, indicate that the interviewee is deemed to possess a valuable perspective on the subject program or other evaluand, review the prior agreements under which the interview will be conducted, state appreciation for the interviewee's participation, reiterate how much time the interview will require, and invite and respond to any questions from the interviewee. Usually this initial orientation and exchange are sufficient to establish rapport for a productive interview.

When the interviewer proceeds to conduct the interview, some means should be provided to record the interviewee's responses. The interviewer might check multiple-choice options on the interview protocol as the interview proceeds (especially in the case of telephone interviews), write out the interviewee's responses, or tape-record the session if prior permission has been obtained from the interviewee. When feasible, it can be especially productive to have two members of an interview team. One conducts the interview, and the other keeps notes and, as appropriate, interjects follow-up questions, especially when responses were not clear. In successive interviews, the interviewees can intermittently exchange interviewing and note-taking roles. As an interview proceeds, the interviewer should, as needed, ask the interviewee to clarify or elaborate on unclear or incomplete responses . At the end of the interview, it is a good idea to invite interviewees to add any information they view as important. Finally, the interviewer should thank the interviewee for her or his valuable contribution to the study.

Following an interview, it is important to review the written record of the responses as soon as possible, while the memory of the session is fresh. Since a written record of the interview is likely to be cryptic, this is the time to add details that one remembers but did not write down. Clearly this point has implications for scheduling when multiple interviews are involved. If possible, the evaluator should schedule time following each interview to scrutinize the results and flesh out the record. This activity may not be necessary if the full interview session was tape-recorded. In that event, the tape should be transcribed for review and analysis. The preceding discussion is intended to apply generally to all types of interviews. However, different types have some unique requirements worth mentioning:

- *Telephone interviews.* Typically multiple interviewers conduct the interviews within a phone bank and code responses as they are received. The interview protocols need to be scripted carefully so that all interviewers will obtain comparable data that can be aggregated and analyzed. The interviews must be administered according to a standard protocol. The interviewers should be thoroughly trained, calibrated, and supervised. Usually the interviewees in telephone interviews are selected randomly or systematically in order to ensure that they are representative of a population of interest. An advantage of tightly scripted telephone interviews is that they are quite amenable to scoring, aggregation, and statistical analysis. A disadvantage is that they are not sufficiently open-ended and flexible to obtain in-depth information that capitalizes on the idiosyncratic insights of different respondents.
- *Loosely structured, flexible interviews.* These interviews are much harder to summarize, aggregate, and subject to statistical analysis than telephone interviews. Nevertheless, they can yield invaluable qualitative information, and their results are amenable to qualitative analysis and identifying important themes. In using this approach, the investigator usually wants to gain insights into the strengths and weaknesses of a program from a wide range of perspectives. At the outset, he or she may have in mind a set of questions and persons who could answer them. However, too much structure might prevent the evaluator from obtaining a rich set of insights from parties other than those on the initial list of interviewees. Such respondents might identify key issues in a program that the evaluator has not thought to investigate previously. Thus, the evaluator might start by contacting a few known stakeholders. In the initial interviews, the evaluator might ask the respondent to identify and discuss what he or she considers to be the most important issues in the subject program. Near the end of the session, the interviewer would ask the interviewee to identify anyone who might have additional insights into the issues discussed. Subsequently, the evaluator would follow the obtained leads and contact the identified persons. They also would be asked to identify issues and other persons who could shed light on them. From interview to interview, the evaluator would review and keep a record of what is being learned. At the end of the process,

he or she would have a rich set of information to examine, analyze, and synthesize. This approach employs snowball sampling to choose interviewees.

• *Structured but flexibly administered interviews.* In this approach, the evaluator prepares a structured set of questions. If possible, these questions might be on a single sheet of paper. The interviewer might provide a copy of the interview questions to the interviewee as an agenda and a heuristic. The interviewer then starts the process by asking the first question. As the interviewee responds, he or she may expand beyond stated questions and begin to answer other questions further down the list. As long as responses are relevant to the established questions, the interviewer allows the respondent to move through them in any sequence that helps him or her get the message across. In this approach, the interviewer is concerned with obtaining in-depth, coherent responses to all the questions, but is not concerned about the sequence of responses. In some cases, the evaluator might not employ a printed list of the questions but instead hold the set of questions in her or his mind . In this case, a skillful interviewer asks a question to start the interview and then engages in a free-flowing discussion with the interviewee. The evaluator keeps mental track of the extent to which all the questions are being addressed in whatever sequence and steers the discussion to make sure that all questions are answered. In this approach, it is desirable that the session be tape-recorded or that a second interviewer keeps notes. If tape-recording is not agreed to in this type of interview, we have found it advantageous to have two interviewers in an interview session: one to administer the questions and the other to keep detailed notes and ask follow-up questions.

Interviewing is one of the most pervasive, adaptable, and valuable procedures for gathering evaluative information. Although there are alternative acceptable approaches to interviewing, all forms of the procedure should be applied with careful planning and rigor. (For additional information, see Bradburn & Sudman, 1980; Czaja, Blair, & Sebestik, 1982; Dillman & Tarnai, 1978; Eder & Ferris, 1989; Kvale, 1996; Lavrakas, 1986; and Sudman & Bradburn, 1982.)

Focus Groups

A variation of the interview is the focus group procedure, a group interview approach developed by the consumer research field and widely used during the 1950s and 1960s. Since then, the technique has been adapted and applied for several different purposes. After (or preceding) elections, focus groups often are seen on television in which a moderator engages voters or likely voters to discuss election issues or results. Evaluators frequently use the technique to obtain and analyze the views of stakeholders about the merit and worth of a subject program or pertaining to given evaluation questions.

Originally researchers employed this technique to engage a sample of consumers to judge a consumer product or service. As a usual procedure, the researchers recruited about a dozen consumers—usually in a typical community, such as Columbus, Ohio—and interviewed them as a group to hear their individual and collective judgments of a product or service they had tried. The interviews would last up to two hours and focus on questions of particular interest to those who develop and market the product or service. In starting the session, the moderator would stipulate that each person's perception is important, that there are no right or wrong answers, that participants should feel free to agree or disagree, and that they should probe each other's responses in the interest of providing in-depth understanding and revealing key areas of agreement and disagreement. Especially, the focus group members were asked to be advocates for the potential consumers of the subject product or service. Accordingly, they were expected to send a message to developers concerning what people like themselves need and expect of the product or service and what they saw as good and bad about the one they had tried. The moderator's responsibilities were to draw all panelists into the ensuing discussion of each question, keep the interview moving, ask follow-up questions to promote clear and in-depth responses, and prevent any one member from dominating the discussion. An observer would make a written record of the interchange, and the session likely would be tape-recorded or videotaped. The investigator subsequently would analyze the focus group record to identify areas of agreement and disagreement and discern important themes. The target audience would use the focus group findings along with other information to make decisions related to modifying, packaging, advertising, and selling the subject product or service.

The evaluation field adapted and began using focus groups in the 1970s. Evaluators had begun to expand their methods into the realm of qualitative methods. In the early stages of this movement, evaluators mainly borrowed qualitative methods from other fields, including jurisprudence, sociology, psychology, ethnography, and consumer research. In the focus group procedure, evaluators found a ready-made tool for systematically obtaining multiple perspectives on given evaluation questions. This technique provided some of the benefits found in individual interviews and provided insights based on the interplay among multiple respondents during a single session. It is noteworthy that an evaluation might employ multiple focus groups—for example, one for staff, one for beneficiaries, one for policy members, and one for subject matter experts. Generally the membership of each focus group should be homogeneous.

Evaluators have tended to stay true to the original intent and procedures of focus groups but also have made some changes in the technique. Drawing from our experience in using the technique, we offer the following recommendations for selecting and engaging focus groups to help evaluate programs:

1. Determine a homogeneous class of potential members of the focus group.
2. Stipulate the issue that the focus group will address.
3. Determine a sequence of questions designed to move the group's discussion toward the issue of interest.
4. Select seven to ten members to participate; they should share a common perspective, such as that of beneficiary, but otherwise reflect the diversity of the larger group that shares their perspective on such matters as gender, age, education, and ethnicity.
5. Allot one to two hours for the session.
6. Hold the meeting in a setting that is comfortable, free from distractions, and conducive to discussion. It might be a round table or a circle of easy chairs in a quiet room.
7. Make a record of the group discussion using a tape recorder, video recorder, or written notes.
8. Provide all members of the group with a common orientation to the meeting's objective, agenda of questions, relevant background information, structure, the role they will play, and time allotment for the session.
9. Stress that each person's perception is important, that participants should feel free to agree or disagree, and that they should probe each other's responses in the interest of providing in-depth understanding and revealing key differences of opinion.
10. Conduct the session within a permissive, nonthreatening atmosphere.
11. Skillfully keep the discussion focused on the meeting's objectives; move the conversation through the agenda of questions; ask follow-up questions to promote clear, in-depth responses; and prevent any one member from dominating.
12. Ensure that all group members are given the opportunity to participate and are encouraged to do so.
13. In concluding the session, invite each member to state what he or she judges to be the one or two most important points made during the session.
14. Thank everyone for participating, and adjourn the meeting.
15. Following the meeting, prepare a transcript of the exchange.
16. Analyze the focus group record to identify areas of agreement and disagreement and to discern important themes.

Traveling Observers and Resident Researchers

The traveling observer (TO) technique, developed at the Western Michigan University Evaluation Center, involves the training and assignment of a field researcher to conduct preliminary investigations in advance of subsequent primary evaluations by a panel of experts. Typically, the TO travels from site to site to contact and develop rapport with data providers, collect preliminary information, and work out a plan for a follow-up site visit team. The TO next provides orientation and training to the site visit team prior to its site visits and may support the team during its on-site investigations. Usually the TO is a relatively junior investigator, with members of the follow-up team being more senior. Often the TO spends considerably more days in gathering preliminary data than will the follow-up site visit team. Compensation for the TO usually is paid at a considerably lower rate than the rate for members of the site visit team. Thus, an advantage of the technique is that it saves money for a sizable part of the needed field research.

A variation of the technique is the resident researcher technique, which essentially is the application of the TO approach at a single site. (The traveling observer technique is described more fully in Chapter Fifteen.)

Advocacy Teams Technique

The advocacy teams technique was developed at the Evaluation Center when it was located at the Ohio State University. It was created and applied in 1969 to help the Texas-based Southwest Regional Educational Laboratory identify and assess alternative strategies for serving the acute education needs of migrant children. This technique was created because the methodology of evaluation lacked procedures for identifying and assessing competing strategies for addressing high-priority needs and problems.

The advocacy teams technique has five main steps. The first is to stipulate a target group of beneficiaries and identify objectives to be achieved in meeting this group's assessed needs. The second step is to create alternative strategies for achieving the stipulated objectives. The evaluator establishes two or more advocacy teams, and each team is provided with the subject objectives, pertinent needs assessment information, criteria for assessing proposed program strategies, and a structure for writing up a proposed program strategy. Next, each advocacy team studies the needs assessment data and pertinent literature, brainstorms toward inventing an appropriate program strategy, and writes up its proposed program strategy. In the fourth step, an independent panel evaluates the advocacy teams' proposals against the predetermined criteria and ranks them on overall merit. The client then chooses a strategy for implementation or may assign a convergence team to merge the best features of the competing plans into a hybrid plan. The technique is keyed directly to a decision-making group's needs for creative solutions to high priority needs and problems. (Additional information about this technique appears in Chapter Fifteen.)

Additional Techniques

In addition to the techniques reviewed here, we recommend that evaluators be resourceful in searching broadly for techniques that will address the information needs of their studies effectively. Some of these techniques are discussed in other chapters in this book, including the success case method (Chapter Seven), case study (Chapter Fifteen), and goal-free evaluation (Chapter Seventeen). Other techniques, such as questionnaires and rating scales, are treated in a wide range of research and evaluation methodology textbooks (for example, see Bickman & Rog, 1998; Rossi & Freeman, 1993; Wiersma & Jurs, 2005; and Fitzpatrick, Sanders, & Worthen, 2004).

Summary

The collection of sound information is essential to the success of any program evaluation. Evaluators must obtain a sufficient range and depth of appropriate and reliable information if they are to reach valid conclusions about a program's merit and worth. The Joint Committee's *Program Evaluation Standards* (1994) provides authoritative, useful advice for carrying out sound processes of information collection; evaluators are advised to master and regularly apply these standards. Use of the standards can be helpful in determining what information to collect, upholding the rights of human subjects, studying the program's context, fully describing program operations, using appropriate sampling methods, checking and enhancing the reliability of evidence, validating instruments, and maintaining the integrity of obtained information. Because of the practical constraints in almost all program evaluations, evaluators often have to apply less-than-perfect instruments. They are advised to employ multiple methods in order to provide crosschecks in their search for consistent findings and also to report the limitations of the information they obtain. Evaluators should plan their data collection efforts to fulfill the study's information requirements and also to uphold the rights of respondents and not impose undue burdens on program participants. The research and evaluation fields have produced a wide range of information collection techniques, and evaluators are advised to make good, selective use of the available information collection tools and strategies—both quantitative and qualitative.

Review Questions

1. The validity of evaluative conclusions depends heavily on the adequacy of the information used to reach the conclusions. In general, what requirements should be met by the information that an evaluator uses to judge a program's merit and worth?

2. This chapter discusses the relevance of certain Joint Committee standards for guiding and assessing the collection of information in an evaluation. Explain

the relevance of each of the following standards to the information collection task: Information Scope and Selection, Rights of Human Subjects, Program Documentation, Context Analysis, Defensible Information Sources, Valid Information, Reliable Information, and Systematic Information.

3. Why is it misleading or even incorrect to state that a given evaluation instrument is valid?

4. Distinguish between the terms *valid information* and *reliable information,* and explain why validity is dependent on reliability.

5. What is the basis of the recommendation that evaluators often should employ multiple methods?

6. List steps you would follow to validate a data collection instrument to be used in a particular evaluation.

7. What are the main benefits and also some of the hazards of obtaining and studying existing information as a partial basis for judging a program?

8. What is the role of the literature review in program evaluations?

9. What is the traveling observer technique? How is it used in a program evaluation? What are some advantages of employing this technique in a program evaluation?

10. What is the focus group procedure, and what are its uses in program evaluations?

Group Exercises

Exercise 1. Define each of the following techniques, and then develop an example of how you might beneficially apply each of the techniques in an evaluation: random sampling, stratified random sampling, purposive sampling, snowball sampling, and study of an entire population.

Exercise 2. Develop an illustrative case showing the relevance and process involved in applying the advocacy teams technique.

Exercise 3. Develop a checklist of points to observe in planning and conducting sound interviews of a program's beneficiaries.

Exercise 4. A small county hospital has been in the news for all the wrong reasons: two forced resignations of chief administrators within the past three years, high staff turnover based on what appears to be legitimate grievances, evident shortage of funds to meet some basic medical requirements, and a series of minor scandals involving medical and nursing staff. This sad chronicle of events was capped by the death of two patients resulting from salmonella contamination in the hospital's kitchen. County taxpayers, the hospital's stakeholders, could endure these catastrophes no further. They called a special general meeting that forced the hospital board to initiate immediate evaluation of the institution's procedures, finances, culture (including its effectiveness as a health service), and future viability for the community. The board issued a general request for proposal, part of which required implementation of the focus group procedure in order to obtain stakeholder input.

Your group decides to respond to this RFP. Your assignment in this exercise is to answer the following questions concerning the focus group component convincingly:

a. What perspectives will be important to include in the members of the focus group? Justify your response.

b. How many persons would you include in the group, and why?

c. In selecting the members of the focus group, what sampling procedure would you use, and why?

d. What evaluator roles would you employ to conduct the focus group? What responsibilities would you assign to each role? Justify your answers.

e. Outline the main questions to be addressed in the focus group session. Justify your response.

f. To what extent would you follow a strict agenda versus a totally free-flowing discussion? Justify your answer.

g. Outline an agenda for this session. Justify your plan.

h. How much time would you allow for conducting the session? Justify your response.

i. Outline the contents of your projected report of the focus group session, and justify your plan for this part of the overall evaluation report.

j. List criteria for assessing the focus group segment of the proposed evaluation and justify these criteria.

Conclude this group discussion exercise with each group member briefly stating a known situation where the focus group procedure would be an appropriate technique to use for collecting information for an evaluation.

References

Bickman, L., & Rog, D. J. (1998). *Handbook of applied social research methods.* Thousand Oaks, CA: Sage.

Bradburn, N. A., & Sudman, S. (1980). *Improving interview methods and questionnaire design.* San Francisco: Jossey-Bass.

Czaja, R., Blair, J., & Sebestik, J. P. (1982). Respondent selection in a telephone survey: A comparison of three techniques. *Journal of Marketing Research, 21,* 381–385.

Dillman, D. A., & Tarnai, J. (1978). *Mail and telephone surveys: The total design method.* Hoboken, NJ: Wiley.

Eder, R. W., & Ferris, G. R. (Eds.) (1989). *The employment interview: Theory, research, and practice.* Thousand Oaks, CA: Sage.

Fitzpatrick, J. L., Sanders, J. R., & Worthen, B. R. (2004). *Program evaluation: Alternative approaches and practical guidelines.* Needham Heights, MA: Allyn and Bacon.

Henry, G. T. (1990). *Practical sampling: Applied social research methods series.* Thousand Oaks, CA: Sage.

Joint Committee on Standards for Educational Evaluation. (1994). *The program evaluation standards.* Thousand Oaks, CA: Corwin Press.

Kish, L. (1965). *Survey sampling.* Hoboken, NJ: Wiley.

Kvale, S. (1996). *Interviews: An introduction to qualitative research interviewing.* Thousand Oaks, CA: Sage.

Lavrakas, P. (1986). *Telephone surveys.* Thousand Oaks, CA: Sage.

Rossi, P. H., & Freeman, H. E. (1993). *Evaluation: A systematic approach.* Thousand Oaks, CA: Sage.

Sudman, S., & Bradburn, N. M. (1982). *Asking questions.* San Francisco: Jossey-Bass.

Wiersma, W., & Jurs, S. G. (2005). *Research methods in education: An introduction.* Needham Heights, MA: Allyn and Bacon.

CHAPTER TWENTY-FIVE

ANALYZING AND SYNTHESIZING INFORMATION

The objectives of collecting information in an evaluation are to provide an evidentiary basis for answering priority questions and ultimately judging the program or other object of interest. To finalize an evaluation, the evaluators need to proceed beyond the collection of information and work through the subsequent processes of analyzing and synthesizing the information and ultimately reporting and supporting use of the findings.

This chapter presents a perspective and practical advice on the analysis and synthesis tasks. By *analysis,* we mean identifying and assessing the constituent elements of each set of obtained information and their interrelationships in order to clarify the information's dependability and meaning for answering particular questions. By *synthesis,* we mean combining analysis findings across information collection procedures and devices in order to discern their validity and aggregate meaning for answering the audience's questions and judging the value of the object of interest. For purposes of explanation and illustration, analysis and synthesis are presented in this chapter as independent stages in the evaluation process. In reality, these processes are dependent on and party to the other evaluation processes—design and preparation, collection of information, and reporting—and should be considered and planned throughout the entire evaluation process. We have organized our discussion in this chapter around professional standards for quantitative analysis, qualitative analysis, and justified conclusions (Joint Committee, 1994).

We believe that evaluations should include divergent as well as convergent stages and typically, but not always, culminate in bottom-line conclusions. Thus, most evaluations should not end on a note of multiple or conflicting answers and interpretations. Summative evaluations that leave conclusions to the eye of the beholder mainly add to confusion and controversy. Open-ended evaluation findings often baffle audiences and leave clients and sponsors wondering why they commissioned and funded the summative evaluation. Our position is that evaluators initially should search out multiple findings and interpretations (in the evaluation's divergent stage) but subsequently work (in the convergent stage) toward delivering the best answers they can find. They should justify their conclusions by documenting the assumptions, rules, and procedures used to analyze and synthesize information. In addition, they should buttress their conclusions with appropriate caveats concerning any deficiencies in the obtained information and possible disagreements about value bases for interpretation. Exceptions to conclusions-oriented evaluations are studies commissioned mainly to provide ongoing formative feedback and not result in a final summative evaluation report and studies that do not succeed in producing sufficient evidence to justify the issuing of conclusions. It is bad evaluation practice to present conclusions that reflect only the evaluator's intuition and judgment and are not based on a foundation of relevant information.

Regarding summative evaluations that end by noting that conclusions are open to the readers' interpretations and that they might justifiably judge the assessed program as either good or bad, we identify with an expression attributed to President Harry S. Truman. It went something like this: *I am tired of hearing economists conclude that, on the one hand, the economic outlook is such and such, but, on the other hand, it is very different.* Reportedly Truman commented further that *he was seeking a one-handed economist*—one with willingness and competence to determine and commit to a particular interpretation of the available evidence. Regarding an evaluator's risk of possibly making a wrong interpretation, we think another Truman saying has relevance. He was famous for stating, "If you can't stand the heat, get out of the kitchen." Evaluators who seek and present firm conclusions often face opposition and criticism and sometimes are wrong. However, if they ground their conclusions in systematic analysis and synthesis of a sufficient set of appropriate evidence and report appropriate caveats, we think they will be correct far more often than those who fail to practice systematic, conclusion-oriented evaluation and will be instrumental in helping their audiences make sound decisions and improve programs. Systematic evaluation is not and never will be an exact science, but it is an invaluable guide to progress. Evaluators who are steadfastly afraid of being wrong and consequently equivocate or exercise undue caution probably should seek other worthwhile work, such as bookkeeping, proofreading, window washing, watch repair, or house painting.

Standards for Analyzing and Synthesizing Information

The tradition of evaluation is focused heavily on analysis techniques, especially descriptive statistics and tests of statistical significance. Such techniques have been employed to characterize groups and their program-related experiences and outcomes, examine and judge the significance of changes in various indexes over time, contrast and judge the significance of the outcomes of competing programs, identify and assess relationships between variables, and extrapolate findings in order to predict future outcomes. Beyond statistical analysis, methodologists have advanced procedures for qualitative analysis and final synthesis of findings. Moreover, the art and science of combining quantitative and qualitative methods of data gathering, analyzing, and synthesizing have progressed remarkably in the past two decades. Mixed-method evaluation design and practice is increasingly employed rather than distinctive quantitative or qualitative designs. In this book, we have consistently advocated a broad range of methodologies to develop a foundation of factual evidence to begin responding to clients' questions. Such procedures are the essence of the divergent phase. Using the mixed-method approach, evaluators may well give greater emphasis to quantitative rather than qualitative procedures, or vice versa, depending on the kind and quality of information that will give validity to responses to evaluation questions, and ultimately to reporting and decision making.

Qualitative analysis techniques are needed to mine and interpret the meaning of such information as testimony, interviews, news accounts, and photographic records. Synthesis techniques are required to converge information from a wide range of quantitative and qualitative analyses into bottom-line judgments. Evaluators need to develop facility in selecting and employing procedures for quantitative and qualitative analysis and synthesis in order to answer the questions of their audiences and reach defensible conclusions about the value of programs or other objects of evaluations. Apt summaries of analysis and synthesis concepts are found in the following three Joint Committee (1994) standards: Qualitative Analysis, Quantitative Analysis, and Justified Conclusions. These standards provide a good foundation for discussing the principles and procedures of analysis and synthesis.

Analysis of Quantitative Information

The standard states, "Quantitative information in an evaluation should be appropriately and systematically analyzed so that evaluation questions are effectively answered" (Joint Committee, 1994, p. 165).

Evaluations may encompass a wide range of quantitative information. Examples include age, height, and weight; duration, funding level, expenditure reports, and ratings of the subject program or other object of the evaluation; and indicators of program outcomes, such as blood pressure readings, weight gain or loss, scores on attitude inventories, number of school years completed, achievement test scores, annual income, and number of traffic violations. When such data are involved, evaluators should employ systematic, rigorous, relevant methods of quantitative analysis. However, evaluators should keep in mind that not all evaluations require quantitative analysis.

Quantitative Analysis Techniques

Evaluators may choose from a wide range of analysis techniques to examine and interpret quantitative information. These include, among others, frequency counts; percentages; histograms; pie charts; trend lines; means and medians; variances and standard deviations; correlations; coefficient of contingency; multiple regression; *t*-tests; chi-square tests; test of concordance; analysis of variance; multiple analysis of variance; analysis of covariance; a posteriori significance tests; Delphi technique and Q-sorts; gain score analysis; value-added analysis; cost-utility analysis; trend analysis; time-series analysis; pattern analysis; cluster analysis; effect parameter analysis; factor analysis; and norm-referenced, criterion-referenced, objectives-referenced, and domain-referenced approaches to analyzing achievement test scores. Information on such techniques is readily available in a wide range of textbooks on statistics and research methods. Some examples are Bryk and Raudenbush (1992), Freed, Ryan, and Hess (1991), Goldstein (1987), Hopkins and Glass (1978), Jaeger (1990), Hinkle, Wiersma, and Jurs (2003), Wiersma and Jurs (2005), and Winer (1962). Applications of complex quantitative analysis techniques are facilitated by the use of computers and applicable software. Among the many available statistical packages are Excel (available at www.Microsoft.com/office/Excel), Statistical Analysis System (SAS, available at www.SAS.com), and Statistical Package for the Social Sciences (SPSS, available at www.SPSS.com.)

Evaluators must not merely apply their favorite technique and should not allow familiarity with certain techniques and easy access to computer programs to dictate the analysis process. In approaching a data set, the evaluators should consider what the intended audience wants and needs to learn from the data and then choose analysis methods that will best address the focal questions and fit the characteristics of the data. The selection of such methods may involve qualitative as well as quantitative techniques and sometimes should include either one of these but not the other or, alternatively, predominantly one of these techniques.

An issue in many evaluations is that the quantitative data sets fall short of meeting assumptions underlying many of the available quantitative analysis techniques. The obtained measures may not meet the assumptions of interval or ratio scales required by some statistical analysis techniques, and in many cases the employed data may have only marginal reliability and validity. Also, program participants rarely are selected randomly from a defined population. This complicates the aim of drawing inferences from the obtained analyses to some population of interest. Moreover, in many evaluations, the data respondents are the total population of interest, and there is no issue of using inferential statistics to generalize findings to a larger population of interest. The evaluators need to keep in mind and honestly report limitations and weaknesses in the data that underlie the quantitative analyses. They should employ inferential statistics only when they are relevant to the evaluation questions and should employ only those analysis techniques whose assumptions are met by the data.

Quantitative Analysis Process

Evaluators should start the analysis process by exploring and gaining an understanding of the data set, identifying strengths and weaknesses in the data, making needed corrections, and discerning which of the desired questions can be addressed appropriately with the data. In this process, they should look for data that lie outside the bounds of reasonable expectation and appear to be in error. The point in identifying and analyzing such outliers is to confirm the validity of the measures or disconfirm and delete or correct them.

Often a surfeit of data accumulates, which can too easily lead to fuzzy or even useless interpretations. Thus, the main aim of the quantitative analysis process is to reduce and synthesize information so that the evaluation questions may be addressed rigorously and concisely. There always must exist a close correlation between these questions, planned collection of data, and the methodology used to collect data appropriate to the questions. We deliberately have used the term *reasonable expectation* to give advance warning that data analysis must lead toward interpretations that are credible to clients who proposed the questions that triggered the study. This audience needs to grasp the import of the gathered data and particularly how these data relate to their concerns.

The evaluators should follow the start-up, exploratory analysis stage with more systematic, often increasingly complex analyses aimed at providing clear results and warranted interpretations. However, they should avoid using complex statistical techniques when the audience would be served better by straightforward, simple communicative methods. To help the audience understand and appreciate the analysis results, evaluators should provide visual displays, such as cross-break tables, bar charts, and graphs, examples of which are readily available in appropriate texts. We add one further word of advice to evaluators who are uncertain about the relative importance and suitability of descriptive or inferential statistics: it is advisable to first explore the utility of descriptive statistics and graphics such as the examples we have given. Whether inferential or statistical methods are used, it is essential that these are preceded by a thorough knowledge of collected data and their limitations.

Quantitative Analysis in Comparative Studies

Often evaluation audiences want to know whether one treatment is better than another or whether an innovative program is superior to the existing program. In such situations, evaluators may design evaluations to compare different groups in different programs. For practical reasons, the comparison groups seldom are formed by random assignment, a problem that calls into question the equivalence of the groups.

Nonrandom assignment of subjects to comparison groups introduces a host of difficulties in discerning whether observed between-group differences in outcomes were due to differences in treatments. The different outcomes might reflect only original differences between the groups. Also, complications that impede interpretations of outcome differences arise when treatment and control groups are influenced differently, not only by the treatments they received but also by factors in their separate environments. As another example, differential dropouts of experimental and control subjects might be as influential (or more so) in producing outcome differences as the administered treatment and control conditions. When there are no observed outcome differences, it is possible that the experimental treatment was not carried out as planned.

These examples of difficulties in conducting comparative studies underscore that quantitative analysis in such studies is a daunting task that requires care, resourcefulness, incisive investigation (and associated costs), multiple methods, documentation of procedures and difficulties, and a good measure of circumspection and caution in interpreting findings. And even when subjects are assigned to treatment and comparison groups randomly, many intervening factors as outlined above—such as differential attrition, inadequate implementation of treatment plans, and contextual influences—can confound the obtained outcome measures. In their classic book *Experimental and Quasi-Experimental Designs for Research*, Campbell and Stanley (1963) enumerated threats to internal and external validity in a wide range of research designs. To overcome such difficulties, evaluators often are wise to supplement their statistical analyses with descriptive, in-depth case studies of the experiences and outcomes of the comparison groups.

Testing Statistical Hypotheses

When conducting comparative experiments, evaluators state and test hypotheses based on data obtained from experimental and control groups. A statistical test is a set of rules for deciding whether to accept or reject a hypothesis. According to Winer (1962, p. 9), "A statistical hypothesis is a statement about a statistical population, which on the basis of observed data, one seeks to support or refute." Typically, there are competing hypotheses—for example:

H1: The difference between the assessed outcomes of treatment and control conditions is zero.

H2: The difference between the assessed outcomes of treatment and control conditions is greater than zero.

The rules for testing such hypotheses require a basis for expressing the accuracy of the evaluator's decision. The measure of accuracy is a probability statement of making the decision that agrees with the true conditions in the population of interest. The decision rules depend partly on what the client group considers the critical boundary needed to guard against arriving at the wrong decision. This boundary determines the alpha level, such as a .05 probability of rejecting the H1 hypothesis when it is in fact true, and the beta level, such as a .10 probability of rejecting some alternative H2 hypothesis when it is true. Wherever the evaluator sets the significance level, there is a risk of arriving at the wrong decision. This risk involves both type 1 error and type 2 error. Therefore, in setting the boundaries, the evaluator and client group need to consider both types of potential error carefully.

Type 1 and 2 Errors

The alpha level of significance that the evaluator sets is the upper bound on the probability of rejecting H1 when in fact H1 is true. This kind of mistake is known as a type 1 error, and the probability of making such an error is controlled by where the evaluator sets the alpha level of significance. By setting a small alpha level, such as .01, the evaluator minimizes the type 1 error of rejecting HI when it is true. However, the smaller numerically one sets the alpha level (type 1 error), the greater the probability is of making a type 2 error. A type 2 error occurs when the decision rule does not reject H1 although a certain alternative H2 is true. The potential size of a type 2 error depends on both the level of significance and which alternative H2 is in play. The size of a type 1 error for an H1 hypothesis is represented by alpha, and the size of the type 2 error for a given alternative hypothesis (H2) is designated by beta. The definitions of type 1 and type 2 errors are summarized in Table 25.1.

The concepts of type 1 error and type 2 error are important in evaluation work because small differences in treatment effects can be practically important. If the evaluator sets a very small alpha level and a relatively large beta level, a small but important effect might be dismissed. For example, early research investigating the link between cigarette smoking and lung cancer used small alpha levels and tended to dismiss small indications of a causal link between tobacco use and lung cancer. The H1 hypothesis that cigarette smoking had no effect on lung cancer was not rejected in such early research. Failure to accept the H2 hypothesis linking cigarettes to lung cancer proved to be a quite serious type 2 error.

Single-Group Evaluations

In addition to comparative studies, many evaluations look only at the program experiences and outcomes of a single group. Evaluators may design such single-group studies to compare pre- and postprogram measures, or they may employ this approach to gain an in-depth understanding of how a program operates and what it produces. In the latter case, it is important to supplement quantitative data

TABLE 25.1. DEFINITIONS OF TYPE 1 ERROR AND TYPE 2 ERROR.

Decision	True State of Affairs	
	H1 is true	**H1 is false H2 is true**
Reject H1 Accept H2	Type 1 error (alpha)	No error
Do not reject H1 Do not accept H2	No error	Type 2 error

with in-depth qualitative information about the implementation of the program and the recipients' experiences, outcomes, and judgments. Variations of the single-group approach could include time-series studies that look for trends in outcome measures associated with receipt of the program.

Single-group studies are vulnerable to a range of difficulties that complicate analysis and interpretation. With no comparison group, it can be difficult to establish whether gains in criterion measures were due to the program or other factors. In such studies, evaluators should provide descriptive statistics, buttress these with qualitative information and analyses, and advise the audience to be cautious in interpreting the findings.

Determining Consistent, Replicable Patterns of Results

As feasible, evaluators should employ different methods of analysis to determine whether a consistent and replicable pattern of results is present. They might apply parallel parametric and nonparametric techniques, quantitative as well as qualitative techniques, and interpretations against individual scores as well as group means. In many comparative evaluations, the treatment is applied to intact groups, and the group is the correct unit of analysis. However, given that the number of such treated groups often is small, the resulting analysis of group means will lack power to detect small but important differences (and thus carry a high risk of type 2 error). In such a case, the evaluator can gain statistical power by using individual scores to check for significant differences. In the area of exploring the data, we think such a check is appropriate, although the individual is not the statistically correct unit of analysis.

Use of multiple techniques can help overcome some of the deficiencies in the data and assist the audience to see how much they should trust the reported findings. Evaluators should produce overall statistics such as group means, medians, and standard deviations, but also should look more deeply into the data. Determining only the average performance of program participants might mask important positive or negative effects on subgroups or individuals. In comparative analyses, evaluators often should follow up statistical tests of main effects with tests for statistical interactions and subsequent a posteriori tests for simple effects on subgroups. Analytical methods such as analysis of covariance might be used to adjust for initial differences between nonequivalent groups, but it is often difficult to meet the assumptions underlying these tests. Evaluators must not assume or imply to their audiences that such techniques as gain scores, matching, or analysis of covariance will necessarily adjust sufficiently for preexisting differences between comparison groups.

Testing Practical Significance of Findings

Beyond tests for statistical significance, evaluators also should examine the practical significance of findings. This can entail further quantitative analysis, such as computing an omega-squared statistic, but it often requires exchange with stakeholders, which can be pursued through focus groups, interviews, hearings, or other qualitative techniques. This possibility underscores the point already made that quantitative and qualitative analyses often complement each other and should be used together in reaching defensible interpretations and conclusions. Clients who are unfamiliar with quantitative methodologies and inferential statistics may be unconvinced by determinations emanating only from data interpreted in this fashion. However, description and graphics can be both illuminating and reassuring.

Documenting and Validating Quantitative Analyses

Ultimately evaluators should ensure that their analysis techniques and calculations are defensible. They should document the procedures they employed, state the assumptions required by these techniques, report the extent to which the assumptions were met, and justify (and, as appropriate, qualify) their interpretations of the results of their analyses. They should report potential weaknesses in the evaluation design or data analysis (for example, violation of scaling or randomization assumptions, program participants' dropping out) and discuss their possible influence on interpretations and conclusions. They should accord importance to both rigor and relevance and should not assume that statistically significant results are necessarily practically significant. Evaluators also should not credit nonsignificant statistical results because stakeholders judge them as practically significant unless there is evidence that the small but practically important difference is replicable. Again, we emphasize that evaluators and their clients should set the level of statistical significance in consideration of the potentials for and importance of types 1 and 2 error.

Evaluators should bear in mind that quantitative analyses often fail to provide sufficient insight into the most important questions. A former president of a major university often assessed statistical comparisons of universities by saying "Statistics are like bikinis; they reveal a great deal but always conceal the essentials." Although statistical analyses are often important, many require follow-up qualitative analysis.

Analysis of Qualitative Information

The Joint Committee (1994) states, "Qualitative information in an evaluation should be appropriately and systematically analyzed so that evaluation questions are effectively answered" (p. 165).

Michael Patton (1990) stated that a qualitative inquiry has a foundation built on several interconnected themes. In this section, we present some of these themes as we develop various strategies of qualitative inquiry:

- Naturalistic inquiry: A nonmanipulative study of situations as they unfold naturally.
- Inductive analysis: Immersion in details of data to delineate categories or sets of information and their interrelationships.
- Holistic perspective: Studying the whole phenomenon of an evaluand that may not be reduced to discrete variables (as occurs commonly with quantitative analysis).
- Qualitative data: Arising from and encompassing a range of techniques that capture perspectives and experiences through personal contact of the evaluator with study subjects and their actual situations.
- Case study orientation: Captures the true nature of individual, unique cases. Endeavoring to be as objective as possible, the evaluator does not advance personal views or agendas. (For an in-depth study of the case study methodology, see Chapters Fourteen and Eighteen.)

It is difficult to imagine any evaluation study not including some qualitative information.

Evaluations typically acquire and analyze a wide range of qualitative information—for example: proposals and accountability reports; staff résumés; meeting minutes; correspondence files; beneficiaries' judgments of services; letters to the editor; site visit reports; participant observers' reports; case study reports; newspaper articles; public relations brochures; interview responses; independent observers' field notes; oral testimony; written complaints; award documents; photographs; video- and audiotapes; focus group transcriptions; public forum reports; proceedings of hearings; conference reports; various kinds of records; and unsolicited comments, accounts, and judgments. Qualitative information often is collected by design, but some of it may appear unexpectedly or be discovered through exploratory investigation. It may concern a wide range of program variables, such as beneficiaries' needs and wants, how and why a program got started, goals and plans, schedules and budgets, personnel and procedures, equipment and facilities, operations and expenditures, and intended and unintended outcomes. Descriptive studies—such as documentation of a program's activities, definition and description of the program's stakeholders, and description of staff credentials—rely heavily on qualitative data and attendant information.

When qualitative information is collected, which is the case in most program evaluations, evaluators should employ systematic, rigorous methods of qualitative analysis. The Joint Committee (1994) defines qualitative analysis as "the process of compiling, analyzing, and interpreting qualitative information about a program that will answer particular questions about that program" (p. 171). Such analyses culminate in narrative presentations, such as summaries of main outcomes, discussion of the extent to which program plans were well executed, major and minor themes running through stakeholder inputs, identification of inconsistencies as well as consistencies in different sets of obtained information, contrasts of findings from different stakeholder viewpoints, contrasts of findings at different points in time, and interpretations of cause and effect relationships.

Qualitative information has many benefits in an evaluation. These include providing breadth of perspectives and depth of information, buttressing and complementing quantitative findings, confirming or disconfirming quantitative findings, rounding out the full countenance of a program, and helping the audience perceive a program's essence and nuances. Also, pertinent quotations may be reported along with quantitative results to illuminate the latter. In qualitative analyses, it is essential to consider alternative and possibly conflicting perceptions of reality as well as different values from which to judge programs.

Qualitative Analysis as a Discovery Process

In contrast to quantitative analysis, qualitative analysis often evolves in a discovering mode rather than following a predetermined analysis plan. In the course of qualitative analysis, evaluators often have to generate information collection devices, category systems, and methods of summarizing and displaying information throughout the evaluation. Whereas quantitative analysis typically focuses on information that was collected from a predetermined sample, qualitative analysis often uses information from snowball samples that grow and take direction based on successive exchanges with key informants. As the Joint Committee (1994, p. 171) states, "Qualitative analysis often involves an inductive, interactive, and iterative process whereby the evaluator returns to relevant audiences and data sources to confirm and/or expand the purposes of the evaluation and test conclusions. It often requires an intuitive sifting of expressed concerns and relevant observations."

In applying qualitative analysis techniques, evaluators should allow emergent questions to shape the collection and analysis of qualitative information as the evaluation proceeds. For each set of qualitative information, the evaluators should choose an analytical procedure and plan for summarizing findings that are appropriate for addressing part or all of the evaluation's questions and that suit the nature of the information to be analyzed. They should define the boundaries of the information to be examined in such terms as targeted beneficiaries, geographical location, time period to be examined, financial sponsors, and program budget. By identifying pervasive themes in the information, the evaluators should ferret out meaningful categories of information, such as innovative methods, undue control by administrators, democratic leadership, motivated staff, personality conflicts, value conflicts, inadequate (or adequate) supervision, goal drift, and community involvement. In communicating findings to audiences, the evaluators might extract certain findings from the qualitative analysis and embed them in the presentation of quantitative findings.

Practical Steps in the Qualitative Analysis Process

Initially it can be useful to analyze information obtained from each qualitative method separately, for example, interviews, open-ended questionnaires, focus groups, or documents. Each such set of information might be examined to address each evaluation question concerning such matters as beneficiaries' needs; program implementation; intended effects; side effects; and judgments of quality, utility, and significance. In general, any one set of qualitative information has been sufficiently and appropriately analyzed when the evaluator has derived a set of categories that unambiguously account for the obtained information and amplify and address the evaluation questions; when the information has been parsimoniously grouped into the categories; when the categories have been verified as reliable and valid; when the categories of information have been applied to produce meaningful inferences and conclusions; when the qualitative analysis process has been documented and validated; and when the evaluator has forthrightly reported any potential weaknesses in the information and its analysis.

The general process we have found useful in analyzing given sets of qualitative information can be summarized in the following steps:

1. Compile a set of documents for each type of qualitative information, such as correspondence, newspaper clippings, transcriptions of focus group meetings, and notes from interviews.
2. Mark each document in each set with a unique identification number, for example, for correspondence, Cor-1, Cor-2, Cor-3, and so on.
3. Read through a random sample of the documents in each set, making marginal notes on points that seem relevant to the evaluation's purposes and questions; examples are characteristics of beneficiaries, needs of beneficiaries, how and why the program was launched, strengths of the program design, innovative methods, program detractors, staff competence, indications of graft, program implementation, program costs, program outcomes, and side effects. Such marginal notes provide a grounded basis for generating categories for use in the qualitative analysis. Note that these are not preconceived categories

but those that occur to the analyst when first studying random samples of materials in each set.

4. In each set of materials, group the marginal notes into an efficient set of categories in order to eliminate minor, trivial differences between voluminous marginal notes.

5. Contrast the derived sets of categories, and synthesize them into a coherent set of categories that is faithful to what was obtained for each set and is as efficient as possible.

6. Contrast the derived set of categories with the conceptual framework and main questions guiding the evaluation, and develop a standardized set of categories for the subsequent analyses of qualitative information. This finalized set of categories should reflect the previous empirically derived categories, the guiding evaluation approach, and the evaluation's main questions. This is the stage in which an evaluation approach such as Scriven's Key Evaluation Checklist (see Chapter Sixteen), Stake's countenance approach (see Chapter Eighteen), or Stufflebeam's CIPP model (see Chapter Fifteen) can be especially useful.

7. Apply the standardized set of categories to analyzing each set of qualitative information. Continue reading the material in each set until a relevant category has been attached to each noteworthy segment of each document.

8. For each set of information, summarize what has been learned in relation to each category of findings, for example, the program's costs, community support and opposition, conflicts of interest, main effects, and side effects. Also annotate the summary with the identification numbers of the relevant source documents. This is important preparation for answering later questions from recipients of the eventual evaluation report.

9. Looking across the summaries for the different sets of information, write findings in relation to each evaluation question—for example, To what extent did the program reach all the intended beneficiaries? To what extent were the outcomes worth the effort and cost? To what extent was the program institutionalized? This procedure will help clarify issues relating to evaluation questions, as well as help shape the content and nature of the final report.

10. Subject the results of the qualitative analysis to independent critiques, and resolve any identified deficiencies.

Table 25.2 summarizes these ten steps. It highlights the salient features of each step (both purpose and process) and can serve as a ready reference when qualitative methods are contemplated or used in an evaluation.

As reflected in step 9, after analyzing individual sets of qualitative information, the evaluators should look at the different sets—first individually and then in combination—to determine areas of agreement and disagreement. Such contrasts should take into account the different methods applied, different sources of

TABLE 25.2. PRACTICAL STEPS IN THE QUALITATIVE ANALYSIS PROCESS.

Step	Purpose	Process
1	To select the type of qualitative information needed	Compile a set of documents for each type of information needed in the study.
2	To identify selected documents	Mark each document with a distinguishing code (for example, interview 1.4, correspondence 1.3).
3	To prepare a grounded basis to generate categories for later use in analysis	Study a random sample of the various document sets, making marginal notes relevant to the evaluation's purposes and questions.
4	To eliminate trivialities	Group marginal notes into efficient, tight categories, discarding minor differences.
5	To reduce derived sets of categories to efficient proportions	Contrast developed sets of categories, and synthesize them to a new coherent group that retains the essence and meaning of original category sets.
6	To develop a standardized set of categories for analyzing qualitative information	Contrast and compare the new set of categories with the evaluation's conceptual framework and questions, and develop a standardized set of categories for subsequent analysis. (This final set of categories should reflect previously empirically derived categories.)
7	To analyze each set of qualitative information	Apply the developed standardized set of categories to each set of qualitative information, and continue the analysis process by further reading until a relevant category emerges for each salient section of each document.
8	To detail what each category of findings reveals and to annotate these with identification tags in anticipation of questions from report recipients	Summarize each category of findings (for example, costs, likely impediments, positive effects, sources of support), and identify these with a code to respond more easily to questions raised by report audiences.
9	To examine the various summaries, recording findings in relation to each evaluation question (for example, what intended and unintended effects obtain)	Address each evaluation question by synthesizing relevant information from the summaries of findings for the different categories of information.
10	To seek independent assessment of the analyses contained in steps 5 to 9 (in particular) so that weaknesses are identified and resolved before the study moves to conclusions and reporting	Subject main aspects of qualitative analysis to independent observation, and carefully note and resolve any weaknesses that are exposed by this type of examination.

information, and different times of information collection. In addition, as seen in step 10, the evaluators should document their qualitative information, analysis procedures, and findings and subject them to careful scrutiny and verification. We stress that evaluators should document the entire qualitative analysis process, including annotating each qualitative analysis finding by identifying the reference numbers of the documents that formed the basis for the finding. This is a strong means of accountability and allows inspection and possible replication by other evaluators. Moreover, the evaluator should obtain critiques of the qualitative analysis from such sources as evaluation experts, relevant subject matter experts, and members of the client group.

Qualitative Analysis Techniques

Qualitative information may be analyzed appropriately through a wide range of techniques. In addition to the method summarized of reading and annotating text, other methods may include uses of computers and a variety of software programs. In one of our evaluations, we sought to determine whether stock phrases (that on their face were positive or at least innocuous) were being embedded in personnel evaluation reports as codes to surreptitiously steer decision makers to promote or not promote the employee. A computer word processing program was used to search for the stock phrases in a computer file of the efficiency reports of previously promoted employees and also in a computer file of the efficiency reports of employees previously denied promotion. The evaluators had uncovered these phrases in an unofficial manual for guiding evaluations being conducted by supervisors. The message accompanying the phrases essentially was that certain of the phrases could be embedded in the evaluation report to cue decision makers to promote an evaluee, while other provided phases could be presented to surreptitiously advise against promoting an evaluee. In this way, the evaluators could get their message through without leaving a record indicating their harsh (or positive) judgment of an evaluee. It was found that supposedly positive or neutral stock phrases that actually conveyed a negative message were highly prevalent in the reports of employees who had been denied promotion but were almost nonexistent in the files of the promoted employees. One implication of these findings was that the supervisors who were preparing the efficiency reports were not doing a good job of providing decision makers with candid assessments of an employee's performance of job responsibilities, the essence of a sound personnel evaluation; instead, they were inserting code phrases to tip off decision makers as to who should not (or should) be promoted. Moreover, on the other end, the decision makers seemed to be looking for the presence or absence of the stock statements instead of looking for evidence about an evaluee's performance of job responsibilities. The use of a word processing program greatly facilitated this analysis, which in part led to a reform of the subject personnel evaluation system.

Qualifications Needed to Conduct Qualitative Analyses

Those who practice qualitative analysis need appropriate training and an appreciation for rigor as well as relevance. They should be proficient in such tasks as interviewing stakeholders, developing focus group questions, recording fieldwork data, interpreting historical information, taking accurate notes, conceptual analysis, text analysis, computer-assisted content analysis, historical analysis, videotape analysis, audiotape analysis, coding and classifying information, grounded theory analysis, and writing qualitative research reports, particularly in conjunction with outcomes from quantitative research. Especially, they should be adept in identifying themes and majority and minority positions in a body of information. Information on qualitative analysis techniques, including uses of computer software, is available in a wide range of publications. Some examples are Crabtree and Miller (1992), Denzin and Lincoln (2000), Fetterman (1998), Fielding and Lee (1991, 1998), LeCompte and Goetz (1982), Leninger (1985), Mabry (2003), Miles and Huberman (1984), Patton (1987, 1990), Strauss (1987), Tesch (1990), Wolcott (1995), and Yin (1991).

Despite the importance of qualitative analysis, evaluators should not become overzealous in conducting qualitative analyses. They must not get carried away with the emergent, divergent, and in-depth features of qualitative analysis. They should not overstress the details of program circumstances and as a consequence obscure the more general pervasive findings that are likely to be of interest to their audience. They should not be so enticed by interesting new questions that they neglect to address the evaluation's main questions. They should be judicious and parsimonious in collecting qualitative information so that they do not make the evaluation too expensive and time-consuming. Moreover, we cannot overemphasize that quantitative and qualitative information are complementary and should work together to support the evaluation's findings and conclusions.

Validating Qualitative Analyses

Whatever methods of qualitative analysis are employed, the evaluators should ensure the accuracy of findings by seeking confirmation from quantitative information and verify the resulting inferences and conclusions. They should judiciously examine different sources of evidence on such bases as verifiability, credibility, and degree of contact with the assessed entity. Evaluators should closely examine the validity of preconceptions, working hypotheses, generally accepted past practices and beliefs, and cited past evaluation conclusions. To test the consistency of categories, themes, and conclusions, it is a good idea, whenever possible, to engage two or more independent evaluators to analyze the same set of information. Also, it is good practice to subject qualitative analysis results to an independent audit. In addition, evaluators should engage representatives of stakeholders to review and give their assessments of the validity and meaningfulness of drafts of qualitative analyses. Ultimately the evaluators should document the qualitative analysis process and report this documentation along with the results of having the analysis validated.

In general, the purpose of qualitative analysis is to enrich an evaluation's message and prevent invalid conclusions. When evaluators meet the Joint Committee's Qualitative Analysis standard, they avoid using inappropriate methods of analysis; carefully document, cross-check, and evaluate their findings; safeguard their audience from reaching premature closure or misinterpreting the results; and keep the evaluation within reasonable bounds of time and cost.

Justified Conclusions

The Joint Committee (1994) states, "The conclusions reached in an evaluation should be explicitly justified, so that the stakeholders can assess them" (p. 177).

The roles of quantitative and qualitative analyses are to provide bases for reaching justified conclusions, which are the evaluation's final judgments and recommendations. They offer audiences a foundation for judging and making decisions about a program or other object of interest. The evaluation's conclusions must be carefully derived and shown to be sound. They must be both defensible and defended. They should be appropriately qualified in terms of the applicable time periods, contexts, activities, persons, purposes, and supporting evidence.

Evaluators should base their conclusions on all pertinent information collected; on appropriate analyses and logic; and on a systematic, defensible synthesizing process. They should show how this information relates to the conclusions. In reaching conclusions about a program's effectiveness, evaluators should identify side effects as well as main effects. As feasible, evaluators should present not only their bottom-line conclusions, but also plausible alternative conclusions along with an explanation of why they were rejected. While evaluators should attempt to address the audience's questions, they should be careful not to present conclusions that extend beyond the limits of their data. On the other hand, they should not be overly cautious in interpreting the evaluation's findings. A report that leads to effective decision making is devoid of exaggeration and pretension, but replete with justified statements of the evaluand's merit and worth.

In justifying conclusions, evaluators should supply the audience with full information about the evaluation's design, procedures, information, analyses, synthesis, and underlying assumptions. As feasible, evaluators should solicit feedback from a range of program stakeholders concerning the clarity and credibility of judgments and recommendations. As appropriate, they should advise their audiences of any equivocal findings in the evaluation report and warn them to be cautious in applying those findings. Faulty and unexplained conclusions or ones that reach beyond the data may mislead audiences or cause them to disregard the evaluation.

A key process related to the Joint Committee's Justified Conclusions standard is that of synthesis: combining the study's values base, information, and analyses into a unified set of conclusions. In line with the mixed-method approach advocated in this book, and particularly in this chapter, the synthesis process involves information arising from both quantitative and qualitative inquiries.

The synthesis component is a highly challenging activity. It requires a determination of whether the audience requires a final synthesis; critical review of the available information and analyses to determine whether a final synthesis is feasible; rigorous application of logic and justifiable decision rules in relating the findings to evaluation questions and bottom-line areas of judgment; creativity in conceptualizing pertinent judgments; pragmatic thought plus reference to supporting evidence in developing actionable recommendations (if such are warranted); solicitation and use of critical reactions to draft judgments and recommendations; and proficiency in writing clear, substantiated, and properly qualified judgments and recommendations. Also, the evaluator should support the synthesis of evaluation findings with a detailed appendix that documents the evaluation design, information, and quantitative and qualitative analyses.

In the synthesis process, evaluators should focus front and center on the audience's questions and issues related to the program's value. They should draw together relevant quantitative and qualitative analysis results pertaining to each evaluation question and areas for judgments and recommendations. The CIPP model provides a convenient advance organizer for grouping the audience's questions and the essential elements of a sound, comprehensive set of evaluation conclusions. The model's generic questions pertain especially to beneficiaries' needs, appropriateness of program plans, adequacy of program implementation, reach to the intended beneficiaries, amount and quality of outcomes, side effects, sustainability of the program, and transportability of the program. Main categories of bottom-line judgments are merit, worth, significance, and probity. In the context of the CIPP model, a good synthesis will provide an informative, justified response to each of these matters. Each such response might start with the quantitative or qualitative results and subsequently might buttress these results with the other type of information. The write-up of each conclusion, as appropriate, should include areas of agreement across information sources, but also should point out areas of contradictory evidence. Moreover, the synthesis process should be documented and subjected to independent assessment.

Michael Scriven noted that a final synthesis not always is needed or feasible (see Chapter Sixteen). He also stressed that evaluators must not recklessly state a judgment based only on personal judgment rather than on a logical link to solid, relevant evidence. Nevertheless, he stated that an evaluator should proceed toward a final synthesis if the client requires one and, if so, as far in that direction as is technically defensible. In order to synthesize obtained evaluative information and reach defensible conclusions, we suggest that evaluators carry out the following steps (which are roughly but not totally consistent with the steps recommended by Scriven):

1. *Compile evidence on the assessed needs of the program's targeted beneficiaries and assess the extent to which program goals are reflective of the assessed needs.* If the answer is affirmative, the goals can be used as criteria for assessing the worth of outcomes. If the answer is negative, then the assessed needs should be employed to assess the worth of program outcomes.

2. *Determine appropriate rules for reaching justified conclusions.* A few examples are that a housing program for the working poor is at least partially meritorious if the different aspects of house construction passed all official city inspections, that the program is at least partially worthy if the projected number of members of the targeted group of working poor obtained high-quality houses and that at least 90 percent of them lived in the housing and kept up mortgage payments for at least four years, that the program has significance beyond the local application if it was replicated by other community development groups, and that it meets specified probity requirements if its books were audited and there were no indications of fraud or graft and if it got a good report from program supervisors on its ethical treatment of program participants.

3. *Select or derive defensible criteria for applying the decision rules.* Example criteria of merit include the codes city inspectors use to approve electrical and plumbing installations; criteria of worth include those used to determine housing needs of the targeted beneficiaries plus the program's goals if they reflect assessed needs of the targeted beneficiaries; criteria of significance include the facts of successful replications of the project; and criteria of probity include the professional standards of the auditing and accounting fields.

4. *Retrieve appropriate quantitative and qualitative evidence for applying the determined criteria of merit, worth, significance, and probity.* Evidence of merit in the housing example employed in this section could include city inspectors' reports and approvals or disapprovals of different aspects of each constructed house; evidence of worth

could be records of the program's beneficiaries residing in their houses over time, caring for their property, meeting mortgage payments, and contributing to the health of their community; evidence of program significance could be reports of site visits to projects that successfully replicated the subject housing project. Note that the evaluator would retrieve both quantitative analyses and qualitative analyses and apply them together in applying the evaluative criteria.

5. *Determine if there is reliable and valid evidence for a sufficient range of criteria of merit, worth, significance, and probity to proceed with a determination of justified conclusions.* Such determinations may be made for each of the four dimensions of value. It is possible that the client group might not be interested in the dimension of significance, and although no particular data may have been collected on probity, there may be no issue in this area. However, in most cases, a decision to proceed with the synthesis task should be supported by adequate evidence at least in the areas of merit and worth. At this point, the effort to synthesize information and reach justified conclusions appropriately would be aborted if there is not adequate evidence to proceed. This could be the case when the client and evaluator had previously agreed that the evaluation would be a limited effort focused, for example, on only a few formative evaluation issues.

6. *Determine with stakeholders if the criteria for merit, worth, significance, and probity should be weighted differently.* For example, some criteria in each set might be weighted as essential, while others could be weighted as important. In the ensuing analysis, the evaluator should judge the program a failure if it failed any criterion designated as essential, no matter how well the program performed against the other criteria.

7. *Use relevant evidence to rate the program as 4 (strong), 3 (adequate), 2 (weak), 1 (unacceptable), or 0 (unratable) on each criterion.* The evaluator should judge the program a failure if it received a score of unacceptable on a criterion designated as essential. It is desirable to engage multiple raters who have successfully completed training and calibration to accomplish this rating task.

8. *Develop a bar graph of the rating results for each involved dimension, for example, merit, worth, significance, and probity.* Each bar graph should array the employed criteria, identify those that are essential, and provide a bar reflecting the score for each criterion.

9. *For each dimension of value, provide a narrative conclusion about the extent to which the evaluand satisfied the associated criteria and justify the conclusion with reference to the supporting quantitative and qualitative evidence.* The evaluator should judge the program as failing any dimension for which an essential criterion was not met.

10. *Looking across all the dimensions of value, write an overall summary statement that assesses the evaluand's value.* This should be prepared essentially in the form of an executive summary that reviews the synthesis process, presents the main conclusions,

documents the decision rules, references the supporting evidence, and references the obtained independent assessments of the conclusions.

11. *In consideration of the evaluative conclusions and supporting evidence, determine if useful recommendations can be presented and justified with supporting evidence.* Recommendations should not be tendered if they are only intuitive. However, in some cases, the obtained evidence and relevant literature can be used to offer relevant, defensible recommendations. In other cases, it may be appropriate to propose a follow-on study designed explicitly to identify and evaluate alternative courses of action; related to the CIPP model, such a recommendation is tantamount to proposing that the client contract for an input evaluation.

Throughout the synthesis process, it is desirable to obtain critical reactions to the various formulations. Reactions should be obtained from independent evaluation specialists, the client, and stakeholders. The reactions should be employed to guide the synthesis process and should be summarized for inspection by members of the evaluation audience.

Summary

Evaluation relies on principles of research—as in quantitative analysis and qualitative analysis—but also requires values analysis. Because the state of the art in the latter area is primitive compared with qualitative and quantitative research methodology, some have advised evaluators to collect, analyze, and report only solid evidence. Accordingly, they have recommended that evaluators leave matters of synthesis and interpretation of findings to the evaluation's client. Such conservative, technically oriented practice is intended to keep evaluators from advancing into areas where they might make mistakes. However, it falls short of being evaluation—the assessment of value. In this chapter, we have departed sharply from the value-free line of advice. We believe that evaluators should make the client and other stakeholders a party to the synthesis process, especially in clarifying decision rules, criteria, and weights for criteria. However, we posit that the essence of a professional evaluator's role is to conduct quantitative analysis, qualitative analysis, and synthesis toward the goal of reaching bottom-line, value- and evidence-based judgments and, as warranted, providing actionable recommendations.

Review Questions

1. Construct a matrix, and fill in the cells to define, compare, and contrast the concepts of quantitative analysis, qualitative analysis, and synthesis of evaluation findings.

2. List the practical steps you would follow in analyzing a set of quantitative information, and explain why it is important to begin this process by exploring the data.

3. Identify some of the reasons that make it important for evaluators to employ multiple analysis techniques, including problems an evaluator could encounter while obtaining information most relevant to the research questions. What are the benefits of employing multiple analysis techniques?

4. Define the concepts of type 1 and type 2 errors, explain why these concepts are important in evaluation work, and give three examples where a type 2 error would be more important than a type 1 error.

5. In comparative analyses, why should evaluators often follow up statistical tests of main effects with tests for statistical interactions and subsequent a posteriori tests?

6. Compare and contrast the concepts of statistical significance and practical significance, give an illustration of why a finding might be statistically significant but lack practical significance, and identify some ways that the evaluator can examine a finding's practical significance.

7. List criteria for judging whether a set of qualitative information has been sufficiently and appropriately analyzed.

8. What is meant by the term *evaluative conclusions*? What is their role in an evaluation? How are evaluative conclusions appropriately justified, and what kind of information should an evaluator present to a client in order to justify a set of evaluative conclusions?

9. Characterize the process involved in synthesizing sets of quantitative and qualitative information. List as many steps as you can in this chapter's recommended process for synthesizing obtained evaluative information.

10. What is the rationale for Michael Scriven's position that a final synthesis is not always needed or feasible? How does this claim relate to his concepts of formative and summative evaluations?

Group Exercises

Exercise 1. Critique the statement that all evaluations should include convergent as well as divergent stages and that every evaluation should culminate in a bottom-line set of conclusions.

Exercise 2. Discuss and defend the claim that quantitative analysis and qualitative analysis are complementary processes. In your discussion, explain and illustrate how these processes support each other in the presentation of findings.

Exercise 3. Identify and define at least five threats to the internal validity of comparative evaluation studies, whether or not subjects were randomly assigned to treatment and control groups. Discuss how such threats can be addressed through both quantitative and qualitative analysis.

Exercise 4. Identify a comparative study that is familiar to at least one member of your group. Discuss this study in terms of what alpha and beta levels make sense in terms of the possibilities of type 1 and type 2 errors. Identify examples of type 1 and type 2 errors where the type 2 error is more important than the type 1 error. What are the implications of these examples for setting the critical, or alpha, level on type 1 error?

Exercise 5. Develop a checklist of sources of qualitative information that are often relevant in program evaluations. You might list the sources within groups; provide a brief definition for each source; and indicate its relevance for different bottom-line criteria, such as merit, worth, significance, and probity.

Exercise 6. Consider that your group has obtained a set of interview responses to a standard set of questions from different interviewees. List the steps your group would follow to analyze this set of qualitative information with special reference to possible pitfalls the evaluator might encounter and must consider.

Exercise 7. Suppose your group was assigned to develop a short course to train evaluators in the procedures of qualitative analysis. What procedures would you include in this course? Place the identified procedures into three groups: essential, important, and marginally important. (Group members could address this question individually, and then compare and discuss your answers.)

Exercise 8. Under what conditions can an evaluator appropriately present the client with a set of recommendations? Under what conditions is this not appropriate? If the evaluator has too weak a basis for offering recommendations but the client still wants them, what course of action available from the CIPP model might the evaluator suggest to the client?

References

Bryk, A. S., & Raudenbush, S. W. (1992). *Hierarchical linear models: Applications and data analysis methods.* Thousand Oaks, CA: Sage.

Campbell, D. T., & Stanley, J. C. (1963). *Experimental and quasi-experimental designs for research.* Boston: Houghton Mifflin.

Crabtree, B. F., & Miller, W. L. (1992). *Doing qualitative research.* Thousand Oaks, CA: Sage.

Denzin, N. K., & Lincoln, Y. S. (2000). *Handbook of qualitative research* (2nd ed.). Thousand Oaks, CA: Sage.

Fetterman, D. M. (1998). *Ethnography: Step by step* (2nd ed.). Thousand Oaks, CA: Sage.

Fielding, N. G., & Lee, R. M. (1991). *Using computers in qualitative research.* Thousand Oaks, CA: Sage.

Fielding, N. G., & Lee, R. M. (1998). *Computer analysis and qualitative research.* Thousand Oaks, CA: Sage.

Freed, M. N., Ryan, J. M., & Hess, R. K. (1991). *Handbook of statistical procedures and computer applications to education and the behavioral sciences.* New York: Macmillan.

Goldstein, H. (1987). *Multilevel models in educational and social research.* New York: Oxford University Press.

Hinkle, D. E., Wiersma, W., & Jurs, S. G. (2003). *Applied statistics* (5th ed.). Boston: Houghton Mifflin.

Hopkins, K. D., & Glass, G. V (1978). *Basic statistics for the behavioral sciences.* Upper Saddle River, NJ: Prentice Hall.

Jaeger, R. M. (1990). *Statistics: A spectator sport* (2nd ed.). Thousand Oaks, CA: Sage.

Joint Committee on Standards for Educational Evaluation. (1994). *The program evaluation standards.* Thousand Oaks, CA: Corwin Press.

LeCompte, M. D., & Goetz, J. P. (1982). Problems of reliability and validity in ethnographic research. *Review of Educational Research, 52,* 31–60.

Leninger, M. (Ed.). (1985). *Qualitative research methods in nursing.* Orlando, FL: Grune & Stratton.

Mabry, L. (2003). In living color: Qualitative methods in educational evaluation. In T. Kellaghan & D. L. Stufflebeam (Eds.), *International handbook of educational evaluation* (pp. 167–188). Norwell, MA: Kluwer.

Miles, M. B., & Huberman, A. M. (1984). *Qualitative data analysis: An expanded sourcebook* (2nd ed.). Thousand Oaks, CA: Sage.

Patton, M. Q. (1987). How to use qualitative methods in evaluation. In J. L. Herman (Ed.), *Program evaluation kit* (2nd ed.). Thousand Oaks, CA: Sage.

Patton, M. Q. (1990). *Qualitative evaluation and research methods.* Thousand Oaks, CA: Sage.

Strauss, A. L. (1987). *Qualitative analysis for social scientists.* Cambridge: Cambridge University Press.

Tesch, R. (1990). *Qualitative research: Analysis types and software tools.* Bristol, PA: Falmer.

Wiersma, W., & Jurs, S. G. (2005). *Research methods in education: An introduction* (8th ed.). Needham Heights, MA: Allyn and Bacon.

Winer, B. J. (1962). *Statistical principles in experimental design.* New York: McGraw-Hill.

Wolcott, H. F. (1995). *The art of fieldwork.* Walnut Creek, CA: AltaMira.

Yin, R. K. (1991). *Case study research: Design and methods.* Thousand Oaks, CA: Sage.

CHAPTER TWENTY-SIX

COMMUNICATING EVALUATION FINDINGS

Previous chapters have provided the background theory, standards, and practice for effective evaluations to be undertaken. Certainly, with larger evaluation studies in particular, a great deal of planning and expenditure of time, money, and other resources will be needed. An effective evaluation will have an impact on decision makers and intended users so that the full potential of programs will be realized, including changes that stakeholders may well find daunting. Despite the thoroughness of planning and execution of an evaluation, it is quite possible for the exercise to stumble, or even fail, at the last, vital hurdle. Unless evaluation outcomes are presented to client audiences in a systematic, convincing, and ethical fashion, the entire enterprise, however excellent the data gathering and analysis have been, is likely to be of little avail. In fact, our observations indicate that apart from wasted resources, lasting damage to the program may be a reality. Thus, the importance of strong communication of evaluation findings cannot be overemphasized. Reporting is an integral part of planning, even before data are gathered. During this early stage, the format, style, and content of the final report (if there is to be one) should be negotiated with stakeholders, including funding groups, together with a defined audience for the report. This chapter covers these and other issues, such as future implications of recommendations, related to reporting and using evaluation information.

It is a basic requirement for evaluators to be sensitive to clients' needs with respect to program improvement and skilled in communicating evaluation outcomes through clear and cogent written and oral presentations. Then the chances that the report and its recommendations (if required) will be effectively received, disseminated, and used are enhanced.

Let us review some basic aims of good evaluations such as those presented in Chapters Thirteen through Eighteen. They should stimulate and even excite stakeholders' insights into their own programs and enlighten all involved in the program about its true merit, worth, and potential for improvement. Program evaluations should inform, educate, and convince decision makers about various pathways and choices leading to program strengthening. Realities of the program must be exposed so that those involved in leadership roles will be helped in making decisions regarding whether to sustain, expand, reduce, or terminate the program. Sound evaluation procedures may also lead to decisions about purchasing and adopting a new program or adapting one currently being used to meet the requirements of revealed circumstances. Moreover, if there has been substantial investment in a program, there will be accountability requirements for records and reports. The evaluator must be heavily involved in such accountability issues and clear reporting about them. Finally, field-based program evaluations may seek to inform a wider public about a program's background, structure, cost, implementation, and outcomes. In this constructive sense, evaluation is often a public relations service. In all of these procedures, communication and reporting skills are essential. Such skills will ensure open disclosure of findings during and following program implementation, leading to potential program improvement, acceptance of a successful program, or termination of a failed effort.

Inadequate reporting is a pervasive shortcoming in program evaluation, perhaps mainly because it is seen to be of less importance than planning, data collecting, and analysis. Another reason is that effective communicating and reporting are demanding tasks. Indeed, the communication process is not simple or always predictable in practice. Often evaluators need to interact with the client group and provide them with formative feedback throughout an evaluation and beyond, and often this leads to immediate decisions to improve a program whether currently in use or at a developmental stage. Different segments of the audience may require or be entitled to different amounts and levels of information. In controlling the release of information, the evaluator often has to deal effectively and diplomatically with contractual and legal constraints and sometimes with pressures from the media or political interest groups for premature or inappropriate release of findings. The life of an evaluator is not meant to be easy!

Fundamentally, evaluators must be masters of written and oral communication. They need to make their presentations factual, interesting, and persuasive. Often they must make complex technical procedures understandable to those with little background in evaluation methodology. The needed communication process may encompass both informal exchanges and formal reports. Employed media may be oral or printed, textual or graphical, presentational or interactive, published or unpublished, and delivered simply or by complex technology. The process may be open and public or restricted to certain approved audiences. Whatever the nature of the audience and employed media, the reasons to communicate evaluation procedures and findings are to secure understanding and appropriate uses and impacts of the evaluation findings.

Beyond preparing and communicating clear reports and assisting audiences to use the findings, evaluators must deal effectively with the psychological and political aspects of evaluation as a change process. Clearly, sound evaluation is a change process because evaluators aim to convince their clients and other audiences to respect, understand, and use evaluation findings in order to make and implement appropriate decisions, especially those oriented to improving programs. It is a well-known axiom of any change process that meaningful involvement in crafting and understanding change activities inclines participants to support a program of change, Chapter Eighteen underlines the significance of this. Evaluators need to be skilled in appropriately involving program stakeholders to help plan, conduct, and report evaluations so that stakeholders will understand, respect, and use the findings.

In addition to developing psychological support for an evaluation, evaluators need skills in the political aspects of evaluation. In many evaluations, the audience includes subgroups with different, often conflicting interests. Not infrequently, one group will seek to exploit the evaluation process and findings to gain or maintain an advantage over one or more other groups. Moreover, it is common for stakeholder groups to engage in heated exchanges about the meaning and practical implications of evaluation reports. The evaluators must be even-handed and scrupulously ethical in serving the evaluation needs of all the right-to-know audiences. Evaluators should not take sides in disputes between stakeholder groups. Also, they should give voice to all the interest groups in appropriate matters for stakeholder inputs. Often it is wise to engage representatives of the different interest groups to critique evaluation plans and draft instruments and reports, discuss with each other their different judgments of the evaluation work, and convey both their agreements and disagreements to the evaluators. The evaluators should respectfully consider inputs from all stakeholder groups. While showing due respect for stakeholders' efforts to offer feedback, evaluators can (and should) disagree with inputs that lack logic and merit, and they must not give away their evaluation responsibilities, authority, and independence. Moreover, evaluators should demonstrate that they value and make appropriate use of critical feedback about evaluation plans, draft reports, and other evaluation materials. To effectively address political threats to an evaluation's success, evaluators especially need skills to organize and chair discussions among a program's stakeholders. They should be adept at anticipating, forestalling if possible, and, as necessary, managing conflict. If organizational and personnel conflicts exist, these should be recognized as very much a part of an evaluation and be recorded in interim and final reports. Such conflicts will impinge on programs and have been known to prevent the achievement of intended outcomes. Reporting of debilitating organizational conflicts is a professional duty of evaluators and should not be evaded.

This chapter provides an orientation and practical information for equitably and skillfully involving stakeholders in the evaluation process, addressing psychological and political threats to the evaluation's success, and effectively reporting and promoting the use of sound evaluation information. Our presentation is designed to be consistent with the Joint Committee's *The Program Evaluation Standards* (1994), one of the most comprehensive and authoritative sources of practical advice for securing use of evaluation findings. It stresses and explains that evaluation reports should be relevant, sufficiently comprehensive, balanced, clear, timely, impartial, defensible, politically viable, and effectively delivered and disseminated. The Evaluation Impact standard states that "evaluations should be planned, conducted, and reported in ways that encourage follow-through by stakeholders, so that the likelihood that the evaluation will be used is increased" (p. 59).

We have divided this chapter into four sections: arranging and applying conditions to foster use of findings, providing interim feedback, preparing and delivering the final report, and providing follow-up assistance to enhance the evaluation's impact. Within each, we have summarized and elaborated relevant information from selected Joint Committee (1994) standards, added insights and examples gleaned from our evaluations, and used the discussion to generate practical advice.

Establishing Conditions to Foster Use of Findings

Evaluators should not expect that their intended audience will automatically make appropriate, informed use of the evaluation findings. Instead, they should work with the client to determine the need for evaluation service following submission of the final report. Such planning has implications for budgeting the evaluation work beyond the collection and reporting of information, so that the evaluator then will be available to promote and support use of the findings. The evaluator should help the client consider areas of postreporting service. These could include interpreting findings pertaining to new questions from the audience, identifying training needs of program staff, helping the client assess whether a new budget sufficiently addresses issues found in the program, increasing public understanding and acceptance of a successful program, or planning for a follow-up investigation to address identified issues. The evaluator can help members of the client group look into the data produced by the evaluation for relevant, valid information pertaining to such matters and can assist in disseminating findings. However, the evaluator must not assume the role of the client.

In preparing for a possible evaluation study, evaluators should and can do much to promote use of evaluation findings. An especially valuable step is to arrange for the involvement of stakeholders from the start of deliberations to decide whether to undertake an evaluation. Subsequently evaluators should maintain a close association with stakeholders throughout and even after completion of the study. Once evaluators and clients have decided to proceed with an evaluation, they should negotiate a contract with strong provisions—budgetary and otherwise—for promoting effective, proper use of evaluation findings. We have often found it advantageous to establish and obtain the services of a broadly representative evaluation review panel throughout an evaluation. Such a panel can be engaged to review and give feedback on draft evaluation plans, tools, and reports. We think there is no more powerful means to promote uses of evaluation findings than in involving users in the process of producing those findings and that reviewing evaluation materials is an appropriate way to accomplish this. Following are discussions of four important means to foster use of evaluation findings that often can and should be employed in the process of launching an evaluation.

Involve Stakeholders in the Evaluation

A key principle to follow is that one's involvement in a process such as evaluation can strongly influence one's understanding of, respect for, and use of the results of the process. Thus, so far as is feasible, it is wise to involve members of the evaluation's audience in reviewing and reacting to evaluation plans, draft reports, and other evaluation materials. The client most likely is but one part of the right-to-know audience. The evaluators should consider a wide range of potentially interested parties and identify all those who need and have the right to receive evaluation reports. The evaluators should project how the identified audience could use the evaluation findings beneficially and should engage its members in helping to make such determinations. Helping a group early in the evaluation process to focus on evaluation questions and consider how they might respond to answers is a good way to promote their interest in the study and their eventual use of findings.

Determine Audiences and Their Potential Use of Evaluation Findings

Implicit in such evaluation user involvement is the important task of identifying the audiences for reports. To be effective, a report must target those involved in the program who at least initially are best placed to propose questions for the study and who logically will be most concerned about evaluation outcomes. This strongly accords with our often-stated contention that any useful evaluation should have impact. Unfortunately, it is common for evaluators to ignore some audiences that not only could give clarity and definition to the evaluation, but also could act against the best interests of the study's purposes out of understandable chagrin. Moreover, such personnel, lacking program insights arising during the evaluation and becoming confused about aspects of reports, may make decisions of their own accord, to the detriment of program development. In selecting audiences for the report (often in conjunction with a client), there is the ever-present difficulty of pinpointing the most appropriate people. A sound rule of thumb is to select those persons and groups who will use the evaluation's outcomes to strengthen the program and often the organization itself. In this audience identification process, depending on the circumstances, the evaluation review panel may be approached to review evaluators' audience selections for the report so that all pertinent stakeholders are represented. The next section deals with this topic in considerable detail.

Exhibit 26.1 provides a framework for identifying members of the audience and analyzing their potential uses of evaluation findings. The row headings list a wide range of potential members of the audience, and the column headings identify typical uses of findings. The first use involves program leaders and staff in applying findings to focus and develop a program, as occurs in the context and input stages of the CIPP model (see Chapter Fifteen), and also the staff's ongoing improvement of the program, as occurs in Scriven's formative role of evaluation and the CIPP model's process stage. In a second use of findings, those responsible for program operations and results compile evaluative information into accountability reports and present these to the program's financial sponsors and other interested parties, such as beneficiaries. The exhibit's third use of findings focuses on groups that may want to adopt the program and apply it elsewhere. In the exhibit's fourth use of findings, various groups, such as the program's staff, a professional organization, or a professional journal, may want to publish the findings and distribute them broadly. The fifth noted use involves studying findings in order to become better informed about the involved phenomena. Among the groups who merely want to study the program's findings are researchers, college and university instructors, graduate students, and other members of the scientific community. Clearly, many evaluations have a diverse audience with varied interests in the findings. Evaluators are advised to analyze the audience carefully at the outset and throughout a study to provide a basis for communicating findings effectively and receiving feedback of use in making the evaluation a high quality, respected enterprise.

We suggest that evaluators use this matrix to make an initial approximation of the audience to be served and how the different parties could be expected to use the evaluation's information. This initial approximation could be represented by checkmarks in the appropriate cells. After the evaluators interact with program stakeholders to validate and finalize such approximations, they can apply the analysis, along with other information, to decide what reports would make the most impact, what persons and groups should receive which reports, how the reports should be tailored to the different parties' interests, and when and how the reports should be delivered.

In order to make such determinations, the evaluators should learn as much as possible about the evaluation assignment. When feasible, they should do so before they agree to do the study, complete a design, and negotiate a contract. They should explore with the client the question of appropriate report recipients and their needs for information from the study and should obtain and study relevant documentation, especially the program proposal. Other relevant background materials could include the needs assessment that led to the development of the program, a request for proposal that led to the submission of a proposal, pertinent correspondence, minutes of meetings, press clippings, and other pertinent materials. The evaluator should also contact representatives of different segments of the evaluation's audience, ask them to identify issues that they believe should be studied, invite their identification of sources of relevant information, and ask them to identify other persons who should be interviewed.

In the course of gathering background information about the program from a wide range of stakeholders and a wide range of materials, the evaluators especially should find and interact with anyone who might be harmed as a consequence of the evaluation. They should be invited to state any concerns they have about the potential fairness of the evaluation and what they think should be done to protect the evaluation's integrity.

We emphasize that, if possible, the evaluator should perform background investigation before agreeing to do the study. Such investigation is invaluable for deciding whether to conduct an evaluation and, if so, how to design, conduct, and report the study so that it will be fair to all parties and effective in promoting the use of its findings. Preliminary background investigation has special value for identifying all segments of the audience, engaging representatives to help focus the study, convincing them that the study is worth doing, convincing them that it would not be a witch hunt or whitewash, and determining with their help how they might use the evaluation findings.

EXHIBIT 26.1. FORMAT FOR IDENTIFYING AND ANALYZING THE NEEDS OF AN EVALUATION'S AUDIENCE.

Potential Members of the Audience	*Potential Uses of Evaluation Reports*				
	Program Development and Improvement	Program Accountability	Program Adoption Decisions	Dissemination of Information	Increased Understanding of Involved Phenomena	Other
Client						
Funder						
Program administrators						
Program staff						
Policy board						
Program advisory committee						
Beneficiaries						
Minority group stakeholders						
Persons who might be harmed as a consequence of the study						

Potential adopters of the program					
Personnel of competitive programs					
Scientific community					
Instructional and training staffs					
Government programs					
Foundations					
Legislators					
General public					
Media					
Libraries and archives					
Evaluation review panel					
Legal community					
Others					

Build Trust and Viability Through Evaluation Contracting

Evaluators are wise to negotiate appropriate contractual agreements that safe-guard the evaluators' ability to interact equitably and appropriately with all stake-holders and ensure the study's integrity. Contracts provide a basis for settling disputes about such matters as which groups should receive which reports, who will help edit the reports, who will have final editorial authority, how the reports will be evaluated and finalized, and how and when they will be disseminated. We believe that the evaluator should insist on final editorial authority and release of findings in accordance with advance agreements.

Negotiating a sound evaluation contract helps set the conditions for effectively disseminating evaluation findings. Such contracts should clearly define the evaluation's right-to-know audience, the evaluation questions, interim and final reports, which reports will be provided to each segment of the audience, opportunities that stakeholders will have to contribute to the evaluation, authority for editing and disseminating reports, any provisions for prerelease review of reports, opportunities for program personnel to rebut reports, and provisions for reviewing and updating contractual agreements as needed. While the evaluators will contract with the client, before signing the agreement, they at least should consult with representatives of groups that will be directly affected by the evaluation. Clearly, reaching and making public an appropriate set of advance evaluation agreements does much to build trust with program stakeholders and can incline them to respect the evaluation and make use of its findings.

As a practical matter, the evaluation contract should provide for financing evaluation services related to promoting and supporting appropriate use of findings following delivery of the final report. In many evaluations, there is only a vague notion that evaluators will assist users in interpreting and applying evaluation findings after they have been reported. If the evaluation contract and budget do not provide for funding the evaluators' follow-up involvement, the evaluators will be unlikely to assist users to understand, interpret, and apply the findings. The lack of such assistance can render an otherwise sound evaluation relatively cost-ineffective. Failure to budget for such follow-up assistance can be penny-wise and pound-foolish. It is in an evaluation client's interest to anticipate the need for and fund the follow-up service of evaluators so that there will be a maximum return of evaluation use for the typically much larger investment in collecting and reporting evaluation findings. (For a broader discussion of evaluation contracting, see Chapter Twenty-Three.)

Establish an Evaluation Review Panel

In proceeding with an evaluation, we have often found it important to appoint and engage the services of an evaluation review panel that includes representatives of the different segments of the evaluation's audience, as illustrated in Exhibit 26.1. The panel's role is to review and provide critical reactions to draft evaluation designs, schedules, instruments, reports, dissemination plans, follow-up plans, and the like. The panel should be charged with assessing the draft materials for clarity, feasibility, relevance, importance, and likely impact on program users.

We stress that this panel should be labeled a review panel, not an advisory panel or a steering committee. A role of providing critical reviews is within the capabilities of a wide range of stakeholders. It is also a vitally important formative metaevaluation role, as discussed in Chapter Twenty-Seven. However, such a group typically lacks, within its membership, sufficient capability to suggest how deficiencies in evaluation materials should best be overcome. Also, steering an evaluation is the evaluator's sphere of responsibility and authority. Evaluators must not give away this role to a stakeholder panel, as is wrongly advocated in the pseudoevaluation approach labeled *empowerment evaluation* (see Chapter Six). We have seen disastrous consequences when an evaluator delegated authority to a steering committee essentially to direct the evaluation work. Results can be confusion, conflict, and filibustering among members of a heterogeneous group who believe they can and should decide how an evaluation should proceed or not proceed. Another possible counterproductive effect is role conflict between the evaluator and the steering committee. Panelists' judgments on how evaluations should be carried out and on what findings and conclusions should and should not be reported are all too easily influenced by members' vested interests related to the program. While the evaluators should be open to suggestions from the review panel, they should emphasize that the panel's main role is to critique, not to engineer, evaluation activities. Given this stance, evaluators can receive possibly contradictory critiques from different stakeholders with different points of view and assess and use these inputs on their merits. Of course, the evaluators should inform the panel periodically about how plans and evaluation tools may have been modified in response to the panelists' inputs.

An Example of an Evaluation Review Panel

In an evaluation of a state's teacher evaluation system, we benefited by appointing and using the inputs of a review panel that was broadly representative of groups with interests in the state's education system. The state superintendent of public instruction chaired this panel. Two members of the evaluation team served in the role of the panel's client. They provided the panel with advance evaluation materials for review, attended panel meetings, listened to the panel's critiques of evaluation materials, asked questions as appropriate, responded to panelists' questions, prepared reports of each panel meeting, and used the panel's critiques to strengthen the evaluation and promote use of findings.

The panel members were commanding officers of the state's two large military posts (since many children of servicepersons attended the state's public schools), the president of the state teachers' union, an elementary school teacher, a middle school teacher, a secondary school teacher, an elementary school principal, a middle school principal, a secondary school principal, the director of the state's teacher evaluation system, a member of the state board of education, the director of the federally supported educational research and development center located in the state, a dean of an area college of education, an educational measurement specialist, a data processing specialist, a representative of the state chamber of commerce, a representative of the state office of the National Association for the Advancement of Colored People, the majority leaders of the state's senate and house of representatives, a representative of one of the state's largest industries, two high school students, a parent with children in an elementary school and a middle school, and a parent of a high school student. This panel was broadly representative of those who could be expected to be interested in seeing the state's teacher evaluation system strengthened, and it included persons with relevant substantive and technical expertise.

The panel met for about ninety minutes approximately every six weeks throughout the eight-month evaluation. About ten days prior to each meeting, the evaluator supplied the panelists with materials to be critiqued plus an agenda (prepared with the panel's chairperson) and asked each panelist to review the materials prior to the meeting. During the meeting, the state superintendent led the panel through the agenda, which consisted mainly of hearing panelists' critical reactions to the subject evaluation materials and their responses to questions posed by the evaluation team. A special responsibility of the chairperson was to ensure that all panelists had the opportunity to be heard and that no panelist dominated the discussion. An especially effective technique for managing discussions in a large group is to place a tented name placard in front of each participant and ask anyone who wants to speak to place the placard on its end. The chairperson can then recognize each person who has something to say in the sequence in which placards were turned up.

One evaluation team member kept notes of the meeting. As needed and requested by the chairperson, the evaluators helped keep the meeting focused on its agenda items. Although there was never an attempt to force a consensus, each meeting was concluded by inviting each panelist in turn to state what he or she considered the most important point for consideration by the evaluation team. At their option, group members could pass on this opportunity to speak. Following each meeting, a member of the evaluation team prepared and distributed copies of the minutes of the meeting.

This use of the evaluation review panel proved to be highly effective. The panel provided valuable critiques and related information to the evaluation team.

The team used these inputs to address issues in the evaluation as appropriate. They also kept the review panel apprised of how their inputs were being used to strengthen the evaluation. In the process of reviewing evaluation materials, the panelists became familiar with the evaluation process and eventually its findings. They also came to understand and respect the different points of view represented by the panelists. To be sure, issues were raised and debated. However, from meeting to meeting, the panelists found it increasingly easy to reach and express consensus opinions. Without question, members' participation on the panel inclined them to respect the evaluation findings and support their use for reforming the state's teacher evaluation system. Moreover, through their critiques, the panel contributed to the evaluation's quality and impact. Following delivery of the final report, panelists were also helpful in disseminating findings to their reference groups.

Providing Interim Evaluative Feedback

Once an evaluation has been contracted and funded, the evaluators conduct the data collection and analysis activities. Throughout this process, the client group often requires interim reports. This is especially so when the evaluation is oriented to supporting program development and improvement, often called the *formative role*. Not all evaluations serve formative roles; those that are exclusively summative in their orientation may have little or no need for interim reports other than progress reports given to the client to show that the evaluation is on track.

In some cases, an interim report is mainly an early approximation of the eventual final report. This is especially so in applying Scriven's consumer-oriented approach to evaluation. Under this approach, an interim report addresses those bottom-line questions for which data are currently available. Successive interim reports will have gaps where data are not available, but over time the reports will become increasingly complete in addressing all the items in Scriven's Key Evaluation Checklist (see Chapter Sixteen and www.wmich.edu/evalctr/checklists).

Evaluators may determine contents for the interim reports by employing other evaluation models or approaches. For example, in applying the CIPP model, successive reports may be structured to answer questions about context, inputs, process, and products as discussed in Chapter Fifteen and detailed in the CIPP Evaluation Checklist (www.wmich.edu/evalctr/checklists).

Beyond addressing the requirements of an employed evaluation approach, the evaluators should also consider and, as feasible, be responsive to stakeholders' questions as they emerge. This requires ongoing interactions between the evaluators and stakeholders (as might be involved in an evaluation review panel). Such ongoing interactions are strongly present in the CIPP model, Stake's responsive evaluation approach (see Chapter Seventeen), and Patton's utilization-focused evaluation (see Chapter Nineteen and his checklist at www.wmich.edu/evalctr/checklists).

In our CIPP model–oriented evaluations, we have developed and applied an interim reporting approach that we labeled the *feedback workshop technique*. This is a method for systematically conveying draft interim findings to a program's leaders and staff, guiding their discussion of the findings, obtaining their critical reactions to the draft report, supporting their use of findings, and using their feedback to strengthen evaluation plans and materials. In applying this procedure, evaluators send a draft report (and possibly drafts of other evaluation materials) to a group as jointly determined by the program director and the evaluation team leader. Typically this group comprises key program staff members and may have a broader composition.

The evaluators send an interim report to the designated group approximately ten days in advance of a feedback workshop and ask the members to review the findings prior to the workshop. The evaluators ask members of this group to identify any factual errors and ambiguities that they see in the reports (and other materials that may have been sent). It is appropriate to solicit and consider critiques regarding clarity and defensibility of conclusions. However, the evaluators should not invite program staff members or others in attendance to change evaluative conclusions, since these are the evaluators' responsibility. While the evaluators should listen to critiques of draft conclusions, they must not relinquish any of their authority for determining conclusions. Maintaining control over the statement of conclusions is essential for maintaining the evaluators' credibility as independent investigators.

At the workshop, the program director presides and leads the group through an agenda. Basically, it includes the following items:

1. The program director summarizes the workshop agenda and engages those present to finalize and approve it.
2. The evaluators brief those at the meeting on the draft evaluation report and any other associated materials (using either overhead projector transparencies or a PowerPoint presentation with associated handouts). They then invite attendees to identify factual errors and ambiguities in the draft. They note that as independent evaluators, they have to maintain authority over the evaluation's findings and conclusions and are not asking those present to amend either of these.
3. The program staff members and others present offer critical reactions to the draft evaluation report and other materials that may have been provided. The reactions may be oral, written notes handed to the evaluators or copies of the draft materials with marginal notes.

4. The program's representatives subsequently discuss the relevance of findings to possible program improvement initiatives.

6. As appropriate, the program director may engage the staff in formulating program improvement decisions.

7. The program director invites each attendee to identify the most important point that surfaced in the meeting.

8. The evaluators brief the attendees on upcoming evaluation activities and may request assistance in carrying them out, such as helping with distribution of questionnaires or arranging access to program files.

9. The evaluators invite attendees to identify any new evaluation questions that should be addressed in a subsequent interim report.

10. The evaluators engage the program's representatives in planning and scheduling the next feedback workshop.

11. The program director summarizes and adjourns the meeting.

12. Immediately after the feedback workshop, evaluators may meet informally with the program's director and some staff members, perhaps over lunch. Experience indicates that parties have found such informal exchanges valuable for applying the interim findings to program improvement, strengthening the evaluation, and strengthening communication between the evaluators and the client group.

Following each feedback workshop, the evaluators prepare a set of minutes of the meeting and send it to the program's director for distribution to staff and others as appropriate. The evaluators also use information from the workshop to correct any factual errors and ambiguities in the draft evaluation report and other evaluation materials that may have been critiqued. They finalize the report and accompanying materials and send the updated versions to the program director for distribution, as appropriate based on advance agreements.

The feedback workshop technique is keyed to effecting two-way communication about interim findings between evaluators and a program's staff and possibly other members of the client group. The technique has proved effective for keeping interim feedback focused on program improvement needs and assisting a client group to make relatively immediate use of findings for program improvement decisions. The technique also is invaluable for providing evaluators with critical feedback of use in strengthening draft reports and other materials. These exchanges have value for keeping interim feedback relevant to emergent program developments, updating evaluation plans as appropriate, and obtaining program staff assistance in subsequent data collection activities. This technique has proved so useful that we advocate its use in any evaluation that involves the provision of interim feedback. (A checklist by Gullickson and Stufflebeam for applying this technique is available at www.wmich.edu/evalctr/checklists.) Although the technique is geared to providing feedback to a program's staff and other authorized users, its basic format is also applicable to interacting with the program review panels discussed previously in this chapter.

Preparing and Delivering the Final Report

Most evaluations culminate in a final report. Multiyear evaluations typically require annual evaluation reports as well as the ultimate final report. Basically, the annual or final reports should be comprehensive yet reader friendly. This often means that the evaluators should provide different versions of the report—for example, an executive summary; a full report of findings and conclusions; and an extensive technical appendix of procedures, tools, and data. Such reports may be printed or included on a computer Web site. They may be supplemented with audiovisual materials for use in presenting and discussing the findings in group settings.

The examples we provide or report should be useful as evaluators consider how to organize their own culminating reports. However, we emphasize that reporting needs of different evaluations will vary and that no one outline is appropriate for structuring all evaluation reports. Instead, evaluators should carefully study the needs of their audience and exercise responsiveness and creativity in crafting responsive and effective reports.

Formats for Evaluation Reports

Formats for culminating reports vary according to the evaluation model or approach being followed, the requirements of the evaluation's sponsor, the nature of the evaluand, the homogeneous or heterogeneous nature of the audience, and stakeholders' particular evaluation questions and special information needs. The format of some reports will array and assess the relative merits of alternative programs, services, or products. Other reports will focus on the background, structure, costs, implementation, and outcomes of a single program or other object. No matter the form of reporting, it should conform to advance agreements on reporting.

Consumer Reports. Consumer reports that assess alternative objects focus on classes of objects that are available to consumers, alternatives within each class, and the relative costs and merits of objects within each class. *Consumer Reports* magazine is the gold standard for reports that inform consumers about the relative merits of alternative products and services. Any issue of that magazine provides excellent examples of such reports. Within this book, Chapter Eleven is an example of a consumer-oriented evaluation report since it critically examines the relative merits of eight alternative evaluation approaches against 30 standards for evaluations.

Another example appears in Exhibit 26.2. It is an outline for a hypothetical evaluation report focused on assessing alternative computers for classroom use. As this outline illustrates, consumer-oriented evaluation reports are keyed directly and concisely to serving consumers' decision needs. Such reports focus on a particular need of consumers such as selecting a type and brand of computer for use in classrooms. They array a reasonable range of decision alternatives—as determined in the evaluation's original design—and classify them into types, for example, laptops versus desktops and Mac versus Windows based.

Clearly, a consumer report format is useful when helping an audience critically contrast and compare alternatives in order to reach an adoption or purchasing decision. Often such alternatives are in the form of products such as vacuum cleaners, refrigerators, or textbooks. The alternatives can also be softer, as in different approaches to delivering reading instruction or, as seen in Chapter Eleven, different approaches to evaluating programs. Clearly an evaluator's repertoire for conveying evaluation findings should include the consumer report approach.

Single-Object Reports. In contrast to consumer-oriented evaluations, many evaluations focus on a single program or other object. Rather than serving adoption or purchasing decisions, the final reports of these studies typically sum up the nature and accomplishments of the given object. Decisions to be served may include deciding to continue, reduce, expand, improve, or terminate a program. These final reports often are keyed to informing a broad audience about the program's background, structure, implementation, costs, main effects, and side effects.

Exhibit 26.3 contains the contents page for a summative evaluation that focused on a single project. It is the self-help housing project described in Chapter Twelve and referenced in a number of subsequent chapters. The final report of this evaluation is noteworthy for its unique organization. Like most other final evaluation reports, all the contents of this report (except for a detailed technical report) are inside one pair of covers. However, this report essentially was three reports in one. The intention in using this format was to provide different reports for study by different segments of the audience and to make it easy for each segment to locate quickly and read the part of the presentation that most interested them.

Another unique feature of this composite report is that each individual report concluded with a photographic retelling of the report's story. This was feasible in

EXHIBIT 26.2. ASSESSING COMPUTERS FOR CLASSROOM USE.

Introduction

Recent developments in Windows-based and Macintosh desktops and laptops

History of use in classrooms

What the future holds for new hardware

Will today's machines soon be obsolete?

Basic contrasts

How to choose

Laptops versus desktops

Macs or Windows based

Dependability and service

Discounts for schools

School needs and availability of programs for education applications

Compatibility with other hardware

Cost

Warranties

Graphic comparisons of ten brand-name laptops on:

Frequency of repairs

Users' ratings of technical service

Teachers' ratings of classroom utility

Graphic comparisons of ten brand-name desktops on:

Frequency of repairs

Users' ratings of technical service

Teachers' ratings of classroom utility

Tabular comparisons of five low-budget laptop machines on:

Cost

Six technical criteria

Memory and RAM

Advantages

Disadvantages

Overall merit

EXHIBIT 26.2. ASSESSING
COMPUTERS FOR CLASSROOM USE, Cont'd.

Tabular comparisons of five moderate- to high-budget laptop machines on:

Cost

Six technical criteria

Memory and RAM

Advantages

Disadvantages

Overall merit

Tabular comparisons of five low-budget desktop machines on:

Cost

Six technical criteria

Memory and RAM

Advantages

Disadvantages

Overall merit

Tabular comparisons of five moderate- to high-budget desktop machines on:

Cost

Six technical criteria

Memory and RAM

Advantages

Disadvantages

Overall merit

Best buys

For classroom use in a low-budget laptop

For classroom use in a moderate- to high-budget laptop

For classroom use in a low-budget desktop

For classroom use in a moderate- to high-budget desktop

The methods behind the ratings

EXHIBIT 26.3. CONTENTS PAGE
FOR THE SELF-HELP HOUSING EVALUATION.

Executive Summary
Prologue
Introduction

Report One: Project Antecedents
    1. Consuelo Foundation
    2. Genesis of the Project
    3. Project Context
    [Photographic Reprise]

Report Two: Project Overview
    4. Project Overview
    5. Recruitment and Selection of Project Participants
    6. Home Financing and Financial Support
    7. Construction Process
    8. Social Services and Community Development
    [Photographic Reprise]

Report Three: Project Results
    9. Evaluation Approach (initial planning grant, audiences and reports, purposes, design, evaluation questions, basis for judging the project, data collection, environmental analysis, program profiles, traveling observers, case studies, interviews, goal-free evaluations, feedback workshops, synthesizing findings, personnel, constraints, cost of the evaluation, metaevaluation)
  10. Evaluation Findings (context, inputs, process, impact, effectiveness, sustainability, transportability)
  11. Conclusions (project strengths, project weaknesses, key lessons learned, bottom-line assessment)
    [Photographic Reprise]

Epilogue
Acknowledgments
References
About the Evaluators
Appendixes
    A. Evaluation Reports
    B. Traveling Observer's Handbook
    C. Case Study Participants
    D. Case Study Interview Protocol
    E. Builder Interview Protocol
    F. Evaluation Personnel
    G. Metaevaluation: Attestation of Adherence to Professional Evaluation Standards
    H. CIPP Evaluation Model Checklist

this evaluation because of the visible nature of a host of vital project elements. Photographs pertaining to Report One on project antecedents included the beauty of nearby mountains and ocean beaches; the rundown nature of area neighborhoods; the presence of squatters on area beaches; a village of small, two-room structures for homeless people; area schools and recreation facilities; area stores and restaurants, including boarded-up buildings; leaders of the project's sponsoring foundation; and project staff in their planning sessions at foundation headquarters. Photographs recapping the Report Two story of project implementation portrayed the project's staff; vacant building plots prior to construction; contractors providing beneficiaries on-the-job instruction in construction procedures; beneficiaries at work building their houses, including women and men operating power equipment with which they were previously unfamiliar; the project's community center and playground; the variety of types of houses built; houses in various stages of construction; cul-de-sacs designed to foster community cohesion; landscaping around houses and the community at large; expensive stone walls and heavy iron gates that home owners had erected to mark off their property and keep it secure; the celebration and blessing that followed each construction cycle; happy families inside or outside their just-completed houses; and participation of children and their parents in educational and social support activities. Photographs reprising the Report Three story of evaluation results confirmed that after seven years, the foundation and beneficiaries had produced a wonderful community that was populated with a diverse population of grateful, low-income home owners.

The photos showed happy children—in front of their attractive houses, at play, and at study; attractively landscaped properties; happy couples proudly standing in front of the house they had built; community picnics and parties; an impressive center designed to house community activities; and large groups of home owners in group meetings. This set of photos was concluded with two adjacent photos intended to sum up what had been accomplished. One showed the project's benefactor, Consuelo Zobel Alger, who, prior to her death, had declared, "I want to spend my heaven doing good on earth." The other concluding picture was a panoramic view of the beautiful, child-friendly new community, named "The Spirit of Consuelo."

In this evaluation, the sequence of photographs at the end of each report had a number of advantages for the readers. It helped them better assess and appreciate why and how the project was started, where it was conducted, whom it served, who led the project, who performed the various tasks, how the project was designed and carried out, how it progressed over time, and what it accomplished. We observed that review of photographs stimulated some readers to return to certain sections of the report to deepen their understanding of project implementation and accomplishments. The pictures also stimulated and aided discussion about certain issues in the project, such as the values underlying the project and home owners' propensity to mark off their individual properties with impressive stone walls and gates. Some readers of the report told us they would have been skeptical about its printed claims of high project success had they not seen the successes vividly displayed in photographs. Based on our experience in this evaluation, we strongly recommend the use of photographic reprises when a project's characteristics are highly visible, and especially when a project's progression and success (or failure) can be demonstrated in an appropriate sequence of pictures. Now we look more closely at the composition of The Spirit of Consuelo evaluation report (available at www.wmich.edu/evalctr).

Report One was aimed at audiences who had no prior knowledge of the project, its sponsor, or its environment. This report presented information on the Consuelo Foundation, the values it imparts to its projects, why and how this organization started the self-help housing project; the assessed needs of working poor and homeless people in the area; the project's environment of mountains, seacoast, and poverty-stricken neighborhoods; and its economic, demographic, and social characteristics. This report addressed each of these matters in some detail. Persons from around the world who had expressed interest in this project wanted such background information. However, the evaluation's client group was already well informed on these matters and needed only to skim the contents of Report One.

Report Two presented the details of project implementation. It was especially addressed to persons and groups that might be interested in replicating the project's unique approach to values-based, self-help housing and community development. This report presented an overview of the project's rationale, values, targeted beneficiaries, goals, structure, staff, operations, and financing. Especially, this overview explained how, during each of seven annual increments, six to seventeen pairs of cobuilders had worked together on weekends over a ten-month period to build their houses. The report presented the criteria for choosing project participants and explained how they were recruited and chosen. It described the selected cobuilders, including their backgrounds, demographic characteristics, ethnic composition, education level, areas of employment, and especially their children. It explained the approach to helping project participants obtain mortgages and related loans. It described the foundation's investment in the project and how it would recoup some of the investment. It explained how project participants built their own houses, how they were trained and assisted to do so, and how they were supervised. It described the roles of the contractors who trained the project participants and those who did the specialized electrical, plumbing, and concrete work. It described the state's role in constructing and maintaining roads and infrastructure and inspecting the various stages of construction. It reported on why and how the foundation erected a community center and explained the covenants and rules for living in this community. Report Two also discussed how the foundation's staff delivered social and community development services throughout the life of the project. Clearly, this second report was intended to inform interested parties about the project's nuts and bolts and what would be required to mount and conduct similar projects.

Report Three presented the project's results. These were assumed to be of interest to all segments of the evaluation's audience. This report summarized the details of the employed evaluation approach. Especially, these details included the initial grant to plan the evaluation; the audience, its information needs, and the reports that were tailored for use by different groups; purposes and intended uses of evaluation findings; value bases for judging the project; the data collection tools and activities; plans for synthesizing and reporting evaluative information; evaluation personnel and costs; constraints on the evaluation, such as prohibitions against recording interviews with beneficiaries; and provisions for evaluating the evaluation. The core of Report Three included findings divided according to the different components of the CIPP model and focused especially on the assessed needs of targeted beneficiaries and the local area. The findings were presented in terms of the project's context, structure, process, reach to the targeted beneficiaries, effectiveness in addressing beneficiaries" needs, sustainability, and transportability. Report Three's ensuing conclusions were divided into the project's strengths and weaknesses, key lessons learned, and a bottom-line assessment. The last focused on the project's quality; worth to beneficiaries, the local area, and community developers around the world; and unfulfilled needs and objectives.

Following presentation of the three core reports, the overall document concluded with an epilogue, recognition of those who contributed to the evaluation, references to the interim reports that led to the final document and relevant publications, information about the evaluation contracting organization and staff, an executive summary, and appendixes. The appendixes contained interim evaluation reports and tools, information about project beneficiaries and evaluation staff, a self-assessment metaevaluation by the staff, and a copy of the CIPP Evaluation Model Checklist. The metaevaluation was keyed to the thirty Joint Committee *Program Evaluation Standards* (1994). The appendixes provided a modicum of information about the design, tools, and implementation of the evaluation that likely would satisfy the interests of most members of the audience. However, technical specialists in the evaluation community likely would require much more detail about the evaluation's methodology than could reasonably be contained in one document designed to serve the evaluation's diverse audience. Therefore, in evaluations such as this example, we advise evaluators to prepare a separate detailed technical report on how the evaluation was designed, instrumented, carried out, and assessed.

Another feature of this final report was that we placed a pullout, laminated, single-sheet copy of the executive summary within it. It supplemented the other copy contained within the report and provided readers a convenient means to view the executive summary while looking through the complete report.

Presentation of Evaluation Reports: Decisions About Conclusions and Recommendations

Final reports may be presented in a number of ways and forms. Above all, what is presented must be clear to relevant program stakeholders; otherwise, much of the purpose of the evaluation will be lost. Thus, the interpretation of outcomes is vital to the presentation. To achieve the desired outcome of sound interpretation and strong stakeholder desire to use the evaluation's findings, careful planning must be given to the form or forms of presentation. Whatever these are, they must be attractive and even exciting. Evaluation judgments, an essential part of the evaluator's task, need to be clearly related to the evaluation questions and subsequent findings; these in turn need to be related to data gathering, analysis, and synthesis. If the advice given in this chapter is followed, there should be no unjustified surprises arising from conclusions and their presentation. In summary, presentation of findings and evaluator judgments and conclusions must be well organized, logically developed on the basis of the evaluation's planned progress, and so convincing that the evaluation has an impact on users relative to program change and development. The closing stages of the evaluation should continue to encompass a shared understanding of the study's purposes and findings. The report becomes a means to an end—that is, the actual use of findings by program personnel.

Readers may have noted from our depiction of The Spirit of Consuelo evaluation that no mention was made of recommendations. Practitioners and theorists of evaluation differ markedly in their opinions about the place and worth of recommendations. In the past, almost all evaluations concluded with a series of these. Indeed, clients expected that recommendations would appear to provide guidelines for future decision making and changes or substantiation of present practices. Provided that recommendations arise from logically developed evaluator judgments based on techniques and warranted assumptions with a foundation in widely accepted standards and relevant information, it is likely that future evaluation reports could continue to give advisory recommendations. But caution is needed.

Let us consider the wider implications of evaluation recommendations. Will these provide sure safeguards against future implications arising from the ways they are interpreted? The answer to this question is no. Michael Patton (1997) stated, "Recommendations have long struck me as the weakest part of the evaluation" (p. 328). His opinion is that despite huge strides in studying programs and in methodological development, evaluation has lagged behind in the development of recommendations. Moving from data-gathering analysis to making recommendations is not to Patton's way of thinking "a simple, linear process" (p. 328). Readers and users of evaluation reports have every right to know and understand on what bases recommendations were compiled. Michael Scriven (1993) placed a clear warning that it is potentially fallacious to draw a nexus between determining the merit, worth, and value of an object and making recommendations. His contention is that while good evaluators may develop soundly based judgments, too often they are ill equipped and lack the necessary experience and data to formulate defensible recommendations.

There are, however, other views about the presentation of recommendations. For instance, Michael Hendricks and Elizabeth Handley (1990) have stated their view that "evaluators should almost always offer recommendations" (p. 110). Others, such as Worthen, Sanders, and Fitzpatrick (1997), advocate organizing evaluation judgments into somewhat of a blunt dichotomy, that is, strengths and weaknesses (or limitations). They see sound elements in this approach, such as attention being focused on positive and negative elements of evaluator judgments in a fashion understandable to audiences.

In our opinion, however, any display of strengths and weaknesses must be underpinned by clear and valid information if there is to be any possibility of audience acceptance of recommendations thereafter. Worthen et al. (p. 419) ambiguously conclude their discussion on the inclusion or otherwise of recommendations in reports. On the one hand, they "strongly prefer the inclusion of recommendations," and on the other, they see that "there are times when they might be appropriately omitted."

Our view is that a responsible evaluator must consider the possibility of including recommendations. The decision to have recommendations or not should be discussed with the client and stakeholder group at the early planning stage. A decision to consider recommendations must always be qualified by caveats. For example, the study should proceed only to the point of evaluator judgments if the obtained data pertain exclusively to the program's merit and worth. In such a case the evaluator appropriately would leave it to the client and other stakeholders to decide how best to respond to the evaluation's findings. However, if the evaluation includes systematic follow-up study to identify and assess alternative responses to the evaluation's conclusions, then the evaluators appropriately can identify and recommend a sound course of action.

One primary criterion for judging the worth of an evaluation is its utility (Joint Committee, 1994). Allied to this is the need to provide reports to decision makers in a timely fashion. It is of little use to clients to have reports provided after the period when decisions for program improvement have to be made. Formative evaluation reports designed to help program personnel during the development stage of a program clearly are needed before the program is completed (although these reports may constitute sections of the final report). Both formative and final reporting should be undertaken after relevant discussions with program users so that they have the desired impact. One aspect of evaluation impact is the extent to which the study saves client resources and thus is seen to help provide cost-effective measures.

Providing Follow-Up Support to Enhance an Evaluation's Impact

The completion and submission of evaluation reports lay the foundation for subsequent efforts to apply the findings. Recipients of evaluation reports need to study, assess, and make sound interpretations and applications of the findings, especially those in annual and final reports. Provided that the advance evaluation agreements include follow-up functions for the evaluators and resources to support the work, evaluators can help groups understand and consider how they might appropriately use reports. To the extent that evaluators are able to do so, their follow-up efforts can increase an evaluation's impact.

We reiterate that evaluators should not in any way take over the role of their decision-making clients. It is proper for evaluators to promote and assist appropriate uses of evaluation findings. However, it is inappropriate for them to make program decisions based on the findings or to exert undue pressure for certain choices. Appropriate ways evaluators can foster proper use of findings are to (1) help users interpret findings and see their implications for decisions and actions, (2) help them avoid misinterpreting findings, (3) caution against making inappropriate inferences and applications, (4) assist potentially contentious groups to deliberate civilly and constructively about the findings; and, as appropriate, (5) help the client group plan for needed follow-up investigations.

Leading Discussions and Managing Conflict

Dissension about how findings can and should be applied often occurs when an evaluator meets with stakeholders to promote and assist their uses of the final report. Consequently, evaluators need to be adept at coordinating group discussions and also at managing conflict when it arises in feedback sessions. This is especially important when, in the course of presenting and leading discussions of evaluation findings, heated exchanges arise over the meaning and importance of the findings. Among the critical skills of conflict management are those involved in engaging "combatant" groups to discuss and resolve their disagreements about the meaning and appropriate uses of evaluation reports. As a discussion leader, the evaluator needs skill to:

- Propose and reach agreement with the evaluation client and others on goals for group discussion
- Help a group of stakeholders settle on an agenda and rules for group interactions
- Coordinate or assist coordination of exchanges among group members
- Initially foster divergent thinking and deliberation
- Ensure that all participants have opportunities for input
- Prevent overzealous participants from dominating the exchange
- Listen and take notes
- Ask clarifying questions
- Summarize areas of agreement and disagreement as they emerge
- Help the group try for consensus
- Engage all participants in summarizing what they see as the outcome of the discussion
- Engage the group to decide on next steps
- Prepare and distribute a summary of the meeting

As evident in this list of discussion leadership tasks, an evaluator can play a valuable mediation role in helping a diverse stakeholder group understand and appropriately use evaluation findings. To do so, evaluators should develop their abilities to be effective discussion leaders.

Helping a Client Group Interpret and Apply Evaluation Findings

In our experience, evaluators' follow-up activities typically are conducted according to agreements reached with the subject program's director. Together, the evaluator and program administrator will define the audiences for follow-up support, for example,—program staff, a program advisory panel, beneficiaries, interested community members, the program's policy board, and others. Separate meetings may be slated for each of several key groups. It can be important to meet with such groups separately, since program-related responsibilities and interests may vary considerably from group to group. To foster impact, evaluators should tailor follow-up exchanges over evaluation reports to the program-related responsibilities of each group and their particular interests and questions.

The preparation for and conduct of each follow-up meeting can employ the general approaches outlined earlier in this chapter. These focused on meetings with evaluation review panels and feedback workshops with program staff and others. Again, we suggest that evaluators and their clients will find the Evaluation Feedback Workshop Checklist (available at www.wmich.edu/evalctr/checklists) highly useful. Other approaches to providing follow-up assistance for interpreting and using evaluation reports may include focus groups, public forums, socio-dramas, journal articles, Web sites, and simulation exercises based on the evaluation findings.

A Sociodrama Example of Evaluation Follow-Up Assistance

One of the most interesting follow-up approaches we have observed was a socio-drama designed and conducted by the University of Illinois' Robert Stake. He had directed an evaluation of a state's educational accountability system and is-sued a comprehensive, largely critical report of the system's procedures and find-ings. The lengthy technical report was of interest and use to a narrow group, including especially state education accountability staff members and account-ability specialists. However, a much broader audience of educators, policymak-ers, and citizens was interested to learn and deliberate about the involved policy issues without having to study the detailed technical report.

To respond to this diverse group, Stake conducted a series of public meetings in large auditoriums. Each person in attendance was provided a single sheet that, in matrix form, identified the study's conclusions about the state's new educational testing and accountability system. Conclusions presented on the sheet included strengths and weaknesses of the accountability system and issues of concern at local as well as state levels.

The riveting factor of the meetings was a sociodrama enacted on the audi-torium's stage. Five chairs were arranged as if they were the seats in an automo-bile. Persons sitting in the "automobile seats" represented a group that had just left a meeting where the evaluation of the educational accountability system had been presented. The five stakeholders—a teacher, a school principal, a school board member, a member of a local parent-teachers association, and the school district's director of testing—were returning to their home city on the other side of the state.

During their journey, these persons reflected on and discussed what they had heard at the meeting. They mainly discussed issues seen in the accountability sys-tem that they judged especially relevant to their school system and community. One topic was the fairness and quality of the state's tests. While they acknowl-edged that a reputable testing company had produced the tests, they also ques-tioned whether the company had been given sufficient time and resources to validate the tests. In fact, the testing company had issued strong caveats in this regard. The discussants thought the pass-fail standards attached to the tests probably were arbitrary and unrealistic. They were highly skeptical about the use of single test scores to promote and graduate students and to reward or sanction schools. They projected that this high-stakes use of a test would generate unjust decisions about students, teachers, and administrators and likely would create much conflict. On the other side, they considered that there were some advantages of employing the same test in every district in the state, especially that a common state testing program would be welcomed by the state's lay public. However, they worried that a single set of state tests might have an adverse, narrowing effect on their local curriculum, especially since the tests did not cover all curricular areas. Another worry was that teachers and students would spend inordinate amounts of time practicing and preparing for the state tests. Moreover, they worried that this testing program could spawn possible cheating by teachers, who might feel pressure to make sure that all students' test scores were in the acceptable range. Still another concern was that the state would take so long in scoring tests that results would be returned too late to be of much use to teachers and students. Concerning the state level, the discussants wondered whether this new testing program would sap the state's scarce resources for education or, if not, whether the state would be able to revise the tests regularly and keep them up to date.

The actors raised a number of provocative issues. Following the dramatization, Stake would add some comments and brief the audience on the summary of program strengths, weaknesses, and issues on the single sheet that had been distributed. He then would open the public meeting to comments, questions, and discussion. Invariably, this sociodrama format spawned a substantive, provocative exchange among those in attendance.

Helping Policy and Administrative Groups Understand and Apply Findings

Evaluators often have to serve the information needs of policy bodies as well as program administrators. In serving these different audiences, the evaluators need to be sensitive and appropriately responsive to a number of issues. Especially, they should be mindful of and attentive to the client group with whom they have contracted. Typically, this group is the program's administrator, but it might be the program's policy board. In either case, the evaluator and client need to plan together on how to contact and serve the different audiences.

In such planning, the evaluators should be mindful and respectful of differences in the evaluation needs of policymakers and administrators. The evaluator should not fall into the situation of aiding and abetting policymakers to usurp program administrators' authority. The potential for misuse of evaluation findings emerges when a policy board inappropriately delves into the area of administrative decision making and wants the evaluators to give them information of use in directing the day-to-day program operations and, possibly, making personnel decisions. Evaluators should not steer policymaking groups in the direction of taking over administrative decisions. Also, they should not become party to a policy board's decisions to hire or fire a program's administrator or other staff members. The guiding principles here are that a program's staff should have authority that is commensurate with its areas of responsibility and that evaluators should provide evaluative information and follow-up service to policy boards and program staffs that are commensurate with their areas of policy responsibility and authority.

Clearly, evaluators have to walk a fine line and exercise utmost professional integrity when serving both policy and administrative groups. Ideally, policymakers set program goals and priorities, assign responsibilities to administrators to carry out the program, and give them commensurate authority to make and implement the day-to-day program implementation decisions. While evaluators have no authority to differentiate a program's policy and administrative roles, they can and should be sensitive to potential problems in this area and not exacerbate them. They should avoid focusing a policy group on a program's day-to-day administrative matters. In general, it is appropriate to focus the attention of policy boards on needs assessment data of use in affirming or revising program goals and priorities, cost-effectiveness information of use in assessing the adequacy of program resources and the return on investment, process information of use in determining whether a program is a high-quality effort that is focused on intended outcomes, and outcome information of use in deciding whether a program is achieving its goals and is worthy of continuation.

Planning and Conducting Follow-Up Input Evaluations

When promoting the impact of an evaluation report, it is wise to consider the particular study that generated the report in a broad improvement-oriented context. Whereas evaluations often raise more questions than they answer, the unanswered questions can provide valuable leads to needed follow-on studies. This is especially the case in using the CIPP model (see Chapter Fifteen), where an input evaluation might be launched to help the client group solve problems identified in the original evaluation. When a product evaluation identifies issues and problems in a program, the evaluator and client appropriately should consider whether a problem-solving study should be conducted. If so, they are wise to plan and launch an input evaluation aimed at identifying or developing, then assessing alternative solution strategies.

An Example of Using the CIPP Model to Reform a System

In our work for the U.S. Marine Corps, we employed an input evaluation to help the Marine Corps leaders reform its personnel evaluation system. Our initial evaluation found that the existing system for evaluating officers and enlisted personnel was in need of reform. The leaders of the Marine Corps agreed with our conclusion. However, our evaluation had not culminated in recommendations for solving the identified problems. Clearly, the study had produced no appropriate information base for solving the identified problems. Any recommendations we would have made would have been strictly armchair and not defensible. An acceptable solution to the problems we found had to be located outside the bounds of the original study. Accordingly, with the Marine Corps' buy-in, we conducted a follow-on input evaluation.

That study identified about ten alternative personnel evaluation systems being used in other military services and industry. We critically examined these against the Marine Corps' twenty-two standards for sound personnel evaluation systems and found that none was acceptable for solving the problems in the Marine Corps' current system. Collectively, however, these different systems had some promising features.

Subsequently, we used the results of this initial input evaluation as a basis for creating plans for three new personnel evaluation systems. This was accomplished by engaging three independent teams, each to generate the best possible personnel evaluation system for the Marine Corps. Each team reviewed the results of our previous evaluation of the existing personnel evaluation system plus the information we had gathered about other personnel evaluation systems, including our ratings of those systems. One team was assigned to use this information to generate a system that built on and reformed the existing personnel evaluation system. The second team was assigned to design a system based on the outside system we had rated highest. The third team was assigned to exercise utmost creativity to design a creative new system.

The three teams designed these systems as competing approaches to reforming the Marine Corps personnel evaluation system, and they took advantage of what we had learned through evaluating the ten alternative systems. We evaluated the three invented systems against the twenty-two standards and reported the results to the Marine Corps hierarchy. The top generals chose one of the systems for development and implementation. It turned out to be the system that was a reform of the current system and not the one we rated best overall. However, we had rated the plan for reforming the current system highest on feasibility.

We then provided a plan for constructing and pilot-testing the new system. The pilot-test plan was patterned after the process and product components of the CIPP model. The Marine Corps proceeded to develop, pilot-test, and install the new personnel evaluation system. We see this experience as a cogent example of how an evaluation can be planned and carried out interactively with a client group to produce a valuable outcome.

Summary

This chapter is titled "Communicating Evaluation Findings," but more than that, it is about securing impacts of evaluation studies. Without proper uses of findings, an evaluation can be no more than an academic exercise. The concern for impact should be pervasive throughout the process of planning, budgeting, conducting, and reporting an evaluation. Typically, evaluations should yield interim feedback, as well as annual and final reports. As feasible, evaluators should support client groups' uses of reports following their delivery. Clearly, the needs and interests of the full range of stakeholders should be considered when promoting use of findings. Involving stakeholders in the evaluation process is a vital way to secure their interest and stimulate them to value and use evaluation reports. In so doing, evaluators need sensitivities and skills in the psychological, political, policy, and administrative aspects of programs and communication processes.

We have presented sample formats for consumer reports and single object reports. We have warned that evaluators must not take over the client's decision-making role, and we have discussed some of the difficulties in serving policy bodies as well as administrators. We have also issued cautions about the complexities and difficulties in rendering recommendations. Often follow-on studies such as input evaluations are needed to generate defensible, actionable recommendations. We have suggested a range of techniques for promoting evaluation impacts: evaluation review panels, feedback workshops, public forums, Web sites, focus groups, journal articles, and sociodramas. Especially, we have illustrated that the CIPP model is focused heavily and practically on promoting evaluation impacts.

Review Questions

1. State what you consider an evaluation review panel to be. Then check the definition in the Glossary at the back of this book.
2. What is the feedback workshop technique as presented in this chapter? Check your response with the definition in the Glossary.

3. Why is the Joint Committee's Standard U1-Stakeholder Identification so important in evaluation reporting processes?
4. Reacquaint yourself with Standard U5-Report Clarity, and list essential elements for any evaluator to observe.
5. What is the value of an evaluator's presenting findings derived from formative evaluation to a program's right-to-know audiences?
6. Give five reasons that the evaluator should be available, if required by program decision makers, to support and promote the use of findings.
7. Give as many reasons as you can explaining why culminating reports will vary according to the evaluation model or approach being used.
8. What is a consumer report? Quickly review Chapter Eleven, and state why it is an example of a consumer-oriented evaluation.
9. Why should an evaluator never assume the role of his or her clients with respect to decision making?
10. Under what circumstances would an evaluator and client consider implementing input evaluation as a follow-up study, and how would such a follow-up study respond to issues involved in presenting recommendations based on the original evaluation?

Group Exercises

Exercise 1. Discuss the relevance to the success of an evaluation study of identifying and involving right-to-know audiences for both interim and final reports. What are the functions of the evaluator and these program personnel in these aspects of the evaluation, and where do these differ and overlap?

Exercise 2. Exhibit 26.1 provides a format for identifying and analyzing the needs of an evaluation's audience. Study this exhibit, and then decide as a group the extent to which you find it useful in delineating potential uses of evaluation reports. Are there any other categories of member audiences or potential evaluation uses you would include?

Exercise 3. Many, but not all, evaluations culminate in a final report. Discuss types of evaluation studies that logically require formal written reports, those that seldom need such formality, and those where the decision about reporting is left open at the planning stage. In each instance, give reasons for decisions about reporting.

Exercise 4. There are numerous ways in which evaluators are able to provide follow-up support to clients to enhance the findings contained in reporting. Discuss this statement, with special emphasis given to helping client groups interpret and apply evaluation findings.

Exercise 5. What are the issues in developing recommendations based on an evaluation of a program? Under what circumstances should an evaluator decline to present recommendations? Under what circumstances can evaluators develop and report defensible recommendations?

Exercise 6. Recapitulate and react to the contention in this chapter that an evaluation's sounding board should be labeled a review panel but not an advisory committee or steering committee. How is this position reflected in their assessment of empowerment evaluation in Chapter Six?

References

Hendricks, M., & Handley. E. A. (1990). Improving the recommendations from evaluation studies. *Evaluation and Program Planning, 13,* 109–117.

Joint Committee on Standards for Educational Evaluation. (1994). *The program evaluation standards.* Thousand Oaks, CA: Corwin Press.

Patton, M. Q. (1997). *Utilization-focused evaluation.* Thousand Oaks, CA: Sage.

Scriven, M. (1993). *Hard-won lessons in program evaluation.* New Directions for Program Evaluation, 58. San Francisco: Jossey-Bass.

Worthen, B. R., Sanders, J. R., & Fitzpatrick, J. L. (1997). *Program evaluation: Alternative approaches and practical guidelines.* New York: Longman.

CHAPTER TWENTY-SEVEN

METAEVALUATION

Evaluating Evaluations

E valuation is of fundamental importance to society, and the evaluation field has advanced substantially in its professional organizations, standards, approaches, methodology, experience, and public service. Nonetheless, due to a host of technical, political, organizational, and psychological complications, many things can and do interfere with and threaten the success of evaluation work. A compromised evaluation might yield invalid conclusions and mislead its audience. Other evaluations operating under severe resource and time constraints may generate findings that are sound but with highly restricted applicability. Clearly it is in the professional and public interests that evaluators subject their evaluations to rigorous metaevaluation. Fundamentally, a metaevaluation is an evaluation of an evaluation. Systematically evaluating evaluations is profoundly important, because it helps evaluators detect and address problems, ensure quality in their studies, and forthrightly reveal an evaluation's limitations; moreover, metaevaluation reports assist audiences to judge an evaluation's relevance, integrity, trustworthiness, cost-effectiveness, and applicability.

This book is designed to provide evaluators, evaluation students, and other interested parties with a comprehensive perspective on the professional practice of evaluation, including ways and means of evaluating evaluations. Before we proceed in this final chapter to discuss metaevaluation in depth, we think readers will find a reprise of the book's major themes useful.

Our orientation has been both theoretical and practical. These two factors are intertwined throughout the book and are underlined by six themes. The first two themes are that (1) increasingly, the evaluation discipline is being grounded in sound theory, that is, a coherent set of conceptual, hypothetical, pragmatic, and ethical principles forming a general framework to guide the study and practice of evaluation; and (2) society needs and is using evaluations to inform decisions and hold service providers accountable for the value of their services. To these ends, evaluators are developing and deploying a responsive, distinctive evaluation methodology. The chapters in Part One present the fundamentals of evaluation by discussing the evaluation field's history and current state, the nature of evaluation theory, professional standards for evaluations, and personnel evaluation as well as program evaluation.

Part Two is a consumer report examination of twenty-six approaches often used to evaluate programs, including both illicit and defensible approaches. The assessments in this part are keyed to the book's third and fourth themes: (3) evaluators can choose from a range of defensible evaluation approaches, and (4) evaluators should employ professional standards to ensure and assess the quality of evaluation approaches and particular evaluations. Part Three extends the development of these two themes by providing details, procedures, and examples of application for six especially noteworthy evaluation approaches. In Part Four, we have presented procedures that possess general applicability across evaluation approaches. We have discussed these procedures in a sequence that proceeds through an evaluation's start-up, design, budgeting, contracting, information collection, analysis, synthesis, reporting, and follow-up.

Part Four emphasizes the book's fifth theme: (5) evaluators should involve stakeholders in the evaluation process to hear and consider their inputs and enhance prospects for their wise use of findings. Part Four now turns, in this culminating chapter, to the book's sixth theme.

This final theme, labeled the metaevaluation imperative, stresses that (6) as professionals, evaluators must subject their evaluations to evaluation. They should do so to guide evaluation planning and implementation and to report the evaluation's strengths and weaknesses publicly. This chapter is an update and amalgam of Stufflebeam's *Meta-Evaluation* (1974), "The Methodology of Meta-evaluation" (2000a), and "The Metaevaluation Imperative" (2001c). This chapter provides a rationale for metaevaluation, a conceptualization and operational definition of metaevaluation, metaevaluation contrasted with meta-analysis, an illustrative case, eleven steps in the metaevaluation process, selected metaevaluation procedures, and checklists for use in metaevaluations. We have structured the chapter to instruct in both the theory of metaevaluation and its practical application.

A Rationale for Metaevaluation

Metaevaluations are in public, professional, and institutional interests to ensure that evaluations provide sound findings and conclusions, that evaluation practices continue to improve, and that institutions administer efficient, effective, ethical evaluation systems. Evaluation has developed as a vital area of professional service as societal groups increasingly engage evaluators to investigate and pass judgment on many and varied consumer programs, projects, products, organizations, and services.

Metaevaluation is a professional obligation of evaluators. Achieving and sustaining the status of a profession requires subjecting one's work to evaluation and using the findings to serve clients well and over time to strengthen services. This dictum pertains as much to evaluators as to accountants, architects, engineers, lawyers, postal officials, hotel and restaurant administrators, judges, public safety officials, school and university administrators, air traffic control officials, construction contractors, emergency care workers, religious clerics, nurses, physicians, dentists, pharmacists, psychologists, teachers, national defense leaders, and other service providers. It means that evaluators should ensure that their evaluations are themselves evaluated. Moreover, metaevaluations are needed in all types of evaluation, including evaluations of programs, projects, products, services, budgets, expenditure reports, equipment, systems, organizations, theories, models, research designs, artistic works, conferences, students, and personnel.

Apart from needing metaevaluations to ensure the quality of their evaluations, evaluators, as professionals, should use metaevaluations to provide direction for improving individual studies as well as their developing evaluation approaches and tools and to earn and maintain credibility for their services among client groups and other evaluators. Consumers need metaevaluations to help decide whether to accept and act on evaluative conclusions about products, programs, services, and other evaluands they are using or considering for use. They need metaevaluation reports to identify sound evaluations, use their findings with confidence, and discard corrupt or faulty reports. Basically, cogent metaevaluations assist users in avoiding acceptance of invalid evaluative conclusions and instead to make measured, wise use of sound evaluation information. Those who may not aspire to be professional evaluators but who house and oversee evaluation systems need metaevaluations to help ensure that their institution's evaluation services are relevant, ethical, technically sound, practical, usable, timely, efficient, and worth the investment. Also, the subjects of evaluations—including program staff members, various professionals, and students—have the right to expect that the systems used to evaluate their aptitudes, educational qualifications, experience, competence, and performance meet appropriate standards for sound personnel evaluations or student evaluations. Clearly, metaevaluations are in the best interests of a wide range of parties who may be served or affected by evaluations.

As with other professional enterprises, an evaluation can be excellent, poor, or mediocre. Many things can and do go wrong in evaluations. They might be flawed by, for example, inadequate focus, inappropriate criteria, poor designs, unreliable measuring devices, deficient contracts, insufficient resources, an unrealistic time limit, incompetent personnel, participants with serious conflicts of interest, poor oversight and coordination, uncooperative program personnel, subterfuge or even sabotage by program stakeholders, invalid information, recording or analysis errors, excessive costs, late reports, ambiguous reports, biased findings, unsupported conclusions, unwarranted recommendations, or corrupt or misguided use of findings. Such problems may occur in evaluations of programs, products, equipment, personnel, students, institutions, and other evaluands and across a wide range of disciplines and service areas.

If such problems are not detected and addressed in the evaluation process and if the evaluation survives to a conclusion, evaluators may present erroneous findings; deliver services that are overly expensive, ineffective, or unfair; become complicit in unethical or misguided uses of findings; and likely will impair their credibility. If flawed reports are issued without being exposed by sound metaevaluations, evaluation audiences may make bad decisions based on the erroneous findings. As Scriven (1994) reported, even the highly respected and widely used *Consumer Reports* magazine should be independently evaluated to help readers see the limitations as well as the strengths of the many product evaluations published in this magazine. Invalid personnel evaluations can have unfair or inappropriate consequences for employees or, conversely, for an institution and its clients. Similarly, evaluations that accredit unworthy programs or institutions are a disservice to potential students or other constituents. In addition, professional standards and principles for evaluations will be little more than rhetoric if they are not applied in the process of judging and improving evaluation services.

Proactive metaevaluations are needed to help evaluators focus, design, budget, contract, and carry out sound evaluations. Retroactive metaevaluations are required to help audiences judge completed evaluations. In the evaluation literature, these two kinds of metaevaluation are labeled *formative metaevaluation* and *summative metaevaluation*.

A Conceptualization and Operational Definition of Metaevaluation

The practice of evaluating evaluations has quite a long history in fields related to evaluation, although the label *metaevaluation* was applied to this area only recently.

Over the years, evaluation reports on national issues such as racial segregation, surreptitious evaluation of the long-term effects of syphilis on African American military personnel, the "tyranny" of achievement testing, benefits of preschool education, the link between smoking and lung cancer, the link between asbestos and lung cancer, the safety of mining practices, the safety of thalidomide, the quality of schools, and the link between paper mills and water quality in rivers and the Great Lakes have spawned great societal debates, especially concerning needs for new laws and regulations. In turn, these debates have led to evaluations of the subject evaluation reports. Clearly such metaevaluations have been crucially important in helping public officials and the public adjudicate the validity of various evaluations' reported conclusions and recommendations and sometimes to help government enact responsive legislation or take other corrective actions.

Michael Scriven introduced the term *metaevaluation* in 1969 in the *Educational Products Report*. He employed this label to refer to his evaluation of a plan for evaluating educational products. Essentially Scriven defined a metaevaluation as any evaluation of an evaluation, evaluation system, or evaluation device. He argued that issuance of inaccurate or biased reports could seriously mislead consumers to purchase unworthy or inferior educational products and then use them to the detriment of children and youth. Thus, he stressed, the evaluations of such products must themselves be evaluated and such metaevaluations are critically important to the welfare of consumers. Although Scriven initially focused the term *metaevaluation* on the narrow sphere of evaluations of educational products, it is clear that the underlying concept is applicable to the widest possible range of evaluations. Every evaluation study should be sound, and its soundness should be ensured and enhanced through formative metaevaluation and verified or discredited through one or more defensible summative metaevaluations.

An Operational Definition

Operationally, we define metaevaluation as the process of delineating, obtaining, and applying descriptive information and judgmental information—about pertinent criteria—including the evaluand's utility, feasibility, propriety, and accuracy and its systematic nature, competent execution, integrity, respectfulness, and social responsibility—in order to guide the evaluation and report its strengths and weaknesses. This definition is designed particularly to serve the needs of evaluators who choose to adhere to the standards issued by the Joint Committee on Standards for Educational Evaluation (1981, 1988, 1994, 2003) and the American Evaluation Association's *Guiding Principles for Evaluators* (2003). The definition is consistent with metaevaluation applications of the U.S. Government Accountability Office *Government Auditing Standards* (2003). (See Chapter Three for detailed information on alternative sets of standards that have applicability to metaevaluations.)

It is instructive to consider the main elements of the definition of metaevaluation. The process elements of this definition include both group process and more discrete technical tasks. The group process tasks of delineating and applying denote the metaevaluator's interactions with the client and other stakeholders of the evaluation being assessed. In planning the metaevaluation, the evaluator identifies, communicates, and negotiates with the client and other stakeholders, as appropriate, to reach mutual understandings on the important metaevaluation questions, how they are to be addressed, how and when the findings are to be reported, areas of responsibility and authority for different aspects of the work, resources for the engagement, and the metaevaluation standards. In the metaevaluation's concluding stages, the metaevaluator meets or otherwise communicates with the client and other stakeholders to help them understand, correctly interpret, and apply the metaevaluation findings. In presenting the findings, the metaevaluator should help the audience draw justified conclusions and should caution them against overgeneralizing or otherwise making inappropriate interpretations and uses of findings.

The obtaining elements in the definition of *metaevaluation* are the technical tasks required to collect, analyze, and synthesize the information needed to judge the target evaluation. Especially involved are the collection and assessment of the evaluation's plans, budget, contract, instruments, data, computer programs, implementation records, interim and final reports, and expenditure reports; evaluator credentials; and evidence of uses of findings. In addition, the metaevaluator may interview, survey, or otherwise collect information and perspectives from persons involved in or affected by the evaluation process. As the definition notes, the metaevaluation should be informed by both descriptive and judgmental information. Descriptive information may include statistics and other quantitative information and qualitative information as might be gathered from interviews and content analysis. Pertinent judgmental information includes judgments by stakeholders and other interested parties of any and all aspects of the subject evaluation and might be obtained through focus groups, interviews, hearings, newspaper editorials, and the like.

Our definition's bases for judging evaluations are the standards for program, personnel, and student evaluations developed by the Joint Committee on Standards for Educational Evaluation (1988, 1994, 2003) and the AEA *Guiding Principles for Evaluators* (2003). In addition, we advise evaluators to use other professionally developed standards that are appropriate in particular evaluations. Especially these could include the *Government Auditing Standards* (U.S. Government Accountability Office, 2003) for evaluating evaluations of government programs and the American Psychological Association's *Standards for Educational and Psychological Testing* (1999) for evaluating educational achievement tests and psychological instruments. In some situations, it will be instructive to employ more than one set of standards for assessing an evaluation. Sanders (1995) showed that the Joint Committee standards and the AEA *Guiding Principles* are compatible and complementary. Grasso (1999) merged and jointly applied both sets of requirements. (Again, Chapter Three provides detailed information on professional standards for evaluations.)

Qualifications to Undertake Metaevaluations

Professionally recognized standards provide the foundation for sound metaevaluations. However, the irksome question lingers: Who is qualified to carry out such an important task?

We believe that the following qualifications are essential:

• *A working knowledge of alternative sets of professional standards for evaluations together with an ability to choose and apply standards that fit particular evaluation assignments.* Without such a sure reference point, the metaevaluator's decisions will appear arbitrary and lack credibility. Moreover, the metaevaluator and audience will lack a common, valid basis for adjudicating findings and conclusions. (The next section underlines serious, potential faults resulting from deficiencies in the understanding, use, and appropriate application of standards, and also emphasizes that pertinent adaptations to standards may occur if circumstances so warrant.)

• *A combination of methodological expertise and comprehension of the subject program or other evaluand.* The metaevaluator must be qualified to investigate and judge the technical aspects of the subject evaluation and also should possess or develop substantial knowledge of the substantive domain of the subject program or other evaluand. Of course, the metaevaluator must be capable of judging an evaluation's quantitative and qualitative methods. The metaevaluator also must possess or acquire a modicum of familiarity with the relevant content area. Without adequate grounding in an evaluation's substantive domain, the metaevaluator is prone to produce findings that are superficial, invalid, or viewed with suspicion. However, since metaevaluators perform their services across a wide spectrum of evaluations and substantive areas, they cannot be expected to enter every metaevaluation assignment with the needed level of content expertise. More often than not, a metaevaluator will begin a metaevaluation assignment with limited knowledge of the evaluand on which the target evaluation is focused. Therefore, metaevaluators must excel in making quick, extensive studies of pertinent subject matter domains. Moreover, they should often engage a team that possesses the needed combination of methodological and content area expertise.

• *Sufficient experience and competence to fulfill clients' needs for metaevaluations.* Evaluators should provide evidence of competent performance as metaevaluators or present credentials that they are well trained in the concepts, standards, and methods of metaevaluation. In either case, they should present credentials affirming that they possess the knowledge and ability needed to meet clients' needs for metaevaluations. Skills and experience in undertaking evaluations confidently are essential, basic requirements.

• *Honesty, integrity, and respect for individuals and society generally.* These qualities are essential for all evaluators and have special significance for metaevaluators. Most metaevaluations culminate in a final judgment of an evaluation. At stake are uses of the subject evaluation and also the reputations of evaluators of the program or other evaluand and of program leaders, managers, and staff. Especially affected are decisions based on the subject evaluation, which, because of metaevaluation findings, may be overturned or sustained. The consequences of a metaevaluation's misrepresentation for whatever reason may be dire. The metaevaluator's craft involves validly substantiating or discrediting an evaluation's findings and conclusions, while respecting and guarding against bringing undue harm to the dignity and self-esteem of involved parties. Complex issues often are involved because of the diversity of stakeholders and their interests. This fact underscores the imperative that metaevaluators be sensitive, ethical, and competent.

• *Skills in negotiating formal metaevaluation contracts.* Such contracts should include clarification of the metaevaluation's client, appropriate audiences, budget, standards and methodologies to be employed, and responsibility and authority for editing and distributing reports. Other contractual factors may include follow-up services to help ensure that the metaevaluation has an impact. (See Chapter Twenty-Three for details on contracting.)

• *Ability to effectively communicate and collaborate with other parties to the metaevaluation.* Typically a metaevaluator or metaevaluation team will have involvements with a wide range of persons and groups: the program's evaluator, administrator, staff, and beneficiaries, among others. Metaevaluators require skills to communicate forthrightly and diplomatically with this full range of persons. Especially, they should be skilled in putting at ease and having substantive exchanges with persons who might well be threatened by the metaevaluation or intimidated by external metaevaluators. Metaevaluators should show respect for the full range of parties to the metaevaluation and deal evenhandedly with all of them. Moreover, they should be able to stimulate interest in the metaevaluation and generate a spirit of cooperation among the entire group toward obtaining valid, useful findings. They should be skilled in developing rapport with contributors to the metaevaluation and in asking incisive initial and follow-up questions. Above all, metaevaluators must be excellent listeners.

Caveats in Applying Standards and Principles

Some caveats are in order regarding the use of standards and guiding principles. The Joint Committee standards are focused on evaluations of education and training programs, education personnel, and students and are not designed for use in evaluating programs and other objects outside the fields of education and training. Moreover, the Joint Committee expressly developed these standards for use in the United States and Canada and pointedly cautioned against uncritical use of these standards outside this context. In this regard, it should be remembered that the Joint Committee defined a standard as a principle commonly agreed to by the parties whose work will be evaluated against the standard. The committee argued that evaluators in other countries should carefully consider what standards are acceptable and functional within their cultures and should not uncritically adopt and apply the Joint Committee's standards. There are definite problems in transferring North American standards on human rights, freedom of information, rights to privacy, and other matters covered by the Joint Committee's standards to cultures outside the United States and Canada (Beywl, 2000; Jang, 2000; Smith, Chircop, & Mukherjee, 2000; Taut, 2000; Widmer, Landert, & Bacmann, 2000). Nevertheless, evaluators in a number of countries have adapted the Joint Committee's standards to their situations and secured agreements among their colleagues to apply the standards. Also, evaluators often have adapted the Joint Committee's standards and used them to conduct evaluations outside the fields of education and training. When the evaluators and their client groups agree that the Joint Committee's standards are applicable to their noneducation evaluations, we see no problem with pertinent adaptations and applications. We are glad the Joint Committee's standards have provided useful models for adaptation outside the fields of education and training and outside North America.

The AEA's *Guiding Principles* (2003) also have an American orientation. It is noteworthy, however, that AEA's membership includes evaluators from many countries. AEA seems to espouse the reasonable position that its members and other evaluators, wherever they may be conducting evaluations, should adhere at least to the *Guiding Principles* if they intend to claim consistency between their evaluations and what AEA recommends for conducting sound evaluations. It is noteworthy that the Joint Committee standards provide extensive detail beyond what is included in the AEA *Guiding Principles* but that the *Guiding Principles* are designed for use across a wide array of disciplines and service areas. It often makes sense to apply both the Joint Committee's standards and the AEA *Guiding Principles* in metaevaluations, thus taking advantage of their complementarities.

The U.S. Government Accountability Office has shared its *Government Auditing Standards* (2003) with government accounting organizations and accountants throughout the world, for whatever considered use they might make of these American standards. The GAO standards are referenced and used, at least as a model, in a wide range of countries. We perceive that many auditors throughout the world view the GAO standards as the best available model for setting and applying standards of financial accounting in government programs.

The point of this discussion of caveats is that standards for use in given metaevaluations should have been validated for such use. Clearly, metaevaluators can choose from alternative sets of standards for sound evaluations. In Chapter Three, we presented the standards that we recommend for consideration and have advised that these standards be used in accordance with their stated purposes and spheres of applicability. Although these standards provide excellent examples of essential aspects of standards, they are not intended for universal applicability. Evaluators outside North America should carefully determine the standards that are professionally and politically acceptable in their context. These might or might not reflect the contents of the standards that have been developed and adopted for use in the United States and Canada.

The final part of this chapter's operational definition of metaevaluation notes its basic purposes as guiding the evaluation and reporting its strengths and weaknesses. Like any other kind of evaluation, metaevaluations may have a formative role in helping an evaluation succeed and a summative role in helping interested parties judge the evaluation's merit and worth.

Metaevaluation in Relation to Meta-Analysis

In contrast to our conceptualization of metaevaluation, it is instructive to contrast metaevaluation and meta-analysis. Although these terms refer to quite different concepts, they are often inappropriately equated. A metaevaluation assesses the merit and worth of a given evaluation, evaluation system, or evaluation device. A meta-analysis is a form of quantitative synthesis of studies that address a common research question. In program evaluation research contexts, this usually involves a comparison between treatment and control (or treatment A and treatment B) comparison. Across a selected set of similar studies, the investigator calculates and examines the magnitude and significance of effect sizes.

Although metaevaluation and meta-analysis are different activities, metaevaluations have applications in meta-analysis studies. Metaevaluations are used first to evaluate and determine which candidate comparative studies qualify for inclusion in a defensible meta-analysis database. Also, a metaevaluation can and should be conducted to assess the merit and worth of the completed meta-analysis study. The meta-analysis technique is rarely applicable in a metaevaluation, since most evaluations do not involve multiple comparative studies in a particular program area.

The following example describes a metaevaluation that adhered quite closely to the preceding conceptualization of metaevaluation. Our presentation of this metaevaluation is intended to help readers identify the main tasks that are present in most metaevaluations.

An Illustrative Case Employed to Reveal Main Tasks in Metaevaluations

This illustration is a metaevaluation of the teacher evaluation system previously employed by Teach for America (TFA), an organization that recruits, trains, and certifies graduates of various baccalaureate programs for service as teachers in inner-city schools. These teacher trainees had four-year degrees grounded in an arts and sciences discipline, but most had no university-based teacher education. TFA's role was to recruit able students desiring to serve inner-city students; provide them a year of on-the-job, supervised teacher training in inner-city schools; rigorously evaluate their performance and potential during and immediately following this probationary period; and subsequently recommend only satisfactory performers for certification as effective teachers.

The metaevaluation function was important to TFA's sponsors, administrators, certifying bodies, constituent school districts, and teacher trainees. TFA's leaders needed to demonstrate the program's quality, integrity, and ability to produce and recommend only competent teachers, since the program was an innovative, radical alternative to traditional programs for educating and certifying teachers. Those programs involved teacher trainees in a four- or five-year on-campus college or university baccalaureate program. Some members of the teacher education establishment charged that TFA's program was inferior to traditional college and university teacher education programs, because the students had not received sustained instruction from teacher educators in school functioning, teaching techniques, classroom management, assessment techniques, and characteristics of children and youth. Such criticisms are ironic since traditional teacher education programs have been severely criticized for failing to produce sufficient quantities of keenly intelligent, effective instructors with substantial foundation in course content. Clearly the traditional programs had not met inner-city school districts' needs for certified teachers, as evidenced by the large numbers of vacant teaching positions, employment of many teachers with emergency, provisional certificates, assignment of teachers to teach subject matter outside their college majors, and the heavy use of substitute teachers.

Urban school districts have had great difficulties in hiring and retaining competent teachers to fill needs in the various subject matter and specialty areas and across grade levels. With the advent of TFA, many inner-city schools were understandably interested in the possibility that they could hire TFA graduates to fill their staffing needs, especially since these graduates had majors in subject matter areas such as mathematics, physics, biology, chemistry, history, English, modern languages, and geography. Their desire and availability to teach in inner-city schools would be a plus if they also possessed skills of classroom management, instructional planning, effective communication, motivating students, using technology, achievement testing, and teamwork. Urban school districts potentially were an important market for TFA.

Understandably, the school districts required solid assurances that TFA's graduates were well trained and appropriately equipped to deliver excellent teaching services to inner-city students. State bodies that certify teachers also needed evidence that TFA's teacher candidates had developed the needed teaching competencies. The teaching candidates themselves needed assurances that they would be functioning in a profession for which they were well suited and appropriately prepared and would be welcomed and respected. They also deserved to be credentialed or screened out based on fair, valid, impartial assessments. If TFA could expect state government to approve, trainees to enroll, and schools to employ the graduates, it needed to achieve and maintain credibility for the soundness of its bold alternative to traditional teacher preparation and certification programs. Fundamentally it needed to do an excellent job of preparing the teachers and also conduct and report a rigorous, credible evaluation of the postpreparation qualifications of each TFA student. TFA's evaluation of the teacher trainees was a crucial task in awarding certification and getting only qualified teachers into the schools. Its system for evaluating the probationary teachers was labeled the performance assessment system (PAS).

In 1995, TFA commissioned a metaevaluation to help ensure that PAS was providing a credible, technically sound basis for assessing the competence of TFA's teacher candidates. The metaevaluation was also deemed important to convince interested parties that PAS had been subjected to an independent metaevaluation. TFA engaged William Mehrens from Michigan State University, Jason Millman from Cornell University, and Daniel Stufflebeam from Western Michigan University to serve as the metaevaluation team. All three were extensively published experts in evaluation theory and methodology and collectively possessed specialized expertise in state teacher certification systems, measurement and statistics, evaluation standards, and metaevaluation procedures. TFA assigned this team to determine whether the PAS, in design and execution, fairly, reliably, and accurately evaluated beginning teachers.

The five main components of PAS were a teacher-compiled portfolio, portfolio assessors, a system of training and calibrating the assessors, systematic examination and assessment of portfolios, and certification recommendations derived from the assessments. The evidence in each teacher's portfolio included teaching plans, videotaped teaching, the teacher's assessment devices, students' work, and an analysis of the students' academic growth. The portfolio also included survey results from the teacher's principal, other supervisors, teacher colleagues, parents, and students.

Two specially trained assessors independently evaluated each portfolio according to preestablished rubrics and produced subscores for the specified certification criteria. A third assessor resolved any unacceptable discrepancies between the first two sets of ratings.

The metaevaluators assessed whether each of the following was sound: the performance assessment design and criteria, assessors' selection and training, implementation of the portfolio review process, assessments of teachers' impacts on students' learning, quantitative analysis of the assessors' ratings of probationary teachers, legal defensibility of the PAS, and implications for PAS's wider use. The metaevaluators also assessed the PAS against the requirements of the Joint Committee's *Personnel Evaluation Standards* (1988) to reach judgments about PAS's utility, feasibility, propriety, and accuracy.

The metaevaluators first obtained from TFA and studied documents related to the targeted metaevaluation questions and the twenty-one Joint Committee standards. Among others, these documents included the teacher trainees' academic records, the credentials of the assessors assigned to evaluate the evidence on each probationary teacher, and the TFA plan and associated recruitment, training, and assessment criteria and devices. The metaevaluators observed and prepared field notes on the training of assessors and examined a sample of the beginning teachers' portfolios. Subsequently they observed the assessors' actual assessments of the teachers' materials and analyzed the ratings and resulting certification recommendations, especially for reliability of subscores and agreements on final recommendations. Throughout the process, the metaevaluators conducted both telephone and face-to-face interviews with a range of participants. Examination of the obtained evidence was used to judge whether TFA's performance assessment system met, partially met, or failed to meet each of the Joint Committee standards. They also referenced pertinent policies, statutes, and laws to assess the legal viability of TFA's assessment structure and process. Finally, they produced an executive summary, a full-length report, and a technical appendix for the completed metaevaluation. In accordance with the metaevaluation contract, these reports were delivered to TFA for its discretionary use. The metaevaluation contract included no provision for follow-up work by the metaevaluators, a limitation, if not a deficiency, of the metaevaluation.

The basic findings were that TFA's evaluation team performed creditably and legally in conducting and reporting summative evaluations of the TFA probationary teachers. Also, TFA was judged to have performed professionally in informing its state department and school district clients about the evaluation findings. The metaevaluation identified areas where TFA needed to improve the PAS, especially in providing less hurried training for the assessors, strengthening the assessments of the teacher trainees' effects on student learning, and better matching of assessors and trainees on content areas and grade levels taught.

Metaevaluation Tasks

The preceding TFA example points up main tasks that should be considered in planning a metaevaluation process. Basically, these are generic tasks. Because metaevaluation is only a special type of evaluation, readers should not be surprised that the identified tasks apply to evaluations in general and not only to metaevaluations. Readers should keep in mind that these tasks were derived from a particular metaevaluation case; not all the tasks would necessarily apply in all formative and summative metaevaluations, and additional tasks sometimes are needed. The following tasks, then, are suggested mainly as a heuristic for use in planning metaevaluations and selecting appropriate methods.

The client commissioned qualified metaevaluators. Beyond having previous similar experiences in evaluating teacher evaluation systems, TFA selected Millman, Mehrens, and Stufflebeam to address three specialized areas. Millman, a past president of the National Council on Measurement in Education, focused especially on technical measurement questions, a topic on which he had published much and was eminently qualified. Mehrens examined PAS's legal viability, reflecting his extensive experience in assessing the legal viability of state teacher certification systems. Stufflebeam assessed PAS against the twenty-one Joint Committee standards, whose development he had led. These considerations aside, clearly TFA did not select these team members for their gender or racial diversity, although these are often relevant considerations. Presumably this team was selected to provide expertise that the client group lacked and to provide an independent, credible perspective on TFA's evaluation process. However, evaluators will not always be able to or need to engage an independent metaevaluator. In some resource-poor evaluations and especially in formative evaluations, the evaluators appropriately might do much or all of the formative metaevaluation themselves. Such self-metaevaluation practice is better than conducting no metaevaluation at all, provided it systematically addresses and adheres to appropriate professional standards for evaluations.

In contemplating conducting a metaevaluation, the metaevaluator should clearly identify the client and other appropriate audiences for the metaevaluation reports. In the TFA case, the client group included TFA's leaders and staff. The metaevaluation included many additional stakeholders, among them TFA's teacher trainees and the participating state education departments and school districts. Other audiences were teachers, school board members, administrators, and students in the involved school districts.

Another early task in the metaevaluation process is to clarify in writing the agreements needed to guide the metaevaluation and often to negotiate a formal metaevaluation contract. Among the important agreements reached in the TFA case were clarification of the metaevaluation issues and questions, the standards to use in judging the evaluation system, guaranteed access to the needed information, substance and timing of reports, designated responsibility and authority to edit and release the metaevaluation reports, and provision of the required resources. Formal contracts are not always required, especially in small, formative, internally conducted metaevaluations. In general, though, it is wise and can prove important to clarify and record as much as feasible the basic agreements that will guide and govern the metaevaluation, including provisions for subsequently modifying the agreements by mutual consent, as needed. In the contracting process, the metaevaluators and client should carefully consider whether the metaevaluator should help the metaevaluation audience interpret and apply findings following delivery of the final report. If an agreement is reached to obtain such follow-up metaevaluation service, the metaevaluation budget should include funding for this activity.

The next task in the TFA metaevaluation was to compile the available, relevant information. Often the evaluator can collect such information at a program's central office or even have such information delivered by mail. The initial information collection process typically culminates in a desk review of relevant documents and filed information. Following this work, the metaevaluator often must collect additionally needed information on site, especially information that can be obtained only where program activities are under way. For example, the TFA metaevaluation included telephone and on-site interviews, observations of assessor training sessions, and study—in a secure setting—of portfolios collected from TFA trainees. To reach valid conclusions, metaevaluators need access to all the relevant available information and authorization to collect any additionally needed information. Basically the metaevaluator should obtain the full range of information required to address the metaevaluation questions and apply all the applicable standards and principles.

After compiling the needed information, the metaevaluator should analyze and synthesize the information, determine conclusions, and (usually) write up the metaevaluation findings. The TFA metaevaluators presented tables showing both quantitative and qualitative analyses and formulated judgments of TRA's adherence to each of the Joint Committee's twenty-one standards. The metaevaluators then divided the writing assignments, produced draft sections for the report, and reviewed and discussed the report's draft components. Subsequently one member compiled the entire report and submitted the semifinal draft to the client for review. After considering critiques from the client and other stakeholders, the metaevaluators finalized their report and transmitted it to the client. As with other tasks, the need for extensive work in reporting depends on the metaevaluation context. For example, if the metaevaluation is sensitive, large scale, and summative, formal written reports of findings will be required along with supporting technical appendixes. However, in more formatively oriented metaevaluations, findings may appropriately be conveyed by oral communications, e-mail messages, letters, telephone calls, discussion sessions, and so forth.

Following delivery of the final report, the TFA metaevaluation team stood ready to help the client and other stakeholders interpret and apply the findings. Such follow-up activity can be crucially important to help (1) the client strengthen an evaluation system, (2) the client disseminate the metaevaluation findings, (3) the interested stakeholders use the metaevaluation findings appropriately and productively, and (4) help ensure that various report recipients do not misinterpret, misrepresent, or misapply the findings. Metaevaluation follow-up procedures will not always be desired by the client or feasible. Clearly, metaevaluators cannot be expected to wait on the client following completion of the metaevaluation if there has not been a prior agreement and associated funding to make this feasible. We recommend that in the initial contracting process—especially in large, summatively oriented metaevaluations—the metaevaluator and client carefully consider the possibility of engaging the metaevaluator to provide service following delivery of the final report. Often such follow-up service can contribute importantly to the metaevaluation's impact, but this contribution is unlikely to occur if the client has not planned and budgeted for the metaevaluator's follow-up involvement.

This analysis reveals that a metaevaluation (or, for that matter, evaluations of other stripes) may be divided into eleven main tasks. These are summarized in Exhibit 27.1 as a structure for identifying alternative procedures.

Metaevaluation Arrangements and Procedures

Using the eleven metaevaluation tasks in Exhibit 27.1, we next look at some of the specific arrangements and procedures that have proved useful in ten metaevaluations: two of personnel evaluation systems, five of program evaluations, one of a needs assessment system, one of alternative theoretical approaches to evaluation, and one of a large-scale student assessment system. One of the personnel evaluation-related metaevaluations focused on the system the U.S. Marine Corps used prior to the mid-1990s to evaluate the performance of officers and enlisted personnel, and the other addressed the system that the Hawaii Department of Education had been using to evaluate Hawaii's public school teachers. The examples of evaluations of program evaluations were the New York City School District's testing of the Waterford Integrated Learning System, a computer-based

EXHIBIT 27.1. STRUCTURE FOR IDENTIFYING
ALTERNATIVE METAEVALUATION PROCEDURES.

1. Staff the metaevaluation team with one or more qualified evaluators.

2. Identify and arrange to interact with the metaevaluation's stakeholders.

3. Define the metaevaluation questions.

4. Agree on standards, principles, or criteria to judge the evaluation system or particular evaluation.

5. Issue a memo of understanding or negotiate a formal metaevaluation contract.

6. Collect and review pertinent available information.

7. Collect new information as needed.

8. Analyze and synthesize the findings.

9. Judge the evaluation's adherence to appropriate standards, principles, or criteria.

10. Convey the metaevaluation findings through reports, correspondence, oral presentations, and other ways.

11. As appropriate, help the client and other stakeholders interpret and apply the findings.

skills program for elementary school students (Finn, Stevens, Stufflebeam, & Walberg, 1997); an evaluation of programs at the Appalachia Regional Educational Laboratory; an evaluation of the Reader Focused Writing program for the Veterans Benefits Administration (Datta, 1999; Grasso, 1999; Stake & Davis, 1999); an evaluation of Australia's national distance baccalaureate program. Open Learning Australia; and a small-scale, modest formative metaevaluation of Michael Scriven's first goal-free evaluation (of an early childhood program in a southern California school district). The needs assessment example was a metaevaluation conducted by the U.S. Army Command in Europe to assess needs assessments it was using in the mid-1980s to plan and offer courses to soldiers based in Europe. The metaevaluation of theoretical approaches was Stufflebeam's (2001a) assessment of alternative program evaluation models. The metaevaluation of a large-scale assessment system focused on an attempt by the National Assessment Governing Board to set achievement levels on the National Assessment of Educational Progress (Stufflebeam, Jaeger, & Scriven, 1992; Vinovskis, 1999).

Space limitations prohibit in-depth discussion of any of these cases. Instead, we cite them for particular arrangements and procedures that proved useful in conducting the eleven tasks identified in Exhibit 27.1 and for their relevance to the different types of metaevaluation. Our intent is to help readers consider arrangements and procedures that might aid the conduct of the eleven metae-valuation tasks and, where feasible, to show optional ways of approaching differ-ent tasks. Clearly, a metaevaluation's context is important in determining when a procedure is or is not applicable and likely to be effective. In discussing these pro-cedures, we offer caveats and commentary to help readers maintain circumspec-tion as they consider whether, when, and how to apply the cited arrangements and procedures. Following a restatement of each of the eleven tasks, we discuss the arrangements and procedures that we judge to have been useful in the refer-enced metaevaluations.

Task 1: Staff the Metaevaluation with One or More Qualified Metaevaluators

Clients should engage metaevaluation teams whose members have the needed technical qualifications, content knowledge, and credibility. The members should be respected and trusted by the stakeholders. In setting up the metaevaluation team for the Marine Corps, it was important to include persons with military per-sonnel evaluation experience, as well as expertise in the different aspects of a metaevaluation. The metaevaluation for the New York City School District's com-puter-assisted basic skills program included the perspectives of educational re-search, program evaluation, educational policy, and school district operations, as well as the perspectives of men, women, and minorities. This team also could have used additional perspectives representing school and classroom-level operations, computer technology, and possibly others. Generally the metaevaluation team's leader should clarify the required work and involve the client and stakeholders in appointing a qualified team.

In some situations, the client can afford to employ only a single metaevalua-tor and should then engage the most credible, capable metaevaluator one can find. For example, over a period of years, the Western Michigan University Evaluation Center employed William Wiersma to conduct the center's annual metaevalua-tions of Appalachia Regional Educational Laboratory project evaluations. He met this need exceptionally well because of his stature as an eminent educator, re-searcher, and author of widely used educational research methodology textbooks. He is thoroughly familiar with professional standards for evaluation and educa-tional measurement. His more than forty years of research on schools and teacher education programs equipped him to understand education at all levels and to re-late effectively to teachers, school administrators, policymakers, researchers, teacher educators, parents, and students. Wiersma's impressive credentials give an indication of the characteristics one should seek for a "lone ranger" meta-evaluator assignment. The published metaevaluations by Datta (1999) and Grasso

(1999) of the Stake and Davis (1999) evaluation of Reader Focused Writing program also illustrate the engagement of single, credible metaevaluators.

Even in the face of restricted resources and a formative metaevaluation orientation, the evaluator can sometimes obtain metaevaluation service from a colleague at little or no cost. For example, Stufflebeam's assessment of Scriven's goal-free evaluation referenced above involved a fee of only a hundred dollars. Upon reviewing Scriven's initial evaluation plan, Stufflebeam judged that Scriven's plan to observe mainly classroom activities would miss program effects occurring on the school's playground and elsewhere outside the school. Following a revised plan, the program's main effects were identified—and not in classrooms but on the playground.

Sometimes the evaluator cannot or need not engage even a single independent metaevaluator, especially when the target evaluation is internal, small scale, and informal. Even then, the evaluator usefully can self-assess evaluation plans, operations, and reports against pertinent professional principles and standards.

Task 2: Identify and Arrange to Interact with the Evaluation's Stakeholders

The metaevaluation for the U.S. Marine Corps was instructive regarding the identification and involvement of stakeholders. Prior to contracting for the metaevaluation, the Marine Corps leadership established two stakeholder panels and arranged for systematic interaction between them and the metaevaluators. On the executive-level panel were eleven generals, four colonels, the sergeant major of the Marine Corps, and some other officers. The second-tier advisory panel included about twenty representatives from different ranks of officers and enlisted personnel. In setting up and arranging for systematic inputs from these broadly representative panels, the Marine Corps sought to ensure that the metaevaluation would be relevant and credible to all levels of marines.

A Marine Corps management office scheduled monthly meetings between the metaevaluators and each panel, with each meeting scheduled for at least two hours. The metaevaluators were contractually required to deliver printed reports at least ten working days in advance of the meeting, and the panelists were expected to read and prepare to discuss the reports. Collectively these reports spanned all major tasks in the metaevaluation: selection of standards for judging the Marine Corps' personnel evaluation system; plans and instruments for obtaining information; diagnoses of strengths and weaknesses in the current personnel evaluation system; assessments of alternative personnel evaluation systems used in business, industry, and six other military organizations; generation and evaluation of three alternative new evaluation plans; and a plan for operationalizing and testing the selected new personnel evaluation system. For both groups, a designated general officer presided over each meeting.

Every meeting began with a briefing by the metaevaluators using an overhead projector, with copies of the transparencies distributed to all persons present. A period of questions, answers, and discussion followed. In concluding each meeting, the presiding general officer asked each panelist to address a bottom-line question. This general then summarized the meeting's main outcomes. Subsequently an assigned officer prepared and distributed a report of the discussion and conclusions reached at the meeting. These meetings were highly substantive and productive, with one lasting more than five hours without a break. We judge these Marine Corps panels to have been exemplary of the demeanor and contributions of evaluation clients; they were consummately professional, substantively engaged, and ultimately well-informed decision makers.

A limitation was that the stakeholder panels were top heavy with high-ranking officers, a significant limitation, considering that they had all been promoted by the personnel evaluation system under investigation. Also, all of the panelists worked in the Washington, D.C., area, not, for example, in California, Hawaii, Montana, Russia, Saipan, or Okinawa. There was a risk that voices and concerns of rank-and-file members throughout the Marine Corps would not be sufficiently represented and heard. The metaevaluators had to strive mightily to convince the Washington-area generals of the need for additional inputs from outside the Washington, D.C., area and from the full range of marine ranks. With this accomplished through surveys and site visits, the stakeholder involvement aspect of this metaevaluation improved. We are confident that the structure involved in this project for the Marine Corps could be beneficially applied in metaevaluations set in school districts, foundations, businesses, and other nonmilitary settings.

Nevertheless, this example's stakeholder involvement procedures were largely dictated by the culture of the Marine Corps and the fact that the commandant had mandated the metaevaluation and associated reform of the Marine Corps' performance review system. In other less structured institutions, a more flexible process of identifying and interacting with stakeholders might be better. Also, metaevaluators should keep in mind that some important metaevaluation stakeholders are identifiable only as the metaevaluation unfolds. In such cases, the metaevaluator and client should consider keeping open the question of who should be involved and informed throughout the metaevaluation and engaging them over time as appropriate. To pursue the most effective process of interaction, the metaevaluator should carefully study and take into account the metaevaluation's context and the client organization's culture and preferred style of communication and involvement.

Not all metaevaluations need heavy involvement of stakeholders. As an example, there was minimal involvement of stakeholders in Stufflebeam's (2001a) metaevaluation of alternative theoretical approaches to evaluation. He engaged the authors of a number of the approaches evaluated to react critically to his characterizations and assessments of their approaches, obtained critiques of the draft manuscript from colleagues, and had extensive exchange with Gary Henry who was coediting the New Directions for Program Evaluation volume where the metaevaluation report, titled "Evaluation Models," appeared (Stufflebeam, 2001a). Although some metaevaluations will require extensive, more or less formal interactions with stakeholders, others require little, if any, interaction with either a narrow or wide range of stakeholders. The metaevaluator should carefully consider the study's setting and exercise judgment in deciding how best to involve stakeholders.

Task 3: Define the Metaevaluation Questions

In selecting questions for a metaevaluation, the fundamental considerations are to assess the evaluation for (1) how well it meets the requirements of a sound evaluation (merit) and (2) the extent to which it meets the audience's needs for evaluative information (worth). Fundamentally, the metaevaluator should assess the extent to which the evaluation conforms to professionally determined requirements of a sound evaluation, for example, the AEA *Guiding Principles for Evaluators* (2003) and the Joint Committee's *Program Evaluation Standards* (1994). It follows that the metaevaluator should address the client group's particular questions.

Illustrating the latter point, the National Assessment Governing Board (NAGB), in concert with its contracted metaevaluators, defined more than twenty questions concerning its attempt to set achievement levels of "basic, proficient, and advanced" on the National Assessment of Educational Progress.

Two examples illustrating clients' specific questions are as follows:

- Is the membership of NAGB duly constituted, sufficiently representative of the National Assessment's constituencies, and effectively in touch with stakeholders so that it enjoys sufficient authority and credibility to set and secure use of achievement levels on the National Assessment?
- Are NAGB's policy framework and specifications for setting achievement levels sufficiently clear and consistent with the state of the relevant measurement technology to ensure that an appropriately representative group of standards formulators can consistently and effectively set sound achievement levels on the National Assessment?

In general, the metaevaluator should ensure that the metaevaluation will determine the quality and overall value of the target evaluation and also address the audience's most important questions. Because some important metaevaluation questions may not be clear at the outset, the metaevaluator and client should consider the desirability of keeping open the possibility of identifying and addressing additional questions as the metaevaluation unfolds. Balance between the evaluation's initial structure and openness to consider emergent questions is desirable.

Task 4: As Appropriate, Agree on Standards, Principles, or Criteria to Judge the Evaluation System or Particular Evaluation

Evaluation is a professional activity. As such, often it is appropriate and helpful to judge evaluations against the professional standards and principles of the evaluation field. Indeed, the need to invoke professional standards for evaluations is one of this book's key themes. Harmonious conduct and potential impact of the evaluation are enhanced when metaevaluators and their clients reach a clear, advanced understanding of the standards, principles, or criteria to be applied in evaluating the target evaluation. Depending on particular situations, evaluators and clients may choose from among a range of published standards and principles pertaining to evaluation. Some examples follow and, of course, Chapter Three deals in depth with standards and principles for evaluations.

The APA *Standards for Educational and Psychological Testing* (1999) is especially useful for assessing educational testing programs (for example, NAGB's attempt to set achievement levels on the National Assessment of Educational Progress) and particular assessment devices. Such applications of the "APA test standards" to metaevaluate measurement devices are seen in the various volumes of the *Buros Mental Measurements Yearbooks*. Other potentially useful standards include the National Center for Education Statistics' *Statistical Standards* (1992), its *SEDCAR Standards* (1991) for conducting large-scale surveys, the U.S. Government Accountability Office's *Government Auditing Standards* (2003), and the AEA's *Guiding Principles for Evaluators* (2003).

The standards most used in our metaevaluations are the personnel, program, and student evaluation standards issued by the North American Joint Committee on Standards for Educational Evaluation (Joint Committee, 1981, 1988, 1994, 2003). They have been applied widely in American educational evaluations. For example, the Hawaii State Board of Education adopted the Joint Committee's program and personnel evaluation standards as state policy, stipulating that these standards be used to assess and strengthen Hawaii's system of educational accountability.

Although the Joint Committee's standards were developed for use in evaluating North American educational evaluations, certain groups have found them appropriate and useful in other areas. For example, with minor modifications, the U.S. Marine Corps adopted the Joint Committee's Personnel Evaluation Standards for use in assessing and reforming its system for evaluating officers and enlisted personnel. Similarly, General Motors (Orris, 1989) used the Joint Committee's *Personnel Evaluation Standards* to evaluate executives. The U.S. Army applied the Joint Committee's (1981) *Standards for Evaluations of Educational Programs, Projects, and Materials* to evaluate needs assessments conducted to help determine what courses the army should provide to U.S. soldiers stationed in Europe.

In metaevaluations of the Stake and Davis (1999) evaluation, Datta (1999) employed the AEA *Guiding Principles,* and Grasso (1999) mainly applied the *Guiding Principles* but also referenced the Joint Committee's *Program Evaluation Standards* (1994).

We acknowledge that metaevaluators and client evaluators need not always reach an advanced agreement on an explicit set of standards, principles, or criteria for judging an evaluation. Such formal negotiation of the bases for judging an evaluation tend to be unnecessary to the extent that only the evaluator needs the feedback, the orientation is formative rather than summative, the target is a draft evaluation plan or a particular issue in the evaluation, and the need for feedback is immediate. In such cases, an experienced evaluator's professional judgment may suffice. Metaevaluators should formally invoke pertinent evaluation standards, principles, and criteria when the evaluation would be strengthened thereby and when doing so is feasible. This will usually be the case in summative metaevaluations and often so in formative metaevaluations of fairly broad scope and large size.

Experience with and research on metaevaluation is too limited to yield definitive advice on weighting different standards for judging evaluations. In general, we advise metaevaluators to begin by assuming that all the involved standards should be accorded equal importance. Following deliberation with stakeholders and careful thinking about a particular metaevaluation, if appropriate, one should differentially weight the standards. Sometimes it will be clear that some standards are not applicable in the particular metaevaluation. For example, the U.S. Army command in Europe decided that all of the Joint Committee's accuracy, feasibility, and utility standards were highly applicable for judging the target needs assessment system but that there was no need to invoke the propriety standards. If more were known about this case, one might justifiably disagree with the army command's decision to exclude the propriety standards. However, it is nevertheless true that metaevaluators have to make choices about assigning relative importance to different standards. In doing so, a metaevaluator should exercise careful judgments and document the basis for those judgments. In general, fewer standards will be applicable and important to the extent that the target evaluation is small, formative, and directed only to the evaluator or a small audience.

Large-scale, summative evaluations employing the Joint Committee's standards often require that all the standards be applied. In such situations, one might decide justifiably that certain standards are so important that a failing grade on any of them will cause the evaluation to fail, even though high marks were attained on the other standards. In the case involving evaluation of alterative evaluation models, the metaevaluator decided that no model should receive a passing grade if it failed any of the following standards: Service Orientation, Valid Information, Justified Conclusions, and Impartial Reporting. The stated rationale for this was that a model would be an unacceptable guide to evaluations if it did not assess a program's service to beneficiaries, answer the evaluation's questions, present defensible conclusions, and issue unbiased findings.

Task 5: Issue a Memo of Understanding or Negotiate a Formal Metaevaluation Contract

As with most other evaluations, typically a metaevaluation should be grounded in a sound memorandum of agreement or formal contract. According to the Joint Committee (1994), evaluators and their clients should negotiate and document evaluation agreements that contain "a mutual understanding of the specified expectations and responsibilities of both the client and the evaluator" (p. 87). Such an agreement clarifies understandings and helps prevent misunderstandings between the client and metaevaluator and provides a basis for resolving any future disputes about the metaevaluation. Without such agreements, the metaevaluation process is vulnerable to misunderstandings, disputes, efforts to compromise the findings, attacks, or the client's withdrawal of cooperation and funds. As the committee further states, "Having entered into such an agreement, both parties have an obligation to carry it out in a forthright manner or to renegotiate it. Neither party is obligated to honor decisions made unilaterally by the other" (p. 87). Written agreements for metaevaluations should be explicit but should also allow for appropriate, mutually agreeable adjustments during the metaevaluation. Checklists by Stake and Stufflebeam designed to help evaluators and clients identify key contractual issues and make and record their agreements for conducting an evaluation or metaevaluation are available for downloading (www.wmich.edu/evalctr/checklists). Also see Chapter Twenty-Three. These checklists are designed to help evaluators or metaevaluators and their clients launch, stand by, and, as appropriate, modify the agreements required to guide and govern an evaluation or metaevaluation.

In the metaevaluation of an evaluation of the Waterford Integrated Learning Systems project in the New York City School District (Miller, 1997), the metaevaluation team (Finn et al., 1997) was contracted not by the primary evaluators or the program directors but by an independent foundation. This helped the meta-evaluators maintain their independence and issue sometimes unwelcome judgments without concern about having their contract canceled. Many metaevaluations have the potential for conflict; when feasible, obtaining a contract and funds from a third party strengthens the metaevaluation's contractual grounding and viability.

An example of the hazards of proceeding without clear, advance written agreements is seen in the metaevaluation for NAGB (Stufflebeam, Jaeger, & Scriven, 1992; Stufflebeam, 2000b). Following completion of the contracted for-mative metaevaluation, the metaevaluators agreed to the client organization's ur-gent request, motivated by congressional pressure, for an immediate follow-up, summative metaevaluation. In view of the urgency of Congress's demand for a summative metaevaluation, the metaevaluator agreed to proceed with this follow-up metaevaluation before NAGB could formally process a contract through the federal bureaucracy. When NAGB subsequently was offended by the draft report and refused to pay for the summative evaluation work, there was no formal writ-ten agreement with which to press the issue. The metaevaluator's university never received payment for the summative metaevaluation work that had been agreed to informally but not in a written contract. The ensuing controversy over the draft summative metaevaluation findings stimulated a congressional investigation and almost resulted in cancellation of NAGB's funding. Much of this unfortunate con-troversy likely would have been avoided if the metaevaluators had insisted on reaching clear understandings and recording them in a signed contract before proceeding with the summative metaevaluation.

Task 6: Collect and Review Pertinent Available Information

After agreeing on the terms to govern the metaevaluation, the metaevaluator needs to examine the target evaluation against pertinent evidence. Initially this involves collecting and assessing existing information. In some metaevaluations, this is the only information needed to reach the metaevaluation conclusions. Legitimate reasons for collecting additional information are that the existing information is technically inadequate, insufficient, or insufficiently credible to answer the meta-evaluation questions and earn the report recipients' confidence in the findings and conclusions. When the existing information is fully acceptable for producing a sound metaevaluation report, further data collection can be wasteful.

Datta (1999) and Grasso (1999) referenced both the Stake and Davis (1999) published summary of their evaluation of the Reader Focused Writing program and their full-length report. A key lesson for evaluators seen in the Datta and Grasso metaevaluations is that evaluators and their clients can facilitate the conduct of metaevaluations by placing evaluation reports and supporting materials on a Web site for independent study and assessment of the completed evaluation. When negotiating the metaevaluation contract, evaluators and their clients are advised to consider making their study findings and procedures accessible on an appropriate Web site.

Stufflebeam's metaevaluation of the evaluation of the Open Learning Australia distance education program is instructive about the kinds of extant information from which to begin a metaevaluation and how to handle that information. It was in the interest of Open Learning Australia to control the metaevaluation's costs, since travel from the United States to Australia entails sizable expense. Thus, it was agreed that Open Learning Australia would send pertinent information to Kalamazoo about both the program and the external evaluation being conducted by evaluators at Melbourne University. It was agreed that the metaevaluator would reference this material in reaching at least tentative judgments about the adequacy of the Australia-based evaluation of this program. A wide array of documents was sent to Kalamazoo: letters, plans, budgets, contracts, brochures, data collection forms, journal and newspaper articles, minutes of meetings, field notes, reports, and responses to reports. The metaevaluation's foci were the nature of Open Learning Australia, the background of the evaluation, the evaluation plans and procedures, the evaluation process, the data, the conclusions, publicity for the program, and guidelines for the metaevaluation.

The metaevaluator's client emphasized that all judgments of the evaluation should be grounded in references to pertinent evidence. This, they stated, would distill any stakeholder notions that the remotely conducted metaevaluation was only a set of vaguely informed opinions. Accordingly, the metaevaluator catalogued every piece of information used in the metaevaluation, giving its year of origination and a unique number within that year. In reporting a judgment for each of the thirty Joint Committee program evaluation standards, the metaevaluator referenced each catalogued information item used in reaching the judgment. Thus, the client group and its constituents could review essentially all the evidence used to reach the metaevaluative conclusions. In other metaevaluations, this documentation procedure has been useful not only for bolstering the metaevaluation report's credibility, but also for maintaining a quite definitive history of the metaevaluation that can facilitate revisiting and studying the metaevaluation in later years, as might occur in doctoral dissertations.

Task 7: Collect New Information as Needed

While the extant information for evaluating the evaluation of Open Learning Australia (OLA) was substantial, the metaevaluator and client agreed that the information that had been mailed to Kalamazoo was insufficient to generate and support metaevaluation conclusions. Thus, the metaevaluator traveled to Australia to fill in some important information gaps. In addition to talking with OLA's leaders and participating faculty, he also met with several OLA students and with leaders and faculty in the more traditional higher education programs. This additional information led the metaevaluator to conclude that the assumed need—within Australia—for Open Learning Australia was questionable. Most of the nation's colleges and universities had many vacancies and were seeking students. Moreover, almost all of the OLA students lived not in the remote areas of Australia but in close proximity to institutions with openings for new students. Also, the quality of OLA offerings was highly variable, and there was unevenness in controlling exams against fraud. The metaevaluator's findings were at variance with the highly positive Australia-based evaluation of OLA. The metaevaluator concluded that the additional information obtained by making an on-site investigation proved essential to preparing and submitting a valid metaevaluation report. Such on-site investigation often is crucially important in metaevaluations, if for no other reason than to validate the information that has already been collected.

Another example of supplementing existing information with new information to reach metaevaluation conclusions occurred in this chapter's assessment of Hawaii's teacher evaluation system. Jerry Horn first used extant information to judge the Hawaii system against each of the twenty-one personnel evaluation standards (Joint Committee, 1988). He then supplemented this information with surveys of stratified random samples of Hawaii's public school teachers and administrators. The survey items were keyed to the twenty-one standards. The additional information not only corroborated the initial judgments but also provided an even stronger and more credible case that the existing teacher evaluation system was in serious need of reform.

Task 8: Analyze and Synthesize the Findings

The wide array of information used in various metaevaluations requires a variety of quantitative and qualitative analysis procedures and tailored approaches to synthesis. In our metaevaluations, we have used line and bar graphs, pie charts, reanalysis of data from the target evaluation, and computer-assisted content analysis among other analytical techniques. Often we have let analysis results stand without converging them into a supercompressed grade. In these studies, we have usually presented separate results for an evaluation's utility, feasibility, propriety, and accuracy, followed by a narrative summary and discussion. As illustrated later in this chapter, sometimes we have combined scores on utility, feasibility, propriety, and accuracy into an overall score for an evaluation and also judged the overall evaluation to be excellent, very good, good, fair, or poor.

In her metaevaluation of the Stake and Davis (1999) evaluation of the Reader Focused Writing program, Datta (1999, p. 350) employed a cross-break table to contrast the topics addressed in each of five case study reports. Based on this analysis, she observed, "Because there seemed to be only a few common elements reported on in each site . . . the reliability in areas such as productivity seems uncertain. Sorting out idiosyncratic findings from incomplete inquiry is a bit difficult." In such a situation it would be a mistake to attempt a synthesis, which could only mask the idiosyncrasies of the different case study reports.

In a reanalysis of cost and effectiveness data for two alternative reading improvement programs (which we label Program A and Program B), Stufflebeam arrived at conclusions that strongly contradicted the conclusion of the primary evaluation's draft report. That report had concluded that Program A was more cost-effective than Program B, basically because Program A spent less than Program B on each student being served and because it was assumed that the two programs were equally effective for the served students. The assumption that the two programs were equally effective was not supported and was a basic flaw in this analysis.

A key issue concerned what number of students should be included in the denominator used to determine each program's annual per pupil cost. Program A purported to serve every student in each participating school, and the evaluator had thus divided the sizable total annual program cost for each school by the number of students in the school. This analysis yielded a quite low per pupil cost for each school receiving Program A. Program B, which concentrated its reading recovery resources on students with substantial reading improvement needs, theoretically was less expensive and potentially more cost-effective for a school as a whole than Program A. Also, Program B sought to serve each targeted student only until her or his reading proficiency was satisfactory and sustainable. For this program, the evaluator divided the total annual program cost for each school by the relatively small number of students this program served. Thus, each school's cost was high for each student served by Program B—about $8,000. On the basis of the different analyses for the two programs, Program A's per pupil cost for each school was much lower than that for the schools served by Program B. The evaluator had gone on to suggest that Program A potentially was more cost-effective than Program B, considering that they were assumed to have comparable student achievement outcomes.

These conclusions were erroneous on both effectiveness and cost analysis grounds. Program B, which concentrated its reading recovery resources on only those students with reading deficiencies, argued that its program theoretically was less expensive and potentially more cost-effective for a school as a whole than Program A. This was so because year after year, Program A spent a large amount of money but spread its services thinly across all students in the school. Program A thus extended remedial services to many students who did not need such service and watered down the resources it might have concentrated on students with di-agnosed reading deficiencies.

School district decision makers needed to know which program was more cost-effective for a school as a whole in helping its students with reading deficiencies become good readers. A fairer cost analysis procedure would have divided each program's total annual cost by the total number of students in the involved school. This would have produced comparable schoolwide per pupil costs for each program. Over time, the evaluator might assess each program's cost-effectiveness by annually identifying the number of students in each school not requiring remediation in reading, then dividing this number into the school's annual expenditure for reading remediation. The lower the quotients over time, the greater the indication that the program was attaining cost-effectiveness. This procedure could work provided that the student populations for schools receiving each program were comparable at the evaluation's outset. While we do not have data to determine whether Program A or Program B would win in such a comparative study and analysis, we would bet on Program B. This is so because that program concentrates its resources on students with assessed needs for remedial reading instruction and is designed to serve each targeted student only until his or her reading achievement is satisfactory and sustainable.

Task 9: Judge the Evaluation's Adherence to Appropriate Standards, Principles, or Criteria

Following analysis and display of the obtained information, the evaluator should judge the target evaluation. Particularly important is the approach to judging the evaluation against the employed standards. Datta (1999) and Grasso (1999) basically keyed their narrative assessments of the Stake and Davis (1999) evaluation to an outline of the main standards in the AEA's *Guiding Principles* (2003) and subparts of each.

Typically we have keyed our metaevaluations to each of the twenty-one standards in the Joint Committee's *Personnel Evaluation Standards* (1988) or the thirty standards in the Joint Committee's *Program Evaluation Standards* (1994) and, more specifically, to six to ten specific points (depending on what published checklist is used) associated with each standard. To support narrative judgments, we usually score the target evaluation on all points for each standard and then assign a predetermined scaled value meaning (for example, excellent, very good, good, fair, poor) to the evaluation's adherence to each standard. Sometimes we subsequently have followed a set procedure to aggregate the scores across standards and produce judgments of the evaluation on each of the main requirements of utility, feasibility, propriety, accuracy, and overall.

Tables 27.1 and 27.2 illustrate how we and colleagues developed and presented judgments of the Marine Corps' personnel evaluation system. The rubrics

TABLE 27.1. RUBRICS USED TO DETERMINE WHETHER A MILITARY BRANCH'S PERSONNEL EVALUATION SYSTEM SATISFIES THE CONDITIONS OF UTILITY, FEASIBILITY, PROPRIETY, AND ACCURACY.

Categories of Standards	Degree of Fulfillment of Requirements[a]		
	Not Met	Partially Met	Met
Utility	1. Three or more standards are not met.	2. At least three of the five standards are met or partially met, and at least one standard is not met. Or 3. Fewer than four standards are met, all five are either met or partially met, and no standard is unmet.	4. At least four or five standards are met, and none is unmet.
Feasibility	5. Three or four standards are not met.	6. At least two of the four standards are met or partially met, and at least one standard is not met. Or 7. Fewer than two standards are met, and no standard is unmet.	8. At least two of the four standards are met, and none is unmet.

Propriety	9. Three or more standards are not met.	10. At least three of the five standards are met or partially met, and one or two standards are not met. Or 11. Fewer than four standards are either met or partially met, and no standard is unmet.	12. At least four of the five standards are met, and none is unmet.
Accuracy	13. Four or more standards are not met.	14. At least five of the eight standards are met or partially met, and at least one standard is not met. Or 15. Fewer than five standards are met, at least four are either met or partially met, and no standard is unmet.	16. At least five of the eight standards are met, and none is unmet.

Note: This form is designed for use in judging the overall utility, propriety, feasibility, and accuracy of an evaluation. Use of the decision rules on this form requires that the user first judge whether the evaluation meets, partially meets, or fails to meet the detailed requirements of each of the twenty-one standards as they appear in Joint Committee on Standards for Educational Evaluation (1988) and an additional standard (Transition to the New Evaluation System) developed for this project.

[a] In some cases, a standard appropriately may be judged as not applicable, and such standards would have no impact on determining which of the rubrics fits the pattern of judgments.

TABLE 27.2. CONCLUSIONS ON THE DEGREE TO WHICH A MILITARY BRANCH'S PERSONNEL EVALUATION SYSTEM SATISFIES STANDARDS OF UTILITY, PROPRIETY, FEASIBILITY, AND ACCURACY.

Category of Standards	Conclusion	Rubric[a]
Utility	Not met	1
Feasibility	Partially met	6
Propriety	Partially met	10
Accuracy	Not met	13

[a] See Table 27.1 for the rubrics.

in Table 27.1 were used to determine the degree to which the personnel evaluation system had satisfied standards in the four categories—of utility, feasibility, propriety, and accuracy. All available relevant evidence was then used to identify the personnel evaluation system's strengths and weaknesses related to each standard. Using these lists, judgments were formed about whether the system met, partially met, or failed to meet each standard. To summarize the results, the rubrics from Table 27.1 were used to prepare the summary matrix in Table 27.2. Based heavily on this analysis, the U.S. Marine Corps decided to replace its personnel evaluation system with one that would better meet the standards.

Task 10: Convey the Findings Through Reports, Correspondence, Oral Presentations, and Other Ways

Throughout most metaevaluations, there are important occasions for preparing and submitting evaluation reports. Typical reports include an initial metaevaluation plan, interim reports keyed to the evaluation's important aspects, the final report, and a technical appendix. For each report, it is usually advisable to prepare and submit a draft, follow this up with a feedback workshop designed to orally communicate and discuss the draft reports, and subsequently complete and submit the finalized version of the particular report (see Chapter Twenty-Six). The core contents of the reports can be keyed to the guiding standards and principles for evaluations. Tables 27.1 and 27.2 illustrate ways to display the rationale for and results of standards-based judgments of evaluations. For many reports, it is often appropriate to prepare an executive summary, a set of supportive transparencies or a computer-projected presentation, a full-length report, and a technical appendix. Depending on advance agreements, it may also be appropriate to post the metaevaluation report on a Web site, submit an executive summary for publication in a professional journal, or both.

Task 11: As Appropriate, Help the Client and Other Stakeholders Interpret and Apply the Findings

Throughout the metaevaluation process, it is desirable for the metaevaluator to have regular, periodic exchanges with representatives of the key audiences. The evaluation for the Marine Corps is illustrative of an extensive, functional, tightly scheduled reporting process. At the beginning of the metaevaluation, the Marine Corps established two client panels and issued specifications and a tight schedule for delivering reports. The reporting deadlines were closely linked to the Marine Corps' need to make decisions for reforming its personnel evaluation system and to do so promptly. A key determinant of the deadline for delivering the final metaevaluation in six months was the commandant's mandate that a plan for reforming the personnel evaluation system must be submitted and approved before his fast-approaching retirement from the position of commandant. This constraint had serious implications for the metaevaluation's work schedule and the level of needed resources. Under the study's severe time limit, it was especially crucial that the metaevaluators and Marine Corps leaders met regularly and often to review findings and apply them to the ongoing process of reforming the personnel evaluation system.

Our experience with the Hawaii Department of Education was similar in some respects to the experience with the Marine Corps. At the outset of the metaevaluation, the department appointed a review panel that represented the various interests in the state's public education system. The panel included a broadly representative group of persons with interests in the state's teacher evaluation system. The metaevaluator and members of the Hawaii Department of Education met regularly with this group to discuss and obtain input for the ongoing metaevaluation of Hawaii's systems for evaluating teachers. The panel was charged to receive, critique, discuss, and help the department use the findings. The review panel helped clarify the questions, provided valuable critiques of draft reports, and used the findings to generate recommendations for improving the state system of teacher evaluation. By being involved in the metaevaluation process, the review panel developed ownership of the findings and became a powerful, informed resource for helping to chart and obtain support for the needed reforms.

It was important that this group was labeled a "review panel" and not an "advisory panel." The orientation was that the panel's members were qualified to critique draft plans, schedules, interview protocols, and reports from their perspectives and on such matters as feasibility and clarity. The panel members were not necessarily qualified to provide technical advice for improving such meta-evaluation aspects as the design, instruments, and analysis procedures. In our experience, reference groups sometimes become dysfunctional and counterproductive when they are accorded an aura of unmerited expertise by virtue of being labeled an advisory panel.

Parallel to the involvement of the review panel, the metaevaluators engaged Hawaii educators to help carry out the metaevaluation. They were especially helpful in obtaining relevant documents, files, and data tapes and in arranging for other Hawaii educators to participate in interviews, surveys, and focus group meetings.

Metaevaluation can and often should be a collaborative effort, especially when the aim is to help an organization assess and reform its evaluation system. When the aim is to protect the public from being misinformed by evaluations of specific entities, the evaluator must maintain proper distance to ensure an independent perspective. Even then, metaevaluators should communicate appropriately with audiences for the metaevaluation reports to secure their confidence, interest, assistance, understanding, and informed uses of findings.

Comparative Metaevaluations

Sometimes a metaevaluation involves a comparative assessment of a number of evaluations. For example, professional societies such as the American Evaluation Association and the American Educational Research Association do so when they rate evaluations as a basis for making awards to outstanding evaluations. Table 27.3 provides an example of how nine hypothetical candidate evaluations might be subjected to a comparative metaevaluation. The hypothetical evaluations are listed in order of judged merit. The ratings are in relationship to the Joint Committee's *Program Evaluation Standards* (1994) and hypothetically were derived by using a special checklist keyed to the *Standards*.

Assume that each evaluation was rated on each of the thirty Joint Committee program evaluation standards by judging whether the study met each of ten key features of the standard (as defined in Stufflebeam's *Joint Committee Program Evaluation Standards Checklist*, available at www.wmich.edu/evalctr/checklists). Further assume that each evaluation was then judged as follows: 9–10 Excellent, 7–8 Very Good, 5–6 Good, 3–4 Fair, and 0–2 Poor. The score for each evaluation on each of the four categories of standards (utility, feasibility, propriety, accuracy) could then be determined by summing the following products: 4 times the number of Excellent ratings, 3 times the number of Very Good ratings, 2 times the number of Good ratings, 1 times the number of Fair ratings.

TABLE 27.3. RATINGS OF CANDIDATE PROGRAM EVALUATIONS.

Evaluation Approach	Graph of overall merit 0 100 P F G VG E	Overall Score and Rating	Utility Rating	Feasibility Rating	Propriety Rating	Accuracy Rating
Evaluation 1	———	92 (VG)	90 (VG)	92 (VG)	88 (VG)	98 (E)
Evaluation 2	———	87 (VG)	96 (E)	92 (VG)	81 (VG)	79 (VG)
Evaluation 3	———	87 (VG)	93 (E)	92 (VG)	75 (VG)	88 (VG)
Evaluation 4	———	83 (VG)	96 (E)	92 (VG)	75 (VG)	69 (VG)
Evaluation 5	———	81 (VG)	81 (VG)	81 (VG)	91 (VG)	81 (VG)
Evaluation 6	———	80 (VG)	82 (VG)	67 (G)	88 (VG)	83 (VG)
Evaluation 7	———	80 (VG)	68 (VG)	83 (VG)	78 (VG)	92 (VG)
Evaluation 8	———	72 (VG)	71 (VG)	92 (VG)	69 (VG)	56 (VG)
Evaluation 9	———	60 (G)	71 (VG)	58 (G)	58 (G)	50 (G)

Note: P = Poor, F = Fair, G = Good, VG = Very Good, E = Excellent. Within types, listed in order of compliance with the *Program Evaluation Standards* (Joint Committee, 1994).

Judgments of each evaluation's strength in satisfying each category of standards could subsequently be determined according to percentages of possible quality points for the category of standards as follows: 93 to 100 percent, Excellent; 68 to 92 percent, Very Good; 50 to 67 percent, Good; 25 to 49 percent, Fair; and 0 to 24 percent, Poor. This was accomplished by converting each category score to the percentage of the maximum score for the category then multiplying by 100. In the table the four equalized scores were next summed, divided by 4, and compared with the total maximum value of 100. The evaluation's overall merit was then judged as follows: 93 to 100, Excellent; 68 to 92, Very Good; 50 to 67, Good; 25 to 49, Fair; and 0 to 24, Poor. Regardless of each evaluation's total score and overall rating, we would judge any evaluation as failed if it received a Poor rating on the vital standards of P1 Service Orientation, A5 Valid Information, A10 Justified Conclusions, and A11 Impartial Reporting.

This procedure unequally weights different standards in the process of computing a total score and overall rating. This is because there are unequal numbers of standards in the four categories. An alternative means of determining a total score and overall rating is to sum and average the thirty individual standard scores. We advise metaevaluators to compute, assess, and discuss the extent of agreement between the two total score and overall rating approaches.

Checklists for Use in Metaevaluations

Checklists can be useful in metaevaluations. The Evaluation Contracting Checklist and the Joint Committee Program Evaluation Standards Checklist plus additional checklists may be accessed at www.wmich.edu/evalctr/checklists. Included in that repository are checklists designed for use in evaluating personnel, program, and materials evaluations. They are applicable to the conduct of primary evaluations and metaevaluations. Among others, these checklists include Michael Scriven's Key Evaluation Checklist, a checklist by Ernest House and Kenneth Howe for guiding and assessing deliberative democratic evaluations, Lorrie Shepard's Checklist for Assessing State Educational Assessment Systems, Stufflebeam's personnel and program evaluation checklists keyed to the Joint Committee's evaluation standards, and others of his that focus on the tasks in the evaluation process and on the AEA *Guiding Principles for Evaluators.* (For a general discussion of evaluation checklists, see Stufflebeam, 2001b.)

The Role of Context and Resource Constraints

The preceding discussion of metaevaluation needs to be tempered by considerations of the reality constraints in evaluation work. It will not always be important or feasible to do a formal metaevaluation. Especially, the client may be unwilling to commission and fund an independent metaevaluation. All the cases referenced in this chapter are examples where a client requested and funded a metaevaluation. Even then, the cases varied considerably in the client's need for extensive, formal feedback and the size of the budget. The amounts of money invested generally were in the range of $10,000 to $30,000, but the smallest metaevaluation cost only $100, and the metaevaluation for the U.S. Marine Corps cost more than $450,000. Generally the small, formative target evaluations required much less money and effort for metaevaluation than did the large-scale, summative metaevaluations. Usually cost should not be a deterrent to obtaining some level of metaevaluation. Typically the size of budgets for metaevaluations is minuscule compared with the cost of the target evaluation—often less than 2 percent of the target evaluation's budget. Moreover, in large-scale, high-stakes evaluations, metaevaluations often can be judged cost free when their costs are compared with the value of the benefits they produce.

Nevertheless, sometimes evaluators will not request or need a formal metaevaluation. Examples are evaluation systems that have been subjected to a metaevaluation relatively recently and that subsequently have operated relatively free of complaints and observed problems. Also, individual personnel evaluations typically require no metaevaluations, except when one is triggered by an appeal of the findings. Many government agencies, accrediting organizations, and charitable foundations seek no metaevaluations of the evaluations they sponsor, presumably because they trust their system of monitoring and oversight (although such trust is not always justified). Very small-scale, formative evaluations, as when one evaluates a small project or a course for purposes of improvement, might not need or be amenable to any kind of formal metaevaluation.

Nevertheless, despite evaluations that require little or no metaevaluation, it is always appropriate for an evaluator to plan and carry through even small-scale formative evaluations with a metaevaluation mind-set. One of the best ways to do this is to thoroughly study and internalize the key messages of the Joint Committee's standards, the AEA *Guiding Principles for Evaluators,* or other relevant standards. Having the underlying metaevaluation principles in mind is invaluable in planning evaluations, dealing with issues and problems as they arise, advising evaluation participants regarding the dilemmas they face, and—after the fact— taking stock of what the evaluation accomplished.

Summary

Metaevaluations serve all segments of society. They help ensure the integrity and credibility of evaluations and are thus important to both users and producers of evaluations. Metaevaluations often are needed to scrutinize evaluations of charitable services; research and development projects; equipment and technology; state assessment systems; new, expensive curricula; policies and strategic plans; automobiles and refrigerators; hospitals and other organizations; and engineering plans and projects. They are also needed to assess and help improve the systems used to evaluate physicians, military officers, researchers, evaluators, public administrators, teachers, school principals, students, and others. In cases of appeal, metaevaluations are needed to assess the soundness and fairness of evaluations of individual employees. As seen in these examples, metaevaluations are in public, professional, institutional, and personal interests.

Examples of the societal value of metaevaluations abound. Purchasers of consumer products need assurance that evaluations of alternatives are sound and safe. Taxpayers, needing to decide on levels of support for public services intelligently, require assurance that they are getting dependable information on the needs of beneficiaries and performance of government services. Parents need to know whether they are getting reliable and valid evaluations of their children's academic progress and of the colleges where they might send their children. In cases of high-stakes evaluations, students and their parents are entitled to know whether the students' efforts and achievements have been graded fairly, accurately, and validly. School board members and school administrators need assurances that they are getting relevant and technically defensible evaluations of schools, programs, and personnel. Politicians and their constituents need to know whether international, comparative evaluations of educational achievements in different countries are valid and defensible for use in reviewing and revising national education policy. In all of these examples, users of evaluations need sound metaevaluation information to help them assess the relevance, dependability, and fairness of the evaluative information they are receiving.

As professionals, evaluators themselves need to regularly subject their evaluation services to internal and independent review. Sound metaevaluations provide evaluators with a quality assurance mechanism they can use to examine and strengthen evaluation plans, operations, draft reports, and means of communicating the findings. The prospect and fact of metaevaluations should help keep evaluators on their toes, push them to produce defensible evaluation services, and guide them to improve their services over time.

Metaevaluation is as important to the evaluation field as auditing is to the accounting field. Society would be seriously at risk if it depended only on accountants for its financial information without acquiring the scrutiny of independent auditors. And parents, students, educators, government leaders, businesspersons, and consumers in general are at risk to the extent they cannot trust evaluation findings.

Despite the strong case that can be made for metaevaluation, not all evaluations require or merit a metaevaluation. Small-scale, locally focused, and improvement-oriented evaluations may not require any special metaevaluation. Making such determinations is a matter for careful judgment by the evaluator and client; they should take into account the local setting and especially the audience for the target evaluations. The many evaluations that do merit a special metaevaluation vary considerably concerning the type and level of needed effort. In general, whatever the type and level of evaluation to be conducted, evaluators should bring a strong metaevaluation orientation to their work. Small, improvement-oriented evaluations often should employ a modicum of formative metaevaluation. Large-scale, summative evaluations usually should secure at least a formal, summative metaevaluation and often a formative metaevaluation as well. In deciding whether to commission or conduct a metaevaluation, evaluators and their clients should keep in mind that a metaevaluation's cost is typically small compared with the cost of the target evaluation and that the value of the metaevaluation's benefits can far outweigh the metaevaluation's costs.

We defined *metaevaluation* generally as an evaluation of an evaluation and operationally as the process of delineating, obtaining, and applying descriptive information and judgmental information about pertinent criteria—including the evaluand's utility, feasibility, propriety, and accuracy and its systematic nature, competent execution, integrity, respectfulness, and social responsibility—in order to guide the evaluation and report its strengths and weaknesses. Based on these definitions, we presented a general, eleven-task methodology for metaevaluation. We referenced example metaevaluations to identify key metaevaluation arrangements and techniques of use in carrying out each metaevaluation task. The examples included evaluations of program and personnel evaluations, alternative evaluation models, assessment devices, a needs assessment system, and a state accountability system. Among the procedures presented for use in metaevaluations were review panels; a contracting checklist; when feasible, contracting for a metaevaluation with a third party; a range of checklists for judging evaluations; rubrics and analysis protocols for judging evaluations; and feedback workshops. Readers can access and download a range of checklists designed for use in metaevaluations at www.wmich.edu/evalctr/checklists. Also included on this Web site are a paper by Michael Scriven (2000) and one by Stufflebeam (2000c).

Undergirding this chapter is the strong recommendation that evaluators should ground their metaevaluations in professional standards and principles for evaluations. For evaluators working in North America, we recommended the use of the AEA's *Guiding Principles for Evaluators;* the Government Accountability Office's *Government Auditing Standards;* and the professional standards for evaluations of programs, personnel, and students issued by the Joint Committee on Standards for Educational Evaluation. Applying parallel, systematic methodologies and checklists for more than one set of standards is consistent with the virtue of applying multiple methods and perspectives in evaluation work to foster rigor and reproducibility of judgments and to identify discrepancies that should be taken into account.

As seen in this chapter and the book as a whole, evaluators are making progress in conducting evaluations and metaevaluations. Sustaining and increasing efforts to systematize and increase the rigor, relevance, and contributions of the full range of evaluation efforts are in the interest of professionalizing the evaluation field and serving society well. It seems fitting that we conclude this book with a discussion of metaevaluation. It is one of many forms of evaluation and goes to the heart of evaluators' ongoing quest to professionalize their services, strengthen their discipline, and contribute through sound and accountable evaluation to strengthening all aspects of society.

Review Questions

1. List at least five reasons an evaluator could give a client to justify the expense of contracting for an independent metaevaluation of an evaluation system, such as a state's teacher evaluation system.
2. Compare and contrast the concepts of metaevaluation and meta-analysis.
3. List this book's six major themes.
4. What is this chapter's operational definition of *metaevaluation*? How would you explain this definition to a colleague who is unfamiliar with metaevaluation?
5. According to this chapter, what are the eleven main tasks of a metaevaluation?
6. What advantages does a metaevaluator attain by contracting with a third party to conduct a particular metaevaluation?
7. Why might it be inappropriate for evaluators in Malaysia to adopt and apply the Joint Committee's *Program Evaluation Standards*?
8. Under what circumstances is it likely to be inappropriate or unnecessary to conduct a metaevaluation of a particular evaluation?
9. What are the pros and cons of applying the Joint Committee's *Program Evaluation Standards* and the AEA's *Guiding Principles for Evaluators* in combination?
10. List at least ten things that can go wrong in an evaluation, and discuss how a sound metaevaluation could be designed to prevent or expose these.

Group Exercises

Exercise 1. Compare and contrast formative metaevaluation and summative metaevaluation in terms of purpose, timing, and audiences.

Exercise 2. Ask one member of your group to describe an evaluation with which he or she is familiar. As a group, list at least eight features of this evaluation that should be assessed in a metaevaluation.

Exercise 3. Visit the www.wmich.edu/evalctr/checklists Web site, and review the checklists your group might use to conduct a metaevaluation of the evaluation your group identified in response to question 2. Which one or more checklists would your group choose to conduct the metaevaluation? Justify your choice.

Exercise 4. Consider whether all of the features your group identified in response to question 2 would be covered in an application of your group's chosen checklists.

Exercise 5. This chapter lists skills required by a competent metaevaluator. Discuss these skills, with a frank assessment of your ability to undertake a metaevaluation effectively. If you acknowledge deficiencies, what actions could you take to attain the needed competency?

References

American Evaluation Association 2003 Ethics Committee. (2003). *Guiding principles for evaluators.* http://www.eval.org/Guiding%20 Principles.htm.

American Psychological Association. (1999). *Standards for educational and psychological testing.* Washington, DC: Author.

Beywl, W. (2000). Standards for evaluation: On the way to guiding principles in German evaluation. In C. Russon (Ed.), *The program evaluation standards in international settings* (pp. 60–67). Kalamazoo: Western Michigan University Evaluation Center.

Datta, L. (1999). CIRCE's demonstration of a close-to-ideal evaluation in a less-than-ideal world. *American Journal of Evaluation, 20,* 345–354.

Finn, C. E., Stevens, F. I., Stufflebeam, D. L., & Walberg, H. J. (1997). A meta-evaluation. In H. Miller (Ed.), The New York City public schools integrated learning systems project. *International Journal of Educational Research, 27,* 159–174.

Grasso, P. G. (1999). Meta-evaluation of an evaluation of reader focused writing for the Veterans Benefits Administration. *American Journal of Evaluation, 20,* 355–371.

Jang, S. (2000). The appropriateness of Joint Committee standards in non-Western settings: A case study of South Korea. In C. Russon (Ed.), *The program evaluation standards in international settings* (pp. 60–67). Kalamazoo: Western Michigan University Evaluation Center.

Joint Committee on Standards for Educational Evaluation. (1981). *Standards for evaluations of educational programs, projects, and materials.* New York: McGraw-Hill.

Joint Committee on Standards for Educational Evaluation. (1988). *The personnel evaluation standards.* Thousand Oaks, CA: Corwin Press.

Joint Committee on Standards for Educational Evaluation. (1994). *The program evaluation standards: How to assess evaluations of educational programs.* Thousand Oaks, CA: Corwin Press.

Joint Committee on Standards for Educational Evaluation. (2003). *The student evaluation standards.* Thousand Oaks, CA: Corwin Press.

Miller, H. L. (Ed.). (1997). The New York City public schools integrated learning systems project: Evaluation and meta-evaluation. *International Journal of Educational Research, 27,* 159–174.

National Center for Education Statistics. (1991). *SEDCAR (Standards for Education Data Collection and Reporting).* Washington, DC: Westat.

National Center for Education Statistics. (1992). *NCES statistical standards.* Washington, DC: Author.

Orris, M. J. (1989). *Industrial applicability of the Joint Committee's Personnel Evaluation Standards.* Unpublished doctoral dissertation, Western Michigan University.

Sanders, J. R. (1995). Standards and principles. In W. R. Shadish, D. L. Newman, M. A. Scheirer, & C. Wye (Eds.), *New directions for program evaluation* (pp. 47–52). San Francisco: Jossey-Bass.

Scriven, M. (1969). An introduction to meta-evaluation. *Educational Products Report, 2,* 36–38.

Scriven, M. (1994). Product evaluation: The state of the art. *Evaluation Practice, 15,* 45–62.

Scriven, M. (2000). *The logic and methodology of checklists.* www.wmich.edu/evalctr/checklists/.

Smith, N. L., Chircop, S., & Mukherjee, P. (2000). Considerations on the development of culturally relevant evaluation standards. In C. Russon (Ed.), *The program evaluation standards in international settings* (pp. 60–67). Kalamazoo: Western Michigan University Evaluation Center.

Stake, R., & Davis, R. (1999). Summary evaluation of reader focused writing for the Veterans Benefits Administration. *American Journal of Evaluation, 20,* 323–344.

Stufflebeam, D. L. (1974). *Meta-evaluation.* Kalamazoo: Western Michigan University Evaluation Center.

Stufflebeam, D. L. (2000a). The methodology of metaevaluation. In D. L. Stufflebeam, G. F. Madaus, & T. Kellaghan, *Evaluation models.* Norwell, MA: Kluwer.

Stufflebeam, D. L. (2000b). Lessons in contracting for evaluations. *American Journal of Evaluation, 21,* 293–314.

Stufflebeam, D. L. (2000c). *Guidelines for developing evaluation checklists.* www.wmich.edu/evalctr/checklists/.

Stufflebeam, D. L. (2001a). *Evaluation models.* New Directions for Evaluation, no. 89. San Francisco: Jossey-Bass.

Stufflebeam, D. L. (2001b). Evaluation checklists: Practical tools for guiding and judging evaluations. *American Journal of Evaluation, 22,* 71–79.

Stufflebeam, D. L. (2001c). The metaevaluation imperative. *American Journal of Evaluation, 22*(2), 183–209.

Stufflebeam, D. L., Jaeger, R. M., & Scriven, M. (1992). *A retrospective analysis of a summative evaluation of NAGB's pilot project to set achievement levels on the National Assessment of Educational Progress.* Paper presented at the annual meeting of the American Educational Research Association, San Francisco.

Taut, S. (2000). Cross-cultural transferability of *the program evaluation standards.* In C. Russon (Ed.), *The program evaluation standards in international settings* (pp. 60–67). Kalamazoo: Western Michigan University Evaluation Center.

U.S. Government Accounting Office. (2003, June). *Government auditing standards.* Washington, DC: Author.

Vinovskis, M. (1999). *Overseeing the nation's report card: The creation and evolution of the National Assessment Governing Board (NAGB).* Washington, DC: National Assessment Governing Board.

Widmer, T., Landert, C., & Bacmann, N. (2000). Evaluation standards recommended by the Swiss Evaluation Society (SEVAL). In C. Russon (Ed.), *The program evaluation standards in international settings* (pp. 60–67). Kalamazoo: Western Michigan University Evaluation Center.

GLOSSARY

Accountability/payment by results approach   Uses a questions-oriented methodology, focusing on questions about outcomes by employing external perspectives.

Accreditation   The assessment of an evaluand or evaluee against formally established standards.

Accreditation/certification evaluations   A system and process of reviewing and assessing an institutional program or personnel against accepted standards for the purpose of certifying program or personnel credentials.

Accuracy   A government reporting standard for performance audits that states that reports should provide evidence that is true, findings that are correctly portrayed, and a report that is credible and reliable in all matters. The report should clearly indicate limitations of the data and contain no unwarranted conclusions or recommendations based on those data. As a personnel evaluation standard, accuracy demands that evaluations should provide sound information about a person's qualifications and performance.

Accuracy standard   A program evaluation standard that states that an evaluation should ensure that it can determine the worth or merit of the program being evaluated.

Active-reactive-adaptive process of evaluation   Interactive discussion, advice, and general consultation that continues throughout a utilization-focused evaluation between the evaluator and the intended users. Michael Patton states that utilization-focused evaluators must be active in purposefully identifying intended program users and formulating questions with these users that will shape the study. Evaluators are reactive in focusing on the thinking of users and responding to their ideas. As the process unfolds, the evaluator responsively adapts aspects of the evaluation to accommodate situational dynamics and increased understandings by both evaluators and users.

Advance organizers   Types of variables used to determine information requirements.

Advocacy teams technique   A technique for use in input evaluations in which teams generate competing proposals for meeting targeted needs and an independent team evaluates the alternative proposals against established criteria.

Alpha   The magnitude of a type 1 error for an H1 hypothesis. For example, if the level of statistical significance has been set at .01, then across a large number of replications of the study, 1 percent of them would be expected to reject H1 when it is true.

Alpha level of significance   The upper bound on rejecting a hypothesis when it is true. For example, if the significance level is set at .05, then across a large number of replications of the study, 5 percent of them would be expected to reject H1 when it is true.

Amateur evaluation   Evaluation by persons with minimal evaluation expertise but striving to conduct a credible study.

American Evaluation Association (AEA)   An association formed in 1986 from the Evaluation Research Society and the Evaluation Network.

American National Standards Institute (ANSI)   The organization recognized to set standards for educational evaluations in the United States.

Analysis of information   The method or methods used to identify and assess the constituent elements of each set of obtained information and their relationships in order to clarify the information's dependability and meaning for answering particular questions.

Antecedents   Relevant background information, including any conditions existing prior to the evaluation that may relate to outcomes.

Applying   The use of evaluation findings. Although this step is under the control of clients, the evaluator should at least offer to assist in the application of findings.

Apportionment   A process that allocates a finite set of resources to alternative evaluands in consideration of their relative merits and importance.

Assets   Accessible expertise and services, usually in the local area, that could be used to help fulfill the targeted purpose.

Audit documentation   A government fieldwork standard for performance audits that states that auditors should prepare and maintain documentation related to planning, conducting, and reporting on the audit. This documentation should contain sufficient information to enable an experienced auditor who has had no previous connection with the audit to ascertain from the documentation the evidence that supports the auditors' significant judgments and conclusions. Audit documentation should contain support for findings, conclusions, and recommendations before auditors issue their report.

Audit objectives   A government reporting standard for performance audits that states that the purposes of the audit should be clear, specific, neutral, measurable, and feasible.

Audit scope   A government reporting standard for performance audits that states that the depth and coverage of the audit work should explain the relationship between the population of items sampled and the sample examined; identify organizations, geographical locations, and the period covered; and explain and document problems. Auditors also are expected to report significant constraints on the audit.

Benefit-cost analysis   As applied to program evaluation, a set of largely qualitative procedures used to discover the cost of a program and to determine what program investments returned in terms of economic objectives attained and broader social benefits perceived.

Beta   The magnitude of a type 2 error for a specified H2. For example, if the beta level is set at .10, then across a large number of replications of the study, 10 percent of them would be expected to erroneously accept H1 as true.

Case study evaluations   Focus on in-depth depiction, description, analysis, and synthesis of a particular program or other evaluand in progress (or, occasionally, as it has occurred in the past). The focus of the case study is the case itself.

Case study evaluator responsibilities   Bounding and conceptualizing the case; selecting phenomena, themes, or issues to study; seeking patterns of data to develop issues for study; triangulating key observations and bases for interpretation; selecting alternative interpretations to pursue; and developing assertions or generalizations about the case.

Catalytic authenticity   An evaluation's fostering of an event or events in which stakeholders took appropriate action.

Checklists   Lists of items, such as tasks or criteria, to consider when undertaking an evaluation or some aspect of an evaluation.

CIPP model for evaluation   A comprehensive approach for conducting formative and summative evaluations in which evaluators, in conjunction with stakeholders, seek clear, unambiguous answers to pertinent questions about an enterprise's context, inputs, process, and products. A central theme is to assist and assess the extent to which a programmatic effort effectively serves targeted beneficiaries and does so within a framework of defined, appropriate values. Operationally a CIPP evaluation delineates, obtains, reports, and applies descriptive judgmental information about an object's merit, worth, significance, and probity in order to guide decision making, support accountability, disseminate effective practices, and increase understanding of the involved phenomena.

Clarification hearing   A form of judicial approach to program evaluation, with a program placed clearly in a legal focus procedurally. Evidence and arguments both pro and con the program are judged in a formal legal setting, exposing the program's strengths and weaknesses.

Clear   A government reporting standard for performance audits requiring reports to be easy to read and understand and prepared in as simple, straightforward, nontechnical language as the subject permits.

Collective case study   A case study in which evaluators move further away from the particular case as they study a number of cases together, so that they can inquire into the phenomenon or population.

Communication specialist   A person with excellent communication skills and technical skills who ensures that evaluation reports are relevant to the interests of their target audiences and understood by them.

Competence   A government auditing standard that states that the staff assigned to perform the audit or attestation engagement collectively should possess adequate professional qualifications for the tasks required. In more general terms, competence is a guiding principle requiring evaluators to provide skilled, effective service to stakeholders.

Concise   A government reporting standard for performance audits requiring reports not to be longer than necessary to convey and support the message.

Congruence analysis   Questions whether what was intended occurred, based on observations and logical conclusions displaying discrepancies with expectations.

Constructivist evaluation An evaluative approach that rejects any aspects of experimental design, while emphasizing that the truth of a program is constructed by a paradigm of individuals who work within it and for it. Constructivist evaluation employs a subjectivist epistemology.

Consumer reports   Assess alternative objects by focusing on classes of objects available to consumers, alternatives within each class, and the relative costs and merits of objects within each class.

Consumer-oriented evaluations   An approach in which the evaluator is the enlightened surrogate consumer, drawing conclusions about the merit and worth of the program being assessed. The consumer's welfare is the focus of, and justification for, the evaluation.

Context evaluation   Assesses needs, problems, assets, and opportunities to help decision makers establish defensible goals and priorities and help relevant users judge goals, priorities, and outcomes.

Convergent stage of evaluation planning   The stage when the evaluator works with clients and stakeholders and selects questions from the divergent stage to be the basis for the evaluation. *See also* Divergent stage of evaluation planning.

Convincing   A government reporting standard for performance audits requiring audit results to be responsive to the audit objectives, presented persuasively, and conclusions and recommendations to follow logically from the presented facts.

Cooperative evaluation agreement   An arrangement for the evaluator and sponsor to collaborate in conducting the evaluation.

Cost-plus evaluation agreement   Includes the funds required to conduct an evaluation assignment, plus an additional agreed-on charge for the evaluator's services outside the sphere of the contracted evaluation. A cost-plus budget can be built into a grant, a fixed-price agreement, or a cost-reimbursable agreement. There are three types: (1) *Cost-plus-a-fee budget:* the additional funds used to help sustain the contracting organization; (2) *cost-plus-a-grant budget:* the additional funds used to support program functions, such as supporting graduate students, research on evaluation, or an evaluation conference; (3) *Cost-plus-profit budget:* typically employed by for-profit evaluation organizations in order to make financial gain from contracted evaluations.

Cost-reimbursable evaluation contract   An agreement that the evaluator will account for, report, and be reimbursed for actual evaluation project expenditures.

Critical competitors   Well-performing alternatives to an evaluand that might be less expensive or more effective.

Criticism and connoisseurship   An approach to evaluation, arising from methods used to assess artistic and literary works; assumes that experts in a given area offer capable analyses in a way impossible by any other methodology.

Decision/accountability–oriented evaluations   Evaluations that emphasize that program assessments should be used proactively to help improve a program as well as retroactively to judge its value.

Defensible purpose   A desired end that has been legitimately defined consistent with a guiding philosophy, set of professional standards, institutional mission, mandated curriculum, national constitution, or public referendum, for example.

Deliberative democratic evaluation   A process that emphasizes a democratic, equitable, and principled approach to program evaluation and strives to produce valid, reliable, and defensible information about the program's merit and worth.

Delineating   Effective, two-way communication involving evaluator, client, and other interested parties and culminating in negotiated terms for the evaluation.

Descriptive information   The part of a final evaluation report that objectively describes the program's goals, plans, operations, and outcomes and discovers insights and judgments of potential concern (often expressed as questions to be answered) that come from a reasonable array of relevant sources.

Divergent stage of evaluation planning   An early stage when an exploratory inquiry discovers issues, insights, and judgments of potential concern (often expressed as questions to be answered) from a reasonable array of relevant sources.

Eclectic approaches   Evaluative approaches that pragmatically draw from and selectively apply a wide range of methods and concepts to address the questions of designated stakeholders.

Eclectic evaluation   An evaluation that pragmatically draws from and selectively applies principles and procedures from a wide range of evaluation sources.

Empowerment evaluation   While the evaluator offers technical assistance, this approach gives authority for the process, outcomes, and reporting of an assessment to stakeholders.

Empowerment under the guise of evaluation   An external evaluator helps a client develop evaluation expertise, but allows the client to write, edit, and then release a report in the name of the external evaluator.

Environmental analysis   Involves gathering contextual information in the form of available documents and data concerning such matters as area economics, population characteristics, relevant projects and services and political dynamics, and the needs of the targeted population.

Equity   Assessment of an evaluand's affirmative and reasonable conformance to principles of justice, freedom, equal opportunity, and fairness for all involved personnel without imposing bias, favoritism, or undue hardships on anyone.

Ethical principles   A set of codes or standards that govern the behavior of evaluators.

Evaluability assessment   Developed as a particular methodology for determining the feasibility of progressing with an evaluation of a program; informal, qualitative data are collected to determine if the program will be served productively by systematic, quantitative evaluation.

Evaluand   The object of an evaluation, especially a program, project, organization, or person.

Evaluation   The systematic process of delineating, obtaining, reporting, and applying descriptive and judgmental information about some object's merit, worth, probity, feasibility, safety, significance, or equity. The result of an evaluation process is an evaluation as product.

Evaluation agreements   May take the form of a formal contract (applicable to external agreements) or a less formal memorandum of agreement (better suited to internal evaluations). Both forms of agreement should provide a framework of mutual understanding for proceeding with the evaluation work.

Evaluation approach   A broad conceptualization of evaluation methodology and practice, encompassing evaluation models.

Evaluation bidders' conference   A conference that provides all potential bidders with an equal opportunity to receive background information about the needed evaluation and to address questions to the sponsor's representatives.

Evaluation budget   A detailed estimate of financial and associated resources required to implement the full range of proposed tasks within a given time period that convinces the sponsor the study is affordable, feasible, and would be performed at a high level of quality and professionalism.

Evaluation by pretext   Begins with preferred conclusions and arranges data supporting predetermined outcomes.

Evaluation caseworker   A person who periodically interacts with clients, reviews program documents, observes program activities, interviews and otherwise gathers information from participants, drafts reports, and assumes primary responsibility for writing up the findings.

Evaluation client   A person or group that will use the results for some purpose such as program selection, program improvement, or accountability to a sponsor. The client group includes the person who commissioned the evaluation, as well as those who will attend to and use its results.

Evaluation constraints   The practical constraints of many evaluation assignments preclude or make it extremely difficult to fully meet the standards associated with sound information collection or analysis.

Evaluation contract   A legally enforceable written agreement between the evaluator and client regarding the evaluation's specifications and both parties' responsibilities.

Evaluation contracting   Establishes a trusting relationship between an evaluator and a client and formalizes their agreements in a written statement for holding each party accountable and for resolving disputes.

Evaluation coordinator   A person who manages the work effort, usually of several evaluators or evaluation projects.

Evaluation design   The set of decisions required to carry out the needed evaluation.

Evaluation designer   A person who designs an evaluation to respond to a client's information requirements.

Evaluation developer   A person whose role has at its base the function of helping evaluators collectively attain and maintain the status of a profession.

Evaluation grant   A financial award to support a qualified evaluator to conduct a study that is of interest to the evaluator, contains social value, lies within the sponsor's mission, and is seen to be at a fundable level.

Evaluation ideologies   According to Michael Scriven in Chapter Sixteen, all of these are flawed:

> **Management**   Michael Scriven's well-managed evaluation requires more than guidance from a competent administrator, because "self-serving, indulgent" managers and evaluators may impose rigid controls that would distort evaluation procedures, outcomes, and subsequent decision making.

Positivism   Applies to evaluators who, in their attempts to remove bias from scientific works, overreact and portray science in general, and evaluation in particular, as value free.

Relativism   Viewed as an overreaction to problems associated with a positivist ideology; relativists hold that everything is relative, and there is no objective truth—a position that may deny the possibility of determination of merit.

Separatism   The separatist ideology is rooted in the denial or rejection of the proposition that evaluation is a self-referent activity, perhaps best reflected in the proposition that evaluators should be totally independent of what is evaluated.

Evaluation research   A special kind of applied research whose goal, unlike nonevaluation research, is not to discover knowledge but to test the application of knowledge.

Evaluation researcher   A person who studies evaluation-related needs and problems, theorizes about professional services, examines practices in the light of knowledge and principles from relevant disciplines, considers work in its historical context, and moves knowledge about evaluation forward through structured examination of the field's guiding assumptions and hypotheses.

Evaluation respondent   A person who filled out the forms, answered the test questions, responded to interview questions, submitted her or his work products, and allowed her or his work to be observed.

Evaluation request for proposal   An organization's or sponsor's published or direct mail request for proposals to conduct a particular evaluation.

Evaluation sponsor   An individual, institution, or organization that initiates an evaluation and provides financial and other resources to ensure its satisfactory conduct.

Evaluation review panel   A representative group from an organization and its environment whose functions include reviewing evaluation plans, assessing the progress of the study as it evolves, perusing and commenting on draft interim and final reports, and facilitating the collection of information and dissemination of findings.

Evaluation stakeholders   Individuals or groups closely identified with a program and likely to be affected by changes arising from the evaluation.

Evaluation standard   A principle commonly agreed to by experts in the conduct and use of evaluation for the measure of the value or quality of an evaluation.

Evaluation trainer   A person who teaches evaluation to potential evaluators.

Evaluee   The person who is the object of an evaluation.

Evidence   A government fieldwork standard for performance audits requiring the obtaining of sufficient, competent, and relevant evidence to provide a reasonable basis for the auditors' findings and conclusions.

Experimental studies   Designed to determine the effects of a program or other planned intervention. They employ random assignment or matching procedures to assign beneficiaries or organizations to experimental or control groups, administer a treatment to the experimental group, contrast outcomes for the involved groups, and make inferences about the intervention's effects.

External impairment   A government auditing standard charging audit organizations to identify possible external impairments and ways of addressing them in internal policies and procedures for reporting and resolving external impairments.

Feasibility   A personnel evaluation standard stating that evaluation procedures should be efficient, politically viable, relatively easy to implement, and adequately funded.

Feasibility standard   A program evaluation standard stating that an evaluation should be realistic, prudent, diplomatic, and frugal.

Feedback workshop technique   A method for systematically conveying draft interim findings to a program's leaders and staff (and possibly other designated stakeholders), guiding their discussion of the findings, obtaining their critical reactions to the draft report, supporting their use of findings, and using their feedback to update or strengthen evaluation plans and materials.

Fieldwork standards for performance audits   Government auditing standards pertaining to planning the audit; supervising staff; obtaining sufficient, competent, and relevant evidence; and preparing audit documentation.

Final synthesis According to Michael Scriven (Chapter Sixteen), includes searching for appropriate decision rules; deriving prima facie criteria admissible in probative judgments; deriving criteria of goodness inherent in the classical definition of the evaluative object; assessing the needs and preferences of the client and beneficiaries; obtaining evidence of each object's status on the criteria of merit, worth, and significance; weighing the criteria; profiling the result; deciding whether to try for a final synthesis; and, if warranted, combining the results to reach an overall conclusion.

Finding A government reporting standard for performance audits stating that results should be keyed to the audit objectives and supported by sufficient, competent, and relevant evidence.

Focus group technique A group interview approach developed by the consumer research field and used by evaluators predominantly to obtain and analyze the views of stakeholders about the merit and worth of a program or obtain multiple perspectives on a given evaluation question. The function and expertise of the group moderator are central to the successful outcomes of the interview.

Form A government reporting standard for performance audits stating that auditors should prepare audit reports that communicate the results of each audit.

Formal evaluation An evaluation that is relevant, rigorous, designed and executed to control bias, kept consistent with appropriate professional standards, and otherwise made useful and defensible.

Formative evaluation An evaluation that assesses and assists with the formulation of goals and priorities; provides direction for planning by assessing alternative courses of action and draft plans; and guides program management by assessing implementation of plans and interim results.

General theory of a program area A conceptual framework that covers a wide range of program evaluations, denotes their modal characteristics—including logic and processes of evaluative discourse—and describes in general how program evaluations should be assessed and justified.

Goal and role of evaluation All evaluations have a unitary, unchanging goal (to determine value as objectively as possible); however, their roles may vary widely in the pursuit and clarification of constructive uses of evaluative data.

Two prevalent roles are formative evaluation (to assist in developing programs or other objects) and summative evaluation (to assess the object's value once it has been developed).

Goal-free evaluation   An evaluation in which the evaluator is kept ignorant of a program's goals so that he or she can uncover the full range of program outcomes regardless of what was intended. The goal-free evaluator searches for all effects of the object being evaluated and examines them against the assessed needs of the relevant consumers.

Government auditing standards   A set of standards developed by the U.S. General Accountability Office to help auditors assess and ensure the validity of reported information on the results of government-funded programs and the soundness of related systems of internal control.

Grading   Judging an evaluand's merit by assigning it a grade, such as A, B, C, D, or F, or a rating, such as outstanding, excellent, good, fair, poor, or very poor.

Grounded theory   A conceptual framework based in systematic, rigorous documentation and analysis of actual program evaluations and their particular circumstances.

Guiding principles for evaluators   A set of five principles and twenty-three underlying normative statements adopted by the American Evaluation Association to guide evaluation practice.

Hermeneutic approach to evaluation   The process of exploring and interpreting a program's salient endeavors and accomplishments as they occur by collecting and describing alternative individual constructions on the matters of interest and ensuring that each respondent approves what was attributed to her or him.

Hypothetical principles   Research-based principles for conducting program evaluations.

Improvement/accountability approaches   Focus on determining an evaluand's merit and worth; their functions are to foster program improvement and accountability, assist consumers to make wise choices among optional programs and services, and certify meritorious programs and institutions for use by consumers.

Independence   A government auditing standard requiring in all matters relating to the audit work, the audit organization and the individual auditor, whether government or public, to be free in both fact and appearance from personal, external, and organizational impairments to independence.

Informal evaluation   An evaluation that is unsystematic, lacks rigor, and may be biased.

Information scope   Evaluators should collect information that has sufficient breadth to address the audience's most important information needs and to support a judgment of merit and worth; typically, evaluators should obtain information on all important variables.

Information specialist   A person who provides library services for an organization and is proficient in information sciences and computer technology.

Input evaluation   Assesses alternative approaches, competing action and staffing plans, and budgets for their feasibility and potential cost-effectiveness in meeting targeted needs and achieving goals.

Instrumental case study   A case study that provides insight into an issue or a theory needing refinement.

Integrity/honesty   A guiding principle for evaluators stating that evaluators should display honesty and integrity in their own behavior and attempt to ensure the honesty and integrity of the entire evaluation process.

Internal evaluation   Work within organizations to address evaluation needs such as conducting studies of the organization's externally funded projects or assessing the merit and worth of planned or operating organizational programs.

Interviewing imperatives   These entail experience of the interviewer, preparation, clear understanding of the program, purpose of the interview, and rapport with the respondent.

Intrinsic case study   A case study undertaken to give a better understanding of the inner nature of a particular case, irrespective of its possible extrinsic value.

Intrinsic evaluation   Assesses an evaluand's inner quality, regardless of its effects on beneficiaries, by assessing such aspects as policies, goals, structure, facilities, equipment, plans, procedures, staff qualifications, and communications.

Judgmental information   Provides an evaluative conclusion based on a set of values or standards plus discussions of an evaluand's strengths and weaknesses, and may include recommendations for improvement.

Key Evaluation Checklist   A practical tool developed and continually refined by Michael Scriven for applying his evaluation approach; can be adapted for use in particular evaluations, including metaevaluations. The rationale of the checklist is that evaluation is essentially a data-reduction process, whereby large amounts of data are obtained and assessed and then synthesized in an overall judgment of value or at least a profile keyed to selected checkpoints.

Legitimate private evaluation feedback   Occurs only when the evaluation is sound and conforms to relevant laws, policies, and appropriate contractual agreements.

Management information systems   Used to supply managers with information needed to conduct and report on their programs, but political control may lead to the provision of information that aims to give political advantage.

Meta-analysis   A form of quantitative synthesis of studies that addresses a common research question and yields a composite effect size across studies. In the program evaluation research context, this usually involves a treatment and control comparison.

Metaevaluation   An evaluation of an evaluation to help detect and address problems, ensure quality, and reveal an evaluation's strengths and limitations. It is the process of delineating, obtaining, and applying descriptive information and judgmental information—about the utility, feasibility, propriety, and accuracy of an evaluation and its systematic nature, competent execution, integrity and honesty, respectfulness, and social responsibility—to guide the evaluation and report its strengths and weaknesses. Metaevaluation is a professional obligation of evaluators.

Metaevaluator   A person who conducts metaevaluations. The role can be extended to assessing the worth, merit, and probity of all that the profession is and does, evaluation services, use of evaluations, evaluation training, evaluation research, and organizational development.

Methodology   A government reporting standard for performance audits charging auditors to clearly explain what was done to achieve audit objectives.

Method-oriented program evaluation   An approach that typically uses a particular method to determine the nature of the program (quasi-evaluation).

Mixed-method studies   Program evaluations that employ a range of quantitative and qualitative methods.

Modular evaluation budgets   Budgets that delineate the funding requirements for each part of a designed evaluation project or for each project year.

Naturalistic inquiry   A procedure and process for studying a program as it unfolds, paying close attention to context, internal dynamics, and insights of stakeholders. It imposes no controls on the development and delivery of the program or assignment and involvement of participants. It employs investigatory categories and variables that unfold during the course of the study. Thus, the approach minimizes investigator manipulation of the study setting and places no constraints on what the outcomes of the research will be. Typically, naturalistic studies employ heavy use of qualitative methods while also using quantitative techniques.

Need   Anything essential for a satisfactory mode of existence. It follows that anything without that condition would fall below a satisfactory level.

Needs   Those things necessary or useful for fulfilling a defensible purpose.

Needs assessment   A study to determine deficiencies in the wellbeing or performance of targeted beneficiaries or in the instrumentalities needed to prevent beneficiaries from suffering bad consequences. Determinations of such outcome and treatment needs provide a basis for setting goals and determining criteria for judging a program's outcomes.

Numerical weight and sum (NWS)   A relatively common approach to reach evaluative conclusions requiring computing an overall score on an evaluation object by summing across all criteria the products of each criterion's weight times the object's score on the criterion. (This procedure could erroneously give a passing grade to an object that failed or did poorly on the most important criteria but scored high on less important or even trivial criteria.)

Objectives-based evaluation   A classic example of question-oriented evaluation that determines whether the program's objectives have been achieved; especially applicable in assessing tightly focused projects that have clear objectives.

Objective testing programs   Employ standardized procedures, such as multiple choice questions, to assess achievements of individual students or groups of students compared with the norms, standards, or previous performance.

Objectivist evaluation   An evaluation based on the theory that moral good is objective and independent of personal or merely human feelings. Fundamentally, these evaluations are intended to lead to conclusions that are correct—not correct relative to an evaluator's or other party's predilections, position, preferences, or point of view.

Objectivity   A government reporting standard for performance audits stating that the entire report should be balanced in content and tone; shortcomings should be set in an appropriate context; and evidence should be presented in an unbiased, fair manner so that users can be persuaded by the facts.

Obtaining   The work involved in collecting, correcting, organizing, analyzing, and synthesizing information.

Ontological authenticity   An evaluation's success in helping stakeholders surface and understand their unconscious or unstated beliefs and values concerning the evaluand.

Opportunities   Advantageous circumstances, especially including funding programs that could be used to help fulfill targeted needs.

Organizational impairment   A government auditing standard stating that audit organizations need to be free from impairments to independence attendant to their place within or relationship to the organization that houses the entity to be audited.

Outcome need   A level of achievement or outcome in a particular area required to fulfill a defensible purpose.

Pandering evaluations   Informing a client of what he or she wants to hear (often evading the truth of a program) toward the goal of winning the client's favor.

Payoff evaluation   Concerned not with the structure or process of a program or any other object but with its effects on beneficiaries (for example, test scores, employment, physical fitness, home ownership, or financial gains).

Performance testing   With emphasis on reality, requires students to demonstrate their achievements by producing authentic responses to evaluation situations, such as written or spoken answers, personal presentations, or portfolios of work.

Personal impairment   A government auditing standard charging audit organizations to maintain internal quality control systems to detect whether auditors have any relationships and beliefs that might cause them to be partial or give the appearance of partiality.

Personnel evaluation   The systematic assessment of a person's qualifications or performance in relation to a role and defensible purpose of an institution, profession, program, or other entity.

Personnel evaluation standards   A set of standards developed by the Joint Committee on Standards for Educational Evaluation and approved by the American National Standards Institute. The twenty-one standards are grouped according to four essential attributes of a sound evaluation: utility, feasibility, propriety, and accuracy.

Phenomenology   Pertaining to outward manifestations, that is, things perceptible by the senses, while embracing systematic scientific study of relationships between organizations (and their constituent individuals) and their environment.

Planning   A government fieldwork standard for performance audits that directs auditors to define audit objectives, scope, and needed methods.

Politically controlled studies   Those that seek the truth of a program but may inappropriately control the release of findings.

Posttest-only designs   An experimental design that randomly assigns participants to intervention treatments, followed by posttreatment assessment and interpretation of outcomes. Random assignment is assumed to strengthen equivalence between groups and support the drawing of defensible causal inferences.

Pragmatic principles   Procedural guidelines for conducting evaluations that have been shown to work well in evaluation practice.

Preordinate evaluation   Usually focused narrowly on examining the extent to which preestablished objectives are achieved.

Pre-post designs   Experimental designs in which participants are randomly assigned to treatment and control groups, and measures are taken before and after the treatment.

Prescriptive theory   A conceptual framework proposed by an evaluator— based on reflections on and critical analyses of a wide range of evaluation experiences—and intended to act as a guide for other evaluators.

Probative inference   Prima facie conclusion about an evaluand's value based on close study of relevant facts and context.

Process evaluation   Assesses the implementation of plans to help staff carry out activities and thereafter to help the broader range of users judge program implementation and interpret outcomes. Through documentation of the process and reporting on progress to appropriate program staff and other interested parties, a judgment is made about the extent to which planned activities are being (or were) carried out on schedule, as planned, and efficiently.

Product evaluation   In general terms, product evaluation identifies and assesses outcomes—intended and unintended, short-term and long-term—to help staff keep an enterprise focused on achieving agreed-on, important outcomes and ultimately to help relevant users gauge the success of the effort in meeting targeted needs. In a different sense, product evaluation refers to the evaluation of tangible products such as computers, automobiles, and cameras. In all product evaluations it is important to identify and validate criteria of merit, weight their relative importance, assess the product on each criterion, and, where possible, reach an overall conclusion.

Professional evaluation   Undertaken by trained evaluators possessing high-level technical skills, knowledge of evaluation theory and methodology, and a commitment to meet the evaluation field's standards.

Professional judgment   A government auditing standard requiring auditors to assess situations or circumstances and draw sound conclusions in order to serve the public interest effectively and maintain utmost integrity, objectivity, and independence.

Program context analysis   (1) Formative evaluations require contextual information to help a program take account of local circumstances and respond to beneficiaries' needs and problems. (2) Summative evaluations require contextual information to help audiences understand why a program succeeded or failed and to prevent erroneous interpretations that the findings have wider applicability than the context justifies.

Program evaluation   Systematic collection, analysis, and reporting of descriptive and judgmental information about the merit and worth of a program's goals, design, process, and outcomes to address improvement, accountability, and dissemination questions and increase understanding of the involved phenomena.

Program evaluation model   An evaluation theorist's idealized conceptualization for conducting program evaluations.

Program Evaluation Standards   A set of standards developed by the Joint Committee on Standards for Educational Evaluation and approved by the American National Standards Institute. The thirty standards are grouped according to four essential attributes of a sound evaluation: utility, feasibility, propriety, and accuracy.

Program evaluation theory   A coherent set of conceptual, hypothetical, pragmatic, and ethical principles forming a general framework to guide the study and practice of program evaluation.

Project profiles   Characterize the project, including items such as mission, constituents, needs, plans, resources, and accomplishments to date.

Propriety standards   Evaluation standards requiring evaluations to be conducted legally, ethically, and with due regard for the welfare of the affected parties, including beneficiaries as well as the service providers.

Pseudoevaluations   Purposely produce and report invalid assessments or withhold or selectively release findings to right-to-know audiences. They do not adhere to professional standards for evaluation. Five predominant types are public relations, politically controlled, pandering, evaluation by pretext, and empowerment under the guise of evaluation.

Public relations studies   Studies in which the emphasis is placed not on truth seeking but on the acquisition and broadcasting of information that provides a favorable, but often spurious, impression of the program.

Purposive sampling   Sampling that allows the evaluator to focus on key informants to obtain information. In such situations, random sampling would not be applicable. However, purposive sampling may lead to snowball sampling, where initial interviewees identify others who could provide relevant information.

Qualitative analysis   The process of compiling, analyzing, and interpreting qualitative information to answer particular questions about a program.

Quality control and assurance   A government auditing standard stating that each organization performing audits or attestation engagements should have an appropriate internal system in place for maintaining a high degree of excellence and should undergo an external peer review.

Quantitative analysis   A wide range of concepts and techniques for using quantitative information to describe a program and study and communicate its effects. The process involves compiling, exploring, validating, organizing, summarizing, analyzing, synthesizing, and interpreting the quantitative information. Most quantitative analysis techniques are classified as descriptive or inferential statistics.

Quasi-evaluation   Legitimate evaluative studies that sometimes are too narrow in questions addressed or methods employed to support an assessment or assumption of merit and worth.

Quasi-experimental designs   Employed when there is a causal intent to the evaluation but random assignment is not feasible. These approaches include various safeguards to counter threats to internal validity.

Questions-oriented program evaluation   Addresses specified questions, often employing a wide range of methods; this approach is considered to be a quasi-evaluation study.

Random sampling   A type of probability sampling in which each individual or unit in the population has an equal and independent chance of being selected for data collection. This method maximizes the chances that the sample will be representative of the population and thus permits generalization to the population. This procedure allows the evaluator to set acceptable confidence intervals and draw a sample of sufficient size to achieve the desired level of precision of estimate. If the requirements of random sampling are met (and valid measures are obtained), the evaluator can reach defensible inferences about certain features of the population of interest.

Ranking   Involves placing different evaluands in an ordered list according to their scores on a criterion of merit.

Realist evaluation   A concept of evaluation calling for sustained, long-term study of a particular social intervention—such as Head Start—to develop explanations of why, how, where, and for whom the approach works or fails to work.

Regression-discontinuity design   A quasi-experimental design in which subjects who meet a certain criterion are compared with those who failed to meet that criterion. A difference in the regression line for the two groups suggests a program effect.

Relativistic evaluation   Directed toward a pluralistic, flexible, interactive, holistic, subjective, constructivist, and service-oriented approach. No final, authoritative conclusions are sought. Responsive evaluation is a leading case in point. Beauty is in the eye of the beholder.

Reliability   Information that is free from internal contradictions and when repeated information collection episodes yield, as expected, the same answers.

Report contents   A government reporting standard for performance audits stating that the audit report should include the objectives, scope, and methodology; the audit results, including findings, conclusions, and recommendations, as appropriate; a reference to compliance with generally accepted government auditing standards; the views of responsible officials; and, if applicable, the nature of any privileged and confidential information omitted.

Report issuance and distribution   A government reporting standard for performance audits stating that auditors should submit reports to the appropriate officials of the audited entity and the appropriate officials of the organizations requiring or arranging for the audits.

Report quality element   A government reporting standard for performance audits stating that the report should be timely, complete, accurate, objective, convincing, clear, and as concise as the subject permits.

Reporting   Effectively and accurately communicating the evaluation's findings in a timely manner to interested and right-to-know audiences.

Reporting standards for performance audits   A government auditing standard that pertains to the form of reports, report contents, report quality, and report issuance and distribution.

Respect for people   A guiding principle for evaluators stating that evaluators respect the security, dignity, and self-worth of the respondents, program participants, clients, and other evaluation stakeholders.

Responsibilities for general and public welfare   A guiding principle for evaluators stating that evaluators articulate and take into account the diversity of general and public interests and values that may be related to the evaluation.

Responsive (client-centered) evaluation   A relativistic, social advocacy approach where the evaluator interacts with clients (often a diverse group) to support and help develop, administer, and improve programs in a nondirective, counseling manner. The approach employs descriptive and judgmental information to examine a program's background, rationale, transactions, standards, and outcomes. Special features are searching for side effects, representing the inputs of diverse stakeholders, and issuing holistic reports.

Safety   Assessments of the risks associated with the implementation and operation of the evaluand.

Scoring   Involves assigning a number to an evaluand; such numbers represent a sum of quality points that usually are assumed to be equal in value and additive.

Self-referent nature of evaluation   As professionals, evaluators must evaluate and improve their services. This requires regularly evaluating their own work against professional standards and obtaining independent assessments of their evaluations.

Significance   The evaluand's potential influence, importance, and visibility.

Significance of evaluation   The importance of the extent to which the evaluative field is contributing to the welfare of society.

Simple object evaluation reports   Reports that focus on a single program or other object; typically, the final reports are keyed to informing a broad audience about the program's background, structure, implementation, cost, main effects, and side effects.

Social agenda/advocacy approaches to evaluation   Studies directed at increasing social justice through program evaluation, seeking to ensure that all segments of society have equal access to educational and social opportunities and services.

Social system   An interrelated set of activities that ideally function together to fulfill a mission and achieve defined goals within a certain context.

Specific program evaluation theory   A conceptual framework of program evaluation that has many of the same characteristics as a general theory but is delimited to account for program evaluations that are restricted to particular substantive areas, locations, or time periods.

Stakeholders   Those who are intended to use the findings, others who may be affected by the evaluation, and those expected to contribute to the study. These persons help affirm foundational values, define evaluation questions, clarify evaluative criteria, contribute needed information, help interpret findings, and assess evaluation reports.

Standards-based evaluation   An evaluation that incorporates fundamental principles recognized by the profession.

Statistical hypothesis   A statement about a population that one seeks to affirm or reject based on data from a sample of the population.

Statistical test   A set of rules for deciding whether to accept or reject a hypothesis.

Statutory provisions re: auditing   Safeguards that protect against abolition of the audit organization by the audited entity; require transparency of reasons for removing the head of the audit agency; prevent the audited entity from interfering in the audit; require the audit organization to report to a governing body that is independent from the audited entity; give the audit organization sole authority over staffing the audit work; and guarantee access to records and documents needed to complete an audit.

Structured observations   Studies where investigations systematically focus on and record observations of specific behaviors or characteristics of program personnel.

Success case method of evaluation   A questions-oriented approach based on emphasizing illuminated instances of program success, which are contrasted with failing or failed elements of the program.

Summative evaluation   Helps consumers decide whether a developed product or service—refined through development and formative evaluation—is a better buy than other alternatives. In general terms, summative evaluation typically occurs following development of a product, completion of a program, or end of a service cycle. It draws together and supplements previous information and provides an overall judgment of the evaluand's value.

Supervision   A government fieldwork standard for performance audits stating that staff are to be properly supervised.

Synthesis of information   The method or methods used to combine analysis findings across information collection procedures and devices in order to discern their validity and aggregate meaning for answering an audience's questions and judging the value of the object of interest.

Systematic evaluation   Standards-based evaluation that is conducted with great care, not only in collecting information of high quality, but also in clarifying and providing a defensible rationale for the value perspective used to interpret the findings and reach judgments and in communicating evaluation findings accurately to the client and other audiences.

Systematic information control   An information process to ensure that an evaluation's information is regularly and carefully checked, made as error free as possible, and kept secure.

Systematic inquiry A guiding principle for evaluators stating that evaluators conduct systematic, data-based inquiries.

Tactical authenticity A study's success in advocating for all stakeholders, especially those with little power.

Technical support specialist A person with technical expertise whose work supports the evaluation efforts. This group of experts could include test development specialists, sampling specialists, computer specialists, statisticians, case study specialists, and technical writers.

Telephone interviews A form of interview, typically where multiple interviewers conduct the interview within a phone bank and code responses as they are received. The interview protocols need to be scripted so that all interviewers will obtain comparable data that can be aggregated and analyzed.

Theory of evaluation A coherent set of conceptual, hypothetical, pragmatic, and ethical principles that form a general framework to guide the study and practice of evaluation.

Theory-based evaluation An evaluation that begins with a well-developed and validated theory of how defined programs operate to produce outcomes or with an approximation of such a theory at an initial stage of a particular program evaluation.

Transdiscipline A discipline comprising a core field together with a number of independent applied fields. Its principal mission is developing procedures and tools for the use of a wide range of applied fields and disciplines. Statistics, measurement, logic, and evaluation are some of the more important examples.

Transdiscipline of evaluation A conceptualization of the evaluation field as encompassing evaluations of various entities across all applied areas and disciplines. It comprises a common logic, theory, and methodology that transcend specific evaluation domains that also have unique characteristics.

Traveling observer technique A procedure developed by the Evaluation Center at Western Michigan University that directly addresses process evaluation data requirements while also providing information useful in context, input, and product evaluation. A preprogrammed investigator, working on site, investigates and characterizes how staff members are carrying out a project before reporting findings to other evaluation team members during feedback sessions.

Treatment need   A certain service, service provider, or other helping agent required to meet an outcome need.

Triangulation   Reaching conclusions about the consistency of outcomes from varying sources and methodologies for measuring a particular construct.

Type 1 error   The probability of rejecting a given hypothesis (for example, the difference between assessed outcomes of alternative treatments is zero) when the hypothesis is in fact true.

Type 2 error   The probability of not rejecting an H1 hypothesis when a given alternative hypothesis is true.

Unstructured observations   Information obtained from loosely controlled, unobtrusive surveillance of program operations designed to help focus and structure later, more systematic observations.

Utility   A category of personnel evaluation standards stating that evaluators should issue results that are credible, informative, timely, and influential; the results should help individuals and groups improve their performance and help superiors make needed personnel decisions and guide staff development and other personnel actions.

Utility standards   A set of program evaluation standards stating that an evaluation should serve the information needs of its intended users.

Utilization-focused evaluation   A form of eclectic evaluation developed by Michael Patton, geared to ensure that evaluations have an impact by guiding the process in collaboration with an identified group of priority users, with focus placed squarely on their intended uses of the evaluation.

Validating information-gathering processes   Focuses on the soundness and defensibility of inferences or conclusions that are drawn from the information-gathering processes and products. Processes should be selected and used to produce information that is relevant to study questions, reliable, and sufficient in scope and depth to answer all the evaluation's questions.

Validation   The process of compiling evidence that supports the interpretations and uses of the data and information collected using one or more instruments and procedures. Validity resides not in any instrument or procedure but in their use in generating inferences and conclusions in a particular study.

Value   A defensible guiding principle or ideal that should be used to determine the evaluand's standing and therefore is any of a range of ideals held by a society, group, or individual. As the root term in *evaluation*, value is central to the determination of criteria for use in judging programs or other entities.

Value-added assessment   A form of outcome evaluation depending on systematic assessment coupled with hierarchical gains-score analysis to assess the effects of programs and policies. Emphasis is often on annual testing of students at various grade levels to assess trends and partial out effects of the different components of an education system (for example, individual schools, groups of schools, and individual teachers).

Worth   A program's combination of excellence and service in an area of clear need, within a specified context.

NAME INDEX

SUBJECT INDEX